MEDIASCAPES

NEW PATTERNS IN CANADIAN COMMUNICATION

Fourth Edition

EDITED BY

LESLIE REGAN SHADE

University of Toronto

NELSON EDUCATION

NELSON EDUCATION

Mediascapes: New Patterns in Canadian Communication, Fourth Edition
by Leslie Regan Shade

Vice President, Editorial Higher Education:
Anne Williams

Executive Editor:
Laura Macleod

Marketing Manager:
Terry Fedorkiw

Developmental Editor:
Jessica Freedman

Photo Researcher:
Sandra Mark

Permissions Coordinator:
Sandra Mark

Content Production Manager:
Hedy Sellers

Production Service:
Cenveo Publisher Services

Copy Editor:
Karen Rolfe

Proofreader:
Jitendra Kumar Das

Indexer:
BIM Indexing Services

Senior Production Coordinator:
Ferial Suleman

Design Director:
Ken Phipps

Managing Designer:
Franca Amore

Interior Design:
Peter Papayanakis

Cover Design:
Trinh Truong

Cover Image:
pated/iStockphoto

Compositor:
Cenveo Publisher Services

Printer:
RR Donnelley

Printed and bound in the United States of America
1 2 3 4 16 15 14 13

For more information contact Nelson Education Ltd., 1120 Birchmount Road, Toronto, Ontario, M1K 5G4. Or you can visit our Internet site at http://www.nelson.com

Library and Archives Canada Cataloguing in Publication Data

Mediascapes: new patterns in Canadian communication / edited by Leslie Regan Shade. — 4th ed.

Includes bibliographical references and index.
ISBN 978-0-17-650864-7

1. Mass media—Canada—Textbooks. I. Shade, Leslie Regan, 1957–

P92.C3M46 2013
302.230971 C2012-906720-2

ISBN-13: 978-0-17-650864-7
ISBN-10: 0-17-650864-3

CONTENTS

PREFACE

Mediascapes was originally conceived and created by the late Paul Attallah and I to serve what we saw as a growing need for an undergraduate textbook in communication studies with a "clearly Canadian" approach. This was over a decade ago, when we were both teaching large undergraduate introductory courses—Paul at Carleton University, and I at the University of Ottawa. Little did I imagine then that I would now be composing the preface to the Fourth Edition in the summer of 2012!

The various editions of *Mediascapes* have always strived to present an overview of historical and contemporary trends in Canadian communication studies, covering a range of topics while focusing on media institutions, media and digital policies, and social and cultural issues. The title *Mediascapes* derived from conversations between the two of us about what word or series of words could best convey a rapidly converging media landscape characterized by the convergence of digital technologies and accelerating global politics surrounding the social, economic, and cultural impacts of these palpable shifts. The brilliant scholar Arjun Appadurai coined the term "mediascapes" in his 1990 article, "Disjuncture and Difference in the Global Cultural Economy."[1] This referred to the ways that information and communication products (films, newspapers, television shows, etc.) were distributed via electronic means to global audiences and to the various representations and images created by these diverse media. Appadurai also devised other dimensions of global cultural flows (ethnoscapes, technoscapes, financescapes, and ideoscapes), some of which are also relevant to the spirit and context of the book. So we could say that while Paul and I loosely borrowed the term "mediascapes" from Appadurai, for us its usage was meant to convey the innumerable and innovative ways that media technologies were becoming embedded in the everyday lives of Canadians. And now, it seems that with this Fourth Edition, the term *Mediascapes* is its own brand!

This Fourth Edition continues to provide a critical look at media institutions and policies in Canada. Communication trends identified in the Third Edition are still evident with this edition: innovations in digital and wireless technologies, leading to cross-platform convergence, consumption, and delivery platforms that are both personalized and mobile; globalization, wherein flows of knowledge, capital, and people challenge national and global regulatory systems and media policies; and changing audience structures, wherein media publics are increasingly multicultural, sophisticated, and able to choose from a palette of media content from mainstream, alternative, and user-generated sources.

NEW TO THIS EDITION

Thanks to the excellent feedback from reviewers of the Third Edition, the Fourth Edition is more streamlined, with five sections comprising four chapters each for a total of 20 chapters. Sections are arranged thematically, and while they are intended to be used in order of appearance, the sections and individual chapters can be used interchangeably.

The first section, "Theoretical and Methodological Approaches to Canadian Communication Studies," provides an intellectual history of communication studies in Canada and distinct approaches to analyzing media texts from critical, feminist, and postcolonialist perspectives. Included are chapters by Sheryl Hamilton (critical perspectives in communication studies), Amin Alhassan (development communication and postcolonialism), and Kim Sawchuk (feminist perspectives) that have been updated from the Third Edition, and a new chapter written by Mark Lipton on media studies pedagogy and literacy.

The second section, "Media Regulation and Policies in Canada" looks at how various media and cultural institutions are regulated. A new chapter by Jeremy Shtern and Sylvia Blake examines the role of the Canadian Radio-television and Telecommunications Commission (CRTC) with reference to recent case studies in broadcasting regulation. Ira Wagman and Ezra Winton's chapter on Canadian cultural policy is updated for this Fourth Edition, as is Russell Johnston's on advertising in Canada. New to this edition is Philip Savage's chapter on audiences, in which he looks at the historical and current conception of the audience in communication studies.

The third section, "Media Institutions" presents an overview of discrete media industries: Zoë Druick updates her chapter on film and mockumentaries, as do Leslie Shade and Michael Lithgow in their discussion of media ownership trends and issues. Josh Greenberg's chapter on public relations (PR) in this edition provides an overview of the industry, its representation in popular culture, and the relationship of PR and journalism. A new addition to this edition is Mia Consalvo's chapter on the video game industry in Canada, represented by the major Canadian technopoles of Vancouver, Toronto, and Montreal.

"Social Media," the fourth section of the book, examines a range of technological and policy issues that were subsumed under the term "new media" in the Third Edition. Updated chapters by Valerie Steeves on privacy and Judith Nicholson on mobiles are complemented by new chapters by Meera Nair examining fair dealing in Canadian copyright legislation and an examination of the commodification and surveillance attributes of social media from Kenneth Werbin.

The final section of *Mediascapes*, "Media Diversity," provides updates by David Skinner on alternative media, First Nations mediascapes by Lorna Roth, and children's media by Natalie Coulter. New to the Fourth Edition is Faiza Hirji's chapter on media portrayals of race and representation in the news media.

Each of the five major parts of the book opens with an introduction that identifies salient themes addressed in the chapters. Each chapter concludes with questions that reinforce the main ideas presented in the chapter and a references list. Some chapters also include end-of-chapter notes.

Acknowledgments

Again, I offer kudos and gratitude to my fantastic colleagues, old and new, who responded enthusiastically to my request for collaboration with (once again!) their exciting and smart chapters.

Special thanks to the always supportive, encouraging, and professional staff at Nelson Education: Laura Macleod, Executive Editor, Higher Education; Hedy Sellers, Production Systems Specialist; Jessica Freedman, freelance developmental editor; and Karen Rolfe, freelance copy editor. Thanks as well to Rajachitra, Project Manager—Books at Cenveo Publisher Services for conscientious and pleasant attention.

MEDIASCAPES ONLINE RESOURCES

http://www.nelson.com/mediascapes4e

The book support website contains student and instructor resources. Students and instructors can link directly to relevant websites associated with each of the book's chapters, and can also access a variety of media profiles and updates, as well as a glossary of media terms.

Leslie Regan Shade
Faculty of Information
University of Toronto
leslie.shade@utoronto.ca

NOTE

1. Appadurai, A. (1990, Spring). Disjuncture and difference in the global cultural economy. *Public Culture* 2(4): 1–11.

INTRODUCTION

INTRODUCTION TO *MEDIASCAPES: NEW PATTERNS IN CANADIAN COMMUNICATION*, FOURTH EDITION

Leslie Regan Shade
University of Toronto

In this introduction to *Mediascapes*, I present an overview of theoretical and methodological approaches to Canadian communication studies. This introduction is certainly not meant to be an exhaustive overview but rather suggestive of the historical influences that have characterized communication studies as a field and the dynamic scholarship that has been generated. I also provide a brief overview of new trends and approaches to communication studies research in Canada.

One can argue that Canadian communication studies is characterized by its critical sensibility, cultural policy focus, and orientation toward social justice. While these are not the sole defining elements, they do resonate throughout most of the chapters in this Fourth Edition.

One key quality of communication studies is its interdisciplinarity; the inherent flexibility of communication studies in linking to and adopting from the fields of sociology, women's studies, international development, political science, history, science and technology studies, cultural studies, information studies, and other humanities and social science disciplines lends itself to innovative and energizing research that draws from diverse methodological perspectives. In turn, communication studies has infiltrated into other disciplines (such as sociology and English), reinvigorating these scholarly domains.

As Table 1 illustrates (Major Canadian Communication Studies Programs), broadly speaking, the field is dominated by critical approaches to communication and culture, with an emphasis on media institutions and policies, media creation and practices, and technology studies. That new departments of communication studies have been flourishing in Canada in the last decade alone, with a particular increase in graduate programs, points to its popularity with students and recognition from academic administrators.

One can further argue that communication studies in Canada is distinguishable from the mainstream of American communication studies in its critical orientation; this claim is addressed in Sheryl Hamilton's first chapter in this book. A critical stance encompasses both political economy and cultural studies—orientations that were dogmatically opposed (most floridly in the United States) during scholarly debates in the 1980s and early 1990s, but which have been increasingly reconciled by recent intellectual détentes (Mosco, 2004; Babe, 2009). This critical sensibility is, as Hamilton observes, taken for granted in Canada; it is, however, still contested and highly politicized in the United States (McChesney, 2008) where administrative research (primarily quantitative and empirical research that seeks to answer clearly identifiable problems, often financed by and for media corporations and state agencies) reigns, such that critical research and scholars are often marginalized in the academy.

Both political economic and cultural studies perspectives characterize critical communication studies. Political economy examines the relationships between media and communication systems and broader social structures within society, interrogating how media systems and policies reinforce, challenge, or influence existing class and social relations. The interrelationships among media ownership, government policies, and support mechanisms that influence media content and behaviour are examined, as are structural and labour practices in the production, distribution, and consumption of media (Mosco, 2009).

Cultural studies analyzes the diverse ways that media construct meaning, how audiences engage with media, and the social role of the state in developing cultural policy. Canadian cultural studies is specifically interested in the relationship of Canadian cultural industries within a globalizing mediascape (Mookerjea, Szeman, & Faurschou, 2009). It is no surprise then that Canadian communication studies arose as a response to various royal commissions studying media—in particular, the role of Canadian media in forging a distinct Canadian identity counter to the powerful influence of American media (Robinson, 2000).

Much research in Canadian communication studies focuses on technology; evident since the early 1990s has been a flurry of research on various forms of digitization, and the social and policy aspects of the internet (Shade, 2007), and now, as Part IV will explore, social media. Querying the impact and imbrication of technology and social change is indeed a distinguishing feature of Canadian communication studies, reflecting a "paradoxical relationship" (Eid & Paré, 2008) regarding the sustainability of Canadian identity and inherent notions of technological sovereignty.

There are two other areas of communication studies research that need to be mentioned, but which *Mediascapes* does not focus on. One strand is interpersonal and organizational communication and some forms of audience research, deriving from the cognitive sciences and closely aligned to psychology (Sévigny and Humphreys, 2007). Focusing more on the perceptual dimensions rather than the societal dimension of communication, a classic example is from the work of Marshall McLuhan (2001), especially in relationship to the perceptual impact of technologies such as television or the telephone. Rhetoric, the use of language for persuasion and public presentation, is another minor strand in Canadian communication studies. Rhetoric is much more important in U.S. universities; the reasons for its marginalization in Canada deserve to be further investigated. Michael Dorland and Maurice Charland (2002) argue that the lack of a Canadian rhetorical tradition is both because of the

TABLE 1 Major Canadian Communication Studies Programs

University	Faculty	Degrees Offered	Home School	Area of Focus
University of **Alberta**	Extension	M.A.C.T. (MA in Communication and Technology)	Communications and Technology http://www.mact.ualberta.ca/	Communications & technology; human communication; organization communication; knowledge management
Brock University	Social Sciences	B.A., M.A. in Popular Culture http://www.brocku.ca/social-sciences/undergraduate-programs/cpcf	Department of Communication, Popular Culture & Film http://www.brocku.ca/social-sciences/graduate-programs/ma-in-popular-culture	Business communication; media & communication studies; film Studies; popular culture
University of **Calgary**	Faculty of Arts	B.A., M.C.S., M.A., Ph.D. (Graduate Program in Communication and Culture)	Communication Studies http://comcul.ucalgary.ca/ http://comcul.ucalgary.ca/graduate	Communication studies; film studies; science technology & society (BA). Social contexts of science and technology; media & film studies; sociocultural approaches to communication; critical health studies; social & global justice (MA & Ph.D.)
University of **Cape Breton**	School of Arts and Social Sciences	B.A., B.A.C.S. (BA in Communication and Community Studies)	Communication Department http://faculty.capebretonu.ca/communication/	Interpersonal communication; public communication; media studies; rhetoric; social change; health communication
Carleton University	Faculty of Public Affairs	B.A., M.A., Ph.D.	School of Journalism and Communication; http://www1.carleton.ca/communication/about/	History and theory; policy and political economy; socio-aesthetics; technology; journalism; politics and persuasion; communication and identity; law; feminism
Concordia University[a]	Arts and Science	B.A., Graduate Diploma, M.A., Ph.D.	Department of Communication Studies http://coms.concordia.ca/	Media practice; research creation; documentary film; game studies; intermedia; sound studies; cultural studies; feminism; rhetoric; critical race studies; policy & political economy; international; critical technology studies; history
University of the **Fraser Valley**	Faculty of Arts	B.A., Media & Communication Studies	Communications http://www.ufv.ca/cmns.htm	Organizational communication; intercultural communication; professional communication

Huntington University		B.A.	Communication Studies http://huntingtonu.ca/programs/communication-studies/	Communication theory; mass media; rhetorical studies; communication policy
Université **Laval**	Lettres	B.A., M.A., Graduate Diploma	Département d'information et de communication http://www.com.ulaval.ca/	Industries culturelles; médias; communication publique; journalisme
McGill University	Arts	B.A., M.A., Ph.D.	Department of Art History & Communication Studies http://www.mcgill.ca/ahcs/	Visual culture; new media; sound studies; feminism; political economy; global media policy; media & public policy; critical technology studies;
McMaster University	Humanities	B.A., M.A. in Communication and New Media; Master of Communication Management	Communication Studies and Multimedia Program http://csmm.mcmaster.ca/	Cultural studies; media, culture & technology; digital culture; multimedia design; professional communication
Université **Montréal**[a]	Arts et Sciences	B.A., B.Sc., M.Sc., D.É.S.S (Diplome d'études superieures spécialisées) en communication organisationnellle, communication politique; Ph.D.	Département de communication http://www.com.umontreal.ca/	Médias de masse/nouvelles technologies; aspects sociaux, culturels, juridiques, et institutionnels des médias; organisationnel; communications politique; féminisme
University of **New Brunswick at Saint John**	Faculty of Arts	B.A.	Information and Communication Studies http://www.unb.ca/saintjohn/arts/depts/socialsciences/ics/index.html	Information and communication technologies and practices; media & culture; information gathering, governance & policy
University of **Ontario Institute of Technology** (UOIT)		B.A.	Communication http://www.socialscienceandhumanities.uoit.ca/programs/bachelor_of_arts_in_communication/index.php	Science and technology; digital media; health science; commerce and marketing

(Continued)

TABLE 1 Continued

University	Faculty	Degrees Offered	Home School	Area of Focus
University of **Ottawa**	Arts	B.A., B.A. Journalism, Public Relations (La Cité Collégiale, Algonquin); M.A., M.C.	Department of Communication http://www.communication.uottawa.ca/eng/	Organizational; media studies; critical technology; cultural studies; health communication
Université **Québec à Montréal**[a]	Faculté de communication	B.A., B.J., M.A., Ph.D.	Département de communication sociale et publique http://www.dcsp.uqam.ca/Profil/professeurs.aspx	Médias; culture; communication de groupe;sociopolitique; psychosociologique; sémiotique; anthropologique; ergonomie cognitive; technologie
Royal Roads University	School of Communication and Culture	B.A. and M.A. in Professional Communications, M.A. in Intercultural and International Communication	Program in Communications http://communication-culture.school.royalroads.ca/studies-communication-and-culture	Applied & professional communication; organizational; public relations; intercultural; international
Ryerson University[b]	Faculty of Communication & Design; RTA School of Media; School of Graduate Studies	B.A., M.A., Ph.D.	B.A., Radio & Television Arts; Master of Media Production; M.A. and Ph.D., Joint Graduate Program in Communication & Culture http://www.ryersonrta.com/ http://comcult.yorku.ca/	Media and culture; broadcasting & interactive media production; television studies; politics and policy; cultural studies
Simon Fraser University	Faculty of Comm-unication, Art & Technology	B.A., M.A., Graduate Diploma; Ph.D.	School of Communication http://www.cmns.sfu.ca/	Media and cultural studies; history & theory of communication; social theory; globalization, social change & social justice; political theory; cultural policy and politics; policy & political economy; book publishing; health communication; feminism; critical technology studies
SFU - **Great Northern Way** Campus		MA in Digital Media	UBC, SFU, Emily Carr University of Art & Design, BCIT, Centre for Digital Media http://mdm.gnwc.ca/program/mdm	Professional program in digital media production

Université de **Sudbury**	Département de communication publique	B.A., Certificate en Journalisme	Études Journalistiques http://usudbury.ca/index.php/en/programs/communication-publique-fr	Journalism
University of **Toronto, Mississauga**	Institute of Communication, Culture, & Information Technology	B.A.	Communication, Culture, and Information Technology Interaction Digital Media (with the iSchool (Faculty of Information)) Professional Writing & Communication http://www.utm.utoronto.ca/iccit/programs/programs-offered/ccit-major	Media studies; knowledge management; surveillance studies; policy issues; digital media studies; professional communication
Trent University		B.A. (Honours, Media Studies) B.A., Ph.D. (Cultural Studies)	Media Studies http://www.trentu.ca/mediastudies/ Cultural Studies http://www.trentu.ca/culturalstudies/	Media studies; popular culture; history theory; documentary practices; new technologies; cultural studies
University of **British Columbia, Okanagan**	Faculty of Creative and Critical Studies	B.A.	Media Studies http://www.ubc.ca/okanagan/critical/options/cultural/mediastudies.html Cultural Studies http://www.ubc.ca/okanagan/critical/options/cultural.html	Visual culture; television studies; popular culture; video game culture; documentary; social justice; intercultural perspectives
Western University (formerly University of Western Ontario)	Faculty of Information & Media Studies	B.A., (Media Information & Technoculture; Media Theory & Production) M.A., Ph.D. (Media Studies); M.A. (Pop, Music & Culture); M.L.I.S. , Ph.D.(Library & Information Science) M.A.J. (Master in Journalism) MHIS, Ph.D. (Master of Health Information Science)	Information & Media Studies http://www.fims.uwo.ca/	Policy & political economy; critical technology studies; feminism; international; library & information studies; popular culture & music; journalism; law; health information

(Continued)

TABLE 1 Continued

University	Faculty	Degrees Offered	Home School	Area of Focus
University of **Waterloo**	Faculty of Arts	B.A., M.A.	Digital Media Studies Specialization (B.A.); Experimental Digital Media (M.A.), English Language and Literature http://english.uwaterloo.ca/Digital_Media_Studies_Specialization.html http://english.uwaterloo.ca/MA-XDM.html	Digital humanities; information design; visual rhetoric; electronic imaging
Wilfrid Laurier University	Arts	B.A., M.A.	Communication Studies http://www.wlu.ca/homepage.php?grp_id=286	Media industries and contemporary culture; theory and criticism; technology & culture; visual communication & culture; feminism
University of **Windsor**	Arts & Social Sciences	B.A., M.A. (Communication & Social Justice)	Department of Communication, Media & Film http://www.uwindsor.ca/communications/	Media practices; theory and criticism; policy and systems; social justice; feminism
York University[b]	Arts	Diploma, B.A., M.A., Ph.D.	Department of Communication Studies Joint Graduate Program in Communication & Culture M.A. and Ph.D., http://www.yorku.ca/laps/comn/ http://comcult.yorku.ca/	Traditional forms of mass communication (print, radio, film, television); new media; policy; political economy; international; critical technology studies; feminism

Note. This is an overview of communication programs; any omissions are unintentional. For further information on communication studies programs see the Academic Programs listing at the Canadian Communication Association: http://www.acc-cca.ca/Default.aspx?pageId=612862

[a]The Ph.D. is offered jointly by Concordia University, Université du Québec à Montréal, and Université de Montréal.

[b]The M.A. and Ph.D. are offered jointly by Ryerson and York.

weakness of Canadian civil society (the sphere of social relations ungoverned by the state) and the disposition of our political institutions. Paul Attallah (2005) observes that "the rhetorical tradition may perhaps be observed in the role that schools of journalism play in Canada," and in departments of linguistics concerned with rhetoric, broadly conceived, and discourse and sociolinguistics phenomena.

In the decade in which *Mediascapes* has been produced, there have been major shifts in the Canadian mediascape, especially around the rapid development and use of communication technologies. As many of the chapters in this Fourth Edition illustrate, digitization and convergence (both technological and across multiple content and distribution mechanisms) have accelerated, such that we now no longer think of "information highways" but rather take for granted an integrated social media landscape, characterized by personalized mobile devices through which we communicate and access diverse content. Media ownership in Canada is even more consolidated than before, and regulatory structures have become more politicized. Along with the ubiquity of social media are a host of policy issues, privacy and copyright in particular, and an attendant desire by Canadians to participate in structures of policymaking and, particularly for many young Canadians, to be involved in digital policy activism.

As the chapters in *Mediascapes* attest, Canadian communication studies takes account of these ever-evolving developments in technology, policy, and ownership structures. It does so with a critical orientation and a sensibility toward the role of communication technologies as an essential and integrated component for active citizenship.

There are several exciting issues and trends in Canadian communication studies to briefly highlight here. One is the integration of science and technology studies (STS) and communication studies. Here, a critical and exploratory lens is placed on media and information technologies, paying particular attention to their historical context, their infrastructures, their material dimensions, and the interplay between their materiality and the creation of symbolic content and meaning (Boczkowski & Lievrouw, 2008). A recent development in STS extends to a move from studies of technological production to actual creation and experimentation of technological materiality through what Matt Ratto (2011) terms "critical making." Ratto explains that "critical making emphasizes the shared acts of making rather than the evocative object. The final prototypes are not intended to be displayed and to speak for themselves. Instead, they are considered a means to an end, and achieve value through the act of shared construction, joint conversation, and reflection" (p. 253).

Related to critical making is an emergent category within the humanities and social sciences: research-creation. Integral to such scholarship is a creative dimension via the production of digital media and arts technologies through innovative aesthetic explorations. As Owen Chapman and Kim Sawchuk describe, "In research-creation approaches, the theoretical, technical, and creative aspects of a research project are pursued in tandem, and quite often, scholarly form and decorum are broached and breeched in the name of experimentation" (2012, p. 6). Institutionally, funding for research-creation has been codified under the three main research funding bodies in Canada and Quebec: the Canada Council (which funds fine arts), the federal Social Science and Humanities Research Council (SSHRC), and Quebec's Fonds Québécois de la recherche sur la Société et la Culture (FQRSC).

Communication studies has also been enriched by a focus on the various labour dimensions of the communication and media industries, and their products, services, production elements, and consumer uses. Research straddles domestic/national perspectives as well as the transnational dimensions of producing media products. For too long, as Catherine McKercher and Vincent Mosco contend (2006), labour has been a conspicuously missing element of political economy. To rectify this gap, McKercher and Mosco have produced and edited a body of scholarship that provides both historical and contemporary studies on trade labour unionization; the challenges of new media workers, often working in contingent and contractual conditions; and the feminization of labour (Mosco, McKercher, & Stevens, 2008).

Aligned with these interrogations into labour is the field of production studies, which investigates how media is produced and how media makers produce culture. Production studies consider the many hierarchical layers of labour in the production of media content—not just an examination of the "top tier" of the directors, producers, and star-studded actors, but the distinct productive labour that goes into producing content—camera operators, script doctors, costume designers, etc. It examines the political economy of the media products and the policies that promote or inhibit the creation of media products (Mayer, Banks, & Thornton, 2009).

As you read through the various chapters in this Fourth Edition of *Mediascapes*, I hope you will discover and share with me the conviction that communication studies in Canada is characterized by a spirit of critical enquiry, creativity, and intrepidness.

REFERENCES

Attallah, P. (2005). Introduction to Part I, Institutional Context. In P. Attallah & L. R. Shade (Eds.), *Mediascapes: New patterns in Canadian communication* (2nd ed.) (pp. 1–8). Toronto: Nelson Thomson.

Babe, R. E. (2009). *Cultural studies and political economy: Toward a new integration.* Lanham, MD: Lexington Books.

Boczkowski, P., & Lievrouw, L. A. (2008). Bridging STS and communication studies: Scholarship on media and information technologies. In E. J. Hackett, O. Amsterdamska, M. Lynch, & J. Wajcman (Eds.), *The handbook of science and technology studies* (3rd ed.) (pp. 951–977). Cambridge, MA: MIT Press.

Chapman, O., & Sawchuk, K. (2012). Research-creation: Intervention, analysis and "family resemblances." *Canadian Journal of Communication 37*, 5–26.

Dorland, M., & Charland, M. (2002). *Law, rhetoric, and irony in the formation of Canadian civil culture*. Toronto: University of Toronto Press.

Eid, M., & Paré, D. (2008). Editorial: Mapping communication and media studies in Canada. *Global Media Journal—Canadian Edition 1*(1), 3–7. Retrieved August 24, 2012, from http://www.gmj.uottawa.ca/0801/inaugural_eid%20and%20pare.pdf

Mayer, V., Banks, M. J., & Thornton, J. (Eds.). (2009). *Production studies: Cultural studies of media industries*. New York: Routledge.

McChesney, R. (2008). *Communication revolution: Critical junctures and the future of media*. New York: The New Press.

McKercher, C., and Mosco, V. (Eds). (2006.) The laboring of communication. Special issue: *Canadian Journal of Communication 31*(3). Retrieved August 24, 2012, from http://www.cjc-online.ca/index.php/journal/article/view/1841/1942

McLuhan, M. (2001). *Understanding media: The extensions of man*. New York: Routledge (orig. published 1964).

Mookerjea, S., Szeman, I., & Faurschou, G. (2009). *Canadian cultural studies*. Durham, NC: Duke University Press.

Mosco, V. (2009). *The political economy of communication* (2nd ed.). Thousand Oaks, CA: Sage Publications.

———. (2004). *The digital sublime*. Cambridge, MA: MIT Press.

Mosco, V., McKercher, C., & Stevens, A. (2008). Convergences: Elements of a feminist political economy of labor and communication. In K. Sarikakis & L.R. Shade (Eds.). *Feminist interventions in international communication: Minding the gap* (pp. 207–240). Lanham, MD: Lexington Books.

Ratto, M. (2011) Critical making: Conceptual and material studies in technology and social life. *The Information Society* 27(4), 252–260.

Robinson, G. J. (2000). Remembering our past: Reconstructing the field of Canadian communication studies. *Canadian Journal of Communication 25*(1). Retrieved August 24, 2012 from http://www.cjc-online.ca/index.php/journal/article/view/1145/1064

Sévigny, A., & Humphreys, K. R. (2007). Cognitive science and the future of communication studies in Canada. In J. Greenberg & C. Elliott (Eds.), *Communication in question: Competing perspectives on controversial issues in communication studies* (pp. 344–351). Toronto: Nelson Higher Education.

Shade, L. R. (2007). Focus on the field: A look at the historiography and role of media in communication studies. In J. Greenberg & C. Elliott (Eds.), *Communications in question: Canadian perspectives on controversial issues in communication studies* (pp. 334–343). Toronto: Thomson Nelson.

PART I
Theoretical and Methodological Approaches to Canadian Communication Studies

Introduction

Leslie Regan Shade
University of Toronto

This first section of *Mediascapes* consists of four chapters that provide an overview of theoretical and methodological approaches to Canadian communication studies. The intention is to provide students with a panoramic overview of the intellectual origins of communication studies, a sense of how and why Canadian communication studies is distinct from communication studies in the United States, and a "tool-kit" of concepts, frames, and approaches to studying mediascapes. These four chapters interrogate the dimensions of critical communication research (Hamilton), approaches to critical engagement with media and elements of media literacy (Lipton), the development of postcolonialist theories in development and international communication (Alhassan), and feminist approaches to communication and media studies (Sawchuk).

In her chapter, Sheryl Hamilton provides an historical and contemporary look at the development of communication studies as an intellectual discipline in North America. She argues that while it is difficult to map the field of Canadian communication studies, one taken-for-granted assumption from some Canadian scholars is their implicit stance that Canadian research is "critical," referring to a more politicized attitude toward the subject matter of the research and its use for social change. But, as Hamilton cautions, by relying on geography and national identity to harness this critical sensibility, Canadian scholars may be limiting their critical imagination. Instead, she urges scholars to take more risks: methodologically, via newer incursions into interdisciplinarity, by a deeper understanding of historical influences, and through more self-reflexivity.

Mark Lipton's chapter investigates what it means to "do" media studies, and the fusion of pedagogy and practice for students. He asks us to think carefully about how our personal interests and social background influence our critical engagement with diverse texts and different modes when we take a stance on a media issue, policy, or piece of entertainment or news content. He provides an overview of the origins of media literacy (Canada—particularly Ontario—has been an innovator in promoting media literacy in schools) and how its approaches have been necessarily transformed in the transition from a more static broadcasting model to participatory and asynchronous digital modes of communication. He also sketches out the intellectual antecedents of contemporary media studies and how it has been influenced by approaches from early cultural studies scholarship in Britain. Finally, he provides some examples of thinking critically about media in our everyday lives, emphasizing that the mundane, or banal, can be fodder for further fertile interrogations.

Critical communication studies have been influenced by postcolonial thought and feminist media studies, the topic of the next two chapters in this section. Amin Alhassan provides an historical overview of development communication in the 1960s and its role in furthering Western-style modernization in the formerly colonized countries in the Global South. The role of communication technologies (from radio to the internet) in fostering this development, and the often technologically determinist assumptions by government policymakers and NGO organizations, is highlighted. From social marketing precepts in the 1970s to programs promoting information and communication technologies for development in the new millennium, development communication has been contentious. Critical perspectives on development communication have offered nuanced critiques of cultural and media imperialism, highlighting the imbalance of North–South information flows, political economic assessments of the development industry, and the role of the major supranational organizations, such as the United Nations family, as well as incorporating participatory approaches, involving projects funded by development organizations with the active research involvement of the citizens whom the research is meant to impact. Alhassan highlights the Fogo Island process in the 1960s as emblematic of the use of participatory media to effectuate change; later attempts by Canadian development organizations such as the Canadian International Development Agency (CIDA) and the International Development Research Centre (IDRC) in the area of information and communication technologies for development have been internationally successful but often tend to replicate earlier administrative interventions. In his conclusion, Alhassan challenges us to question who development *really* benefits.

The F word. We all know what that refers to. So do my students. In my undergraduate and graduate teaching at two Canadian universities over the last decade and a half, feminist perspectives and scholarship are readily integrated into a variety of courses I teach, broadly centred on media institutions and communication policy. That feminist communication studies research is now, more than ever, a focus of dedicated and regular academic journals, integrated into more course syllabi, and central to much graduate student research is heartening. Kim Sawchuk provides a pioneering overview of feminist media studies in Canada, detailing its lively attention to issues of power, race, class, social justice, sexuality, and sexualities, but also questions why feminism is still, in 2013, a contested terrain inside and outside the university. Detailing feminist paradigms; the interrelationships between gender, sex, and sexuality; how feminism is framed in the media; and feminist media scholarship, Sawchuk challenges us to continue to "do feminism" in our academic and everyday lives.

1

CONSIDERING CRITICAL COMMUNICATION STUDIES IN CANADA

Sheryl N. Hamilton[1]
Carleton University

On his return to Simon Fraser University in the mid-1970s, **communication** scholar Dallas Smythe, disheartened by his experience in communication studies in the United States, called for Canadian communication thought to distinguish itself from American approaches through its *critical* stance. He clearly hoped that Canadian communication research would not reproduce what he considered to be the errors of much American scholarship in its turn to *administrative* research. This happened in the time period when many communication studies programs were being established in the Canadian university system and Smythe's appeal seemingly resonated. The notion of defining Canadian communication studies through its criticalness took hold. This chapter considers this inherited distinction between critical and administrative approaches to communication studies, suggests a set of criteria by which to understand critical research in general, and then examines how "critical" has served as an uninterrogated trope in Canadian communication studies, in particular. Ultimately the chapter suggests that in order to disrupt its smug complacency and *be* critical, Canadian communication studies needs to stimulate its critical imagination through its embrace of a broader range of theoretical approaches, self-reflexivity, and historical understanding.

CRITICAL VERSUS ADMINISTRATIVE: THREE FRAMING EVENTS

Any attempt to define "critical" inherits the troubled distinction between administrative and critical communication research from the United States. Despite its inaccuracy and simplicity, "critical versus administrative" continues to be one of the central frames through which scholars have aligned, organizations have developed, and the history of the field is taught and understood.

I suggest that three American communications events established the distinction between critical and administrative as a founding narrative. The *first* is Paul Lazarsfeld's 1941 article, "Remarks on Administrative and Critical Communication Research," which names the distinction and maps its parameters. The second is

Todd Gitlin's scathing critique of the dominance of administrative research in the American study of media and communication in his 1978 watershed article, "Media Sociology: The Dominant Paradigm." It politicizes the distinction between administrative and critical and poses a serious challenge to the administrative approach. The third formative event is the special issue of the *Journal of Communication*, published in 1983, intended to be an appraisal of the state of the field, but that exposes significant tensions, reveals key gaps, and, most importantly for our purposes, generates the frames in which subsequent debate would take place. From this third event, we can more richly map the characteristics of a critical approach, or at least its aspirations.

Paul Lazarsfeld is held to be one of the founding fathers of communication studies. With his colleagues, he pursued quantitative research using large-scale surveys and statistical analysis to explore the effects of media on people's behaviour. The research was funded through alliances between philanthropic foundations, universities, and interested corporations with the ultimate goal of making media more effective.

In the late 1930s, this approach was challenged by a group of émigré Jewish scholars who fled Nazi Germany to settle in the United States and came to be known as the **Frankfurt School.** Trained in European schools of thought, heavily influenced by Marxism, and deeply concerned about what they saw as the industrialization of culture, scholars such as Max Horkheimer, Theodor Adorno, and Herbert Marcuse both enriched, and came into conflict with, the approach of Lazarsfeld and his colleagues.

This conflict, and his desire to resolve it, motivated Lazarsfeld to write his 1941 article. He could not have realized that he would make a distinction about types of communication research that would organize professional and intellectual practice in the field for at least the next 50 years. In grappling with the clash of approaches, he labels his own *administrative* and the Frankfurt School's *critical.*

Administrative research, he suggests, is conducted in the service of a public or private administrative agency (Lazarsfeld, 1941, p. 8). Viewing media as useful tools, administrative researchers pose questions such as "Who are the people exposed to the different media? What are their specific preferences? What are the effects of different **methods** of presentation?" (Lazarsfeld, 1941, p. 3). Lazarsfeld (1941) recognizes the limitations of administrative research approaches, noting that they may not take full account of history and that "they solve little problems, generally of a basic character, when the same methods could be used to improve the life of the community if only they were applied to forward-looking projects related to the pressing economic and social problems of our time" (p. 8).

In contrast, **critical research** assumes that "prior and in addition to whatever special purpose is to be served, the general role of our media of communication in the present social system should be studied" (Lazarsfeld, 1941, p. 9). It therefore differs from administrative work in two respects: "it develops a theory of the prevailing social trends in our times, general trends which yet require consideration in any concrete research problem; and it seems to imply ideas of basic human values according to which all actual or desired effects should be appraised" (Lazarsfeld, 1941, p. 9). Thus, critical research begins with social theory, contains normative values, and places communication in the larger social context. Its research questions include "How are these media organized and controlled? How, in their institutional set-up, is the trend toward centralization, standardization and promotional pressure expressed? In what form, however disguised, are they threatening human values?" (Lazarsfeld, 1941, p. 10).

Lazarsfeld is suggesting that the purpose and methodologies of the research, the moral commitment of the scholar, the relationship between theory and empirical reality, and the place of values in research are crucial lines of distinction between critical and administrative research. In his view, critical research assumes the task of revealing how media function in order to reproduce dominant **ideology** in their given social context. Further, he recognizes that such an approach is essentially theoretical because it makes certain assumptions (e.g., about the power of media, the susceptibility of audiences, the nature of the media–audience contact) that are not always empirically verifiable. Finally, it is this very embrace of theory without concern as to its "prove-ability" that Lazarsfeld (1941) also sees as the primary weakness of critical approaches (pp. 12–13).

While both research traditions were present in the United States, it was the administrative orientation that seemed to resonate most with the times, characterized in part by the rise of commercial television, the support of big-money research in the social sciences, and a general postwar optimism in American thought and culture. This dominance of a pluralist, administrative outlook is what media sociologist, Todd Gitlin, coined the "dominant paradigm" in 1978—the *second* event in the distinction between critical and administrative communication research. Gitlin was concerned primarily with the increasing failure of media to engage effectively with politics and with the persistent failure of what he calls "media sociology" to engage with the power implications of the contemporary media environment.

He faults the majority of research for a focus on not only the effects of media, but also for defining effects so narrowly as to be incapable of supporting an understanding of the social impacts of media. He argues methodology has trumped theory, and that administrative research not only asks the wrong questions, but also has the even more problematic consequence of diverting attention from "larger social meanings of mass media production" (Gitlin, 1978, p. 206). He adds, "... by taking for granted the existing institutional order, the field has also been able to skirt the substantive questions of valuation. ... But of course in failing to ask such questions, it has made itself useful to the networks, to the market research firms, to the political candidates" (ibid.). He feels administrative research poses its questions from the perspective of the stakeholders and powerbrokers, thus serving a legitimating function for capitalist relations.

He claims that a paradigm is a "tendency of thought" recognized by its area of investigation, its methodology, and its results. However, he notes that a paradigm is generated not only by and through its producers but also by its consumers—"the profession that accords it standing as a primary outlook" (Gitlin, 1978, p. 208). In an attempt to illuminate the shortcomings of this paradigm to the profession of communication researchers who accord it that standing, he then systematically dismantles the claims of *The People's Choice* (1948) and *Personal Influence* (1955), as well as challenging the effects of the charismatic figure of Paul Lazarsfeld, himself, as an "institution man."

Interestingly, while Gitlin's is a damning critique, his image of the critical approach is only alluded to, as a more critical other, posing questions of ownership, influence, power, and politics. It is in the *third* structuring event of the administrative versus critical origin story that we get more specific detail on what terrain is staked by critical communication scholars in the 1980s.

In the 1983 special issue of the *Journal of Communication*, titled *Ferment in the Field*, editor George Gerbner gathered 35 original articles from 41 international scholars from both traditions to reflect on the distinction that Lazarsfeld had advanced 42 years earlier. As Gerbner (1983a) wrote in his introduction, "This volume represents the first time that so many internationally prominent scholars have examined and commented upon communications as a field of study in one publication" (p. 4). It catalyzed deliberations on critical approaches in the field more broadly (see, for example, the special issue of the *Canadian Journal of Communication* in 1985 that focused on teaching critical communication studies or the special issue on critical communication research of *Media, Culture and Society* in 1984).

Ferment in the Field was a revealing expression of tensions within the field of communication studies at the time. Ongoing tensions between critical and administrative approaches (identified by Gitlin) were spurred on by the translation of the work of European Marxist thinkers such as Antonio Gramsci and Louis Althusser, the development of women's studies and cultural studies programs, and the radical shifts in the social, economic, and cultural context of mass media and their study in the post–World War II period.

The authors vociferously debate the validity of the administrative and critical approaches, with almost no one stopping to interrogate the starting premise of the distinction. In 2009 Todd Gitlin, Jostein Gripsrud, and Michael Schudson were invited to reflect on the impact of *Ferment in the Field* 26 years after its publication. Gitlin is cynical, but Schudson suggests that "it became a kind of milestone, a marking point, a points [sic] of reference of some kind ..." (Sjovaag and Hallvard, 2009, p. 132). I would argue, more specifically, that it served then as an articulation of the nature of the challenge to the dominant paradigm, but more importantly to us now, is a catalogue of the characteristics of an archetypical understanding of critical communication studies in North America—an archetype to which both American and Canadian scholars have been talking back ever since.

DEFINING CRITICAL COMMUNICATION STUDIES

The attributes mapped by the scholars in *Ferment in the Field* in the early 1980s have been echoed and developed in subsequent work continuing in the critical tradition across a wide range of scholarly trajectories. In recent years, too often critical communication research has been conflated with Marxist-influenced theory, but no one school of thought can claim critical research as its own. Critical communication studies has been shaped by political economy, but also by cultural studies, Marxist sociology, **semiotic analysis,** institution studies, dependency theory, international communications, and in more recent years, by feminist and sexuality studies, post-colonial thought, critical race theory, poststructuralism, diaspora studies, and governmentality studies, among others. This section examines the shared characteristics of critical communication studies, shaped by these approaches, in the following categories: research problem, social power, methodology, researcher orientation, theoretical influences, and knowledge claims.

Research Problem

How does critical communication studies define its research problem? Critical communication scholars have generally focused on the relations between communication and social power. This focus has been variously framed as a question of (1) social control and power (Halloran, 1983); (2) concern with structures of power (Gerbner, 1983b); or (3) an investigation into domination, contradiction, and struggle (Mosco, 1983). The central unit of knowledge is society rather than the individual, and communication practices are considered within their various social contexts.

Simply stated, critical communication research takes on the "big issues." As Rogers (1982) notes, "Critical scholars believe that a theory of communication is impossible without a theory of society, so their scope of analysis is much wider than that of empirical scholars" (p. 125). Therefore, critical researchers ask questions such as, Who controls the media? How can media be used by a greater diversity of people? How do we negotiate our roles within and between social groups through practices of communication? How do communication structures work with other social, economic, and cultural structures to order society?

Generally, this focus has meant a shift in emphasis from the effects of media on individuals to analyses that are more historically grounded and socially situated. Critical communication research has concentrated on ownership and control of media systems, the linking of media structures to other larger social structures, and analyses of the institutional aspects of communication. When considering individuals, critical scholars view them as members of groups, or as subjects, navigating positions shaped in part by hierarchically organized social power arrangements.

Social Power

Critical researchers ask the questions they do because they hold a particular understanding of the relationship between communication and power. Bailie (1997) suggests that "critical communication scholarship is rooted in the assumption that social institutions and human relations are relations of history, power and struggle" (p. 33). Critical scholars therefore view social power as unequally distributed and generally subscribe to a conflict-based model of social relations that focuses on struggle and difference rather than on agreement and consensus. Indeed, critical communication studies rejects the linear model of causality at work in administrative research and replaces it with more complex forms of social determination. Consequently, administrative research is content to study, for example, the impact that radio advertising might have on listeners. Critical research, in contrast, wants to investigate the historical origin of radio advertising, the type of interest that tends to use radio advertising, the ways in which the advertising binds listeners to the capitalist system, and so on. It is precisely because the study of complex forms of social determination can lead in so many directions that distinctions among critical scholars have emerged. However, despite their differences, all critical thinkers share an opposition to the *liberal pluralist* notion of social power, which sees power as neutral and potentially equally shared.

While advancing a more diverse and less idealistic understanding of social power and how it intersects with communication structures and practices, in the 1980s not all instances of power seemed to be on the research agenda. For example, feminist scholars working within the critical tradition suggested at the time, "if the question of social and economic power is central to any critical perspective ... then the failure of such work to come to terms with sex-based power differentials and their role in cultural production and reproduction is symptomatic of serious flaws in our theoretical traditions" (Saunders, 1985, p. 35). Thus there were power differentials within the critical communication studies field itself that needed to be recognized and addressed.

And this continued. Later in the 1980s and into the early 1990s, the influence of *poststructuralist* and *postmodernist* theory would produce a nasty and divisive split within critical communication scholarship between American cultural studies and political economy, culminating in the mud-slinging special issue of *Critical Studies in Mass Communication* in 1995, pitting advocates of the two approaches against each other. These ongoing internal divisions illustrate two key points. First, that the critical versus administrative distinction obscures, and may even prevent, a more sustained inquiry into the ways in which critical research is implicated in certain formations of power. And second, the ways in which assumptions about how social power operates shape conclusions about what types of actions to take, what types of outcomes are appropriate, how power should be wielded, and who should wield it.

Methodology and Methods

Much of the debate between the critical and administrative approaches played itself out in disputes over **methodology**, particularly in the 1980s and into the 1990s. In fact, the administrative approach is sometimes called the **empirical** approach because it studies immediately observable phenomena using "scientific" methods. In contrast, critical research is often seen as methodologically unrigorous because it rejects empirical approaches to knowledge and is not concerned with demonstrating its theoretical claims through scientifically verifiable data.

Critical researchers have pointed out, however, that critical research frequently uses empirical methods (Mosco, 1983; Habermas, 2006). As well, a number of scholars have observed that critical research is compatible with empirical methods (Allen, 1999; Elasmar, 1999; Gerbner, 1964; Halloran, 1983; Rogers, 1982). Sterne (2005) demonstrates that critical research legend, C. Wright Mills, in fact, built his critical inquiry upon a foundation of administrative research conducted by others, further illustrating some of the inaccuracies, and problematic effects, of the distinction between administrative and critical research.

The framing of the debate between critical and administrative approaches as between qualitative and quantitative research methods or between science and the humanities, has resulted in three unproductive lines of discussion. First, it has led to claims of moral superiority by both sides of the debate. For critical scholars, the moral superiority derives from a sense of the importance of the work being done; according to Halloran (1983), "we have to accept that it is more important to be important than to be impeccable" (p. 278). For administrative scholars, claims to moral superiority are grounded in science and "pure" knowledge untainted by ideology.

The second unproductive debate results from the fact that no distinction is being made between *empirical* and ***positivist***. This can result, and some argue has resulted, in an avoidance of empirical research by critical communication scholars (for fear of reproducing administrative work) and a similar and related avoidance of policy work (Abramson, et al., 2008). Empirical methods seek to describe, through the application of established procedures, an aspect of material reality; positivist methods emerge out of a belief that objective truth can be rendered through the **scientific method.** Although the methods employed by critical researchers can certainly produce empirical results, critical researchers make no claim to produce positivist (i.e., objective) results. On the contrary, they would argue that the claim to objectivity or **value neutrality** is itself a value-laden claim.

Third, debates about methodology have led to attempts to find a "middle ground," a strategy that often favours the empirical perspective. This approach fails because the debate has never really been about methodology; everyone can use a range of methods. The debate has really been about differing ontologies and epistemologies—what does the world consist of and how can we know it? Fundamentally conflicting ontologies and epistemologies cannot be brought together onto a middle ground.

This reduction of more important issues to disputes about methodology has limited the scope of critical communication research. In rejecting positivism, too often critical researchers do not reflect adequately on methodological rigour. However, the solution is not to be found in a turn to positivist or quantitative methods, but rather in a more sustained exploration of the relationship between theory and our ability to describe lived reality and human experience.

Researcher Orientation

The first three tenets of critical research are (1) the appropriate object of study is the relationship between communication and power; (2) social power is unequally distributed; and (3) questions of theory supercede questions of methods. Following from these is the fourth assumption advanced by critical researchers, which addresses the relationship between the researcher and who or what is being researched. It describes the orientation of the researcher to her or his work. It asks what it means to do ideological research. Interestingly, both proponents and critics of the critical approach to communication research have labelled critical approaches "ideological." For critics, this label means that critical research is unscientific, polemical, and simply reflective of the beliefs of the researcher.

For its proponents, however, the term *ideological* is a way to show that research not only analyzes ideology as an object (i.e., it demonstrates the symbolic traces of social power) (Sholle, 1988) but also is political in itself because it is committed to the disruption of the status quo (Blumler, 1983; Mosco, 1983, 1996; Smythe and Van Dinh, 1983; Straw, 1985). Both sides of the debate therefore agree that critical communication research is not value free; it is guided by its values in its selection and treatment of research questions. Critical researchers feel that recognizing and incorporating values is an inevitable part—and, indeed, a positive aspect—of doing research. Administrative scholars, on the other hand, would argue that values corrupt the objectivity of research and need to be controlled. A critical approach counters that even if the administrative school of thought does not acknowledge its values (objectivity, truth, science, utility, pluralism), those values are still reflected in the choice of research questions and methods.

While critical scholars have been willing to acknowledge the existence of values in their research, they have become increasingly circumspect about what those values are. It is often assumed that critical researchers are on the "left" in political terms, but this orientation is not often enough defined. Scholars such as Hanno Hardt (in McLuskie et al., 2004) and Eileen Meehan (2004) encourage critical scholars to reflect upon what a critical communications practice might mean in the contemporary political, economic and institutional climate of media industries, politics, and universities.

Theoretical Influences

A *fifth* basis on which to understand critical communication research is to ask what are its theoretical influences. The theoretical legacies of critical communication research that are acknowledged within the field include European critical theory, American pragmatism and the **Chicago School** of symbolic interactionism, and Marxist theory.

One of the distinguishing aspects of critical approaches is their recognition of the influence of European critical theory—specifically, the Frankfurt School. European critical theory includes the work of first-generation Frankfurt School members such as Theodor Adorno, Max Horkheimer, and Herbert Marcuse, as well as second-generation thinkers such as Jürgen Habermas. The influence of European critical theory has been to frame critical communication research in relation to larger critiques of modernism, to explore the specificity of commodity culture, and to offer a stinging critique of the industrialization of the cultural domain. It also advocates for greater democratization of the means of communication and their separation from the mode of industrial production.

The theoretical influence of American pragmatism and Chicago School symbolic interactionism comes from the work of John Dewey, Kenneth Burke, George Herbert Mead, and Herbert Blumer. Emerging from this work is a concern with the practice of communication in relation to progressive social change and a shift from one-way models of communication to interactive models of meaning making and identity formation.

The third major theoretical influence on critical communications is Marxist theory. This can be mapped through the shifting theorization of ideology and culture from more simple deterministic models ascribed to Marx to approaches from Althusser and Gramsci. The influence of Marxist thought is also strongly apparent in the political economy stream of critical communication thought. As a result, critical communication attaches great importance to ideology, to debates about questions of determination with the related question of where to locate culture, and to a shared recognition that one cannot consider communication messages and practices outside their socioeconomic contexts.

All three theoretical influences have enriched the field of communication studies, but critical communication scholars have been slower to recognize the value of other critical approaches not growing directly out of class-based analysis. For example, feminism, queer theory, and postcolonialism have produced deeply interesting critical theory that could enrich the field of critical communication studies as a whole. While this work is accepted within the field, its applicability has tended to be seen as specific to issues of gender, sexuality, race, and ethnicity, as opposed to offering rich theoretical resources for critical communication studies more broadly. Recently Kent A. Ono made an impassioned appeal for not limiting the notion of critical to work shaped by Continental philosophy. He argued instead for a definition that "addresses power as a constitutive dimension of public life" (Ono, 2011, p. 94). He encouraged communication studies to take advantage of the "various and diverse critical positions as potential starting points for theorization" (ibid.), rather than beginning only from class-based and antifascist positions.[2] He would include in this feminist, queer, third world (including third cinema), race and ethnicity, transnational, postcolonial, and diaspora studies (ibid.). While some may feel this too greatly diffuses the "critical project," I would argue that these approaches are linked in their understanding of the significance and diversity of modes of social power as a starting place for theory and research, as well as in their commitment to social transformation.

Knowledge Claims

The *sixth* and final shared assumption of critical research answers the question: what kinds of knowledge claims can and do critical communication researchers make? Critical communication seeks both to engage critically with existing social relations and to change those relations. Critical communication scholars work to produce "research that both advances criticism of the existing world system and promotes the 'critical state' that would transform it" (Mosco, 1983, pp. 245–246). Research should therefore offer resources to effect positive social change (Halloran, 1983).

Whether seen as creating conditions for free (or freer) communication, social democracy, or unfettered expressions of self, critical research sets as one of its central objectives the production of intellectual and political resources for social transformation and individual and collective emancipation (Bailie, 1997; Gerbner, 1964; Haight, 1983; Halloran, 1983; Jansen, 1983; Splichal, 2008). Ramsey (2011) goes so far as to posit being critical as almost utopian, suggesting "... being critical shall have to articulate the conditions for the possibility of taking a step beyond from out of our having been" (Ramsey, 2011, p. 89). Consequently, not only must communication be thought about more critically, but so too must the place of the researcher and her or his work in society. It is in this way that critical research understands itself as political.

For example, Splichal (2008) describes critical communication research as "emancipatory." He argues, "it is inseparably connected to politics ... because it focused on contradictions and conflicts in contemporary societies, which are often rooted in the alienating conditions of individuals and social groups" (p. 20). Too often, however, critical scholars assume the progressive and political nature of critical communication studies, rather than arguing, investigating, or labouring over it (see Straw, 1985 for an early critique of this tendency).

Thus, from the encounter between the critical and administrative research traditions, a set of shared ontological and epistemological assumptions emerges through which we can begin to see what a critical approach to communication studies might look like. Critical communication studies (1) takes as its primary question the relationship between communication and social power; (2) understands social power as a dynamic structuring force and recognizes that power is unequally distributed within society; (3) privileges theory over method and is more concerned with producing social critique than objective knowledge; (4) embraces the role that values play in producing knowledge; (5) has its theoretical roots in American and European radical thought but can access a much wider range of critical theorizing; and (6) seeks to produce knowledge that will effect positive social change.

Interestingly, American communications scholarship since *Ferment in the Field* seems to have an uneasy relationship with the notion of critical. Since 1983, there has been regular and frequent intellectual hand wringing as American communication studies has tried to sort out what doing critical communication research might (or should) mean. To note merely a few examples, the *Journal of Communication* dedicated another special issue to "The Future of the Field—Between Fragmentation and Cohesion" in 1993 featuring a section titled "Rethinking the Critical Tradition." There has been a revival of the Frankfurt School thinkers, particularly Adorno (see Kalyvas, 2004). A Festschrift[3] in honour of Hanno Hardt organized in 2003 took up the question of what is critical communication studies in "A Conversation with Hanno Hardt on the Future of Critical Communication Studies" (see McLuskie et al., 2004). The discussion persists in a 2011 forum "Being Critical" in the journal *Communication & Critical/Cultural Studies*. And a 2011 edited collection, *A Moment of Danger: Critical Studies in the History of U.S. Communication Since World War II* offers an "alternative" history of communication research in the United States, focusing on critical interventions as a corrective to dominant narratives (Peck and Stole, 2011).

CRITICAL COMMUNICATION STUDIES IN CANADA

So where does Canada fit into this ongoing American meta-narrative? Because of its **marginality** to American communication scholarship, its particular history of institutionalization, and its intellectual history, Canadian communication studies sees itself as always already critical. "Critical" functions as an underlying and almost always uninvestigated *assumption* in Canadian communication studies. In Canada, the question has not been whether or not Canadian communication studies is critical, but rather in what ways communication studies in Canada is distinctly Canadian.

The Ghost of Innis: Critical-Ness Assumed

Writing that "Canada has a rich heritage of communication thought" (p. 19), Robert Babe (2000a) traces the foundations of Canadian communication thought through the work of ten scholars: Graham Spry, Harold Innis, John Grierson, Dallas Smythe, C.B. Macpherson, Irene Spry, George Grant, Gertrude J. Robinson, Northrop Frye, and Marshall McLuhan. At its very foundations, he states, Canadian communication thought is **dialectical**, holistic, ontological, oriented to political economy, and concerned with mediation. Most significantly for our purposes, he argues it is critical.

Babe sees Canadian communication thought as operating within the critical tradition, in opposition to administrative or pluralist approaches. By critical research he means "evaluative research presuming enduring criteria for judging policies, activities, events, human relations, institutions, and so forth, and as well enduring goals towards which we should strive" (Babe, 2000a, p. 16). It is this ability to evaluate critically that marks Canadian scholars as critical in the American sense of the term. Indeed, there is general agreement that, in its historical origins, Canadian communication thought, and particularly the work of Innis, is critical (Acland & Buxton,

1999; Carey, 1975, 1983; Grosswiler, 1996; Hardt, 1992; Kroker, 1984; Robinson & Theall, 1975).

What has been the legacy of these foundational thinkers in terms of understanding what critical communication studies means in Canada? According to the few scholars considering it, the question, like its American counterpart, takes as its central concern larger issues about the ways in which power and communication intersect. Power in the Canadian context is understood with an attention to history and the interplay of historical forces (Kroker, 1984; Theall, 1975; Tremblay, 1981). It shares assumptions with other critical communication approaches about the nonpluralist nature of social power, but theorizes that power in a specifically dialectical model (Babe, 2000a; Kroker, 1984; Theall, 1975). In other words, history is produced through the encounter of contradictory social forces. Furthermore, the historical legacy of foundational communication thought has offered some significant attempts to think through the place of technologies of communication (rather than only mass media) in processes of modernization (Carey, 1983; Kroker, 1984). Finally, it has placed at the forefront values having to do with human emancipation and exploring the conditions of a better life (Babe, 2000a; Kroker, 1984).

Interestingly, a majority of the thinkers identified as foundational were developing their communication ideas before the **institutionalization** of the field of communication studies in Canada. While most observers would agree that these were critical thinkers who contributed to the foundation of Canadian communication thought, it is less clear how their ideas have played out in communication studies as a discipline in Canada since the 1960s. According to Robinson (2000), "While the general outlines of Innis' and McLuhan's work are known, whether they have inspired a unique kind of Canadian scholarship is much more difficult to determine" (p. 122).

HURDLES TO UNDERSTANDING THE FIELD

Part of the difficulty in knowing if or how Canadian communication studies is critical is knowing the field at all. Any appraisal of Canadian communication scholarship as a field of study or discipline is hindered by the striking lack of any well-detailed maps of its emergence and development. When and how did communication studies become institutionalized within Canadian universities? When were the first professional associations established and with what effect? What journals serve this academic community? How can one characterize the work done in the field? Can we identify generational patterns? Who has been theorizing since McLuhan, Innis, et al.?

The *first* hurdle in answering these questions is the diffuse nature of Canadian communication scholarship. In the early 1980s, Salter (1981) noted that much work in communication studies was appearing in the journals of other disciplines or was being published in communication journals in the United States or Europe. More than three decades later, Salter's claim remains true. In 2000, the then editor of the *CJC* expressed regret that Canadians cannot look to the ***Canadian Journal of Communication*** (Canada's only English-language academic journal devoted to communication) to map the history, development, and trends of communication studies in Canada (Lorimer, 2000a). Canadian communication scholars continue to publish in international journals or in contexts outside the discipline altogether, and many do not identify strongly with Canadian communication studies.

The *second* hurdle in mapping the field is the lack of a comprehensive and accepted historical account of its development. The special issue of *CJC* published in 2000 was intended to do this but does not. One might also look to undergraduate communication textbooks for such an overarching narrative. Yet a review of current undergraduate texts in use in Canada over the last decade comes up empty.

Without a recorded history, myths of origin are necessarily weak. Perhaps it has been this lack of well-established, historical narratives that has structured the attempts to define Canadian communication studies into its predictable identity crisis: Is Canadian communication uniquely Canadian? It is through this issue that the critical elements of Canadian communication studies have been negotiated, articulated, and ultimately constrained.

Uniquely Canadian

The debate about Canadian national identity, which is at the heart of so much substantive Canadian communication research and policy, also plays itself out in the consideration of the discipline as a whole. For example, a key goal of Babe's (2000a) book is "to discern whether there exists a mode of communication inquiry that might be termed 'quintessentially Canadian'" (p. 4). He is not alone in this pursuit. Kroker (1984) attempts to map a distinctly "Canadian mind," while Robinson and Theall (1975) suggest that Canada can claim a "unique communications philosophy" (p. 1).

Claims to a specific Canadian approach to communication studies rest on two central arguments. *First*, Canadian communication studies is unique because it is critical. Critical functions as a largely undefined marker of distinction from the American administrative approach. It also casts Canadian communication studies research as morally superior to its American counterpart. *Second*, Canadian communication studies is framed as unique because of its distinctive epistemological position—one of in-betweenness or marginality.

Babe (2000a) argues that it is the values of Canadian scholarship that make it critical: "the fact that most of these theorists are able to contemplate a superior human nature, that is, to compare things as they should be with things as they are, qualifies them as critical theorists in the tradition acknowledged by Lazarsfeld" (p. 316). He recognizes the role of religion in foundational Canadian communication thought and suggests that it may be responsible for the "high moral standard" of these thinkers (Babe, 2000a, p. 308). The overtones of moral superiority or a location outside ideology are also present in Kroker's (1984) claims that "the Canadian discipline ... represents a courageous, and creative struggle to think outside of and against the closed horizons of technological society" (p. 13).

These claims abound in Canadian communication conferences, analyses, and classrooms. The chain of reasoning proceeds as follows. Canadian communication thought is unique (i.e., non-American) because it is critical. It is critical now (in the present) because it was critical then (when Innis was writing). And because it is critical, ultimately it is better than communication studies in the United States.

Unfortunately, these assumptions have a number of negative consequences for knowledge. First, there is a lack of considered attention to what critical might mean now, as opposed to when Innis was writing. Second, it sets as the standard the distinction between critical and administrative research articulated by Lazarsfeld, rather than the complex history of debates within American, European, and Canadian communication studies. Therefore, it does not engage with a more sophisticated understanding of what critical communication studies might be. Finally, it reduces the important question of what critical might mean to the less interesting question of how we are different from our American counterparts.

Canadian communication studies research is assumed to be *already* within a critical paradigm, and that paradigm is often conflated with political economy. Unfortunately, such assumptions do not do justice to the diversity of work being produced under the name "critical," including policy studies, institutional analyses, feminist research, industry analysis, postcolonial studies, **queer theory**, and technology studies.

As noted earlier, the second major defining characteristic of Canadian communication studies that has been identified is its in-betweenness and marginality. Canadian political, social, geographic, and economic marginality (mostly in relation to the United States) is seen as producing an **epistemology** of the margins. A number of scholars identify Canadian communication scholarship as unique in that it draws on both European and American traditions. Kroker (1984) sees Canadian communication thought as an oppositional mode between European and American perspectives; he feels it is characterized by its location "in-between." He defines this as "a restless oscillation between the pragmatic will to live at all costs of the American and a searing lament for that which has been suppressed by the modern, technical order" (p. 7). From this position of in-between, Canadians offer a unique, critical perspective.

Some scholars go further than in-betweenness and claim that a defining characteristic of Canadian communication thought—and, indeed, of all Canadian intellectual and cultural development—is its marginality (Babe, 2000a, 2000b; Carey, 1975; Robinson and Theall, 1975; Theall, 1975). The belief that a critical stance emerges from a sense of marginality is echoed in claims made by American and British critical scholars (Carey, 1982; Garnham, 1983; Hardt, 1992; Smythe & Van Dinh, 1983). According to Robinson and Theall (1975), "Canada's geopolitical marginality on the fringe of the North American continent seems to have given rise to two distinct outlooks: a particular perception of this country's cultural mission and a unique communication studies philosophy" (p. 3). Babe (2000a) argues that "people at the margins can see things differently, that is, dialectically: unable to escape exposure to dominant discourses, they nonetheless understand that these discourses are not their own" (p. 23).

Yet what are the limits of this epistemological positioning on the margins? The claim to criticality through marginality again rests on the examples of the canonical Canadian communication thinkers: Harold Innis, Marshall McLuhan, George Grant, and Northrop Frye. But how pertinent is the sense of geographical marginality expressed by a few great thinkers to our definition of "the margins" today? How does marginality play itself out in relation to the globalizing context of the early 21st century? Furthermore, how can marginality function as a self-conscious characteristic? Theall (1975) claims that "this phenomenon of marginality provides a natural negative perspective" (p. 20). But how can a phenomenon that has been thus articulated be considered natural? As Briankle G. Chang recently noted, "nothing seems more banal and easy than being critical today" (Chang, 2011, p. 85).

BANAL AND EASY

What can be seen from the foregoing analysis is that the critical-ness of Canadian communication studies has been mapped onto discourses of the ongoing search for a unique Canadian national identity. Indeed, the search for Canadian uniqueness has derailed a sustained interrogation of what a critical approach to communication might entail and whether or not it is even present in the Canadian field. In short, the field has not been critical enough. Lorimer (2000b) criticizes generations of communication scholars in Canada for not moving past Smythe's limited "political economy" understanding of critical communications; he suggests, as have others, that as the discipline has matured, its critical edge has dulled (see also Salter, 1987).

The mapping of a critical disciplinary identity onto a national identity has also produced certain blind spots. As Meisel (1987) notes, "the questions asked by researchers—and the questions not asked—are greatly conditioned by their societal and national setting" (p. 57). The cultural nationalist position, for example, has always accepted a strong, legitimate state presence. Yet is approval of an interventionist state consistent with an approach that defines itself as critical and therefore as being in opposition to the normalizing power of any state? Although communication studies in Canada did not become institutionalized in the university system as a result of a close relationship with media industries (as in the United States), it did do so in close relationships with government. In fact, a significant number of scholars attribute the rise of communication studies in Canada to the needs of royal commissions studying media (Robinson, 2000; Salter, 1987; Tate et al., 2000). Tate et al. (2000) regard this as a positive development:

> What tends to be invisible in the equation is precisely the important role which royal commissions and other government-created study groups and task forces have tended to play in our scholarly life. Focused stimulus, funding, and collegiality are generated that tend to give structure to new and emerging areas of organized scholarship. Arguably, it is not coincidental that the CCA [Canadian Communication Association] and the *CJC* (in its evolved form as a peer-reviewed scholarly journal) were established in the wake of the LaMarsh Commission. (p. 86).[4]

Yet one of the hallmarks of critical research, even as Lazarsfeld framed it, was its intellectual independence. Gerbner (1983b) reminds us that "critical inquiry is the distinguishing feature of a discipline and the hallmark of independent scholarship" (p. 355). Others have urged more caution regarding this close relationship with the government's research agenda (de la Garde, 1987). Salter (1987) suggests that "the influence of government funding on the research programs of a discipline should never be underestimated" (p. 35). She goes on to remark that "there are some dangers in relying upon the needs of government to create the research foci within a discipline" (p. 41). If we are to follow Gerbner's call for critical inquiry, it would seem that this relationship with the interests and agenda of the Canadian state requires more scrutiny—a scrutiny that will not take place if we do not recognize our institutional history and if we do not abandon the assumption that we are *already* critical.

NOT ENOUGH FERMENT IN THE FIELD

Critical communication studies can be described through a series of commitments to the question of the intersection of communication and power in society, to a recognition of social inequity, to nonquantitative methods, to an epistemological position that recognizes the place of values in research, to theoretical roots in radical thought, and to the production of knowledge that contributes to a broader project of human emancipation. However, rather than understanding critical communication studies as an ongoing practice requiring self-reflexivity, the embrace of new theories and approaches, and constant vigilance against complacency, these six values too often become assumed rather than reflected upon and adapted in relation to historical change. More specifically in Canada, the claim to automatic critical status, anchored in geography and national identity, reproduces the dated and problematic distinction between critical and administrative research. As Jonathan Sterne (2005) writes of the use of the labels *critical* and *administrative* in the 1950s: "... using these labels to describe mid-century research is destructive of both historical memory and future imagination" (p. 87). Our contemporary and future imagination more than half a century later continues to suffer.

Bailie (1997) suggests that "critical communication studies are intricately linked to a project that promotes a critical imaginary: the ability to think beyond present social, political, and economic conditions to participate in the construction of alternative futures" (p. 33). Carey, too, uses the language of imagination when he argues that "a critical theory of communication must affirm what is before our eyes and transcend it by imagining, at the very least, a world more desirable" (1982, p. 33). The times in which we live are marked by an increasing concentration of media, daily incursions into our privacy by corporate and state actors, and increasing wealth disparities. However, we also see the rise of global social movements, increased public awareness of media power and communication rights, the explosion of interesting uses of social media and digital technology for creative and political practices, and regular examples of prodemocratic social action on the part of diverse coalitions of social actors. These attributes of our contemporary moment suggest that the time may never be better, as communication scholars, to explore the possibilities of an unfettered critical communication imagination.

QUESTIONS

1. What are the major differences between administrative and critical research as defined by American communication studies?
2. What are the six shared assumptions of critical communication research?
3. Why is it difficult to determine if Canadian communication studies is critical?
4. How does Canadian communication studies define itself as unique (i.e., distinct from U.S. communication studies)?
5. Discuss the ways in which Canadian communication studies is and is not critical.
6. Select a current communication phenomenon. How would you analyze it as a critical communication scholar? What kinds of questions would you ask?

NOTES

1. The author wishes to thank Jessica Wurster for her invaluable research assistance and McGill University for its support of the original research for this chapter. The anonymous reviewers' comments over the years have been, and continue to be, constructive and informed. Leslie Regan Shade is a generous and thoughtful editor; the work has improved with her ongoing commitment and interest in the piece. Finally, this chapter would never have happened without the support and nudging of Paul Attallah. Despite its changes over numerous editions, it still bears the traces of our lively discussions. Thanks, Paul.
2. It should be noted that not everyone agrees with the author and Ono (2011). Christian Fuchs, for example, makes an equally passionate plea for critical

media and communication studies "remembering the Marxian roots of this field" (Fuchs, 2009, 6).

3. A Fetschrift is a way that academics pay tribute to a particular scholar and her or his body of work, either through a publication or through a scholarly event.
4. The LaMarsh Comission was the Ontario Royal Commission on Violence in the Communications Industry, 1977.

REFERENCES

Abramson, B. D., Shtern, J., & Taylor, J. (2008). "More and better" research? Critical communication studies and the problem of policy relevance. *Canadian Journal of Communication 33*(2), 303–317.

Acland, C. R., & W. J. Buxton. (1999). *Harold Innis in the new century: Reflections and refractions.* Montreal and Kingston: McGill-Queen's University Press.

Allen, M. (1999). The role of meta-analysis for connecting critical and scientific approaches: The need to develop a sense of collaboration. *Critical Studies in Mass Communication, 16*, 373–379.

Babe, R. E. (2000a). *Canadian communication thought: Ten foundational writers.* Toronto: University of Toronto Press.

———. (2000b). Foundations of Canadian communication thought. *Canadian Journal of Communication, 26*, 19–37.

Bailie, M. (1997). Critical communication pedagogy: Teaching and learning for democratic life in democratizing communication? In M. Bailie & D. Winseck (Eds.), *Democratizing communication? Comparative perspectives on information and power* (pp. 33–56). Creskill, NJ: Hampton Press.

Blumler, J. G. (1983). Communication and democracy: The crisis beyond and the ferment within. *Journal of Communication*, 33(3), 166–173.

Carey, J. (1975). Canadian communication theory: Extensions and interpretations of Harold Innis. In G. J. Robinson & D. F. Theall (Eds.), *Studies in Canadian communications* (pp. 27–60). Montreal: Graduate Program in Communications.

———. (1982). The mass media and critical theory: An American view. In M. Burgoon (Ed.), *Communication yearbook 6* (pp. 18–34). Beverly Hills, CA: Sage.

———. (1983). The origins of the radical discourse on cultural studies in the United States. *Journal of Communication, 33*(3), 311–313.

Chang, B. G. (2011). Introduction: Sixteen and a half questions on 'being critical.' *Communication and Critical/Cultural Studies, 8*(1): 85–87.

de la Garde, R. (1987, Winter). The 1987 Southam lecture: Mr. Innis, is there life after the "American Empire"? *Canadian Journal of Communication*, 7–21.

Elasmar, M. G. (1999). Opportunities and challenges of using meta-analysis in the field of international communication in critical studies. *Mass Communication, 16*, 379–384.

Fuchs, C. (2009). A contribution to theoretical foundations of critical media and communication studies. *Javnost—The Public*, *16*(2): 5–24.

Garnham, N. (1983). Toward a theory of cultural materialism. *Journal of Communication*, *33*(3), 314–329.

Gerbner, G. (1964). On content analysis and critical research in mass communication. In L. A. Dexter & D. M. White (Eds.), *People, society and mass communication* (pp. 476–500). New York: Free Press.

———. (1983a). Introduction. *Journal of Communication*, *33*(3), 1–4.

———. (1983b). The importance of being critical—In one's own fashion. *Journal of Communication*, *33*(3), 355–362.

Gitlin, T. (1978). Media sociology: The dominant paradigm. *Theory & Society*, *6*(2), 205–253.

Grosswiler, P. (1996). The dialectical methods of Marshall McLuhan, Marxism, and critical theory. *Canadian Journal of Communication*, *21*(1), 95–124.

Habermas, J. (2006). Political communication in media society: Does democracy still enjoy an epistemic dimension? The impact of normative theory on empirical research. *Communication Theory*, *16*, 411–426.

Haight, T. R. (1983). The critical researcher's dilemma. *Journal of Communication*, *33*(3), 226–236.

Halloran, J. D. (1983). A case for critical eclecticism. *Journal of Communication*, *33*(3), 270–278.

Hardt, H. (1992). *Critical communication studies: Communication, history & theory in America*. London and New York: Routledge.

Jansen, S. C. (1983). Power and knowledge: Toward a new critical synthesis. *Journal of Communication*, *33*(3), 342–354.

Kalyvas, A. (2004). Back to Adorno? Critical social theory between past and future. *Political Theory*, *32*(2): 247–256.

Katz, E., & Lazarsfeld, P. F. 1955. *Personal influence: The part played by people in the flow of mass communications*. Glencoe, IL: Free Press.

Kroker, A. (1984). *Technology and the Canadian mind: Innis/McLuhan/Grant*. Montreal: New World Perspectives.

Lazarsfeld, P. F. (1941). Remarks on administrative and critical communication research. *Studies in Philosophy and Social Science*, *9*(1), 2–16.

Lazarsfeld, P. F. (1948). *The people's choice: How the voter makes up his mind in a presidential campaign*. New York: Columbia University Press.

Lorimer, R. (2000a). Editorial: The genesis of this issue—Twenty-five years of the CJC. *Canadian Journal of Communication*, *25*, 3–7.

———. (2000b). Introduction: Communications teaching and research—Looking forward from 2000. *Canadian Journal of Communication*, *25*, 9–17.

McLuskie, E., Hegbloom, M., & Woodfin, F. (2004). In the company of Hanno Hardt: A festschrift on the future of critical communication studies. *Journalism*, *5*(2): 227–241.

Media, Culture and Society (1984), 6(3).

Meehan, E. R. (2004). Moving forward on the left: Some observations on critical communications research in the United States. *Javnost—The Public*, *11*(3): 19–30.

Meisel, J. (1987, Winter). Some Canadian perspectives on communication research. *Canadian Journal of Communication*, 55–63.

Mosco, V. (1983). Critical research and the role of labour. *Journal of Communication*, *33*(3), 237–248.

———. (1996). *The political economy of communication: Rethinking and renewal.* London and Thousand Oaks, CA: Sage Publications.

Ono, K. A. (2011). Critical: A finer edge. *Communication and Critical/Cultural Studies*, *8*(1): 93–96.

Ramsey, E. (2011). Somehow, learning to live: On being critical. *Communication and Critical/Cultural Studies*, *8*(1): 88–92.

Robinson, G. J. (2000). Remembering our past: Reconstructing the field of Canadian communication studies. *Canadian Journal of Communication*, *25*, 105–125.

Robinson, G. J., & Theall, D. F. (Eds.). (1975). Introduction. In G. J. Robinson & D. F. Theall (Eds.), *Studies in Canadian communications* (pp. 1–6). Montreal: Graduate Program in Communications.

Rogers, E. M. (1982). The empirical and critical schools of communication research. In M. Burgoon (Ed.), *Communication yearbook 5* (pp. 125–144). New Brunswick, NJ: Transaction Books.

Salter, L. (Ed.). (1981). Editor's introduction. In L. Salter (Ed.), *Communication studies in Canada/Études Canadiennes en communication* (pp. xi–xxii). Toronto: Butterworths.

———. (1987, Winter). Taking stock: Communication studies in 1987. *Canadian Journal of Communication*, 23–45.

Sholle, D. J. (1988). Critical studies: From the theory of ideology to power/knowledge. *Critical Studies in Mass Communication*, *5*, 16–41.

Sjovaag, H., & Hallvard, M. (2009). From fermentation to maturity? Reflections on media and communication studies: An interview with Todd Gitlin, Jostein Gripsrud and Michael Schudson. *International Journal of Communication*, *3*, 130–139.

Smythe, D. W., & Van Dinh, T. (1983). On critical and administrative research: A new critical analysis. *Journal of Communication*, *33*(3), 117–127.

Splichal, S. (2008). Why be critical? *Communication, Culture & Critique*, *1*(1), 20–30.

Sterne, J. (2005). C. Wright Mills, the Bureau for Applied Social Research, and the meaning of critical sociology. *Cultural Studies, Critical Methodologies*, *5*(1), 65–94.

Stole, I. L., & Peck, J. (Eds.). (2011). *A moment of danger: Critical studies in the history of U.S. communication since World War II.* Milwaukee: Marquette University Press.

Straw, W. (1985). Teaching critical media analysis. *Canadian Journal of Communication II(1)*, 5–16.

Tate, E. D., Osler, A., Fouts, G., & Segal, A. (2000). The beginnings of communication studies in Canada: Remembering and narrating the past. *Canadian Journal of Communication, 25*, 61–103.

Theall, D. F. (1975). Communication theory and the marginal culture: The socio-aesthetic dimensions of communication study. In G. J. Robinson & D. F. Theall (Eds.), *Studies in Canadian communications* (pp. 7–26). Montreal: Graduate Program in Communications.

Tremblay, G. (1981). Préface. In L. Salter (Ed.), *Communication studies in Canada/ Études Canadiennes en communication* (pp. vii–x). Toronto: Butterworths.

2

DOING MEDIA STUDIES

Mark Lipton
University of Guelph

I JUST SAW *THE IRON LADY*; IT WAS GREAT!

I hate Meryl Streep. I know, for some of you that must seem like a crazy proposition. *Hate* is a bad word. But I hate her. I hate her like I hate cats. And I'm allergic to cats. I know she's won every acting trophy. Yet I have a strong reaction to seeing Meryl Streep as a popular culture text and I've been conditioned to reinforce my reaction in the years since I've been watching her on the Hollywood scene. Maybe you like her. That's okay. I don't mind. You're entitled to your opinion. I like to say to my students that freedom of expression in the classroom is an undeniable right. I may disagree with you, but I will defend to the death your right to your opinion. So you like Meryl. Go ahead. She still bugs me. Nonetheless, I was dragged to see the latest biopic *Iron Lady* where I got to see Meryl slowly losing her marbles, as the character emerges with Alzheimer's disease. The character in this film is Margaret Thatcher, known to many as the longest serving prime minister of the United Kingdom from 1979 to 1990; she was the first female prime minister as well as the first female leader of the Conservative party. Thatcher, however, is not one of the United Kingdom's most cherished prime ministers. Thatcher was expelled from office, forced out of government by her own cabinet members and succeeded by John Major. Perhaps it was because of her ultra conservative values; maybe it was due to a public backlash against many of her policies (particularly an unpopular Poll Tax). Nonetheless, this Thatcher is a sad lady. And there is Meryl. Good old Meryl. Meryl now has another gold trophy. Lucky her. I begin my chapter here with this story of Meryl, Margaret, and the movie because the film's author (screenwriter Abi Morgan) penned some powerful lines of dialogue that encapsulate some of my pedagogical practice when it comes to doing media studies.

In the film, an elderly Thatcher remarks to her doctor, "People don't think any more; they feel. One of the greatest problems of our age is that we are governed by people who care more about feelings than they do about thoughts and ideas. Now, thoughts and ideas, that's what interests me." Thatcher continues, "Watch your thoughts, for they become words. Watch your words, for they become actions. Watch your actions, for they become habits. Watch your habits, for they become character. Watch your character, for it becomes your destiny."

I repeat these spoken lines of dialogue throughout the semester, using my worst possible Meryl Streep accents. My point is to introduce to media students a critical principle when taking up the challenge of doing media studies. Here it is: when looking at media messages, or texts, your brain generally engages in two actions: you either ignore the text (because it doesn't matter to you) or you *react* to the thing: Oh, there's Meryl again; I hate her. I am responding uncritically. This is simply how I feel. I want to offer two axioms of communication about the ways in which humans *respond* to media texts and messages. First, your response will most likely be analogous to the way you responded to a similar text in your past. Second, the way you respond to any text will say a lot more about *you* then the actual text. These two axioms about response are how I introduce students to critical analysis.

To reiterate: I hate Meryl Streep. Not because she's a good or bad actor. Her skill at her craft has nothing to do with my response. Hate is a feeling. I'm not engaging in thoughtful critical analysis when I write how I hate Meryl. I am feeling. To some, my feelings are funny; to others insulting, rude, vacuous, insincere. Please don't think Ms Streep's ability as an actor has anything to do with my personal feelings. My feelings are based on an entirely different set of personal connotations that, at this point, I'd like to remain a mystery. There are more interesting questions to ask that redirect my response away from feelings toward critical analysis—thinking. In forming a critical analysis of Meryl one might ask: Why has Meryl won all those awards? What is it about her performance in this film that led her peers to celebrate her achievements? What evidence can you discover that reveals how she embodies a character? What are the criteria for outstanding actors? My feelings, however, prevent me from careful analysis that would provide me with an exacting answer to these questions.

The point I need to make is that feelings don't help me as a student of media when formulating opinions about texts. When I want my opinions to count, they need to be based on a solid foundation of reading texts and constructing meaning in significant ways. By significant ways, I refer to the process of **critical thinking**.

> Critical thinking is the intellectually disciplined process of actively and skillfully conceptualizing, applying, analyzing, synthesizing, and/or evaluating information gathered from, or generated by, observation, experience, reflection, reasoning, or communication, as a guide to belief and action. In its exemplary form, it is based on universal intellectual values that transcend subject matter divisions: clarity, accuracy, precision, consistency, relevance, sound evidence, good reasons, depth, breadth, and fairness. (Scriven & Paul, 1987)

When doing media studies, begin by noting the intellectual differences between feeling and critical thinking. I cannot say I really hate Meryl Streep when I apply critical thinking to her as a *text*. I notice, for example, her ability to adopt the verbal and nonverbal distinctiveness of a character; Meryl captures the qualities of a frail old lady with a twitch of her chin while reflecting the character's hot temper by regulating the tenor of voice. When I watch this actor on screen, Meryl Streep (the human, the celebrity) disappears and I am welcomed into the world of the film.

This chapter continues by applying critical thinking and approaches to meaning making associated with students of media studies. Then, to provide greater context, I reflect on the historical approaches to media education. These historical approaches situate the state of media studies and media education today. And today, I argue, media students are adopting this critical approach as vital, given our state of media ecology. Finally, I suggest and probe possible projects media students might encounter in ways that apply these lessons of doing media studies in the 21st century.

What is a Text? Medium Versus Media

So far I have been writing this word *text* and I want to take a moment to critically analyze how I am applying its meaning. In high school the word "text" most likely referred to textbooks (math, science, geography, French, etc.) or the texts you were reading in English class (novels, poems, plays, Shakespeare, etc.). Media students extend their understanding of the term **text** to include a vast range of approaches, from the study of phenomena in general to include everyday objects of perception (things, works, objects, artifacts, etc.). The word "text" is broadly defined so as to acknowledge how all media construct and carry meaning; as a result, all media can be subject to analysis and critical thinking. Just as you are able to analyze how a print-based text (such as a novel) was written at a specific time period for a certain audience, so too can you analyze how a film was created for an intended audience during a particular decade.

A distinguishing feature of this new use of text is that it is informed by the Latin word *texere* (to weave) and *textum* (a web; texture). Texts are acknowledged as woven, and readers join authors as the weavers. That is, the emphasis is on the text as an open and perhaps even unfinished process in which the reader has some specific and symbolic work to do. Doing media studies requires students to apply critical thinking in symbolic ways such that texts are interrogated to reveal greater understandings, meanings, and if possible, a revelation of what's at stake for humans, society, the environment, and so on.

The word "text" is useful for students of media because it allows us to ask questions about our everyday lives in informal culture. There are few limits to what qualifies as a text when doing media studies: a picture from a magazine, a television show, a face, a YouTube video, a painting, a dress (or pair of shoes), a hockey game, an arrangement of flowers, a city, Disney princesses, Nicki Minaj's hairstyle, comic books, Iron Man's costume, a video game, office design, a pair of jeans, makeup, corporate internet sites, a webpage, this book you are reading right now—these are all examples of texts that are open to investigation for students of media. When doing media studies, the word "text" helps to identify an object of inquiry; text can work simultaneously as a set of forms, an effect, a practice, an outcome, a structure.

For students of media, please recognize that the word "text" is a kind of shorthand for identifying a **medium** of communication. Any text that conveys meaning can be considered a medium of communication. **Media**, the plural form of the word "medium," makes explicit that more than one form or mode of communication is necessary to convey a message. A text may rely on multiple forms or modes of communication to convey its message. This book, for example, relies on the form of letters, paper, and so on. A film is a complex set of forms of media that include things like sound, lighting, editing, scriptwriting, costume design, oh – and acting ... The notion of **multimodalities** helps define the way that media works within communication systems. Ergo, this expanded definition of text introduces media students to a much larger set of questions about the complex nature of communication systems. Thinking about texts is just the first step.

RESPONDING AS READING

In order for my critical reading of a text to say something about that text's intrinsic value or worth, I must engage in some form of symbolic work. Reading or **decoding** refers to the symbolic work that readers must engage in to arrive at a meaning. Stuart Hall (1980) defines reading in semiotic terms when he writes:

> By the word *reading* we mean not only the capacity to identify and decode a certain number of signs, but also the subjective capacity to put them into a creative relation between themselves and with other signs: a capacity which is, by itself, the condition for a complete awareness of one's total environment. (p. 135)

Hall is a founder of the Birmingham Centre for Cultural Studies, and cultural studies has also played a major role in contemporary theories of texts and meaning by calling attention to the sociopolitical aspects of reading. Hall identifies three broad kinds of "reading" that students of media applied to texts: first, "dominant readings" occur when readers recognize, as Cook (1995) says, "what a [text] is saying and broadly agree with it" (p. 162); second, "oppositional readings" occur when readers recognize the dominant meanings of a text but reject them for cultural, political, or ideological reasons; and third, "negotiated readings" occur when readers accept, reject, and/or refine elements of a text in light of their own views and assumptions. Hall's definition of reading makes reference to traditions in semiotic theory, known as the "science of sign systems." Media studies scholars interested in the construction of meanings have taken up this tradition of semiotics. Semiotics begins by deconstructing texts into component parts and analyzing the specific elements that are applied in constructing or weaving meaning. Given several names by various scholars,[1] these elements always include a reader (or meaning maker), a text (or object of perception), and the cognitive processes by which meanings of the thing perceived are made. In Hall's view, these cognitive processes have to do with one's capacity to relate one text to experiences with other sign systems. So, for example, you (a reader) will make (weave) meaning of my essay (a text) based on your experiences with language, other essays, other texts, and a multitude of experiences that may influence the meanings you make of my words. Decoding or reading, then, is a process of meaning construction arising out of a negotiation between the reader and the text. Textual signs are activated by readers who decode these signs according to and by following their own subjective experiences. In other words, readers' intentions with regard to media texts are multiple and do not work uniformly.

Following semiotic theory, when I "read" the text of *The Iron Lady*, I decode the actor Meryl Streep as a sign and I activate what she "means" based on my subjective experiences. As a student of media studies, my reading must be informed by an understanding of media systems, codes, and structures. This information is what makes up media studies curriculum. Curriculum, simply put, is the content of an academic course. Students who specialize in media studies often take a number of classes, each with its own focused curriculum. In classroom settings, it is also important to note the various approaches to teaching; different teachers approach the task of teaching with particular pedagogical styles. Pedagogy refers to the method or process of instruction. I introduce these ideas about curriculum and pedagogy because they are fundamental concepts to media educators in formulating an approach to doing media studies. The introduction to critical thinking, texts, and reading establishes elements applied in various approaches to doing media studies in various classroom settings. Now I examine the various means by which media studies has been taken up in classroom settings. Though my scrutiny follows an historical frame, many of these approaches are still applied in classrooms today.

A BRIEF HISTORY OF MEDIA EDUCATION: MEDIA IN THE CLASSROOM

While there is widespread agreement among educators and media scholars alike that contemporary schooling should include media education, there is very little agreement on what should be the objectives of such education, or how they would be best achieved. The work of Neil Postman, for example, has long stressed the need for education about technology. Such education, according to Postman (1985, 1995), would involve "how the meanings of information and education change as new technologies intrude upon a culture, how the meanings of truth, law and intelligence differ among oral cultures, writing cultures, printing cultures, electronic cultures" (p. 191). Postman's argument for what ought to be included in a media studies curriculum is but one voice among many who have suggested ways in which schools can help students (actively) deal with today's media-saturated environments.

Early ideas about media education stem from suspicions and fears of the power of early mass media and their uses for propaganda before and during World War II, from concerns about the emergence of market-driven, consumer culture following the war, and from the high/low culture debates of the 1930s to 1950s. Cultural critics F. R. Leavis and Denys Thompson (1933) held a highly influential position that wanted to protect young people against the effects of the media. Similarly, work emerging from the Frankfurt school marked the products of mass media and popular culture as dangerous. In their celebrated essay *The Culture Industry: Enlightenment as Mass Deception* (1944), Theodor Adorno and Max Horkheimer assert that Western education systems function as conduits for the culture industry, deceiving all consumers. These critics celebrated the German education system as enjoying "protection" (p. 132) from market mechanisms that further the culture industry. Adorno and Horkheimer's definition of the culture industry included the ideological consequences of the products of mass media and popular culture. By objectifying these products, the authors assumed that protection from them would foster what they deemed to be proper cultural growth. It is no surprise then, as Halloran and Jones (1986) note, that media education "arose from a deep concern among educators and literary critics that young people needed to be protected against what were considered to be the very harmful and powerful influences of the mass media" (p. 10). It is important to note that this **protectionist** approach to education is still in use by educators today. Protectionist in attitude, there are still some educators who insist that media act as agents of distortion; media are deceptive; media promote aggression; the commercial media industry structures communication environments; and finally, media habits consistently need to be re-evaluated.

By the 1950s, however, attitudes began to shift because protectionist views of media education were identified with elitist attitudes toward "high" and "low" culture. British educator Richard Hoggart (1957) argued that in democratic societies, "the activity of producing a culture ceases to be exclusive to one particular privileged group, and becomes instead an integral part of all social groups" (Hoggart, cited in Murdock & Phelps, 1973, p. 14). Hoggart's evaluation of the rigid hierarchical division between the elite culture of the literary tradition (high culture) and newer media-based cultural forms (low culture) led to a proposal that ranged all cultural artifacts along a continuum marked "authentic" at one end and "phony" at the other. This research into what the "masses" read about (and sang about) supported a belief that popular literature was associated with the life and values of the people for whom it was produced. Viewing texts or media in this way allowed the question of the impact of media to shift from a protectionist stance, (e.g., What does the material do to the people who consume it?) to a more discriminatory perspective (e.g., What do people of different sociocultural backgrounds do with the material they select?). A new **discriminatory** approach to doing media studies posed the following question: "What critical standards can help people distinguish the good texts from bad texts?" Approaches to media in the classroom that followed in the 1960s and 1970s explored such questions by looking at film. Cinema, according to Whannel (1969), is "a significant feature of contemporary culture representing the most developed and distinctive form of art produced by technology with the unique feature that its growth, from its most primitive beginnings, is preserved for study on celluloid" (p. 21). Moreover, film was a major form of media at the time, especially relevant to the lives of young people. Film also lent itself to systematic study in school because, like literature, film had generated a body of theory and a set of critical standards by which good work could be distinguished from poor work. Other forms of media, such as television, were not considered as useful to the development of critical sensibilities among the young because, as Cook and Hiller (1976) point out, these media lacked "any distinct theory and/or critical tradition" (p. 20). In this view, then, the objective of media education was to teach students to discriminate among the wide range of newer aesthetic texts by learning the standards and criteria that distinguished good from poor. Again, it is important to note that many educators continue to insist that a discriminatory stance is necessary when teaching about media.

If these first two approaches developed as ways to teach *about* media, another strain of media education evolved in an attempt to justify teaching *through* media. In this approach, media are viewed as instructional tools. The clearest application of this approach is to the training in the use of information and communication technologies (ICTs). The "how to" class in communications technology (e.g., the teaching of spreadsheets, file management, power point, web design, or other media skills) usually takes the form of narrow training in technical skills where media function as the instruments of instruction. One also gets a sense of this method when an English teacher uses a film and/or television text as a reward for hard work, as a lure for unmotivated students, or as a means to visualize literary texts, supplementing the learning of narrative devices and literary techniques. In this instrumentalist approach, note how media is both part of the school curriculum (what is taught) and the educator's pedagogy (how it is taught). Many media education curricula (textbooks) contain lists of activities that use media texts to develop thinking skills. The **instrumentalist** approach, where media texts are merely instruments or tools that supplement learning, often reinforces the protectionist method. For example, in an English curriculum where the goal is to provoke reading and writing through critical analysis and interpretation, reading media texts is often akin to what Robert Morgan (1998) sees as "code-cracking" (p. 166). Media studies is less frequently about media use or media production but about developing a "resistant, self-defensive posture" so as not to succumb to media messages (p. 164).

Until the 1980s, these three approaches—the *protectionist*, the *discriminatory*, and the *instrumentalist*—dominated most media curricula and pedagogical practices involving the use of media in education. Today, doing media studies resists and criticizes these approaches, identifying various problems. For example, these past approaches make the assumption that media use is inherently passive and harmful and that learning about media means giving up those pleasures established and reinforced by experiences outside the classroom. Doing media studies should begin with students' current media habits, thereby bridging the gap between what students do outside the classroom and what they do inside. This has led to today's **critical** approach to doing media studies. What I describe in the next section is a synthesis of this approach; there are no singular aspects that educators must follow to meet the criteria of teaching media today. My description of today's critical approach is open for discussion, appropriation, and a variety of applications.

DOING MEDIA STUDIES: TODAY'S CRITICAL APPROACH

To formulate a critical response, students of media analyze the historical, cultural, and social dimensions of media texts. Andrew Higson and Ginette Vincendeau (1986) describe two contrary tendencies of media critics' responses; on the one hand, media texts have "the status of a mind-numbing drug"; on the other, and in intense reaction to this attitude, media critics find meaning in the "parodic play with form," seeing pleasure within "the realm of social relations" (p. 2). In either case, media students engage in reading in a way that is infused with textual analysis so as to formulate an argument about selected texts. To reach this goal, media students often examine many levels of resistance and appropriation that occur within media traditions. In other words, an understanding of history and theory is vital to formulating a critical response; media students demonstrate an understanding *about* media texts by researching, reading, analyzing, writing, and rewriting. Thinking about media requires work. Paul Willis (1980), a cultural studies scholar, names this thinking "symbolic work." Another way for students of media to think about this work is by taking responsibility for developing their own cultural knowledge and their own educational outcomes.

For Willis, media education gives students control of the "conditions, production, and consumption of their own symbolic resources" (p. 129); this, in turn, increases "the range, complexity, elegance, self-consciousness and purposefulness of [students'] involvement" (p. 131) in symbolic work and learning. Willis marks a difference between formal, school culture and informal, common (media) culture. Willis would say, for example, textbooks at school are "owned" by the teacher; media texts are "owned" by their readers (users, audiences, participants). As a result, media texts can be manipulated through acts of creative symbolic thinking. For these reasons, creative symbolic work within media studies offers important possibilities for "oppositional, independent or alternative symbolizations of the self" (p. 150).

David Buckingham (2003a), perhaps the world's leading media education scholar, summarizes the *critical* approach to media education:

> As media educators, we set out to produce well-informed responsible citizens who will be able to take a distanced stance toward the immediate pleasures of the media. We want to give our students the *critical* knowledge and the analytical tools that we believe will empower them, and thereby enable them to function as autonomous, rational social agents. (p. 313)

As a student of media, I look at the concepts "social agent," "social power," or "agent of change" with a serious eye—as fundamental goals of doing media studies. I do not want students to be subjects of the media, but agents of change. Are you using media, or being used by media?

Students of media see a relationship between media and culture; we often connect media change to social, political, economic, personal (and other) transformations that have radically altered our world. "The telephone, for example, was celebrated for the way in which it could make business more efficient and facilitate more democratic forms of social life, yet it was also condemned for its disruption of intimate relationships and its unsettling of established social hierarchies" (Buckingham, 2003b, p. 11). In another example, I look to my bike. I like my bike. People bike for work, utility, recreation, and fun. I also think about bicycles within a larger historical, social, and cultural context by researching the early beginnings of bicycle production. Though first invented in the early 19th century (1817 by all accounts), during the second bicycle craze of the 1890s bikes provided one of the few means for women to find independence outside the home, yet bikes were still considered immoral. (See, for example, Smith, 1972; Henderson et al., 1989.) Your bike (a media text) represents women's agency, quest for mobility, and emancipation into the public sphere of the late 19th and early 20th century. (Picture Meryl Streep on a bike.)

There are divergent positions to take about the impact of media: hard technological determinism describes a direct and causal relationship between a new technological form and its effects on various elements of culture. The physical form of a medium impacts the material requirements for encoding, transmitting, storing, retrieving, decoding, and distributing information. This, in turn, biases, constrains, controls, and limits the content of the form. Marshall McLuhan's (1964) "the medium is the message" encapsulates this hard determinist position (p. 7); for McLuhan, media change has social and personal consequences.

Today's critical approach to doing media studies begins by addressing these complex relationships about media's power. A lot of students want to know, "How does this media impact me? Why should I care?" To this end, students of media often look to the responses, media texts, or other cultural formations of displaced people or how audiences of media texts respond (or perform or live through their response) as outsiders. There is a long and rich history in the disciplines of anthropology and sociology, to study culture so as to understand the nature of social relations, order, and action as it unfolds in the mundane, taken-for-granted aspects of our daily lives. Media studies also looks to the field of cultural studies as producing pressing interdisciplinary theoretical scholarship and research that is both analytically sound and socially concerned. For example, some of this work brings together voices from different marginalized groups—groups that are often isolated from each other as well as from the dominant culture; students of media look to research that joins issues of gender, race, sexual diversity, disability, and class in one forum but without imposing a false unity on the diverse cultures represented. This important line of inquiry for understanding media's social power is frequently termed *identity politics*. For Buckingham (2008), "the term *identity politics* refers primarily to activist social movements" (p. 7), which seek to challenge oppressive accounts of identities that have been constructed by others (e.g., media systems) that hold power. Put another way, one's identity is often constrained and controlled by media institutions, structures, and systems. As a result, our subjective responses often conform to rigid social rules. By applying a critical approach, media students can both locate and direct how **quotidian** (i.e., everyday) practices manifest patterns of structure and agency.

PRACTICAL WORK: THINKING AND DOING

One of the greatest challenges and goals for media students at this historical moment is to keep apace with the rapidly changing face of media use, production, and practices. The recent explosion of new information and communication technologies, mobile media, and social media forms is undeniable. To address the changing nature of technological change, the *critical* approach to doing media studies seeks to strike a balance between theory and practice. Following a basic premise of media education, media students engage in modes of inquiry that rely on practical work or media production. Many education theorists have long argued, "If students are to understand media texts ... then it will obviously be helpful if they have first-hand experience of the construction process from the inside" (Masterman, 1985, p. 26). Len Masterman's (1985) *Teaching the Media* had "an enormous influence on scholars and practitioners with interests in media literacy education because it articulated the unique configuration of challenges and opportunities associated with teaching and learning both media analysis and media production" (Hobbs, 2005, p. 866). In the years since Masterman first articulated this argument, students of media have taken up the challenge of media production, recognizing its educational potential, and celebrating the creative play and symbolic work without suspicion.

Ethnographic researchers, artists, and activists were some of the early pioneers in the uses of experimenting with media texts as both a method and a construct. For example, media students today owe a debt to the research and creative practices of the Situationist International (SI) movement (Debord 1957, 1967) whose revolutionary ideas addressed the power dynamics separating intellectual and artistic creations. Guy Debord's (1957) *Psychographic Guide of Paris* remixes satellite maps of Paris by rearranging cutouts of neigbourhoods according to political and intellectual ideology. The Situationalist International movement includes a body of work ranging from essays to activist actions.

By 1975, researchers working at the Centre for Contemporary Cultural Studies at the University of Birmingham were applying and representing a radical cultural landscape when they undertook detailed studies of cultures, subcultures, and class (Jefferson, et al., 1975). Members of this school engaged in ethnographies about political and social identities, including subjects such as the Teds, Mods, Skinheads, drug users, black music, and street-boy culture. Through ethnographic research, these researchers recognized how subcultures and their acts of "resistance through rituals" function through particular creative practices in the form of **bricolage**, i.e., ideological play with the form and thus meaning of particular texts (etymologically from French: to fiddle, tinker and, by extension, to make creative and resourceful use of whatever materials are at hand regardless of their original purpose). From this, creative practices enter the academic halls as a viable means for uncovering important intellectual projects such as new methodological frameworks, theoretical trends, textual interpretations, political implications, and critical approaches. In fact, bricolage itself is a theoretical apparatus in many qualitative and ethnographic handbooks as a starting place for engaging in a research practice.

David Buckingham (2007) describes how bricolage is becoming a quotidian practice for today's youth accustomed to sampling and remixing existing media (without thought of copyright and intellectual property): "Students will increasingly be developing customized media environments, in which they take it as their right to select and use media to suit their individual needs. Increasing number of students are likely to have access to media production technologies outside the classroom" (p. 116). With access to a range of information and communication technologies, young people are remixing, appropriating, and sampling texts to create new forms of expression. Kirsten Drotner (2008) suggests that "young people's digital practices promote the formation of competencies that are absolutely vital to their future, in an economic, social, and cultural sense" (167). Drotner considers the relationship between these digital practices and the challenges to education. For students of media, it is vital to understand the tools with which we work. We use media production tools not just for leisure or pleasure, or for the sake of playing with tools in and of itself, but with the intention of applying critical thinking and symbolic work. The critical approach to media education takes up the challenge of using the tools of production to critique, explore, examine, and analyze media texts of all kinds.

Not all scholars are as optimistic as Drotner about the potential of integrating media tools into school curriculum. There is clearly a digital divide between those who have access to media tools and those without. Further, as Darin Barney (2005) explains, "for some people access to the internet is a source of empowerment, autonomy, and agency, for many it simply means connection to a technological infrastructure in relation to which they remain significantly disadvantaged and powerless" (pp. 155–156). Students of media work to redress this imbalance; an objective is to seek greater understanding of the terms "empowerment," "autonomy," and "agency."

Megan Boler (2008) emphasizes the view that media students understand the concept of agency by calling for attention to the social, civic, and cultural implications of our symbolic work. She writes, "We need more than new theoretical frameworks and concepts to help us understand what is happening and how to intervene. We also need to know what interventions are happening and how they are working" (p. 31). Boler's attention to **interventions** is a plea to media students to consider how the critical approach might lead to change for improved social justice, fairness, and the greater good. In this way, media students do research that inevitably and itself can be seen as a political act.

Today's "new digital media enable us to tell many more stories that may actually assist us to better govern ourselves. But to have such stories told, we have to ensure that our new digital communications readily permit such messages to be meaningfully heard" (Chester, 2007, p. xix). The critical approach to doing media studies takes a position that the integration of theory and practice is one of the best ways to be *meaningfully heard.* Media students take up Boler's call for attention to interventions and their inner workings. A crucial goal is to be heard and to intervene.

In sum, there are three elements to the critical approach that media students need to consider in their work. First, students of media apply symbolic work and critical thinking to selected texts. This work requires critical thinking, research, writing, more thinking, more research, and more writing (rewriting, revisions, editing). Our goal is to read and then develop an argument about a media text in order to uncover its significant meaning. In this way, we apply critical strategies in our approach to meaning making. Second, doing media studies asks students to consider media tools as functional objects that can aid in the development of our arguments. We use tools not just in and of themselves, but because they are the best means for developing, making, and circulating our arguments and messages. Digital practices are exploited so that competencies are augmented and, quite possibly, new meanings are discovered. Finally, in this work, students of media are asked to consider the *value* of their work. It is possible to create media messages that explicitly and implicitly seek to change current media systems for great social justice.

STUDENTS DOING MEDIA STUDIES: SOME EXAMPLES

In the final section of this chapter I describe a few particular instances of student practical work that follow this critical approach. My examples are selected not for their spectacular results, but because of their mundane qualities that are repeated on a daily basis by students. In each example I present a sample of a routine response, activate symbolic work, illustrate introductory practical work, and explain student interventions. These are narratives of work produced in my media studies classroom and are, by no means, intended as prescriptions. The point of these examples is to activate your thinking to consider the range of possible work students of media can create. You are only limited by the limits of your imagination.

BLACKBERRY OR APPLE?

I notice the first day in my lecture hall that almost every student has a mobile device. This device—the ubiquitous cellular phone—either sits on the desk in front of the student or the student holds it closely in hand ready to respond to its immediate command (e.g., a text message). I ask the question, "Are you a BlackBerry or an Apple?" Students tell me why they prefer one device to the other: "I'm a Mac" or "I like it." These are not critical responses. Students of media ask questions about their media choices. For example, since Research in Motion (RIM), the company behind BlackBerry, is based in Canada, does the selection of device impact Canada's economy? Do the devices' functions (e.g., graphical interfaces) impact use, cognition, or productivity? What are the unique features of the device that make it capable of engendering new social, cultural, or personal behaviour? I ask all students to place their mobile device on the desk in front of them; I then ask them to password protect their phone. If they do not know how to manage this operation, there are sufficient students with the competency to assist. I argue that everyone should understand both how to lock one's mobile device and why such protections are important. Learning how to lock one's device is an introduction to practical work. Devices that students treasure as part of a quotidian practice require particular technical competencies. It may seem simple to some, or bizarre to others, but locking one's phone is a vital skill for students of media. Once every student is confident with this skill, we discuss how a mobile device can contain as much information as a filing cabinet. Students began to articulate why individuals should password protect their phones: some fear losing the device, others discourage friends who snoop through applications, and others raise issues about privacy. In the wake of the Occupy movement, many students worry that police can search through the entire contents of their device without a warrant. This potential intrusion on privacy is augmented by the fact that many students download (pirate) music without concern for copyright. Media students discovered the importance of Canada's Online Security Bill, dubbed *Protecting Children from Internet Predators Act.* Stephen Harper's Conservative government introduced this proposed amendment to the *Criminal Code of Canada* on February 14, 2012, during the 41st Parliament. This proposed law grants police departments access to personal information about Canadian internet users without a warrant. Following this bill as it moves through parliament (see for example, http://www.openparliament.ca) gave students access to civic information that allowed opportunities to voice their concerns to government officials. Students were encouraged to write to public officials; as a result of public backlash, the bill was referred back to the House Standing Committee on Justice and Human Rights for possible amendments. Media students with the basic digital competency of password protecting their mobile device have a resistance strategy. Students involved in protest movements shared this knowledge and their digital competency with other young activists.

PROFESSIONAL TWEETS

Students of media should not resist the social media application Twitter, a fast growing microblogging and social networking site. In fact, I argue one's Twitter feed functions as a kind of curriculum vitae (résumé). As libraries expand digital missions and goals, the U.S. Library of Congress signed a formal agreement with Twitter to archive every public tweet. When entering the professional world, a potential employer will "look you up" on Linked In and Facebook: however, Twitter tells a story about its users' lives. Tweeting about political unrest or useful resources for learning narrates a very different story than tweeting about what you ate for breakfast. In this vein, media students need to consider critical tweeting. By this, I mean using Twitter as a critical tool for building social and cultural capital. As students look at sample tweets, we examine differences between mundane and banal tweets as opposed to people who use Twitter in more critical ways. Critical uses of this tool are described within the context of the Arab Spring uprising. In 2009, international media were banned from the streets of Tehran in the wake of recent elections; many Iranians turned to Twitter as a means to ensure facts were communicated. As a result, the world learned about political unrest, military brutality, and electoral reform. Twitter functions as a vehicle for public journalism. Media students are asked to take up the challenge of using Twitter as a public mode of communication. To this end, students learn the functional elements of Twitter and its related services and applications. There is an unwritten "twitiquette" or conventions and rules that one needs to learn in order to build a following. Students learn about the conventions of finding like-minded people to follow, using hashtags and direct messages, posting links with shortened URLs, discovering effective third-party applications (e.g., TweetDeck, HootSuite, and Twitterific), and retweeting. By focusing and narrowing tweets to a particular topic, many students of media are representing their identity online in a controlled manner while building a solid foundation in their uses of this social media platform. The goal is to develop digital competency with Twitter in order to create a feed that has value. For example, one student's interests focused explicitly on sports. She considered herself a hockey fan and dreamed of a career as a sports broadcaster. Her Twitter account, as a critical practice, reflected her interests. She posted hockey scores. She also posted critical commentary about the games. For example, she noticed how Canada as a nation was represented through various iconic symbols; she questioned the politics of women's hockey as represented through ice time; she evaluated broadcasters' language when narrating the game. Soon, this student built a large following and understood how her Twitter feed (and archive) functioned as both a calling card and a political act. Politically, this media student's practical work raised awareness about gender inequalities and national symbols; socially, she found her voice for communicating in the social media world by responsibly adding to and commenting on the public discourse of sports; and personally, the student accumulated an archive of messages on the topic of sports that represented an identity that she hoped to use professionally.

SEMIOTIC GUERRILLA WARFARE

Umberto Eco (1979) used the term "semiotic guerrilla warfare" to describe a tactic for reading texts against "pre-established plans" (p. 150) or dominant messages;

this term is a method for oppositional decoding as a political act. As media systems encode messages with symbolic codes, these texts can function as a form of domination exerting social control. Advertising, for example, collects aesthetic forms to attract the eye; however, the dominant message is to sell goods or services. Students of media engaged in semiotic analyses of texts employ meaning-making strategies by isolating component parts of texts for additional scrutiny. As students write their analyses, I encourage practice work by asking students to remix these messages using the tools at their disposal. Some students create collages of images and text to intentionally change (and challenge) dominant messages. Other students demonstrate a growing competence in the uses of digital imaging tools (e.g., Photoshop, InDesign, etc.) to demonstrate control over design, typography, and message. Semiotic guerrilla warfare is also known as subvertising, culture jamming, and others. It is sometimes confused with street art, vandalism, or other forms of artistic appropriation. The goal for media students is not to engage in acts of destruction but to illustrate through practical work a disruption or subversion of mainstream institutions. Examples of student work can be found among the many "anti-ads" targeted at conspicuous consumption. One student took the symbol for an expensive car brand (BMW) and used digital tools to replace the type with subversive letters (BUY). In this way, ordinary symbols are made extraordinary, and this student's work draws attention to significance beyond what is expected. The student decided to print a number of these remixed symbols onto stickers; he then placed stickers around town to circulate his message. Another student found inspiration in Dove's (2004) Campaign for Real Beauty, which features real women, not models, advertising the company's products. To resist the beauty industry's assertion of women who are unrealistically thin if not unhealthy looking, this media student took an old Barbie doll and wrote the word "fat" across its body several times. She then filmed this doll using stop-motion animation engaging in typical activities including buying fast food, eating junk food, watching television, etc. As the video progressed, the student demonstrated competency in digital editing techniques as this doll's body began to morph into a larger, fatter woman. She ends the short video with text on the screen that reads "Fat Is Beautiful." In both examples, students illustrate the workings of semiotic guerilla warfare, how it works as a strategy for reading media texts, as a means for developing competency in digital tools for creating media messages, and as an intervention for changing how media institutions represent society.

CONCLUSION: DOING AND CREATING

There is something missing in these examples. In each case, students also engage in traditional academic scholarship. This is demonstrated by critical thinking, reasoned responses, and academic writing. In other words, students of media connect practical work and traditional scholarship so as to encounter new questions, problems, or issues. I have described three elements in a critical approach to doing media studies.

First, students identify media texts that require substantive study. We create arguments about dominant, negotiated, and oppositional readings of these texts. Second, by applying knowledge about digital tools, we further investigate our arguments by creating our own media texts in ways that support our arguments. Finally, students of media consider how our readings and creations work as interventions within society and culture; doing media studies interrogates sites of struggle and advocates for change. Given these elements, I am calling for a new kind of "digital essay" that employs both scholarship and digital practice. There are many other examples to draw from for inspiration. Students have geotagged global maps to provide information about media ownership; written and produced public service announcements about online bullying; and logged social media usage followed by a week-long effort of refusing and resisting social media. I encourage students to follow their interests, to ask questions, to do, and to create.

QUESTIONS

1. How would you classify your educational interests in terms of reading and writing? Are you more "reader" or "writer" when encountering print-oriented texts? What if you are reading and writing media texts?
2. Explain the terms "empowerment," "autonomy," and "agency." Provide examples of your media use and its relation to your explanation.
3. How is bricolage similar or different from culture jamming, remixing, and sampling?
4. How might an intervention work as a political act?
5. What kind of practical work could you apply to your questions about media?

NOTE

1. For example, C. S. Pierce's (1839–1914) representamen, object, interpretant; C. W. Morris's (1901–1979) sign vehicle, designatum, interpretant; and F. de Saussure's (1857–1913) sign, signifier, signified. For a full account of each scholar's work, as well as the approaches of other major figures in the field of semiotics, see Winfried Noth (1995), *Handbook of Semiotics*, Bloomington and Indianapolis: Indiana University Press.

REFERENCES

Adorno, T. & Horkheimer, M. (1944). The culture industry: Enlightenment as mass deception. In *Dialectic of enlightenment*. Trans. J. Cumming. New York: Continuum, 120–167.

Barney, D. (2005). *Communication technology*. Vancouver: UBC Press.
Buckingham, D. (2003a). Media education and the end of the critical consumer. *Harvard Educational Review* 73(3), 309–327.
Buckingham, D. (2003b). *Media education: Literacy, learning and contemporary culture*. Cambridge: Polity Press.
Buckingham, D. (2007). Media education goes digital: An introduction. *Learning, Media and Technology* 32(2), 111–119.
Buckingham, D. (2008). Introducing identity. In D. Buckingham (Ed.), *Youth, identity, and digital media*. (pp. 1–24). The John D. and Catherine T. MacArthur Foundation Series on Digital Media and Learning. Cambridge, MA: The MIT Press.
Chester, J. (2007). *Digital destiny: New media and the future of democracy*. New York: New Press.
Cook, J. (1995). The interpretative tradition. In M. Alvarado & O. Boyd-Barrett (Eds.), *Media education: An introduction*. (pp. 155–167). London: British Film Institute.
Cook, J. & Hiller, J. (1976). The institutionalisation of film and television study. In M. Alvarado & O. Boyd-Barrett (Eds.), *Media education: An introduction*. (pp. 18–20). London: British Film Institute.
Debord, G. (1957). *Psychographic guide of Paris*. (Ed.), The Bauhause Imaginiste, Denmark: Permild and Rosengreen.
Debord, G. (1967). *Society of the spectacle*. Trans. D. Nicholson-Smith. New York: Zone.
Drotner, K. (2008). Leisure is hard work: Digital practices and future competencies. In D. Buckingham (Ed.), *Youth, identity, and digital media*. (pp. 167–184). The John D. and Catherine T. MacArthur Foundation Series on Digital Media and Learning. Cambridge, MA: The MIT Press.
Eco, U. (1979). *A theory of semiotics*. Bloomington: Indiana University Press.
Hall, S. (1980). Encoding/decoding. In S. Hall, D. Hobson, A. Lowe, and P. Willis (Eds.), *Culture, media, language*. (pp. 128–138). Cambridge, UK: Unwin Hyman.
Hall, S. & Jefferson, T. (Eds.). (1975). *Resistance through ritual: Youth subcultures in post-war Britain*. Birmingham: Taylor and Francis.
Halloran, J. D. & Jones, M. (1986). The inoculation approach. In M. Alvarado & O. Boyd-Barrett (Eds.), *Media education: An introduction*. (pp. 10–13). London: British Film Institute.
Henderson, K. A., Bialeschki, M. D., Shaw, S. M., & Freysinger, V. J. (1989). *A leisure of one's own: A feminist perspective on women's leisure*. State College, PA: Venture Publishing.
Higson, A. & Vincendeau, G. (1986). Melodrama: An introduction. *Screen* 27(6). London: The Society for Education in Film and Television.
Hobbs, R. (2005). The state of media literacy education. *Journal of Communication*, 55(4), 865–871.
Hoggart, R. (1957). *The uses of literacy*. London: Chatto & Windus.

Iron Lady, The. (2012). Dir. P. Lloyd. Screenwriter Abi Morgan. Perf. Meryl Streep. The Weinstein Company. Film.

Jefferson, T. et al. (Eds.). (1975). *Working papers in cultural studies* 7 & 8. Birmingham: University of Birmingham.

Leavis, F. R. & Thompson, D. (1933). *Culture and environment*. London: Chatto & Windus.

Masterman, L. (1985). *Teaching the media*. London and New York: Routledge.

McLuhan, M. (1964). *The medium is the message: The extensions of man*. New York: Random House.

Morgan, R. (1998). Media education in Ontario: Generational differences in approach. In A. Hart (Ed.), *Teaching the media: International perspectives*. (pp. 145–167). New Jersey: Lawrence Erlbaum.

Murdock, G. & Phelps, G. (1973). Teachers in the classroom: Using mass media material. In M. Alvarado & O. Boyd-Barrett (Eds.), *Media education: An introduction*. (pp. 14–17). London: British Film Institute.

Noth, W. (1995). *Handbook of semiotics*. Bloomington and Indianapolis: Indiana University Press.

Postman, N. (1985). *Amusing ourselves to death: Public discourse in the age of show business*. New York: Penguin.

Postman, N. (1995). *The end of education: Redefining the value of schools*. New York: Knopf.

Scriven, M. & Paul, R. (1987). Critical thinking as defined by the National Council for Excellence in Critical Thinking. Proc. of 8th Annual International Conf. on Critical Thinking and Education Reform. Retrieved July 30, 2012, from http://www.criticalthinking.org/pages/defining-critical-thinking/766

Smith, R. (1972). *A social history of the bicycle: Its early life and times in America*. New York: American Heritage Press.

Whannel, P. (1969). Film education and film culture. *Screen 10*(3), 49–59.

Willis, P. (1980). *Common culture: Symbolic work at play in the everyday cultures of the young*. Boulder, CO: Westview Press.

3

POSTCOLONIALISM AND COMMUNICATION STUDIES

Amin Alhassan
University for Development Studies, Ghana

Scholarly interest in communication studies in what is today known as the Global South evolved and developed immediately after World War II around two main factors. First was the popularly expressed need for nation building in the former colonies in Asia, Africa, Latin America, and the Caribbean. Independence from colonialism meant these former colonies had to modernize their societies in order to participate in the international comity of nations. In this particular framework, communication studies scholarship became part of the international and national agenda of facilitating development and modernization. The second factor was a postwar international search for alternative means of influence in international relations. The war taught world leaders the painful lessons of the use of military force in international relations. Thus, the search for alternative means of influence—soft power—was at the heart of the founding of what was initially labelled *international communication* and subsequently qualified as *development communication*.

Prior to the war, the paradigm of international relations was founded around the concept of imperial realms of control, generally known as colonialism. The big powers, notably, Britain, France, Spain, Belgium, and Portugal, had colonies and those who controlled the largest piece of the colonial pie were considered the most powerful. The war not only weakened the key actors economically and militarily, but also transformed international relations around two blocs of West and East. The Axis powers of Germany, Italy, and Japan lost the war to the Allied powers of Britain, France, the Soviet Union, and the United States. But within the Allied powers, differences of systems of governance and political ideology became the defining fault lines that were to reshape the world into the American-led Liberal Democratic and capitalist regimes of the West, and the Soviet Russian-led Socialist and Communist regimes of the East.

Given the hard lessons of the use of military force, evident in the destruction of Europe and the decimation of Hiroshima and Nagasaki, the quest for soft power as the medium of control rose high on the agenda of the emerged big powers of the United States and Soviet Russia. It was against this background that United States President Harry Truman spelled out his new doctrine of international solidarity in March 1947, in which he argued that American assistance to Greece and Turkey would prevent those countries from falling to Communist Russian influence. When he was re-elected in 1949, in his inaugural address, he rearticulated his philosophy of containment from Communism by asking his country to champion the eradication of poverty, which according to him, was affecting two-thirds of the world. He told Americans that their country had the requisite scientific and technological means to alleviate global poverty in other countries, as their "poverty is a handicap and a threat to both them and the more prosperous areas" such as the United States (Truman, [1949] 1964). The **Truman Doctrine** then can be described as the ideological foundation of international development assistance between developed countries in the West and the former colonized countries of Asia, Africa, Latin America, and the Caribbean. It is generally considered to be the genesis of the new language of diplomacy, in which international development assistance became the means to win allies and containment from Communism, the newfound enemy of the West after the defeat of the Axis powers. However, in a more critical sense, it inaugurated a new form of soft power for controlling countries in what is sometimes called the Third World (Escobar, 1995).

The idea of international development that evolved from these two factors was based on the assumption that the Western countries' status of being "modern" explained their "developed" condition. The countries of the **Global South**, according to the Truman Doctrine, were poor because they were not modern. Thus the challenge was to transfer the modernist way of doing things, in areas such as health, education, governance, industry, and agriculture, for instance, to the Global South. This understanding of *transfer* as development was crucial in making *communication* and *media* the centrepiece of what was to become known as modernization and development (Lerner, 1958; Schramm, 1964). The communicative turn in modernization theory and practice meant that if only the right messages about development were transmitted through the right channel to the right target with maximum effect, development could be accomplished. This technocratic understanding of development, premised on the transmission model of communication, went in tandem with the strategic understanding from the corridors of power in developed industrialized countries that development and modernization, framed through international development assistance, was the "soft power" to control the postcolonial nation-states into the realm of influence of the West. Development communication as an area of expertise and as an academic field of inquiry became attractive to both the strategic minded (see Samarajiva, 1987; Simpson, 1993) and the charitably altruistic internationalist scholars, philanthropists, and activists who took the Truman challenge literally and have since gone out to the Global South to help with international development work, often as volunteers or within the institutional framework of nongovernmental organizations (NGOs), international multilateral organizations such as United Nations branches, or state organizations such as the Canadian International Development Agency (CIDA).

DEVELOPMENT COMMUNICATION THEORY

The technocratic understanding of the use of communication to enhance modernization gave rise to a new area of study called **development communication**, initially in the United States and later in Canada and Europe. Waisbord (2000, p. 1) defines development communication as the "application of communication strategies and principles in the developing world. It is derived from theories of development and social change that identified the main problems of the post-war world in terms of lack of development or progress equivalent to Western countries." While this definition encapsulates the general framework of development communication, Waisbord elaborates that how this is actualized in detail depends on the ideological and political position of the implementers. Against the multiplicity of theories that have been developed from different ideological and political positions, the field of development communication can be mapped around the following three main approaches: the modernization and behaviourist approach, the dependency school and its affiliate cultural imperialism thesis, and the more radical participatory approach.

The Modernization and Behaviourist Approach

This is sometimes referred to as the dominant paradigm of development communication because, ideologically and philosophically, it reflects the founding ideas of the Truman Doctrine, the transmission model of communication, a stage theory of world history espoused by Walt Rostow (1960), and strategically depends on marketing methods for social change. The founding text in this approach is Daniel Lerner's *The Passing of Traditional Society: Modernizing the Middle East* (1958). This book and subsequent ones in this tradition of scholarship rely on behavioural psychology of attitudinal change, personal influence, and motivation as the means to achieve social change and national development (Kunczik, 1984; Melkote and Steeves, 2001). The dominant paradigm ssumes a linear history of the world where progress through a lower level of human achievement to a higher level is the only means of individual and social development (Rogers, 1976). National development starts from individual behavioural modification from traditional conservativism to a more mobile and cosmopolitan outlook. The task of national development then is one of getting communication and the transmission of messages right so that people and society can move up the ladder of human civilization (Schramm, 1964).

It is against this philosophical understanding of development that Everett Rogers's *Diffusion of Innovations*, first published in 1962 and currently in its fifth edition, is considered the quintessential guide to promoting social change through the transfer of development messages from the developed countries to the developing ones. Essentially, it argues that any new idea or technology that needs to be adopted to improve on the conditions of a people goes through five stages of adoption: awareness, interest, evaluation, trial, and adoption or rejection. Thus the task of the communication specialist is to work through this model to enhance the adoption process.

Another transmission-oriented modernization approach to development communication is social marketing, where techniques of advertising are used to promote the adoption of what are considered to be development-oriented practices. For instance, in the fight against HIV/AIDS infection in the Global South, social marketing approaches are used to promote the use of condoms and other safe-sex practices. Social marketing, defined as "the design, implementation, and control of programs calculated to influence the acceptability of social ideas and involving consideration of product, planning, pricing, communication, distribution, and marketing research" (Kotler and Zaltman, 1971, p. 5) was first introduced into the field of development communication in the 1970s. For a more accessible and recent explanation of social marketing see Kotler et al. (2002).

A third behaviourist model under the dominant paradigm of modernization is *edutainment*, the combination of education and entertainment to influence human actions. This neologism is sometimes written as entertainment-education. Both designations refer to what Singhal and Rogers (1999, p. xii) define as "the process of purposely designing and implementing a media message to both entertain and educate, in order to increase audience knowledge about educational issues, create favourable attitudes, and change overt behaviour." Theoretically, it builds on Stanford Professor Albert Bandura's (1977) social learning theory, where the point is made that people learn through role models and the entertaining process. Both entertainment-education and social marketing models are commonly used in promoting cultural behavioural change projects such as encouraging the adoption of modern agricultural techniques or encouraging parents to send their female children to school.

But the challenge of doing development for which communication theory has been mobilized to help is more than just behavioural change. Beside the programmatic challenges of specific development initiatives such as health promotion and cultural and social change, communication is implicated in more complex ways than just fixing local problems. Some scholars have pointed out that if developing countries are simply to replicate the experience of **modernity** that characterizes the historical trajectory of Western nations, then what the modernization-as-development paradigm aimed at was simply westernization as development for the countries of the Global South. It focused on further integrating these countries into the economies of the developed Western countries that slavery and colonialism had inaugurated. Slavery and colonialism started the process of linking the economies of the Western countries and Africa in particular, where the latter was to produce free human labour for the agricultural and industrial needs of the West. With the end of slavery, the African continent, like the rest of Asia, the Caribbean, and Latin America, was to serve as a source of raw materials for the industrial needs of the West within a colonial framework. The end of colonialism required the invention of a new framework for controlling these countries. Thus, critical communication scholars have theorized the modernization-as-development paradigm as the latest reinvention of the colonial relationship (Luke, 1990). Communication scholars working to ensure effective transmission of development messages to bring about modernization were to some extent similar to the religious missionaries of the 18th and 19th centuries whose work paved the way for formal colonialism. If the missionaries of yesteryear worked ostensibly to save souls for heaven above, their modern-day counterparts are working to save souls from poverty for the heaven on earth called modern society or as Schramm puts it, "the Great Society" (Schramm, 1964).

In addition, the focus on individual behavioural factors and locality under the modernization paradigm implied that the problem of underdevelopment or lack of development was due to internal factors such as culture, personal attributes such as laziness, and psychological factors such as lack of empathy or need for achievement. The modernization theory thus bracketed out historical relations of exploitation and the wider political economic issues from the explanatory framework of development.

Dependency Theory and Cultural Imperialism

In response to the limitation of modernization as development, a new wave of scholarly currents emerged, especially from Latin America, that pointed out that there was a dialectical relationship between the developed status of the Western countries and the underdevelopment of the Global South (Gunder Frank, 1969; Amin, 1976). This was not only caused by historical factors of slavery and colonialism, but also was an ongoing process through trade and cultural relationships. These supporters of **dependency theory**, sometimes referred to as the dependency school, proved their thesis by showing how unequal trade relations between developing countries and the developed ones were the main source of exploitation. Most of the developing countries contributed to international trade as producers of raw materials whose prices were determined by markets in the developed countries. For instance, while Brazil and Ghana produced cocoa beans used in making chocolate, these beans were traded in commodities markets in London, UK, where the world prices were determined. In addition, factories where these cocoa beans were transformed into chocolate were located in Europe. In the end, the developed countries had the power to determine the value of the labour of the cocoa farmers in Ghana and Brazil, while the countries of the Global South had no control of the prices of industrial goods such as cars and refrigerators they imported from Europe.

Theoretically, dependency theory was developed out of the Marxist theory of imperialism. The focus was economic. But the conceptual resources of the political economy of imperialism were soon mobilized to describe what was considered a cultural dynamic that mimicked the economic logic of imperialism. This approach became known as **cultural imperialism** (Schiller, 1976; Hamelink, 1983). In offering a summary of its meaning, Kunczik (1984, p. 195) writes that "Cultural imperialism is in operation, as the dependency theorists see it, when the culture of a nation at the center is unilaterally imposed on the peripheral countries at the expense of their cultural integrity." Such an imposition occurred through the global media, whose extension across countries is justified on the democratic ideals of the "free flow of information." But as the dependency theorists pointed out, the idea of the free flow of information was used as an ideological smokescreen to culturally dominate countries whose media industries were not yet developed. In addition, the dependency theorists argued, solving development problems was essentially a political question and not just a matter of information transmission.

At the international and diplomatic level, the main contribution of the dependency theorists and cultural/media imperialism scholars was in the UNESCO-sponsored debates on the **New World Information and Communication Order (NWICO)** in the 1970s and 1980s. These debates focused on the need for a fair exchange of culture and information, occasioned by the mainstreaming of satellite technology that for the first time made it possible to transmit information across national borders without state control. Developing countries felt overwhelmed culturally by this technology that multinational corporations had. Media corporations, all predominantly Western and symbolized by Hollywood and international news agencies, dominated the international flow of cultural products such as news and movies. It was against this background that developing countries came together under the umbrella of the **Non-Aligned Movement** to demand a global agreement on curbing the dominance of Western media corporations in the name of cultural autonomy and integrity of developing countries. But the United States and Britain defended the status quo by saying this was antidemocratic and an ideological battle against the Western democratic principle of the free flow of information. When both the United States and Britain withdrew from UNESCO in 1985, Canada chose the neutral position of neither being for the position of the Non-Aligned bloc nor approving of the Western boycott. The United States, which was the single largest contributor to UNESCO's budget, returned in 2002. Its flexing of diplomatic muscle contributed to the collapse of the Non-Aligned Movement demand for equity in global cultural flows.

Participatory Approaches

Apart from the critical language developed under the rubric of cultural imperialism to interrogate the dominant paradigm, another intellectual movement that emerged, especially in the 1970s and 1980s, became known as **participatory theories and approaches** to communication and development. Paulo Freire made a seminal contribution to this thinking with his book *Pedagogy of the Oppressed*, published in Portuguese in 1968 and translated into English two years later. For Freire, the challenge of development is communicational and not informational. He develops his idea from the etymological understanding that communication is about communion and community, while information transmission is about power and control as understood in the sender and receiver transmission model of communication. In addition, empowerment is the basis of development and it is achieved first and foremost through the facilitation of the powerless to reclaim their power to name the world. Thus development starts at the discursive level of naming one's world. Freire labelled the process whereby the expert acts as a teacher who imparts knowledge or expertise *domination*. Thus the process in which the teacher/expert gives knowledge to students who then regurgitate the knowledge and repeat it in an exam, he called *banking education* and further argued that this model is complicit in the disempowerment of the poor. His alternative to banking education is called *problem posing education* whereby the poor are encouraged to recover their voices and collaborate with the teacher/facilitator to name their world by first defining their problems and then working to offer solutions. Such a process of asking the dispossessed to be part of a solution and not just be at the receiving end of prescriptive solutions is the crux of participatory communication and development. This approach thus seeks to close the distinction between theory and practice. Participatory communication and development revolves around the philosophical concept of *praxis*, simply defined as reflexive practice.

Freire developed his revolutionary thinking and theory of participation while working with Brazilian peasants. His rethinking of participation has inspired several development interventions framed as *participatory*. However, like all revolutionary concepts with a high promise, the Freirean concept of participation has recently been invoked to legitimize projects that are anything but *participatory*. In effect it has become a buzzword.

THE FOGO PROCESS IN CANADA

Despite the abuse of the conceptual promise of participation, one remarkable example that was initiated in Canada and has now become a global benchmark on the use of film or video as a participatory medium of development is called the **Fogo process**. Named after Fogo Island, located on the northwest coast of Newfoundland, the Fogo process refers to the process of using video to enable people categorized as poor to rename their world and offer their own perspectives on why they are said to be poor and what can be done about their poverty. To be precise, both the Fogo process and Freire's work on participation are contemporaneous. In 1965, the Economic Council of Canada issued a *Report on Poverty in Canada*. The then Director of the Extension Department at Memorial University, Donald Snowden, was enraged because to him the report was a classic case of using urban values to misrepresent rural problems and describe some rural communities in Canada as beyond economic redemption. It was a good example of how expert opinion—in this case, experts of economic development from Ottawa—had gotten it wrong. Snowden's point was that the rural areas of Canada were poor because of isolation and a lack of communication infrastructure to access information (Quarry, 1984; Williamson, 1990).

To demonstrate his idea, Snowden chose Fogo Island, a community that was suffering serious economic decline. The community, made up of ten separate settlements totalling 5,000 people, had for some 300 years depended on fishing as the mainstay of the local economy. But the declining fishing stock led to about 60 percent of the population living on government social assistance. The Canadian government's response to what it considered to be unsustainable fishing communities, such as Fogo Island, was to relocate the people to places in Newfoundland where the economy was vibrant. But for the Fogo Islanders, development was not just an economic decision; it was cultural. They had been used to Fogo Island as home and were not willing to be relocated. Snowden pointed out the situation occurred because the communities were not communicating horizontally among themselves as well as vertically among themselves and government or policymakers. The task of development communication was to provide these horizontal and vertical channels. Thus, Snowden collaborated with Colin Low, a filmmaker at the National Film Board of Canada, and initiated a project of filming community meetings and interviews to discuss community problems and what the people thought. These short films, 27 in total, were then screened for the community members to view their neighbours expressing their problems and opinions. This allowed the members to discover that they shared a common predicament. The films were then shown to provincial government officials, including the premier. The politicians were also given the opportunity to reply through film. The process triggered local energies among community members and created governmental attention to the people's problems. The idea of relocation was dropped and new ways of revamping the island were initiated, including massive government infrastructural expenditure on the area. The use of film or video to trigger social activism and development has come to be known as the Fogo process in development communication theory. It is also marked as the dawn of activist documentary media at the National Film Board of Canada as the period from 1967 to 1980 saw radical experimentation with the use of the moving image in social change (see Waugh et al., 2010). A 41-minute feature video documentary *Fogo Project—Memo from Fogo* that presents the Fogo process can be viewed online (Extension Service, 1972).

Since then, the Canadian success story of participatory video for development has been replicated in poor neighbourhoods of the United States and several countries in the Global South. However, a point to note is that these attempts outside Canada have yielded mixed results of modest successes and many disappointments, and exemplify the key point about development communication interventions that are based on participatory epistemology. Each context differs and any attempt to generalize from one success story may very well lead to disappointment. Here then is the reason that, despite its emancipatory promise, participation as a paradigm of development communication has failed to displace the dominant paradigm of modernization premised on behavioural change. As with the dependency theorists, and the cultural imperialism framework, participation has strong theoretical resonance but remains as a complement to mainstream modernization theory.

In recent times, the reduction in the cost of audio-visual media equipment and indeed the sheer ubiquity of digital photographic equipment (as in for instance the convergence of the camera and the cell phone) has made possible various innovative projects in media and civic participation. In following the Freirean philosophy of participation and the Fogo process principles of subject-produced media, these recent initiatives have relied on the power of the camera to amplify the voice of those at the margins of society, or as an instrument of recording evidence of abuse.

There are several international and local examples using subject-produced media for emancipatory or policy advocacy purposes. For instance, the international non-governmental organization Witness (http://www.witness.org) has acquired a global reputation for facilitating the generation and circulation of human rights videos. In some situations, subaltern or marginalized subjects have been able to document abuses and bring them to the attention of the international community for action. *Mapping Memories* is a local example of a collaborative project that empowers minority immigrant youth in Montreal to produce creative work aimed at positively impacting on policies and educational practices of their communities (see Miller et al., 2011). The possibility of uploading subject-produced media onto YouTube and the power of building communities of interest through avenues such as Facebook strongly suggest that the future of communication and development theory and practice may as well be tied to increased democratization of access to communication and information technologies.

Feminist Contributions

Apart from dependency theory and the participatory turn in development communication, another scholarly stream that has contributed in rethinking the role of communication in the emancipatory project in the Global South has been feminist theory. Despite their radical posture, dependency and participatory critiques of modernization could not really unpack the fact that mainstream development communication approaches were gendered in ways that are subtly patriarchal even as they promise emancipation to all. Given the fact that women and children have tended to be most affected by poverty in the Global South, many development initiatives were framed around their economic empowerment. But after some decades of intervention, some feminist scholars questioned the strategies and approaches used in executing social change initiatives. For instance, one particular enduring approach to development has been to seek to control population growth by introducing contraception services in developing countries. The idea that population growth should be regulated to correspond to resource availability is traced to Thomas Robert Malthus (1766–1834). In applying the Malthusian theory of population growth and economic development to the Global South, the assumption has been that providing women with family planning resources automatically empowers them. Given the historic role that the oral contraceptive pill as a revolutionary reproductive technology played in the emancipation of women in the developed Western countries, it appeared sound reasoning to conclude that it could be of great benefit to women in the Global South.

However, after several years of implementing family planning initiatives through diffusion of innovation, social marketing, and edutainment approaches, feminist scholars brought new illuminating perspectives to argue that governmental family planning programs in many developing countries were not really emancipatory. On the surface, making available reproductive technologies to women appears to be empowering. But on a critical examination, critics argued that women were introduced into development discourse because of their fertility and not as subjects requiring resources to become productive members of society (Greene, 2000). Greene articulates the argument that the mainstream Malthusian understanding of the need to control population growth is a particular form of rationality used to govern women's lives. In some countries of the Global South, governments used this conceived Malthusian population panic as an excuse to usurp women's right to choose when to have children. In Puerto Rico, for instance, by 1968, about 35 percent of Puerto Rican women of child-bearing age had been sterilized, often without their knowledge (Einsiedel, 2000, p. 177). An alternative feminist rationality is not to consider women and their reproductive capacities as objects for manipulation by external forces, but rather to consider them as subjects requiring economic, cultural, and political rights. These rights should include the power to choose on matters of reproduction and access to productive resources. Thus the Puerto Rican example contrasts with the experience of Sri Lanka where government family planning programming was embedded in broader universal education and primary health care policies, leading to a significant 52 percent drop in fertility (Einsiedel, 2000, p. 178). Thus the widening of the population and development debate to go beyond access to reproductive technologies and to include social, economic, and political rights of women has been considered one of the remarkable contributions from feminist scholarship to the theory and practice of communication and development.

INFORMATION AND COMMUNICATION TECHNOLOGIES

One of the means by which the modernization paradigm renews itself to play upon utopian promises is through the rhetoric of new technologies as a panacea for development. Mass communication theory or communication studies as a field of expertise has always been attracted to the issue of the development of the Global South for two reasons. First is the issue of communicativeness as a necessary ingredient of successful development, where the focus is on how to effectively carry out communication. The second has to do with the lure of technologies of communication when they are first introduced into society. Each time a new technology of communication is introduced, promises of social change are often proclaimed as anticipated benefits. And these expectations are often exaggerated within the area of international development. For instance, in the 1960s and 1970s when UNESCO was the leading UN agency in the field of development communication, it believed developing countries could speed up development by increasing the availability of mass media facilities. Thus it recommended that, at a minimum, every developing country should aim to provide for every 100 persons ten copies of a daily newspaper, five radio receivers, two cinema seats, and two television sets as a guarantee for successful modernization (Schramm, 1964; Melkote and Steeves, 2001). Some countries managed to achieve these statistical benchmarks, but failed to achieve "developed" status.

Despite the fact that this approach to development was misdirected, it fed into a renewed thinking of modernization as a project of communication; this time, not just as a transmission problem, but a case of **"information poverty."** If only the potential of new communication technologies could be unleashed in the Global South, development will happen, so the thinking went. The untested notion of "information poverty" received a new lease of life with the advent of digital communication technologies. The era of networked computer communication, and the convergence of telecommunication with the computer, revamped waning enthusiasm on international development, especially with the coinage of the term **digital divide**. The new information and communication technologies (ICTs) were considered to be capable of facilitating the speedy solution to development problems.

In Canada, the **International Development Research Centre (IDRC)** and CIDA, both federal government organizations, continue to invest many resources in this area through direct programmatic intervention such as IDRC's Acacia project (http://www.idrc.ca/acacia). The Acacia project is both a research and demonstrative project aimed at assisting "countries in Africa [to] apply information and communication technologies (ICTs) to social and economic development." One remarkable success of this project is the number of research publications that has resulted since 2005. However, the focus of both CIDA and IDRC on the latest technologies makes critical scholars question the motive for such ventures. Notably, critical scholars have questioned the reduction of the complex nature of development to just an issue of the digital divide, as if this latest divide is not a function of other older forms of divides, such as economic and literacy divides (Gandy, 2002; Shade, 2003; Gunkel, 2004). A recent Senate report from Ottawa evaluating CIDA's record of work in Africa concluded that after spending $12.4 billion of Canadian taxpayers' money in Africa over a period of 40 years, the agency did not have any tangible results to show as success (Senate of Canada, 2007). Part of the problem, the report noted, was that 81 percent of CIDA's staff were based in Ottawa, with only 19 percent working in the field. The story of CIDA as a development organization that has a big budget and delivers very little has led some critics to point out that international development intervention has led to what can be described as the development industry, dominated by politicians engaged in pork-barrel politics, technical experts, and NGO officials, with the actual target of development—the poor—losing out.

Despite the challenges that characterize institutionalized intervention in ICT for development, there are several instances of digital dividends from the spread of ICTs in the Global South apart from the use of video as an instrument of participatory media production as discussed earlier. In many developing countries the diffusion of mobile telephony in itself is a remarkable story of national and international development. About 1 percent or less of the people of the Global South had access to telephones in 1994 before the spread of mobile digital telephony (Alhassan, 2004). By 2010, mobile telephony networks had covered 90 percent of the world's population (ITU, 2010). It is significant to note that for the majority of people in the Global South, their first computer will be a smart phone, and not a laptop or desktop. Their first internet banking or online money transfer is likely to be done through a Web-based phone application.

What is remarkable is that the democratization of access to telephony and indeed the internet are not facilitated by international development assistance from the developed world to the developing world. They are mainly driven by the private sector in search of profit. Thus, despite the fact that the field of communication and development was founded as part of international development assistance, recent developments call for a rethinking of the field from a framework of aid and development assistance, to one of trade and investment.

POSTDEVELOPMENT AND POSTCOLONIAL LAMENTATIONS

The various attempts at critiquing modernization as development were aimed at causing a paradigmatic change. While this shift has not actually happened, the critiques have resulted in the development of the scholarly trajectories of dependency and cultural imperialism, as well as participatory approaches. As bodies of theories, these critiques have sometimes been appropriated into renewing modernization theory and practice, as evident in the adoption of the vocabularies of these critiques by institutions that symbolize the modernization approach. Institutions such as the World Bank, CIDA, the U.S. Agency for International Development (USAID) (all of which are institutional manifestations of the modernization paradigm) often appropriate the language of participation, community involvement, and local initiatives into their operations without actually following their original critical perspectives. Because these organizations are also the main employers and funders of international development initiatives and NGOs, the challenge for many scholars is not to fix development and make it work; rather, it is to rethink the whole project of international development as a mechanism of power and domination.

It is against this background that Michel Foucault's (1980) insight on how discourse and power represent reality and make certain truths visible while occluding others has been mobilized by a number of scholars of postcolonial theory to explain frameworks of global power relations and how the language of help, rescue, emancipation, and development are inventions of power to continue the process of governmentalization and domination. In this direction, the works of Edward Said (1979),V.Y. Mudimbe (1988), Chandra Mohanty (1991), Homi Bhabha (1990), and Arturo Escobar (1995) are exemplary of this tradition of scholarship. However, a distinction needs to be made between *postcolonial theory* and *postdevelopment theory*. While postcoloniality is concerned with the legacy of colonialism as it is textually manifested in film, literature, and other forms of representations, postdevelopment is concerned with development as a mechanism of governmentality invented and deployed to continue from where direct colonial subjection left off. Thus postcolonial theory has a wider scope than postdevelopment theory. But beyond these initial differences of scope, both share the same epistemological framework of employing discourse, knowledge construction, and power to interrogate social formations (Alhassan & Chakravartty, 2011).

If you have lived with the assumption and belief that international development, for which communication scholarship was implicated to help achieve its goals, is aimed at the economic, political, and social emancipation of the countries of the Global South, Arturo Escobar's (1995) **Foucauldian analysis** of development as an invention will lead you to a rethinking. By arguing that discourse is about the establishment of a set of relationships that make certain truths evident while denying other truths, categories such as "poverty" and "malnutrition" for instance, around which the whole enterprise of development is based, become questionable as absolutes. They are human constructions that have come about through the knowledge–power relations. In retrospect then, we can reflect on how the Fogo Islanders disproved the government of Canada's economic experts who had described them as poor. Through the medium of film, they recovered their voice to speak for themselves and redefined their situation as not being poor. Discourse then is not just about language that reflects reality out there; discourse has the primary function of inventing reality.

From such a radical perspective, Escobar reminds us that when Truman described two-thirds of the world as being poor, he actually imposed his version of reality on two-thirds of the world. In the process of privileging his truth, the World Bank (then called the International Bank for Reconstruction and Development (IBRD), the postcolonial state as a vestige of colonial domination, and the academic disciplines of economics, nutrition, and agricultural sciences were all implicated in this process of the "problematization of poverty" that needed intervention (Escobar 1995, p. 21).

Foucauldian analysis of discourse–power–knowledge as a mechanism for establishing a "regime of truth" requires that we map out the post–World War II historical conjuncture around which Truman made his proclamation. He was concerned with global domination and access to vital and strategic resources that needed to be within the reach of the Western economies and away from the reach of the then Soviet Union. But the era of direct colonialism was over. Thus the discourse of development was invented as soft power to control the Global South. If this perspective sounds convincing, you may ask yourself: who needs development? Is it the countries of the Global South or developed countries such as the United States, Britain, and Canada, to mention a few, who have established large bureaucracies of international development as part of their Ministries or Departments of Foreign Affairs?

Some critical scholars at the extreme left end of postdevelopment theory have called for abandoning any discussion of international development (Esteva, 1985). Others, including Escobar, have used the occasion of the deconstruction of development to propose alternatives to development (Ziai, 2004; Pieterse, 1998; and Matthews, 2004). A common feature of these new directions is a push for locality, participation, and self-initiative. Several NGOs have taken on the challenge to translate these revolutionary ideals into practice. It remains to be seen, however, whether these laudable approaches will survive the enduring hegemonic embrace of the dominant paradigm of modernization as development.

QUESTIONS

1. Why is communication theory relevant to development practice defined as an institutionally planned effort to bring about social change and progress in the Global South?
2. What accounts for the continued dominance of the "modernization as development" paradigm? Why are paradigms resilient?
3. Why has the participatory approach, which mobilizes local people in responding to their own developmental needs (e.g., the Fogo process), garnered less attention than the modernization or behaviourist approach?
4. Is providing information and communication technologies (ICTs), such as computers, cell phones, and digital cable, a viable response to development issues in the Global South? What aspects of this developmental practice might be subjected to criticism by adherents of the participatory, dependency, postcolonial, and/or postdevelopment schools of thought?
5. What is a discourse and how can this concept aid us in thinking about development communication and the realities of inhabitants of the Global South?

REFERENCES

Alhassan, A. (2004). *Development communication policy and economic fundamentalism in Ghana*. Tampere, Finland: Tampere University Press.

Alhassan, A. & Chakravartty, P. (2011). Postcolonial media policy under the long shadow of empire. In R. Mansell & M. Raboy (Eds.), *The handbook of global media and communication policy* (pp. 366–382).West Sussex, UK: Wiley-Blackwell.

Amin, S. (1976). *Unequal development: An essay on the social formation of peripheral capitalism*. New York: Monthly Review Press.

Bandura, A. (1977). *Social learning theory*. Eaglewood Cliffs, NJ: Prentice Hall.

Bhabha, H. (1990). The other question: Difference, discrimination and the discourse of colonialism. In R. Ferguson, M. Gever, T. T. Minh-Ha, and C. West, (Eds.), *Out there: Marginalization and contemporary cultures* (pp. 71–87). New York: New Museum of Contemporary Art/Massachusetts: MIT Press.

Einsiedel, E. F. (2000). Border crossing: Gender, development, and communication. In K. G. Wilkins (Ed.) *Redeveloping communication for social change: Theory, practice, and power* (pp. 175–183). Lanham, MD: Rowman & Littlefield.

Escobar, A. (1995). *Encountering development: The making and unmaking of the Third World*. Princeton: Princeton University Press.

Esteva, G. (1985). Beware of participation and development: Metaphor, myth, threat. *Development: Seeds of Change, 3*, 77, 78–79.

Extension Service. (1972). *Fogo Project—Memo from Fogo*. National Film Board of Canada/Memorial University of Newfoundland. Retrieved July 31, 2012, from http://collections.mun.ca/cdm4/item_viewer.php?CISOROOT=/extserv&CISOPTR=122&CISOBOX=1&REC=4

Foucault, M. (1980). *Power/Knowledge*. New York: Pantheon Books.

Frank, A. G. (1969). *Latin America: Underdevelopment or revolution*. New York: Monthly Review Press.

Gandy, O. H. (2002). The real digital divide: Citizens versus consumers. In L. Lievrouw & S. Livingstone (Eds.) *Handbook of new media: Social shaping and consequences of ICTs* (pp. 448–460). London: Sage.

Greene, R. W. (2000). Governing reproduction: Women's empowerment and population policy. In K. G. Wilkins (Ed.) *Redeveloping communication for social change: Theory, practice, and power* (pp. 27–38). Lanham, MD: Rowman & Littlefield.

Gunkel, D. J. (2004). Second thoughts: Towards a critique of the digital divide. *New Media & Society 5*(4), 499–522.

Hamelink, C. (1983). *Cultural autonomy in global communication: Planning national information policy*. New York: Longman.

ITU. (2010). *World telecommunication/ICT Development report 2010*. Paris: ITU.

Kotler, P., Roberto, N., & Lee, N. (2002). *Social marketing: Improving the quality of life*. Thousand Oaks, CA: Sage Publications.

Kotler, P. & Zaltman, G. (1971, July). *Social marketing: An approach to planned social change*. Journal of Marketing, 3–12.

Kunczik, M. (1984). *Communication and social change: A summary of theories, policies and experiences for media practitioners in the Third World*. Bonn, Germany: Friedrich-Ebert-Stiftung.

Lerner, D. (1958). *The passing of traditional society: Modernizing the Middle East*. New York: The Free Press.

Luke, T. W. (1990). *Social theory and modernity: Critique, dissent, and revolution*. Newbury Park: Sage Publications.

Matthews, S. (2004). Post-development theory and the question of alternatives: A view from Africa. *Third World Quarterly, 25*(2), 373–384.

Melkote, S. R. & Steeves, H. L. (2001). *Communication for development in the Third World: Theory and practice for empowerment*, 2nd Edition. London: Sage Publications.

Miller, L., Luchs, M., & Dyer Jalea, G. (2011). *Mapping memories: Participatory media, place based stories & refugee youth*. Montreal, QC: Concordia University. Retrieved July 31, 2012, from http://storytelling.concordia.ca/refugeeyouth/book

Mohanty, C. (1991). Cartographies of struggle: Third world women and the politics of feminism. In C. Mohanty, A. Russo, & L. Torres (Eds.), *Third world women and the politics of feminism* (pp. 1–47). Bloomington: Indiana University Press.

Mudimbe, V. Y. (1988). *The invention of Africa*. Bloomington: Indiana University Press.

Pieterse, J. N. (1998). My paradigm or yours? Alternative development, post-development, reflexive development. *Development and Change, 29*, 343–373.

Quarry, W. (1984). The Fogo process: An interview with Donald Snowden. *Interaction* 2(3), 28–63.

Rogers, E. (1976). Communication and development: The passing of the dominant paradigm. *Communication Research 3*(2), 213–240.

———. (2003). *Diffusion of innovation* (5th ed.). New York: The Free Press.

Rostow, W. W. (1960). *The stages of economic growth: A non-Communist manifesto.* Cambridge, UK: Cambridge University Press.

Said, E. (1979). *Orientalism*. New York: Vintage Books.

Samarajiwa, R. (1987). The murky beginnings of the communication and development field. In N. Jayaweera & S. Amunugama (Eds.), *Rethinking development communication* (pp. 3–19). Singapore: AMIC.

Schiller, H. I. (1976). *Communication and cultural domination*. White Plains, NY: International Arts and Sciences Press.

Schramm, W. (1964). *Mass media and national development*. Stanford, CA: Stanford University Press.

Senate of Canada. (2007). *Overcoming 40 years of failure: A new road map for Sub-Saharan Africa*. Ottawa: Government of Canada.

Shade, L. R. (2003). Here comes the DOT Force!: The new cavalry for equity? *Gazette: the International Journal for Communication Studies 65*(2), 107–120.

Simpson, C. (1993). Mass communication research, counterinsurgency, and scientific "reality." In W.S. Solomon & R.W. McChesney (Eds.), *Ruthless criticism: New perspectives in U.S. communication history* (pp. 313–348). Minneapolis, MN: University of Minnesota Press.

Singhal, A. & Rogers, E. M. (1999). *Entertainment-education: A communication strategy for social change*. Mahwah, NJ: Lawrence Erlbaum.

Truman, Harry. ([1949]1964). *Public papers of the President of United States: Harry S Truman*. Washington, DC: US Government Printing Office.

Waisbord, S. (2000). *Family tree of theories, methodologies and strategies in development communication*. New York: Rockefeller Foundation.

Waugh, T., Baker, M. B., & Winton, E. (Eds.). (2010). *Challenge for change: Activist documentary at the National Film Board of Canada*. Montreal; Ithaca: McGill-Queen's University Press.

Williamson, H. A. (1990). The Fogo Process: Development support communication in Canada and the developing world. In F. L. Casmir (Ed.), *Communication in development: A multinational perspective* (pp. 270–288). Norwood, NJ: Ablex Publishing.

Ziai, A. (2004). The ambivalence of post-development: Between reactionary populism and radical democracy. *Third World Quarterly*, 25(6), 1045–1060.

4

BEYOND THE F-WORD: A CONSTELLATION OF FEMINIST CONCEPTS FOR MEDIA RESEARCHERS

Kim Sawchuk
Concordia University

I have intentionally called myself a feminist since my late teens. I am now in my venerable 50s and my allegiance to and appreciation of feminism as fundamental to communication research and media activism hasn't wavered. Feminist literature, theory, culture, and politics are very much present in Montreal, my home town, including a recent conference of young feminists (*Rebelles*) that has led to an ongoing national listserv of events, alternative radio shows such as *Ladies Home Electronics Companion*, *Venus*, and *Dykes on Mykes*; the ongoing success of digital media arts organizations such as MAWA (Winnipeg) and Studio XX (Montreal); and the creation of a Canada Research Chair in Feminist Media Studies.

Yet in the midst of this *camaraderie*, and arguably vibrant feminist culture, there have been moments when I have had the distinct feeling that to speak from a feminist standpoint in settings that are not overtly feminist is either surprising or just plain unwelcome. Raised eyebrows that quietly ask, "What, you're still a feminist?" are occasionally accompanied by remarks that interrogate feminism's relevance in these "postfeminist" neoliberal times, which assert the values of hyperindividualism over collective actions and identities. This general indifference or even overt hostility to feminism can, I will admit, lead to an uncomfortable self-silencing in academic and social situations. The fear of recrimination may lead one to decide it is prudent to hold back from overtly naming oneself, or one's research, feminist for fear of being misunderstood, pigeon-holed into what a colleague once quipped was "a niche market," or even having one's research proposal laughed at or rejected.

I want to better comprehend these fears of feminism and to affirm the ongoing intrinsic relevance of feminism to the intertwined fields of media, communication, and cultural studies. To do so, I reflect upon the opening anecdotal observations, which intentionally highlight the quizzical and sometimes abject affective responses to the "f-word," detailing some of the historical representations of feminist issues, goals, and values in the media, as they have been analyzed by feminist media critics. This is followed by a discussion of the distinction between feminism as a paradigm consisting of identifiable *frameworks* and a feminist paradigm as a *constellation of concepts*. Three concepts central to feminism—gender, sex, and sexuality—are featured in this discussion. Following this, feminism's alliance with critical race studies and queer theory is articulated. I end with a brief reflection on my desires for a feisty feminist future. As I am arguing, a conceptual approach to feminist theorizing allows for a critical flexibility that is capable of adapting and responding to both persistent *and* new social, political, cultural, and intellectual challenges in our discipline. It asserts a way of finding feminism.

FEMINISM IN THE MEDIA

Let me be clear. There are two separate but interrelated issues at stake here: the syndrome that one can name as "fear of feminism" and the fear of naming oneself a feminist because of a sense that it is just not welcome. The latter is not for mere lack of courage, but can be understood as part of a systemic or historical set of conditions that create, as Raymond Williams would say, "a structure of feeling" (1977, p. 127): a wonderful oxymoron that combines an analysis of both thought and emotion in a given historical moment within a particular set of conditions. What, then, has contributed to a structure of feeling, institutionally and culturally, that can breed a fear of feminism?

Let us begin with the presentation of feminism in the news media. As research on the depiction of feminism in the news has indicated (Tuchman, 1978; Freeman, 2001, 2011; Hinds & Stacey, 2001), feminism doesn't get much press and, when it does, it isn't always great. Hilary Hinds and Jackie Stacey have analyzed how British news coverage has historically painted feminism and feminists as "bra burners" and "career-driven superwomen" and contemplated trends of reconciling feminism with femininity, as in the case of images of Princess Diana, as well as a fascination with "women who kill." Canadian newspaper accounts describing the "new wave of feminism" in the late 1960s and early 1970s implied that those participating in the "women's liberation movement," as it was often termed at the time, were simply being carried along by a faddish force outside either thought or a conscious assessment of systemic and structural inequities between men and women, such as persistent differences in wages even when the two sexes occupy the same job (Johnson, 1969, p. W5).

In 1970, a strike by teachers in Ontario was discussed as being supported by a wave of feminism sweeping the country (Johnson, 1970, p. 11). This was accompanied by another report on feminist activities in Australia, whose headline conveyed the warning that "feminism spreads" (ibid, p. 11). Women, it was assumed, were being seized by a kind of mob mentality, devoid of rational thought, and brainwashed by a manipulative and vindictive elite vanguard of troublemakers (Sawchuk, 2008b). This media discourse on the viral spread of feminism from all quarters of the globe was used to conjure the specter of the bra-burning, man-hating women's libber, a caricature of feminism's underlying sophistication as a theory and complexity as a political practice.

Canadian communication scholars, such as Barbara Freeman (2001) and Valerie J. Korinek (2000), have looked carefully at these representations of women's issues, and feminism, in the media. Freeman has noted the ways that the 1970s *Report on the Royal Commission on the Status of Women in Canada* orbited the main pages of the news, instantiating women as "the satellite sex" whose concerns were secondary to the "real" political issues of the day. This tendency has a long history within news reporting on women's issues, in which a traditional distinction has existed between stories assumed to cater to women and stories oriented to men (Van Zoonen, 1988). The sections in the news for women pejoratively were known as "the pansy patch" and covered concerns associated with femininity and the domestic sphere: the house, gardening, shopping, children, cooking (Tuchman, 1978), while stories associated with the public sphere of politics and business were assumed to be of interest to men (Holland, 1998).

Such assumptions may correspond to the interests of "real" women and men, but what such a persistent division between "soft" and "hard" news ignores is how these activities become associated with one sex or the other, and how real men or women come to accept these subject positions as their own and psychically "invest" in them (Henriques et al., 1998). *Normative* assumptions about ideal forms of femininity and masculinity—that is, implicit messages of right and wrong behaviour that are assumed to be the purview of one sex or the other—are not only represented but also perpetually encoded in these small but persistent ways: such encodings have what might be called a *performative* effect on bodies and subjects (Butler, 1990; de Lauretis, 1987), as Iris Marion Young explores in *Throwing Like a Girl* (1990). One can take the marketing of colour-coded diapers for babies as a prime example of the ways that powerfully gendered messages are emitted from the moment that a child is born (Sawchuk, 1992) and continue on into adulthood. In *Pink Ribbons, Inc.* (2006), Samantha King has written cogently and critically about the marketing strategies behind the "pink-ribbon" campaigns for breast cancer research, questioning how much campaign money actually goes to research while pointing out the inculcation of a what she calls a "tyranny of cheerfulness" (Fillion, 2006).

However, all is not so simple or closed off to either negotiation or overt change. Korinek's *Roughing It in the Suburbs* (2000), on the Canadian women's magazine *Chatelaine*, highlights the surreptitious ways that feminism was presented in its pages, particularly with the rise of Doris Anderson to the position of editor. Korinek's research demonstrates that even when it was not overtly articulated, classical feminist issues (abortion, lesbianism, violence against women, pornography) acquired a popular representational presence in the traditional women's media of the weekly glossy magazine.

In the context of North America, perhaps the most infamous portrayal of feminism in the media was the June 29, 1998, *Time* magazine cover with the bodiless heads of Susan B. Anthony, Betty Freidan, Gloria Steinem, and Calista Flockhart (as Ally McBeal) on a black cover accompanied by the provocative question "Is feminism dead?" While the article itself was slightly more complicated—it questioned feminism's connection to the mores of celebrity culture—the image implied something quite different. The selection of heads representing the history of feminism as a succession of icons from a first wave of suffragettes, to the second wave of the 1960s, to an excessively skinny, neurotic television character of the 1990s is telling. In this imaging of a lineage of feminism, all of the women are white, evidencing a colour-blindness to the contributions of women like Angela Davis, Alice Walker, Audre Lord, June Jordan, Trinh T. Minh-ha, Chandra Mohanty, and Gloria Anzuldua to the movement. African-American, First Nations, Asian, and Latina women are absented from this depiction of the history of American feminism. This is consolidated, visually, by the use of a white face on a black background.

Such an image, promoted as "North American," likewise obliterates feminism's different heritages in specific national contexts: for example, in Canada one might have included the images of Nellie McClung, Judy Rebick, Rosemary Brown, Lee Maracle, and Alanis Morrisette. One of the key points for feminism in Canada is how easily we may accept American popular culture or traditions as our own, while the obverse is not necessarily the case. And while feminism is an international movement that spills over borders (Sarikakis & Shade, 2008; Mohanty, 2003), I would argue that it is paramount that we pay attention to our local histories, and by local I do not just mean the products of Canada's major media industries or our cadre of home-grown international celebrities. As important are the myriad of ways that a feminist presence is maintained at the grassroots in a variety of arts and cultural institutions; and here Sharon Fernandez's documentation of the story of the Desh Pardesh video and film festival (a Toronto-based arts festival bringing forward "the voices of those who are most silenced inside the South Asian community and society at large: gays, lesbians, bisexuals and trans-gendered people" [2006]) is exemplary. More work and research on the connections between activism and the arts in Québec and Canada are necessary and would reveal the deep connections between the history of feminism and cultural activism, a history touched upon in the recent exhibit WACK! Art and the Feminist Revolution at the Vancouver Art Gallery (2008–2009).

Even if one imagines a Canadianized version of the *Time* cover, such a picture accepts much of what feminism counters: the idea that a single individual Caucasian female can stand in for a social movement. In this way, such an image brought to the fore anxieties about a future for feminism and its ability to regenerate itself. The question "Is feminism dead?" rhetorically implies its own answer: the possibility that indeed it was sucked into a vortex of celebrity postfeminism that made previous generations seem, well, old and dated. And, after all, who wants to belong to a dead movement?

"YOU'RE ALL A BUNCH OF FEMINISTS"

I want to return to my initial questions but in another manner. Feminist fears for the physical well-being of women are borne out by statistics that indicate the presence of ongoing violence committed against women by men (Beres, Crow, & Gotell, 2009). This doesn't mean that women are incapable of violence, as Yasmin Jiwani's analysis of the racially motivated murder of Reena Virk by a gang of teenage girls forcefully brings home (2006). From this perspective, it is not a given that men are inherently or *essentially* violent, any more than it is an inevitable given that women are kind and nurturing. One of the assumptions of a feminist analysis is that one is not born a woman, one becomes a woman: in other words, biology aside, we learn the cultural mores of acceptable femininity and masculinity.

Declaring oneself a feminist or simply being labelled a feminist can be risky, as one is reminded every December 6. This is the day in 1989 that a lone gunman entered Montreal's *L'école polytechnique* and murdered 14 young engineering students, all of them women. In his murderous rampage he shouted "you are all a bunch of feminists." His suicide note, reprinted on the pages of newspapers worldwide, explicitly blamed feminists for instigating policies that made it more difficult for men, like him, to enter into their traditional professions, like engineering, which had opened its doors to women: never mind, of course, that women are still underrepresented in the sciences. He also iterated his contempt for 19 public women named as feminists, including Francine Pelletier, an outspoken francophone journalist. One would think that such an event would have simply made evident what many women have felt at intermittent moments when walking down a dark street alone or in the confines of their homes: misogyny (the hatred of women), homophobia (the hatred and fear of homosexuality), and sexism (the systemic perpetuation of gendered injustices) exist and can have deadly consequences.

For many feminists at the time this was not an isolated event and was instead a sign of a broader malaise. Maureen Bradley's video *Reframing the Montreal Massacre* (1995, 2006) takes a critical look at the media coverage of the Polytechnique to question the denials in the media that this was a misogynistic attack connected to structural issues of violence against women. Bradley's video pays particular attention to the way that Canada's pre-eminent female reporter at the time, Barbara Frum, underscored the attack as a more general human tragedy and chastised the feminist movement for wanting to seize the moment to address these issues publicly (Bradley, 2006).

As these examples of the depiction of feminism in the media remind us, feminism is sometimes treated with a dread and horror that can have terrible and tragic consequences. But such media treatments also point to some of the issues that are important to consider *for* feminism. It is first and foremost a reminder that being female, biologically, is not the same as being a feminist, nor does one guarantee the other. Barbara Frum, a successful woman in the media, dismissed and denied feminism in her coverage of the event, asserting that this was a human tragedy and not just one affecting women.

Feminist research on power, class, gender, and politics has looked at the careers and policies of conservative women in positions of political power, such as Margaret Thatcher or Australia's Pauline Hanson, to make this point (Schreiber, 2008). In a more contemporary context, the distinction is evident in the example of former American vice-presidential candidate turned celebrity, Sarah Palin, whose agenda was to consolidate very traditional family values that run counter to feminist politics (Douglas, 2008). Palin used her image of traditional femininity to advocate for restrictive definitions of "family" that were to include only heterosexual married couples as legitimate: in this case, a woman is promoting a very powerful message about **hetero-normativity** (heterosexuality is a given, as are all the values associated with male–female couples). Wrapped in a blanket of unabashed patriotism, this hetero-normative political strategy has since been picked up by Michele Bachmann in the United States, as well as the Wildrose campaign, led in Alberta by Danielle Smith. Critiques of the patriarchal basis of unquestioning allegiances to the state, a legitimation of the violence wrought in the name of the defence of the fatherland, and an identification of the citizen as consumer (as in the Wildrose Campaign) constitute but one of the many key contributions of feminist communication scholars to analysis of power relations (Razack, 2004). Given this context, being feminist does not mean promoting all who are female; however, it does entail an examination of women because of a history of their exclusion from the research agenda within the social sciences. Gayatri Spivak once termed this historically and contextually contingent concern as one of "strategic essentialism" (1990).

At the same time, Frum's position in 1989 is a reminder why feminists who have examined the numbers of women getting positions in the media (or university departments) are careful to not simply end the struggle at better representation for females in organizations. Better representation can be a part of the initial feminist agenda in organizations: that has been the point of affirmative action programs that try to rectify gender biases in a particular field (van Zoonen, 1995; Steiner, 1998). Such statistical analyses can reveal systemic inequities of power based on assumed differences between the capacities of men and women: one need only look at the persistent wage differentials between men and women in all occupations to understand this point. Yet the inclusion of women into the media or university will not *per se* make a difference to the media representations (or the curriculum) that are then produced and circulated within an institution. While individual women may have gained from the feminist struggle to allow women access to the public sphere, this does not mean that women who enter into any profession either have a knowledge of their indebtedness to these past struggles, nor are they necessarily carrying the torch of feminism. Further, the "un-coupling" of feminism from biological sex opens the door to the participation of "men in feminism" (Jardine & Smith, 1987).

This complex situation of feminist politics leads me to agree with Frum in one respect. In moments such as the Polytechnique attack, it is important to remember those individual lives involved and ask when, strategically, the time is right to make an issue feminist. As I recall, these points *were* debated within the feminist community at the time (if not the press). A feminist analysis of the news, such as Bradley's, recuperates the identities of the murdered women, examining how their names, Geneviève Bergeron, Hélène Colgan, Nathalie Croteau, Barbara Daigneault, Anne-Marie Edward, Maud Haviernick, Maryse Laganière, Maryse Leclair, Anne-Marie Lemay, Sonia Pelletier, Michèle Richard, Annie St-Arneault, Annie Turcotte, and

Barbara Klucznik Widajewicz, were often obliterated into the general category of "14 young women" or "victims" in news reports, while the name of the killer was repeated, earning him a place in the hall of infamy.

It is important to acknowledge that despite its complex iterations and contrary to media representations, feminism may hold a core set of values: to end all forms of gender injustice, including the tyranny of the concept of a universal subject in which "man" can stand in for "woman." Yet while this may signal a minimal commonality, feminists do deliberate and may agree or disagree on the appropriate course of action to take. Feminism may be a paradigm within media studies, but this does not mean that feminists are a homogeneous group. But what does one mean by a paradigm?

PARADIGMS AND KEY CONCEPTS

I once wrote, in a set of lecture notes for a course on Media and Feminist Theory, that "Feminism was not a paradigm but a field of inquiry." In retrospect I think that feminism can be thought of as a paradigm. By **paradigm**, I draw upon the work of Thomas Kuhn, who defined paradigms in the structure of scientific revolutions as intellectual worldviews that offer both everyday but also scientific explanations of how things operate (1962). Kuhn uses the example of how Nicolaus Copernicus upset European understandings of the cosmos by asserting that the earth rotates around the sun rather than the obverse. Marketing researchers speak of a paradigm shift that made the consumer, as opposed to the product, the centre of contemporary marketing research. Computer geeks speak of a paradigm shift from one technology to another. Embedded in both academic and popular uses of the term *paradigm* is the idea that a revolutionary movement of one sort or another has taken place.

Almost every textbook on feminism will proclaim the difficulty of defining feminism (Gatens, 1991; Van Zoonen, 1994) yet it is arguable that feminism has created a paradigm shift in disciplines such as communication and media studies. The paradigm of feminism has usurped a biologically deterministic patriarchal logic that proclaims a natural order to the universe where men are assumed to be inherently superior (mentally and physically) to women because of biological differences. Feminism upsets the presupposition and hierarchical notions embedded in hegemonic or common-sense understandings of biological difference. Biological determinism presupposes that biological sex is stable and unassailable and that social behaviour or psychological identification (gender) is merely a consequence of naturally occurring differences between the sexes. Defenders of a biological determinism make a strict division between males and females, and then assume that this accounts for different behaviours instantiating a kind of gender script. I have a uterus, therefore I am girl, therefore I shall find a suitable man to reproduce the species. I am a man, therefore I am under the sway of testosterone, therefore my aggressive behaviour is not my fault. This perspective, full of contradictions, tends to accord women superiority in terms of the emotions, while men are seen as inherently rational, except in moments when violent action is called for to protect themselves, the family, or the nation.

Texts such as *Men are from Mars, Women Are from Venus* (Gray, 1992) and television shows like *Brain Sex* (Moir & Jessel, 1989) are emblematic of popular representations of the biologically deterministic position that seems to operate as "common sense." In media and communication theory this assumption lurks in classical theories, such as that of Harold Lasswell (1960) in which there is an assertion that the precondition of democracy is rationality and "sentiment aggregates" are depicted as a threat to the realization of a truly rational public. Feminist media studies does not deny that biology matters, although *how* it matters is debated. Indeed, a significant body of feminist media research has been to explore how we communicate with more than words (Marks, 2002; Probyn, 1992) as well as to examine the representations of the body in media texts. The cult of beauty, fashion, sexuality, eating, and health are all areas where a feminist reconceptualization of the body enters into media studies (Bordo, 1993; Davis, 1997; Marchessault & Sawchuk, 2000; Nadeau, 2001). Feminist political theory challenges the primordiality of rationality as either the purview of men or, in some instances, the strict division between rationality and sentiment. This concern with the body and embodiment historicizes, contextualizes, and challenges biological determinism and a logic that proclaims the natural inferiority of women to men.

While feminists might agree with an analysis of gender injustice, the conclusions drawn and the solutions found to rectify such a situation are not always unified. For some, this means usurping gender binaries by understanding the fluidity of gender roles (Bell, 2010; Bornstein, 1993; Devor, 1989). For others, such as those who identify with the eco-feminist movement, this means accepting these binaries and revaluing the traditional strengths of women (Griffin, 1978/2000). This is often the distinction between a feminist studies focused on gender and the processes of gendering, and a feminist studies predicated on the study of women. What they have in common, minimally, is a will to disrupt hierarchies of power that are based on sex and gender difference. And here a quick dip back into terminology and a few core concepts.

By *sex* I mean one's supposed biological sex; by *gender* I mean the social and cultural adoption of behaviours, attitudes, and perceptions of what is or is not appropriate for persons of a particular sex. Emblematic of this position, which questions the relationship between sex and gender and their conflation, is Simone de Beauvoir's *The Second Sex* (1949/1989), which claimed that "one is not born a woman; one becomes a woman." This proclamation challenges the idea that "human beings" are undifferentiated, universalizable subjects. De Beauvoir forcefully makes the case that this lack of acknowledgment often made woman subservient to man. However, this distinction between biology and culture or sex and gender is not so clear-cut.

The term *sex* has two significations. First, it can be an act or action that denotes one's sexual orientation or sexuality whereby one comes to understand one's self as lesbian, gay, bisexual, heterosexual, or homosexual. In this respect, traditional research distinguishes between sexual identity and sexual role: the first denoting what a person may identify as, the other term referring to how that person publicly enacts his or her sexuality. Second, sex can refer to one's biological sex. One of the fundamental questions for feminist researchers of the biological basis of sex is how we come to understand biology and what biology we are speaking of when conceptualizing sex: is it chromosomal, hormonal? Is it based on secondary sexual characteristics: what if one has a hysterectomy? Small breasts? A mastectomy? Are you less than or no longer a woman? What of a small penis? Are you less a man? Researchers studying human biology contend that there is much more variation within the sexes than is commonly acknowledged precisely because of the comfort and promotion of a dualistic sex-gender dichotomy (Devor, 1989; Fausto-Sterling, 1992). As well, those who are transgendered complicate our common-sense understandings of the biology as firm ground (nature), upon which is built gender (culture) (Rubin, 2003).

Gender itself is a complicated concept: for those who study gender there is a basic distinction between gender roles, for example, and gender identity: gender identity may be how one individually sees oneself while gender roles denote the expectations, practices, and performances of that identity. Feminist researchers in media studies deploy this language. As Dorothy Smith (1993) cogently writes: "Introducing the concept of gender into feminist thought was an important political move. It meant that we did not have to argue our way at every step out of the biological connections implicit in the concept of sex" (p. 159). This doesn't mean taking gender as a "given determination as a discursive entity" (p. 120) as Smith suggests. It is a "phenomenon" and not just a "variable."

Feminist research examines these questions and sets of concepts, looking at their circulation in media texts, organizations, and practices in everyday life. These concepts aren't just given but always up for debate and discussion. As Smith (1993) illuminates, "Taking up 'gender' from within, exploring social relations gendering the particular local historical sites of women's experience, means attending to specificities, not gender in the abstract, not as total, but as multiple and sometimes contradictory relations" (p. 159). This analysis, which takes up the specific processes of *gendering* the media's interplay with these issues is vital to comprehend and is at the core of feminist media studies. This initial cluster of concepts is at the heart of that constellation known as feminism and part of what we might call the feminist paradigm in media studies. And here I want to return to the distinction I suggested between a paradigm and a framework.

FEMINIST FRAMEWORKS

I addressed the ways that feminism is framed within the press as something to be feared. This idea of framing is distinct from understanding feminism as a series of frameworks. If a paradigm is a kind of overarching position constituted by interrelated concepts, a framework designates a way to classify different branches of feminism into subcategories within a broader paradigm. A **framework**, as a term, tries to identify the specific epistemological or ontological assumptions that lie beneath the walls of a particular subcategory, which provide an invisible scaffolding for an analysis or an argument. There have been a number of ways that feminism has been thought of as a framework that is of relevance to communication, media studies, and cultural studies.

One predominant framework for understanding feminism in the academic and the popular press is as a series of waves. This metaphor of the wave can be understood as demarcating a series of feminist positions, or frameworks, that are numerically ordered as first, second, and third. These numberings correspond to both historical periods and a set of perspectives that are aligned with a particular political agenda. First wave feminism, it is said, is allied with the suffragette movement and begans at the turn of the 20th century until well after World War I, when women earned the right to vote in the United States. The second wave of feminism is assumed to begin in the 1960s (after the presumed dormancy of feminism in the 1950s). This feminist period is characterized by a concern with finding solidarity between women and the fight for equal rights in the workplace. The third wave of feminism, it is suggested, was launched by a younger generation of women dissatisfied with what was perceived as the dogmatism of second wave feminists who were seen as having a unified conception of sex and gender that was blind to race, ethnicity, sexuality, and other forms of difference within the broader category of "woman." We have seen this vision of feminism on the pages of *Time*, but it is something that one encounters in discussions, for example, of feminist topics such as "girl power" often associated with third wave feminism (Mitchell, 2002; Nicholson, 1987).

A feminist analysis from within the perspective of communication does not merely accept these categories as a given, but looks at the language, or rhetoric, used by feminists to narrate their own history (Richardson, 1994). A wave, for example, implies that a social movement gathers momentum, crests or peaks, then abates and dies. It assumes that one wave follows another. These forms of analysis do provide a general sense of historical change. Yet as scholars of the wave have noted, such a breakdown of feminism into periods and waves can falsely represent the modern history of feminism as having a single point of origin (the United States) and tend to cover up the incredible heterogeneity within each wave.

Within communication and media studies, there have been attempts to offer a reading of feminism through other classificatory schemes, or frameworks. In their examination of feminism in Lana Rakow's ground-breaking anthology *Women Making Meaning*, Kathyrn Cirksena and Lisa Cuklanz (2002) provide a guided tour through "five feminist frameworks for communication studies": liberal feminism; socialist feminism; radical feminism; psychoanalytic feminism; and cultural feminism. These frameworks seem a strange basis for comparison: liberal and socialist feminism are overtly ideological political categories; psychoanalytic feminism is part of a scholarly epistemological tradition; cultural feminism, which isn't equivalent to cultural studies, seems to cut across the different frameworks (Cirksena & Cuklanz,

1992). This attempt to create a way to classify different trajectories within feminism indicates the difficulty of solidifying what is a dynamic movement into a subset of stable, identifiable forms. A framework is a metaphor drawn from the world of construction, but it also suggests, visually, that the goal of a theory and of the practices is to provide a solid foundation on which to stand.

There is something immovable and inflexible about such understanding of theory, feminist or otherwise, as building a framework to contain and explain events, phenomena, or lived experience in such broad abstract categories. The search for frameworks transforms feminism into a static entity that will always leave one wondering how one actually fits into a rigid schema.

A CONSTELLATION OF CONCEPTS

Another approach to understanding the contribution of feminism to communication, media studies, and cultural studies is to celebrate it as a series of interrelated concepts: women, woman, feminine, femininity, female, gender, sex, sexuality, sexual orientation, masculinity, femininity, the gendered division of labour, patriarchy, heterosexuality, hetero-normativity, queer, lesbian, gay, straight, bisexual, transsexuality, trans-gendered, sexism. These are but some of the interrelated concepts that create a veritable galaxy of themes and issues giving feminist media studies an identifiable shape, which is in constant motion and mutation. These themes are particular to a location and a temporal or historical moment when different issues warrant attention. From within this perspective, **feminism** is an approach to analyzing the world that pays attention to the specificity of the subjects in media and communication as subjects always and already constituted within a sex-gender system, but not in ways that are completely predictable.

As the visual theorist Meike Bal (2002) has written, **concepts** are not merely words. Concepts are intersubjective and performative (p. 24). Concepts move between disciplines and people. They come to rest in certain fields. They instigate dialogue. The ever-expanding constellation of concepts that composes the feminist universe and any feminist analysis of the media assumes a familiarity with these terms and grapples with their implications for our ability to communicate with each other and the generic and institutional forms within which communication occurs. These concepts invite a way of reflecting upon the ethical decisions we make on a daily basis and, as such, they inform our study of communication, culture, and the media. They assert the specificity of a powerful dimension of our social and personal existence to open up new universes of critique, exploration, and reflection on this existence. They can change our perception of our practice, and they transform other concepts once they are taken into account.

For example, one of the concerns within communication is on the nature of citizenship and media democracy. A standard concept of citizenship looks at political participation as the formal dimensions of practices such as voting. A feminist notion of citizenship (Lister, 2003) is attentive to the split between the public and private spheres. It radically transforms the idea of citizenship and citizenship studies by examining a range of policies and practices in locations that are connected to media governance (Armatage et al., 1997). The amount of television watching or the various practices of internet usage that parents enforce in the home have a bearing on public policy that inextricably articulates parental decision making to citizenship (Shade, Porter, Sanchez, 2005). Media discourses on hypersexualization in Quebec, for example, blame girls for being "too sexy," which in turn affects the imposition of dress codes in home and school (Caron, 2006). A feminist perspective on citizenship doesn't merely add women or girls into the equation, but articulates an understanding of citizenship and media governance as intimately connected to daily life.

FEMINISM AND THE STUDY OF THE MEDIA

A feminist reading of media studies may look at the processes of encoding of gendered messages in these texts and media formats, using these concepts to better understand how they are operating within a specific set of social relations. This has produced a rich body of research. One part of this program has been to critique the perpetuation of sex-role stereotyping of masculinity and femininity, and by stereotype I mean images that uncritically perpetuate restrictive notions of appropriate gender behaviour (Trimble, 1990). Freeman's (2006) work for example, examines the representation of lesbians in *Chatelaine* magazine, while her more recent work (2011) provides biographical studies of Canadian women media workers from the late 19th century to the early 21st century. Yasmin Jiwani and Mary Young (2006) have examined the news coverage of the trial of the murder of women in Vancouver, many of them Aboriginal. Yasmin Jiwani and Hooma Hoodfar's (2012) recent interventions into news media discourse inserted a powerful questioning of the media coverage of the "Shafia trials" and the media's use of the term *honour killings* to describe what Jiwani and Hoodfar reframe as the *femicide* of Zainab, Sahar, and Geeta Shafia, as well as Rose Amir Mohammed. Indeed, one of the latest developments from within feminist media studies is the creation of a series of workshops, targeted to women, on how to write such op-ed pieces for newspapers (see the Op-Ed Project in the United States at http://www.theopedproject.org and Informed Opinions in Canada at http://www.informedopinions.org).

Feminist media studies does not take the occurrence of gendered messages as an inevitable "given." Instead the question is how such images and narrative positionings are associated with a very naturalized understanding of male and female, or masculinity and femininity within feminist media studies. What is unravelled in the analysis is how these very categories become a part of the "natural order of things" and thus remain unquestioned. Such a position also focuses on the processes of textual production and enactment and the relationship between, as Eileen Meehan and Ellen Riordan (2001) have said, "sex and money." It examines the ways that readers, spectators, or audiences consume the preferred reading of these texts and it also studies how various industries work to create images (see Mayer, 2005). These issues have been put on the table for discussion at conferences such as Sex, Media and Money, organized by Alison Beale and Catherine Murray (Murray & Beale, 2011). They have also been examined as part of recent studies of labour in a transnational context and the shift toward digital media production (Gajjala & Oh, 2012). Closer to home, the 2012 strikes by students in Québec have been articulated in terms of the impact of neoliberal educational policies on women and girls in a series of cogent policy analyses and statements issued by Concordia University's Simone de Beauvoir Institute.

As a major contributor to the studies of audiences in both communication and cultural studies, feminist media analysis of Harlequin romances, soap operas, and women's magazines has examined how female and male readers and viewers negotiate these messages, which may be at once pleasurable and problematic. This research tries to understand how individuals and communities actively engage with preferred readings, sometimes building alternative fan cultures or subcultures around them (Radway, 1987; Ang, 1985; Hermes, 1995; Stacey, 1994).

In the Canadian context, Mary Bryson (2004) has examined how different communities and constituencies of queer women use the digital space, not only as a means of consumption, but also to create connection. Others have been concerned with the production of gendered forms of media that cater to female and male audiences (Korinek, 2000). This **ethnographic research** (Bryson et al., 2006) and **reception research** (Korinek, 2000) counter the media image of women as brainwashed by popular cultural representations of femininity and masculinity. It tries to comprehend how the media fits into the everyday routines and practices found within the home, and in some instances how these representations have created our very notion of home (Spigel, 1992). Other feminist studies of the media, mostly affiliated with science and technology studies (STS) examine the way that we may conceive of a media format or a technology as masculine or feminine, the processes by which different genders use technology, and the ways that cultural technologies become gendered (Shade, 2002; Peddle, Powell, & Shade, 2008; Balka, 2001; Tremblay, 2008). Such questions are seen as both local and connected to a broader set of concerns that may traverse boundaries.

As mentioned earlier, a concern of feminist scholars, such as Tuchman, Hinds and Stacey, Freeman, and Korinek, has been the representation of feminism within the media, work that has parallels in American feminist research (Faludi, 1991; Douglas, 1994). This analysis of the representation of feminism *in* the media is distinct from a feminist analysis *of* the media that looks at how media representations work to consolidate, subvert, or negotiate our dominant understandings of the social and individual capacities of men and women.

Feminist work on the media located in Canada engages with and has contributed to the broader dialogue within feminism and within communication, cultural studies, and media studies. Here it is worth mentioning the critical work on a number of feminist topics: sexuality and sexualities (Cossman et al., 1997; Namaste et al., 2007; Nadeau, 2001, 2006; Pidduck, 2004; Fleras, 2011); religion and media (Sullivan, 2005; Couture, 2009); the representation of racism in the press and public culture (Gagnon, 2000; Razack, 2004; Jiwani, 2006a; Jiwani and Young, 2006; Perley, 2009; Eid & Khan, 2011), telecommunications policies on sex and sex role stereotyping (Trimble, 1990) and the gendering of cultural policy (Beale, 1998; Cairns, 2010). Feminists in Canada have also examined, theoretically, the processes and language of gender and sex (Saunders, 1985; Probyn, 1993; Smith, 1993) reflecting on the conceptual issues at stake in the advancement of a rigorous and insightful feminist media studies.

Feminist researchers in Canada have examined the practices of media production (Hogan, 2009; McCartney, 2006; McKercher, 2009), articulating feminism to political economy (Shade, 2002) and the law (Hamilton, 2009; Craig et al., 2011). They have queried the question of the nation and nationalist discourses in the media (Razack, 2004; Armitage et al., 1999; Brun, 2009; Austin-Smith & Melnyk, 2010; Grandy, 2010) and explored issues of violence (Burfoot & Lord, 2006; Jiwani, 2006. Workers in information and communication technologies (ICTs) have comprised areas of more recent interest (Gabrielle Tremblay, 2008; Shade & Crow, 2004), as well as women's participation in and relationship to a range of digital technologies (Crow & Petty, 2008; Magnet & Rodgers, 2012). Girls' culture and media uses and practices is a new and emergent area in the field (Reid-Walsh & Mitchell, 2000; Jiwani, Steenbergen, Weber, & Mitchell, 2000; Caron, 2006; Keller, 2012), which is complemented by a range of work that is historical in focus (Kinahan, 2007; Martin, 1991).

Within the Canadian context, the study of media must also include community-based media (Hogan, 2009) including video distribution and production centres and the digital media arts (Sawchuk, 2008b), where feminism thrives. One of the peculiarities of the Canadian context is the incredible amount of local activity that is out there to explore and, as feminist media critics, for us to write about. This brief overview is but a very small sampling of the contributions of feminism to media studies. It is indexical in nature, pointing to areas and issues, rather than comprehensive.

Feminism continues to both flourish and be challenged by other social movements that are contending with unequal hierarchies of power and striving to find new and creative ways to open up the world for a variety of other subjects. Within the broader universe of communication studies, the current feminist galaxy intersects with two other areas of critical inquiry. Within the past ten years, two of feminism's allies have been located in queer media studies and critical race theory. **Queer theory** has drawn upon feminist analyses of gender, and contributed back to feminism but offering expertise and insight into the place of sexuality and homophobia in our current context (Nadeau, 2006). This intersection with queer studies has also enlivened traditional feminist debates on pornography and the representation of sexuality in the media (Cossman et al., 1997). These programs of research complicate feminism and challenge it.

Feminists working in **critical race theory** may have a distinct and different understanding of what feminism can contribute to their own lives: Alice Walker, for one, insisted that she was a "womanist," not a feminist. First Nations women often refer to what may be seen from a contemporary feminist perspective as traditional categories of mother, father, earth, and sky (Valiskakis, 1992, 2005). What is crucial here is that as a feminist one does not judge these different positions, but rather asks how different cultures understand gender and sexuality, how this is communicated, and what mediated forms this takes.

FEMINIST FUTURES

Feminism as paradigm and practice has outlived both *Time* magazine's dire prediction on the death of feminism and the television show *Ally McBeal.* Feminism is being nurtured by new generations of media scholars and gender activists who are working within this dynamic universe of ideas, and this legacy of critical inquiry. And here, I offer a word on finding feminism in the current conjuncture.

While there are many critical feminist journals that publish articles on women and the media—*Atlantis*, *Signs*, *Genders*, *differences*, *Feminist Review*, *Girlhood Studies*, and *Representations*—there is but one journal devoted explicitly to feminism and communication: *Feminist Media Studies.* There are also a number of journals open to publishing feminist work, including *Canadian Journal of Communication*, *Topia*, *Cultural Studies*, and *Critical Studies in Mass Communications* and *Communication.* There are alternative publications, such as the bimonthly magazine *No More Potlucks*, a beautifully designed and innovative forum for an array of feminist writings. The recent creation of *ADA: A Journal of Gender and Technology* by Carol Stabile is not only exploring the potential of multimodal publishing for feminism, but also acting as a generative platform for creating trans-border connections, and questioning the limits of traditional forms of peer review. Within the Canadian academic context, there are those of us who explicitly work from within a feminist framework and whose primary engagement and intervention is in the long conversation that is feminism. There are those who are allied with feminism but who may do other teaching or research. There are those, male and female, who teach traditional subject areas and find ways to support feminist research in the field by including it in course outlines, citing it in their own work, and acknowledging its contributions. These efforts recognize that issues such as gender representation in courses, on syllabi, at meetings, and in departments, are still ongoing and valid concerns in universities. All of these are ways of "doing feminism."

Doing feminism is, as I have been suggesting, a recognition and analysis of existing power differences and a dynamic galvanizing force of productive and creative action that promotes individual and collective empowerment, rather than power as domination over others (Bowes, 1996). Feminism is not simply an extraneous add-on to the media agenda, but is intrinsic to the study of communication

(Alhassan, 2007). It allows us to see and identify, with a critical eye, gender injustices. However, even more so, it allows us to imagine other possibilities for engaging in social relations with each other and the possibility to do research that is both different and makes a difference. And here I signal the exemplary work undertaken by Gail Guthrie Valaskakis (2005), whose complex readings of Aboriginal culture and technology included storytelling and the voices of her participants (including her grandmother) in a most ethical and inspiring manner. Feminism, as such, offers a series of critical tools and imaginative concepts to critique and enliven media and communication studies.

QUESTIONS

1. Why does feminism matter to communication studies? What does feminism reveal that other political and theoretical frameworks do not?
2. What are two original feminist projects that you might undertake?
3. Where have you encountered feminist research in your courses? What have you encountered?
4. Is it necessary to be a woman to be a feminist?
5. Find a recent news story that deals with an issue relevant to feminism and analyze its language.

REFERENCES

Alhassan, A. (2007). The canonic economy of communication and culture: The centrality of the postcolonial margins. *Canadian Journal of Communication, 32*(1), 103–118.

Ang, I. (1985). *Watching* Dallas*: Soap opera and the melodramatic imagination*. London: Routledge.

Armitage, K., Banning, K., Longfellow, B., & Marchessault, J. (Eds.) (1999). *Gendering the Nation: Canadian women's cinema*. Toronto: University of Toronto Press.

Austin-Smith, B., and Melnyk, G. (Eds.) (2010). *The gendered screen: Canadian women filmmakers*. Waterloo: Wilfrid Laurier University Press.

Bal, M. (2002). *Travelling concepts in the humanities: A rough guide*. Toronto: University of Toronto Press.

Balka, E. (2001). The invisibility of the everyday: New technology and women's work. In E. Riordan & E. R. Meehan (Eds.), *Sex and money: Feminism and political economy in the media* (pp. 60–75). Minnesota: University of Minnesota Press.

Beale, A. (1998). Cultural policy as a technology of gender. In A. Beale and A. Van Den Bosch (Eds.), *Ghosts in the machine: Women and cultural policy in Canada and Australia*. Toronto: Garamond Press.

Beauvoir, S. de. (1949; 1989). *The second sex*, trans. H.M. Parshley. New York: Random House.

Bell, S. (2010). *Fast feminisms*. New York: Autonomedia.

Beres, M., Crow, B., & Gotell, L. (2009). The perils of institutionalization in neoliberal times: Results of a national survey of Canadian sexual assault and rape crisis centres. *Canadian Journal of Sociology, 34*(1), 135–164.

Bordo, S. (1993). *Unbearable weight: Feminism, western culture and the body*. Berkeley: University of California Press.

Bornstein, K. (1997). *My gender workbook*. New York: Routledge.

Bowes, A. (1996). Evaluating an empowering research strategy: Reflections on action research with South Asian women. *Sociological Research Online, 1*(1). Retrieved August 1, 2012, from http://www.socresonline.org.uk/home.html

Bradley, M. (1995). *Reframing the Montreal massacre*. (video). Retrieved September 4, 2012, from http://vimeo.com/6996357

Bradley, M. (2006). Reframing the Montreal massacre: Strategies for feminist media activism. *Canadian Journal of Communication, 31*(4), 929–936.

Brun, J. (2009). Le site internet des archives de Radio-Canada et les femmes en 2007: Une présence limitée, une histoire partiellement racontée. *Recherches féministes, 22*(1), 105–122.

Bryson, M. (2004). When Jill jacks in: Queer women and the net. *Feminist Media Studies, 4*(3), 239–254.

Bryson, M., MacIntosh, L., Jordan, S., & Lin, H-L. (2006). Virtually queer? Homing devices, mobility, and un/belongings. *Canadian Journal of Communication, 31*(4), 791–814.

Burfoot, A. & Lord, S. (2006). *Women: Gender, violence and representation*. Waterloo: Wilfrid Laurier University Press.

Butler, J. (1990). *Gender trouble: Feminism and the subversion of identity*. New York: Routledge.

Cairns, K. (2010). "Thinking beyond borders"? A transnational feminist critique of discourses of internationalism in Canada. *Atlantis: A Women's Studies Journal, 35*(1), 25–35.

Canada. (1970). *Report of the Royal Commission on the Status of Women in Canada*. Retrieved September 4, 2012 from http://epe.lac-bac.gc.ca/100/200/301/pco-bcp/commissions-ef/bird1970-eng/bird1970-eng.htm

Caron, C. (June 2, 2006). Too sexy to go to school: A media discourse analysis of the recurring public debate on girls' dress. *Canadian Communication Association Conference*, York University, Toronto, Ontario, June 1–3.

Cirksena, K. & Cuklanz, L. (2002). Male is to female as ___ is to ___: A guided tour of five feminist frameworks for communication studies. In L. Rakow (Ed.), *Women making meaning: New feminist directions in communication* (pp. 18–44). New York: Routledge.

Cossman, B., Bell, S. Gotell, L., & Ross, B. L. (1997). *Bad attitude/s on trail: Pornography, feminism and the Butler decision*. Toronto: University of Toronto Press.

Couture, D. (2009). La corporéité chez Karl Rahner: Lecture féministe. In M. Allard, D. Couture, et J-G Nadeau (Eds.), *Pratiques et constructions ducorps en christianisme* (pp. 225–246). Montréal: Fides, Collection Héritage & Projet 75.

Craig, C. J. & Turcotte, J. F., with Coombe, R. (2011). What's feminist about open access?: A relational approach to copyright in the academy. *feminists@ law*, *1*(1). Retrieved August 1, 2012, from http://journals.kent.ac.uk/index.php/feministsatlaw/article/view/7/54

Crow, B. & Petty, S. (Eds.). (2008). Digital feminisms. Special issue of *Atlantis: A Women's Studies Journal*, *32*(20), 1–91.

Davis, K. (1997). My body is my art: Cosmetic surgery as feminist utopia? *The European Journal of Women's Studies*, *4*(1), 23–38.

Devor, H. (1989). *Gender blending*. Bloomington: Indiana University Press.

Douglas, S. (1994). *Where the girls are: Growing up female with the mass media*. New York: Random House.

Douglas, S. J. (2008, September 10). Feminism without feminism. *In These Times*. Retrieved August 1, 2012, from http://www.inthesetimes.com/article/3898/feminism_without_feminism

Eid, M. & Khan, S. (2011). A new-look for Muslim women in the Canadian media: CBC's *Little Mosque on the Prairie*. *Middle East Journal of Culture and Communication*, *4*(2), 184–202.

Faludi, S. (1991). *Backlash: The undeclared war against American women*. New York: Doubleday.

Fausto-Sterling, A. (1992). *Myths of gender: Biological theories about women and men*, rev. ed. New York: Basic.

Fernandez, S. (2006). More than an arts festival: Communities resistance and the story of Desh Pardesh. *Canadian Journal of Communication*, *31*(1), 17–34.

Fillion, K. (October 3, 2006). Interview with Queen's University Professor Samantha King. Retrieved August 1, 2012, from http://www.macleans.ca/culture/books/article.jsp?content=20061009_134235_134235

Fleras, A. (2011). *The media gaze: Representations of diversities in Canada*. Vancouver: University of British Columbia Press.

Freeman, B. (2001). *The satellite sex: The media and women's issues in English Canada, 1966–1971*. Waterloo: Wilfrid Laurier Press.

———. (2006). From no go to no logo: Lesbian lives and rights in *Chatelaine*. *Canadian Journal of Communication*, *31*(4), pp. 815–842.

———. (2011). *Beyond bylines: media workers and women's rights in Canada*. Waterloo: Wilfrid Laurier University Press.

Gagnon, M. K. (2000). *Other conundrums: Race, culture and Canadian art*. Vancouver: Arsenal Press.

Gajjala, R. & Oh, Y. J. (Eds.). (2012). *Cyberfeminism 2.0*. New York: Peter Lang Publishing.

Gatens, M. (1991). *Feminism and philosophy: Perspectives on difference and equality*. Cambridge: Polity Press.

Grandy, K. (2010). Busy bee, tough mom, farmer's daughter: The Canadian business press portrayal of Annette Verschuren. *Canadian Journal of Communication*, *35*(1), 49–62.

Gray, J. (1993). *Men are from Mars, women are from Venus: A practical guide for improving communication and getting what you want in your relationship*. New York: HarperCollins.

Griffin, S. (1978/2000). *Woman and nature: The roaring inside her*. California: Sierra Club Books.

Hamilton, S. N. (2009). "Not a sex victory": Gendering the person. In *Impersonations: Troubling the person in law and culture* (pp. 69–104). Toronto: University of Toronto Press.

Henriques, J., Holloway, W., & Couze, V. (1998). *Changing the subject: Psychology, social regulation and subjectivity*. London: Taylor & Francis.

Hermes, J. (1995). The research (as) process: A methodological account. In *Reading women's magazines* (pp. 176–208). Cambridge: Polity.

Hinds, H. & Stacey, J. (2001, July). Imaging feminism, imaging femininity: The bra-burner, Diana and the woman who kills. *Feminist Media Studies, 1*(2), 153–177.

Hogan, M. (2009). Dykes on Mykes: Podcasting and the activist archive. *Topia, 20*, 199–215.

Holland, P. (1998). The politics of the smile: "Soft news" and the sexualization of the popular press. In C. Carter, G. Branston, & S. Allan (Eds.), *News, gender, and power* (pp. 17–33). London: Routledge.

Jardine, A. & Smith, P. (1987). *Men in feminism*. New York: Routledge.

Jiwani, Y. (2006). *Discourses of denial: Mediations of race, gender and violence*. Vancouver: University of British Columbia Press.

Jiwani, Y. & Hoodfar, H. (2012, January 31). Should we call it "honour killing"? *Montreal Gazette*. Retrieved from http://www.montrealgazette.com

Jiwani, Y. & Young, M. (2006). Missing and murdered women: Reproducing marginality in News Discourse. *Canadian Journal of Communication 31*(4), 895–917.

Jiwani, Y., Steenbergen, C., & Mitchell, C. (2006). Girlhood: Surveying the terrain. In Y. Jiwani, C. Steenbergen, & C. Mitchell (Eds.), *Girlhood: Redefining the limits* (pp. ix–xvii). Montréal: Black Rose Books.

Johnson, W. (1969, May 1). The wave of feminism opposes motherhood, marriage: Traditional role rejected. *The Globe and Mail*, W5.

———. (1970, August 31). Can Ontario teachers federation meet challenge of reforming negotiations? *The Globe and Mail*, 11.

Keller, J. M. (2012). Virtual feminisms: Girls' blogging communities, feminist activism, and participatory politics. *Information, Communication & Society, 15*(3), 427–447.

Kinahan, A-M. (2007). Cultivating the taste of the nation: The National Council of Women of Canada and the campaign against "pernicious" literature at the turn of the twentieth century. *Canadian Journal of Communication, 32*(2), 161–179.

King, Samantha. (2006). *Pink Ribbons, Inc.: Breast cancer and the politics of philanthropy*. Minneapolis: University of Minnesota Press.

Korinek, V. J. (2000). *Roughing it in the suburbs: Reading* Chatelaine *Magazine in the fifties and sixties*. Toronto: University of Toronto Press.

Kuhn, T. (1962). *The Structure of scientific revolutions*. Chicago: University of Chicago Press.

Lasswell, H. (1960). The structure and function of communication in society. In W. Schramm (Ed.), *Mass communication* (pp. 117–130). Urbana: The University of Illinois Press.

Lauretis, T. de. (1987). Technologies of gender. In *Technologies of gender* (pp. 1–15). Bloomington: University of Indiana Press.

Lister, R. (2003). *Citizenship: Feminist perspectives*. New York: New York University Press.

Magnet, S. & Rodgers, T. (2012). Stripping for the state: Whole body imaging technologies and the surveillance of othered bodies. *Feminist Media Studies, 12*(1), 101–118.

Marks, L. (2002). *The skin of the film: Intercultural film, embodiment and the senses*. Durham: Duke University Press.

Martin, M. (1991). *Hello Central?: Gender, culture and technology in the formation of telephone systems*. Montreal: McGill-Queen's University Press.

Mayer, V. (2005). Softcore in TV time: The political economy of a cultural trend. *Critical Studies in Media Communication, 22*(4), 302–320.

McCartney, A. (2006). Gender, genre, and electroacoustic soundmaking practices. *Intersections: Canadian Journal of Music, 26*(2), 20–48.

McKercher, C. (2009). Writing on the margins: Precarity and the freelance journalist. Commentary. *Feminist Media Studies, 3*(9), 370–374.

Meehan, E. & Riordan, E. (Eds.) (2001). *Sex and money: Feminism and political economy in the media*. Minneapolis: University of Minnesota Press.

Mitchell, A. (2002). "talkin' 'bout my generation." *herizons magazine*.

Mohanty, C. T. (2003). *Feminism without borders*. Durham: Duke University Press.

Moir, A. & Jessel, D. (1989). *Brain sex: The real difference between men and women*. London: Penguin.

Murray, C. & Beale, A. (2011). Sex, money, media: A tribute and political reflection. *Canadian Journal of Communication 36*(1), 179–184.

Nadeau, C. (2001). *Fur Nation: From beaver to Brigitte Bardot*. New York: Routledge.

———. (2006). L'urgence-désir comme engagement. *Canadian Journal of Communication, 31*(4), 919–928.

Namaste, V., Vukov, T. H., Saghie, N., Jean-Gilles, J., Lafrenière, M., Leroux, M. -J., et al. (2007). HIV and STD prevention needs of bisexual women: Results for Projet Polyvalence. *Canadian Journal of Communication, 32*(3/4), 357–383.

Nicholson, L. (Ed.) (1987). *The second wave: A reader in feminist theory*. New York: Routledge.

Peddle, K., Powell, A., & Shade, L.R. (2008). Bringing feminist perspectives into community informatics. *Atlantis: A Women's Studies Journal, 32*(2), 33–44.

Perley, S. (2009). Representation and participation of First Nations women in online videos. *Journal of Community Informatics, 5*(2). Retrieved August 1, 2010, from http://www.ci-journal.net/index.php/ciej/article/view/559/453

Pidduck, J. (2004). *Contemporary costume film: Space, place and the past.* London: British Film Institute.

Probyn, E. (1992). Theorizing through the body. In Lana Rakow (Ed.), *Women making meaning* (pp. 83–99). New York: Routledge.

Probyn, E. (1993). *Sexing the self: Gendered positions in cultural studies.* New York: Routledge.

Radway, J. (1987). *Reading the romance: Women, patriarchy and popular literature.* Raleigh: University of North Carolina Press.

Razack, S. H. (2004). *Dark threats and white knights: The Somalia affair, peacekeeping, and the new imperialism.* Toronto: University of Toronto Press.

Reid-Walsh, J. & Mitchell, C. (2000). "Just a doll": Liberating accounts of Barbie-play. *The Review of Education/Pedagogy/Cultural Studies, 22*(2), 175–190.

Richardson, L. (1994). Writing: A method of inquiry. In N. K. Denzin & Y. S. Lincoln (Eds.), *Handbook of qualitative research* (pp. 516–529). Thousand Oaks, CA: Sage Publications.

Rubin, H. (2003). *Self-made men: Identity and embodiment.* Nashville: Vanderbilt University Press.

Sarikakis, K. & Shade. L. R. (Eds.) (2008). *Feminist interventions in international communication: Minding the gap.* Lanham. MD: Rowman and Littlefield.

Saunders, E. M. (1985). Teaching media and gender. Special issue on teaching critical communication studies. *Canadian Journal of Communication, 11*(1), 35–50.

Sawchuk, K. (1992). Le marketing du corps: Les couches jetables. *Sociologie et sociétés, XXIV*(1), 103–112.

———. (2008a). Artificial life and lo-fi embodiment: An interview with Melanie Baljko and Nell Tenhaaf. *Atlantis: A Women's Studies Journal, 32*(2), 6–17.

———. (2008b). Feminism in waves: Re-imagining a watery metaphor. In L. Gotell & B. Crow (Eds.), *Open boundaries: A women's studies reader*, 3rd ed. (pp. 58–63). Toronto: Pearson/Prentice Hall.

Schreiber, R. (2008). *Righting feminism: Conservative women and American politics.* Oxford: Oxford University Press.

Shade, L. R. (2002). *Gender and community in the social construction of the Internet.* New York: Peter Lang.

Shade, L. R. & Crow, B. (2004). Canadian feminist perspectives on digital technology. *Topia, 11*, 161–176.

Shade, L. R., Porter, N., & Sanchez, W. (2005). "You can see anything on the internet, you can do anything on the internet": Young Canadians talk about the internet. *Canadian Journal of Communication, 30*(4), 503–526.

Smith, D. (1993). *Texts, facts and femininity: Exploring the relations of ruling.* London: Routledge.

Spigel, L. (1992). Television in the family circle. In *Make room for TV: Television and the family ideal in postwar America* (pp. 36–72). Chicago: University of Chicago Press.

———. (2004). Theorizing the *Bachelorette*: 'Waves' of feminist media studies. *Signs: Journal of Women in Culture and Society 30*(1), 1209–1221.

Spivak, G. C. (1990). *The post-colonial critic*, S. Harasym (Ed.). Chicago: University of Chicago Press.

Stacey, J. (1994). Feminine fascinations: Forms of identification in star-audience relations. In *Star gazing: Hollywood cinema and female spectatorship* (pp. 141–163). London: Routledge.

Steiner, L (1998). Newsroom accounts of power at work. In C. Carter et al. (Eds.), *News, gender and power* (pp. 145–159). London: Routledge.

Sullivan, R. (2005). *Visual habits: Nuns, feminism and American postwar popular culture*. Toronto: University of Toronto Press.

Tremblay, D-G. (2008). Permeability between work and non-work: The case of IT self-employed workers. *Canadian Journal of Communication, 33*(4), 701–720.

Trimble, L. (1990). Coming to a station near you: The CRTC policy on sex-role stereotyping. *Canadian Public Policy, 16*(3), 326–338.

Tuchman, G. (1978). *Making news: A study in the construction of reality*. New York: Free Press.

Valaskakis, G. G. (2005). *Indian country: Essays on contemporary native culture*. Waterloo: Wilfrid Laurier University Press.

———. (1992). Sacajawea and her sisters: Images and Indians. In *Indian princess and cowgirls* (pp. 11–49). Montreal: Oboro.

Van Zoonen, L. (1988). Rethinking women and the news. *European Journal of Communication, 3*(1), 35–54.

———. (1994). *Feminist media studies*. London: Sage.

———. (1995). Gender, representation, and the media. In John Downing et al. (Eds.), *Questioning the media: A critical introduction* (pp. 311–328). Thousand Oaks, CA: Sage Publications.

Williams, R. (1977). *Marxism and literature*. Oxford, U.K.: Oxford University Press.

Young, I. M. (1990). *Throwing like a girl and other essays in feminist philosophy and social theory*. Bloomington: Indiana University Press.

Media Regulation and Policies in Canada

Introduction

Leslie Regan Shade
University of Toronto

The four chapters in this section of *Mediascapes* explore the myriad ways that Canadian media and cultural institutions are regulated via policies and regulatory systems that have been developed, refined, and, in many instances, contested, over the years. This section also examines how, in a predominantly commercial media environment, we conceptualize and measure media audiences, and how advertising structures media and in turn how the advertising industry is regulated. As we will see in this section, regulating the media can be incredibly fraught as media convergence implicates Canadians as active critics and sense makers of cultural and media content, troubles the boundaries of broadcasting and telecommunication policies (Shtern and Blake), connects Canadians as members of diverse audiences (Savage), allows for citizens to interact and often reshape these cultural products (Wagman and Winton), and structures how Canadians receive and react to marketing messages (Johnston).

In their chapter, Jeremy Shtern and Sylvia Blake provide us with a very useful historical synopsis of media regulation in Canada, with specific attention to the role of the Canadian Radio-television and Telecommunications Commission (CRTC). They provide a series of broadcasting regulatory vignettes to situate and examine the complex political dynamics inherent in the regulatory process, where a diverse array of stakeholders seek to shape the outcome of regulatory decisions. Through recent case studies on media diversity and media concentration and ownership, vertical integration, the regulation of "new media," and foreign ownership levels in telecom, Shtern and Blake highlight the tensions inherent in a regulatory environment that seeks economic prosperity for media industries while at the same time upholding notions of social well-being for the Canadian citizenry. The authors also question, in the context of highly charged and politicized environments, whether or not the

CRTC is still a relevant regulatory institution, and conclude that a revision and merging of the *Broadcasting* and *Telecommunication Acts* could make the CRTC a more viable staple organization for regulatory matters.

The centrality of cultural policy in the Canadian mediascape is the subject of Ira Wagman and Ezra Winton's chapter. As they point out, evoking "cultural policy" is awkward, given that Canada does not have a Department of Cultural Policy per se, although various provincial and federal departments and ministries are responsible for various aspects of cultural policy—sports, broadcasting, film, heritage festivals, online digital content, etc. Formative Canadian communication studies research focused on analyzing cultural policies that attempted to achieve nationalistic objectives of fostering Canadian content, very often to counter the dominant influence and power of cultural content from the United States. Rather than exhaustively delineating cultural policies from the last century to now, Wagman and Winton instead provide a few case studies that illustrate key concepts for cultural policies and the maintenance of Canadian cultural industries: geographic, economic, and social well-being at local, provincial, and national levels, through the creation of various cultural policy apparatus: legislation (such as the *Broadcasting Act*), the creation of cultural institutions (notably, the CBC), and policy techniques (funding sources for cultural industries, such as the Canada Council for the Arts). Two new challenges are identified by Wagman and Winton: digitization, which alters classic distribution techniques and traditional audience measurement, and the increasing politicization of cultural policy (and consequently underfunding of various programs), particularly under the Conservative majority government of Prime Minister Stephen Harper.

Philip Savage's chapter provides an overview of the often-elusive and taken-for-granted notion of the audience. Audiences, Savage remarks, can be "slippery" because they are definitionally diffuse, dynamic, and diverse. As he illustrates, however, in communication studies, audience models have been well entrenched in three theoretical strands: mass communication, political economy, and cultural studies. The former perspective reflects an administrative orientation (as per Hamilton's chapter) while critical orientations emanate from political economy (in particular, Canadian Dallas Smythe's famous construction of the audience commodity) and cultural studies. Savage reflects on his professional experience working in CBC Radio as an audience researcher in his discussion of the operations of applied audience research, particularly the nuances of rating structures. He also discusses innovative digital forms of audience research and proposes an audience massage model, which utilizes *rhetoric*, *frames*, and *structures* to shape favourable outcomes for entities that finance or regulate broadcasting.

How advertising structures assorted media operations, historically and at present, is the topic of Russell Johnston's chapter. Surveying 250 years, Johnston documents the creation of the advertising industry and its permutations through technological innovations, the standardization of agencies, the creation of marketing research as a science to dissect consumer behaviour, and industry regulation and policies (laws, regulations—including self-regulation, and codes). He also looks at new challenges to traditional advertising given globalization, new and plentiful media channels including social media platforms, and targeted mechanisms to attract fickle consumers, particularly young people. Certainly the ethical implications of guerilla and viral marketing, and indeed, the ability of social media to capture and monetize the personal information of its users through sophisticated data mining and the targeting of personal ads, is perhaps one of the most vexing challenges for policy.

5

POWER AND POLITICS AT THE CRTC: THE RECENT PAST AND UNCERTAIN FUTURE OF CANADA'S COMMUNICATIONS REGULATOR

Jeremy Shtern
Department of Communication, University of Ottawa

Sylvia Blake
School of Communication, Simon Fraser University

"COMM'N CANADA!"

During the fall of 2009, Canadians were bombarded with advice on the future of their media system. It was not necessarily the most useful advice. Consider, for example, that separate video clips featured:

- Passing YouTube meme and singer/songwriter Dave Carroll, who was commissioned to produce a song and video called "The Cable Song" to underline the importance of "saving local television." The imagery providing the backdrop to this acoustic folk-rock piece included footage of a comical cable "big boss" dressed in a cow costume, illustrating the extent to which the Canadian cable industry represents a "cash cow"[1];
- A Rick Mercer episode with a staged "man on the street" interview, where he plays an individual who, upon being informed of possible rising costs of Canadian television services, measurably responds: "This is not a world in which I would want to raise a child... I'm glad I'm sterile";[2] and
- A 20-something faux journalist (whose conspicuously casual jacket comes off as a brazen attempt to put a youthful face on an appeal to populist sentiments) implores: "Comm'n Canada, enough is enough! Stop the TV Tax!"[3]

Each vignette was produced in the effort to mobilize public opinion one way or the other around a 2009 Canadian Government regulatory proceeding that sought to reconsider the billing relationship between certain broadcast networks and Canada's cable oligarchy. Most remarkably, only the second of the three was actually intended as parody.

While we can take for granted that this was not a high point of democratic discourse in Canada, this debate, commonly referred to as the "save local TV/stop the

TV tax" or "fee for carriage/value for signal proceeding," is but one small episode within the ongoing history of media regulation in Canada. This is a history that dates back at least to the introduction of radio broadcasting in the 1920s. On closer inspection, such proceedings are snapshots. They can be used to illustrate the functioning of media regulatory processes in Canada and are, in various ways, emblematic of both the politics that surround Canadian media regulation and of the power relations and political economies that shape them at a given moment.

This chapter examines the reasoning behind and methods for regulating broadcasting in Canada, as well as the challenges that regulators face in negotiating the industry's economic needs and social responsibilities. It begins with a brief description of Canada's regulatory framework and its complex responsibilities, and then draws from a few key recent regulatory proceedings to further illustrate the rationale for and challenges of regulating broadcasting. It is formatted as an anecdotal description of "how things work,"[4] with a focus on underlining some of the fundamental challenges that emerge from a series of case studies. These include concentrated media ownership; internet protocol-based content; politicized decision making; and lobbying and superficial public engagement.

We conclude the chapter by arguing that fundamental reform to Canada's media regulation is required. Though it makes no pretence about being an exhaustive or even detailed study, this chapter hopes to make a modest contribution by introducing some key themes and processes, stimulating critical reflection on the structure of Canada's media system and its future, and directing interested readers toward a more comprehensive base of references and resources.

INTRODUCTION: MEDIA AS SOCIAL ACTORS; MEDIA AS ECONOMIC ACTORS

In contrast to the simplistic populist messages featured in the fee for carriage/value for signal videos mentioned above, the Canadian media are a key part in a very complex cultural system. Generally speaking, the cultural industries, including broadcast and communications, are considered to be "both industry and art" (Grant & Wood, 2004, p. 23)—that is, these industries are both significant *economic actors* and *social actors*.

Media organizations can be described as *social actors* in that they "are able—and even expected—to influence public opinion, government policy, and citizen voting behaviour" (Napoli, 1997, p. 207). They can also be described as *economic actors* in the sense that they employ people, generate revenue, and bear responsibility to shareholders. In the processes of informing and entertaining, they seek investment, innovate, and respond to the ebb and flow of the marketplace.

Around the world, the media's social and economic imperatives often overlap and are in a constant tension with one another. The governments in all developed countries regulate the media to varying degrees in order to define the social role for media and to ensure that social objectives are not sacrificed to the bottom line of industry profitability.

In comparison to most countries, the relationships between the economic and social roles for Canadian media are highly complex, and the role of government regulation in negotiating these relationships is even more pronounced. Given Canada's cultural and linguistic divides; large, often sparsely populated territory; and proximity to Hollywood and other American cultural industries, the typical social role of the media is accentuated by a series of Canadian cultural policies designed to deploy mass communication to support Canadian identity and to protect Canadian industries from cultural imperialism.[5]

While all Canadian media organizations take in revenue and most exist to turn a profit, government regulatory intervention structures the economic role for Canadian media almost as much as the social role. The Canadian media operate in a heavily regulated rather than free marketplace. In broadcasting, for example, audiences have largely tuned out English-language Canadian television shows. Yet subsidy programs that help pay for production, and Canadian content **(Can-con)** regulations that require Canadian broadcasters to feature a certain percentage of domestically produced content help keep independent producers in business and recover broadcaster loses. At the same time, policy intervention supports the highly profitable practice of **simulations substitution**, allowing Canadian networks to sell advertising on American network programming. On the telecommunications side, private firms receive subsidies to ensure **universal service** delivery in sparsely populated areas, and historically, non-Canadian firms have been permitted only limited access to the Canadian market.[6]

The "Stop the TV Tax" campaign attempted to tap into the frustration with government intervention in the Canadian media marketplace that occasionally bubbles to the surface of public discourse. Yet, this economic regulation is fundamental to the achievement of ambitious social policy goals linked to Canada's system of mass communication. In a truly free marketplace, Canada's media industry would not exist, or at least would not be likely to exist in a form that was capable of providing the kind of less profitable public service functions that it is mandated to present. In other words, Canadian communication regulations assign a social mandate to media organizations and, at the same time, strive to ensure that the industry is sufficiently stable, accountable, and responsibly managed to be capable of fulfilling those obligations.

In short, broadcast and telecommunications are complex industries that not only effect economic well-being in Canada, but also impact cultural and national identity and unity, promote the democratic process, and shape social values. Weighing industrial economic needs and the public good is a constant balancing act for media and telecom policymakers.

Within the Government of Canada, policy making in broadcast and telecommunications is shared by the Department of Canadian Heritage and Industry Canada. However, because mass communication is so crucial to elections and democratic deliberation, it is important to have visible and functional separation between the government of the day and public authority over the mass communication system. Thus the day-to-day monitoring and management as well as certain policy development functions for communication regulation are vested in an independent regulatory body called the ***Canadian Radio-television and Telecommunications Commission* (CRTC)**. The CRTC operates at arm's length from the government in developing and enforcing significant portions of media and communications policy.

THE CANADIAN RADIO-TELEVISION AND TELECOMMUNICATIONS COMMISSION

The current iteration of the Canadian Radio-television and Telecommunications Commission (CRTC) was effectively established by the *Canadian Radio-television and Telecommunications Commission Act* in 1976. The 1976 *CRTC Act* assigns the commission responsibility for monitoring and regulating telecommunications as well as broadcasting in Canada. The CRTC is charged with enforcing various pieces of legislation and policy, particularly the *Broadcasting Act* and the *Telecommunications Act*.

The *Broadcasting Act*, 1991

The *Broadcasting Act* is the ultimate authority governing Canadian broadcasting. It defines broadcasting as any transmission of programs by radio waves or other means of telecommunication, for public reception through a receiving apparatus (such as a radio or television). The first *Broadcasting Act* (the *Canadian Radio Broadcasting Act*) received royal assent in 1932, and experienced its most recent major revision by Parliament in 1991.

The act sets out the policy for the Canadian broadcasting system, establishes the role and powers of the CRTC, and sets out the mandate and requirements of the Canadian Broadcasting Corporation (CBC). It also offers some guidance for policymakers in navigating the tensions between the social and economic elements of broadcasting, requiring first and foremost that the Canadian broadcasting system be owned and controlled by Canadians, and that it "serve to safeguard, enrich and strengthen the cultural, political, social and economic fabric of Canada" (3.1).

The *Telecommunications Act*, 1993

The 1993 *Telecommunications Act* is the telecom counterpart of the *Broadcasting Act*. It defines telecommunications as "the emission, transmission or reception of intelligence by any wire, cable, radio, optical or other electromagnetic system, or by any similar technical system" (2.1). In a similar manner to the *Broadcasting Act*, the *Telecommunications Act* defines the objectives of the national telecommunications system, including policy objectives, Canadian ownership requirements, and regulatory procedures.

While the *Broadcasting Act* sets out a framework for broadcasting policy and the *Telecommunications Act* sets out a framework for telecom policy, these frameworks are intentionally very general, and CRTC regulatory decisions need not be submitted to the House of Commons as part of a full legislative process. Furthermore, the commission has authority to "issue guidelines and statements with respect to any matter within its jurisdiction" (5.6), but these guidelines and statements are not binding on the commission's later activities. This provides the CRTC room to respond to trends in a rapidly changing technological, economic, and social environment by granting it some autonomy in interpreting the act, and establishing and enforcing regulations.

However, it is not surprising that in such a large and multifaceted policy arena as communications, the CRTC shares certain regulatory responsibilities with other organizations and government departments. For example, Industry Canada is responsible for most technical issues, including spectrum allocation; Heritage Canada shapes Canadian broadcasting through its cultural policies, funding programs, and legislative proposals; various broadcasting standards organizations complement the CRTC's role in regulating and monitoring program content; and the Canadian court system addresses individual issues related to slander and libel in broadcast content. Parliament also maintains the right to amend broadcasting frameworks such as the *Broadcasting Act* and the *Canadian Radio-television and Telecommunications Act*, as well as the right to nominate members of the CRTC, issue general policy directions to the commission, review individual CRTC decisions, and influence broadcast content through funding structures such as subsidies and tax credits.

Despite the level of relative autonomy that the CRTC has been given to monitor and regulate the aspects of broadcast and telecom under its jurisdiction, the commission nevertheless experiences several significant challenges to its authority. The following sections examine four of these challenges through the lens of mini case studies that illustrate some of these issues, and how the commission attempted to respond to them. The first looks at the commission's "Diversity of Voices" and "Vertical Integration" proceedings as an attempt to deal with media concentration. The second examines the challenges of regulating in light of new media and "over-the-top" services such as Netflix. The third case study considers the distance between the commission and government (the length of the commission's "arm") given the recent tendency of government to overrule the CRTC, as well as politicized commissioner appointments. Finally, we consider issues related to lobbying and superficial public engagement, such as the **fee for carriage/value for signal** debate discussed in the introduction to this chapter.

CHALLENGE 1: DIVERSITY OF VOICES AND "VERTICAL INTEGRATION"—MAINTAINING SOCIAL OBJECTIVES AMID MEDIA CONCENTRATION

Canada has among the highest levels of concentration in media ownership in the Western world (Hurtig 2008; Raboy 2010; Skinner & Gasher 2005). Among the issues outlined by Shade and Lithgow in Chapter 9, highly concentrated media ownership challenges the social objectives of media regulation by limiting the number of sources of information available to consumers (Baker, 2006; Murdock, 1990). Concentrated ownership also undermines the economic regulation of mass communication in Canada by creating powerful media conglomerates that, with every merger and accusation, drift closer to being "too big to fail." As real competition diminishes in the consumer marketplace, the lobbying power of communication firms increases at the expense of the real-politic leverage that the CRTC and other government agencies once held over a field of smaller, more interchangeable incumbents. In other words, the players in Canadian media and telecom are now fewer in number and more politically powerful than ever before, leading to a lack of competition and consumer choice, and creating a situation in which the failure of any one major communications company would put Canada's broadcast and telecom oligopoly one step closer to a total monopoly.

While it does not set out clear guidelines for what a truly "diverse" broadcasting system would look like, the *Broadcasting Policy for Canada* within the *Broadcasting Act* sets out a series of guidelines that define several of the elements that should be present in a diverse broadcasting system, including requirements for source diversity (local, national, and international sources; community programming; and contributions from independent producers) as well as content diversity (programming that is "varied and comprehensive," including opportunities for exposure to "the expression of differing views"). Within these guidelines, we once again see an acknowledgment of the social role of the broadcasting system and the importance of ensuring that Canadians are able to inform and entertain themselves by choosing from the broadest possible range of content.

However, here (as elsewhere) the guidelines in the *Broadcasting Act* are vague about implementation of such principles, and it is largely left to the CRTC to interpret the act, and develop and enforce specific regulations to ensure that broadcasters follow the rules. Indeed, even the act's use of the word *should* instead of *must* in outlining elements of the broadcasting policy leaves space for interpretation by framing these elements as lofty goals that the broadcasting system must strive for, but is not necessarily expected to achieve.

Ensuring an adequately diverse broadcasting system has proven a key challenge for the commission, particularly because of uncertainty over the definition of diversity. A wide range of actors weigh in on diversity debates with viewpoints stemming from different ideologies, premises, and semantic understandings of the term. Depending on who you ask, diversity in broadcasting can refer to concerns about media ownership consolidation and vertical integration; editorial diversity/diversity of opinion on the airwaves; inclusion of traditionally marginalized voices in broadcasting (such as visible minorities, First Nations, people with disabilities, and women); assured shelf space for Canadian cultural expression; or the development of a system that is free from any government control.

Diversity of Voices (2007)

In March 2007, the CRTC announced its plans to hold a series of public hearings to review its approaches to issues related to diversity of voices in broadcasting. The CRTC accepted written comments from industry stakeholders and interested members of the Canadian public for the CRTC 2007-5 Proceedings on Diversity of Voices until July 2007. That September, the commission held a series of public proceedings allowing interested parties to present their arguments before the commissioners in person. Among the organizations and individuals submitting interventions were various broadcasting networks (including the CBC), industry lobby groups and professional associations, civil society groups such as "Friends of Canadian Broadcasting," and various individual Canadian citizens speaking from perspectives ranging from "regular" audience members to confirmed experts on the subject. In its call for comments, the commission chose not to define *diversity*, and the resulting 162 written interventions and 52 presentations therefore stemmed from a variety of premises and conceptions of what *diversity* means, different perspectives on the current state of diversity, and different solutions to develop an ideally diverse system.

When it came time to draft a summary and make regulatory decisions based on the proceedings, the commission chose only to address issues related to ownership diversity, stating that "[a]lthough terminology varies and various parties to the proceeding provided a range of perspectives and understanding of the term 'diversity of voices,' the common objective appears to be to ensure the provision of a diversity of viewpoints either through ownership regulations or by means of programming obligations" (CRTC, 2008). In the policy decisions that it derived from the proceedings (CRTC 2008-4), the commission modelled a new set of competition thresholds for private media based on the thresholds established by the Competition Bureau for banking in Canada. The 2008 regulations prevent post merger combination market shares of more than 45 percent in a single market, and require that mergers that would lead to combined market shares of between 35 and 45 percent be more closely monitored, while those involving less than 35 percent be approved more quickly. The other significant regulatory change that emerged from the proceedings prevents companies from holding assets in more than two of three major media formats (newspapers, television, and radio) in a single market, although this ruling did not include free daily newspapers or those considered to cover "national" issues, most notably *The Globe and Mail* and the *National Post.*

Then Chairperson of the CRTC Konrad von Finckenstein argued that the measures represented "an approach that will preserve the plurality of voices and the diversity of programming available to Canadians, both locally and nationally, while allowing for a strong and competitive industry" (CRTC, 2008). The spokesperson for Friends of Canadian Broadcasting, Ian Morrison, welcomed the decision, citing it as evidence that the CRTC recognizes the risk that media concentration poses to diversity, stating that "although I would quibble on some of the details, I think this is an example of the CRTC doing its job" (Canadian Press, 2008).

However, the regulations were met with criticism from several industry associations and unions, which argued that the new regulations would do little to prevent further industry consolidation. The Canadian Media Guild argued that the CRTC had "blown a chance" with a weak ruling that "essentially embodies the status quo," while the Communications, Energy and Paperworkers Union condemned a policy that "does nothing about media empires that currently have a stranglehold on some large markets, such as Vancouver, or what happens on the national level" (The Canadian Press, 2008).

While the CRTC may in many cases have only a small margin for manoeuvre around the status quo, its arm's-length status, practice of informal brokering, and mandate to proactively investigate emerging problems can allow the commission to think progressively and make surprisingly agile moves for reform. One small victory that came out the 2007 Diversity of Voices hearing was the eventual establishment of a community radio fund that gained momentum when interventions repeatedly underlined both the potential role that community broadcasting could play in interjecting diversity into Canadian broadcasting and the sorry state of contemporary support for the sector.[7] In this case, the commissioners were listening, and at least to some extent trying to respond to what was said at the Diversity of Voices hearing.[8]

CRTC 2010-783 Review of the Regulatory Framework Relating to Vertical Integration

Approximately two years after releasing the policy based on the 2007 Diversity of Voices proceedings, the CRTC announced that it would be conducting another review of regulatory frameworks relating to industry consolidation, this time focusing specifically on issues related to vertical integration in broadcast and telecom industries.

Vertical integration describes a process in which a single company gains ownership or control over several aspects of a product or service's production and distribution process. The form of vertical integration that is most discussed within communication industries occurs when the same firm controls both content creation and distribution properties. For example, Rogers Communications owns the Rogers Centre in Toronto (formally the Sky Dome), the Toronto Blue Jays baseball team, and SportsNet radio, television, website, and magazine, while also offering cable television and internet services in the Greater Toronto Area. For fans, this means that Rogers Communications can have a hand in every step of their Blue Jays experience, from control over the team itself and the building in which it plays, to broadcasting games and producing sports commentary, and even owning the telecommunications infrastructure that allows fans to connect to the internet to look up sports statistics or connect to other fans. There are currently numerous other examples of Canadian firms that control some combination of production companies or facilities, newspapers, magazines, internet portals, sports properties and other venues for creating entertainment and information programming, as well as broadcasting licences, internet service providers, mobile phone service providers, and cable companies. Figure 5.1 shows a visualization of some of Rogers Communications' vertically and horizontally integrated assets in Toronto.

The commission launched the vertical integration proceedings the same day it approved Shaw Communications' takeover of the insolvent Canwest Global Communications, citing both the Canwest takeover as well as other recent cases in the trend toward consolidation as reason for the policy review. The public proceedings were conducted in May 2011; however, they received much less attention in the popular press than the 2007 Diversity of Voices proceedings, and accordingly, also received fewer public interventions.

Bell, Rogers, Shaw, and Quebecor Media (QMI), sometimes referred to as the "big four" vertically integrated Canadian media companies, argued that there is no

FIGURE 5.1 Vertical and Horizontal Integration of Some of Rogers Communications' Assets in Toronto

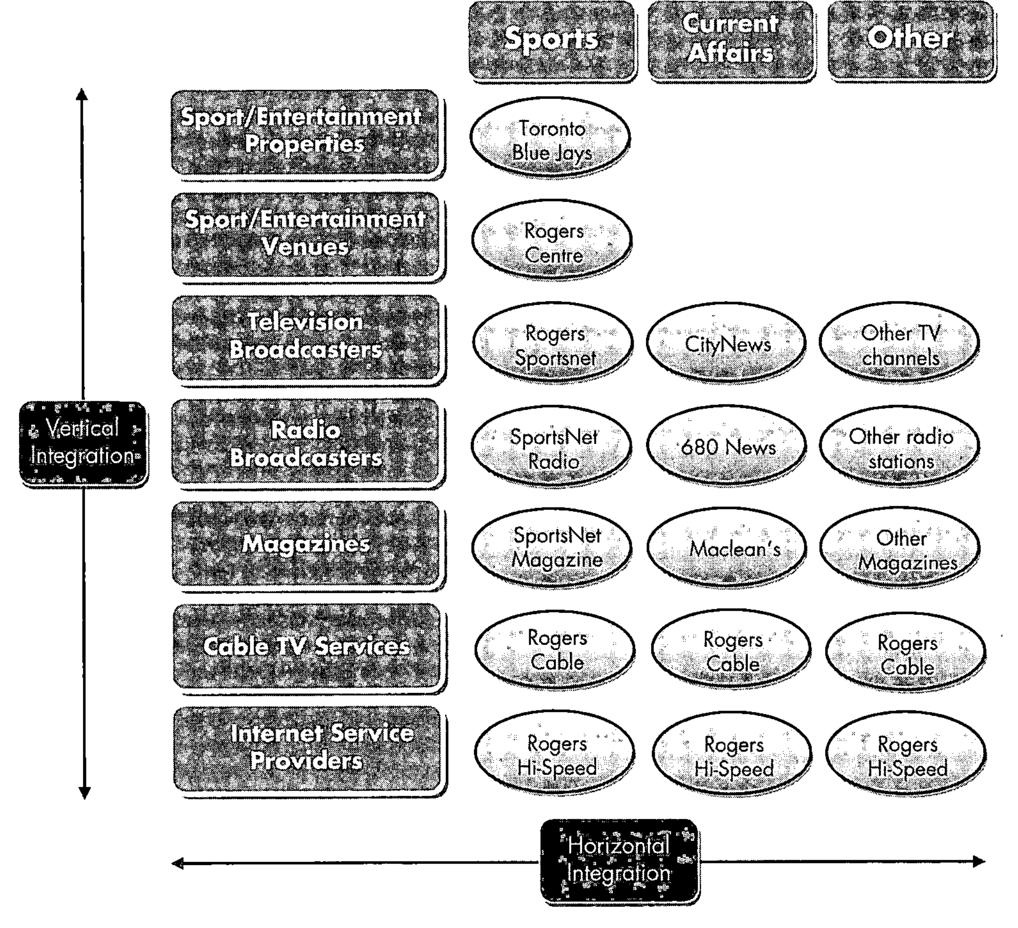

Source: Image by S. Blake, 2012.

evidence that vertical integration poses a threat to competition in broadcast and telecom industries, and could in fact benefit Canadian media industries by stabilizing struggling services such as conventional television, providing the financial certainty companies need to innovate and launch new services, and ensuring that Canadian companies are able to compete in the emerging global economy. Small markets, they argue, require large and stable companies that can compete with unregulated internet-based media services, and, without vertical integration, it would be impossible to do so.[9]

The rest of the intervening parties—including smaller broadcasters and telecom companies, industry associations and unions, public interest groups, and the CBC—disagreed, pointing to rising costs for consumers, declining diversity in journalism, and anticompetitive practices on the part of vertically integrated companies that "self-deal" their own content to gain competitive advantage.

While the commission did recognize the benefits of the cost savings and efficiencies associated with vertical integration in its determinations, it also noted that vertically integrated entities may partake in anticompetitive behaviour since they "have both the opportunity and incentive to give undue preference by providing themselves with exclusive access, on various distribution platforms, to content that they control" (CRTC, 2011a). In other words, vertically integrated companies have a strong incentive to deny competitors the opportunity to distribute popular content that they control because they benefit when consumers wishing to access it have to subscribe to their services to do so. This form of exclusivity could have negative effects for consumers, who would have no choice but to subscribe to services through certain companies in order to access the content they want. It could also harm smaller service providers, which may be denied the opportunity to offer certain popular programming to customers. As then Chairperson of the CRTC Konrad von Fickenstein stated, "Canadians shouldn't be forced to buy a mobile device from a specific company or subscribe to its internet service simply to access their favourite television programs" (CRTC, 2011b).

Based on this conclusion, the commission stated that it would address exclusivity and anticompetitive behaviour by deciding to (1) prohibit companies from offering TV programs exclusively to their mobile or internet subscribers, *except for* programming produced specifically for an internet portal or a mobile device; (2) adopt a code of conduct to prevent anticompetitive behaviours among distributers, broadcasters, and online programming services; and (3) implement measures to ensure that independent distributors and broadcasters are treated fairly by large integrated companies. The latter will be done in part by requiring that at least 25 percent of specialty services distributed by a large integrated company be owned by an independent broadcaster, and requiring broadcasters launching new pay or speciality services to make them available upon request to all distributors as an individual service (CRTC, 2011b). The commission also encouraged vertically integrated companies to offer customers greater flexibility in selecting and paying for just the services they want as part of their packages, and required them to report on their progress by April 2012.

Overall, the commission seemed to recognize that vertical integration is a problem because it can lead to anticompetitive behaviour and deny consumers choice in which company they get their services from (leading to challenges for nonvertically integrated companies, and the risk of more consolidation). The commission has taken some steps to help ease that, and also promised to address some other concerns if the vertically integrated companies fail to do so on their own.[10] We can certainly conclude that *not* having these measures would be worse than having those that were offered. However, the measures do little to address the underlying cause of these problems, which is a lack of ownership diversity, leading to a situation in which four major companies exercise considerable control over Canada's broadcast and telecom systems.

CHALLENGE 2: NEW MEDIA

Advancing technologies and new media also present a significant challenge to the CRTC's position as broadcast and telecom regulator, as audio and video content on the web bear increasing resemblance to content that exists on the regulated airwaves. The CRTC decided not to regulate the internet in 1999, determining that the internet was meeting the objectives of the *Broadcasting Act* and *Telecommunications Act*, and stating that "both creativity and innovation grew in an environment without regulation" (CRTC, 2012a). At the time, most internet services were text based; however, recent years have seen a shift in which more and more Canadians are accessing audio and video content through new unregulated **"over-the-top" (OTT)**[11] **services,** such as YouTube, Apple TV, and Netflix.

In making the case for vertical integration, the "big four" are quick to point out the ways in which new OTT services challenge the current broadcast and telecom environment in Canada. These services, they argue, threaten Canadian broadcasting and cable companies by competing for scarce advertising and subscription dollars and encouraging consumers to leave the regulated system by offering inexpensive or free niche and on-demand content (Standing Committee on Canadian Heritage, 2011). They also argue that these services hurt Canadian production because their parent companies do not make any financial contributions to the Canadian production industry, and they are not bound by Canadian content regulations. For instance, Shaw has insisted that "consumers will ultimately suffer, with fewer Canadian choices" (Standing Committee on Canadian Heritage, 2011). Ironically, the "big four" have historically resisted Canadian content regulations and requirements that they invest in Canadian production.

Other stakeholders (Netflix, the independent ISP Teksavvy, Apple, and the Canadian Internet Policy and Public Interest Clinic) disagree with this apocalyptic view for Canadian broadcasting, arguing that OTT services are complementary to the existing regulated broadcasting system, and can foster innovation leading to greater consumer choice. Many licensed companies are also taking the opportunity to launch OTT services of their own, and the CBC has argued that OTT offers another platform that can enable consumers to access a range of Canadian programming (CRTC, 2011c).

At the time of writing, the commission has opted to "allow the OTT market to continue evolving" rather than regulate the services or respond to the concerns of large broadcasting distribution undertakings (**BDUs**) by easing regulation in the traditional broadcast system (CRTC, 2011c). However, some commentators have argued that through certain telecom decisions that affect the cost of bandwidth (such as the usage-based billing decision, discussed in some detail below), the commission has the ability to partake in de facto cultural policy affecting the success of OTT services by influencing the cost of the bandwidth that consumers need to access these services (Winseck, 2011). That is, while the commission does not actively regulate content or cost structures for OTT services, it does bear some responsibility for influencing consumers' ability to access them through the decisions that it makes regarding the relationships between major telecom providers (most of which, such as Bell and Rogers, also hold assets in the traditional broadcast market) and the smaller, independent internet service providers not linked to the incumbent telecoms conglomerates that compete by offering large quantities of broadband to consumers at lower prices.

What this leads to is a broadcasting system in which some broadcasters are licensed and directly regulated by the commission (traditional broadcasters), and some are permitted to operate without licences, but are indirectly affected by CRTC decisions regarding telecom issues (OTT services). Even if the CRTC does eventually choose to regulate OTT services, it may be difficult to impose the same rules on these services as it does to players in the traditional broadcast environment, since they do not operate on scarce Canadian airwaves.

CHALLENGE 3: HOW LONG IS YOUR ARM?

As we have discussed, the CRTC was designed as a regulatory body that operates at arm's length from government and enjoys relative autonomy in interpreting the *Broadcasting Act* and the *Telecommunications Act*, and regulating and monitoring the broadcast and telecom environments. However, the Canadian government can influence the commission's behaviours and decisions, either directly by issuing general policy directions and reviewing individual CRTC decisions, or indirectly by appointing members to the commission. This can influence the degree of autonomy that the commission has to pursue policy directions independent of government influence; in other words, the length of the arm that separates the commission from government. In recent years, the commission's arm has appeared to shrink, particularly due to politically motivated appointments to the commission and the government's tendency to overrule certain CRTC decisions.

Since 2006, government intervention into CRTC decisions has occurred with unprecedented frequency. These interventions have generally moved toward liberalization and deregulation in telecommunications, including overturning a decision to regulate some telephone services offered through broadband internet connections (VoIP) (CBC News, 2006a), as well as easing regulation on pricing for local phone services (CBC News, 2006b). In two high-profile cases, the government's decisions to overrule CRTC regulations were made at least partly in response to public outcry about the commission's rulings: in 2009, the reversal of the CRTC's ruling not to grant a licence to the Egyptian-backed communications company Globalive (Longford, 2011), and in 2011, the decision to send back the CRTC's ruling on a much-publicized internet usage-based billing (UBB) proposal.

In the first case, cabinet overturned the CRTC's decision not to grant a licence to a new cellular provider—Wind Mobile—due to concerns that the parent company (Globalive) did not adequately meet the requirements for Canadian ownership and control. The Toronto-based company purchased the rights to establish a new wireless network at a government auction in 2008, under the initial approval of Industry Canada. In October 2009, the CRTC refused to grant the company a licence to operate in Canada, stating that since the greater share of the company's debt and equity was owned by Egyptian billionaire Naguib Sawiris, Globalive did not meet requirements for Canadian control (CBC News, 2009; CRTC, 2009b; Sturgeon, 2009).

Then Industry Minister Tony Clement overturned the CRTC decision and granted approval to Globalive without requiring any changes to ownership structure, describing the Canadian ownership requirements as a "subjective test," in which "two branches of government could reasonably come to different conclusions" (Vieira, 2009). Clement's decision was initially overturned by the Federal Court of Canada, but later reinstated by the Court of Appeals. While Wind Mobile does currently operate in several major Canadian cities, Globalive's competitors are expected to appeal the decision to the Supreme Court of Canada. In the meantime, current levels of competition between existing Canadian firms leave Canadian consumers struggling with some of the highest prices in the world and, in many cases, notoriously draconian contracts and poor customer service (cf Geist, 2008).

More recently, Clement sent the commission back to the drawing board after a much-publicized ruling on internet usage-based billing (data caps on internet service). The primary concern was that the UBB model was too inflexible, and if primary internet service providers (ISPs) such as Bell were able to apply UBB rates to independent ISPs (such as Teksavvy), the smaller competitors would have to impose UBB on their customers, making it difficult for them to differentiate their services from other providers based on price and generous bandwidth. In response to widespread outcry about the decision, spearheaded in large part by the group OpenMedia.ca, Clement tweeted his intention to ensure that the CRTC either reverse its decision or face direct government intervention (CBC News, 2011). When questioned about his perspective on the CRTC's relevance as an arm's-length regulator, Clement stated:

> Certainly there is a role to have an independent set of ears and eyes to look at some of these regulatory issues, but I also believe ... the government ... has a role to play to set the

policy that is going to make sure that Canada remains relevant and competitive in the Internet age."(CBC News, 2011)

Then Chairperson of the CRTC Konrad von Fickenstein responded that the commission had already decided to review the decision before hearing about Clement's tweet in the newspaper, and expressed annoyance that Clement had chosen to announce his decision through social media rather than speaking directly with the commission.[12]

The government's tendency to shorten the CRTC's "arm" by sending rulings back for review or overruling decisions has both advantages and disadvantages. On the one hand, broadcast and telecom industries are facing unprecedented change in a rapidly globalizing and technologically advanced world. The way Canada chooses to adapt to technological change and globalization in communications industries can have significant economic and social impacts. It is therefore very important that the CRTC be held accountable to the Canadians who will be affected by its decisions, and one way to do this is by making the commission accountable to the government that Canadians elect.

On the other hand, if government overrules the CRTC too often, the commission risks losing its value as an arm's-length regulatory body altogether. If the government of the day is overly bold in ensuring that the commission put forward only rulings that it finds favourable ("do as we want, or we'll overrule you"), then the CRTC will no longer operate separately from government and will effectively lose its ability to make controversial, unpopular, or progressive rulings when it is necessary to do so.

POLITICIZED COMMISSIONER APPOINTMENTS

Another significant way that the government can indirectly influence the CRTC's direction is through the selection of commissioners. There can be up to 13 commissioners, all of whom are appointed by cabinet, including the three senior roles of chairperson, vice-chairperson of Broadcasting, and vice-chairperson of Telecommunications. At the time of writing, 11 of 13 commissioners were appointed by the current Conservative cabinet (the other two by the former Liberal government), eight commissioners are male and four are female, and none of the commissioners belong to an ethnic or visible-minority group.[13]

While the government's power in selecting CRTC commissioners need not be a source of controversy in itself, recent politicized appointments have drawn criticism from opposition MPs, who argue that inappropriate appointments could lead to a breakdown in the regulator's independence from government. In particular, the appointment of lawyer and former radio DJ Tom Pentefountas to the post of CRTC vice-chair of Broadcasting in 2011 sparked controversy, with critics describing Pentefountas as "unqualified" since he lacked the in-depth knowledge of media convergence and the broadcasting industry required for the position. Opposition members also suggested that Pentefountas's appointment might have been a reward for being "a friend of the Conservative Party," since Pentefountas was a former president of Quebec's conservative Action démocratique du Québec party and an acquaintance of then-PMO spokesman Dimitri Soudas (Galloway, 2011).

Besides the problem of how the inclusion of relatively unqualified and allegedly politically motivated commissioners could affect the CRTC's decision-making process, politicized commissioner appointments can also harm the commission's public reputation as a nonpartisan organization. The appointment of commissioners with clear political ties and little knowledge of communications industries call into question the commission's authority to regulate and monitor communications industries. Inappropriate commissioner appointments can increase public skepticism about the CRTC and its agenda.

CHALLENGE 4: LOBBYING AND SUPERFICIAL PUBLIC ENGAGEMENT

Broadcast and telecom policy issues are often both complex and politically charged, with actors including large broadcast and telecom companies, smaller broadcasters, community media, civil society groups, trade unions, and advocacy groups, many of whom lobby for support from the public, government, and the regulator itself. On top of the lobbying from industry stakeholders, additional commentary on communications issues is added by journalists, bloggers, and academics who vary in their levels of broadcast and telecom expertise, as well as the detail and accuracy with which they report on communications issues. Often, the mishmash of competing interests results in messages to the public, government, and commission that are neither clear nor entirely accurate, leading to confusion and frustration among a Canadian public that is left to either wade through dense and sometimes esoteric CRTC documentation, or piece together a series of oversimplified and/or politically fraught accounts from the news media and lobby groups.

Our introductory anecdote about the value for signal/fee for carriage issue offers a strong illustration of this sort of oversimplification and politically charged rhetoric. In May 2009, the commission announced that it would hold a proceeding that would address, among other topics, "providing revenue support for conventional broadcasters," including "exploring a mechanism for establishing, through negotiation, fair market value for signals of the conventional television stations distributed by broadcasting distribution undertakings"(CRTC, 2009a).[14] Previously, cable and satellite companies were required to offer certain local channels to customers, but were not required to pay for these services as the broadcasters were thought to receive sufficient revenue through advertising. However, by 2009 the commission found that, in an increasingly fragmented television market, local broadcasters were no longer able to compete on an advertising-based revenue model alone. The proposed value-for-signal (VFS) model would allow local broadcasters to supplement their advertising income by negotiating a fee for distributers to carry the local signals. The proceedings began in the fall of 2009, and the commission heard the arguments for and against the proposed VFS model from broadcasters and distributors.

After receiving an Order-in-Council[15] (2009-1569) requiring it to report on the impact that the VFS proposal could have on customers and the communications industry as a whole, the commission announced that it would accept written and online submissions from the public as well as industry stakeholders, and would hold a public hearing to offer stakeholders and interested citizens the opportunity to comment on the issue (CRTC 2009-614). In response, cable and satellite distributors and local broadcasters organized parallel public campaigns related to the VFS proposal (including those mentioned in the introduction to this chapter), with both sides presenting highly rhetorical partisan cases designed to raise the public's ire without explaining the proposal's cause or function. The cable and satellite distributors framed the proposal as the introduction of a new "TV tax" that Canadians would be forced to pay to greedy broadcasters trying to maximize their revenues (Stop the TV Tax, 2009). The broadcasters' campaign, entitled "Local TV Matters," attacked broadcast distributors for "runaway cable bills," intentionally rolling together the rising costs of cable and satellite with the distributers' purported failure to "pay their fair share for local TV."[16] In fact, the VFS proposal was neither the introduction of a "TV tax," since the decision to raise the cost of cable packages in response to the VFS negotiations would be left entirely to the discretion of the distributor, nor would a favourable decision lead to the cap on cable fees that the "Local TV Matters" campaign called for. Both campaigns were based almost entirely on alerting Canadians to the other side's supposed greed, while neglecting to explain the VFS proposal or direct viewers to the actual discourse put forward by the CRTC.

Nonetheless, the campaigns were successful in motivating Canadians into action. In total the commission received 173,000 comments submitted through various campaigns, dwarfing the mere 16,700 comments that respondents posted directly on the CRTC website.[17] Since then, similarly rhetorical and intentionally vague campaigns by industry or special interest groups have received up to 500,000 responses. In some cases, the CRTC has been forced to act in response to these consumer demands, despite the known power of lobbying and superficial citizen engagement driving the campaigns.

IS THE CRTC STILL RELEVANT?

If we take a moment to consider the overall cumulative impacts of these trends toward media conglomeration, changing technology, politicized commissioner appointments, government interference in decision making and the increasing power of lobbying and superficial public engagement, it is clear that the CRTC is currently facing a number of major challenges and constraints on its role as an autonomous arm's-length regulatory agency. Critics within the government, industry, and media have been outspoken about the commission's challenges and called loudly for its disbandment since the 1990s. Given the many serious issues discussed in this chapter, there is real cause for discussion about whether the commission is still able to fulfill its monitoring and regulatory roles. The remainder of this chapter considers whether or not the CRTC is still relevant in today's social, economic, and political climate, and what changes may be needed to current regulatory frameworks to prepare broadcast and telecom industries for further technological advances and globalization.

The case for the CRTC's relevance is not an easy one to make. On the surface, technological advances would seem to pose a challenge to the CRTC's raison d'être because there is no longer the same scarcity of channels for mass communication in Canada. Indeed, the very idea of a government administering licences rests on an increasingly antiquated premise that the limited supply of airwave frequencies requires a detached, public-interest-focused steward to ensure that the demands of audiences and national goals are met. Technological advances and consumer behaviour are leading us toward an almost laughable situation in which the same content is delivered over networks to screens that are highly regulated (television) as is delivered over networks to screens that are not regulated at all (the internet). The dominance of a small group of vertically integrated media conglomerates that verge on being "too big to fail" combined with the repeated efforts by the current government to overrule CRTC decisions is seriously undermining any leverage that the regulatory agency might have once had to challenge the status quo and push for much-needed policy change. The appointment of unqualified government boosters to crucial commissioner posts that demand certain skills and specialist knowledge raises fundamental questions about the moral authority of the organization to do so in the first place. While the Canadian citizenry is arguably more engaged and mobilized around communications regulatory issues now than it ever has been, various stakeholders have been highly successful in simplifying and manipulating issues through their public opinion mobilization campaigns. In the short term, the CRTC is suddenly challenged to manage public expectations, raise public media literacy, and deal with unprecedented levels of often misguided interventions while also accepting the traditional burdens of monitoring, analysis, and policy development of its role (for which it is arguably already under resourced). Yet, conversely, the CRTC is more relevant now than it has ever been.

Over the past few years the CRTC has been forced to reluctantly embark on nothing short of a programmatic reorientation of Canada's system of mass communication that will continue into the foreseeable future. It is being asked to draw lines in the sand around fundamental questions such as the extent to which our system of mass communication will remain Canadian in content and ownership, the extent to which cultural policy will prop up unprofitable Canadian media, and how a half century of thinking about media regulations will apply (or not apply) to digital technologies. It is being asked to pick winners and losers among cable companies and broadcasters, and between incumbent and insurgent firms, and to predict the geometry of which hypothetical conglomerates might eventually be the most globally competitive national champions. All the while, it does so on the basis of two separate pieces of antiquated legislation (the *Broadcasting Act* and *Telecommunications Act*) that predate the digital technologies that are redefining communications, and amid unprecedented levels of media attention, public engagement, and political scrutiny.

All of which is to say, the role of the CRTC as a forward-looking, expert-driven, independent ombudsman for mass communication that is consciously situated at arm's length from the government of the day is more important now than ever. Arguably, the first step that is required to take us from the CRTC we have to the CRTC we need is to revise the pieces of major legislation on which it operates.

CONCLUSION: MERGING THE *BROADCASTING ACT* AND THE *TELECOMMUNICATIONS ACT*

In response to the erosion in the distinction between broadcasting and telecommunications industries, the last decade has seen repeated calls to merge the *Broadcasting Act* and the *Telecommunications Act* both from government reports (Industry Canada, 2006; Standing Committee on Canadian Heritage, 2003), as well as international organizations (OECD, 2002). Indeed, Canada is perceived as lagging behind many states that have already moved toward integrated frameworks for communications industries: the European Commission policy does not distinguish between the regulation of telecom networks that emerged as telephone networks and those that began as cable TV networks, and several Organisation for Economic Co-operation and Development (OECD) member countries as well as several developing states have moved to merge their regulatory frameworks for broadcast and telecom (while separating carriage and content regulations), while the United States has had a single *Communications Act* governing broadcast and telecom since 1934 (Industry Canada, 2006).

Given that broadcast and telecom industries are undeniably converging, there are many reasons that it might make sense to merge the *Broadcasting Act* and the *Telecommunications Act* into a single communications act. In the 2006 *Telecommunications Policy Review Panel* (TPRP) report, the panel argued that a single regulatory act would allow for more symmetrical and "technology neutral" regulation, which would permit greater investment and innovation by allowing network operators "the freedom to invest in and develop the IP network infrastructure in the most efficient and effective way possible in response to market demand" (Industry Canada, 2006, p. 11-9). An integrated communications act could also allow for policies to focus on the best solutions for the new network environment. On a practical level, communications companies are already involved in both broadcasting and telecom services, consumers are increasingly accessing broadcast content through telecom platforms such as computers and smart phones, and the old corded home phone appears to be going the way of the dodo. At best, these trends make the division between broadcast and telecom technologies seem increasingly artificial and archaic while, at worst, critics argue that policies that insist on dividing the increasingly merged industries could throttle innovation among broadcast and telecom companies.

On the other hand, one might argue that, while they may be converging, broadcast and telecom industries are not yet sufficiently merged to justify a single regulatory framework, particularly given the greater social objectives vested in the Canadian broadcasting system than in telecommunications. In 2010, the Government of Canada announced its intention to liberalize foreign ownership rules in telecom with the goal of "strengthening market competition and attracting new capital and innovative ideas from abroad"(Industry Canada, 2010). In its discussion, however, the government stated that it would not yet apply similar liberalization to broadcasting industries, describing the policy objectives and legislative authorities under the *Telecommunications Act* and *Broadcasting Act* as "distinct," and stating that "[w]ith respect to broadcasting content and culture, the government will not consider any action that could impair its ability to pursue Canadian culture and content policy objectives" (p. 10). In April 2012, the government introduced legislation that would amend the *Telecommunications Act* to allow non-Canadian entities to launch new telecommunications carriers, or acquire current telecom carriers that hold a market share of less than 10 percent of total Canadian telecom service revenues (CRTC, 2012b). However, in keeping with its 2010 comments on the importance of broadcasting for Canadian cultural expression, the government chose only to relax ownership regulations in telecom, and has not yet proposed modifications to ownership requirements in broadcasting.

Regardless of whether the acts are merged, they undoubtedly need to be revisited to account for the changing technological and political environment. This would include providing greater transparency in selecting CRTC commissioners; outlining limits on Parliament's ability to overrule CRTC decisions; recognizing and dealing with convergence issues; dealing fundamentally with media consolidation and vertical integration; and translating social policy objectives into the less-regulated marketplace of new media services. This is a complex conversation, but democracy demands that such important questions be considered in their full complexity, and not simplified and obfuscated. Comm'n, Canada!

QUESTIONS

1. What is vertical integration? Can you think of any current examples of vertical integration (other than the example provided in this chapter)?
2. Explain the role of the CRTC as an arm's-length regulator for broadcasting and telecommunications. Do you think the CRTC's role is still relevant? Why or why not?
3. Examine publicly available copies of the *Broadcasting Act* and *Telecommunications Act* (available at http://laws-lois.justice.gc.ca/PDF/B-9.01.pdf and http://laws-lois.justice.gc.ca/PDF/T-3.4.pdf). Do you think the two acts should be merged? If you were in charge of amending the acts, what would you change?
4. In this chapter, we have discussed some of the ways that Canadian broadcasting and telecommunications have evolved in recent years. How do you think these

industries are going to evolve and change in Canada in the next five years? The next 10 years?

5. What is the ideal role for the voice of the Canadian public in the regulation of Canadian media? Is it better for public opinion to be apathetic to media policy issues or highly mobilized by the sort of partisan campaigns that we have referred to in this article?

NOTES

1. The Cable Song, Dave Carroll. Uploaded by localtvmatters, October 7, 2009. Retrieved August 1, 2012, from http://www.youtube.com/watch?v=uKLS6sNKRGU&feature=related
2. Rick Mercer: Stop TV Tax. Uploaded by CBCtv on December 9, 2009. Retrieved August 1, 2012, from http://www.youtube.com/watch?v=ojFj17_acMU&feature=related
3. Cable vs TV Part 2: Rogers Claim. Uploaded by CrewRite on October 18, 2009. Retrieved August 1, 2012, from http://www.youtube.com/watch?v=ZdaEOwoAiZA&feature=relmfu
4. For more detailed descriptions of how things work, see Salter & Odartey-Wellington, 2008; Raboy, 1990, 1995.
5. For a comprehensive audit of such policies, see Grant and Wood (2004) part 2, and Raboy and Shtern (2010), chapter 3.
6. In April 2012, the Government of Canada introduced legislation to amend the *Telecommunications Act* to allow for greater foreign investment in telecommunications. The amendments will allow non-Canadian entities to launch new telecommunications carriers, or acquire Canadian telecommunications companies that have less than 10 percent market share, as determined by the CRTC.
7. The CRTC Structural and Operational Plan for the Community Radio Fund is at http://www.crtc.gc.ca/eng/archive/2011/2011-431.htm. See the Community Radio Fund of Canada website at http://www.communityradiofund.org
8. In its public notice, the commission stated that it would once again review "information and trends with respect to the sources of news and information used by Canadians" no later than 2013, when it would make adjustments to the policy if necessary.
9. All of the interventions for proceeding CRTC 2010-783 can be viewed at https://services.crtc.gc.ca/pub/ListeInterventionList/Default-Defaut.aspx?en=2010-783&lang=e
10. The commission has warned that it will hold more proceedings and regulate more strictly if companies cannot show that they have made progress toward offering consumers more flexibility in choosing services.
11. The CRTC defines an "over-the-top" service as a service that is "independent of a facility or network dedicated to its delivery (via, for example, cable or satellite)" (CRTC, 2011c).

12. In November 2011, the CRTC released a ruling that rejected the UBB model in favour of a capacity-based model preferred by the independent internet service providers (ISP). The commission acknowledged that the UBB model was too inflexible, and ruled that the capacity-based model would be more consistent with how providers plan their networks, and would be less susceptible to billing disputes. The full ruling is available at http://www.crtc.gc.ca/eng/archive/2011/2011-703.htm
13. The profiles of current CRTC commissioners can be found at http://www.crtc.gc.ca/eng/about/commissioners.htm
14. The commission had considered retransmission negotiations previously in 2007 (CRTC 2007-53) and 2008 (CRTC 2008-100), but in both instances had determined that broadcasters did not need assistance from retransmission consent at those times.
15. An Order-in-Council is a decision taken by cabinet that has not been approved in the legislature, but still has the force of law. Thousands of Orders-in-Council are issued each year, and are published in the *Canada Gazette.*
16. While the localTVmatters website has been removed, several of the ads and videos are still available on YouTube by searching "Local TV Matters."
17. Following the public proceedings, the commission created a VFS regime (CRTC 2010-167), but also referred the case to the Federal Court to determine if implementing the VFS regime was within its authority as granted under the *Broadcasting Act.* The case is currently awaiting consideration by the Supreme Court. The full list of interventions can be viewed at http://www.crtc.gc.ca/4250/eng/ipp16.htm#a2009614

REFERENCES

Baker, E. (2006). *Media concentration and democracy: Why ownership matters.* New York: Cambridge University Press.

CBC News. (2006a, November 15). *Conservatives overrule CRTC on regulation of internet phones.* Retrieved August 1, 2012, from http://www.cbc.ca/news/business/story/2006/11/15/berniervoip.html

———. (2006b, December 11). *Ottawa accelerates deregulation of local phone service.* Retrieved August 1, 2012, from http://www.cbc.ca/news/canada/story/2006/12/11/phones.html

———. (2009, December 11). *Globalive says wireless network launch imminent.* Retrieved August 1, 2012, from http://www.cbc.ca/technology/story/2009/12/11/clement-crtc.html?ref=rss#socialcomments

———. (2011, February 3). *CRTC must reverse internet usage ruling: Clement.* Retrieved August 1, 2012, from http://www.cbc.ca/news/canada/story/2011/02/03/crtc-internet-clement.html

CRTC. (2008, January 15). *CRTC establishes a new approach to media ownership*. Retrieved September 3, 2012, from http://www.crtc.gc.ca/eng/com100/2008/r080115.htm

———. (2011a, September 21). *Broadcasting Regulatory Policy CRTC 2011-601: Regulatory framework relating to vertical integration*. Retrieved August 1, 2012, from http://www.crtc.gc.ca/eng/archive/2011/2011-601.htm

———. (2011b, September 21). *CRTC takes action to ensure a wide choice of television programming on all platforms*. Retrieved August 1, 2012, from http://www.crtc.gc.ca/eng/com100/2011/r110921.htm

———. (2011c). *Results of the fact-finding exercise on the over-the-top programming services*. Retrieved August 1, 2012, from http://www.crtc.gc.ca/eng/publications/reports/rp1110.htm#ftn2

———. (2012a). *Frequently Asked Questions*. Retrieved August 1, 2012, from http://www.crtc.gc.ca/eng/faqs.htm

———. (2012b). *Speech*. Retrieved August 27, 2012, from http://www.crtc.gc.ca/eng/com200/2012/s120605.htm

Canada. (1991). *Broadcasting Act* (S.C., c.11). Retrieved August 1, 2012, from http://laws-lois.justice.gc.ca/eng/acts/B-9.01

———. (1993). *Telecommunications Act* (S.C., c.38). Retrieved August 1, 2012, from http://laws-lois.justice.gc.ca/eng/acts/T-3.4

Canadian Press. (2008, January 15). *CRTC imposes cross-media ownership restrictions*. Retrieved August 1, 2012, from http://www.cbc.ca/money/story/2008/01/15/crtc.html

Galloway, G. (2011, February 4). *CRTC appointment smacks of cronyism, NDP says*. *The Globe and Mail*. Retrieved August 1, 2012, from http://www.theglobeandmail.com/news/politics/ottawa-notebook/crtc-appointment-smacks-of-cronyism-ndp-says/article1895426/

Geist, M. (2008, May 6). Arrival of iPhone trains spotlight on Canada's wireless crisis. *The Ottawa Citizen*. Retrieved August 1, 2012, from http://www.canada.com/ottawacitizen/news/bustech/story.html?id=3fb80bcf-bc8f-49c9-b9fc-27328503415c

Grant, P. S., & Wood, C. (2004). *Blockbusters and trade wars: Popular culture in a globalized world*. Vancouver: Douglas & McIntyre.

Hurtig, M. (2008). The press vs. the people: Media ownership in Canada one of the world's most concentrated. *CCPA Monitor*, *15*(2), 6–8.

Industry Canada. (2006). *Telecommunications Policy Review Panel final report*. Ottawa: Government of Canada.

Industry Canada. (2010). *Opening Canada's doors to foreign investment in telecommunications: Options for reform*. Ottawa: Government of Canada.

Longford, G. (2011).Spectrum policy: Squandering the digital dividend? In M. Moll & L.R. Shade (Eds). *The internet tree: The state of telecom policy in Canada 3.0*. (pp. 123–135). Ottawa: Canadian Centre for Policy Alternatives.

Murdock, G. (1990). Redrawing the map of the communications industries: Concentration and ownership in the era of privatization. In M. Ferguson (Ed.), *Public communication: The new imperatives* (pp. 1–15). Beverly Hills, CA: Sage.

Napoli, P. M. (1997). A principle-agent approach to the study of media organizations: Toward a theory of the media firm. *Political Communication*, 2, 207–219.

Organisation for Economic Co-Operation and Development. (2002). *Regulatory reform in Canada: From transition to new regulation challenges*. Retrieved August 17, 2012, from http://www.oecd.org/regreform/1960562.pdf

Raboy, M. (1990). *Missed opportunities: The story of Canada's broadcasting policy*. Montreal and Kingston: McGill-Queen's University Press.

Raboy, M. (1995). Influencing public policy on Canadian broadcasting. *Canadian Public Administration* 38(3): 411–432.

Raboy, M. (2010). Media. In M. Raboy & J. Shtern (Eds.). *Media divides: Communication rights and the right to communicate in Canada*. Vancouver: UBC Press, 91–119.

Raboy, M., & J. Shtern. (2010). *Media divides: Communication rights and the right to communicate in Canada*. Vancouver: UBC Press.

Salter, L. & Odartey-Wellington, F. (2008). *The CRTC and broadcast regulation in Canada*.Toronto: Thompson.

Skinner, D., & Gasher, M. (2005). So much by so few: Media policy and ownership in Canada. In D. Skinner, J. R. Compton, & M. Gasher (Eds.), *Converging media, diverging politics: A political economy of news media in the United States and Canada* (pp. 51–76). Lanham, MD: Lexington Books.

Standing Committee on Canadian Heritage. (2003). *Our cultural sovereignty: The second century of Canadian broadcasting*. Ottawa.

Standing Committee on Canadian Heritage. (2011, March). *Impacts of private television ownership changes and the move towards new viewing platforms*. Retrieved August 1, 2012, from http://publications.gc.ca/collections/collection_2011/parl/XC61-403-1-1-03-eng.pdf

Stop the TV Tax. (2009). Retrieved April 24, 2012, from http://www.stopthetvtax.ca

Sturgeon, J. (2009, November 23). *Stakes high as rivals await fate of Globalive. The National Post*. Retrieved September 2, 2012, from http://www.canada.com/nationalpost/financialpost/story.html?id=d91ac7a5-fc7a-4b20-a4cc-3577f7838e77

Vieira, P. (2009, December 11). *Globalive's entry boon for consumers: Clement. Financial Post*. Retrieved December 20, 2009, from http://www.financialpost.com/story.html?id=2329655

Winseck, D. (2011, November 29). *Dead horses and Internet policy: The CRTC's usage-based billing and vertical integration decisions as lost opportunities*. Retrieved August 1, 2012, from http://dwmw.wordpress.com/2011/11/29/dead-horses-and-internet-policy-the-crtcs-usage-based-billing-and-vertical-integration-decisions-as-lost-opportunities

6

CANADIAN CULTURAL POLICY IN THE AGE OF MEDIA ABUNDANCE: OLD CHALLENGES, NEW TECHNOLOGIES

Ira Wagman and Ezra Winton
Carleton University

To some degree the notion of "cultural policy" is problematic. Few political parties have ever declared a formal cultural policy as part of a political platform and the federal government does not have a Ministry of Culture. The government agency responsible for Canada's cultural sector, the Department of Canadian Heritage, also oversees the country's amateur athletics program, the status of women, and issues associated with human rights and multiculturalism. Cultural issues also fall under the purview of a range of federal government departments, such as the Department of Foreign Affairs and International Trade and Industry Canada. Even Canada's provinces and some of its municipalities have policies directed at Canada's cultural sector.

We associate some institutions as being closer to cultural policy than others, such as the National Film Board of Canada, or the Canada Council for the Arts, but many institutions and individuals are affected by cultural policies in this country. A 2008 report from the Conference Board of Canada points out that the cultural industries in Canada contribute nearly $85 billion into the national economy, employing over a million Canadians in the process (Conference Board of Canada, 2008). It is easy to think that the cultural sector is a small part of Canadian life, even if the numbers show something very different. We can understand cultural policy, then, as a container term that refers to the portfolio of legal, regulatory, and technical instruments that structure and support artistic activities from broadcasting to ballet.[1]

At the heart of these policies are competing sets of values; one is *aesthetic*, the other is *economic*. Cultural works are seen by many to possess a transcendent quality, as representations of a nation's creative energies, as a comment on social or political issues, or as material judged in aesthetic terms (such as "beautiful" or "sublime"). These qualities are often difficult to justify in economic terms, which privilege profits, competition, and efficiency. As Tyler Cowen explains, understanding the way we resolve those "potential clashes" between economic and aesthetic values is a central question for cultural policy analysts (Cowen, 2006, p. 4).

While the specific orientation of cultural policies may change over time, we can say that the Canadian government has always managed those "potential clashes" by stressing the *national* significance of its cultural policies for almost a century.

We routinely hear how the history of cultural policy has allowed "Canadian stories" to be shared among Canadians from coast to coast to coast and allowed for a vibrant cultural sector to flourish. Such policies are necessary, we are told, to ensure national cohesiveness and citizen participation across a large and historically fragmented Canadian society. However, such policies have also been framed in a language of national defence; Canada needs cultural policies, we are told, to protect its citizens from overexposure to "American culture" and to ensure Canada's cultural sovereignty.

In this chapter we argue that any study of cultural policy in Canada has tended to be about the managing of tensions from these three areas—artistic, nationalistic, and economic. To make sense of this we pose three questions: Why do we make cultural policies? How are those policies put into action across a range of cultural activities? Have those policies been successful? Our account here is not intended to offer a history or a catalogue of Canada's cultural policies; instead, we draw on selected examples, primarily from the areas of film, broadcasting, and digital media to illustrate key concepts that can be applied across the cultural sector. We conclude by suggesting that although new media technologies offer new possibilities for cultural production, distribution, and exhibition, issues that have framed previous policies will remain central to future policies affecting the cultural sector.

THE RATIONALE FOR CULTURAL POLICIES

Why do we "do" policy for cultural purposes? Policies regulating the automotive industry, health care, or the environment may intuitively make sense, when we consider the need for government to manage and organize social and economic activities that affect the wider public good. Policies that regulate the water industry are necessary to ensure that drinking water in Canada remains safe and free of unwanted chemicals or pollution. But what about policies that regulate a documentary film about the water industry? Why would we need policy on something that is clearly expressive in nature? In this section we briefly provide four reasons for the state to intervene in the cultural realm.

Geographic Reasons

The physical and geographical terrain of Canada is an important factor in both the development and implementation of the country's cultural policies. It is useful to think of geographic rationales for cultural policy through two opposing ideas: distance and proximity.

First, there is the issue of Canada's tremendous size and its diversity. The country is a large, sprawling landmass, one whose provinces touch the Atlantic and Pacific Oceans as well as the Arctic Circle. Canada is also a regionally diverse country, with geographical differences serving as physical markers that point to the cultural and sociopolitical diversity that is found in the many folds of its population. Regionalism also means different language groups, so a one-size-fits-all approach needs to be discarded if policy is to account for cultural expression that comes in French, English, Nsyilxcen, Cree, and more. Considering these geographic reasons, cultural policies are necessary to overcome distances and differences to ensure exchange as well as access to a range of cultural works, whether one is in urban, rural, or northern settings. Since many cultural works travel through communications technologies, the issue of distance calls for policies that ensure the existence of a solid technological infrastructure—of radio transmitters, cable systems, or broadband—that can ensure access to those cultural materials.

While the difficulty in overcoming Canada's vast landmass is representative of the challenge of distance, other rationales for cultural policy concern the challenge of geographical proximity, namely to the United States. For all its size, the majority of Canadians live within 200 kilometres of the United States border. In the early years of radio and television, this proximity meant that Canadians could easily access American radio and television stations, and Canadian-produced television did not emerge until many years after Canadians had been watching television from U.S. border stations (Jeffrey, 1996, p. 207). Over the years many politicians and policymakers have expressed concerns that this kind of proximity facilitates easy access for American popular culture and considerable competition for airtime or space on the magazine stand for Canadian expressions. What this also meant, however, was the need to establish policies that would ensure that Canadians could gain access to their own creative works, an act that could be made possible only by providing structural and institutional support for the development of what we now call the "cultural industries."

Economic Reasons

The tension between art for art's sake and art for money's sake, or intrinsic value versus exchange value, cuts to the heart of why cultural policy is shaped with economics in mind: the state is seen to be an arbiter of culture, free of pure profit or market incentives, and a creator of policies that allow for the production and dissemination of art and culture that is not driven by a market logic. In assessing Canadian magazine policy, Imre Szeman writes: "The cultural significance of magazines lies not in the printed text collected between its covers, but in what the existence of such a cultural form suggests about the relationship between culture and economics in a society like ours" (Szeman, 2000, pp. 222–223). While some argue against the commodification of culture, cultural nationalists have argued that it is up to the government to ensure a robust environment is created that engenders the production and dissemination of art and culture not solely dictated by the market. The need for immunity from market forces is important to understanding the second feature of the economic rationales for cultural policies. In one sense, cultural works can be expensive to produce; given Canada's relatively small population and given that there is little additional cost to import American products into

Canada, cultural policies need to be put in place to encourage cultural production. In another sense, some forms of cultural expression may be controversial in nature; as a result, it may be difficult for artists to find a "market" for art works that may not have a commercial benefit. The recognition of the distinctive economic characteristics of Canadian cultural production calls attention to the need for policies that can correct market irregularities, thus facilitating both the production and distribution of Canadian art works, regardless of their "market value" or commercial worth. This is not only for aesthetic purposes. The cultural industries in Canada—as in many other countries—translate into jobs and dollars. Although arts organizations employ a number of people, the large-scale operations of a television or film production involve an impressive number of technical staff, construction workers, caterers, advertisers, publicists and more. Referencing the ways the government develops policies to encourage other economic activities, such as automotive production, many argue that the economic contributions of cultural production are evidence that cultural policies not only help the artistic community, but also Canadian society at large.[2]

Social Reasons

Whether one is discussing policies for museums, documentaries that explore social issues, or directives aimed at managing social spaces created around cultural production, cultural policies in Canada nearly always have the social in mind. This element of cultural policy sees citizenship as entailing more than political acts, such as voting, or civic acts, such as volunteer work, but measures membership in the nation-state by the level of access and participation individual citizens have in their culture and arts. Seen from this perspective, then, the structure and quality of communication systems is related to the quality of Canadian democracy. Media technologies play a central role in the framing and exchange of information and ideas, and are part of the ways in which Canadians learn about themselves and others. As a result, cultural policies are needed to provide both the structural foundation and to encourage the development of content to allow for these kinds of information exchanges to take place.

National(istic) Reasons

The Hollywood blockbuster film *Avatar* was written and directed by a Canadian, James Cameron. Despite this fact, few would call the film Canadian. Why? This question—a question of origin—is tightly welded with questions of identity and nationality. Benedict Anderson (1991) has famously argued that the nation is imagined, and that the nation-myth is held together through communication and cultural technologies that collapse time and space. Canada, a country founded on the soil of hundreds of First Nations, carved out of conflict between the two colonial powers France and England, and neighbouring the almighty USA, is a problematic national concept to communicate, enforce, and maintain. As Serra Tinic maintains, "... Canada may provide an example of the ultimate modern imagined community. National public broadcasting was intentionally designed to counteract the effects of geographic vastness and provide a sense of national self-consciousness to the diverse regional, linguistic, Native, and immigrant groups within the country's boundaries" (Tinic, 2005, p. 16). Since confederation, governments residing over the dominion of Canada have leveraged cultural policies in order to augment economic, political, and social policies directed at nationhood. The earmarking of federal monies for Canada Day celebrations in a politically volatile Quebec, or the recent emphasis on events celebrating the 200th anniversary of the War of 1812, is only the tip of the national iceberg that is concealed by the murky waters of governmentalism; that is to say, cultural sovereignty is continually entangled and equated with national sovereignty.

CANADA'S CULTURAL POLICIES AT A GLANCE

With an understanding of some of the rationales for making cultural policy, we can now turn our attention to a survey of the range of legal, regulatory, institutional, and instrumental aspects of Canada's cultural policies.

Cultural policy measures come about through a range of different mechanisms. One may be diplomatic in nature, to bring Canada's policies on copyright in line with those of other countries or through international agreements. Another may be more political in nature; the result of intense lobbying by one group or groups within Canada's cultural sector. A third way may be pragmatic; an institution creates policies in order to achieve certain objectives, such as to support the publication of poetry.

However, one of the leading methods of policymaking comes through the consultative process, in which the government calls for public opinion and participation to assist it in making policies for specific cultural industries. Over the past 80 years, Canada has had a number of Royal Commissions to facilitate consultation on cultural issues. Royal Commissions are public inquiries created by the prime minister to investigate matters of public interest or controversy. A group of commissioners are named from outside the government to oversee the inquiry, experts are consulted to provide research and testimony, and members of the public are encouraged to submit opinions to the commission, either in public or in writing.

Royal Commissions have been vital to Canada's cultural policies. The 1928 Royal Commission on Radio Broadcasting, chaired by Sir John Aird, concluded that radio broadcasting was in Canada's national interest and made recommendations that would lead to the establishment of the Canadian Broadcasting Corporation. The 1951 Royal Commission on National Development in the Arts, Sciences, and Letters, chaired by Vincent Massey, underscored the importance of state support for a range of artistic activities and led to the creation of the Canada Council for the Arts (see Litt, 1992 for a full account). The 1957 Royal Commission on Broadcasting, chaired by Robert Fowler, helped to structure Canada's broadcasting industry to include private and public broadcasting. Finally, the 1980 Royal Commission on Newspapers, chaired by Tom Kent, made strong recommendations to the government about the concentration of ownership in the newspaper industry.

We continue in this section by turning our attention toward three specific components of Canada's cultural policy apparatus: legislative actions, cultural institutions, and policy techniques.

Legislative Actions

Acts of the federal parliament have established the legal and regulatory structure for Canada's arts and cultural sectors. Among the legal instruments in place are laws protecting individual privacy, punishing hate speech, ensuring consumer protections, allowing for individuals to access government information, and providing copyright and patent protections (Gasher, Lorimer, and Skinner, 2008, p. 149). There are also laws in place that outline the structural components of certain forms of cultural activity.

One example is broadcasting. Canada's *Broadcasting Act*, last updated in 1991, establishes the rules and regulations for Canada's broadcasting system. The act states who should own broadcasting undertakings; that broadcasting be offered in both of Canada's official languages across the country; that broadcasting should provide a rich and varied amount of programming reflective of the diverse interests, cultural, and ethnic heritages of Canadians; and that the system "should serve to safeguard, enrich, and strengthen, the cultural, political, social, and economic fabric of Canada" (Canada, *Broadcasting Act*, s. 3d). What is striking about the present context, one characterized by the rise of digital media, is that neither this act nor the *Telecommunications Act* have anything to say about computers or about the ways computers are used to do the things that both of the acts oversee, namely distribute content and serve as a platform for new forms of material. Once seen as separate, broadcasting and telecommunications are now very much the same thing, with some companies owning properties across media platforms. Quebecor, for example, now owns a number of major newspapers as well as television networks, and distributes its content through its Videotron service. The fact that the laws have not been updated may well be due to lack of political will, but for our purposes it serves to remind us of the fact that the framework of Canada's digital media environment has been built on a legal structure that preceded many of the major technological and structural developments which characterize the present media landscape.

Another example pertains to the ownership of Canadian media properties. The *Investment Canada Act* limits the extent of the foreign ownership of firms in "cultural businesses," such as newspapers, broadcasting operations, publishing, and film distribution (Government of Canada, 1985). Such policies have been a double-edged sword. Although they maintain the ownership of Canadian media companies within

Canada, such laws seriously limit the number of players that can compete in the Canadian marketplace, producing a media environment dominated by only a few large players. We have already seen the case of Quebecor above, but of course there are others. For example, the proposed merger of Bell Canada with Astral Media would create a media conglomerate comprising 79 television channels, 107 radio stations, and more than 100 websites across Canada (CBC News, 2012). Another company, Shaw Media, provides broadband internet and cable service, as well as owning the Global Television Network, History Television, and many others. A system that was intended to foster strong companies in order to provide a stable environment for the distribution of Canadian content has also produced an environment that is characterized by considerable ownership consolidation across numerous media platforms.

Cultural and Regulatory Institutions

One of the results of a number of legislative actions has been the creation of a number of key institutions to administer over or regulate Canadian cultural activities. The Canadian Broadcasting Corporation was created in 1936 to provide broadcasting services in English and French, first on radio, and then on television. The National Film Board of Canada (NFB) was created in 1939, first as a propaganda organization promoting Canada's war effort, but later became an essential supporter of the production of documentary, animation, and experimental films, and as a leading training institution for Canadian filmmakers. The Canada Council for the Arts was created in 1957 to oversee the production and promotion of the arts in Canada. The council supports a range of artistic activities in Canada, including literature and the performing arts. In addition to cultural institutions, acts of parliament have also created regulatory institutions to oversee adherence to the rules by those participating in cultural activities. **The Canadian Radio-Television and Telecommunications Commission (CRTC)** was created in 1969 and is responsible for overseeing the activities of Canada's radio and television broadcasters, cable and satellite companies, and telecommunication service providers (see Chapter 5).

The move from institutional creation to the creation of regulatory agencies reflects a broader shift in cultural policies. Beginning in the 1960s and 1970s, Canada's policies in broadcasting and film moved beyond support of individual cultural institutions and toward the development of **cultural industries** (Dorland, 1998). In broadcasting, the CBC was once the only national network on radio and in television, and problematically, was also the regulator of all broadcasting activity in Canada. By the 1960s, private networks were permitted to operate, and a new agency was created, the Board of Broadcast Governors (which would become the CRTC) to issue broadcast licences and monitor the activities of private broadcasters on the public airwaves. Government support for movies underwent a similar transformation, moving away from the NFB and documentary film and toward the development of a feature film industry. What emerges, then, is a kind of cultural policy apparatus, one that has established the working environment in which production companies, film distribution undertakings, and book and magazine editors all operate.

Policy Instruments

To satisfy the legal requirements of Canada's cultural policies, cultural institutions and regulatory bodies deploy a range of techniques while achieving policy objectives. For example, there exist a number of organizations and funding sources that support the production of cultural works in Canada. Telefilm Canada supports the production of television, films, and new media. Among its many support initiatives, the Canada Council administers a number of grants to assist theatrical companies to mount productions. The Canada Book Fund supports the publication of Canadian writers by aiding domestic publishers. Organizations such as FACTOR or Musicaction provide funds to assist new musicians to produce master recordings. The Canadian Magazine Fund supports the creation of editorial content and organization support for the country's magazine sector, while the Canada Periodical Fund (CPF) was recently developed with the intention of assisting print magazines, nondaily newspapers, and digital periodicals. The Canada Media Fund focuses on the creation and support of various forms of media content, including software and digital media.

In addition to policies that encourage production, there are instruments that encourage the distribution or exhibition of cultural works. Arguably the best example is Canadian content regulations for the country's broadcasters. The *Broadcasting Act* states that broadcasters have to carry a minimum amount of material deemed to be "Canadian." This is determined by two different measurements. For radio, a song is considered to be Canadian if two of the following members of the production—the composer, performer, lyricist, or place of production—are Canadian. This is known by the acronym "MAPL" (music, artist, production, lyrics). For television, a production is deemed Canadian if a certain percentage of the episode's creative talent is Canadian or a certain percentage of the production's expenses is incurred for services by Canadian companies. Such a system provides the structure to ensure that Canadian productions have "shelf space" on the air.

If such policies represent more direct policy instruments, Canada's cultural sector also relies on a range of different indirect forms of support. The distribution of Canada's magazines is assisted by subsidies to offset postal costs, which make sending magazines through the mail less expensive. Canada's musicians can apply for assistance from a range of different funds to assist in the promotion, marketing, and distribution of musical works, both on- and offline. Until recently, the federal government operated a service that transported artworks between publicly funded Canadian art galleries at a reduced cost. This allowed art institutions to be able to share works more easily. Many film and television productions—either made specifically for Canadian audiences or foreign films shot on location in Canada—rely on tax breaks offered at the federal, provincial, or municipal levels that help to offset or reduce the overall costs of production.

ASSESSING CANADA'S CULTURAL POLICIES: THE PROBLEM WITH "SUCCESS"

If one were to measure success by the existence of a "cultural sector," one could easily conclude that Canada's cultural policies have, over time, achieved their goals. There are numerous theatre troupes, broadcasting companies, publishers, and magazines to serve a diversity of Canadian interests. Whether there should be more outlets is obviously a matter of personal choice, but it is safe to say that the cultural policies have created an environment that exists to facilitate industrial development. The expansiveness of those policies gives Canada's cultural sector a relative level of stability. The term "relative" is important here because as many artists and cultural creators know, Canada's cultural policies are usually in a state of flux. Support funds are sometimes increased, then diminished; programs are created and folded; someone who is awarded support for one project may not win a second or third time.

Some examples may be illustrative here. At one time the Department of Foreign Affairs assisted in the cost of touring exhibitions for artists as well as musicians; that support has since stopped, making it more difficult for some artists to distribute and showcase their work on a global level. A decision by the CRTC to change the rules on what it considers to constitute "Canadian content" can have direct effects on Canada's production community. A decision to count "entertainment news" programming as Canadian content sparked a flurry of production of new programs to fulfill this objective, including shows such as *Entertainment Tonight Canada,* and *eTalk Daily.* At various points in time over the past 25 years, including in the present context, there have been concerns that the funding for the CBC will be cut, affecting its capacity to deliver public broadcasting. Such threats are internal to the logic of cultural policymaking, and a reminder that those who work in the cultural sector in Canada must constantly adapt to changing policy conditions as well as those affecting the specific industry in which they work.

In each of these and many other cases, we can see that the heavy influence of the federal government across an array of policy supports means that those supports—and those affected by them—are usually dependent upon political machinations and subject to a tremendous amount of bureaucracy. In other cases, the fluctuations are economic in nature; for example, changes to the value of the Canadian dollar can either attract or repel foreign film and television productions from shooting in Canada.

Since the cultural industries have evolved over time, putting more and more Canadians on the global scene, and since Canada has had a long history of cultural policies, it is commonplace to assume a direct relationship between the two. Many conclude there is a relationship between the success of a show, book, or piece of art and the policies that provided the infrastructure for that product to enter the marketplace or for that form of cultural expression to be made available to audiences in Canada and abroad. Other examples abound: most notably those that equate the survival of the Canadian music industry to Canadian content regulations on radio.

However, both of these claims rest on a number of problematic assumptions about the effect of policies on artistic production. They assume that there was nothing inherently artistic about the television program or piece of music that resonated with audiences; that none of the other exogenous factors—scheduling, marketing, social or regional context—could have had an impact on the show's success. They also assume that without such a policy framework, the cultural industries would not have developed to the state they are in today. In other words, such conclusions are arrived at through a privileging of policy over other factors (Wagman, 2010).

It would be naïve to suggest that the range of Canada's cultural policies has had little impact on the structure and character of Canada's cultural sector and in the development of its cultural industries. Indeed, those policies provided a framework in which the cultural sector has developed. However, understanding the *extent* of those policies either on individual artists or on cultural sectors is more difficult to prove. Consider the cases of television and film. In the United States, television shows fail frequently; some figures suggest an 80 percent failure rate. In the case of Canadian film, we often argue that the problem is that, especially in English Canada, audiences do not go to see Canadian films. We routinely refer to the failure of Canadian television programs or the paltry percentage of screen time devoted to Canadian movies at the theatres as evidence of problems with the cultural policy apparatus. Some even have suggested that, as is the case for television and radio, Canada's movie theatres operate with content requirements to ensure Canadian movies reach Canadian theatre screens.

One might also argue whether theatrical exhibition should be the appropriate measure of success. What about documentaries or short films, which are rarely shown at theatres, or movies made for television or shown on video-on-demand services (see Acland, 2002)? Should success be measured by audience ratings? DVD sales? Merchandise sales? If we say that the purpose of cultural policy is to create jobs in the cultural sector, then audience size, box office results, or Oscar awards are poor augurs for success. If we say that the purpose of cultural policy is to ensure that Canadians go to see Canadian movies at multiplexes, then perhaps other policies need to be put in place.

However, if we say that the purpose of cultural policies is to train people for careers in the cultural industries, then people working on a television show that fails may gain valuable experience that they can use for future efforts. The creative personnel who worked on television programs we consider to be successful, such as *Corner Gas* or *Les Bougons*, or *Holmes on Homes* did not just walk off the street and into television. Many appeared on television shows or in movies that did not have a long shelf life. On the backs of successes, then, are many failures, unintended consequences, and delightful accidents that may have little to do with specific policy initiatives. One of the key questions to ask when making sense of the success or failure of cultural policies should be, "What is the meaning of success?" Many will acknowledge that a program such as *Little Mosque on the Prairie* constitutes a successful Canadian television show. But what is such a claim based upon? Canadian audience figures for the show were mixed, so this may not be the measurement. The show has been sold worldwide to many countries, reaching a global audience. It attracts considerable scholarly attention, as well as press coverage (for example, Matheson, 2012). If we consider success in terms of moderate local success and great international sales, the show would seem to be a hit. How about Nickelback? The group is a Canadian act that relies very little on the cultural policy apparatus but is very successful in terms of sales, even if the band receives little attention from critics and even derision from certain segments of the public. Determining "success" then means determining first what we mean by success.

NEW MEDIA, OLD CHALLENGES

Canada's cultural policies have always sought to provide resolutions to challenges posed by the introduction of new technologies. In this section we outline how **digitization**, and particularly, the rise of the internet, has challenged some of the existing frameworks that underlie Canada's cultural policies.

Multiple Creators, Global Content

How do you create effective policy for the YouTube generation? And is policy even relevant in such a *multiverse* of creators and content? With advancements in technology, the tools to make media and to disseminate and consume media have proliferated. **DIY** and amateur "do it with others" (**DIWO**) films, music, news, blogs, photography, radio, and more are proliferating in a mediascape that is increasingly globally connecting content producers/users who are altogether unconcerned with a nationalist context. A recent economic report on the Canadian film and television industry states, "the most important developments in 2006 occurred in the emerging alternative platforms and the user-generated content that audiences often find compelling on these new platforms" (*Profile 2007*, 2007, p. 7). In his treatise on "convergence culture" Henry Jenkins states, "This circulation of media content—across different media systems, competing media economies, and national borders—depends heavily on consumers' active participation" (Jenkins, 2006, p. 3). Indeed, the activities of many more operators in the cultural industries have left policymakers scratching their heads. Since so much of this content flows through the internet and across different social media platforms, it is unsurprising that the Canadian government is seeking ways to fold the internet into a policy framework. That said, at this point what we have are starting points. The arrival of streaming video providers such as Netflix raised questions about whether foreign services should be obliged to contribute to funds that support Canadian cultural production. There have also been attempts by those in the creative sector to argue that internet service providers are "broadcasters" and as such should also contribute to the system. This argument appears at numerous public hearings, and even through an unsuccessful case before the Supreme Court of Canada (Ladurantaye, 2012a). Others have suggested that cultural policy mechanisms be put in place to support the production of **user-generated content**. But what are the implications for all these emergent producers and users who are making their own media in their homes, uploading it to the internet, and reaching a global audience that can number in the millions? Justin Bieber did not benefit from Canadian music subsidies; his star rose because of response to his amateur video posts on YouTube, which begs the question, "Where does YouTube fit in a policy framework?" Such policy questions are further complicated by the mass proliferation of media devices.

Abundant Devices/Platforms

As more and more individuals become increasingly "wired," shifting uses of technology and new ways of consuming content emerge. Whether it is machinima (movies made from assembling video game content), viewing content online, or a cell phone deployed for vlogging (video blogging), there is no denying the sheer abundance and multiplicity of media devices and platforms. A 2008 report from Statistics Canada found that over one third of Canadian households are storing "unused or obsolete computers and communication devices" (Statistics Canada, 2008).[3] This is to say nothing of the exportation of e-waste, be it flat-screen televisions or discarded hard drives, to countries in the developing world. **Convergence** has also meant the merging of media delivery systems, such as the phone that records and plays video, the computer that streams television and radio, and the television that streams video from the internet. Media production and consumption—once confined to the dark rooms, living rooms, studios, and theatres of Canada—has gone mobile. The old rubric of media beamed into the home for consumption is exploding into a media environment that has multidirectional content flows. Consider the case of *Trade Centre*, the annual program that airs on sports network TSN covering the NHL trade deadline. The program, once lasting an hour or two, now stretches over the course of an entire day, and users can follow developments either by watching TSN or by visiting the network's website; following its Twitter feed; reading blogs by its contributors and reporters, following development on TSN's radio stations; following trades with iPhone and Android apps; and for those who subscribe to the Bell service, by watching the broadcast live on a mobile device.

This presents obvious challenges for policymakers. Rules and guidelines developed for radio that is produced in Canada and broadcast over the radio airwaves cannot necessarily account for radio that is delivered through the internet and cellular networks to computers and portable media devices. Regulatory measures that qualitatively assess language or hate speech, along with quantitative assessments, such as adding up Canadian content, are less effective in accounting for the diversity and abundance of devices and platforms that transmit media. Cultural policy that ensures that "adult content" is shown on television only during certain hours is equally strained when it is confronted with satellite TV and television that is streamed or downloaded and watched on a computer, cell phone, tablet, or television. For now, the CRTC exempts cellular companies from television regulations,[4] but cultural policy will need to adapt and evolve if the government is to have any say at all in the production, distribution, and consumption of media, especially as new media increasingly push old media to the back of the analogue cupboard.

Multiple Audiences

Cultural policy, like other state interventions in the social life of Canadians, is in theory shaped by the population and its diverse tastes, habits, and cultural sensibilities. Therefore, it has been a challenge for policymakers to write policy for a population whose media consumption habits are difficult to measure. We may have statistics about things such as personal internet use in Canada (the present figure is that Canadians are online for over 40 hours a week, on average—among the most in the world) and we have some insights as to what popular media consumption habits may be, but we remain largely unsure about the nature of that consumption (Ladurantaye, 2012b). In Canada very little research has been conducted into the varied ways individuals consume and experience media, and this problem area is further exaggerated in an era of multiple, or fragmented, audiences. In a study of the international success of Mexican *telenovellas* (similar in some ways to the popular *téléroman* in Quebec), Pastina and Straubhaar write that:

> audience preferences are formed within the overall trend toward cultural proximity within both national and cultural-linguistic boundaries. However, within this logic of cultural proximity, other forces also apply. It is important to understand cultural proximity working not only at the national and supranational levels but also at the subnational and regional spheres. (Pastina and Straubhaar, 2005, p. 271)

Geographic and linguistic proximity is one way to look at audiences in Canada. Francophones and residents of Quebec are more likely to seek out French-language programming than anglophones. However, there are still other forces at play in what determines the tastes and habits of individuals consuming media. Aggregate social categories may have been appropriate for assessing audiences in the 1980s, when the media universe was restricted to fewer channels and producers, but not anymore. In the contemporary context, where multiple producers and endless channels and platforms compete for the attention of consumers, fragmentation is the defining characteristic. To continue with the Quebec example: within *la belle province* there is a tendency toward French-language media, but among francophones there are further audience divisions. In Montreal, there exists a large Haitian population who seek out media that reflects their cultural inclinations. Within that group there are likely some seeking queer content, some seeking out Hollywood, and others seeking out British comedies. In Quebec, as with the rest of the country, there are myriad audiences identifying with and consuming media that reflects their cultural tastes and sensibilities, whether it is along lines of sexual identity, class, diasporic community, or divergent genres. For policymakers, "knowing the audience" is a complicated and opaque task. The current mediascape has teenagers in Winnipeg downloading the latest Bollywood film to a tablet device while streaming an episode of *Breaking Bad* on Netflix; an elderly couple watching the CBC's *Air Farce* on their tube television in Truro; children in Nunavut watching, and singing along to, the latest Lady Gaga music video on MTV via satellite; a group of university students on a bus watching *The Daily Show* on an iPhone; tweens piling into an Imax theatre in Vancouver to watch a 3-D martial arts film; and a married couple in Hull renting the Quebec hit *Incendies* at their local video store. Creating informed and effective policy for these kinds of diverse cultural habits requires an understanding of a population rapidly undergoing media consumption changes. In other words, a shift in policymaking for "the mass audience" to "niche audiences."

Narratives Across Platforms and Markets

Among these changes in consumption is a phenomenon that is steadfastly perfected by media conglomerates: the art and craft of expanding and carrying a narrative across a multiplicity of markets and platforms. Jenkins reminds us that "convergence is both a top-down corporate-driven process and a bottom-up consumer-driven process" (Jenkins, 2006, p. 18) where media producers and audiences both "build" multiple-platform narratives that stretch out and are harvested by fans for creative value and corporations for lengthy cycles of profit, as in cases such as *Harry Potter* or the *Twilight* series of films.

The contemporary mediascape shows little signs of retaining the more static characteristics of older models, but instead the cultural cycle is broken apart and reassembled by producers and consumers multiple times at multiple locations in multiple ways. For example, the Canadian documentary *The Corporation* (2003) was produced; broadcast on television; shown in theatres, festivals, and home parties; and eventually available through DVD sales and rentals. Along the way, the narrative that is explored in the film was expanded and augmented through a website, a book, an "official" **torrent** download, and a classroom version for teachers (see http://www.thecorporation.com). The film narrative no longer lives and dies in the dark space of the movie theatre but instead grows across different formats (discs, digits, paper) in different contexts (public and private places, front rooms, theatres, classrooms) and in different markets (domestic, international, book industry, film distribution, and exhibition). As Jenkins reminds us, this is more than just a plethora of profit-inducing products, it is also a cultural shift in the way we consume and experience media. From online voting for TV's *American Idol* to the short film that accompanies Naomi Klein's bestselling book *The Shock Doctrine* (see http://www.naomiklein.org/shock-doctrine), narratives unfold across time and space in nearly as many ways as there are stories to tell (and sell), presenting new challenges and demands for cultural policy. One emergent genre that confounds both policy and older media models is the webdoc, a way of storytelling that combines cinema, audio, photography, text, and the internet and rekindles the classic "choose-your-own-adventure" book series with digital flare. The NFB has staked its claim as an institution at the forefront of this new genre, and projects such as *Highrise* (http://highrise.nfb.ca), a Webdoc peering into the vertical world of global suburbs, have won praise from artists, audiences and techies alike.

Expansive New Laws

Generally speaking, cultural policies toward Canada's arts and cultural sector have shifted over time, often in response to technological changes. The current context is no different, even if the response has been slower. The proliferation of digital technologies and the rise of the internet offer new ways to become engaged in cultural participation. The internet makes issues about "shelf space" less problematic. The policy challenge, therefore, has to change from simply addressing exposure to an approach concerned with access. Rules on net neutrality (to ensure that every internet user is treated the same, and that others cannot connect faster than others) and copyright are the keystones to that objective. Digital media works, unlike their older analogue cousins, are extremely easy to replicate and disseminate. An entire feature film can be downloaded in just minutes (provided your internet provider isn't engaged in **throttling**). An illegal recording of the newest blockbuster (complete with heads blocking the screen inside the movie theatre) can be distributed via a torrent Weblink to millions within hours of its release. A song can be downloaded and installed as a cellphone ring in seconds. DIY creators can make **mash-ups** from popular culture and distribute their creations through the internet, as seen most recently with the subversive "Pepper Spraying Cop" **meme** (http://pepperspraying cop.tumblr.com) and the playful "Invisible Obama" that followed Clint Eastwood's speech at the 2012 Republican Convention (for more, see Gauntlett, 2011 and search @InvisibleObama and #Eastwooding on Twitter.com).

With this flourishing of creativity, sharing, and selling, new laws have been drafted, and in some cases enforced. Most of the new laws around new media practices are concerned with protecting cultural works such as copyright laws. But others seek to limit how mobile digital works of art are in a world of multiple platforms. For example, the recent passing of Bill C-11 has brought about changes to Canada's copyright law that impinge on the ways in which Canadians make use of digital content. One provision now makes it illegal to move music from a CD to an iPhone if the record company has placed a "digital lock" on the disc (Raj, 2012).

With the rapid and accessible copying and sharing of cultural works, individual artists and corporations are either scrambling for ways to restrict the activity or embrace it, such as the earlier torrent example of *The Corporation*. Other laws address internet use, which has sparked a fevered debate over **net neutrality** (learn more at openmedia.ca). As laws seek to restrict the freedom of internet use under the banner of "protection," many argue that fundamental rights are being impinged upon. The freedom to explore and surf the internet is seen as encroached upon as new laws allow telecommunication companies to work with content producers to "guide" and at times restrict users as they seek out content on the web. This issue was publicized in the early months of 2012 when hundreds of American and Canadian websites "went dark" for a day to protest a proposed, and subsequently shelved, U.S. policy called SOPA (the *Stop Online Piracy Act*). The fight isn't over, however, as the Canadian federal government has its own policy version of restricting net use under the proposed copyright legislation, Bill C-11, a point of debate in 2012. The idea of **fair use** has emerged as a counter to protective laws and policy, and has been championed in mash-up culture. Brett Gaylor explores these issues in his 2008 feature length and **open source** (audiences are encouraged to remix the film from clips put online) documentary *RIP: A Remix Manifesto* (http://www.nfb.ca/webextension/rip-a-remix-manifesto).

The debates, laws, and cultural policies around copyright, privacy, net neutrality, and media rights point to the peculiar nature of cultural works that are often regulated entities in unregulated zones. Many lawmakers and policy writers in Canada consider the internet "unchartered territory" where copyrighted materials flow freely between users. Some creators and consumers counter that this is the fundamental difference between a widget and a work of art—you cannot measure the value of cultural products within a market framework because the value is found in the way the film or song or photograph makes you feel. It is an old debate that has found resurgence inside lawmaking and cultural policy circles grappling with an age of media abundance.

CONCLUSION

In the time in which the Conservative government has been at the head of the Canadian government, both as a minority and now (at the time of writing), in a majority position, numerous policy initiatives proposed by the government have attracted considerable attention and controversy. Early in 2008, it announced changes to the country's tax law that would allow the Minister of Canadian Heritage to deny tax credits to Canadian film or television productions on the basis that they were "contrary to public policy." The Canadian comedy *Young People F-ing* became the poster child film for this controversy in 2006. Just prior to calling the 2008 election, the government announced a number of funding cuts to the arts sector that affected a number of different support programs. The government has recently unveiled a series of budget cutbacks across the cultural spectrum, most notably at the CBC and NFB. There has been much talk as well of other changes coming on the horizon, including a revision of laws restricting foreign ownership of Canadian media.

These cases—the proposed and the already passed—highlight the major themes discussed in this chapter. First, they show the prominent role the federal government has played as a patron of the arts, providing both the technical infrastructure and direct funding support for the production, distribution, and presentation of cultural works. This means that the arts and federal politics in Canada are intertwined. Second, it shows that such policies not only affect the lives of cultural producers but also have an impact on what Canadians see and when we see them. Third, it shows us that the cultural sector represents a large and powerful *industry*, one comprising not only individual artists and small arts collectives, but also large corporations, professional industry associations, lobby groups, and the labour movement. In addition to its industrial components, the cultural sector also comprises a large bureaucracy, made up of government ministries, policy analysts, regulatory bodies, and various granting agencies that administer over cultural activity in Canada. Fourth, it shows that powerful ideas about "American culture" and, more specifically, of an "American" mode of cultural production are shaping the way we talk about Canadian arts policies. Finally, it shows that the emergence of new media forms challenges pre-existing policies and serves as a new way for many to become involved in the policy process.

What these cases also reveal is that the complexities of Canada's cultural polices are in many ways a reflection of Canada's complex society, one which is multilingual, multicultural, and regionally diverse. The challenge for cultural policymakers has always been to find the right means with which to balance the aesthetic characteristics of creative production with broader socioeconomic factors. Understanding both the nature and extent of that balance is not an easy task, because it forces us to engage with questions about the role of the state in cultural production; the need for cultural economies to be managed; the ways in which Canada's books, television shows, films, or public broadcasters rely on state support for their existence; and the reasons we use to support them.

QUESTIONS

1. How has the federal government sought to balance what appear to be the competing interests of aesthetics and economics through its cultural policies?
2. How is cultural citizenship different from national or political citizenship?
3. Why do we need different policies for widgets and the arts?
4. How do issues of distance and proximity affect Canadian cultural policy?
5. Concerning cultural policy, how is the internet different than other forms of dissemination, such as more traditional media such as radio and television?

NOTES

1. Throughout this chapter we intersperse the terms "arts" and "culture" to capture the complex component of human creativity, labour, and expression that has been called, generally, the arts, the arts sector, the culture industries, and the cultural sector. As cultural policy seeks to address the artistic and cultural (not to mention economic) aspects of the creative sector, both terms are appropriate.
2. A study by the Conference Board of Canada found Canada's cultural sector generated $46 billion, or 3.8 percent of Canada's GDP, in 2007. And, according to the Canada Council, in 2003–2004, the sector accounted for an estimated 600,000 jobs (Fleck, 2008).
3. The report also states, "Computers, cellular phones and personal digital assistants (PDAs) have become almost ubiquitous in Canada. Sales of computer hardware and software went from $3.0 billion in 1998 to over $4.2 billion in 2006. Cell phone ownership rose from 22% of households in 1997 to 64% in 2005." More recent studies have confirmed this trend. As of 2011, 78 percent of Canadians own a cellular phone. This development has also meant the decline of landlines, once a staple means of communication for Canadians (Powell 2011).
4. According to the CRTC, cellular companies are exempt, based on "arguments put forth by parties that mobile television broadcasting services, as described in the proceeding, are unlikely to compete significantly with traditional broadcasting ..." (CRTC, February 7, 2007).

REFERENCES

Acland, C. (2002). Screen space, screen time and Canadian film exhibition. In W. Beard and J. White, (Eds.), *North of everything: English Canadian cinema since 1980* (pp. 2–18). Edmonton, AB: University of Alberta Press.

Anderson, B. (1991). *Imagined communities*. New York: Verso.

Canada. (1985). *Investment Canada Act*. Retrieved August 30, 2012, from http://laws-lois.justice.gc.ca/eng/acts/I-21.8/index.html

———. (1991). *Broadcasting Act*. Retrieved August 10, 2012, from http://laws.justice.gc.ca/en/B-9.01

CBC News (2012, August 7). Bell rivals cry foul over Astral Takeover. Retrieved September 1, 2012, from http://www.cbc.ca/news/canada/story/2012/08/07/bell-astral-competitors.html

Cowen, T. (2006). *Good and plenty: The creative successes of American arts funding*. Princeton, NJ: Princeton University Press.

CRTC. (2007, February 7). *Broadcasting Public Notice CRTC 2007-13: Exemption Order for Mobile Television Broadcasting Undertakings*. Retrieved September 4, 2012, from http://www.crtc.gc.ca/eng/archive/2007/pb2007-13.htm

Dorland, M. (1998). *So close to the state/s*. Toronto: University of Toronto Press.

Fleck, J. (2008, September 18). Arts and culture funding: An issue for party leaders. *Toronto Star*. Retrieved August 30, 2012, from http://www.thestar.com/federal%20election/article/501159--arts-and-culture-funding-an-issue-for-party-leaders

Gasher, M., Lorimer, R., & Skinner, D. (2008). *Mass communication in Canada*, 6th edition. Toronto, ON: Oxford University Press.

Gauntlett, D. (2011). *Making is connecting: The social meaning of creativity from DIY and knitting to YouTube and web 2.0*. London: Polity Press.

Government of Canada. (1985). *Investment Canada Act*. Retrieved August 30, 2012, from http://laws-lois.justice.gc.ca/eng/acts/I-21.8/index.html

Jeffrey, L. (1996). Private television and cable. In M. Dorland (Ed.), *The cultural industries in Canada* (pp. 203–256). Toronto: James Lorimer and Company.

Jenkins, H. (2006). *Convergence culture: Where old and new media collide*. New York: New York University Press.

Ladurantaye, S. (2012a, February 9). Supreme Court rules ISPs not subject to broadcast regulations. *The Globe and Mail*. Retrieved August 10, 2012, from http://www.theglobeandmail.com/news/technology/tech-news/supreme-court-rules-isps-not-subject-to-broadcast-regulations/article2332233

———. (2012b, March 1). Canada tops globe in Internet usage. *The Globe and Mail* Retrieved August 30, 2012, from http://m.theglobeandmail.com/technology/tech-news/canada-tops-globe-in-internet-usage/article551593/?service=mobile

Litt, P. (1992). *The muses, the masses and the Massey Commission*. Toronto: University of Toronto Press.

Matheson, S. (2012). Television, nation, and the situation comedy in Canada: Cultural diversity and *Little Mosque on the Prairie*. In M. Bredin, S. Henderson, and S. Matheson (Eds.). *Canadian Television: Text and Context* (pp. 153–172). Waterloo, ON: Wilfrid Laurier Press.

Nowak, P. (2008, June 12). Copyright law could result in a police state: critics. CBC.ca. Retrieved August 10, 2012, from http://www.cbc.ca/technology/story/2008/06/12/tech-copyright.html

Pastina, A. C. and Straubhaar, J. D. (2005). Multiple proximities between television genres and audiences. *Gazette 67*(3), pp. 271–288.

Powell, C. (2011, April 5). Topline: Canadian landlines still in decline. *Marketing Magazine*. Retrieved August 10, 2012, from http://www.marketingmag.ca/news/media-news/topline-canadian-landlines-still-in-decline-25569

Profile 2007: An Economic Report on the Canadian Film and Television Production Industry (listed as *Profile 2007: An Economic Report on the Screen-based Production Industry in Canada*). (2007). Published by the Canadian Film and Television Production Association in collaboration with l'Association des producteurs de films et de television du Québec and the Department of Canadian Heritage, February 2007. Retrieved September 4, 2012, from http://www.nordicity.com/reports/2007%20Profile%20(CMPA)%20%5BEng%5D.pdf

Raj, Althia. (2012, June 17). Bill C-11: Copyright legislation and digital lock provisions face opposition in Canada. Huffington Post Canada. Retrieved September 1, 2012, at http://www.huffingtonpost.ca/2012/06/17/bill-c-11-copyright-modernization-act-canada_n_1603837.html?utm_hp_ref=canada-politics

Statistics Canada. (2008). *Disposal of household special wastes.* Retrieved August 10, 2012, from http://www.statcan.gc.ca/pub/16-002-x/2008001/10539-eng.htm

Szeman, I. (2000, Fall). The rhetoric of culture: Some notes on magazines, Canadian culture and globalization. *Journal of Canadian Studies 35*(3), pp. 212–230.

Tinic, S. (2005). *On location: Canada's television industry in a global market.* Toronto: University of Toronto Press.

Wagman, I. (2010). On the policy reflex in Canadian communication studies. *Canadian Journal of Communication 35* (4), pp. 619–630.

7

AUDIENCES ARE KEY

Philip Savage
McMaster University

INTRODUCTION

Audiences are key, but oh so slippery! In Canada where the notion of national, regional, multilinguistic, multicultural, mass-mediated and socially mediated communities is central, the very definition of ourselves as audience has become more than just a communicative and cultural phenomenon. Audiences can be a political and economic battleground over how people work, receive products and services, and even organize ourselves in time and place. This chapter poses some key questions (the "who, what, when, where, how and why") of audience. My goal is to make it less "slippery" or at least provide some practical ways to approach its complexity:

1. *Who* are audiences: in the past, now, and in the digital future?
2. *What* are the characteristics of audience: size, numbers and demographics as measured by ratings; or levels of engagement and activism of individuals and groups on the cusp of social change?
3. *When* did audiences change: from readers to mass media consumers to digital "prosumers" (and when do they not change)?
4. *Where* are these audiences: in a library reading a book alone, or in a crowded Cairo square retweeting across continents? Are audiences different here in Canada than elsewhere?
5. *How* do we see ourselves as audience and how do others see us; as willing consumers, active citizens, or potential threats to public order?
6. *Why* are people audiences; to laugh, to buy, to stay current with news?

Often people use a shorthand for audiences; referring to things such as ratings to describe the audience experience. For example, I (perhaps like you) was one of over 10 million Canadians who watched on television the final men's hockey game between Canada and the United States at the Vancouver Olympics in February 2010 (CTV, 2010). This quantitative research of large audiences is only one way of looking at the audience experience, yet it dominates media and popular discussions. This is for a number of reasons; including the bottom line of host broadcaster CTV,which sold the Olympic advertising based in large part on commercial ratings measures of you and me as audience.

For Canadian communication scholars and critical practitioners of professional communication it is essential to understand from the inside the various audience research techniques (ratings being one, but one of many). This helps us not only communicate more effectively but also, on an ethical basis, be able to critically appraise and improve the research on audiences so that the measures themselves do not become limits on our notion of ourselves, but rather a series of lenses through which we learn to combine, add, or even delete certain perspectives to provide the most open and interesting view of ourselves as media audience members.

Both traditional media ratings and new measures of engagement with digital and social media have become an information commodity central to a digital economy.

Digital media makes the measure of *how many* and *who* is audience more precise, but the social uses of new digital media have made the *how* and *why* more complicated. In Canada, as in many countries—including some of the fastest growing economies in Africa, Asia, and South America—audiences are ever more key, but even more slippery. This leads to a final and broader question we should explore:

1. Who then gets to measure audience and how does it affect your role as a communicative agent in Canada and the world in the second decade of the third millennium?

Chapter Organization

To help answer these questions I have organized this chapter into five sections: (1) Definitions—tracing both historically and in current usage why the term "audience" has signified very different things to different people (its "slipperiness"; (2) Audience Models—how in the scholarly field of Communication Studies different ideas about how audiences are affected by content or use content have developed over time, including some key Canadian perspectives; 3) Audience Research Practice—to give you a behind-the-scenes look at how professional practitioners of audience research actually work in Canada; (4) Digital Audiences—to explore how starting almost ten years ago the shift to digital media platforms and content changed the way people think about audiences—both in the profession and intellectually (making audience ever more "slippery"); and (5) Audience Massage—tying all of these ideas together with a new discursive model of how the way in which large commercial and government organizations talk about and use audience information has the power to shape key decision making within Canadian society—often with deep impacts on our politics, economics, and culture.

AUDIENCE DEFINITIONS

I make a habit of asking people I work and study with to define audience from their own point of view. At the end of 2011, I asked 40 third- and fourth-year students

TABLE 7.1 Ten Common Audience Synonyms

1. Viewers
2. Listeners
3. Consumers
4. Readers
5. Spectators
6. Users
7. Communities
8. Groups
9. Followers
10. Other: Fans, Congregations, Crowds, Voters, Demographics, Populations

Source: McMaster University Students, 2011

in the McMaster University "Media Audiences" course to come up with their own synonyms and images of audience (see Table 7.1). What they shared is pretty typical of what other colleagues and students say:

Two Found Audience Images

The most frequent and most strongly expressed synonyms suggest an association of audience with the idea of a group of people attending (as viewer/listener/spectator) to a live or media performance, or perhaps reading a book or article. These are among the top five notions of audience in students' minds—although the idea of paying to consume such live or mediated expression is also in the top five (audience as "consumers"). This fits my students' favourite image—a cute one—of the young trumpeter playing to his teddy bear audience. But the second image of a networked audience also is very popular with my students, that is, as users/communities/groups who are brought together as audience around a particular common interest. The image also suggests a less hierarchical relationship; that is, as audience members in these situations they are not just receivers of text, audio, or video from one performer or source. Audience members are users/fans/followers who interact with other users for a range of purposes (as religious congregants, as political voters, as community members, etc.) to communicate back to the source or among themselves.

Dictionary definitions also reflect a dynamic and changing notion of audience but one still rooted in the concept of passive spectators. *The Oxford English Dictionary* defines audience as "the assembled listeners and spectators at an event, especially a stage performance, concert, etc." and secondarily as "the people addressed by a film, book, play, etc." (Thompson, 1995, p. 81). According to the *OED*, the term "audience" derives etymologically from a Middle English and Old French word "audire" that, in turn, is rooted in the Latin "audientia," that is, "to hear" (Ibid).[1]

The other main use of the word "audience" is an archaic concept: "a formal interview with a person in authority" (Ibid); for example, a modern papal audience, which

© Flirt/SuperStock

preserves that older meaning of a pope allowing himself to be an audience to a group of other people. Indeed at one level, this definition sounds particularly old fashioned to the modern ear, as per the example given in the dictionary: "give audience to my plea" (Thompson, 1995, p. 81). But in fact maybe it is increasingly relevant; that is, moving back to the future, away from the image of audience as spectator but a more active or even powerful notion of allowing oneself to be an audience. In the era of internet search and social media, how we as audiences are assembled has become a key driver of our very definition of who we are as consumers, citizens, workers, and participants in a variety of other situations. Increasingly, we do the work ourselves to join various audience or "social" groupings via digital networks to "give audience" to their plea.[2]

Urban studies and communication theorists, namely Peter Hall (1998) and Raymond Williams (1981), have shown how the modern notion of audience began in the 16th century, especially in the Elizabethan era around the rise of Shakespearian drama. An audience began to be associated with larger groups of less participatory, secular spectators. Hall contrasts this with the earliest forms of Western drama among the Greeks in the 5th and 6th centuries B.C. In the fourth century B.C., Greek drama and comedy developed from liturgical events with ongoing audience participation around religious themes. Similarly, much of the drama in places such as England before Shakespeare was extensions of masses or passion plays involving

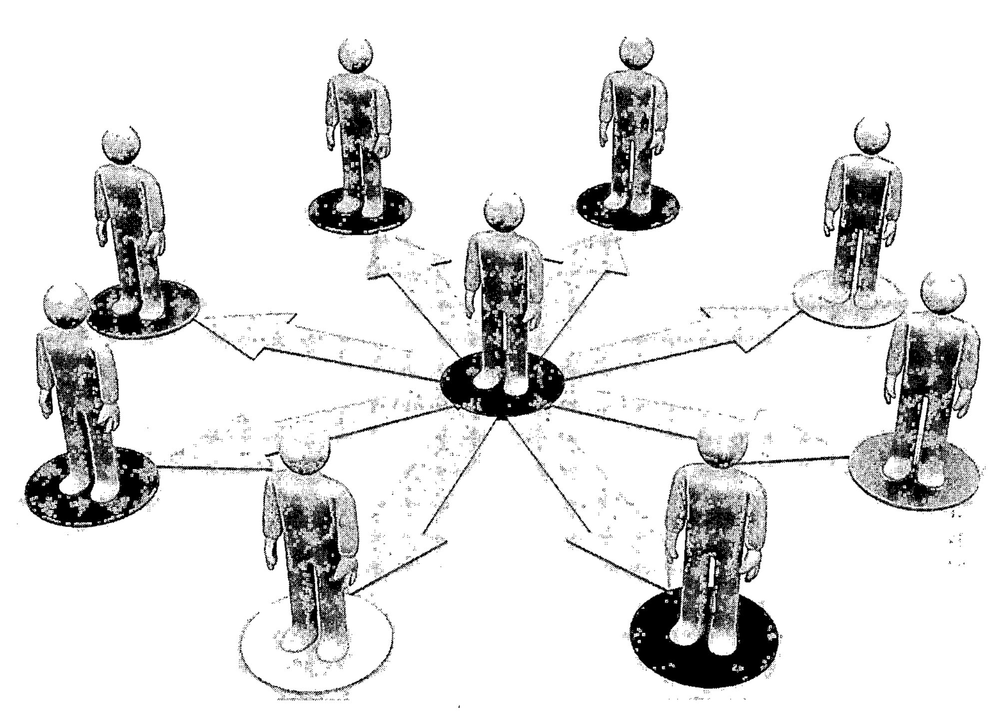

© iStockphoto.com/Palto

a congregation of worshippers who participated in the retelling of biblical or other religious stories.

By the 16th century, according to Raymond Williams, the role of audiences also shifts, to receivers of professional entertainment, usually on a commercial basis. Williams then traces how printed versions of plays and other entertainments rise in the 17th and 18th century to a growing (but still minority) body of readers. The development of mechanized printing presses in the 19th century and electronic communications via radio broadcasting in the early 20th centuries lead to the possibility of readers and listeners joining the majority of any society. But with it comes a further move away from the notion of audience as people involved in the immediate communicative act, and indeed further away from the physical immediacy of spectacle or events themselves.

The new technologies of communication via text, audio, and image permitted geometrically larger proportions of mass audiences to be gathered far away from the original physical site of the message production itself. By the early part of the 20th century there was a grave concern about the power of political parties or commercial enterprises to utilize mass media to effect change almost instantaneously in mass audiences. Research on audiences and mass audiences became an important part of the developing "sciences" of communication, with new models of "mass persuasion."

AUDIENCE MODELS

There are three main groupings of audience models in the modern era linked in turn to the three major theoretical perspectives of communication: (1) mass communication, (2) political economy of communication, and (3) cultural studies. The first perspective has dominated within American media studies (and is sometimes referred to as "administrative communication research"), whereas the latter two "critical" schools are dominant in the contemporary Canadian academic milieu of media analysis.

Mass Communication

Administrative mass communication research can be defined as a study of human communication with a focus on the transmission of messages via mass media and the effects of those messages on society or societal subgroups (McQuail, 1997, pp. 17–19). In terms of its underlying philosophy, it arises from a liberal-pluralist tradition associated with scientific positivism and, more particularly, social behavioural research in the United States in the early part of the 20th century. From early on, its intellectual preoccupation was the formation of **"public opinion"** as it applied to society or individual personal persuasion (Carey, 1989, pp. 45–55). Ironically, the emphasis on public opinion allowed for a shift to a fairly elaborate methodology around audience in institutional mass communication theory. Originally this developed upon fairly simplistic and mechanistic conceptualizations of the communication process; that is, along the lines of a transmission model of communication; the communicative process as information flow from point "A" to point "B." However, mass communication theorists in latter years did adapt and finesse the transmission view; for instance, through models of "uses and gratification" and "**cultivation analysis**." These latter two techniques in fact provide an intellectual legacy that, while useful for critical theorists, especially in cultural studies, also provided practical methodological tools for gathering empirical evidence on the moment of meaning creations by people as audiences.[3] However, critical communication scholars are wary of practitioners who cooperate with (or are coopted by) powerful government, corporate, and even military institutions. In Canada, though, there is a growing body of critical audience scholars who attempt to combine the empirical research of the mass communication approach with the critical insights from the other two schools to create a positive form of democratic intervention into media content creation and communication policy formation (see Table 7.2).

Political Economy of Communication and Cultural Studies

Political economy of communication and cultural studies are the two key critical approaches to understanding communication processes within contemporary societies. Often set up in opposition to each other; in fact, they share many of the same pre-occupations and methodologies.

TABLE 7.2 Audience Models: Mass Communication

Model	Key Authors	Description/Techniques
Direct Effects	Harold Lasswell	Focused on the way effects travelled, or "flowed," from the mass media to their audience and the power of the new mass medium—radio – to overcome individual resistance to the message and the appeal to celebrity (Lasswell, 1927; 1975).
Two-Step Flow	Paul Lazarsfeld	Rather than the mass media "injecting" their messages direct to the population, information was frequently filtered ... through to the "less active" members of the audience via "opinion leaders" (Lazarsfeld and Stanton, 1949).
Uses and Gratifications	Bernard Berelson, Elihu Katz	Audience members are not passive but take an active role in interpreting and integrating media into their own lives. Uses and gratification focus on the consumer, or audience, instead of the actual message itself by asking, "What people do with media?" rather than "What does media do to people?" (Berelson, 1948 Katz, 1959).
Cultivation Analysis	George Gerbner	Media will teach a common worldview, common roles, and common values; over time, cultivation analysts suggest, the media "cultivate" a particular view of the world among users. For example, Gerbner's research found that heavy television viewers overestimated the percentage of Americans who have jobs in law enforcement, and found people, in general, to be less trustworthy than did light television viewers (Gerbner et al., 1988).

Foremost among political economists who pioneered models of audience is Canadian Dallas Smythe. In *Dependency Road: Communications, Capitalism, Consciousness and Canada* (1981), Smythe rested much of his thesis of Canadian cultural and economic dependence on U.S. goods and ideology in term of the theoretical model of a "consciousness industry." Smythe's examination of economic dependence and ideological manipulation rested on a central analysis of the audience work performed by individuals who were increasingly reliant through the 20th century on commercial media both for information and consumer survival:

> The mass media have a more basic influence on our lives and our ideology because they, together with advertisers, take a central part in the process by which the monopoly-capitalist system grows or declines in strength. In the core area, the mass media *produce* audiences and *sell* them to advertisers of consumer goods and services, political candidates, and groups interested in controversial public issues. These audiences *work* to market these things to themselves (Smythe, 1981, p. 5; original italics).

However, it is clear from a full reading of Smythe's analysis of Canadian communications that the power he believes audiences exercise through their work is extremely limited. As current Canadian communication political economist, Vincent Mosco, summarizes it, "For him [Smythe], the process brought together a triad that linked media, audiences and advertisers in a set of binding reciprocal relationships. Mass media programming is used to construct audiences; advertisers pay media companies for access to these audiences; audiences are thereby delivered to advertisers" (Mosco, 1996, p. 148).

According to Mosco, the concept of audience work, while not without flaws in Smythe's original iterations, was useful in order to "think about the analogies between audience activity and the labour process because the latter is a dynamic activity involving complicity and contestation between capital and labour over the control of the process and the product" (Smythe, 1981, p. 149).

Here, though, both Mosco and Smythe reveal their political economy preoccupation with economic structures and class struggle. In short, they are concerned with examining audience work to the degree that it fits a model of human struggle over the means of production. The value of audience activity beyond work, as leisure, enjoyment, or a search for human meaning (values in and of themselves), is largely ignored. And this is a key criticism from cultural studies theorists, who believe the power of audiences to resist manipulation can in certain situations be stronger and more varied than what the political economists describe.

Denis McQuail, professor emeritus at the University of Amsterdam in the Netherlands, has written about the contribution that the cultural studies perspective brings to analysis of audience. In *Audience Analysis* (1997), McQuail points out how the approach to audiences in the cultural studies tradition occupies a "borderland between social science and the humanities" with an approach to media use as "a reflection of a particular sociocultural context and as a process of giving meaning to cultural products and experiences" (McQuail, 1997, p. 18). McQuail goes on to write:

> Reception analysis is effectively the audience research arm of modern cultural studies ... it strongly emphasises the role of the "reader" in the "decoding" of media texts. It has generally had a consciously "critical" edge ... claiming for the audience a power to resist and subvert the dominant or hegemonic meanings offered by the mass media. It is characterised by the use of qualitative and ethnographic methods (Ibid. p. 19).

The Canadian Tradition

The Canadian hybrid of communication research tends in its theoretical perspective to lean somewhat more toward the European approach. According to Paul Attallah and Leslie Regan Shade (in an earlier version of this textbook), Canadian communication research has "tended to identify communication with culture—with a whole way of life—and to examine such questions as how culture embodies values, shapes long term views, or excludes possibilities as well as including them" (Attallah and Shade, 2002, p. 3).

The emphasis on culture in Canadian communication research stems from the fact that Canadian scholars wrestle with larger issues of identity and culture that have not only been at the heart of Canadian communication research but also the overall political project of the country since confederation 140 years ago. This is magnified by the social, political, and economic factors involved in establishing and maintaining a unified political entity over a huge geography among a linguistically and ethnically diverse and regionally based population.

As a result, a typical modern Canadian communication research question—to add to the seven above—might be:

1. What role does the media play in shaping a sense of identity and culture among individuals and communities, especially in a situation where they do not locally control the invention of the media (the technology) nor the production of most of the media messages (the content)?As Liora Salter has said of the Canadian hybrid approach, paraphrased by Sheryl Hamilton: "while it is concerned with social rather than the individual effects and is theoretical like European approaches, it is also more grounded like American approaches" (Hamilton, 2002, p. 19).

As a result, communication researchers like Salter have only just researched policy but also been involved in developing cultural law and policy for Canada through its various cultural agencies, whether the CRTC, the CBC, the Canada Council, or the Department of Canadian Heritage. In light of this, the next section explores how both mass communication and critical models are integrated into practical research used by Canadian media institutions currently, and directions for the future.

AUDIENCE RESEARCH PRACTICE[4]

Applied audience research in Canada "uses social science and market research techniques to study the traits of actual and potential audiences" (LeClair, 2006, p. 3). Popular images of audience research most often relate to ratings research around TV, newspapers, magazines, and radio. The research work is actually broader than that, using many different techniques and looking at a wide variety of events and media that can be thought of in terms of what in broadcasting we see as four key questions:

1. How many and what types of people are watching or listening?
2. Why do people watch or listen to the shows they do, and what kinds of shows do people want?
3. How can I create a show that people will come to?
4. How do I let potential viewers and listeners know about the shows I think they want to use?

It is useful to discuss each of these in turn:

1. How Many People Use the Media?

Ratings are designed to track how programs are performing in terms of attracting different types of people. They are used by:

1. network management to evaluate how their schedules are performing;
2. producers and programmers to judge what types of programming are attractive to viewers.

In broadcasting, the ratings were traditionally collected either through specialized **surveys** called **diaries** or through electronic measurement via devices attached to TV sets. A diary of TV viewing would be sent to over 100,000 Canadians at least twice a year and looked something like this:

BBM TV Diary—Extract

Beginning in the late 1980s the large American audience research firm **AC Nielsen** introduced **people meters** in Canada and eventually formed an agreement with the main Canadian **audience ratings** company, **BBM**, to jointly measure TV viewing nationally in most markets using an electronic device that would track viewing on a daily basis (as opposed to diaries which were collected in sweep weeks and then the results distributed to networks and advertisers a month or two later).

In the late 1990s BBM began an experiment in Montreal with the large U.S. radio rating company Arbitron to record on a more personal and portable manner both radio and TV viewing outside the home (as opposed to the fixed people meter attached to home TV sets). BBM asked a sample of people to use a device called the portable people meter (PPM). A few years later many Canadian cities were measured only by PPMs and by 2010 the PPM was being used to measure national TV network audiences for CBC-TV, CTV, Global, and most specialty channels.

Within broadcasting (and similarly for print media), ratings are designed to track how programs are performing in terms of attracting different types of people. Producers use them to judge what types of programming are attractive to viewers; sales and advertising agencies use them to buy and sell space and time in the media.

THURSDAY

1B Evening

	WHAT CHANNEL?		PVR or VCR DATE RECORDED						THIS TV HAS			Watched TV Out of Home
	STATION NAME OR CALL LETTERS	CHANNEL NUMBER	DATE MM/DD	TIME	AM	PM		NAME OF PROGRAM	Cable	Satellite	Antenna	
4:00-4:14 pm							41					
4:15-4:29							42					
4:30-4:44							43					
4:45-4:59							44					
5:00-5:14 pm							45					
5:15-5:29							46					

Courtesy of BBM Canada.

Outside the broadcasting media there are organizations similar to BBM in Canada: Nadbank for newspapers (http://www.nadbank.com); and the Print Measurement Bureau (PMB; http://www.pmb.ca), for other print publications such as magazines. Increasingly, online versions of media content usage, as well as Web content not affiliated with media per se, are measured by special online subdivisions of the three main media ratings companies (BBM, NadBank, and PMB) or by ratings companies specifically set up for that purpose. The main example of the latter is ComScore (http://www.comscore.com), an American company with specific Canadian online measurement capabilities.

2. Why Do People Use Media?

Ratings tell you who has historically watched or listened, but tell you nothing directly about motivation. Various other methodologies help researchers figure out motivation and therefore help programmers know how to more effectively produce programs appropriate to their audiences. This work is done through three main research methods:

1. surveys
2. **focus groups**
3. **program tests.**

While most communication students will have passing familiarity with the two former techniques, program testing needs a bit of explanation. It usually involves testing video or audio, either existing programs or pilots, using a small sample of people (100–200) by sending them material to watch in their own homes via DVD or online, and then gauging their response through surveys conducted online, over the phone, or in person. It is actually a fairly regimented way of getting at "reception analysis" but in a more consistently measurable manner. This technique has been used in the film industry as well, where auditorium tests bring people to small film screenings and their second-by-second reaction may be measured though dial-testing of enjoyment of particular scenes or alternate film endings (c.f. http://www.asientertainment.com/Dial-Testing.html). The main purposes of this type of research include measuring tastes, attitudes, and motivations for using media; measuring how people react to current and proposed programs; and measuring related lifestyle phenomena.

3. How Do Producers Anticipate Content Production That Attracts Users?

Rather than measuring reaction to existing programs, content producers may wish to try out ideas or concepts prior to production. This is easier in focus groups and program tests than in surveys. In practice ratings, surveys, focus groups, and program tests are all used at different stages of developing new programming and targeting it to appropriate audiences.

4. How Does One Promote and Market Media Content?

Audience research is also used to determine the best ways to publicize new content/programs or new types of media or digital services. Knowing how different people use media helps determine how to construct a campaign to reach specific audiences. In this way one uses audience and market research in a broader context, extending to different vehicles for promotion and advertising such as newspapers, magazines, and billboards.

In a sense, traditional audience research of the late 20th century was trying to formulate a theory and measure the relationship between three key elements of audience attitudes and activities: (1) awareness of content; (2) exposure to content; and (3) behaviour in response to content. The professionals in an audience research department try to break down the elements in that chain. To understand how awareness links to exposure, they attempt to understand how audience interest is developed and can be encouraged. To understand the link between exposure and behaviour (particularly with the dominant commercial media context and how watching advertising links to product purchases), they need to measure not only aspects of attentiveness (in terms of time and frequency watched, etc.) but also aspects of loyalty in their exposure (both to the media content and to the brand of product advertised). Increasingly in the last part of the century the goal was to understand not only the width of the connection between exposure and behaviour but also the depth of that link in terms of what is often called "**audience engagement measures.**"

FIGURE 7.1 Audience Research Revenues in Canada

Source: Savage, P. (2006). *The audience massage: Audience research and Canadian broadcasting policy.* Ph.D. Dissertation. Toronto: York University Graduate Programme in Communication and Culture.

Philip Napoli (2011) writes about specific measures of media audiences in terms of: (1) appreciation, (2) emotional response, (3) recall, and (4) attitudes toward the content. All the traditional methods are used to try to be more precise in measuring these elements of audience connection with media, but in a digital media environment they change in two ways: (1) the specificity of the data provided by audiences in their nature of engagement—with media systems engineered to facilitate instant quantitative and qualitative measures that do not require separate audience research methods; and (2) both the real and imagined sense of audiences as their own content producers that also provide a ready-built market or community (and promotion and wide distribution) of content networks.

DIGITAL AUDIENCES

Time magazine—one of the first and most widely available mass magazines—continues in the digital age an annual tradition to name its "Person of the Year" at the end of December. An interesting thing happened in December 2006 when "you" made the cover—in the role as audience and author simultaneously because, as *Time* wrote, "you control the information age" (Grossman, 2006). Interestingly, four years later *Time* updated the person of the year with the face of Mark Zuckerberg, Facebook inventor and millionaire, for his ability to use the information-age tools to harness for commercial purposes (i.e., control) our power as networked "**prosumers**" to provide to himself and his shareholders a seamless mesh of free content, free marketing and promotion, and freely provided audience data. When Facebook went from a private company to a publicly traded company in 2012, the value of all those audience connections was valued up to $100 billion.[5]

There have always been new media of some sort (printed books in the 15th century, for instance were not just new but revolutionary) but the new digital media of the 21st century is particularly new in the way it combines three technological spheres of human inventions:

1. media content—print, audio, video in various media;
2. communication networks—print and other analogue forms, but also predominantly broadcasting and telecommunications;
3. computing devices—for reasoning and storage and processing (Flew & Smith, 2011, pp. 2–3).

As Terry Flew and Richard Smith point out, up until recently one might see two of the three sectors combined; for example, cable television was a combination of telecom and TV production, or DVDs were a combination of computing devices and TV content. But now the telecom viewing of TV or the computing methods of storing and processing DVDs also happen across a range of communication networks—namely the internet. This is made possible by the digitization of all content into a collection of binary bits of data—almost all books, all audio recordings, and images are available. In turn, the internet's wide reach as a universal platform has led to a range of new applications, or apps, that harness network effects and allow ad hoc groups of users to harness collective intelligence, culture, and labour (Flew & Smith, 2011, pp. 2–3).

In other words, the internet outcome is greater than the sum of the parts—not just use of technology but indeed whole new ways of experiencing the world through the combination of communication networks, computing abilities, and the range of content being produced, shared, and repurposed. Flew and Smith (2011) outline the major characteristics of Web 2.0 as:

- many-to-many connectivity
- decentralized control
- user-focus and easy for new users
- open technology standards
- simple, lightweight, and low cost in design/admin/startup/ongoing development
- expected to evolve with users making new modifications (Flew & Smith, 2011, p. 21).

A number of media scholars have tracked the new role for audiences in a Web 2.0 environment. For instance, Josh Green and Henry Jenkins (2011) talk about the potential for audiences to take advantage of a cultural convergence: "ground-up tactical creativity across different media," as opposed to the technological convergence of "top-down, structured interactivity" (Green & Jenkins, 2011, p. 111).

This is crucial for a proper understanding of the changing nature of audience, but some feel the way Web 2.0 developed is not quite as freeing as its proponents suggest. Green and Jenkins acknowledge that the shift away from a language of audiences or consumers and toward users can be misleading since the latter terms merge passive ("merely clicking") and active ("blogging and uploading videos") (Green & Jenkins 2011, p. 110).

They argue that the various social media networks, especially YouTube, Facebook, and Twitter, are provided "free" to audiences because they not only link audiences directly with advertisers suited to their very specific **demographic** characteristics, but also allow detailed access to an individual's personal data as well as associated data of other potential consumers who happen to be "friends" or "followers": Every mouse click or video view is logged and even these inactive lurkers are ultimately (unwillingly?) generating data to refine content delivery systems or recommendation engines, and ultimately drive up the popularity of the online media business (Green & Jenkins, 2011, p. 111).

Social media in particular allow corporations to have access to whom we are engaged with around content and to assess the depth of that engagement. Content producers can exploit those networks and content that flows particularly well along those networks. This happens in part due to the unique nature of media content that people like to share easily in a Web 2.0 environment, what Green and Jenkins call "spreadable media."

Spreadable media is less of a thing and more of a process by which a large number of people make active decisions to pass along an image, text, song, or bit of video to various friends, family members, or large social networks; therefore, all of us—media producers and consumers alike—are also media appraisers and distributors. This shifts the approach of actually doing audience research; rather than just looking at the effects of new media, we need to understand the characteristics of the new ways of interacting with content in communication networks as a way of understanding the new ways of being audience with the new media.

Philip Napoli weighs in on this as a background to his full 2011 book on "transforming audiences." He believes that a lot of the new audience activism (or limits on it) actually mirrors the approach of audiences prior to mass media standardization. Earlier, audiences were often "very much participatory and active" (Napoli, 2011, p. 12). Drawing on the work of Raymond Williams (quoted above), Napoli describes how the early Elizabethan drama audiences in Shakespeare's England were initially quite raucous: singing songs, and yelling instructions and insults at each other and the actors (until commercial imperatives brought about a demand for a more orderly performance for which money had been paid!). Similarly, the development in the 20th century of community media and film co-ops (often by community groups in

TABLE 7.3 Three Digital Forms of Audience Research

Geo-Targeting	A method of determining the geo-location of a website visitor and delivering different content to that visitor based on his or her location (e.g., country, region/province, city, postal code, organization, IP address, ISP, or other criteria). A common usage of geo-targeting is found in online advertising, as well as internet television with sites such as Netflix restricting content to those geo-located in specific countries (also known as digital rights management).
Internet Search	Google Search, owned by Google Inc., is the most-used search engine, receiving several hundred million queries each day through its various services. The order of search results on Google's search-results pages is based, in part, on a priority rank called a "PageRank." Google places paid advertising alongside the search results of individual users through systems such as AdWords, which allow very targeted advertising and marketing based on the information related to individual search parameters. In this sense it is both geo and topic marketing at the same time.
Social Media Advertising	Social media sites such as Facebook have unique advertising platforms that gather information on users and then automatically place advertising messages on users pages. Facebook allows marketers to target audiences very specifically on the basis of geography, age, gender, education, and relationship status as well as other key words related to users interests. A great deal of personal interest that users provide for their "friends" is data mined by Facebook to provide the most targeted information ever made available through audience research for advertisers. (One marketer sent a message via Facebook advertising to his wife and targeted it so narrowly that she was the only one who saw the ad.).

Source: Carmichael, M. (2012, March 5), They might not get mail every day, but they're sure to be on it, *Advertising Age*, retrieved September 9, 2012, from http://adage.com/article/special-report-american-consumer-project/geotargeting-helping-marketers-find-hard-reach-audiences/233091; Facebook.com Timeline, retrieved September 9, 2012, from http://www.facebook.com/facebook; Google Company, Our products and services, retrieved September 9, 2012, from http://www.google.com/about/company/products; Google.com, Geotargeting, retrieved September 9, 2012, from http://support.google.com/webmasters/bin/answer.py?hl=en&answer=62399; and G. Weinberg (2010, May 14), An FB ad targeted at one person (my wife), retrieved September 9, 2012, from http://www.gabrielweinberg.com/blog/2010/05/a-fb-ad-targeted-at-one-person-my-wife.html

reaction to conglomerate control of those media) shows a combination of audience control over production and distribution.

One example of community members' active role as audiences in a mass media age is the series of Canadian "listener forums" in radio in the middle of the 20th century. The most famous listener forum was "The Farm Radio Forum" that the CBC started in the 1940s in conjunction with farmers' organizations and adult education groups. It continued for almost 20 years—with almost 30,000 average Canadians actively involved in the program each week—giving ideas to programmers for interviews and documentaries, but also using it for listeners' own further education and activism (Savage, 2009).

In a digital media age the process of actually measuring audience has become much more exact because the information about audience behaviour and attitudes is collected more precisely and automatically over a range of internet content and functions.

Listed below are three types of digital audience research that have had the greatest impact.

AUDIENCE MASSAGE

We have looked at the models of audience that dominate in various theoretical streams of thoughts, and we've looked at how some of those models made their way into applied audience research, so we begin to see the potential for gathering huge amounts of information about audiences in the digital communication era. Therefore, I want to return to the Canadian view of the importance of the audience transformation and the larger political and economic transformations that both drive it forward and, in turn, are influenced by audiences. The political economy viewpoint allows us to look at the biases within key institutions—such as media, internet, and audience research companies—that structure or pattern how we act as audiences and indeed how as communicative individuals we are helped or restricted to act freely in our society. The work is often done by, as they say in the movies, "following the money."

FIGURE 7.2 Model of Audience Engagement

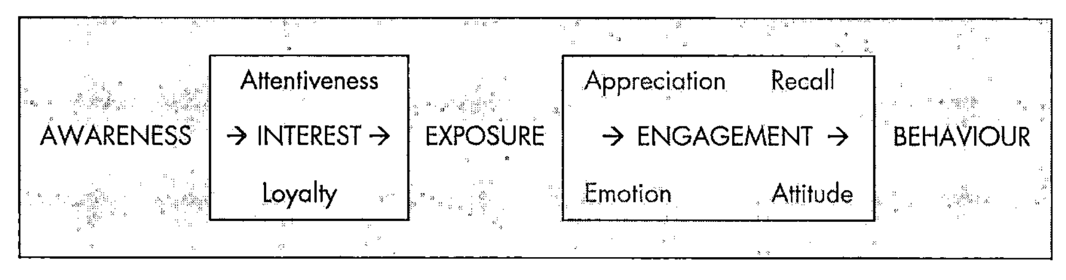

Source: From *Audience Evolution*, by Philip M. Napoli. Copyright © 2010 Columbia University Press. Reprinted with permission of the publisher.

In Canada, audience research has been a useful link between the needs and wants of audiences and the type of media content they receive—but it costs. Each year, approximately $200 million is invested in research as part of the $20 billion-plus media industry.[6] Yet Canadian examples of audience research show how the further development of "scientific" measures of audience are not always an objectively accurate metric for capturing viewer needs and desires. Rather, Canadian evidence suggests that audience measurement in an institutional setting may often be the conscious result of increasingly consolidated, small groups of content producers, distributors, and attendant support workers, including those in commercial ratings firms and other media research agencies.

For Canadians, the reconstitution of audiences is particularly significant. As a national community we have traditionally invested an inordinate amount of cultural energy to reimagine ourselves as unique—closely connected with other countries from whom the current population has immigrated—but separate from them. Key to the project of a Canadian national narrative has been the media and who comprises the audience to the media—analogue, electronic, and digital. Through the state, Canadians traditionally have been less shy than their southern neighbours to invest in, support, regulate, and otherwise collectively shape the extensions of our media.

However, when public institutions—including government bodies, public broadcasters, and civil society groups—are themselves trapped by the sophisticated (and limiting) language of audience, the very vocabulary for reimaging audiences in support of cultural diversity and democratic control is threatened. So that whereas policy and other debates may occur about the "correct" interpretation of audience research studies (content), the deeper research methodologies (the forms) as well as the media firms, advertising agencies, and ratings companies (the institutional structures), which bankroll and support the methodologies, remain largely unexamined. Yet the forms and structures both facilitate and constrain the language used to frame the debate. In fact, in some cases, the forms and structures simply silence or invalidate alternative notions of audience, including those generated by groups of people who define themselves primarily as audiences.

The first university-based Canadian scholarship of the confluence of audience measurement was the work of Ross Eaman in *Channels of Influence* (1994). Eaman offered a focused examination of institutional audience research in Canada, focusing on how national public broadcaster CBC might develop an interpretation of audience research that connected both specific Canadian public policy goals and input from audiences about how they might measure themselves.

According to Eaman, audience research in service of the public interest would combine three roles: (1) information to allow for audience maximization; (2) information to allow for comprehensive audience feedback—quantitative and qualitative—into programming decisions; and, (3) public participation in how the measurement would in fact take place (Eaman, 1994, pp. 198–226). For Eaman, that third role—operationalizing public participation—was crucial to the "cultural

TABLE 7.4 Audience Massage Model

1. Rhetorical (Content/Results)	Research content *results* used to support an *argument.*	e.g., Conservative Party use of ratings and pubic opinion polling to undercut CBC support
2. Framing (Media/Methods)	Research *methodologies* used to support an *approach.*	e.g., discrediting alternative, nonratings based CBC KPI's (qualitative measures of interest and enjoyment)
3. Structural (Discourse/Organizations)	Research *systems* integrated into a way of interpreting a social setting and organizing *action.*	e.g., "triumph of the ratings" within decision-making policy organizations such as the CRTC and Department of Finance

Source: Savage, P. (2006). *The audience massage: Audience research and Canadian broadcasting policy.* Ph.D. Dissertation. Toronto: York University Graduate Programme in Communication and Culture.

democracy" goals of public broadcasting. He argued that the traditional Canadian defence of public broadcasting as a means of alleviating market failure in the production of Canadian program content was no longer sufficient. Through proper audience research, the public broadcaster could evolve into serving a vital democratic function for broad public participation in decision making and identity formation (Eaman, 1994, pp. 198–226).

For professional audience researchers it is abundantly clear that when findings come into contact with public policy, audience research results tend all too often to take on a rhetorical rather than scientific role. To be specific, audience research reports, no matter how scientific or "objective" the researchers may think them to be, become part of the content of rhetorical strategies to influence favourable outcomes in decision-making bodies that fund or regulate broadcasting. We can think of this in terms of an **audience massage** model, which we will briefly explain below in terms of audience *rhetoric*, *frames*, and *structures.*

Audience Rhetoric

Rhetorical massage of *content* is the first level of the massage model. Here, quantitative ratings and public opinion about audience attitudes comprise results that support an argument using the actual content or results from that research. Such results have more to do with the primary interests of the funding source for the research than with the "objective" public interest of audiences. From time to time, obvious research "biases" are exposed and may grab the headlines, especially when direct manipulation of the research is uncovered.

In 2003, during the last major investigation into Canadian broadcasting policy, the Conservative Party—which was then in opposition, but has since formed government—argued in its dissenting chapter to the parliamentary study of broadcasting that "objective" audience ratings demonstrated a precipitous audience share decline for CBC services, specifically for the English-language national CBC-TV network—well below 10 percent in the early part of the millennium (Canada, 2003, Figure 4.16).

In cases like this, the rhetorical debate around audience research and polling deals with a rather transitory concern over the "correct interpretation" of scientific audience research measures. The point to be underlined is that any policy actor's specific use of audience research content in favouring one point of view over another is only the most obvious audience massage that occurs in policy debate, in Canada and elsewhere. Mapping the rhetoric of audience in various policy decisions in itself can be useful, but it is not necessarily the most profound or far-reaching way of examining these decisions.

Audience Frames

At the second level of audience massage, the methodologies used to generate audience results act as the media of research, which are not neutral transmitters of truth. Various forms of audience research methodologies and techniques—diaries, people meters, or PPMs—coalesce into certain historical and institutional patterns of knowing audience, which support a fixed and limiting approach.

Thus, methodologies of audience research prescribe the range of results that are likely to occur, or even be considered worthy of discussion.

In this sense, a good look at the built-in biases of certain methodologies provides a more robust understanding of the limits to notions of audience in various policy contexts. Although many people in the broadcast industry engage in critical discussion of the content and results of audience research studies, at a deeper level fewer people can point to the inherent biases within key measures. The two key points, which the framing critique advances, are:

1. While it seems common sense that "numbers speak for themselves," in fact there is a whole industry set up to demonstrate particularly favourable interpretations based on only certain types of numbers, or indeed numbers rather than other languages of audience;
2. Given the effort required to legitimize nonnumeric understandings of audience, especially the qualitative measures often advanced by public broadcasters or citizens' groups, there is a struggle to include these alternative "measures" of audience in a wider debate about broadcasting goals and policy. This is no accident but, rather, is directly related to the deeper institutional structures and resource allocation that support a narrower view of audience.

Audience Structures

The third and deepest level of audience massage, the structural connections that support a discourse, relate to how entire research *systems* and the research institutions that use them are integrated into dominant, commercial modes of interpreting the role of audience in the "business" of broadcasting. The deepest biases in broadcast players' and regulators' conceptions of audience are macro structures stemming from contradictions that are especially apparent within the mixed Canadian broadcasting system. For instance, the methodological "triumph of the ratings" is used to further entrench a demand-side approach to audience. This tends to oversimplify the broad public interest into simply "eyeballs in front of the screen."

This approach is funded by private Canadian broadcasters that, in almost every case, are consolidated into four major Canadian commercial media-telecommunication conglomerates which dominate newspaper and magazine publishing, radio, TV, cable, satellite, internet provision, mobile telephony, and other telecommunications in Canada: Bell Media (CTV), Quebecor, Rogers, and Shaw (Global). In total these firms represent in their media and telecommunication holdings well over $20 billion (Cdn) in annual revenues (Savage, 2010). They—along with advertising firms—are the principal support for the various television and other audience measurement groups in Canada, and in the case of the main TV (and radio) measurement firm, the Bureau of Measurement (BBM), they sit on the board and make the key decisions about the techniques to be employed.

CONCLUSIONS

Audiences are key, and yet slippery. We started with a series of questions about how to understand media audiences in the Canadian context. By seeing how these questions are asked and answered in different times and different places by people in Canada, we gain understanding of how notions of audience have developed and how institutions, forms, and models of audience affect you as a student and practitioner of communication as well as an audience member. I invite you to continue to ask these questions and explore on your own: Who gets to measure audience and how does it affect your role as a communicative agent in Canada and the world in the second decade of the third millennium?

QUESTIONS

1. Canadian scholars and media professionals spend a lot of time and effort thinking about how audiences act as both citizens and consumers. How do these different audience roles relate to ideas of Canadian identity and independence? In what situations and with what type of media content do you feel yourself a citizen, or a consumer?
2. The early U.S. model of audiences portrayed them as passive receivers of media messages, whereas slightly later European models forced a rethinking of the power of audience to actively decode and re-interpret texts. Think of a situation in your life in which you find yourself largely just letting media content "wash over" you, and other situations in which you are a more active media audience participant. Can you think of a medium in which you move from one role to the other?

3. Why does it matter how we measure audiences in Canada? Number counts of "eyeballs in front of screens" seem to dominate in professional audience research (i.e., the ratings), but what alternatives do you think are important for reconsidering our roles as audience members? How could they in turn affect the type of media we use or even how we use the media?

NOTES

1. In modern Canadian audience research there is an interesting example of how the "audire" sense of the word has fallen away, except in the French-language context. For instance, this author is familiar with the pattern in the CBC audience research department to refer to TV audience members as viewers, as in "BBM reports there were 2.3 million viewers to the Grey Cup." Given the dominance of TV, it is quite common for people to accidentally ask researchers to report on the number of viewers to a radio program. However, on the Radio-Canada side of the house, things are different. My former French research colleagues in Montreal would refer to the number of "auditoires" in reports on both radio and television. Occasionally the term "téléspectateurs" would be used, but that usage was awkward to the ear (let alone the eye) for most in the business.
2. Take the case of Web-lining. Canadian digital media scholars Chung and Grimes (2005) showed how some children's web sites such as Habbo.com and Barbie.com actually entice audiences, but then based on the demographic and spending information collected as the kids interact online, Habbo or Barbie allow them access to less or more products. In that sense, the children are forced to plead for access by giving information about how valuable an audience they are (e.g., where they live, the kinds of services or products they can buy). In some ways it is the modern marketing version of pleading for an audience with the pope, king, or other figure of authority.
3. See, for instance, Berelson (1948) and Gerbner et al. (1988).
4. The material in this section was originally developed when I was head of Audience Research (Radio) at the CBC in the 1990s. My former CBC colleague, Ken LeClair, as CBC's Head of Audience Research (TV), then modified it. Ken LeClair presented some of the material to McMaster University students in 2006 (LeClair, 2006).
5. As *The New York Times* wrote on February 1, 2012, the IPO filing date:

> Facebook, which has more than 845 million users worldwide, said it was seeking to raise $5 billion, according to a figure used to calculate the registration fee ... But many close to the company say that Facebook is aiming for a far greater offering that could value it as high as $75 billion to $100 billion.

At that lofty valuation, Facebook would be much bigger than many longer-established American companies, including [...] Ford Motor. "Facebook's I.P.O. marks another stage of the Internet's evolution," said Charlene Li, founder of the Altimeter Group, a technology consulting firm. "It's so valuable, because it's not just about content, it's about our connections.'" (*The New York Times*, 2012).

6. Annual estimates for 2012 projected from interviews with industry leaders as part of doctoral research (Savage, 2006).

REFERENCES

Attallah, P. & Shade, L. R. (Eds.). (2002). *Mediascapes: New patterns in Canadian communication*. Scarborough, ON: Nelson.

Berelson, B. (1948). *Reader in public opinion and communication*. Glencoe, IL: Free Press.

Canada. (2003). *Our cultural sovereignty: The second century of Canadian broadcasting*. Ottawa, ON: House of Commons Standing Committee on Canadian Heritage.

Carey, J. (1989). *Communication as culture: Essays on media and society*. Boston: Unwin Hyman.

Carmichael, M. (2012, March 5). They might not get mail every day, but they're sure to be on it. *Advertising Age*. Retrieved September 9, 2012, from http://adage.com/article/special-report-american-consumer-project/geotargeting-helping-marketers-find-hard-reach-audiences/233091

Chung, G. & Grimes, S. (2005). Data mining the kids: Surveillance and market research strategies in children's online games. *Canadian Journal of Communication, 30*(4), 527–548.

CTV. (2010). *CAN/USA men's hockey is most-watched sports*. Retrieved August 10, 2012, from http://www.newswire.ca/en/story/635573/can-usa-men-s-hockey-is-most-watched-sports-program-in-canadian-history-with-10-6-million-viewers

Eaman, R. (1994). *Channels of influence: CBC audience research and the Canadian public*. Toronto: University of Toronto Press.

Facebook.com Timeline. Retrieved September 9, 2012, from http://www.facebook.com/facebook

Flew, T & Smith, R. (2011). *New media: An introduction, Canadian Edition*. Don Mills, ON: Oxford University Press.

Gerbner, G., Gross, L., Morgan, M., & Signorielli, N. (1998). Growing up with television: The cultivations perspective. In M. L. DeFleur and S. Lowery (Eds.). *Milestones in mass communication research* (pp. 19–42). New York: Longman.

Google Company. Our Products and Services. Retrieved September 9, 2012, from http://www.google.com/about/company/products

Google.com. Geotargeting. Retrieved September 9, 2012, from http://support.google.com/webmasters/bin/answer.py?hl=en&answer=62399

Green, J. & Jenkins, H. (2011). Spreadable media. In V. Nightingale. (Ed.) *The handbook of media audiences*. London: Blackwell Publishing.

Grossman, L. (2006). *Time: Person of the year: You.* (December 13). Retrieved September 10, 2012, from http://www.time.com/time/magazine/article/0,9171,1570810,00.html

Hall, P. (1998). *Cities in civilization: Culture, innovation and urban order*. London: Phoenix/Orion Books.

Hamilton, S. (2002). Considering critical communication studies in Canada. In P. Attallah & L. R. Shade (Eds.), *Mediascapes: New patterns in Canadian communication*. (pp. 4–26). Scarborough, ON: Nelson.

Lasswell, H. (1927). *Propaganda techniques in the world war*. New York: Knopf.

Lazarsfeld, P. & Stanton, F. (Eds.). (1949). *Communications research, 1948–9*. New York: Harper.

LeClair, K. (2006). An introduction to audience research, McMaster University presentation by the Director of Research, English Services, CBC, March 8, 2006. Toronto: Canadian Broadcasting Corporation, 1–28.

McQuail, D. (1997) *Audience analysis*. London: Sage Publications.

Mosco, V. (1996). *The political economy of communication*. Thousand Oaks, CA: Sage Publications.

Napoli, P. (2011). *Audience evolution: New technologies and the transformation of media audiences*. New York: Columbia University Press.

New York Times. Facebook files for an IPO. Retrieved August 10, 2102, from http://dealbook.nytimes.com/2012/02/01/facebook-files-for-an-i-p-o

Savage, P. (2006). *The audience massage: Audience research and Canadian broadcasting policy*. Ph.D. Dissertation. Toronto: York University Graduate Programme in Communication and Culture.

Savage, P. (2009). Revolutionary radio: Audience models from Canadian public radio in the multimedia era. Presentation to the "Transforming Audiences" Conference. London, UK: University of Westminster, September 3–4, 2009.

Savage, P. (2010). Identity housekeeping in Canadian public service media. In P. Iosifidis (Ed.), *Reinventing public service communication: European broadcasters and beyond*. (pp. 273–286). London: Palgrave Macmillan.

Smythe, D. (1981). *Dependency road*. Norwood, NJ: Ablex Publishing.

Thompson, D. (1995). *The concise Oxford dictionary*, Ninth edition. Oxford, UK: Oxford University Press.

Weinberg, G. (2010, May 14). A FB ad targeted at one person (my wife). Retrieved September 9, 2012, from http://www.gabrielweinberg.com/blog/2010/05/a-fb-ad-targeted-at-one-person-my-wife.html

Williams, R. (1981). *Culture*. Glasgow: Fontana.

8

ADVERTISING IN CANADA

Russell Johnston
Brock University

Advertising is a term with many meanings. It is commonly used as a collective noun to refer to all advertisements. In communication and cultural studies, it refers to a system of communication through which goods and services are brought to the attention of the general public.

Raymond Williams (1987) argues that advertising has two phases. First, the content of advertising has insinuated itself into every medium of communication. Advertisements may be understood as one-way, mediated communication intended for mass persuasion. They manipulate the shared words, images, and symbols of a society to create a favourable impression for a product, service, or cause. For this reason, advertising has been referred to rather poetically as "salesmanship in print." Nonetheless, the barriers to communication that separate advertiser and audience clearly distinguish it from the interpersonal communication that is necessary between sales clerk and customer.

Second, the business of advertising structures media operations in a capitalist economy. It is a common perception that the media serve the public by providing ready access to news and entertainment. In fact, the media serve advertisers first and the public second. Most media outlets face enormous production and distribution costs. The modest fees paid by the public do not cover these costs. Indeed, much radio, television, and internet content is available to the public free of charge. To finance their operations, then, media outlets depend on their ability to attract advertising revenue.

The public is still important to the revenue of media outlets. A media outlet will become financially self-sufficient or profitable only if it attracts an audience desired by advertisers (Smythe, 1981). When an advertiser selects a media outlet to carry its ads, the outlet's value is determined by the size and quality of its audience. "Quality" here is determined by demographic considerations that have an impact on purchasing decisions—things such as age, gender, ethnicity, occupation, and lifestyle choices. Ultimately, advertisers want to reach the highest number of potential consumers at the lowest possible cost.

Advertisers do not need the mass media. They can publicize themselves through event sponsorship, telemarketing, direct mail, flyers, catalogues, billboards, or their own websites. This puts pressure on the mass media to increase their value to advertisers. Some media try to produce the largest audiences possible by appealing to all demographic categories. This is the mass market, and this is the strategy of mainstream outlets such as family newspapers and national television networks. By contrast, specialty media outlets try to produce closely defined audiences similar to the target markets of specific groups of advertisers. For example, *The Hockey News* appeals to hockey fans and attracts advertisements for sporting goods and memorabilia. Either way, whether they chase the mass market or specific target markets, every media outlet tries to produce an audience sought by advertisers. Again, this means that advertising structures media operations. The character and quality of media outlets and their content is driven by the kinds of audiences and advertisers they want to attract.

HISTORICAL BACKGROUND

No one person invented advertising. Unlike film, radio, or television, there is no one person or date to mark its origins. If one accepts that town criers and shop signs are forms of advertising, then advertising is as old as civilization. Modern advertising, however, is integrated with the mass media. Its functions and practices emerged piecemeal over the last 250 years in step with new media technologies.

The first newspaper published in Canada, the Halifax *Gazette* (founded 1752), contained ads for a grocer, a job printer, and a tutor. Over the next century, newspapers across British North America were filled with ads from similar merchants, craftsmen, and professionals who used local papers to reach local audiences. The text of these ads—known as copy—was drafted in a polite style common to business cards. The ads were often set in the paper's own typeface and within traditional column widths. As a result, they could be indistinguishable from news stories. These ads were also indistinguishable from each other.

A second style appeared in the early 1800s. Some companies wanted their ads to stand out from those of their rivals, and to trumpet their goods and services from the printed page. To accomplish this, the polite invitation issued by earlier ads was replaced by the persuasive techniques of salesmanship. Copy was now infused with lavish claims, and boasts on behalf of a company's goods or services. These ads also looked different. They arrested attention with a single, unique font or a jarring variety of fonts. The copy might be enclosed in borders or accompanied by simple iconographic images (for example, the silhouette of a locomotive might illustrate a train schedule.) This style of advertisement grew in popularity as local economies grew and business rivalries intensified through the middle of the century.

1880–1920

Advertising underwent significant changes during the Industrial Revolution. In Canada, these developments led to the organization of advertising as a system of communication. The process took decades to unfold, but by 1920 there was a common set of practices and institutions in place that continue to shape the industry today.

New manufacturing technologies introduced through the 1800s increased the productivity of Canadian industry. With increased productivity, companies expanded their sales territories beyond their local markets into distant regions. Many achieved national distribution by the 1890s. Production and distribution, however, were quite different from selling. Advertising bridged the gap between manufacturers and the public by opening a channel of communication between them. It helped that the printing trades also industrialized during this same period. New cylinder presses and improved imaging techniques allowed newspapers to produce thousands of pages of text per hour with detailed illustrations. Advertisers took advantage of both developments to promote their products (Leiss et al., 2005, 98–101).

A new kind of business emerged to connect advertisers with newspapers: the advertising agency. National advertising campaigns are challenging work. Wherever a company does business, it must identify local media outlets, assess their utility as advertising vehicles, and negotiate their rates. This is called "media buying." When agencies first appeared, it was their only function. They completed these tasks on the advertiser's behalf. In essence, they were and remain consultants with expertise in media, and broker deals between advertisers and media outlets to place ads before the greatest number of potential consumers at the lowest possible cost. Newspapers were the most important advertising medium in Canada until the 1950s, but magazines, catalogues, flyers, posters, transit cards, and billboards were all used as early as the 1860s.

Agencies did not flourish in Canada until the national economy expanded dramatically after 1890. The first known agency, the British American Advertising Agency of Montreal, opened in 1860 and closed soon after. More successful was the Mail Advertising Agency of Montreal, founded in 1878. Anson McKim, its manager, provided astute counsel to the clients of the Toronto *Mail* newspaper, and through his personal efforts he gradually developed confidence in the entire agency business. McKim capitalized on his reputation by opening his own agency in 1889 (Johnston, 2001).

Agencies added a second function in 1900: creative service. By that time, ads already cluttered the visual landscape of cities, and modest ads were not always noticeable. The most effective ads featured both memorable copy and imagery. Agencies supplied these flourishes to their clients' ads by hiring professional copywriters and artists. J. J. Gibbons Ltd. (founded 1900, Toronto) was the first agency in Canada to offer both media buying and creative work. Its innovative approach prompted rival agencies to follow suit by establishing their own creative departments (Johnston, 2001).

Agencies added a third function after 1910: market research. As manufacturers expanded into new markets, their customers grew more remote. Consumer demand in a national market could be more difficult to interpret than in a local market. Manufacturers understandably became anxious, since their business decisions relied on timely, accurate information. Market research addresses these concerns by investigating consumer behaviour. Such information provides reassurance to advertisers; the plans for new products, services, or sales territories can be informed by hard data rather than hunches. Agencies also use this information to inform their media buying and creative services (Leiss et al., 2005).

There are two strands to market research. First, demographic analysis offers an empirical, quantitative picture of consumers. Every media outlet knows the size of its audience, at least roughly. Media buyers, however, want to know how that audience is composed. Are they male or female, young or old? Where do they live? What is their disposable income? To answer such questions, periodical publishers and agencies of the 1910s adapted research techniques from the social sciences to refine the process of media buying. Second, psychological research offers a theoretical, qualitative picture of consumers. American psychologists such as W. D. Scott sought to create more potent ads by investigating the links between advertising and human cognition. In 1910, some believed that effective ads should alter the public's purchasing habits without their knowledge, as if under hypnosis. Today, psychological research makes less sinister claims, but the intent remains the same: to tailor copy and art to the cognitive patterns of consumers. The trade magazine *Marketing* (founded 1908, Toronto) was an early champion of these new techniques. By 1920, all the leading agencies in Canada relied on market research to shape their clients' campaigns (Johnston, 2007).

Taken together, media buying, creative services, and market research provided agencies with a unique set of skills. They also provided agencies with two significant legacies. First, the research methods adapted from the social sciences appeared to have mathematical precision, which bolstered the agents' professional credibility. This credibility, however, was not entirely secure until George Gallup developed reliable public opinion polls in the 1930s (Robinson, 2000). Second, these skills gave shape to agency structures. Major agencies organized their operations by function and divided their core staff into four departments: account management, media research and buying, creative work, and market research. This formal structure has eroded in recent years as agencies move to client-specific teams and flexible workspaces. Nonetheless, such teams retain some element of each function.

1920–1960

After 1920, the advertising industry adapted to broadcasting. Radio became popular after 1922, and Canadian television began in 1952. Both were quickly integrated into the existing structures of advertising.

Nikola Tesla and Guglielmo Marconi did not develop radio for advertising. They wanted to compete with telegraph companies and improve the safety of ships at sea. Talented amateurs, however, became fascinated with the technology and began building sets for their own amusement. In 1919, electronics companies in Canada and the United States realized these amateurs had become a market unto themselves. By airing free programs, electronics companies drew amateurs to their stations, publicized their products, and inadvertently began commercial broadcasting. The federal government wanted to outlaw broadcast advertising, at least initially. Events in the United States changed its mind. There, two major radio networks began soliciting ad contracts in 1926 to finance their programming. Some Americans complained, but most did not. Many listeners felt that an hour of entertainment was worth a few minutes of sales talk. Many Canadian listeners could receive American signals and they grudgingly agreed. Subsequently, Canadian broadcasters demanded similar access to advertising dollars in order to finance their own operations. The federal government acquiesced, and advertising has remained a component of broadcast financing ever since (Johnston, 1997).

Advertising agencies adapted their media buying and creative services to radio. In the periodical press, media buyers pay for space; in broadcasting, they pay for time. There are two ways to handle time. First, "sponsorship" associates an advertiser's name with an entire program. Sponsored programs generally reflect the character and status that the sponsor wants to cultivate in the public mind. For example, MacLaren Advertising (founded 1935, Toronto) developed *Hockey Night in Canada* as an advertising vehicle for Imperial Oil in the 1930s. Announcer Foster Hewitt created a family-friendly atmosphere for fans of the Maple Leafs, while the sponsor's messages portrayed Imperial as a neighbourhood retailer that families trusted with their home heating. Second, "spots" or "commercials" use a brief segment of on-air time for sales talks (usually 15 seconds to 2 minutes long). Although sponsorship was common until the 1960s, spots are now the predominant form of radio advertising.

Television continued these practices. Many radio programs and their sponsors shifted easily to television, including Imperial Oil's *Hockey Night in Canada*. The only major adaptation was the development of stage and film techniques to produce effective visuals in televised ads. Otherwise, media buyers continued to buy time as they had in radio, creative staff continued to write persuasive appeals, and market researchers continued to investigate consumer habits.

1960–2000

The functions of the industry have not changed significantly since 1960. That said, Canadians' gradual acceptance of the country's multicultural heritage altered both media buying and creative services. The change started in Quebec.

Montreal was the country's commercial centre through much of the 20th century. During that time francophones composed roughly 20 to 30 percent of the Canadian market and 80 percent of the Quebec market. Surprisingly, francophones owned and operated few agencies and had little influence within anglophone agencies. This neglect of a massive segment of Canadian society reflected poorly on the entire industry. The situation changed abruptly after 1960 when Quebec francophones demanded greater authority in all aspects of public life. Advertisers responded with French-language campaigns distinct from their English-language campaigns, thereby creating opportunities for francophone agencies. Jacques Bouchard and his agency BCP (founded 1963, Montreal) led the way with a groundbreaking campaign for Labatt's (Elkin, 1973; Côté and Daigle, 1999). Today, agencies embrace multiculturalism and tailor ads to any demographic segment that forms a substantial market.

These changes led to an ironic twist of historical fate. Cossette Communication-Marketing (now Cossette Communication Group) was a graphic design studio founded in 1962 to serve Quebec-based clients. Ten years later, Claude Lessard transformed the studio into an agency. It found early success doing French-language creative work for anglophone agencies and Automobiles Renault. It also caught the attention of McDonald's Restaurants, which contracted the agency for one francophone region of Quebec in 1977. Cossette produced several effective campaigns for the chain and subsequently won the entire national account, in English and French, in 1991. The same strategy won several other blue-chip clients. By 2000 it was the largest agency in Canada and among the top 30 in the world (The rankings, 2006; 64th annual, 2008).

While Quebec nationalists focused on advertising content, English Canadian nationalists were concerned with media buying. As previously noted, advertisers seek to reach the greatest number of potential consumers at the lowest possible cost. Certain American media outlets are attractive because they reach more Canadians than their Canadian rivals. For example, a Detroit radio station may draw more Canadian listeners than similar stations in Windsor. If Canadian advertisers follow listeners to that station, its Canadian rivals would lose revenue and possibly close. Nationalists argue that this tendency necessarily undermines Canadian culture. The federal government agrees and regulates media buying through the *Income Tax Act* and the *Foreign Publishers Advertising Services Act*. Canadian companies may claim the full cost of advertising in Canadian media outlets as a legitimate business expense against income. By contrast, Canadian companies may claim only 50 percent of the cost of advertising placed in foreign outlets (Armstrong, 2000).

2000–present

The most significant change in advertising since 2000 is undoubtedly the explosive growth of digital marketing. In the 1990s, advertisers experimented with the internet to gauge its influence and achieved mixed results. Many companies established websites to accompany their traditional advertising. These websites often replicated the display advertising one might find in a magazine, or the functions of a mail-order catalogue. One innovation, however, was "viral marketing," which relies on peer networks to promote a product, service or website in ways that mimic word-of-mouth recommendations among family and friends. Because digital content is easily copied and shared, it can spread across the country or around the world in a matter of days. Knowing this, companies began to post entertaining content on their websites to attract surfers, and to embed clickable links to facilitate sharing. Caution, however,

TABLE 8.1 Advertising Volume in Canada by Medium (in Millions of Dollars), 1998-2010

	1998	1999	2000	2001	2002	2003	2004	2005	2006	2007	2008	2009	2010
Television	2,330	2,370	2,450	2,553	2,593	2,826	2,963	3,013	3,240	3,299	3,393	3,108	3,390
—national & network	*1,648*	*1,528*	*1,625*	*1,678*	*1,681*	*1,815*	*1,856*	*1,841*	*1,943*	*1,919*	*1,944*	*1,728*	*1,889*
—local & infomerical	*442*	*449*	*445*	*438*	*404*	*406*	*402*	*404*	*416*	*431*	*422*	*375*	*389*
—specialty	*241*	*304*	*381*	*438*	*509*	*607*	*708*	*768*	*882*	*948*	*1,026*	*1,001*	*1,112*
Newspapers*	1,596	1,629	1,731	1,678	1,684	1,697	1,752	1,784	1,768	1,725	1,670	1,380	1,640
—national	—	—	—	*574*	*576*	*580*	*599*	*610*	*605*	*590*	*571*	*406*	*736*
—local	—	—	—	*1,104*	*1,108*	*1,116*	*1,152*	*1,174*	*1,163*	*1,135*	*1,099*	*974*	*631*
—inserts	—	—	—	—	—	—	—	—	—	—	—	—	*273*
Radio	920	953	1,001	1,048	1,080	1,171	1,209	1,313	1,388	1,468	1,558	1,469	1,517
Consumer Magazines	451	460	514	541	558	610	647	665	682	718	692	590	606
Out-of-Home	219	243	263	281	273	284	303	344	370	422	463	416	482
Internet	25	56	110	97	176	237	364	562	1,010	1,241	1,602	1,822	2,232
Other media**	3,276	3,284	3,450	2,659	2,696	2,839	3,006	3,080	3,159	3,146	3,041	2,512	2,595
Other advertising	—	—	—	1,645	1,680	1,743	1,820	1,895	1,855	2,000	2,029	1,805	1,589
Total	8,817	8,995	9,519	10,502	10,740	11,407	12,064	12,656	13,472	14,019	14,448	13,102	14,051

* Newspaper figures do not include revenue for classified advertising.
** "Other media" include direct mail, catalogues, telephone directories, and specialty magazines.
Source: Canadian Media Directors' Council. (2008, 2011). Net Advertising Volume, p. 14 in *Media Digest* 2008/09, 2011/12. Toronto: Marketing Magazine.

was still the strongest driver of internet marketing during this time. In 1999, expenditure on internet marketing in Canada was $56 million, barely 1 percent of total advertising expenditures (Canadian Media Directors' Council, 2008, 14).

Over the next decade, advertisers threw caution to the wind. As more Canadians connected to the internet at home, at work, and through mobile devices, advertisers followed wherever they thought they could find potential customers. By 2010, expenditure on internet advertising had grown to $2.2 billion, or an increase of roughly 3,886 percent. It then represented 19 percent of total advertising expenditures among all mass media in Canada, a share second only to television (Canadian Media Directors' Council, 2011, 14). Table 8.1 provides a graphic illustration of the growth of digital advertising in relation to all other media. Part of this growth reflects the increasing number of companies in Canada with a Web presence, but it is also evident that companies have accepted digital marketing as a necessary component of their marketing strategies.

Internet marketing was enhanced by the development of social networking sites such as Blogger, Facebook, Twitter, and YouTube. Social networking sites provide stable, easily navigated frameworks for internet users to post their own content and invite contributions from others. The ready availability of digital recording technology, especially cameras and mobile phones, meant that individuals could readily include sound, images, and video in their contributions. These sites epitomize Tim O'Reilly's concept of "Web 2.0," a media environment where the barrier between senders and receivers is shattered. This environment is not characterized by publishing but participation, because within it users add value to whatever content is available (O'Reilly, 2005). Any messages "published" by ad agencies and PR firms in traditional marketing campaigns always carry the stigma of self-interest; their work is designed to sell goods. By contrast, conversations among consumers appear to be trustworthy because the participants usually gain no reward. These exchanges are intended to share information although, occasionally, they can reveal some measure of personal investment in a brand that moves beyond mere purchase and consumption.

Many companies have tried to make use of these exchanges on their own websites. One Canadian company that has done so is Canadian Tire. When the retailer posts information about a product on its site, it invites customers to add their own comments about the product, and these comments remain visible for all to read. This practice can result in some surprisingly frank but helpful discussions. In a more aggressive fashion, Facebook has capitalized upon its members' activities through use of the "Like" function that allows individuals to show their appreciation for specific products, services, or companies. Facebook encourages advertisers to make use of this function in order to market themselves through its pages rather than through traditional advertising. As Facebook notes, "People treat Facebook as an authentic part of their lives, so you can be sure you are connecting with real people with real interest in your products" (Facebook, 2012). Notably, it does not have a "Dislike" function (though one was created as a Firefox add-on by developer Thomas Moquet).

INSTITUTIONS

The advertising industry is complex. There are many players, they are highly competitive, and they operate across all media. Institutional structures bring order to this complexity. They were developed as people responded to pressures both inside and outside the industry. That these institutions are necessary and permanent suggests an important point: the issues they address are crucial to the stability of the industry's day-to-day operations (see Table 8.2).

Every sector of the industry has its own association. In each case, rival companies cooperate to promote their common interests. The Canadian Newspaper Association (CNA) is an apt example.[1] It formed in 1858 when several Ontario newspapers lobbied the federal government for lower postal rates. Over time, other issues were raised and resolved cooperatively. The appearance of agencies after 1880, for example, posed several problems for newspapers. The association's handling of these issues attracted new members, and by 1920 it represented daily newspapers across Canada. Today, its mandate is to "to speak with a unified voice when promoting newspaper interests to governments, regulators and the general public" and contribute "to the ongoing evolution of the newspaper industry by raising awareness and promoting the benefits of daily and community newspapers to advertisers, media planners, creative agencies and newspapers" (Newspapers Canada, 2012). In other words, it lobbies the government for policies favourable to newspapers and promotes newspapers as an advertising medium.

The Canadian Community Newspapers Association (CCNA) and Magazines Canada have similar mandates. Both had their origins in the CNA but broke away in 1919 over their competition for advertising dollars. Dailies and magazines competed for the same national advertising contracts; dailies and community papers competed for retail advertising. Eighty years later, however, all three types of publications once again face a common problem with the development of digital news delivery and the growth of internet advertising. Hence, there was a new impetus for publishers to cooperate. In January 2011, the CNA and CCNA agreed to share resources through a new umbrella organization called Newspapers Canada. Although both associations are still governed by their own boards, they share a single chief executive officer who is also the manager of Newspapers Canada. More importantly, the two associations now share research, marketing, and lobbying services to promote all newspapers with a single voice (Newspapers Canada, 2012). Magazines Canada continues to provide its own parallel services to the Canadian magazine industry.

After commercial broadcasting took root in Canada, the Canadian Association of Broadcasters (CAB) formed to establish labour and copyright standards for broadcasting. However, it too was concerned with advertising, and it became an advocate for private-sector commercial broadcasting. By 2010, its membership embraced terrestrial radio and television stations, and cable, satellite, digital, and pay-per view channels in the private sector. That year, however, the association fractured when a dispute arose between terrestrial broadcasters and the cable and satellite companies over a proposed CRTC regulation. The CAB has subsequently reorganized itself as an umbrella organization that maintains research and marketing services for its members, but it no longer serves as an industry lobbyist on regulatory affairs.

The internet Advertising Bureau (IAB) and Out-of-Home Marketing Association of Canada (OMAC) formed to represent the collective interests of Canadian digital media and out-of-home marketing companies, respectively. "Out-of-home marketing" refers to any public media form such as billboards, posters, transit ads, or point-of-sale devices in retail locations. Like the other associations, the IAB and OMAC perform research on the effectiveness of their members' advertising reach, support their members' efforts to attract new business, and lobby all levels of government to produce regulation amenable to their interests.

The Institute of Communication Agencies (ICA) was founded by Anson McKim and J. J. Gibbons, among others, in 1905. Newspapers and advertisers both questioned the value of agencies until 1907, when an agreement between the CNA and ICA formally recognized the value of agents as media buyers. Thereafter, newspapers agreed to accept media buying contracts from the agencies, but in exchange the agencies had to undergo credit checks to demonstrate their fiscal responsibility (Johnston, 2001). Agency accreditation remains a service of Newspapers Canada.

TABLE 8.2 Major Trade Associations Related to Advertising in Canada

Canadian Newspaper Association (CNA): founded 1858; reorganized 1919; reorganized 1996
- represents daily newspapers

Canadian Community Newspapers Association (CCNA): founded 1919
- represents weekly newspapers

Newspapers Canada: founded 2011
- provides research, marketing, and lobbying services to members of CNA and CCNA

Magazines Canada: founded 1919
- represents consumer, business, and cultural magazines

Canadian Association of Broadcasters (CAB): founded 1926; reorganized 2010–2011
- represents radio, television, cable, and satellite channels

Interactive Advertising Bureau of Canada (IAB): founded 1997
- represents internet publishers, advertisers, and service providers

Out-of-Home Marketing Association of Canada (OMAC): founded 2005
- represents billboard, poster, and transit placement agencies

Institute of Communication Agencies (ICA): founded 1905; reorganized 1925
- represents advertising agencies

Canadian Public Relations Society (CPRS): founded 1948
- represents PR firms

Association of Canadian Advertisers (ACA): founded 1916
- represents companies with nationally advertised goods and services

Canadian Marketing Association (CMA): founded 1967
- represents all sectors of the industry

This means all agencies that handle newspaper advertising in Canada must be recognized by this media association.

Advertisers formed the Association of Canadian Advertisers (ACA) in 1916. They wanted proof that advertising actually generated sales. This demand put pressure on media outlets and agencies to produce demonstrable results from their campaigns. This remains the mandate of the association today, to help its members "in maximizing the value of their investments in all forms of marketing communications" (Association of Canadian Advertisers, 2012). The association also lobbies the government on advertising-related issues, particularly to safeguard "commercial free speech."

The members of these sector-specific associations also belong to the broad-based Canadian Marketing Association (CMA). It is the largest association linked to advertising in Canada and provides a forum for all sectors to advance their common interests. It promotes effective marketing practices and represents the industry before government and government agencies such as the CRTC and Industry Canada.

Over the last century, these associations have met with each other to establish common standards for the industry. Their negotiations have usually focused on one of two areas: media buying or creative services. The 1907 agreement between the CNA and ICA was the first of many to regulate media buying; credit checks were designed to ensure the reliability of agencies as buyers. The development of audience measurement ensured the reliability of media outlets as sellers (see Table 8.3). Agencies and advertisers are reluctant to take media outlets at their word; they expect audience research to be verified by an independent auditor. The first such organization, the Audit Bureau of Circulations (ABC), was founded in the United States in 1914 through the cooperation of the press, advertisers, and agencies. Canadian companies participated in its establishment, including the *Toronto Star*, Canadian Pacific Railway, and J. J. Gibbons Advertising. The bureau's audit procedures were designed by representatives from all three sectors to ensure their acceptability. A similar mechanism to measure audience size was developed for each new medium. Some, like the ABC, were created through industry cooperation; examples include the Print Measurement Bureau, the Canadian Out-of-Home Measurement Bureau, and the Bureau of Broadcast Measurement. Others were created by independent entrepreneurs; these include Canadian Facts, which developed the first radio ratings in Canada during the 1930s, and ACNielsen Inc., which developed television ratings in the 1940s and internet ratings in the 1990s (Eaman, 1994).

On the creative side is **Advertising Standards Canada (ASC)**. This nonprofit organization functions as a watchdog, monitoring the content of advertisements. Over the last 40 years, several codes have been developed to govern what advertisers may claim or depict in their ads. In each case, the code was developed voluntarily by the industry in response to public complaints or government pressure (see Table 8.4).

Voluntary participation is key. The Canadian constitution protects freedom of speech. The government and courts, however, insist that protected freedoms not

TABLE 8.3 Audience Research Agencies Operating in Canada

Audit Bureau of Circulations, founded 1914
- audits the circulation of newspapers and magazines

Canadian Circulations Audit Board (a division of BPA Worldwide), founded 1936
- audits the circulation of newspapers and magazines

NADbank, founded 1984
- audits the circulation of daily newspapers

Print Measurement Bureau, founded 1971
- audits the circulation of magazines

Canadian Out-of-Home Measurement Bureau, founded 1965
- audits the visibility of billboards, posters, and transit placements

Bureau of Broadcast Measurement, founded 1942
- audits the audience size of radio and television outlets

AC Nielsen Canada, founded 1944
- audits the audience size of television outlets and the use of internet sites

be abused. For example, federal hate crime legislation places restrictions on speech. Similarly, the government has placed restrictions on commercial speech with regulations governing false advertising and standards of decency. For example, until the 1940s it was illegal to discuss birth control in public; therefore, condom manufacturers could not advertise. Today, alcohol ads may not portray people drinking alcohol. Watch closely—actors may hold open bottles, raise toasts, and clink glasses, but they will never actually drink. The government argues that such regulations protect community standards, but they are driven as much by profits as morals. Individual ads making false claims or promoting controversial behaviours can affect the public's confidence in all advertising. The government tries to protect consumer confidence by discouraging those who abuse the system.

The federal government has enacted several laws regulating the content of ads. Some, such as the *Food and Drugs Act* and the *Consumer Packaging and Labelling Act*, hold companies liable for misleading claims made about their products. Others, such as the *Trade-marks Act* and the *Copyright Act*, protect companies from rivals with unfair marketing practices. Two important laws are designed to uphold community standards. The ***Broadcasting Act*** empowers the CRTC to regulate the character and quantity of all advertising aired by radio, television, cable, and satellite, while the *Canada Elections Act* monitors political advertising by all groups during federal election campaigns.

Under Canada's constitution, the provinces have jurisdiction over trade and commerce. This has created 10 separate legal frameworks that affect advertising. Apart from laws governing general trade practices, there are specific laws that regulate the advertising of pharmaceuticals, alcohol, tobacco, firearms, lotteries, and consumer credit. Several provinces have regulations to prevent billboards from appearing next to major highways. Quebec also has two unique pieces of

TABLE 8.4 Selected Laws, Regulations, and Codes for Advertising in Canada

Government of Canada
- *Broadcasting Act,* 1992, c. 11
- *Canada Corporations Act,* R.S. 1970, c. C–32
- *Canada Elections Act,* 2000, c. 9
- *Consumer Packaging & Labelling Act,* R.S. 1985, c. C–38
- *Copyright Act,* R.S. 1985, c. C–42
- *Food & Drugs Act,* R.S. 1985, c. F–27
- *Foreign Publishers Advertising Services Act,* 1999, c. 23
- *Income Tax Act,* R.S. 1985, c. 1, Suppl. 5
- *Personal Information Protection and Electronic Documents Act,* 2000, c. 5
- *Telecommunications Act* (amendment), s. 41, 2004–05, C–37
- *Trade-marks Act,* R.S. 1985, c. T–13
- Guidelines: Privacy and Online Behavioural Advertising (2011)

Government of Quebec
- *Charter of the French Language,* 1977, c. 5
- Children's advertising provisions, s. 248–249 of the *Consumer Protection Act,* 1978, c. 9

Advertising Standards Canada
- *Canadian Code of Advertising Standards* (2012)

Advertising Standards Canada and Concerned Children's Advertisers
- *Broadcast Code for Advertising to Children* (2010)

Canadian Marketing Association
- *Code of Ethics and Standards of Practice* (2002)

regulation: guidelines governing advertising to children and the *Charter of the French Language.* The provincial government created the charter to protect and promote the French language in Quebec. Its original provisions banned the use of any language other than French on signs posted in public space, thereby affecting the content of billboards, posters, shop signs, and window displays. This provision was struck down by the Supreme Court of Canada in 1988, which held that it violated the Canadian *Charter of Rights and Freedoms,* but the Quebec government invoked section 33 of the *Charter,* the "notwithstanding" clause, to override this decision and maintain the intent of the provision. Now, a second language is permitted on signs only if French appears more prominently.

Advertisers and agents resent state intervention. ASC provides a mechanism for the industry to regulate itself. Its key function is to maintain and administer the ***Canadian Code of Advertising Standards.*** This document, first drafted in 1963, is reviewed annually and revised as necessary. It articulates 14 principles that all advertisers should respect. Its chief concerns are the accuracy and clarity of ad copy; the handling of prices, guarantees, and testimonials; the portrayal of women and visible minorities; and the character of advertising to children. Anyone who objects to an ad in a Canadian media outlet may lodge a complaint with ASC. In 2011, 1809 complaints were received regarding 1153 ads, the majority of which appeared on television (38 percent). ASC reviewed 109 of these ads and found that 83 ads (7 percent) violated the code (Advertising Standards Canada, 2012, 2–4). When this happens, the advertiser is asked to alter the ad or stop it. However, ASC has no recourse to the justice system because it is a private-sector organization. Its sanctions depend on the voluntary cooperation of advertisers, agencies, and media outlets.

The most sensitive reviews concern depiction of sexuality within the bounds of community standards. Two examples may serve as illustrations. In 2010, American Apparel hired adult film performer Faye Valentine to model a unitard. When the images were posted on the retailer's website, they quickly drew a complaint. ASC reviewed the case and noted that "when advertising undergarments, models are often featured in suggestive poses" and "that the majority of the images displayed on the advertiser's webpage did not raise an issue." The images that drew the complaint, however, "appeared to be posed in the advertisement less to demonstrate the unitard's selling features than for the stimulation and gratification of the viewer." As a result, the council ruled that the images contravened public standards (Advertising Standards Canada, 2010). The following year, Virgin Radio had a billboard featuring Usher and the tagline "Shirt On: OMG. Shirt Off: OMFG." Anyone familiar with the vernacular of text-messaging understood that the ad included an implicit profanity. Because the billboard appeared in public spaces and was potentially insensitive to religious beliefs, ASC ruled that this ad also offended public standards (Advertising Standards Canada, 2011). Both examples suggest that aspects of digital culture which are acceptable among private citizens will face scrutiny when adapted for public use by marketers. ASC hopes that its procedures continue to demonstrate the industry's willingness to monitor its own practices both in traditional and digital media.

CURRENT ISSUES

Globalization

Advertising has long been an international industry. Consumer goods manufacturers such as Unilever and Lipton sold their wares throughout the British Empire in the 1800s and advertised accordingly. J. Walter Thompson Advertising, one of the largest American agencies throughout the 20th century, established branch offices wherever its clients sold their goods. By 1930 it was on three continents, including offices in Montreal (established 1929) and Toronto (1930). Clients appreciated that a single agency handled their campaigns worldwide. Other agencies emulated Thompson's model.

In the 1970s, the pace of international expansion intensified when a major American agency, McCann-Erickson, united with a major English agency, Lintas (Mattelart, 1991). Together they formed the Interpublic Group of Companies. The "agency group" model is significantly different from the "international agency" model. Groups recognize that every country has its own marketing challenges created by differences in language, customs, laws, and media use. When agencies from different countries form a group, they offer both convenience and cultural credibility. Through a single company they offer international marketing support that can be implemented anywhere by a local office. In 2007, the four dominant groups were Omnicom Group and Interpublic Group of Companies, both of New York; WPP of Dublin; and Publicis Groupe SA of Paris (Johnson, 2011).

As agency groups extend their reach, they affect smaller, regional agencies. This is particularly true in Canada. The country composes only one small region in the global marketplace, and its manufacturing sector is dominated by foreign-owned companies that produce processed foods, consumer durables, and automobiles—all high-volume advertisers. When the parent companies of Canadian branch plants integrate their Canadian campaigns with their global marketing plans, accounts shift from Canadian agencies to agency groups. For example, McDonald's transferred its media-buying account from independent Cossette to OMD Canada, a division of Omnicom, in 2004.

Few Canadian agencies compete directly with agency groups. Most either join a group or find a niche for themselves within Canada. Some of Canada's oldest agencies took the first path. McKim joined Omnicom, MacLaren joined Interpublic, and BCP sold part of its business to Publicis. Agencies that take the second path generally provide high-quality creative services geared to Canadian audiences—something they claim that groups cannot provide. Rethink Communications (founded 1999, Vancouver) and John St (founded 2001, Toronto) have gone this route. Two notable exceptions follow a third path. Cossette has sought to expand on its own terms. In 2010 it established a new division for its business outside Canada (under the name EDC Communications). By contrast, MDC Partners (founded 1980, Toronto) is a Canadian-owned holding company that has expanded internationally by purchasing relatively small but successful agencies in foreign markets. In 2010, MDC was the tenth largest agency group in the world with more business in the United States than in Canada (Johnson, 2011).

The Death of Advertising?

Industry observers such as Sergio Zyman (2003) suggest big-budget ad campaigns are a casualty of the media-saturated 21st century. Two lines of thought inform this idea. First, the proliferation of new media outlets and audience fragmentation has advantages and disadvantages for advertisers. To remain competitive, media outlets dependent on ad revenue must increase their audience share or reduce their ad rates. This is good for advertisers. However, new media outlets typically focus on narrow target markets that may be unresponsive to traditional mass market campaigns. Advertisers and their agencies are then pressured to create unique ads for each outlet. At the same time, new marketing strategies have allowed advertisers to abandon the traditional mass media altogether by creating their own magazines, digital content, or events. For example, Shoppers Drug Mart produces the magazine *Glow* while CIBC has linked its name to the annual Run for the Cure, a fundraiser for breast cancer research.

Second, the general public has long been cynical of advertising messages. In the past, it was possible to tune out these messages. Radio listeners changed stations, television viewers left the room, and Web surfers ignored banner advertising. Today, digital devices have provided the technology to access media content without advertising, or to eliminate advertising from the content (as with personal video recorders). Advertisers and agencies have responded by making ads more entertaining, controversial, or intrusive in order to capture our attention. Beer ads crafted for the Stanley Cup playoffs and Super Bowl illustrate this trend. Another response is to use technical innovations such as pop-up windows on the internet.

What is the alternative to traditional advertising? Some companies look to public relations and guerrilla marketing. Public relations as an industry has existed since the 1920s and has its own practitioners and institutions. The Canadian Public Relations Society, founded in 1948, serves PR firms just as the ICA serves advertising agencies. Despite their professional separation, however, the function of public relations is the same as that of advertising: to enhance the public's appreciation for companies, their brands, and their products and services. It does this by delivering messages through channels the public generally trusts (Johansen, 2001). One such channel is news organizations. Many people may question a company's advertising but may accept news stories covering that company's affairs. PR firms can generate positive coverage by staging press conferences and spectacles in conjunction with corporate events. PR firms can also boost their clients by sponsoring charitable, cultural, and sports organizations. In times of crisis, it is also the PR firm's responsibility to safeguard a client's reputation (Ries and Ries, 2002).

Guerrilla marketing was a term conceived in the 1980s to describe street-level alternatives to traditional advertising campaigns. While traditional campaigns featured formal, planned strategies and national media exposure, guerrilla marketing tends to use unconventional channels of communication to reach local audiences (Levinson, 1985). This includes packages of coupons delivered door-to-door, "personal" telephone calls known as telemarketing, and contests. Newspapers now use telemarketing and display booths at local festivals and fairs to reach new, local subscribers. Other guerrilla tactics include events and stunts in public places. In June 2002, Nike opened a nightclub in Toronto's Kensington Market district. This neighbourhood, a magnet for artists and students, has street credibility among those who appreciate alternative lifestyles and cultural events. The club's exterior was not branded, but the interior design and employee uniforms were. It was hoped that unsuspecting hipsters would learn to love Nike apparel (Rumack, 2002). During the summer in 2010, McDonald's created beach umbrellas that looked like enormous lids and straws from milk shake cups and then installed them for public use on Toronto beaches. In each of these cases, a company sought to reach its intended market by linking the setting and the medium with the brand in a memorable way.

One other alternative has emerged to challenge traditional marketing, and that is social media. As noted earlier in this chapter, the pervasive influence of social networking sites has provided companies with a structure in which consumers promote the goods and services they like best. Although this once happened innocently through personal exchanges among family and friends interacting online, companies such as Facebook, Twitter, and Klout have found ways to commodify the experience to maximize the benefits for advertisers.

Taken together, audience fragmentation, public relations, guerrilla marketing, and social networking sites have severely challenged the traditional use of mass market advertising. Indeed, this trend has affected Canada's largest agencies. Many have stopped describing their work as advertising, and prefer the terms "marketing" or "communication" (Zyman, 2003). The public simply sees more advertising delivered through more channels than ever before.

Privacy

As noted above, advertising was not welcome on radio when commercial broadcasting began. Similar concerns have dogged the recent development of new marketing practices. Particularly troublesome is the practice of collecting and selling databases of personal information. For decades, periodical publishers have maintained the names and addresses of everyone who subscribes to their magazines. These mailing lists are valuable. In effect, they are databases of individuals who self-identify their lifestyles and spending habits through their choice of reading material. If a magazine reaches a well-defined target market, certain advertisers will want to buy space in it. Direct marketers, however, would rather send their own materials (sometimes called "junk mail") to each subscriber rather than use the magazine itself. Publishers sell their mailing lists to direct marketers for this purpose.

Many other organizations generate similar databases. Digital technologies allow data to be collected across vast networks of businesses. Most prominent is the Air Miles program operated by LoyaltyOne. The program encourages consumers to favour certain retailers, products, and services by rewarding them with points for every purchase. The points can then be used toward air travel. The Air Miles database starts with each person's name and address. It then records each person's purchases, and where, when, and how much was spent. After collating this data, LoyaltyOne can generate highly specialized databases of individuals sorted by their buying habits. For example, it could generate a list of everyone who purchases dog food. With this list, a dog food manufacturer could send a brochure and coupons to everyone on it. Alternatively, the manufacturer could send the same information by email (sometimes called spam). Either way, the manufacturer can be confident that all of the recipients are potential customers because it already knows they buy dog food. This is far more efficient than mass media advertising where 50 to 75 percent of the audience may not even own a dog. Similar databases can be generated by every other loyalty program and credit card offered in Canada.

These practices have fostered anxiety among Canadians. Although consumers provide personal data to companies they trust, they are not willing to have those data shared with a third party. This is apparent in the disdain for junk mail, telemarketing, and spam. Data sharing is unlikely to stop, however; quite the opposite, Facebook has commodified the data its users post to the site to produce one of the most sophisticated and intensive databases ever created about human consumption practices. The estimated value of the company when its shares went public—between $75 billion and $100 billion—was based on its ability to collect and organize personal information for marketing purposes (Avery, 2012). Canadian users were among the first to realize the consequences of their participation, and a Toronto-based campaign encouraged users to delete their personal accounts (Lunau, 2010). More substantially, the federal Office of the Privacy Commissioner investigated Facebook in 2009 and found its data practices problematic when assessed against Canadian privacy law. Facebook subsequently made changes to its global user policies in response to the commissioner's report (Canada, Office of the Privacy Commissioner, 2009; 2011).

Google also offers services to advertisers. Through its AdWords program, Google will associate specific words or phrases with a specific advertiser's website. Then, each time a surfer enters matching words or phrases into the search engine, the search results will prioritize that advertiser's website. Google can tailor its results to the geographic location of anonymous users based upon their IP addresses and to known users through their Google log-in information. For example, a local pizza shop can have its ad prioritized for surfers in its area, while a national pizza chain can have its ad prioritized for surfers across the country. Google then bills each advertiser for every surfer who clicks through from its results page to the advertiser's website. It is Google's ability to collect, retain, and analyze data from searches and click-throughs that raises concerns for privacy advocates. Anyone who has an account with Google, and logs in before every search, will have all of his or her browsing recorded for future use. Google argues that this data is used to improve the accuracy and quality of future searches (Google, 2012). Critics counter that Google retains an unnecessarily detailed level of personal data on its clients.

Equally troubling is the idea that corporate data systems may not be secure. Information contained on electronic databases may be divulged by insiders or hacked by outsiders. In 1997, the Province of Ontario Savings Bank accidentally placed its electronic records for 50,000 customers in the public domain—including their names, addresses, phone numbers, account numbers, and social insurance numbers (Ontario, Information and Privacy Commissioner, 2000). More recently, groups such as Wikileaks and Anonymous have demonstrated their ability to obtain information from supposedly high-security organizations such as the United States military and Federal Bureau of Investigation. Such leaks undermine confidence in all electronic exchanges.

The Canadian federal government cooperated with the CMA to develop legislation governing the use of personal data for advertising and marketing. Both parties sought positive means to bolster the integrity of these databases and to diminish the public's fears. The result of their negotiations is the ***Personal Information Protection and Electronic Documents Act*** (2000, c.5), commonly known as **PIPEDA**. It requires all organizations to obtain the consent of individuals before they collect, store, or distribute personal information. Organizations must also ensure their databases are secure from unauthorized use. For example, under PIPEDA all Canadian periodicals must state whether they sell their subscription lists to other organizations. If a periodical does, it must let subscribers opt out of the list. It was this law that prompted the Privacy Commissioner's investigation of Facebook.

Although the law did not originally apply to telemarketing, the CMA lobbied successfully for its inclusion. Because telecommunications are regulated by the CRTC, however, the government had to empower that agency to take action through an amendment to the *Telecommunications Act*. This passed in 2005. The CRTC then brought into service a mandatory national "do-not-call list" in 2008 that discourages telemarketers from contacting anyone whose number is registered (Canada, CRTC, 2007). The CMA now seeks controls on spam, but a disagreement between the CMA and the government over the implementation of such controls has delayed passage of the relevant legislation (Geist, 2009).

SUMMARY

Advertising in Canada has come a long way from the first newspaper ads in 1752. The creative content of advertising today is colourful and slickly produced, the tone is aggressive, and the technology is stunningly complex. Still, its purpose remains the same: to persuade the public to buy. Less obvious is the effect that advertising has upon our public debates and culture. The influence of industry lobbies such as the ICA, ACA, CPRS, and CMA affects the shape of federal and provincial law. Just as importantly, the logic of media buying affects the nature of Canadian culture as it is produced and distributed through the mass media.

QUESTIONS

1. What is advertising? Has it changed significantly with the advent of digital media?
2. Who has prompted reforms in the advertising industry, and why?
3. Is self-regulation a sound and principled way to regulate the advertising industry?
4. How does media buying affect the content of Canadian radio and television?
5. Why might some observers claim that advertising is either dead or dying? Are they correct?

NOTE

1. Many of the industry associations discussed in this chapter have changed their names since they were founded. Only their current names are used here.

REFERENCES

Advertising Standards Canada. (2010). Ad complaints reports—Q2 2010. Retrieved August 11, 2012, from http://www.adstandards.com/en/Standards/previousReports.asp

———. (2011). Ad complaints reports—Q2 2011. Retrieved August 11, 2012, from http://www.adstandards.com/en/standards/adComplaintsReports.asp?periodquarter=2&periodyear=2011

———. (2012). *2011 Ad complaints report.* Toronto: Author. Retrieved August 16, 2012, from http://www.adstandards.com/en/ConsumerComplaints/2011AdComplaintsReport.pdf

Armstrong, S. (2000). Magazines, cultural policy and globalization: The forced retreat of the state? *Canadian Public Policy, 26*(3), 369–385.

Association of Canadian Advertisers. (2012). The ACA edge. Retrieved August 11, 2012, from http://www.acaweb.ca/en/the-aca-edge

Avery, S. (2012, February 2). How much is Facebook really worth? *The Globe and Mail,* B13.

Canada, CRTC. (2007). Telecom Decision CRTC 2007-48.

Canada, Office of the Privacy Commissioner (2009). Report of findings into the complaint field by the Canadian Internet Policy and Public Interest Clinic (CIPPIC) against Facebook Inc. Ottawa: The Author.

———. (2011). Guidelines: Privacy and online behavioural advertising. Retrieved August 11, 2012, from http://www.priv.gc.ca/information/guide/2011/gl_ba_1112_e.cfm

Canadian Media Directors' Council. (2008). Components of net advertising revenue by medium, p. 14 in *Media Digest 08/09.* Toronto: Marketing Magazine.

———. (2011). Net advertising volume, p. 14 in *Media Digest 2011/12.* Toronto: Marketing Magazine.

Côté, L. and Daigle, J.-G. (1999). *Publicité de masse et masse publicitaire.* Ottawa: Presses de l'Université d'Ottawa.

Eaman, R. (1994). *Channels of influence.* Toronto: University of Toronto Press.

Elkin, F. (1973). *Rebels and colleagues.* Montreal: McGill-Queen's University Press.

Facebook. (2012). Facebook adverts: Case studies. Retrieved January 25, 2012, from http://www.facebook.com/advertising/?campaign_id=40204744918

Geist, M. (2009, 16 October). Canadian Marketing Association attacks anti-spam bill. Retrieved August 11, 2012, from http://www.michaelgeist.ca/content/view/4463/125/.

Google. (2012). Privacy policy, 1 March 2012. Retrieved March 18, 2012, from http://www.google.com/intl/en/policies/privacy

Johansen, P. (2001). Professionalism, building respectability, and the birth of the Canadian Public Relations Society. *Journalism Studies*, *2*(1), 55–71.

Johnson, B. (2011, April 25). Agency report 2011, *Advertising Age*, *82*(17), p. 24.

Johnston, R. (1997). The emergence of broadcast advertising in Canada, 1919–1932. *Historical Journal of Film, Radio, and Television*, *17*(1), 29–47.

———. (2001). *Selling themselves: The emergence of Canadian advertising*. Toronto: University of Toronto Press.

———. (2007). "Partisan politics, market research, and media buying in Canada, 1920." *Journalism & Mass Communication Quarterly*, *83*(4), 917–932.

Leiss, W., Kline, S., Jhally, S., & Botterill, J. (2005). *Social Communication in Advertising*, 3rd ed. London, UK: Routledge.

Levinson, J. C. (1985). *Guerilla marketing*. Boston: Houghton Mifflin.

Lunau, K. (2010, June 3). Facebook update: I quit. Macleans.ca. Retrieved August 16, 2012, from http://www2.macleans.ca/2010/06/03/128651

Mattelart, A. (1991). *Advertising international* (M. Chanan, Trans.). London: Routledge.

Newspapers Canada (2012). About us. Retrieved January 17, 2012, from www.newspaperscanada.ca/about-us

Ontario, Information and Privacy Commissioner. (2000). *A special report to the legislative assembly of Ontario on the disclosure of personal information by the province of Ontario Savings Office, Ministry of Finance*. Toronto: Province of Ontario.

O'Reilly, T. (2005). What is Web 2.0? Retrieved August 11, 2012, from www.oreillynet.com/pub/ a/oreilly/tim/news/2005/09/30/what-is-web-20.html

Rankings, The. (2006, June 19). *Marketing*, *111*(22), 29–34.

Ries, A., and Ries, L. (2002). *The fall of advertising and the rise of PR*. New York: Harper Business.

Robinson, D. (2000). *The measure of democracy*. Toronto: University of Toronto Press.

Rumack, L. (2002, 11 July). Presto! You're cool. *Now Magazine*. Retrieved June 1, 2005, from http://www.nowtoronto.com/issues/2002-07-11/news_story6.php

Smythe, D. (1981). *Dependency road: Communications, capitalism, consciousness and Canada*. Norwood, NJ: Ablex.

Williams, R. (1987). Advertising—The magic system. In *Problems in materialism and culture* (pp. 327–335). London: Verso.

Zyman, S., with Brott, A. (2003). *The end of advertising as we know it*. Hoboken, NJ: John Wiley & Sons.

PART III Media Institutions

Introduction

Leslie Regan Shade
University of Toronto

The four chapters in this section of *Mediascapes* examine various issues and specific case studies of distinct media institutions in Canada—the impact of changing structures of media ownership amid ongoing concentration, convergence, and evolving communication policies (Shade and Lithgow), the often peculiar yet highly creative and popular genre of mockumentaries within the Canadian film industry (Druick), the influence of the public relations industry in shaping media discourse and popular culture (Greenberg), and the video game industry, which has situated Canada as a global leader in design and production of this lucrative business (Consalvo).

Leslie Regan Shade and Michael Lithgow's chapter provides a general introduction to the structural factors surrounding media ownership, both in the global and the national context. As they discuss, the role of media in a democratic society is fundamental. Media serve to enrich, edify, educate, inform, entertain, and illuminate. But as they demonstrate, over the last 25 years, and particularly within the last decade, corporate media have become more powerful in several ways: because of consolidation, vertical integration, and digitization. Corporate media are also influential players in their ability to effectuate and shape communication policy for their interests—which are not necessarily in the public interest. Media ownership matters, as the examples discussed in this chapter illustrate; these include recent debates on foreign ownership in the broadcasting and telecommunication sector and the perceived role and sustainability of public service media such as CBC. Media activism, the goals of which are to reshape media policies and institutions for the continuance of the public interest and ensure a wider diversity of voices, has been re-energized in the last decade, and has coalesced around the media reform movement, which has been active in various national contexts. The chapter reviews several Canadian initiatives, pivotal media reform organizations, and policy moments.

Structures of participation—both in media policymaking and in citizens' cultural engagement and production—are also fundamental issues related to media democracy, and accrue around the notion of cultural citizenship, which Shade and Lithgow discuss in relation to exciting media endeavours that link culture and identity and are truly intended to increase the diversity of voices in the Canadian mediascape.

Canada is well known for its documentary film tradition, with the National Film Board of Canada (NFB) emblematic of this venerable cultural tradition. Referencing this tradition, Zoë Druick examines the rise of Canadian mockumentaries (fake documentary films), characterized by low production budgets, a retreat from the standard format of NFB docs, and an intentional estrangement from the making of feature-length films. Druick argues that mockumentaries are a contemporary cultural form customized for a country that is self-conscious about its ability to make popular and internationally acclaimed films. Through several Canadian and Quebec examples, Druick shows how mockumentaries serve as double-edged texts through parodying documentary conventions (including the NFB sensibility), as well as paying homage to and reinforcing this filmic genre.

Studying public relations and its fascinating industry history is the topic of Josh Greenberg's nuanced chapter. It is often too easy to deride and critique this industry for its shallowness and complicity in pushing "spin," or engaging in ethically dubious practices of deceit, but as Greenberg adroitly demonstrates, PR can and has been used for progressive social ends from its inception to today. PR practitioners and professionals are not only diffuse and situated in a variety of organizational contexts but also guided by professional associations that accredit members, delineate codes of ethics, and engage in professional development activities. Greenberg devotes a section of his chapter to how PR has been portrayed in popular culture, from early cinematic depictions to contemporary films, television shows, literature, and music. Documentary films about the PR industry are also addressed. The relationship between PR and journalism is also explored, an arrangement that has been the subject of much debate particularly as critics contend that it has led to a diminution of journalistic quality and integrity.

A rapidly growing and lucrative media and digital technology sector in Canada is the video game industry. Mia Consalvo's chapter looks at this fertile industry in Canada, where game design and console platforms, as she describes from their early origins to now, have been integrally related to the economic development of the industry. Vancouver, Toronto, and Montreal serve as the major hubs for video game development in Canada, with the well-known companies such as Electronic Arts, Ubisoft, and Eidos receiving lucrative provincial tax breaks in order to compete globally. An available and talented labour pool often educated in digital media arts programs and the allure of residing in hip centres of creative cities has made working for these studios attractive, and thus energized the industry. In order to understand the impact of Canadian studios in the global video game industry, Consalvo situates a case study of Edmonton-based Bioware, whose fame has rested on the creation of popular role-playing games, as it aptly illustrates the coupling of global shifts in the industry and the impact of technological developments. Lastly, the ethical issues surrounding video games—critiques of violent content and legal actions against the industry and the development of content-rating systems by the industry—are addressed, as are more recent debates surrounding labour practices in the industry, where a culture of informality in the workplace can obscure serious issues such as low compensation and arduous hours.

9

MEDIA OWNERSHIP, PUBLIC PARTICIPATION, AND DEMOCRACY IN THE CANADIAN MEDIASCAPE

Leslie Regan Shade, University of Toronto
Michael Lithgow, Carleton University

> As a young journalist, I want to be sure that Canada's media remains a place where the public can hear a wide range of voices. A few giant media corporations controlling journalists will only hurt the spread of information.
>
> As a female professional born and raised in Canada, with ties to the Chinese and Vietnamese communities, I want a choice in what I see on TV, hear on the radio and read in the newspaper and on the internet ... We are already seeing less local content and less diversity of ideas in our media. And there has NEVER been sufficient representation of minority communities in its many varied aspects ... Our future lies in true pluralism, where one voice representing the queer (community), or only one voice representing the Asian community, is not enough. We need to have access to multiple points of view.
>
> Gone, or so it seems, are the days when each paper, each station, each magazine offered a different analysis allowing the citizenry to access a diverse range of opinions and analysis which, in my estimation, is what "fertilizes" a democracy making it possible for it to grow and flourish.
>
> —Campaign for Democratic Media: Excerpts from comments made in the summer of 2007 through "Stop the Big Media Takeover" campaign. Retrieved August 2012, from http://openmedia.ca/sites/openmedia.ca/files/crtcdiversity_commentsCC_0.pdf

These comments reflect just a few of the opinions from Canadian citizens about the state of media ownership and concentration in Canada. In 2007, more than 1,900 Canadians from across the country participated in the Campaign for Democratic Media's "Stop the Big Media Takeover" in response to a CRTC call for comments in its 2007 Diversity of Voices hearing. This review (as described in more detail in

Chapter 5) was initiated after a wave of proposed consolidation in the media industries, alarming many about the healthy fate of local, regional, and national content and raising concerns about whether or not an appropriate diversity of perspectives, including editorial, would be achievable and sustainable without urgent regulatory intervention. The comments also reflect passionate debates about the role of media in a democratic society, and how—and even if—**corporate media** should be held accountable.

Five years after the Diversity of Voices decision, which established guidelines for mergers and acquisitions (deeming that if a single ownership group controlled between 35-40 percent of the market, the proposed acquisition would be subject to review, and rejecting any deal leading to a 45 percent ownership rate as it would constitute excessive concentration), the Canadian mediascape is even more concentrated than before. For instance, the March 2012 announcement of the proposed merger of Bell Canada Enterprises (BCE) and Astral Media Inc. for $3.38 billion would have brought BCE close to the 40 percent threshold with the pay and specialty television holdings. While media mergers need to be approved by the CRTC and the Competition Bureau, in many instances mergers are routinely approved without public scrutiny. In this instance, given the acrimony over the proposed merger (see "Bell, the Behemoth," below) the CRTC held public hearings in Montreal in September 2012. One early dissenting voice was that of political economist Dwayne Winseck, who commented about the proposed merger, "This is truly incredible. If we care at all about the health, diversity and range of voices in the Canadian media, such ventures need to be turned back" (Winseck, 2012). Indeed, in October 2012, the CRTC denied BCE's request to control Astral, with CRTC Chair Jean-Pierre Blais commenting that the deal would "have placed significant market power in the hands of one of the country's largest media companies"; and cited concerns about ownership concentration, vertical integration, and market power in an anti-competitive manner. Further, the CRTC said they were "not persuaded that the transaction would have provided significant and unequivocal benefits to the Canadian broadcasting system and to Canadians sufficient to outweigh its concerns" (CRTC, October 18, 2012).

Media accountability is complex because media serve many masters. Consider for a moment the diversity of media strategies that make up the Canadian mediascape: mobile communication (which includes telephony, advertising, and content distribution); social media including social network sites like Facebook, blogs, and Twitter; podcasts; RSS feeds, email, and listservs; zines; streaming video and video sites such as YouTube; cable and satellite television; community television; commercial radio; campus and community radio; movie theatres; video rentals; magazines and newspapers; and film festivals. Each media strategy has its own social and economic context, including audiences with unique needs and producers with unique goals. Media are used as a source of entertainment, information and news, ideology, history, ideas, and information about products and services. Media are used to achieve political power. Everyone has a stake in the social, political, and economic futures of the places where we live, and in a wealthy and technologically integrated country such as Canada, "the media" are how we collectively engage in these kinds of discussions. Or, in other words, media are at the centre of Canadian democratic reality. Who owns the media raises the rather daunting question of who owns Canada's democracy.

This chapter will provide an introduction to issues, trends, and policy implications surrounding media ownership and democratic outcomes in Canada. It will examine the critical issues of technological convergence, the importance of the public interest, the role of public service media, and the burgeoning media reform movement. We conclude with a brief consideration of the notion of "cultural citizenship" and what it means for Canadians to "own" their own culture through active participation, consumption, and policy reform.

The stakes couldn't be higher. As Canadian communications scholar Marc Raboy writes: "Who decides how issues of media governance get resolved—and, consequently, how media are used—is therefore a question that goes to the heart of how every society in the world today will experience the twenty-first century" (Raboy, 2006, p. 291). Whose culture it is, and ultimately whose democracy, are the questions at stake when we talk about ownership of media in a democratic society.

TRENDS IN GLOBAL MEDIA

There are four main trends in global media: (1) convergence; (2) conglomeration and concentration; (3) globalization; and (4) deregulation. Since the mid-1990s, the global communication sector has undergone a process of rapid neoliberal transnationalization, characterized by increased mergers and acquisitions at national and international levels, and a concomitant global media policy regime that favours market competition, privatization, and a reduction or elimination of foreign ownership restrictions. Capital investment has catapulted the communications industry (broadcasting, telecommunications, newspapers, and advertising) into the largest sector in the global mergers and acquisitions market (Jin, 2008). All these trends characterize **neoliberalism**, which promotes the idea that the marketplace and the accrual of profits should be allowed in all facets of social, economic, and cultural affairs.

Convergence refers to the manner in which digital technologies alter and blur the traditional distinctions between print and broadcasting media. It was widely promoted in the 1990s as the ownership of cross-media platforms and assets, coupled with the integration of digital technologies, produced both vertically and horizontally integrated conglomerates. Proclaimed as "one-stop" shopping for consumers, media behemoths envisioned themselves as providers of information and entertainment, content and distribution, telephone and cable, subscriptions and advertisements. Characteristic convergence mergers in the new millennium included the 2001 acquisition by CanWest Global Communications (Global TV) of Western International Communications (TV stations), Southam (newspapers), Hollinger's Canadian internet properties and the *National Post*, and the 2010 acquisition by Bell Globemedia

(Bell Canada phone company, internet portal Sympatico, satellite distributor Bell ExpressVu) of CTV, the Canadian Television Network, and *The Globe and Mail*.

Convergence strategies shifted from multimedia content convergence for consumers to cross-media opportunities for advertisers. An early example of this was TimeWarner's $1 billion expenditure for cross-platform advertising with companies including Burger King, Kellogg, and Kraft Foods (Powell, 2002). Typical packages in convergence strategies include newspaper and television ads coupled with internet ads, product placements, and even "virtual ads" wherein products are digitally placed into programs or on-air promotions. Another early example was CTV's *Canadian Idol* series, where the integration of makeup and hair products provided by L'Oréal Paris and voting via text messaging (SMS) services provided by wireless companies including Bell Mobility, Microcell, Rogers Wireless, and SaskTel Mobility became an integral component of the cross-platform interactivity that characterized this popular reality television genre (Baltruschat, 2009).

One of the challenges of convergence lies in the policy realm; given the pervasive digitization of media convergence, what regulatory rules should adhere to each medium and which piece of legislation and/or administrative body should be responsible for governance? As François Bar and Christian Sandvig (2008) discuss with respect to the United States, policymakers tend to deal with the challenges of convergence through:

> incremental adaptation of past rules rather than fundamental redesign of the policy regime. They have chosen either to treat a new medium with the policy previously applied to whatever it seemed to resemble, or to adjust through the accretion of exceptions and additions. Thus, policy treats cable television as an extension of broadcast, itself viewed as an extension of radio. (p. 532)

In Canada we see how this emergent techno-policy conundrum plays out in our policy regime. In 1999 when the CRTC ruled on whether internet content should be regulated under the *Broadcasting Act*, it wrote that because everything transmitted over the internet is predominately alphanumeric text, regulation was not necessary (CRTC, 1999). A decade later, the CRTC, in its New Media Project Initiative, grappled with this same issue but with an increasingly sophisticated internet universe consisting of embedded and integrated video streaming, social network sites, and a plethora of user-generated content. The commission's response, once again, was to exempt new media and mobile broadcasting from regulation, and to call for a national digital strategy (CRTC, 2009).

Conglomeration and **concentration** are structural features of the global media system, whereby a small number of media firms end up (through mergers and acquisitions) owning the majority of media products. Conglomerate media firms operate across various media platforms—television, newspapers, satellite, cable, film, publishing, and the internet. There are two main types of ownership concentration in the Canadian media today: horizontal and vertical. **Horizontal concentration of ownership** occurs when a firm in one line of media buys a major interest in another media operation not directly related to the original business, or takes a major stake in a nonmedia company. However, this form of conglomerate ownership has been eclipsed by media companies characterized by **vertical concentration of ownership** (or **cross-media ownership**), which:

> refers to the ownership or control by one entity of both programming services, such as conventional television stations, or pay and specialty services, as well as distribution services, such as cable systems or direct-to-home (DTH) satellite services. Vertical integration also includes ownership or control by one entity of both programming undertakings and production companies (CRTC, 2011, September 21).

Globalization refers to the transformation of communication spaces and social relations occurring across national borders. It is characterized by economic globalization—the integration of the global economy through free-trade mechanisms and international bodies such as the World Trade Organization (WTO); and by cultural globalization—the absorption and integration of global cultural forms into other cultural products and services. Neoliberalism, the dominant political economic system today, inflects globalization with the values (and valorization) of private markets, deregulation, and trade liberalization. Neoliberalism also permeates the ideological undercurrent of recent international ICT (information and communication technologies) policy, notably the 2003 and 2005 **World Summit on the Information Society (WSIS)**, whose multistakeholder approach brought together industry, governments, and civil society to grapple with the issues of global digital divides and information and communication technologies for development (Pickard, 2008).

Finally, **deregulation** is the belief by governments and international trade bodies that competitive markets are fostered by *not* regulating the media. The mantra of market forces weaves itself through industry hype, government rhetoric, and policy documents. But, as Robert McChesney comments, referring to the United States, "while the rhetoric extols small government, free markets, competition, and entrepreneurial risk-taking, the reality is that a large government is doling out crucial contracts, monopoly licenses, and subsidies to huge firms in highly concentrated industries" (2004, p. 51). The same can be said about Canada. Generous corporate tax benefits, government funding programs to encourage and increase Canadian innovation in the ICT sector and make Canada globally competitive, and self-regulatory measures in the ICT sector characterize our current regulatory environment.

CONCENTRATION OF MEDIA OWNERSHIP

Ben Bagdikian, former dean of the Graduate School of Journalism at the University of California at Berkeley, was one of the first media critics to write a full-length study of global media ownership concentration. In the first edition of *The Media Monopoly*, published in 1983, he documented 50 major corporations that controlled the media; by the time of the seventh edition, 21 years later, there were only 5 major media corporations.

> The leaders of the Big Five are not Hitlers and Stalins. They are American and foreign entrepreneurs whose corporate empires control every means by which the population learns of its society. And like any close-knit hierarchy, they find ways to cooperate so that all five can work together to expand their power, a power that has become a major force in shaping contemporary American life (Bagdikian, 2004, p. 4).

"Mediasaurus" is how Dwayne Winseck (2008) describes the state of media ownership, characterized by huge financial mergers, being transnationalist in scope, vertical integration between major U.S. television networks and Hollywood studios, an increased acquisition of independent firms, and being heavily owner-controlled by newsworthy men. Distinguishing between numerical diversity (the number of channels available in any given area) and source diversity (the number of media owners in a given market), Winseck concludes that, at the level of source diversity, markets are indeed becoming more consolidated.

What is perhaps more insidious is not just the symbolic power of transnational media corporations, but also their blatant political power. This is illustrated well by the case of News International, where untrammelled power was accompanied by sheer arrogance, greed, and criminality. In the summer of 2011, News Corporation (headed by CEO Rupert Murdoch) came under intense scrutiny after its British subsidiary News International and its *News of the World* tabloid was accused in a labyrinthine phone-hacking scandal. A five-year investigation by Scotland Yard revealed that hundreds of citizens, politicians, and celebrities had their personal phone records hacked by journalists intent on revealing titillating scoops for their popular readership of 2.8 million a week, and of course, the accrual of profits for the company. The tipping point was perhaps the revelation that reporters had hacked the mobile voicemail of murdered schoolgirl Milly Dowler, compromising the police investigation. The *News of the World* shuttered its operations after 168 years of operation and Murdoch was forced to withdraw his $12 billion bid for control of British Sky Broadcasting (BSkyB). Former journalists, editors, and corporate officers were arrested, police officers involved in the case resigned, and a Parliamentary panel was struck, where Murdoch and his son James (executive chairman of News International) apologized for the unethical nature of the accusations but claimed plausible deniability. In May 2012 the parliamentary committee issued its condemning report, concluding that "Rupert Murdoch is not a fit person to exercise the stewardship of a major international company" (Burns & Somaiya, 2012).[1]

The five major transnational corporations that make up the current global media-entertainment complex are Comcast Corporation, The Walt Disney

Company, News Corporation, TimeWarner Inc., and Vivendi SA. Vertical and horizontal concentration and conglomeration, interlocking boards of directors, mutual promotion and synergy amongst their media products, as well as a surprising and often bland homogeneity of content characterize each corporation (see Table 9.1).

TABLE 9.1 Top 5 Global Media Corporations

Comcast (U.S.)	Founded 1963 CEO: Brian L. Roberts Diversified entertainment, information and communications company. Principle operations are cable through Comcast Cable (operates in 39 states and the District of Columbia). In 2011 the company acquired a 51% stake in NBC Universal from General Electric. Now called NBCUniversal LLC, assets include NBC broadcast stations, cable network properties (including Bravo, CNBC, MSNBC, Oxygen, Weather Channel USA, Golf Channel, Style, and E!), Universal movie studio, Universal theme parks in Hollywood and Orlando. Through Xfinity, it provides video, high-speed internet, and phone services to residential and business customers 2011 consolidated revenue: $55.8 billion (US) Comcast Corporate Information: http://www.comcast.com Comcast Corporation Annual Report 2011: http://www.comcast.com/2011annualreview/?SCRedirect=true Information on the Comcast-NBC deal from FreePress: http://comcast.freepress.net (accessed August 24, 2012)
Walt Disney Company (U.S.)	Founded 1923 CEO: Robert Iger Diversified global entertainment company with media networks (Disney/ABC Television Network, ESPN); 11 parks and 43 resorts located globally; Disney Consumer Products; Disney Interactive Media Group 2011 consolidated revenue: $40,893 billion (US) Walt Disney Company corporate website: http://thewaltdisneycompany.com Walt Disney Company Annual Report 2011: http://cdn.media.ir.thewaltdisneycompany.com/2011/annual/WDC-10kwrap-2011.pdf Free Press Disney Ownership Chart: http://www.freepress.net/ownership/chart (accessed August 24, 2012)
News Corporation (U.S.)	Founded 1922 CEO: Rupert Murdoch Diversified global media company operating cable networks (Fox News Channel, specialty pay TV channels); filmed entertainment (film and television including 20th Century Fox, Fox Searchlight Films); television (Fox Broadcasting Company, Fox Sports); direct broadcast satellite television (BSkyB, SKY Italia, SkyDeutschland, FOXTEL); publishing (including English-language newspapers *Wall Street Journal, The Times, New York Post,* Sunday Mail); other assets (Hulu.com, American Idol.com)

TABLE 9.1 Continued

	Consolidated revenue 2011: $33,405 billion (US) News Corporation website: http://www.newscorp.com News Corporation Annual Report 2011: http://www.newscorp.com/Report2011 Free Press News Corporation ownership chart: http://www.freepress.net/ownership/chart (accessed August 24, 2012)
Time Warner (U.S.)	Founded 1985 CEO: Jeffrey Bewkes Media and entertainment company with television holdings (HBO, Turner Broadcasting System, Warner Brothers Entertainment), magazine holdings (includes *Time, Entertainment Weekly, People, InStyle, Sports Illustrated, Fortune*); Time Warner Global Media Group; online holdings include TMZ.com Consolidated revenue 2011: $28,974 billion (US) Time Warner corporate website: http://www.timewarner.com Time Warner Annual Report 201: http://b2bcdn.timeinc.com/tw/ourcompany/TWX_AR_2011.pdf Free Press News Corporation ownership chart: http://www.freepress.net/ownership/chart (accessed August 24, 2012)
Vivendi (France)	Founded 1853 CEO: Jean-Bernard Lévy Telecommunications and media entertainment company with assets including Groupe Canal (France); Universal Music Group; SFR (French telecommunications group); Maroc Telecom Group (active in Northern Africa); GVY-Brazil; Activision Blizzard (video console games) Consolidated revenue 2011: $28.8 billion euro Vivendi website: http://www.vivendi.com Vivendi Annual Report 2011: http://ir2.flife.de/data/vivendi/igb_html/index.php?bericht_id=1000003&index=&lang=ENGs *Columbia Journalism Review* "Who Owns What" chart on Vivendi: http://www.cjr.org/resources/?c=vivendi (accessed August 24, 2012)

CANADIAN MEDIA OWNERSHIP

Canada's mediascape is characterized by one of the most consolidated media systems in the world, with a high degree of cross-media ownership. What is unique about contemporary media ownership concentration is the dramatic increase in the vertical integration of media companies. And despite warnings (in the media itself!) about an economic crisis of the media industries, they are more than ever resilient and highly profitable. In fact, the Canadian media industry is the eighth largest in the world, and with the emergence of new media, the networked media economy has tripled in the last 26 years while "revenue for internet access rose from $239-million in 1996 to $6.8-billion [in 2010]"... and "online advertising grew from zero to $2.2-billion over the same time" (Winseck, August 23, 2011; see also Winseck, 2011).

The four dominant players in Canada as of Fall 2012 are BCE Inc., Shaw Communications, Quebecor, and Rogers Communications. Figure 9.1 outlines private media ownership as of Fall 2012. This current media configuration, it should be noted, will inevitably change with future buyouts and mergers.

Figure 9.1 illustrates the dominance of the "Cable + Guys" in 2012, with the incredible market power of BCE as a dominant figure in the Canadian mediascape. The rapid change in the media landscape is illustrated well by Figure 9.2 outlining private media ownership in 2009, where a "tri-opoly" of companies CTVglobemedia, Canwest, and Quebecor) reigned. From 2009 to 2012 the Canadian mediascape changed rapidly. Notably, Canwest Global Communication, which was an influential player with significant global broadcasting and publishing assets, went bankrupt in 2009. Founded in Winnipeg in the 1970s, Canwest operated the Global TV network and broadcast holdings and published ten major Canadian daily newspapers, including the *National Post*, which it bought from the (now defunct) Hollinger Inc. The company's newspaper holdings were purchased by a newly formed company called Postmedia Network while its broadcasting holdings were sold to Shaw Communications, now known as Shaw Media.

Bell, the Behemoth

Bell Canada Enterprises (BCE) is by far the largest media company in Canada, and since 2000 it has embarked on a considerable enterprise of consolidation and partnerships to ensure that it can control both content and distribution. Its Bell Media division purchased the CHUM radio stations in 2006, the assets of the CTVglobemedia broadcasting empire in 2010, and in 2012 announced its intent to acquire Astral Media. These acquisitions have been propelled by the need to accumulate content for display on a variety of mobile and wireless devices and as well to strategically position the company in certain geographical markets. For instance, its bid to acquire for $3.38 billion Quebec-based Astral Media was seen as a tangible way for BCE to make lucrative inroads into Quebec and to thus compete with media stalwarts Quebecor and CBC/Radio-Canada, which are dominantly positioned in that francophone market (Rubin & Lu, 2012). The aggregate viewership of Bell and Astral businesses is estimated to be 32 percent (CBC News, 2012, March 16). Three smaller cable companies–Quebecor Inc., Cogeco Cable, and Eastlink—initiated an online campaign (saynotobell. ca) against the proposed merger. The campaign warned consumers of higher costs and lessened Canadian culture should the deal be approved by the government, and urged them to contact the CRTC and the Competition Bureau. To secure exclusive content to be disseminated via its wireless and broadcasting networks, in 2012 Bell also partnered with rival Rogers to purchase for $1.07 billion Maple Leaf Sports and Entertainment, the largest sports franchise company in Canada, which owns the NHL's Toronto Maple Leafs, the NBA's Toronto Raptors, Major League Soccer's Toronto FC, the AHL's Toronto

FIGURE 9.1 Private Media Ownership in Canada, 2012

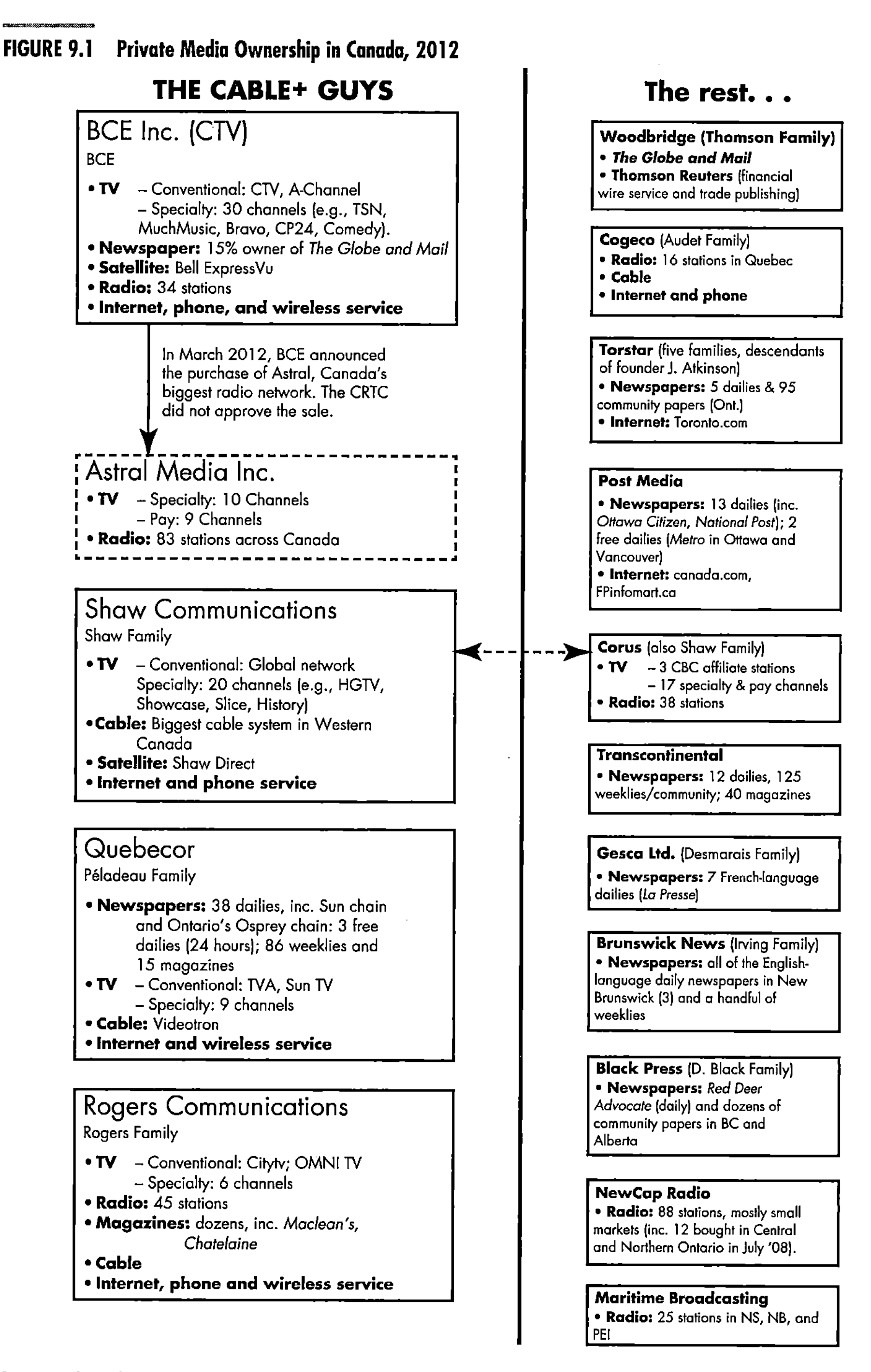

Source: Canadian Media Guild <http://www.cmg.ca/en/wp-content/uploads/2011/06/Media-ownership-chart-2012.pdf> Reproduced with permission.

FIGURE 9.2 Private Media Ownership in Canada, 2009

THE "TRI-OPOLY"

CTV Globemedia
Woodbridge Co Ltd., Teachers Pension, Torstar, BCE

- **Newspapers:** *The Globe and Mail*
- **TV** – Conventional: CTV, A-Channel (6 stations)
  – Specialty: 26 Channels (e.g., TSN, MuchMusic)
- **Radio:** 34 stations
- **Internet:** workopolis.com (40%)

Canwest
Asper Family

- **Newspapers:** 13 dailies (inc. *Ottawa Citizen, National Post*); 2 free dailies (*Metro* in Ottawa and Vancouver)
- **TV** – Conventional: Global (9 local stations, closing or selling five E! stations)
  – Specialty: CW Television (21 channels, e.g., Showcase, HGTV, Discovery, History)
- **Internet:** canada.com, FPinfomart.ca

Quebecor
Péladeau Family

- **Newspapers:** 38 dailies, inc. Sun chain and Ontario's Osprey chain; 3 free dailies (24 hours); 86 weeklies and 15 magazines
- **TV** – Videotron cable
  – Conventional: TVA, Sun TV
  – Specialty: 9 channels
- **Internet:** canoe.ca, jobboom.com (more than 12 sites)

CANADA'S "LARGEST RADIO NETWORK"

Astral Media Inc.
- **TV** – Specialty: 10 channels
  – Pay: 6 channels
- **Radio:** 80 stations across Canada
- **Internet:** TATV

Note: This chart does not include public and public-service media, including CBC/Radio-Canada, TVOntario, Knowledge Network, Télé-Québec, APTN, and Canadian Press, or independents.

The Cable+ Guys. . .

Rogers
- **Cable**
- **TV** – Conventional: Citytv (five stations); OMNI TV in Toronto
  – Specialty: 6 channels
- **Radio:** 45 stations
- **Magazines:** dozens, including *Maclean's, Chatelaine*

Corus/Shaw
- **Cable**
- **TV** – 3 CBC affiliate stations
  – 10 specialty stations
  – 2 pay TV stations
- **Radio:** 53 stations
- **Internet:** corusnouvelles.com
- **Satellite:** Star Choice

Cogeco
- **Cable**
- **TV** – Canal Indigo (32%)
- **Radio:** 2 stations

Waiting to gobble or be gobbled?

Torstar
- **Newspapers:** 5 dailies & 95 community papers (Ont.)
- **Internet:** Toronto.com

– Torstar owns 20% of CTV

Transcontinental
- **Newspapers:** 12 dailies, 125 weeklies/community; 40 magazines

Gesca Ltd. (Power Corp)
- **Newspapers:** 7 French-language dailies (*La Presse*)

Irving (Brunswick News)
- **Newspapers:** all of the English-language daily newspapers in New Brunswick (3) and a handful of weeklies

NewCap Radio
(Newfoundland Capital Corp.)
- **Radio:** 88 stations, mostly small markets

Maritime Broadcasting
- **Radio:** 25 stations in NS, NB, and PEI

Source: Canadian Media Guild. http://www.cmg.ca/Reproduced with permission.

Marlies, and the Air Canada Centre. Rogers also owns the Toronto Blue Jays baseball team, the Rogers Centre, and the Sportsnet broadcaster. The deal, approved by the CRTC in August 2012, highlights how crucial competitive sports and sports franchises are for the profitability of the media industries (CBC News, 2012, May 2). In approving the transaction, CRTC Chairman Jean-Pierre Blais stated that the deal was in the public interest, as it was creating "new home-based sports programming" (Trichor, 2012).

Concerns about media ownership concentration in Canada are not new. In 1970, the Davey Senate Committee on the Mass Media warned that daily newspapers were owned by fewer and fewer owners. The Royal Commission on Newspapers (Kent Commission) reiterated this concern in 1981, at which time the three largest chains controlled 57 percent of the daily circulation. In December 2011 group ownership characterizes newspaper ownership, with the top three groups composed of Sun Media (Quebecor)/Osprey, Postmedia Network Inc. (formerly Canwest), and Médias Transcontinental (Canadian Newspaper Association, 2011). Table 9.2 details these holdings.

In their annual *Communications Monitoring Report* (2011) the CRTC reported that in 2010 the television broadcasting industry delivered over 700 services. The major English-language private conventional companies include BCE (CTV and the A Channel, revenue shares 47 percent), Shaw (Global, revenue share 33 percent), and Rogers (CityTV and Omni, revenue shares 14 percent). In the French-language market the private conventional companies include Quebecor (TVA, revenue share 65 percent) and Remstar (V, revenue share 18 percent). CBC, the national public broadcaster, operates in both the English- and French-language markets. There are also several public provincial broadcasters, such as TVO in Ontario and the Knowledge Network in BC.

In 2010 the radio market industry comprises over 1,200 radio and audio services, with 99 percent of these over the air and 1 percent delivered by **BDU**s (broadcasting distribution undertaking, which can be a cable, satellite, or microwave distributor). Private commercial broadcasters account for 61 percent of radio services, the CBC 8 percent, and 30 percent are from Aboriginal, community, campus, and religious services. The largest English-language private radio operators are Astral, with revenue shares at 21 percent, Corus (16 percent), Rogers (13 percent), BCE (10 percent), and Newcap (7 percent). The largest French-language private radio operators include Astral (44 percent), Corus (22 percent) and Cogeco (17 percent). CBC, the national public broadcaster, operates in both the English- and French-language markets.

It is clear from this brief overview of Canadian media ownership that the terrain shifts dramatically in response to economic and technological trends. Returning to the aforementioned CRTC Diversity of Voices decision, Lise Lareau, president of the Canadian Media Guild, commented that "It doesn't change anything" (Robertson, 2008). The decision "allows the big players to become bigger, and does very little if anything to limit media concentration in Canada," echoed Peter

TABLE 9.2 Canadian Daily Newspaper Ownership

Quebecor/Sun Media/Osprey Media (36)	*Barrie Examiner*
	Beacon-Herald, Stratford
	Brockville Recorder & Times
	Chatham Daily News
	Cornwall Standard-Freeholder
	Daily Graphic, Portage La Prairie
	Daily Miner & News, Kenora
	Daily Observer, Pembroke
	Daily Herald-Tribune, Grande Prairie
	The Daily Press, Timmins
	The Expositor, Brantford
	Fort McMurray Today
	The Intelligence, Belleville
	Kingston Whig-Standard
	Le Journal de Montréal
	Le Journal de Québec
	London Free Press
	Niagara Falls Review
	The North Bay Nuggett
	Northumberlandtoday.com
	The Observer, Sarnia
	Packet & Times, Orillia,
	Peterborough Examiner
	Sault Star
	Sentinel Review, Woodstock
	Simcoe Reformer
	Sudbury Star
	Sun brand: Toronto, Edmonton, Winnipeg, Calgary & Ottawa *Sun*
	Sentinel Review, Woodstock
	St. Catharines Standard
	The Sun Times, Owen Sound
	St. Thomas Times-Journal
	The Tribune, Welland
Postmedia Network Inc. (10)	*Calgary Herald*
	The Gazette, Montreal
	Leader-Post, Regina
	National Post
	Ottawa Citizen
	The Province, Vancouver
	StarPhoenix, Saskatoon
	Vancouver Sun
	Windsor Star

TABLE 9.2 Continued

Transcontinental Inc. (10)	*Amherst Daily News*
	Cape Breton Post
	Evening News, New Glasgow
	The Guardian, Charlottetown
	Journal Pioneer, PEI
	Prince Albert Daily Herald
	Times-Herald Moose Jaw
	Truro Daily News
	The Telegram, St. John's
	Western Star, Corner Brook
Power Corp. of Canada (7)	*Le Droit*, Ottawa/Gatineau
	Le Nouvelliste, Trois Rivieres
	La Presse, Montreal
	Le Quoitidien, Chicoutimi
	Le Soleil, Quebec
	La Tribune, Sherbrooke
	La Voix de l'Est, Granby
Glacier Canadian Newspapers (7)	*Alaska Highway News*, Fort St. John
	Alberni Valley Times, Port Alberni
	The Citizen, Prince George
	Dawson Creek Daily News,
	The Kamloops Daily News
	Nanaimo Daily News
	Times Colonist, Victoria
Torstar (4)	*Guelph Mercury*
	The Hamilton Spectator
	The Record, Grand River Valley
	Toronto Star
Other	Black Press: *Red Deer Advocate, The Trail Times, Cranbrook Daily Townsman, The Daily Bulletin*, Kimberley
	CTVglobemedia: *The Globe and Mail*
	Continental Newspapers Ltd: *Penticton Herald, The Daily Courier*, Kelowna; *The Chronicle Journal*, Thunder Bay
	F.P. Canadian Newspapers LP: *Winnipeg Free Press* *Brandon Sun*
	Glacier Canadian Newspapers/Alta Newspaper Group: *Lethbridge Herald, Medicine Hat News, The Record*, Sherbrooke
	Halifax Herald Inc: *The Chronicle Herald*
	Sing Tao Newspapers Ltd.: *Sing Tao Daily* (50 percent with Torstar)
Independent	*L'Acadie Nouvelle*, Caraquet
	Le Devoir, Montreal
	The Whitehorse Star

Source: From *Canadian Daily Newspaper Ownership* Dec. 2011 <www.newspaperscanada.ca/sites/default/files/Ownership%20Daily%20DECEMBER%202011.pdf> Canadian Newspaper Association.

Murdoch, vice-president of media with the Communications, Energy and Paperworkers union (Trichur, 2008). Their remarks have proved to be prescient, as the current climate of heightened mergers in an era of untrammelled communicative capitalism raises the question of democratic accountability.

A policy concern that has emerged in connection with concentration of media ownership is journalistic freedom. The choice and quality of news can be undermined as controversial topics are deemed too sensitive to explore (Hackett & Uzelman, 2003). Naomi Klein, addressing the ethical implications of journalistic self-censorship, argued that under conglomeration, "the zones where journalists are expected to tread cautiously are also stretching. It becomes awkward to cover not only one's parent company, for fear of being accused of boosterism, but all of their holdings, and their competitors' as well, for fear that it will seem like sour grapes" (Klein, 2000, p. A15). For instance, in 2002 CanWest came under intense criticism from local citizens and national and international newspaper unions for centralizing its editorial policy and in some cases firing editors and columnists who did not conform to ideological prescriptions. The company's actions galvanized local citizens to debate the notion of editorial freedom and media democracy (Shade, 2005). Policy initiatives such as Diversity of Voices seemed expressly positioned to address some of these concerns—even though, according to many, in the end they failed to do so.

Media labour has also attracted attention. With cross-media platforms, what is the responsibility of management to workers in compensating for their intellectual property that can be printed in a daily newspaper and then repurposed to a website? Can employees working in one division of a conglomerate legally do work for another division during a labour dispute? These issues were raised in the longest media strike in a decade, when the Journal de Quebec workers walked out on Quebecor, with the Canadian Union of Public Employees (CUPE) seeking a more balanced and equitable control of its work as the company reorganized for an increasingly digital environment (Surridge & Malhomme, 2008).

Another important policy controversy is foreign ownership in the broadcasting and telecommunications sectors. For as long as there have been broadcasting and telecommunications markets, Canadian regulators and the Canadian public have had concerns about who should be allowed to own the companies that provide these services and fill our airwaves with programming. In recent years there is growing support in some quarters for opening Canadian markets to foreign owned companies. In 2011, the federal government successfully challenged the CRTC's decision to deny an Egyptian-based mobile phone company the right to sell services in Canada (CBC, 2011), as discussed in more detail in Chapter 5. And in 2012, the Canadian government announced plans to lift foreign restrictions altogether for telecommunications companies with less than 10 percent of market share by revenue (CBC, 2012, March 14). Once again, what is at stake depends in large part on whom you ask.

Debates about foreign ownership generally reflect tensions between three dominant stakeholders: industry organizations, the government, and civil society representatives. In Europe and in North America, foreign ownership restrictions tend to reflect three broad areas of concern (Globerman, 1995). The first reflects restrictions intended to protect sovereign power and the ability to control what happens within a national territory by (i) protecting services important to national defence, (ii) maintaining political leverage over telecommunications providers; and (iii) protecting public monopolies. The second set of concerns reflects attitudes toward economic outcomes with policies intended to (i) protect incumbent advantages for domestic companies, (ii) promote regional development, and (iii) preserve domestic monopolies. And third, restrictions are sometimes justified in terms of reciprocity in response to policies restricting foreign ownership in other jurisdictions. We can add to this list the policy objectives that emerge from concerns about **cultural sovereignty** and the degree to which cultural content should reflect the histories, experiences, and concerns of communities within the geographic boundaries of Canada (Raboy, 1990).

It is difficult to argue against the importance of public access to cultural content that reflects local, regional, and national concerns and experiences. And yet, policies that promote and protect cultural sovereignty have come under increasing criticism from various stakeholders who prefer market-based justifications over regulation to address these kinds of concerns. There are no simple solutions. At best, we can identify the range of key issues to consider when questions of foreign ownership restrictions arise in a Canadian context, as detailed in Table 9.3.

With so few media companies dominating so much of the Canadian mediascape, should Canadians be worried about who owns Canadian culture? In an intervention to the CRTC about vertical integration, Karen Wirsig of the Canadian Media Guild and Cathy Edwards of CACTUS (Canadian Association of Community Television Users and Stations) expressed concerns that "broadcasters that are not part of an integrated ownership group—CBC/Radio-Canada, provincial broadcasters, community stations, independent private stations—stand to lose in this brave new world of vertical integration and commercial negotiations" (Wirsig & Edwards, 2011, p. 3).

TABLE 9.3 Considerations Regarding Foreign Ownership in Broadcasting and Telecommunications

Political sovereignty	National defence
	Political leverage over corporations
	Protecting public monopolies
Cultural sovereignty	Problems with national identity and social exclusions (see below)
	Diversity of voices that reflect Canadian demographics
	Developing Canadian cultural expertise and talent
Public interest and democratic governance	Quality local, regional, and national information
	Diversity of stakeholder interests reflected
	Maintaining accountability of public and private institutions and public officials
Economic	Encourage regional development
	Protect incumbent advantages for domestically owned companies
	Consumer prices
Reciprocity jurisdictions	In response to foreign ownership restrictions in other jurisdictions

What then are strategies for safeguarding Canadian sovereignty that Canadian citizens can enact? Reflecting on the impact of the News Corporation hacking scandal, discussed above, Robert Hackett and David Skinner (2012) argue that such media controversies, albeit egregious and detrimental to the public interest, can educate and mobilize the public to counter through responsive policy reactions designed to strengthen media democracy principles. The media reform movement is one example of advocacy for media policies and institutions in the public interest.

MEDIA REFORM IN CANADA

The regulation of media in Canada has a built-in role for the Canadian public. The CRTC oversees the creation of media policy through a process that invites public participation and comment on significant policy changes. Public hearings can attract thousands of submissions. The Diversity of Voices hearings in 2004 received close to 2,000 submissions; policy review hearings for community television in 2010 received over 3,000 submissions; and proposed changes to internet fees for consumers (i.e., usage-based billing) also in 2010, were stopped in part through widespread participation of the Canadian public (a petition against the changes was signed by more than 500,000 Canadians presented by citizen's group OpenMedia). Public involvement is a cornerstone of media policy in Canada.

This does not mean, however, that the policy formation process in Canada is without critics. The Standing Committee on Canadian Heritage, for example (an all-party Parliamentary committee), in its 2003 report *Our Cultural Sovereignty*, expressed concern about conflicts of interest on the part of CRTC commissioners, noting that critics "worry that a revolving door exists which allows those serving on the Commission to come from industry or law firms that deal with the Commission and then go back to industry after their terms are over" (Canada, 2003, p. 568). Citizens groups have also criticized the public hearing process as being onerous and requiring significant commitments of time, resources, and expertise largely out of reach for most Canadians. Throughout the evolution of the Canadian media industries, media reform organizations have emerged to address these kinds of deficits by bringing together scholars, activists, and media professionals with different levels of expertise in an effort to coordinate policy submissions in the public interest. The challenge for these groups, however, has always been sustainability and funding; while industry groups can finance regulatory interventions and contract research with the profits they accrue from their businesses, public interest groups in Canada continue to struggle to finance their efforts and rely on volunteer support. In response to these concerns, in 2012 the CRTC announced the creation of the Broadcasting Participation Fund designed specifically to help public-interest and consumer groups offset the costs of participating in the CRTC's broadcasting proceedings.

The media reform movement in Canada comprises diverse public interest organizations and citizen-based initiatives that aim to conceptualize a vision to reform and reframe media institutions and policies for broader values vital for social well-being and democratic communication. Shade (2011) states that media reform "refers to a social movement, citizen actions countering encroaching media consolidation and commercialization, and policy interventions to protect, promote, and promulgate the public interest" (p. 147) and is "characterized by four often overlapping elements: media criticism, education and literacy; creating, producing, and distributing independent media; media policy activism; and media justice" (p. 150). In the mid-2000s in the United States, buoyed by foundation support and a lively community of activists and momentous policy victories with respect to media ownership caps and low-power FM radio, the movement consisted of an array of groups concerned with media concentration, racial justice, children's rights, gender equity, and digital policy issues such as net neutrality, broadband access, and copyright and digital rights management. Canadian media reform activities coalesced around similar issues, with efforts to reframe policies for the public interest played out in Senate committees, and through Industry Canada, the Department of Canadian Heritage, the Office of the Privacy Commissioner of Canada, and, most intensely, CRTC hearings. Table 9.4 provides a summary of some key Canadian media reform organizations and policy moments.

Labour organizations have also focused on media reform campaigns: the 6,000 member-led Canadian Media Guild has in recent years drawn attention to the impact of strategic cuts in the media industry, (http://www.cmg.ca) and the Communications, Energy & Paperworkers Union concentrates on the impact of increased foreign ownership in the telecom sector (http://www.cep.ca). The gender dynamics of labour in the media industries was the focus of a 2010 conference held in Vancouver; Women in View raised awareness of the paucity of empirical data about the status of women in the film and digital media field as producers, directors, and content creators, and highlighted systemic barriers toward equity (Murray & Beale, 2011). The Toronto-held Making Media Public Conference in 2010 also analyzed the state of labour in the Canadian mediascape, drawing attention to the decline in funding for public service media, the need to improve working conditions for media workers, and the need for policies to protect the intellectual property of freelance journalists working in a media system that digitizes and repurposes their work across different media platforms (Cohen et al., 2011).

PUBLIC BROADCASTING, CULTURAL CITIZENSHIP, AND DEMOCRATIC ACCOUNTABILITY

Media convergence, concentration of ownership, and concern for accountable governance raise questions about Canada's public culture. How can we best ensure that it reflects the public interest values of a democratic society?

The Canadian *Broadcasting Act* is the legislative framework governing broadcast media. Section 3 of the act states that Canada's broadcasting system is made

TABLE 9.4 Media Reform Organizations

Organization	Key People	Policy Issues	Objectives and Results
Canadian Radio League, 1930s	Graham Spry and Alan Plaunt	Lobby for the implementation of the 1929 Royal Commission on Radio Broadcasting (Aird Commission) to advocate for public radio in Canada. What could make it distinct from U.S. radio?	The Canadian *Broadcasting Act* of 1932 created the CRBC (Canadian Radio Broadcasting Commission). This established public broadcasting and eventually the CBC.
Friends of Canadian Broadcasting, founded 1985 http://www.friends.ca	Ian Morrison, spokesperson Support: 66,000 individual volunteer donations; contributions from the CRTC or organizations affiliated with licensees are not accepted.	Defends public, private, and community broadcasting.	Monitors the media, commissions independent research, prepares briefs and CRTC policy submissions. Advocates for CBC funding, influenced direction of *Broadcasting Act* of 1991 and Canadian Heritage study on broadcasting policy.
Canadian Campaign for Press and Broadcasting Freedom, founded mid-1990s	Coalition of academics, activists, and labour/community groups, such as Council of Canadians.	Media concentration and media diversity.	Promoted legislation to address ownership concentration; recommended limiting and reversing levels of media ownership concentration; providing measures to promote diversity in media ownership; and encouraging social responsibility in the media.
Media Action Média (MAM) (formerly MediaWatch), founded 1981. http://www.media-action-media.com	Founded initially under auspices of National Action Committee on the Status of Women. Then independent organization, membership comprising industry professionals, academics, students, and citizens. Now virtual board.	Improve media representations and equity of women in the media industries through research and policy.	Development of CRTC guidelines on sex-role stereotyping guidelines as a condition of licence; undertaking media content analyses on sexism in newspapers, television, magazines, and radio; working with the Canadian Advertising Foundation on the revision of sex-role stereotyping guidelines; and serving as the Canadian representative for the Global Media Monitoring Campaigns (run by the WACC). Currently reports on diversity in Canadian television drama; increasing women's voices in opeds through Informed Opinions.

TABLE 9.4 Continued

Organization	Key People	Policy Issues	Objectives and Results
OpenMedia.ca (formerly Campaign for Democratic Media) 2007 http://openmedia.ca	Steve Anderson, executive director. National, nonprofit, and nonpartisan media reform organization. Membership: network of civil society, consumer, labour and media advocacy organizations, grassroots activists, and academics.	Increase public awareness and informed participation in Canadian media, cultural, information, and telecommunication policy formation. Campaigns advocate for an open internet.	"Stop Big Media" campaign re: 2007 CRTC Diversity of Voices hearing. SaveOurNet.ca campaign on net neutrality, 2010. Petitioning CRTC for licensing of English-language service of Al Jazeera international television news network, 2010. StoptheMeter.ca campaign against usage-based billing, compelling the CRTC to revisit its original decision, 2011. Stop Online Spying, against Bill C-30, a cyber-surveillance bill, 2012.

up of three constituting elements: private media, public broadcasting, and community media. The act sets out goals and objectives for all broadcast media, many of which are specifically aimed at protecting some element of the public interest (See Appendix A). The degree to which these policy objectives are realized is a matter for debate, but the intent behind them suggests a continuing belief in the importance of public interest when making decisions about broadcasting in Canada.

Public Service Broadcasting

The creation of a national broadcaster is one of the ways that the government of Canada has tried to protect public interests within the Canadian broadcasting system. The CBC was created in 1932 to protect Canadian culture from the threat of American radio networks whose programs at the time dominated Canadian airwaves. The CBC's mandate, according to then Prime Minister R. B. Bennett, was to foster "national consciousness" and "national unity" and to ensure that all Canadians, regardless of "class or place" could have "equal enjoyment of the benefits and pleasures of radio broadcasting" (Romanow, 2005). Today, the CBC has grown into a large multiplatform media network encompassing two national television services, 50 regional television stations, two national radio services, and online and satellite services that reach global audiences. CBC's services are offered in English, French, eight Aboriginal languages, and seven languages for international audiences. In its 2010–11 *Annual Report*, the CBC reported its English-language radio audience at 14.7 percent of the national market, and its English-language prime-time television at 9.3 percent; for French-language radio, CBC's share was 19.5 percent and 19.9 percent for prime-time Télévision de Radio-Canada (all figures from BBM Canada). CBC.ca and Radio-Canada.ca reported more than 7.5 million unique visitors per month (CBC Radio Canada, 2011). The CBC continues to be a relevant force in Canadian culture.

Many argue that public-service broadcasting is "a necessary democratic agency" that needs to be invigorated through sustained public support (McChesney, 1999). This is founded on the belief that public broadcasting can fulfill a cultural role that markets are unable or unwilling to provide. Others, however, question the legitimacy of public broadcasting, especially within a context of increasingly disaggregated and global audiences in a digital world.

These questions have had particular resonance recently as the CBC/Radio Canada prepares for its first licence renewal hearings in more than a decade (the hearings are scheduled for November 2012 (CBC, 2012, May 18). The CBC has come under increasing pressure from private-sector stakeholders and conservative detractors. Through a series of high-profile and costly access-to-information requests, Quebecor, one of the largest private media groups in Canada, provoked the CBC into releasing more financial information than required under existing legislation (Allick, 2011). And in 2012, the federal Conservative government made comparatively severe budget cuts to the CBC, decreasing funding by $115 million over a three-year period (CBC, 2012, April 4).

Some of the difficulty in coming to terms with public broadcasting in the 21st century reflects changing expectations about its role. There has always been an expectation that public broadcasting serve in the "public interest," but what this means exactly shifts over time in response to changing public concerns and who the relevant stakeholders are in any given period. The idea of "public interest" can point to policy equanimities—for example, the levels of procedural fairness at work in particular broadcasting policies, how representative they are of public opinion, and the degree to which they articulate commonalities or conciliatory compromise between competing actors (Pal & Maxwell, 2004). "Public interest" can also refer to specific outcomes—from the nationalist aspirations of urban, English-speaking residents of central Canada in the mid-20th century; to a desire for technical and bureaucratic modes of functioning in the 1950s and 1960s; to the accommodation of forms of public discontent in the 1970s; to an emphasis on consumer choice and a neoliberal tendency toward deregulation in the late-20th and early 21st centuries (McCauley, 2003; Raboy, 1990). Civil society advocates in the communications sector have also advanced various and differing claims on behalf of the public, including universal access, privacy protection, and the creation of Canadian content (Shade, 2008); opportunities for self-expression (Napoli & Aslama, 2011); job creation, literacy, health benefits, public safety, and civic participation (Dailey & Powell, 2011); and public broadcasting as an antidote to the power of wealth over the airwaves (Basen, 2003). The "public interest" represents a discursive territory where public 'will' competes for legitimacy with the market demands of the private sector and the regulatory objectives of the state.

One of the hurdles for proponents of public broadcasting in the 21st century is criticism of some of the traditional justifications for state-run media. For example, national broadcasting is generally lauded as a tool for creating and maintaining national identity, but whose identity often reflects social inclusions/exclusions based on race, ethnicity, sexual orientation, gender, and language (Aula, 2000; Clarke, 1997; Dhruvarajan, 2000; Gregg, 2006; Jiwani, 1998). Technological changes are also challenging traditional justifications for public broadcasting. In an increasingly networked and global cultural milieu, cultural protectionism based on terrestrial borders appears in some respects anachronistic. These questions have yet to be resolved.

Another factor to consider in assessing the role of public broadcasting in the 21st century is the failure of market-based strategies in and of themselves to adequately address certain cultural needs. Without regulatory intervention, for example, private broadcasting markets have consistently failed to provide reliable quality local news coverage to all but the largest, urban markets (CRTC, 2009, July 6). Similarly, the high cost of developing Canadian television drama has consistently proven to be an obstacle to its production by private-sector stakeholders without government subsidy or tax incentives. Left to market mechanisms alone, it isn't clear if there would be opportunities for developing Canadian cultural expertise in these areas, or how well the broadcasting system would serve rural, coastal, and northern communities. In recognizing these failures, public interest advocates argue that investing in public broadcasting is one of the ways Canadians can invest in democratic futures. For example, cultural policies that improve public access to reliable information serve democratic goals that are hard to value in market terms (e.g., the provision of reliable and relevant information to citizens making political decisions). Public broadcasting can also play an essential role: in the protection and preservation of cultural memory and heritage; in encouraging diversity of opinions in political discussions; in fostering the development of Canadian talent and expertise; in helping to achieve social justice objectives; and in promoting the accountability of both public and private institutions. These are all worthy objectives, and they elude easy assessment in market terms. Any appraisal of the role of public broadcasting and its continued relevance in Canadian society must take these issues into account or risk ignoring the profound and changing ways cultural production and consumption shape democratic outcomes.

TECHNOPOLES, THE PUBLIC SPHERE, AND CULTURAL CITIZENSHIP

Concerns reflecting the changing expectations for public broadcasting in the 21st century draw attention to more fundamental questions about the importance of public participation in cultural environments. The excitement over digital, networked, and increasingly global cultural and economic flows often obscures their dependence on the material locations and historic conditions on which digital information networks depend. Labour, finance, infrastructure, managerial expertise, and institutional capacity are all required to recreate and maintain what Canadian communications scholar Vincent Mosco calls "technopoles," locations where technical capacities (in relation to global, digital networks for the exchange of information and commerce) have outstripped citizenship capacities in their social importance (Mosco, 1997). Technopoles often emerge in what Saskia Sassen calls "global cities" where, among other things, pools of inexpensive and often socially and politically vulnerable labour can be accessed by those with managerial control over capital to provide the services on which the infrastructures of information depend (Sassen, 2006). The paradox, of course, is that while emergent global information networks offer opportunities for expanding forms of cultural participation, they depend in part on these domains where economic growth supersedes all other social values.

As we saw in a previous section, convergence and technological changes are transforming the mediascape. Big media is getting bigger, more centralized, more hierarchical. Concentration of media ownership is on the increase. But another trend has emerged in connection with new technologies—an unprecedented proliferation of collaborative cultural production through decentralized networks of individuals and groups. As Henry Jenkins (2006) writes: "Patterns of media consumption have been profoundly altered by a succession of new media technologies which enable average citizens to participate in the archiving, annotation, appropriation, transformation and re-circulation of media content" (p. 554). Digital media and new technologies have created infrastructures that allow increased participation in culture through fragmented, bottom-up collaborative efforts, and some scholars have argued that these emerging networks are transforming "the very foundation of how liberal markets and liberal democracies have co-evolved for two centuries" (Benkler, 2006, p. 1) These changes register most loudly in the ways that citizen-led cultural engagement is transforming political landscapes.

Discussions about media ownership and influence over cultural outcomes must take into account the kinds of "ownerships" exercised by individuals and groups through blogging, independent film and documentary, online social networking, streaming video, podcasts, etc., and how these disaggregated cultural efforts are influencing Canada's social and political reality. If big media is one side of the digital coin, then citizen's media is the other.

What makes this significant in democratic terms is the nexus between culture and wider social and political transformations—what some communications scholars refer to as "cultural citizenship" (Stanley, 2006). Cultural citizenship represents the opposite tendency to that of technopoles and describes how cultural participation increases influence over social and political realities. Cultural citizenship, for example, links culture with the political importance of identity. Projects such as the Aboriginal Peoples Television Network (see Chapter 18) allow historically marginalized or excluded communities to assert control over how they are represented in public forums. Cultural participation also brings people together—to share ideas, to celebrate, to express themselves, to create, to be entertained and to learn—which builds networks among strangers and creates opportunities for collective responses to social and political problems. A good example of this is the Dominion Media Co-ops, which maintain a network of websites across Canada (locally based in Halifax, Toronto, Montreal, Ottawa, and Vancouver) where thousands of contributors share citizen journalism, opinion, commentary, video, photos, and audio documentaries, and participate in ongoing conversations about issues of public relevance in Canada and around the world, and often engage in strategic conversations about changing political outcomes (see http://www.mediacoop.ca). Opportunities for collaboration in turn increase levels of social trust, which are essential for establishing senses of belonging and acceptance (Stanley, 2006).

The consumption of culture and its economic outcomes are one aspect of cultural reality in Canadian society, but economic factors describe only a small part of what happens when citizens participate in the technologically diverse mediascapes that make up their day-to-day cultural lives. Cultural citizenship expresses at a more fundamental level the implications of not only media ownership, but also ownership over the processes that give us our collective sense of what it means to be Canadian.

CONCLUSION

Media concentration and cross-media ownership raise important questions about the lack of diversity in news content, a lessening of local coverage, and paucity in the diversity of sources. Are Canadian media providing quality news coverage of international political and social issues? How have economic pressures in Canadian media companies influenced the autonomy and professionalism of journalists? Do convergence and globalization create opportunities for the Canadian media industry, or do they threaten Canadian sovereignty and cultural diversity?

The high levels of concentrated ownership in Canada, some of the highest in the Western world, should have Canadians thinking about the answers to these questions. Convergence, consolidation, deregulation, and globalization continue to be influential trends in the emerging social and economic realities of the 21st century in Canada and elsewhere. Canada's public culture is dominated by large commercial media companies that play an increasingly central role in every aspect of modern, technological society—not least of which is in the formation and exercise of public accountability in democratic terms.

As this chapter highlights, movements and strategies have emerged with an interest in protecting public interest in culture. The CBC, Canada's public broadcaster, has a mandate to nurture Canadian culture. And Canadians have turned to policy reform as a way to ensure public interest concerns are taken into consideration when laws and regulations are formed. Important public issues such as **net neutrality** and the auctioning off of radio spectrum, continue to be unresolved territories where media governance is pitted against private and public interests, with policymakers in between. What is at stake, ultimately, in all of these endeavours, is the degree to which Canadians are allowed to participate in the ongoing formation of Canadian society.

Citizen as consumer is one of the ways that Canadians participate in culture. Undeniably, the ways markets negotiate cultural exchange (i.e., the supply and demand of cultural goods) has a profound impact on our daily lives. But a focus on only consumption obscures other important cultural processes. Canadians *making* culture are involved in shaping Canadian society based on their experiences, histories, and interests. Participation in culture helps determine and define social reality on a day-to-day basis and allows the public to play an important role in exercising "ownership" over Canada's democracy.

Thanks to David Skinner for his astute comments on an earlier version of this chapter.

APPENDIX A

THE CANADIAN BROADCASTING ACT, SECTION 3

(i) the Canadian broadcasting system should be effectively owned and controlled by Canadians;

(ii) the Canadian broadcasting system should provide through its programming, a public service essential to the maintenance and enhancement of national identity and cultural sovereignty;

(iii) the Canadian broadcasting system should serve to safeguard, enrich and strengthen the cultural, political, social and economic fabric of Canada;

(iv) the Canadian broadcasting system should encourage the development of Canadian expression by providing a wide range of programming that reflects Canadian attitudes, opinions, ideas, values and artistic creativity, by displaying Canadian talent in entertainment programming and by offering information and analysis concerning Canada and other countries from a Canadian point of view;

(v) the Canadian broadcasting system should through its programming and the employment opportunities arising out of its operations, serve the needs and interests, and reflect the circumstances and aspirations, of Canadian men, women and children, including equal rights, the linguistic duality and multicultural and multiracial nature of Canadian society and the special place of aboriginal peoples within that society;

(vi) the programming provided by the Canadian broadcasting system should be varied and comprehensive, providing a balance of information, enlightenment and entertainment for men, women and children of all ages, interests and tastes; be drawn from local, regional, national and international sources; include educational and community programs; provide a reasonable opportunity for the public to be exposed to the expression of differing views on matters of public concern, and include a significant contribution from the Canadian independent production sector;

(vii) the Canadian Broadcasting Corporation, as the national public broadcaster, should provide radio and television services incorporating a wide range of programming that informs, enlightens and entertains;

(viii) the programming provided by the Corporation should be predominantly and distinctively Canadian, reflect Canada and its regions to national and regional audiences, while serving the special needs of those regions, actively contribute to the flow and exchange of cultural expression, be in English and in French, reflecting the different needs and circumstances of each official language community, including the particular needs and circumstances of English and French linguistic minorities, strive to be of equivalent quality in English and in French, contribute to shared national consciousness and identity, reflect the multicultural and multiracial nature of Canada.

QUESTIONS

1. Reflect on the policy objectives for the *Broadcasting Act.* Do you agree that these are important objectives? Do you see them reflected in the television that you watch? The radio that you listen to? What goals do you think are missing?
2. Do you think that Canada has a distinct culture? Try to identify specific attributes of Canadian culture and list them. Do you think that these are reflected in public service broadcasting? What *should* a public broadcaster in Canada do? What shouldn't it do?
3. Thinking about the difference between a consumer of culture and a culture maker, identify at least three ways that you consume culture and three ways that you make culture. How are they different? How are they similar?
4. Identify three social identities. Where do they come from? Are they positive or negative? Think of ways that individual Canadians could change the social identities that you identified. In what ways is media ownership significant to your answer?
5. Can you think of one or more examples from your own life where participation in a cultural process (online or otherwise) has led to collaboration, increased social networks, or some kind of group effort? Describe. In what ways do you think your group activities contributed to or influenced Canadian culture?

NOTE

1. For more on "MurdochGate" see a timeframe of events at *The New York Times* (2011, November 29), Anatomy of the News International scandal. Retrieved August 2, 2012, from http://www.nytimes.com/interactive/2010/09/01/

magazine/05tabloid-timeline.html?ref=europe; see also a visual of the players at *Bloomberg Businessweek* (2011), News Corp.'s tangled web. Retrieved August 2, 2012, from http://www.businessweek.com/europe/graphic-news-corps-tangled-web-07142011-gfx.html

REFERENCES

Allick, C. (2011, October 26). War of worlds heats up between CBC, Quebecor. *The Toronto Star*. Retrieved August 2, 2012, from http://www.thestar.com/news/canada/politics/article/1076574—war-of-words-heats-up-between-cbc-quebecor

Aula, A. (2000). Others in their own land: Second generation South Asian Canadian women, racism, and the persistence of colonial discourse. *Canadian Woman Studies, 2*(2), 41–47.

Bagdikian, B. H. (2004). *The new media monopoly*. Boston: Beacon Press.

Baltruschat, D. (2009). Reality TV formats: The case of *Canadian Idol*. *Canadian Journal of Communication, 34*, 41–59.

Bar, F. & Sandvig, C. (2008). U.S. communication policy after convergence. *Media, Culture & Society, 30*(4), 531–550.

Basen, I. (2003). The CBC and the public interest: Maintaining the mission in an era of media concentration. In M.P. McCauley, E. E. Peterson, & B. L. Artz (Eds.), *Public broadcasting and the public interest* (pp. 147–157). Armonk, New York: M.E. Sharp,.

Benkler, Y. (2006). *The wealth of networks: How social production transforms markets and freedoms*. New Haven: Yale University Press.

Burns, J. F. & Somaiya, R. (2012, May 1). Panel in hacking case finds Murdoch unfit as news titan. *The New York Times*. Retrieved August 2, 2012, from http://www.nytimes.com/2012/05/02/world/europe/murdoch-hacking-scandal-to-be-examined-by-british-parliamentary-panel.html?_r=1&hp&pagewanted=print

Canada. Standing Committee on Cultural Heritage. (2003). *Our cultural sovereignty (The Lincoln Report): The second century of Canadian broadcasting*. Retrieved August 25, 2012 from http://www.parl.gc.ca/HousePublications/Publication.aspx?DocId=1032284&Language=E&Mode=1&Parl=37&Ses=2

Canadian Newspaper Association. (2011, December). Canadian daily newspaper ownership. Retrieved August 2, 2012, from http://www.newspaperscanada.ca/sites/default/files/Ownership%20Daily%20DECEMBER%202011.pdf

CBC News. (2012, March 14).Ottawa moves to increase telecom ownership. Retrieved August 25,2012 from http://www.cbc.ca/news/business/story/2012/03/14/paradis-industry.html

———. (2012, March 16). Bell Canada to buy Astral Media for $3.38B. Retrieved August 2, 2012, from http://www.cbc.ca/news/business/story/2012/03/16/astral-bell.html

———. (2012, May 2). BCE-Rogers bid for MLSE won't be reviewed. Retrieved August 2, 2012, from http://www.cbc.ca/sports/story/2012/05/02/competition-bureau-bce-rogers.html

———. (2012, May 18). CBC/Radio-Canada licence renewal hearings set for Fall 2012. Retrieved August 11, 2012 from http://cbc.radio-canada.ca/en/media-centre/2012/05/18

CBC Radio Canada. (2011). *Annual Report 2010-11*. Retrieved August 2, 2012, from http://cbc.radio-canada.ca/site/annual-reports/2010-2011/en/index.html

Clarke, G. E. (1997). White like Canada. *Transition*, *73*, 98–109.

Cohen, N., Macdonald, S., Mazepa, P., & Skinner, D. (2011). Making media public: From discussion to action? *Canadian Journal of Communication*, *36*, 169–178.

CRTC. (1999, May 17). CRTC won't regulate the Internet [news release]. Retrieved August 2, 2012, from http://www.crtc.gc.ca/eng/archive/2000/DB2000-340.htm

———. (2009, June 4). CRTC extends exemption for new media and calls for a national digital strategy. [news release]. Retrieved August 2, 2012, from http://www.crtc.gc.ca/eng/com100/2009/r090604.htm

———. (2009, July 6). Broadcasting Regulatory Policy CRTC 2009-406. Retrieved August 11, 2012, from http://www.crtc.gc.ca/eng/archive/2009/2009-406.htm

———. (2011, September 21). Regulatory framework related to vertical integration. Retrieved August 2, 2012, from http://www.crtc.gc.ca/eng/archive/2011/2011-601.htm

———. (2012, February 1). Postponement of Public Hearing (Broadcasting Notice of Consultation CRTC 2011-379-2). Retrieved August 2, 2012, from http://www.crtc.gc.ca/eng/archive/2011/2011-379-2.htm

———. (2012, October 18). Broadcasting Decision CRTC 2012-574. Retrieved October 18, 2012, from http://www.crtc.gc.ca/eng/archive/2012/2012-574.htm

Dailey, D. & A. Powell. (2011). Towards a taxonomy for public interest communications infrastructure. In P. Napoli & M. Aslama (Eds.), *Communications research in action: Scholar-activist collaborations for a democratic public sphere* (pp. 45–66). New York: Fordham University Press.

Dhruvarajan, V. (2000). People of colour and national identity in Canada. *Journal of Canadian Studies*, *35*(2), 166–175.

Globerman, S. (1995). Foreign ownership in telecommunications: A policy perspective. *Telecommunications Policy*, *19*(1), 21–28.

Gregg, A. (2006, March). Identity crisis. *The Walrus*. Retrieved August 2, 2012, from http://allangregg.com/?p=43

Hackett, R. A. & Skinner, D. (2012). Keeping the Fox at bay: A Canadian perspective on the Murdoch phone hacking scandal. *Television & New Media*, *13*, 1, 31–36.

Hackett, R. A., & Uzelman, S. (2003). Tracing corporate influences on press content: A summary of recent NewsWatch Canada research. *Journalism Studies*, *4*, 331–346.

Jenkins, H. (2006). Quentin Tarantino's Star Wars?: Digital cinema, media convergence, and participatory culture. In M. G. Durham & D. Kellner (Eds.) *Media and cultural studies: Keyworks* (pp. 549–575). Oxford, UK: Blackwell Publishing.

Jin, D. Y. (2008). Neoliberal restructuring of the global communication system: Mergers and acquisitions. *Media, Culture & Society, 30*(3), 357–373.

Jiwani, Y. (1998). On the outskirts of empire: Race and gender in Canadian TV news. In V. Strong-Boag et al., (Eds.) *Painting the maple: Essays on race, gender and the construction of Canada* (pp. 53–68). Vancouver: University of British Columbia Press.

Klein, N. (2000, September 13). One person's synergy is a columnist's nightmare. *The Globe and Mail,* A15.

McCauley, M. (2003). *Public broadcasting and the public interest.* Armonk, New York: M.E. Sharp.

McChesney, R. W. (1999). Graham Spry and the future of public broadcasting: The 1997 Spry Memorial Lecture. *Canadian Journal of Communication, 24*(1). Retrieved August 2, 2012 from: http://www.cjc-online.ca/viewarticle.php?id=504&layout=html

———. 2004. *The problem of the media: U.S. communication politics in the 21st century.* New York: Monthly Review Press.

Mosco, V. (1997). *The political economy of the media.* Thousand Oaks: Sage.

Murray, C. & Beale, A. (2011). Sex, money, media: A tribute. *Canadian Journal of Communication, 36,* 179–184.

Napoli, P. & Aslama, M. (2011). *Communications research in action: Scholar-activist collaborations for a democratic public sphere.* New York: Fordham University Press.

Pal, L. & Maxwell, J. (2004). *Assessing the public interest in the 21st Century: A framework.* Ottawa: Canadian Policy Research Networks. Retrieved August 2, 2012, from http://www.cprn.org/doc.cfm?l=en&doc=508&print=true

Pickard, V. (2008, April). Neoliberal visions and revisions in global communication policy from NWICO to WSIS. *Journal of Communication Inquiry, 31*(2), 118–139.

Powell, C. (2002, February 25). Putting it all together. *Marketing, 107*(8), 15–16.

Raboy, M. (1990). *Missed opportunities: The story of Canada's broadcasting policy.* Montreal: McGill-Queen's University Press.

———. (2006). Making media: Creating the conditions for communication in the public good. (The 2005 Graham Spry Memorial Lecture). *The Canadian Journal of Communication, 31,* 290–291.

Robertson, G. (2008). New rules mean the end of the megamerger. *The Globe and Mail,* January 18, B5.

Romanow, P. (2005). The picture of democracy we are seeking: CBC Radio Forums and the search for a Canadian identity, 1930–1950. *Journal of Radio Studies, 12,* 104–119.

Rubin, J. & Lu, V. (2012, March 16). BCE buys Astral in $3.38 billion media blockbuster. *Toronto Star*. Retrieved August 2, 2012, from http://www.thestar.com/business/article/1147446—bce-buys-astral-in-3-38-billion-media-blockbuster

Sassen, S. (2006). *Cities in a world economy*, 3rd Ed. Thousand Oaks, CA: Pine Forge Press.

Shade, L. R. (2005). Aspergate: Concentration, convergence and censorship in Canadian media. In D. Skinner, J. Compton, & M. Gasher (Eds.), *Converging media, diverging politics: A political economy of news in the United States and Canada* (pp. 101–116). Lanham, MD: Lexington Books.

———. (2008). Public interest activism in Canadian ICT policy: Blowin' in the policy winds. *Global Media Journal (Canadian Edition)*,*1*, 102–121.

———. (2011). Media reform in North America. In R. Mansell & M. Raboy (Eds.), *The handbook on global media and communication policy* (pp. 147–165). Malden, MA: Blackwell Publishing.

Stanley, D. (2006). Introduction: The social effects of culture. *Canadian Journal of Communication*, *31*(6), 7–15.

Surridge, G. & Malhomme, S. (2008, July 3). 438-day Journal de Quebec strike over; Convergence of media in Quebec key issue. *National Post*, FP3.

Trichor, R. (2012, August 16). Ottawa approves Maple Leaf sale, but battle looms over BCE deal for Astral. *The Globe and Mail.* Retrieved August 25, 2012 from http://www.theglobeandmail.com/globe-investor/ottawa-approves-maple-leaf-sale-but-battle-looms-over-bce-deal-for-astral/article4483893

———. (2008). Critics slam CRTC cross-media ownership policy. *Toronto Star*, January 16, B1.

Winseck, D. (2008). The state of media ownership and media markets: Competition or concentration and why should we care? *Sociology Compass*, *2*/1, 34–47.

———. (2011, August 23). Part 1: The growth of the network media economy, 1984–2010. *The Globe and Mail.* Retrieved August 2, 2012, from http://www.theglobeandmail.com/news/technology/digital-culture/dwayne-winseck/part-i-the-growth-of-the-network-media-economy-1984-2010/article2137508

———. (2011). A world on the edge and the "crisis of the media." In M. Moll & L.R. Shade (Eds.), *The internet tree: The state of telecom policy 3.0* (pp. 195–206). Ottawa: Canadian Centre for Policy Alternatives.

———. (2012, March 16). Bell-Astral deal should be stopped in its tracks. *The Globe and Mail.* Retrieved August 2, 2012, from http://www.theglobeandmail.com/news/technology/digital-culture/dwayne-winseck/bell-astral-deal-should-be-stopped-in-its-tracks/article2371806

Wirsig, K. & C. Edwards. (2011, April 27). Letter to CRTC re: CRTC 2010-783 Vertical Integration from Canadian Media Guild and CACTUS. Retrieved August 2, 2012, from http://www.cmg.ca/CRTC-2010-783-vertical%20integration.pdf

10

MAKING A MOCKERY OF CANADIAN CINEMA: INTERPRETING THE RISE OF MOCKUMENTARY

Zoë Druick
Simon Fraser University

Canadian cinema has always struggled with both production and distribution and today it is also a sector being rethought in light of changes being brought about by digital platforms. While Canada is home to what in industrial terms might be considered a large and thriving film and television production industry, its products tend to be geared toward a global film industry rather than creating works that could be defined as Canadian in any meaningful or substantive way. With very few exceptions, our domestic productions still tend to be small in scale, only modestly promoted, and rarely seen. For the most part, history shows that Canadian audiences are likely to forego Canadian fare in favour of bigger budget entertainment with matching publicity budgets made in the United States, or other regional powerhouses such as France, India, China, or Mexico, and utilizing their celebrities. While for many years Canada followed a cultural policy around film that attempted to complement and to some degree question the hegemony of Hollywood and its imperatives of mass audience and profit, a series of shifts in the industry since the 1990s mean that today Canada attempts to compete in a global screen industries marketplace through the production of exportable products and the emphasis on international partnerships for financing and distribution. The logic of making films in order to bolster Canadian identity as well as Canadian industry so common in postwar statements about Canadian culture has all but disappeared, although perhaps its traces remain.

Until the late 1960s, feature films in Canada were almost entirely the domain of the American industry, which also controlled Canadian theatres. Canadian policymakers and opinion leaders took the view that rather than competing, the nation's celluloid products should complement those made by Hollywood. For many years, Canada kept to its strengths: documentary cinema, industrial and sponsored films and, to a lesser degree, animated short films. Fiction films were few and far between. This historical strength was bolstered by policy decisions that allocated funding to the **National Film Board of Canada**, which, since its inception in 1939, has produced over 10,000 films of this sort. Documentaries were seen to be the best way to use cinema: educational and locally made, they put images of Canada and Canadians up on nontheatrical screens outside the mainstream distribution system, and promised to use cinema to improve the population and engage their civic activity.

Around the time of Canada's centenary, feature films became a new policy objective. In 1967, the government established the Canadian Film Development Corporation with $10 million (Dorland, 1998; Magder, 1993). The early 1970s saw a surge of distinctive Canadian features, followed by a cycle of popular, but often tasteless, films made under the tax-shelter policy (Urquhart, 2000).[1] New policy directed at film and television in the 1980s brought about a renewed mandate and an injection of funding to Telefilm Canada (the new name for the CFDC), followed directly by a flowering of art-house fiction features, such as *I've Heard the Mermaids Singing* (1987), *Family Viewing* (1988), *Highway 61* (1991), and *Careful* (1992). However, the signing of the North American Free Trade Agreement (NAFTA) in 1994 brought about a number of significant changes in production objectives and environments in Canada, such as new taxation and labour policies, which encouraged a surge of foreign location and service production, mainly for American film and television, as well as the growth of the video game industry, often at the expense of expensive and risky Canadian features.

In the ledgers, Canada's film industry has steadily climbed since then, both nationally and internationally, and is currently worth $5.5 billion, producing $2.26 billion in export value and an estimated 128,000 jobs (Canadian Media Production Association, 2011, 4). With offices in Montreal, Toronto, Vancouver, and Halifax, Telefilm funds dozens of projects by means of its annual feature film budget of $100 million, as well as upwards of 60 international coproductions each year, mostly with France and the United Kingdom (Telefilm Canada, 2010). Canada plays host to dozens of film festivals, most of which feature a healthy number of Canadian-made films. And Canadian television, long an important venue for a range of Canadian fare, continues to produce original content, all sponsored in part through the Telefilm-administered Canadian Media Fund (Hogarth, 2002). Despite all this activity, however, it would be fair to say that, except for in Quebec, Canada remains a tenuous player in the feature film scene (Canada, 2005). Government funding schemes and industry policies continue to tinker with a delicate cultural sector that is as capital intensive as it is unpredictable. It is in this context that I want to consider the large and growing body of Canadian mockumentaries.

In this chapter, I want to consider the Canadian film sector through the prism of some of its most popular products. I suggest that although mockumentaries have found a prominent place in media culture more generally, their presence in Canada displays particular national characteristics. First, they make a virtue of necessarily low production budgets. In a nation with modest funding for film production and promotion, films that can work with less are at an advantage. The small crews and intimate premises of most mockumentaries make a weakness into a potential strength. Second, they at once engage with and distance themselves from the legacy of the National Film Board. The NFB plays a very significant part in the cultural history of Canada; it has a distinguished reputation around the world. At once a central aspect of Canadian cinema and a restrictive state apparatus, the NFB leaves a complex legacy (Druick, 2007). Third, the strategy of mockumentary often serves to self-reflexively distance filmmakers from the scandalous desire to make feature films. In a country where virtually every feature film requires some public money to be made and therefore is put through an arduous process of funding applications and the vetting of content, all well before the challenging task of finding an audience, feature filmmaking still represents an all-but-impossible task. As texts that make fun of themselves, and often filmmaking as a whole, mockumentaries are, I argue, a cultural form custom made for a nation not sure of its right or ability to make films, especially ones that might be popular.

MOCKING DOCUMENTARY: DOUBLE-VOICED TEXTS

But first a framework for considering the mutability of popular culture. Audience expectations and pleasures are, to some extent, guided by preexisting cultural forms. Film theorists have discussed this cultural process in terms of the concept of **genre**. Although genre has most often been used to distinguish Hollywood films from art films, and low from high culture, it can also be used to characterize the regularities of any type of cultural expression. According to film theorist Steve Neale, genre conventions mobilize audience competences through an "intertextual relay," relating present texts to past experiences (Neale, 2000, p. 2). Despite the fact that documentary is supposed to be a film form about the social world, one in which referentiality overrides semiosis, it is also inevitably a *genre*, or type, of film communication. As such, it is subject to the same parameters as other genres, which alternately excite and bore audiences and the industries creating media fare. If genres are patterns, forms, styles, and structures that transcend individual films and supervise both their construction by filmmakers and their reading by an audience, then the documentary genre may be characterized, like all genres, by particular forms, predictable content, and comfortable modes of reception.

According to John Cawelti (2003) genres have lifespans: inception is followed by conscious self-awareness, and then exhaustion. At that point, genres are ripe for parody and possible renewal. Think of the slasher film's initial reinvigoration of horror, a genre that had become, by the 1970s, locked into clichéd visions of the supernatural and religious. This cycle of films, including *Halloween* (1978) and *Friday the 13th* (1980), in time gave way to its own spate of parodies, such as *I Know What You Did Last Summer* (1997) and *Scary Movie* (2000). *The Blair Witch Project* (1999), which combined horror with amateur style camerawork, capitalizing on the convergence of each style around the point-of-view shot, inspired a cycle of films about the irrational and the unseen, such as *Paranormal Activity* (2007) and *Cloverfield* (2008), ironically returning the horror genre to its earlier supernatural predilections. With the exhaustion of genres, hybrid texts form along generic borders, becoming the testing ground for new cultural forms, which take on provisional stability before they are replaced in their turn. These hybrids are the sites of creative challenges, which are capable of either reinforcing or destabilizing the form as such.

The genre of **documentary** differs from fictional genres in that aspects of its truth-claims are persistently linked to its technology. Its claims for credibility are connected to the verisimilitude of its recording of reality. But more than mere technological guarantor, documentary has actually taken on a range of forms since its inception. According to a taxonomy devised by Bill Nichols (2001, p. 138), a well-known documentary film theorist, there have been six documentary modes since the inception of the genre in the 1920s, all of which continue to operate to various degrees:

- poetic: reassembles aspects of the world poetically; often abstract
- expositional: builds an argument about the social world
- observational: eschews argument; the filmmaker purports to stand by and watch without intervening
- participatory: relies on interviews with witnesses and experts
- reflexive: questions documentary's truth claims while nevertheless attempting to add some form of subjective truth to the subject
- performative: focuses on subjective aspects of experience.

It is worth noting that the more self-reflexive a documentary's form, the harder it is to mock. So expositional, observational, and participatory documentaries, the most dominant forms, are the easiest to mock; while poetic, reflexive, and performative documentaries, already engaged in questioning of the documentary genre, are quite difficult to parody. If the proliferation of border genres does indicate something about the work of genre as a social process, rather than a stable form, we may well ask: what are some of the hybrids that have appeared on the edges of documentary?

One of the earliest and most important is the **docudrama**. A mainstay of television fare since the 1950s, docudrama challenges the fact/fiction distinction, potentially blurring concepts of truth and factuality, bringing aspects of psychology and emotion that audiences are trained to want from melodrama to the authenticity we associate with documentary. They often use sequences of events from real historical occurrence or situation and identities of protagonists to underpin a film script intended to provoke debate about the significance of the events/occurrence. Alternately, they use an invented sequence of events and fictional protagonists to illustrate the salient features of real historical occurrences or situations (e.g., *Titanic* [1997]). The dramatic aspect gives viewers the satisfaction of fiction while the "true story" gives a sense of engagement with reality. Docudramas retell events from history, represent the careers of significant figures, portray recent issues of concern, or focus on ordinary folks thrust into the spotlight for some reason (Paget, 1998). Examples include biopics, historical miniseries, and any acted film billed as based on a "true story." Although often quite different from each other, films in this category usually signal clearly that they are authentic by association with documents and facts, but are not themselves documentaries.

Mockumentary is commonly seen to adopt the "truth-telling" conventions of documentary form in order to pay homage to, parody, and/or reinforce the production of factual discourse. These are fictional texts that imitate documentary codes and take viewers on a journey from fact to fiction (Roscoe & Hight, 2001). The mockumentaries of Christopher Guest, such as *Best in Show* (2000), which start out like documentaries and later take on the emotional verisimilitude of drama, are of this sort.

A **hoax**, by contrast, does not make this distinction. Where most mockumentaries and docudramas will clearly indicate in some way their relationship to the truth, a hoax is a deliberate attempt to fool an audience. It implies that a presumed ethical relationship between filmmaker and audience is transgressed. Although exceedingly rare, the furore triggered by hoaxes indicates the all-important relationship of trust between filmmaker and audience. Famous examples include Orson Welles' broadcast of H.G. Wells' *War of the Worlds* as a news report on radio in 1939 and Costa Botes and Peter Jackson's fake history of New Zealand cinema, *Forgotten Silver* (1995). Hoaxes are useful ways of thinking about the operation of genre. When people find out they have been fooled, they become extremely upset. This is quite the opposite reaction to what audiences experience watching docudramas and mockumentaries. Like all genres existing at the edges of documentary, hoaxes tell us a good deal about the tacit contract of honesty that holds between documentary makers and their audiences.

All of these mobilizations of documentary—as the basis for dramatization, outright fiction, or practical joke—make use of the viewer's presumed knowledge of the form. They are double-voiced discourses that presume familiarity with codes and conventions that paradoxically signify "reality" in order to defamiliarize it. They take advantage of the genre's "intertextual relay" and are fundamentally ironic. Through their form, content, or both, they signal that both truth and fiction are being mobilized. Arguably, this is a complex and satisfying experience for an audience.

As Alexandra Juhasz and Jesse Lerner point out in their collection *F Is for Phony: Fake Documentary and Truth's Undoing* (2006), fake documentaries often do the serious work of pointing out the ruse of authority (pp. 2–3). That said, part of the appeal of mockumentaries is often their humour. At times the strategy is a rhetorical device to travel from fact to fiction, or it may reward the viewer for recognizing cultural codes. The humour often derives from the use of absurd logic, the incongruous combination of elements (such as the bother of documenting life in a tedious workplace whence *The Office* derives its silly premise). At its most pointed, mockumentary will self-reflexively comment on the close connection between documentary and authority, and this premise will be built into the justification for the fake documentary within the film's pretext (e.g. *Borat: Cultural Learnings of America for Make Benefit Glorious Nation of Kazakhstan* [2006]).

Yet, mockumentaries shouldn't be dismissed as one-dimensional or simply parasitic on documentary. Rather, as Craig Hight (2010) argues, mockumentary "does not simply draw from but comments upon and contributes to changes within ...

broader documentary culture" (p. 3). Indeed, Hight suggests that mockumentary, with its knowing winks to its canny audience, "has become just one part of a broader reflexivity toward factual forms within visual culture as a whole" (p. 5). Far from undermining documentaries, the proliferation of mockumentary has paralleled the "rise in popularity and appreciation of feature film documentary itself" (p. 6) and a "broadening of documentary-related media" (p. 29).

MOCKUMENTARIES IN CANADA

Before *The Canadian Conspiracy* (1985), mockumentaries in Canada—and, indeed, anywhere—were rare. A classic of Canadian comedy, *The Canadian Conspiracy* utilizes a traditional expositional form to satirize American Cold War anxieties. Transposing the anxiety from communists to Canadian comics, the film traces the influence—and infiltration—of Canadian comics in Hollywood. Although told from an American point of view, the film also clearly inverts the longstanding Canadian anxiety about not being funny and not producing successful popular culture. We have great comedians, says the film, only they are masquerading as Americans. The film thus succeeds in satirizing a number of nationalist discourses, both Canadian and American, while still maintaining a sense of Canadian superiority, albeit highly ironized.

However the past couple of decades have seen a veritable explosion of mockumentary on Canadian screens. From the observational style of TV shows such as Ken Finkleman's *The Newsroom* (CBC, 1996–7), *Trailer Park Boys* (Showcase, 1999–2008) and *La Job* (Radio-Canada, 2006), to the film festival hits *La moitié gauche du frigo* (2000), *The Delicate Art of Parking* (2003), *The Life and Hard Times of Guy Terrifico* (2005), *Radiant City* (2006), *My Winnipeg* (2007), *Confessions of a Porn Addict* (2008), *Girlfriend Experience* (2008), *The Puck Hogs* (2009), and *The Baby Formula* (2009), and theatrical successes such as *Hard Core Logo* (1996) (with its spinoff *Hard Core Logo 2* [2010], *FUBAR* (2002) (and its spinoff *FUBAR 2* [2010]), *It's All Gone Pete Tong* (2004), *Trailer Park Boys* (2007) and *Trailer Park Boys: Countdown to Liquor Day* (2009), the faux-documentary style has become ubiquitous. This is not even to mention the successful but difficult to categorize animated reality TV parody *Total Drama Island* (Teletoon, 2007–) made in Canada for Warner Entertainment. Achieving levels of popularity rare for Canadian fictional fare, these shows and films utilize the "intertextual relay" of the documentary form, while complicating the national associations with documentary. In what follows, I examine the meaning of mobilizing documentary form in a sampling of these texts, with special attention to the question of how the Canadian context makes specific demands on the parody of documentary form.

Hard Core Logo (1996) is the well-known adaptation of Michael Turner's book of poetry, widely considered to be director Bruce McDonald's most successful film. The film traces the band's desperate Western Canadian reunion tour as they, like punk rock itself, fall apart. In an apparent quest for realism, screenwriter Noel Baker opted for a mockumentary format that allowed him to write in the real director as a self-mythologizing character also named Bruce.[2] The two buddies at the centre of the film routinely criticize "Bruce," as does their idol, fictional punk icon Bucky Haight.

In his analysis of the adaptation, Peter Dickinson astutely notes that the final film produces the effect of a highly characteristic Canadian text combining Canadian cultural institutional traditions and Hollywood: "*Hard Core Logo*, the film, is Julien Temple's *The Great Rock 'n' Roll Swindle* by way of the NFB, Rob Reiner's *This Is Spinal Tap* as funded by Telefilm, Penelope Spheeris's *Decline of Western Civilization, Part 1* as it might have looked on the CBC" (2007, p. 190). The distinctively Canadian aspect is precisely the intertexual combination of American popular culture with Canadian authorized discourse.

Dickinson analyzes the performance of masculinity in the film, a balance between the "hypermasculine erotics of display and exhibitionism on stage" and prototypical "masculine detachment" (ibid, p. 193). As punk rock icons, the boys of *Hard Core Logo* have achieved a certain limited national notoriety and, in the case of Billy Talent, are being sought out by powerful members of the American music industry. Yet, in another way, they emblematize the backwoods antifashion punk sensibility particular to Vancouver, one that distinctively negotiated its identity away from the cross-dressing, urbane, and ironic New York and Los Angeles scenes. So, while Joe Dick and Billy Tallent represent Canadian artists and countercultural figures, they also convey a certain sort of straight-ahead, working-class, small-town, white, rock 'n' roll attitude, a kind of "hyperbolic hoser masculinity," to borrow a phrase from Tom Waugh (2006, p. 203). This kind of cultural homology includes buddies, beer, and loud music, living for the moment without the pretence of educated, cosmopolitan urban life.

Similarly, in Michael Dowse's sleeper hit *FUBAR*, the film's main subjects, Dean and Terry, bond against the filmmaker, Farrel, who has set out to make a documentary about head-banger subculture. From the outset, as Farrel screens his previous film for his new film subjects, the audience is encouraged to identify with Dean and Terry as they request that Farrel "turn down the suck" on his pretentious film full of incomprehensible imagery. By contrast, Dean and Terry's drinking, partying, and head banging seem authentic, if somewhat excessive. The friends are living their lives; Farrel is only "following us around." Moreover, as we soon learn that Dean has testicular cancer, the issue of phallic power is clearly established and Farrel, not Dean or Terry, is the one with something to mock. Finally, on a camping trip to Sasquatch Creek, Farrel shows just how incompetent a Canadian male he is as he refuses to jump into a river, only to finally jump to his death. The film itself continues without the filmmaker, showing just how insignificant he is compared to his film's hard-drinking, dead-end head bangers, who nevertheless know how to live life with gusto. Despite capturing actual documentary footage of recreational parking-lot fights and other facets of small-town partying, the film doesn't achieve any kind of hard hitting exposé of head bangers.

Through the parody of authority and heroism, the mockumentary form is well suited to the satire of masculinity. Where a film like *This Is Spinal Tap* (1984) relentlessly, if lovingly, satirizes the hypermasculinity of heavy metal through a parody of the rockumentary (Plantinga, 1998), both *Hard Core Logo* and *FUBAR* parody the fictional filmmaker's attempt to anthropologically observe the film's subjects who either retain their integrity as characters, or, through an aversion to pretence, are not in a position to be parodied. It is the outsider filmmaker who comes in for ridicule precisely because of his attempt to make a comment on something through the documentary form.

In the Quebec context, mockumentary has also made its mark. Phillipe Faladeau's *Le motié gauche du frigo (The Left-Hand Side of the Fridge)* was a hit upon its release in 2000, winning numerous awards and going on to a successful theatrical release. The film is a mockumentary about the making of a documentary about unemployment. The filmmaker within the film, Stéphane Demers (played by an actor of the same name), is a disappointed actor and playwright who, with the failure to find production outlets for his avant-garde theatre pieces, has turned his hand to a video about his roommate, an out–of-work engineer. Christophe's attempts to find work (and love) become a pretence to explore the state of the unemployment insurance system, the realities of economic globalization, and the implication of engineers in particular with corporate greed (the one job Christophe gets as an engineer is a four-day stint overseeing the disassembly of a factory's machines so that they may be moved to Mexico). Or so it seems. As the film progresses, the viewer becomes aware of the movement away from docudrama (the dramatizing of a typical experience), or even expositional documentary, toward mockumentary. What appears to be a commentary on politics and economy bolstered by documented facts, such as the number of unemployed, or the operation of free trade, becomes more clearly a device to express the preoccupations of one of the central characters, Stéphane.

Even more than the hoser mockumentaries of English-language Canadian cinema, *La motié* parodies sensitive urban men and left-wing politics. Stéphane wants Christophe to become more political about the role of engineers in corporate capitalism, yet the only clearly leftist motif in the film is the fridge, where Christophe's side is always empty, save some carrots and milk. The self-righteous Stéphane's side of the fridge, by contrast, is always well stocked, especially after Radio-Canada starts funding his film within the film. This is a self-reflexive move by Faladeau, as Radio-Canada was, along with Telefilm, one of the real sponsors of the film. At one point a representative of Radio-Canada (presumably fictionalized) is heard in voiceover saying that he'll fund the film despite its depressing subject matter, because it has an engaging personal angle. *La motié* thus enacts through its very form a critique of Quebec broadcasting's turn toward reality-type TV over public service broadcasting.

The mockumentary aspect of the film becomes most pointedly utilized when, approximately halfway through, the camera is turned on the "filmmaker" character and the film takes a turn toward character development over political issues. In this way, the film does indeed move from "reality" to "fiction," as Roscoe and Hight (2001) describe is typical of the genre, involving us in the emotional world of characters rather than developing a discussion about employment and the global economy. By this means, the film mocks the character of Stéphane, the earnest playwright-turned-documentarian with his tedious vision of politicized art, while celebrating apolitical Christophe, who eventually has a falling out with the parasitic Stéphane and turns his career toward his real passion, music.

La motié engages a sophisticated viewer by repeatedly referring to itself as a film. Self-reflexivity is introduced from the outset when Christophe explains the premise of the film to the camera: "The film will end when I get a job. It is like a thriller." In another example, a caseworker Christophe meets with at the Employment Insurance office identifies himself as a former actor, who appeared in Denys Arcand's *Decline of the American Empire* (1986). Arcand's film was an enormous box-office success as well as a critical darling, and Arcand himself is considered one of the most important Quebecois film auteurs of all time. Daniel Brière's appearance in this film, playing an actor who has quit the game, is a good example of self-reflexivity. He is at once lending authenticity to the "documentary" aspect of the film (by playing himself), and sending himself up by presenting himself (falsely) as an out-of-work actor who has become a bureaucrat.

A number of scenes within the film highlight Faladeau's self-reflexive use of the character Stéphane to comment on documentary. For example, when Stéphane ambushes the CEO of a fictitious multinational in the parking lot as he is about to drive away in his SUV, the CEO chastises him for being "ill-informed and late," adding, "you make a poor Michael Moore." When Christophe's girlfriend, Odile, picks up the camera to film him in bed after a night of passion, Christophe says playfully about the constant filming of his most intimate moments, "It's a nightmare." Followed by, "It's better when you're [Odile] behind the camera." This foreshadows Christophe's later wry comment to Stéphane that he feels like he's in *The Truman Show* (1998), a fictional film about a character played by Jim Carrey living in a reality-TV show. Similarly, when Christophe accompanies Stéphane to the lab to drop off his film for developing, the receptionist tells Christophe that all the girls at the lab are hooked on Christophe's life. "It's gripping. Like a soap opera." *La motié* is an example of a film that creatively utilizes the documentary form to create a fictional story that simultaneously references Canadian culture and politics.

In quite a different vein, *Qallunaat! Why White People Are Funny* (2006) engages with the standard ethnographic documentary. First Nations people in Canada have long been the object of the ethnographic gaze, starring in films since the very beginning of documentary when American filmmaker Robert Flaherty made *Nanook of the North* (1922) in northern Quebec. Over the years, members of these ethnic groups have gone on to feature in hundreds of films about First Nations, Métis, and Inuit made by the National Film Board, the CBC, and other broadcasters. *Qallunaat!* utilizes a number of clips from these films in order to acknowledge and subsequently subvert the ethnographic gaze. The acknowledgment comes in the form of Inuit people being interviewed about their perceptions of "qallanaat," the Inuktitut word for "white people."

One of the funniest moments in the film occurs during the mocking of a booklet produced by the Canadian government and distributed to Inuit people in 1947. Entitled "The Book of Wisdom for Eskimo," a woman explains some of its highlights to a group of other Inuit. As she reads from its contents such pearls of wisdom as "if we cannot breathe, we die for lack of air"; "a new baby cannot talk, so it cries"; and "RCM Police [sic], the Eskimo's friend," the group, including the group leader, begins to laugh uncontrollably. The reading of this government document produced by the very people responsible for the attack on Inuit culture by an Inuit voice introduces a second mocking voice to the first, official one. This section documents the use of laughter to subvert official knowledge; the laughter is contagious and destabilizing. However, as with the rest of the film, there is no sustained attack on documentary form as such.

Director Mark Sandiford makes use of many previously filmed documentaries to mobilize a critical discourse of racist forms of knowledge embedded in government apparatus, such as police, education, law, and even filmmaking. In an excerpt taken from the NFB film *Our Northern Citizen* (1956), the narrator lauds the Inuit for their "imitative skills," but suggests that without understanding spoken and written English, they will find only limited success in the modern world. The theme of imitation—a common one in colonial discourse (Taussig, 1993)—is turned on its head by a local comic known for his imitations of government representatives who is documented in the film. The comic is shown making the rounds of a room full of elderly Inuit, gladhanding and speaking a meaningless pastiche of English, French, and Inuktitut. His briefcase heavy with "money" and his wiggling walk make the old folks laugh as much as those who listen to the quotations from the "Book of Wisdom for Eskimo." In both of these sequences, the power of mimicry to embody and expel colonial power is made explicit.

As a parody of ethnographic documentary, the film attempts to do some similar work, imitating the colonial film form just as the mimic imitates the government representative. The film parodically showcases a world where the Inuit are the dominant group, running an institute for the study of white people located "north of the Arctic Circle" and a Department of White Man's Affairs, and making ethnographic films about white people. The film shows Inuit laughing at "qallunaat" (white people), but this is not the same thing as thinking that white people are "funny," as the subtitle of the film puts it. The laughter is an attempt to invert the seemingly intractable relations of power that have racialized the Inuit and forced their assimilation to Euro-Canadian culture. This is not funny so much as it is upsetting. However, parodic documentary is a good fit for satirizing authority and *Qallunaat!* offers some thought-provoking reversals. Making white people funny in the two scenes I described above, forcing the laughter through double-voiced imitations and invocations, involves some important cultural work, for which the mockumentary seems well suited. Unlike the mockumentaries about masculinity discussed above, the filmmaker here is not a featured character. This is not a film about making a film. Rather, the film is part of a larger move to parody the ethnographic documentary and so satirize colonial relations.[3] However, produced by the NFB, whose catalogue the filmmakers raid in order to find objectionable films about the Inuit, the film's critique of official knowledge production in the interest of colonization is perhaps not as strong as it could be. The contemporary Inuit portrayed in the film are all smart and funny, living in safe communities and working at well-funded institutes for the study of white people. The lasting legacies of colonialism are treated as more or less overcome, needing only the fixing of the misconceptions perpetrated by a few Farley Mowat books.

CONCLUSIONS

In this chapter I have tried to provide a context for and establish the meaning of recent mockumentaries in Canada. As double-voiced texts they have proven engaging and meaningful film experiences for funders, filmmakers, and audiences. They have sometimes achieved a level of popularity rare for Canadian cinema. As part of a rise in reflexive media culture and the increasing prominence of the documentary genre, they have been shown on television, and at film festivals, and attained commercial release. But what of mockumentary's formal potential to critique genre and engage in satire? Due to the dominance of documentary-style filmmaking and public-service broadcasting in Canada until the 1980s, and its prominent legacy as an educational and nation-building form, the fatigue of expositional documentary has brought with it exciting potential for parodic engagement. *Qallunaat!*, for example, takes the route of inverting the ethnographic gaze so long directed at First Nations people in Canada.

The utilization of observational documentary as a form in fiction films, however, has not engaged so clearly with Canadian film history or mobilized much of a satire. The films under discussion here seem to be utilizing documentary form to make a virtue of meagre shooting budgets and potentially as a way of building in a self-defensive form of ironized auteurism. You can't make fun of the earnestness of these filmmakers, since the films highlight the failures of Canadian filmmakers. The films' reference point is not so much the social world, or even the documentary genre, so much as it is fictional characters and, sometimes, the world of documentary filmmaking itself. Self-reflexively, these films engage satirically with the act of making a film, rather than with the claims of documentary. They tend not to reference or engage with the more creative uses of documentary film as poetic, self-reflexive, or performative, tending, rather, to represent documentary filmmaking as a purely technological relationship of filmic recording of reality. Indeed, they hardly trouble the dominance of documentary as a media staple. Nevertheless, it is worth considering the ways in which the particular cultural history of cinema in Canada has contributed to the distinctive and ongoing development of new genres that blend fiction and reality such as the mockumentary.

QUESTIONS

1. Do you think that the traditional dominance of Canadian cinema by documentary and realism has led to a distinctive national style of mockumentary?
2. How do new media platforms expand the possibility of mockumentaries?
3. To what degree is satire involved in the act of parodying the documentary genre?
4. How can the mockumentary be used to attract more international audiences to Canadian cinema?
5. Why do you think this kind of humour appeals to audiences?

NOTES

My thanks to Laurynas Navidauskas and Itrath Syed for research assistance.

1. The tax-shelter boom was the result of an attempt by the Canadian government in the late 1970s to encourage capitalization of cinema by making investment in film production a tax write-off. Many dozens of films were made as a result of this policy, most of which were never distributed or exhibited. However, popular results of this policy included the hits *Meatballs* (1979) and *Porky's* (1982).
2. Aaron Taylor (2007) points out that McDonald's screen persona "Bruce" appears in a number of his films (p. 204).
3. Other international films in this vein include *Babakiueria* (Don Featherstone, 1986); *Bontoc Eulogy* (Marlon Fuentes, 1995); and *Mother Dao, the Turtlelike* (Vincent Monnikendam, 1995).

REFERENCES

Canada. (2005). *Scripts, screens and audiences: A new feature film policy for the 21st century*. Report of the Standing Committee on Canadian Heritage (November).

Canadian Media Production Association. (2011). *Profile 2011: An economic report on the screen-based production industry in Canada*. Retrieved August 13, 2012, from http://www.cmpa.ca/industry-information/profile

Cawelti, J. (2003). *Chinatown* and generic transformation in recent American films. In B. K. Grant (Ed.), *Film genre reader III* (pp. 243–61). Austin, TX: University of Texas Press.

Dickinson, P. (2007). *Screening gender, framing genre: Canadian literature into film*. Toronto: University of Toronto Press.

Dorland, M. (1998). *So close to the state/s: The emergence of Canadian feature film policy*. Toronto: University of Toronto Press.

Druick, Z. (2007). *Projecting Canada: Documentary film and government policy at the National Film Board*. Montreal and Kingston: McGill-Queen's University Press.

Hight, C. (2010). *Television mockumentary: Reflexivity, satire and a call to play.* Manchester: Manchester University Press.

Hogarth, D. (2002). *Documentary television in Canada: From national public service to global marketplace.* Montreal and Kingston: McGill-Queen's University Press.

Juhasz, A., & J. Lerner, eds. (2006). *F is for phony: Fake documentary and truth's undoing.* Minneapolis: University of Minnesota Press.

Magder, T. (1993). *Canada's Hollywood: The Canadian state and feature films.* Toronto: University of Toronto Press.

Neale, S. (2000). *Genre and Hollywood.* London: Routledge.

Nichols, B. (2001). *Introduction to documentary.* Bloomington and Indianapolis: Indiana University Press.

Paget, D. (1998). *No other way to tell it: Dramadoc/docudrama on television.* Manchester: Manchester University Press.

Plantinga, C. (1998). Gender, power, and a cucumber: Satirizing masculinity in "This is Spinal Tap." In B. K. Grant & J. Sloniowski (Eds.), *Documenting the documentary: Close readings of documentary film and video* (pp. 318–332). Detroit: Wayne State University Press.

Roscoe, J., & C. Hight. (2001). *Faking it: Mock-documentary and the subversion of factuality.* Manchester: Manchester University Press.

Taussig, M. (1993). *Mimesis and alterity: A particular history of the senses.* New York: Routledge.

Taylor, A. (2007). Straight outta' Hogtown: Sex, drugs, and Bruce McDonald. In G. Melnyk (Ed.), *Great Canadian film directors* (pp. 199–226). Edmonton: University of Alberta Press.

Telefilm Canada. (2010). *Annual Report.* Retrieved August 28, 2012 from www.telefilm.ca/rapport-annuel/2009-2010/english.php.

Urquhart, P. (2000). You should know something—anything—about this movie. You paid for it. *The Canadian Journal of Film Studies 12*(2) (Fall), 64–80.

Waugh, T. (2006). *The romance of transgression in Canada: Queering sexualities, nations, cinemas.* Montreal and Kingston: McGill-Queen's University Press.

11

FLACK ATTACK: THE "PROBLEM" OF PUBLIC RELATIONS

Josh Greenberg
Carleton University

INTRODUCTION

> Public relations was created to thwart and subvert democratic decision making.
>
> —David Miller & William Dinan (2007, p. 1)

> I have no patience for those who try and attribute insidious and mysterious powers to public relations.
>
> —John Hill, co-founder Hill & Knowlton
> (cited in Miller & Dinan, 2008, p. 1)

On September 11, 2001, minutes after the terrorist attack by al-Qaeda on the World Trade Center, Jo Moore, a senior public relations (PR) officer in the British government, sent out a communiqué to other communications advisers suggesting that while the world was distracted by the horror unfolding in the United States, "today is a good day to bury bad news" (Franklin, 2003). Moore's actions were so objectionable that a colleague leaked the memo to the media, exposing a "spin machine that has corrupted the senior civil service" (Jones & Weir, 2002).

In 2006, Britain's national academy of science, The Royal Society, published an open letter to ExxonMobil in *The Guardian* newspaper in which it called on the American oil company to suspend its practice of funding special interest groups that engage in unethical communication about climate change. In the letter, the Royal Society accused Exxon of distributing $2.9 million to 39 organizations in the United States that were misinforming the public about the science of global warming and undermining the notion that there is a scientific consensus on climate change. The Royal Society's actions reflected more than just mounting anxiety about the politicization of environmental policymaking. They reflected a broader concern about the influence of lobby groups and think tanks, and the use of third-party advocacy by multinational corporations to shape public policy and manipulate public opinion (Greenberg & Westersund, 2010).

In 2007, the U.S. Federal Emergency Management Agency (FEMA) was forced to publicly apologize after revelations surfaced that during the height of the California wildfires crisis it held a fake news conference where staff members posed as reporters to ask questions of the agency leadership that would generate answers favourable to the agency's image and reputation (e.g., Kamen, 2007). Public confidence in FEMA's leadership had been badly damaged after the agency mishandled emergency response during Hurricane Katrina two years earlier. The fake news event reinforced perceptions that FEMA was more concerned about its own image than in protecting the interests of the public.

And in January 2012 *The Globe & Mail* reported that Racepoint Group, a Washington-based public relations firm, had been hired by Rwanda's Kagame regime to burnish its international image and reputation. In particular, Racepoint was hired to blunt criticism by journalists and nonprofit groups of the Rwandan government's human rights record (York, 2012). The campaign was intended to create a positive "brand" for the country, infamous for its 1994 genocide, to erect a "wall of defence" on the internet in order to undermine government critics, and to "flood" the media with stories about Rwanda's economic and social progress.

Negative stories about public relations are a common feature of media discourse, whether in the news, movies, television, literature, or music. The dominant narrative about PR portrays a dark art involving **propaganda**, spin doctoring, crisis control, and **reputation management** mostly in service of powerful people and institutions. Public relations practitioners are frequently depicted as either shameless publicists who relentlessly flog and promote the interests of their clients, or secret manipulators who pull the levers of power from behind the scenes.

Despite these negative depictions, some researchers argue there are good reasons to see the expansion of public relations as a boost, rather than a threat, to democracy. Hiebert once wrote that "without public relations, democracy could not succeed in a mass society" (1966, p. 7). By this he meant that if public policy emerges from a competition among different viewpoints, PR can be used to promote the virtues or limitations of those positions and claims. Davis (2002) gives this argument a critical thrust. Even though the political world is shaped by an uneven distribution of power and influence, he argues that a much broader range of policy actors (e.g., unions, NGOs, charities, activists, etc.) are "adopting professional public relations as a means of achieving political and economic objectives" (2002, p. 3; see also Deacon, 2003). From promoting the services they provide (shelter, food, health care, environmental protection, etc.) to advancing public understanding about the contributions they make to politics and public life, increasing numbers of resource-poor organizations, including many charities and NGOs, are making use of PR practices and professionalizing their communication activities to enhance their legitimacy and influence (Deacon, 2003; Greenberg and Walters, 2004; Greenberg and Grosenick, 2008).

Other scholars go further, challenging the depiction of PR as an inherently unethical practice and occupation. To the contrary, they argue that public relations can be the vanguard of ethical action in politics, business, and the public sphere. Current thinking among some academics and advocates is that PR practitioners are best positioned to lead their organizations through a process of consensus building in a way that benefits their stakeholders and society (Grunig, 2001; see also Flynn, 2011). PR should be seen, these advocates argue, as the "ethical guardian" of an organization; i.e., a driving force in establishing the organization's moral conduct and ensuring the delivery of public benefits, whatever those may be (for a critique, see L'Etang, 2003).

This chapter introduces students to public relations as an object of study. It focuses on where PR has come from, the struggle over its meaning, its representation in the mass media, and its relationship to other industries and institutions, particularly journalism.

The chapter is organized in four sections. I begin by sketching the history of public relations as an institution and industry, pointing to how PR was "invented" to help consolidate corporate power and legitimize the role of corporations in the daily lives of the public during the early 20th century. Yet, in addition to this role, public relations was also important in helping to promote progressive politics and social causes. Second, I review the contested definition of public relations and discuss how the PR industry has responded to it. In the third section, I provide an overview of how public relations has been depicted in the mass media, focusing on literature, movies, television, and music. The final section examines the "love–hate relationship" between journalism and PR (White & Hobsbawm, 2007). My hope is that after reading this chapter students will have a more nuanced understanding about public relations and its varied roles in society.

THE BIRTH AND EXPANSION OF PUBLIC RELATIONS

> When an industry has finished its financing, when it has mastered the problems of production, it no longer needs a board of directors where the bankers and production men and engineers dominate. Its major problem for the future will be public relations.
>
> —Bruce Fairchild Barton, 1936
> (cited in Ewen, 1988, xiv)

Although the origins of public relations is a topic of debate (L'Etang, 2003; Brown, 2001), it is generally agreed that the modern PR industry emerged during the late 19th century, primarily but not exclusively in the United States. This was a time of great societal transformation and change: the expansion of the market economy, mass urbanization, and industrialization, the establishment of railroads and other public utilities, rising literacy, and the formation of mass movements for democracy, such as labour and women's rights. According to Ewen (1988), public relations established itself to help political and corporate elites manage and control the challenges posed by universal suffrage and other democratic reforms that were changing society at that time. Key figures such as Ivy Lee, Edward Bernays, Clem Whitaker and Leone Baxter, working at the behest of their government and corporate clients, brought principles of what was then the nascent field of social psychology to bear on campaigns that were designed to manipulate the public into being docile consumers and voters.[1] Where Lee believed in the power of propaganda to tap into the beliefs and ideals of the masses and to then use that access to plant an idea in their minds, Bernays sought to apply to public relations insights from the theory of psychoanalysis, developed by his famous uncle, Sigmund Freud (Ewen, 1988).[2] Whitaker and Baxter, meanwhile brought these practices into the political arena where they toiled tirelessly against liberal causes, keeping Democrats out of government and opposing any nominally progressive initiative that might seek to redistribute wealth and democratize social welfare (Lepore, 2012).

The corporate revolution that took hold in the United States between 1880–1920 provides the context in which the business of public relations emerged. This great transformation gave rise to a new market economy dominated by massive industrial powerhouses, such as Ford and General Motors, General Electric, Standard Oil, and U.S. Steel. In the preceding era, most businesses were run by single persons, families, or partnerships involving several people; these businesses typically had moderate-sized workforces and rather modest levels of investment, from several thousand to several hundred thousand dollars, in the case of larger textile companies. However, by 1880, corporate enterprises had grown substantially in both size and complexity. John D. Rockefeller's Standard Oil Company was reportedly worth approximately $600 million, and when the U.S. Steel Corporation was founded in 1901 it became the largest business enterprise ever launched (Mintz & McNeil, 2012). Founded by some of the biggest names in the history of corporate America (Andrew Carnegie, J.P. Morgan, Charles Schwab, and Elbert H. Gary), U.S. Steel merged approximately 168,000 employees from hundreds of previously independent business units (mines, transportation systems, blast furnaces, rolling mills, etc.) and was reported to be worth about $1.4 billion.

The perception held by most people at the time was that big business was a cold, impersonal monster and a threat to the public interest. This is a view that was promulgated by campaigning journalists (muckrakers) of the era and widely believed by the public. Reflecting on the influence of the muckrakers and their hostility to corporate excess, Walter Lippmann observed, "the sense of conspiracy and secret scheming which transpire is almost uncanny. 'Big Business,' and its ruthless tentacles, have become the material for the feverish fantasy of illiterate thousands" (Lippmann, 1914, p. 1). If for Lippmann the illiterate public and the activist press represented a threat to big business, Peter Garraty argues that the biggest challenge facing giant corporations of the era was not journalism or mass public opinion, but organized labour, and that to increase control over workers, companies such as U.S. Steel (the focus of his case study) would need labour policies that were friendlier

© Bettmann/CORBIS

Edward Bernays (1891–1995) was a member of the U.S. government's WWI propaganda agency, the Committee for Public Information. With his wife Doris E. Fleischman, he launched a highly successful public relations agency in the 1920s. One of his most famous publicity stunts involved recruiting several young women to walk in the Easter Day Parade and light up Lucky Strike cigarettes (a Bernays client) as "torches of freedom." Bernays linked cigarette smoking with the desire of women for independence. Bernays also authored numerous books and articles on democracy, mass persuasion, and public relations.

to the interests of capital: "policy demanded good public relations, this much was clear" (1960, p. 3).

In his book *Creating the Corporate Soul*, Roland Marchand focuses on the public relations industry and its image work for big business at the turn of the 20th century. Marchand argues that while the courts had bestowed legal legitimacy upon the giant corporations of that era, companies such as U.S. Steel, Standard Oil, General Motors, AT&T, and General Electric (among others) "conspicuously lacked a comparable social and moral legitimacy in the eyes of the public" (2001, p. 7). Facing a deeply skeptical public and, in particular, journalists hostile to the so-called robber barons such as Carnegie, Rockefeller, and Schwab, big business needed a new image in order to convince Americans that corporations had a moral purpose and were serving the public good. Recognizing that the negative public perception of corporations would hinder their political and economic ambitions, these giant companies launched a century-long PR campaign to "create the corporate soul."

American Telephone and Telegraph Company (AT&T) was the first company to engage in large-scale corporate PR, embarking on its first major campaign in 1908 to battle the negative portrayal of big business by labour activists and journalists, and to convince the public that private monopolies had virtues and should not be subject to heavy government regulation. To make its case, AT&T's publicity and lobbying efforts stressed the quality and service that the company provided its customers, emphasizing that despite its massive size and scale this did not create an institution that would be out of touch with the needs of the people, but rather allowed for the creation of more customer-friendly services (Marchand, 2001). AT&T's promotional materials stressed customer empowerment, emphasized the dedication of its employees, and focused on the contributions of the telephone to progress in technology and democracy.

AT&T's efforts to convince the public of its beneficence were consistent with the practices of other major corporations during this time. Whether it was telecommunications companies or automotive, steel, or oil corporations, the overriding objective of early corporate PR was to promote business independence by aligning private needs with the public interest in order to attack the regulatory impulse and interests of the state. The promotion of the "corporate soul" and the efforts this represented in terms of establishing a personal relationship between big business, its employees, and customers, was always designed to serve this objective. And while these campaigns met with mostly positive success, they also helped establish a deeply negative view of public relations as a handmaiden of corporate power committed to manipulation and spin (Ewen, 1988; Miller & Dinan, 2008).

Public Relations and Progressive Politics in the Early 20th Century

Notwithstanding the important contributions of studies such as Marchand's for how we understand the origins of PR, it's important to also acknowledge that public relations was integral to the advancement of progressive causes during this era, including women's rights and civil rights. According to Tickner (1988), activists who promoted women's suffrage made regular and effective use of propaganda. Suffrage propaganda was intended "to build up an irresistible pressure of public opinion" to advance women's voting rights, and at the same time to convert support among the political class (ibid, p. 151). Whether it was literature, song, public speeches, posters, periodicals, or political theatre, the media of the suffrage movement selectively arranged evidence and "drew its conclusions on that basis, no more and no less than did the arguments it was ranged against" (ibid, p. 152).

Speeches and patriotic pageants were the most common forms of public address by feminists at the turn of the 20th century. A fascinating collection of articles relating to American "suffrage propaganda plays" shows how the movement for women's equality rights drew heavily on persuasion techniques not unlike those pioneered in the corporate sector to influence policy, public discourse and popular opinion (Friedl, 1990). Suffrage plays were written and performed with an explicit propaganda purpose, reflecting a wide range of controversial topics of the day: not only the importance of winning the right to vote, but also debates about nutrition, alimony, and child support. The play's intention was explicitly ideological: to shed light on the "disparity between idealised bourgeois femininity and the plight of the sweated woman worker" (Tickner, 1988, p. 152). The suffragettes relied heavily on a range of PR strategies and techniques to impugn the motives and undermine the arguments of their opponents.

Public relations also provided a boost to the civil rights movement. Edward Bernays, who mostly applied his rhetorical skills to advance the causes of government and big business, also brought his craft to bear in promoting changes in public opinion about a number of social issues. In 1920 his firm was hired by the National Association for the Advancement of Colored People (NAACP) to handle the media relations for its regional convention in Atlanta, Georgia. The campaign had a simple, progressive agenda: to use the convention as "a springboard for publicity, to make the South and North realize that we are in earnest in battling for the civil rights of the Negro," which included abolishing lynchings and segregationist policies, and promoting equal access to education, employment, and voting rights.

Bernays did not directly tend to the campaign, instead sending his wife and business partner, Doris E. Fleischman (a talented writer and strategist in her own right), to handle all local media outreach and event organizing. The Atlanta conference was the first held south of the Mason-Dixon Line, a symbolic boundary separating the North-east from the southern United States. In the face of insults and threats of violence, Fleischman successfully convinced the Atlanta press to cover the convention as it would other significant social and political events. Bernays eventually joined her and, with the NAACP's tireless advocacy efforts, generated an impressive volume of positive media coverage not only in Atlanta but also across the country, drawing attention "to the progress made by Negroes from the plantation labor to business and the professions."[3]

Over the course of the twentieth century, public relations developed into a much more expansive institution and practice. Sociologist Leon Mayhew argues that techniques associated with corporate PR came to be systematically applied to political communication from the end of World War II through to the 1990s (Mayhew, 1997). Mayhew argues that over this period, political consultants, lobbyists, pollsters, focus group specialists, and other communication professionals burgeoned in size and influence, giving rise to "the often impugned methods of civic persuasion that now dominate public communication" (ibid, p. 4). Mayhew focuses primarily on how professionalized communication has transformed political discourse (mostly for the worse), and his analysis presents a bleak future for how communication can strengthen the public sphere.

Other researchers have come to rather different conclusions. Writing from a "radical pluralist perspective," several studies have challenged the conventional argument that corporate and political power had succeeded on the basis of effective public relations, and was thus impenetrable. These studies examined cases where even in the context of uneven political and economic resources, outsider groups had been successful in applying PR strategies and techniques to their own advocacy efforts, often challenging official accounts. Knight and Greenberg (2002) showed how even though Nike was the world's most visible and successful athletics footwear and apparel company, its PR efforts in the face of accusations about workplace violations had mostly failed against the successful public relations campaigns of students, unionists, church groups, and other human/labour rights advocates. From crime and justice (Schlesinger & Tumber, 1994) to environmental activism (Anderson, 2003) and antipoverty advocacy (Greenberg, May & Elliott, 2006), researchers have shown that groups that do not typically have the ability to define or drive media and policy agendas are utilizing or developing a capacity for instrumentally effective communication, and are showing that public relations can be used to advance progressive causes and policies as well.

DEFINING PUBLIC RELATIONS

Despite the pluralist optimism of recent research and the mixed history of PR practice, the popular image of public relations remains mostly negative: PR practitioners are typically characterized as manipulative, cynical, and driven by their own interests. Even in communication and media studies curricula, public relations remains poorly defined and understood. An early study of mass communication textbooks by Cline (1982) showed that students are frequently given an historically inaccurate account of public relations and are provided with an image of PR that suffers from an "insidious bias."

Yet, despite these negative depictions, practitioners and the professional associations to which they belong see public relations as serving an important and constructive role in society. In 2011, the Public Relations Society of America launched a crowd-sourcing initiative to come up with a baseline definition of PR that "captures the core essence of what it is public relations professionals do" (Rickey, 2012). The impetus for the exercise was to allow the industry to better describe the contributions PR practitioners make in the organizations where they work, and to society broadly. The work of public relations is "so complex and there's so many moving parts that trying to get the most elegant and simple definition is a challenge"(ibid). Is public relations about managing media perceptions? Is it basically an extension of marketing and advertising? Is PR the same as lobbying? If it's different, what makes it so? Is public relations about all of these things? If it is, how can we possibly have a singular definition? These are not easy questions to answer.

Hutton's (1999) review of PR history identifies a number of definitions, metaphors and approaches to the field. Citing research by Harlow (1977), turn-of-the-century public relations emphasized publicity as a way for governments and business to build and sustain goodwill, but this view began to wane by the 1930s and was replaced by a newer, more technocratic vision of PR as a "guide to social conduct" and a vehicle for "social and political engineering" (ibid, p. 200). In the 1950s and 60s, the advocacy view of public relations began to emerge, with practitioners described as "pilots" of public conversation, "interpreters" of stakeholder opinion, and a "devil's advocate" for their clients and employers (Harlow, 1977). This view was eventually eclipsed by a newer technocratic definition that emphasized a normative, managerial perspective. In this view, PR practitioners assist their organizations in maintaining open lines of communication with key stakeholders, manage issues and problems, stay apprised of public opinion, help senior leaders anticipate trends, and advise on evidence-based, ethical communication with the public (Hutton, 1999, p. 200). Ultimately, Hutton distills competing definitions of public relations to argue that it is multidimensional, incorporating elements of advocacy and persuasion, public information and education, cause promotion, reputation construction and repair, and relationship management. In other words, PR is an ever-changing practice that means many things to many people.

Part of what makes defining public relations so difficult is that, unlike formal professions such as medicine, law, architecture, teaching, or accounting, there is no core body of literature, no binding code of conduct, and no formal or official sanctions for violating standards or expectations of practice. Also, people who work in public relations are employed in many different kinds of environments: within agencies, where they typically work for multiple clients and have little control for whom they work and how much they can earn; inside organizations, where they work for only their employer advancing the organization's interests; and as consultants, where they may work for a corporate client one day and a local charity the next but still maintain some control over their working conditions, clients, and rates of pay. Public relations practitioners may also work in government departments, within large, medium, or small-sized companies; in public-sector organizations such as hospitals or universities, or in the public sphere with grassroots advocacy groups. The variability of these settings influences differences in occupational practice and poses a major challenge to the exercise of defining the "core essence" of PR.[4]

This isn't to say that there are no benchmarks for "excellence" in public relations practice, nor that PR does not aspire to professional status (see Grunig, 2001). In many public relations textbooks, students are taught the importance of open, transparent, two-way symmetrical communication as both the most strategic and ethical course of action.[5] So-called "excellent public relations" helps organizations understand the expectations and needs of their stakeholders, and then work to forge consensus about mutually beneficial courses of action (ibid). This view is in keeping with the official statements of professional associations, such as the PRSA and the Canadian Public Relations Society (CPRS), which envision public relations as a management function in which practitioners use communication to align an organization's goals, aspirations, objectives, interests with its stakeholders (e.g., employees, customers, policymakers, media, etc.) to achieve mutual understanding and serve the public interest (Flynn, 2011).[6]

Finally, while normative prescriptions for professional practice are sometimes taught in college or university curricula, they tend more often to be learned on the job and passed on through workplace socialization, where they are either applied directly, modified, or rejected depending on the situation or circumstance.

According to Berkowitz and Hristodoulakis, "organizational constraints often create a disparity between a person's idealized role and the role that is actually being practiced in the workplace setting" (1999, p. 96). And while most national societies offer accreditation programs, these tend to be symbolic rather than required since they are rarely a requirement to securing or maintaining employment.[7]

As a result of its inherently ambiguous nature, people outside PR could be excused for having difficulty understanding what it is that public practitioners do. After all, people in PR can't figure it out either! Amy Thurlow, in an article discussing what she calls the "public relations identity crisis," concluded that in the face of such occupational uncertainty, most PR practitioners just tell their families and friends, "I'm in advertising" (Thurlow, 2009).

PORTRAYING PUBLIC RELATIONS

It has become a truism to say that public relations suffers from bad PR, and to some extent the PRSA initiative was designed to confront and challenge negative perceptions and to promote an image more in keeping with the industry's own interests and goals. Where do these negative perceptions come from?

The dominant representation of public relations comes to us from a variety of media. Although there is not a lot of research on how PR has been depicted in popular culture, the images presented to us through movies, literature, television, and even music provide a lens through which to understand how popular knowledge about public relations is organized and shaped.

Cinematic depictions tend to characterize public relations practitioners as obsequious, cynical, and manipulative, with many of them focusing on the publicity dimension of professional practice.[8] In the 1901 film *Terrible Teddy, the Grizzly King*, Theodore Roosevelt is shown killing a mountain lion in Colorado while his press agent and photographer capture the event on film for posterity. In 1963's *Bye Bye Birdie*, Janet Leigh plays the role of the publicist Rosie DeLeon who concocts a clever stunt that takes a rock singer to a small Ohio town to offer one last kiss to a young fan on the Ed Sullivan Show. Even the classic monster movie, *King Kong* (both the 1933 original and the 2005 Peter Jackson remake), can be seen as a dark tale about the dangers of publicity.

The PR practitioner as crisis manager is also a common character. In the 1938 film, *Four's a Crowd*, Errol Flynn plays PR man Bob Lansford, a former editor and public relations legend; this character was purportedly based on Ivy Lee, who advised the Rockefeller Family through a number of high-profile corporate crises in the 1920s. In the 1988 film *Wag the Dog*, Robert DeNiro's character Conrad Brean is a public relations consultant whose job description essentially boils down to lying, cheating, and doing anything and everything he can to protect the image of the U.S. President. Brean even hires the Hollywood producer Stanley Motss (played by Dustin Hoffman) to manufacture a made-for-TV war in order to cover up a presidential sex scandal. *Thank You for Smoking*, Jason Reitman's 2003 film based on Christopher Buckley's satirical novel, features Aaron Eckhart as Nick Naylor, spin doctor for the tobacco industry. It's a wonderful satirization of the PR industry as a source of public manipulation and deceit. Finally, in the 2006 film *The Queen*, actor Mark Bazelev portrays Prime Minister Tony Blair's infamous public relations advisor Alastair Campbell, who described Princess Diana as "the people's princess" in an effort to help Blair capitalize on the tragedy of her untimely death.

Public relations practitioners have also been featured in popular literature. Kurt Vonnegut's classic 1952 novel, *Player Piano: America in the Coming Age of Electronics*, captures the social consequences of the consumer society and corporate culture in the United States following World War II. Vonnegut had worked as a communications executive at General Electric (one of the titans of modern industry and a pioneer in corporate promotionalism) and it's believed that the book was a fictionalized portrayal of his experiences. In *The Man in the Gray Flannel Suit*, Sloan Wilson's 1955 novel about the alienating effects of a world dominated by corporate interest, the central character, Tom Rath, leaves his job with a nonprofit organization for more pay and a shot at upward financial mobility as a public relations executive for a New York television network. Rath eventually becomes disenchanted by the alienating effects of his new job and describes "the promotion men" as by far "the most cynical of all." Denise Hamilton's 2011 novel *Damage Control* portrays the cunning, clever tactics, and ethical dilemmas, that face elite crisis communications consultant Maggie Silver. Silver is swept up in a murder and scandal involving a wealthy political

Aaron Eckhart as tobacco industry spin doctor Nick Naylor in *Thank You For Smoking*

family and has to constantly balance her personal interests and insecurities against her professional ambitions. The book's depiction of how journalists see public relations is summed up nicely in a line by reporter Fred Sentier, who claims, "You PR hacks are all the same. Cover and duck, dissemble, get your story together. You're sleazy and despicable ... I'd rather starve than work for people like you, hiring yourselves out to the highest bidder" (Hamilton, 2011, p. 85). Hamilton's professional work as a journalist—a long-time staff writer at the *LA Times* and a contributor to *Wired*, *Cosmopolitan*, and *Der Speigel*, among other media outlets—is not insignificant in assessing her characterizations of public relations.

Public relations has figured into numerous television series as well, from highly successful American network programs such as *The West Wing*, *Sex and the City*, and *Spin City* to train-wrecks like Kim Kardashian's reality show *The Spin Crowd*, which revolved around several cast members who all worked in a Hollywood PR firm, and the CBC comedy show *PR*, which dramatized the personal lives of two communications executives. Neither program lasted more than a single season. British television has also taken up the world of public relations. The BBC series *Absolute Power* is set inside Prentice-MacCabe Public Relations, a successful consultancy well known for its loose ethical standards. The show also had a short lifespan, lasting only two seasons. *Absolutely Fabulous*, another BBC production, focuses on the Edina Monsoon Creative Company, a consultancy that specializes in event management. Eddie Monsoon, the show's main character, is frequently shown living the life of a high-flying executive, frequently attending fashion and perfume launches and other celebrity events.

While we have some understanding about depictions of PR on screen and in literature, there is no research to date on its representation in music. Jimmy Buffett's 1998 song "Public Relations" tells the story of Norman Paperman, a Broadway press agent who desires to leave his soul-destroying career in PR to start his life over again on a tropical island after escaping a life-threatening illness:

> Up every morning, out every evening.
> Hustling for the headlines, that's what I do.
> Table at Sardi's, grappling for gossip.
> Working the press for a mention or two.

In the opening verse to its song "Public Relations," punk band Terror of Tiny Town (fronted by Vancouver-based musician Geoffrey Berner) depicts PR as dangerous and manipulative:

> We're not selling a product. We're selling a feeling.
> [Repeat]
> If you got something toxic that you want to sell, you better
> take it to the folks who can do the job well.
> Make it sound sexy, safe and fun, be it cigarettes, pesticides
> or guns.

Hip-hop and electronica artists have drawn on the trope of deception and spin to frame PR in a negative light as well. Vijay Iyer and Mike Ladd's track "Edward L. Bernays Flies the Hintonburg" makes explicit reference to "professional charlatans" and the "masters of sham" who were destroying culture and democracy. And Michael Gilboe's song "Spin Doctor" characterizes PR as a vehicle for escaping responsibility through deception and deceit:

> It's not about telling lies
> Just pull the wool over my eyes
> Ya just sweeten the truth with some juice
> Until you get your head out, out of the tight noose

What do all of these representations mean? Does the fact that popular culture has been generally unkind to public relations mean that people will see PR only as a form of propaganda, manipulation, and spin? Maybe yes, maybe no. While mass media provides cultural cues to help us make sense of the world around us, media audiences are also sophisticated enough to know the difference between entertainment and reality. Yet the extent to which audiences will reach alternative interpretations to those offered in popular culture will be influenced by their direct experiences as well as the availability of competing frames and perspectives. In the case of public relations, there are just too few favourable depictions in popular culture to outweigh the negative ones, and with practitioners unable to do much more than just say "I work in advertising" (Thurlow, 2009) it's debatable whether others will reach competing conclusions.

JOURNALISM AND PUBLIC RELATIONS

> Journalism is printing what someone else does not want printed; everything else is public relations.
>
> —George Orwell

Documentaries have contributed to our cultural catalogue for understanding public relations. One of the best-known documentary treatments of public relations is the 2002 BBC production *Century of the Self.* This series focused on the contributions of Sigmund Freud to public relations, tracing the influence of his theories about human drives and behaviour to his nephew Edward Bernays (discussed earlier in this chapter).

There have been several Canadian documentaries about public relations as well. The first time CBC tackled the topic of PR was in a 1964 documentary called *The Image Makers*, which generated considerable hostility from communication professionals for how it misrepresented the profession's purpose and scope. *Truth Merchants*, a 1998 production from the National Film Board of Canada, focuses on the relationship between journalism and PR through the metaphor of smoke and mirrors. The NFB's description is telling:

> Spin doctors, lobbyists, flaks—they are the sultans of spin. And in today's media-driven age, they exert enormous power, have become important (if often reviled) players in the shaping of public opinion. No major corporation or government body is without them. (Directed by Kevin MacMahon, http://onf-nfb.gc.ca/eng/collection/film/?id=33660)

Canadian journalist Ira Basen's 2007 documentary "Spin Cycles," a six-part series produced for CBC Radio's *The Sunday Edition*, explores "the world of politics, big business, advertising and public relations to find the real message behind all that spin." Although it continues to rely heavily on media spin as a focus of PR work, Basen provides a more comprehensive view of public relations than most other journalistic treatments of the subject. Nevertheless, it too did not escape criticism from some PR practitioners for being overly selective (see Neil, 2009; for a response see Basen, 2009).

The 2003 CBC documentary *Dark Side of the Moon* illustrates "how the truth can be twisted by the manipulation of images." It tells the story of how, in the late 1960s, the Nixon administration enlisted the creative talents of Stanley Kubrick and other Hollywood producers to help the United States build public support for its high-stakes space race against the Soviet Union. The 2006 documentary *The Denial Machine*, produced for CBC's Television's *The Fifth Estate*, emphasizes how fossil fuel corporations have worked with top PR agencies to manipulate public opinion about the "controversy in science" behind global warming. And the series "Love, Hate and Propaganda: The Cold War" shows how the battle for hearts and minds during and after World War II was waged across a variety of cultural institutions, including news, entertainment media, and education. This series focused heavily on media manipulation and finely tuned spin control to "reveal how governments and the industries of persuasion—marketing, advertising and public relations—operate in shaping what we believe."

Outside popular culture, the image we have of public relations is most strongly shaped by the news media. Journalists have described public relations in a predictably negative light: PR practitioners are characterized as "influence peddlers" (Crittenden, 1998) who insinuate themselves into every aspect of politics and society. One well-known Canadian book leaves little to the imagination in describing PR practitioners as *Sultans of Sleaze* (Nelson, 1986). *The Guardian* newspaper was even less reserved when it called public relations "the latrine of parasitic information" (quoted in Farish, 1998). And in March 2012, *The Guardian* ran a story with the headline "Have You Ever Been Lied to by a PR?": "The truth as we [journalists] who try to discover it know only too well, is a moving target. And our chances of hitting the bullseye with a single shot are remote, especially when PRs do their best to obfuscate." Not surprisingly, this report led to considerable eye rolling among PR practitioners, including the vice-president of the PRSA, who argued that aside from "some bad apples in public relations, the vast majority of professionals are ethical and honest. We serve the public interest by acting as responsible advocates for those we represent. We provide a voice in the marketplace of ideas, facts, and viewpoints to aid informed public debate."

Public relations has been an object of journalistic scrutiny and criticism since at least the 1920s when the industry started to take shape in the United States. As DeLorme and Fedler (2003) recount, the hostility between these two occupational groups emerged just after World War I when the press launched a campaign against "space grabbers" (i.e., publicists), whose influence, newspapermen feared, posed a threat to advertising revenue. There is an irony in the strained relationship between these two industries, however. As White and Hobsbawm argue, "in many ways, public relations is a child of journalism, called into being, shaped by, and responding to, journalism" (2007, p. 283). Indeed, many working PR practitioners today started their careers in journalism, only to eventually move over to the "dark side" after finding their news careers limiting or unsatisfying.

As Charron (1989) argues, debates about the relationship between PR and journalism typically focus on a series of normative questions: do public relations officers fulfill a legitimate role in democracy? Does the increased use of PR affect the quality of information that flows from the news media to the public sphere? Is journalistic independence and objectivity threatened by the activities of PR practitioners? Charron conceptualizes the relationship between PR and journalism as "complex and ambiguous," and characterizes it as involving the negotiation of conflict and cooperation: despite their divergent interests, public relations practitioners and journalists are "partners" in an exchange relationship who have to negotiate over resources (publicity and information) and the rules that govern the distribution of those resources.

Negotiating the News

In many ways, the relationship between PR and journalism is about the exchange of resources. Where journalists need substantive content, access to experts, and other kinds of **"information subsidies"** (Gandy, 1982) to put a news report together, public relations officers (or sources concerned about their image, reputation, and relationships) are in search of publicity or the ability to control how their image is depicted. Think of environmental organizations such as Greenpeace, which understand that building advocacy capacity and strengthening public identity as science-based campaign organizations requires an understanding and awareness about how news media operate and what journalists require for getting their own work done. Greenpeace understands the visual bias of mainstream media organizations and thus provides compelling images that are often so strong that they are impossible to ignore. But it also recognizes that effective environmental advocacy requires a foundation in science and so works hard at cultivating relations with environmental reporters to provide the supplementary research materials required to tell their stories about, among other things, the effects of climate change or the threat of offshore drilling. By subsidizing the content of mainstream media reporting, groups such as Greenpeace and the Suzuki Foundation amplify their media exposure, thus allowing them to build and maintain their reputations as credible and reliable news sources (Greenberg and MacAulay, 2009, p. 72).

According to Charron, journalists and PR practitioners "are willing to make certain concessions to obtain what they are looking for" and thus "tacitly coordinate" their activities to ensure they achieve mutually beneficial outcomes (1989, p. 44). Public relations strategists will try to adapt their source's message to both the narrative requirements and structural constraints of news production, while journalists will more likely integrate source material if it addresses certain news values and can be supported by evidence. This isn't to say that journalists and PR practitioners sit down and agree on what a news story will involve, which sources will be included, or what they will say, specifically. Nor is it to say that journalists will automatically and uncritically take what PR practitioners provide them at face value (although many do so). It's to say that there is a mutual recognition that each side has something to offer the other, and that because both occupations operate in an environment of constraint (e.g. deadlines, availability of news gathering resources, client demands/expectations, etc.) they align their occupational activities in such a way that enables them to get their work done.

The relationship between public relations and journalism is thus organized by a combination of opportunities and constraints. The "framework for negotiations" (Charron, 1989, p. 44) between journalism and PR establishes whether one side will be able to effectively influence the conduct of the other. For PR practitioners, sometimes the goal is to influence whether a journalist will be interested in covering a story that can help advance a client or employer's interests, and, if he or she is interested, how that story will be told: which elements will be emphasized, which will be downplayed, what evidence will be brought to bear, etc. Aware of the time pressures journalists face in "putting reality together" (Schlesinger, 1978), PR practitioners seek to leverage journalistic constraints as an opportunity for influencing their actions (whether increasing media attention or reducing it). Tactically, if the objective is to limit the time journalists have for deep investigation, given awareness about their desire to be first in reporting the news, a government agency might call a news conference as close to editorial deadline as possible. If, on the other hand, the goal is to increase knowledge and awareness and promote greater information flow, providing reporters with more time and offering additional resources (e.g., sources with compelling stories, scientific research, testimonials, etc.) can help advance that goal.

CONCLUSION

As a result of how the mass media has portrayed public relations, the sector has been placed into a position of always having to defend its contributions and actions. Where some practitioners have confronted the industry's dark side to demand more transparency, ethical behaviour, and accountability (e.g., Hoggan, 2009), others have challenged the media caricature that PR professionals are a secret cabal of hidden persuaders and accuse journalists who write critically about PR of engaging in a kind of spin doctoring of their own (e.g., Neil, 2009). Many PR practitioners argue that their role is to be an advocate or facilitator of stakeholder and public dialogue, i.e., information brokers who help business, governments, nonprofit groups, and other organizations communicate with one another, the media, and the public about issues and events that are important to all. Ultimately, public relations practitioners prefer to see their industry not as a force of darkness, but as a force for social good that can promote mutual understanding, positive relationships, and contribute to a just society. Yet, as this chapter has documented, this is a view that is subject to considerable contestation and debate.

QUESTIONS

1. In what ways can PR be used to both reproduce and challenge existing relations of power?
2. In what ways has the practice of public relations remained the same and in what ways has it changed since the time of Edward Bernays?
3. What factors account for the significant difference between how mass media depict public relations and how public relations professionals see themselves?

NOTES

1. Jacquie L'Etang argues that this view of public relations suffers from numerous historical blindspots. The notion that PR was invented in America and then exported around the world "is patently not true" and that "in many countries public relations were carried out at various stages" depending on a variety of organizational demands and contexts. (2008, p. 31).
2. Yet as one biographer argues, Bernays' knowledge of psychoanalysis was thin at best, and he should be remembered more for trading on the Freud name as a way to promote his agency than for any contribution he might have made to turning public relations into a science (Tye, 1998).
3. The preceding draws from the Edward Bernays entry at the online Museum of Public Relations. See http://www.prmuseum.com/bernays/bernays_1920.html
4. Indeed, as Berkowitz and Hristodoulakis (1999) argue, the variability in public relations work has led to a low level of consensus about the nature and the characteristics of good PR activities. "Some practitioners see themselves as providing publicity for an organization, whereas others envision their role as maintainers of long-term relationships with an organization's publics ... there is not a broad professional definition of good public relations that spans organizations, and there are not always experienced overseers of public relations practitioners who could ensure a consistent definition of public relations quality" (p. 92).

5. This is the official doctrine taught to students in public relations programs. Students in other disciplines, from communication studies and journalism to sociology and political science, are more likely to be taught that public relations is a tool of official power and an obstacle to democracy.
6. Neither the PRSA's definitional project nor the established view of public relations as a management function are universally supported. Some practitioners see both exercises as unnecessarily limiting and even intellectually dishonest (e.g. Yaxley, 2011).
7. Although public relations is not a profession in the formal sense of the term, it has been subject to ongoing processes of professionalization in the sense that PR industry associations have been concerned for years with establishing standards of integrity and competence, including identifying and demarcating qualified practitioners from amateurs. On public relations and professionalization in Canada, see Johansen (2001).
8. This section on cinematic depictions of public relations draws from Miller (1999).

REFERENCES

Anderson, A. (2003). Environmental activism and news media. In S. Cottle (ed.) *News, public relations and power* (pp. 117–32). London: Sage.

Basen, I. (2009). A response to Boyd Neil. *Canadian Journal of Communication, 34*(2), 311–314.

Berkowitz, D., and Hristodoulakis, I. (2009). Practitioner roles, public relations education, and professional socialization: An exploratory study. *Journal of Public Relations Research, 11*(1), 91–103.

Charron, J. (1989). Relations between journalists and public relations practitioners: Cooperation, conflict and negotiation. *Canadian Journal of Communication, 14*(2), 41–54.

Cline, C. G. (1982). The image of public relations in mass communications texts. *Public Relations Review, 58*(8), 63–78.

Crittenden G. (1998). Flack attack. *The Globe and Mail*, 31 October, p. D1.

Davis, A. (2002). *Public relations democracy*. Manchester: University of Manchester Press.

Deacon, D. (2003). Non-governmental organisations and the media. In S. Cottle (ed.) *News, public relations and power* (pp. 99–116). London: Sage.

DeLorme, D. E., & Fedler, F. (2003). Journalists' hostility toward public relations: An historical analysis. *Public Relations Review, 29*(2), 99–124.

Ewen, S. (1988). *PR! A social history of spin*. New York: Basic Books.

Farish, S (1998). *Managing communication in a changing world*. London: IPR.

Flynn, T. (2011, 7 December.). A defining moment for public relations. *PR conversations: Global discussions of public relations from local perspectives*. Retrieved

August 13, 2012, from http://www.prconversations.com/index.php/2011/12/a-defining-moment-for-public-relations

Friedl, B., Ed. (1990). *On to victory: Propaganda plays of the woman suffrage movement.* Chicago: Northeastern University Press.

Gandy, O.H. (1982). *Beyond agenda setting: Information subsidies and public policy.* Norwood, NJ: Ablex Publishers.

Garraty, J. (1960). The United States steel corporation versus labor: The early years. *Labor History, 1*(1), 3–38.

Greenberg, J., & Grosenick, G. (2008). Building communicative capacity in the third sector: Research from Canada. *Third Sector Review, 14*(2), 51–74.

Greenberg, J., & MacAulay, M. (2009). NPO 2.0? Exploring the web presence of environmental nonprofit organizations in Canada. *Global Media Journal—Canadian Edition, 2*(1), 63–88.

Greenberg, J., May, T., and Elliott, C. (2006). Homelessness and media activism in the voluntary sector: A case study. *The Philanthropist, 20*(2), 131–152.

Greenberg, J., and Walters, D. (2004). Promoting philanthropy? News publicity and voluntary organizations in Canada. *Voluntas, 15*(4), 383–404.

Greenberg, J., & Westersund, E. (2010). Smog and mirrors: Climate change and the Janus face of public relations. In L.R. Shade (ed.) *Mediascapes: New patterns in Canadian communication, 3rd ed.* (pp. 287–306). Toronto: Nelson Canada.

Grunig, J. E. (2001). Two-way symmetrical public relations: Past, present, and future. In R. L. Heath (ed.), *Handbook of public relations* (pp. 11–30). Thousand Oaks, CA: Sage.

Hamilton, D. (2011). *Damage control: A novel.* New York: Scribner.

Harlow, R.F. (1977). Building a public relations definition. *Public Relations Review, 2*(4), 34–42.

Hiebert, R.E. (1966). *Courier to the crowd: The story of Ivy Lee and the development of public relations.* Ames, IA: Iowa State University Press.

Hill Times. (2010). PMO like an iceberg: Only one-quarter showing publicly, rest out of sight. Retrieved August 13, 2012, from http://www.hilltimes.com/news/2010/11/08/pmo-like-an-iceberg-only-one-quarter-showing-publicly-rest-out-of-sight/24851

Hutton, J.G. (1999). The definition, dimensions and domain of public relations. *Public Relations Review, 25*(2), 199–214.

Jones, S., & S. Weir. (2002, February 25). The masters of misinformation. *New Statesman.* Retrieved from http://www.newstatesman.com/200202250020

Kamen, J. (2007, October 26). FEMA meets the press, which happens to be ... FEMA. *The Washington Post.* Retrieved August 13, 2012, from http://www.washingtonpost.com/wp-dyn/content/article/2007/10/25/AR2007102502488.html

Knight, G., & Greenberg, J. (2002). Promotionalism and subpolitics: Nike and its labor critics. *Management Communication Quarterly, 15*(4), 541–570.

Lepore, J. (2012). The life factory: How politics became a business. The New Yorker, (24 September). Retrieved October 15, 2012 from. http://www.newyorker.com/reporting/2012/09/24/120924fa_fact_lepore?currentPage=all

L'Etang, J. (2003). Myth of the "ethical guardian." *Journal of Communication Management*, *8*(1), 53–67.

———. (2008). *Public relations: Concept, practice and critique*. London: Sage.

Lippmann, W. (1914). *Drift and mastery: An attempt to diagnose the current unrest*. New York.

Marchand, R. (2001). *Creating the corporate soul: The rise of public relations and corporate imagery in American big business*. Berkeley: University of California Press.

Mayhew, L. (1997). *The new public: Professional communication and the means of social influence*. Cambridge: Cambridge University Press.

Miller, K. (1999). Public relations in film and fiction: 1930–1995. *Journal of Public Relations Research*, *11*(1), 3–28.

Miller, D., & Dinan, W. (2007). *Thinker, faker, spinner, spy: Corporate PR and the assault on democracy*. London: Pluto.

———. (2008). *A century of spin: How public relations became the cutting edge of corporate power*. London: Pluto.

Mintz, S., & McNeil, S. (2012). "The Corporate Revolution." *Digital History*. Retrieved August 15, 2012 from http://www.digitalhistory.uh.edu

Neil, B. (2009). Spin cycles unspun. *Canadian Journal of Communication*, *34*(2), 307–311.

Nelson, J. (1986). *Sultans of sleaze: Public relations and the media*. Toronto: Between the Lines.

Ponsford, Dominic. (2012, March 6). Have you ever been lied to by a PR? Retrieved August 29, 2012, from http://www.guardian.co.uk/media/greenslade/2012/mar/07/marketingandpr-newspapers

Rickey, David. (2012, February 23). Public relations defined: Our teachable moment. Retrieved August 29, 2012, from http://prsay.prsa.org/index.php/2012/02/23/public-relations-defined-our-teachable-moment

Schlesinger, P. (1978). *Putting reality together*. London: Constable.

Schlesinger, P., & Tumber, H. (1994). *Reporting crime: The media politics of criminal justice*. Oxford University Press.

Thurlow, A. (2009). "I just say I'm in advertising": A public relations identity crisis. *Canadian Journal of Communication*, *34*(2), 245–264.

Tickner, L. (1988). *The spectacle of women: Imagery of the suffrage campaign, 1907–14*. Chicago: University of Chicago Press.

Tromp, S. (2012, February 17). Mayor spent $85,934 on PR consultants. *Vancouver Courier*. Retrieved August 14, 2102, from http://www.vancourier.com/technology/Mayor+spent+consultants/6168176/story.html

Tye, L. (1998). *The father of spin: Edward L. Bernays and the birth of public relations*. New York: Henry Holt & Co.

White, J., & Hobsbawm, J. (2007). Public relations and *journalism. Journalism Practice*, *1*(2), 283–292.

Yaxley, H. (2011). Why I don't care about defining public relations. *PR Conversations*. Retrieved August 13, 2012, from http://greenbanana.wordpress.com/2011/12/05/why-i-dont-care-about-defining-public-relations

York, G. (2012, January 31). Africa on K Street: How a U.S. agency cleaned up Rwanda's genocide-stained image. *The Globe and Mail*. Retrieved from http://www.theglobeandmail.com/subscribe.jsp?art=2322005

12

THE CANADIAN VIDEO GAME INDUSTRY

Mia Consalvo
Concordia University

INTRODUCTION

Video games have become a central part of popular culture, as well as a key economic driver in the media industries. In 2010, sales of hardware and software to play games totalled more than $1.7 billion in Canada, and most expect such numbers to steadily rise (SECOR, 2011). Who's playing all of those games? It depends on what type of game it is, and on what platform, but 59 percent of Canadians say they are gamers, and the average age of a gamer is 33 years old. Overall, 38 percent are female, although the numbers are higher when looking at certain genres, such as mobile, social, and casual games, as well as on certain platforms, such as handheld systems (Entertainment Software Association of Canada, 2011). Almost one-third of Canadians say they play games every day, with the majority (45 percent) picking up a game controller (or using a mouse or touchscreen) a few days a week (Entertainment Software Association of Canada, 2011). As far as popularity of platforms go, consoles aren't the dominant force in gaming that they were less than a decade ago. Just about half of players (49 percent) say they play on a computer, with one-third (34 percent) playing via a console like the Xbox 360, Playstation 3 or Wii, a tenth (10 percent) playing on a handheld system, and only 7 percent on a smartphone or similar device (Entertainment Software Association of Canada, 2011).

Yet where do these games come from? Who's making the games so many of us are playing, and who is profiting? Historically, game development was dominated by companies in Japan and the United States, and the United Kingdom was third in the world in games production. But recently things have shifted, and Canada is now the third largest producer of games. However, although more and more game creation is based in Canada, many of the largest companies doing business here are from somewhere else. As in many other media industries, large publishers control most of the global market for games, determining what is made, for whom, and where it will be created. As Table 12.1 demonstrates, the majority of game companies with the largest revenues and global influence are not from Canada.

Yet even though most of the companies ultimately profiting from the sales of games are from the United States and Japan, there are many small and mid-sized Canadian-owned studios making games for a variety of platforms and in multiple

TABLE 12.1 Game Companies by Revenues

Rank	Name	Revenues, 2009	Country of Origin
1	Nintendo	6,799	Japan
2	Activision Blizzard	4,279	USA
3	Electronic Arts	3,728	USA
4	Sony	1,914	Japan
5	Microsoft	1,741	USA
6	Konami	1,594	Japan
7	Ubisoft	1,249	France
8	Take-Two Interactive	916	USA
9	Square Enix	916	Japan
10	THQ	909	USA

*Revenues are in millions of US dollars; all information from van Kooten, 2010.

Source: Van Kooten, Michel (2010). Top 25 Gaming Companies 2010. *Software Top 100.* Retrieved from http://www.softwaretop100.org/top-25-gaming-companies-2010

genres. This chapter investigates the history of the game industry, including how economic models for selling games have driven game design, as well as how newer platforms for games have challenged traditional business models and introduced new types of players to games. It includes a detailed study of the Canadian firm BioWare and its role-playing-game business and discusses the history of game regulation and labour conditions in the industry. It concludes by speculating on the history of the video game industry in Canada as well as globally, as the two are irreversibly intertwined.

OVERVIEW OF DIGITAL GAME INDUSTRY ECONOMIC MODEL

Although this chapter focuses on the business side of the game industry, it is important to remember that game design has historically been linked with how games are sold. Thus, early games designed to be played in arcades via a cabinet and paid for via quarters or tokens featured escalating difficulty yet open-ended game play—there were rarely, if ever, any endings to games such as *Pac Man*, *Donkey Kong*, or *Centipede*. Instead, players paid for continued access to a game, either buying more lives or extending the time available to play in some manner. Designers were thus trying to encourage players to extend their play experiences, and elite players could play for hours, perhaps finishing only when an unintended **"kill screen"** (signalling an error in the game's code at upper levels) finally put an end to their seemingly endless play session.

That style of play worked well for cabinet-style games played in arcades or other public places. Players were essentially renting access to one or more machines and games for a certain period of time, and the industry was focused on extending that play via continued small payments for as long as possible. Arcades were popular and profitable in North America in the 1980s, and have been continually popular in Japan, only recently beginning a decline in revenue there (Ishaan, 2010). In the west, class-based concerns about who frequented arcades, and the rise of relatively high quality home systems for game play led to the demise in popularity of arcades, and with them, a particular system for generating revenue. Thus the move toward console systems and home-based play led developers to consider how best to sell games in that context, and what those games should be like in terms of their design.

What happened wasn't really a new development—games were already in the home, having been created for home computers at the same time that arcade games were popular. Yet the shift from arcades to home as the locus for now practically all gaming activity meant that more and more play was based on that model. So rather than developers imagining a game with endless play, no save points, and increasing difficulty, different kinds of games could be imagined. Although it would be some time before console games featured the ability to save a player's progress, games with ending points now became more popular, allowing some form of closure or "win state" in counterpoint to simply losing via the loss of lives or points. And with the coming of save points, games that demanded many more hours than a single sitting emerged, allowing a greater complexity to stories and worlds to become possible.

Yet most importantly, a new pricing model was called for with the rise of console games. Arcade games asked for a stream of quarters, and PC games could be based on actual costs of production, and the assumption that players already owned a PC that would run the game in question. Yet for console games, a different model emerged. Often referred to as the **"razor and blades" model,** consoles were usually sold at an initial loss, to allow many potential players to purchase them, in order to create a large "installed base" for purchasing games. Games were then sold at set prices, with a licensing fee paid to the console company to help it recoup its initial R&D and production costs for the console.

For example, when Nintendo created its Nintendo Entertainment System (NES) and sold it in the West, it designed the system to accept only game cartridges that had been approved by Nintendo to run on it. Game developers and publishers were forced to obtain approval from Nintendo to publish games for the NES, and also had to pay them a licensing fee for each copy of the game produced. Nintendo's strict rules for which companies could publish a game on its system and what its content would be like have been criticized but also acknowledged as a practice that ultimately re-established the legitimacy and profitability of the home console industry in North America after the disastrous crash in 1983, when a glut of inferior games causes prices to first sink and then demand to disappear as consumers were unable and then unwilling to distinguish between good and inferior games (Sheff, 1999).

That model has been predominant in the core of the game industry until quite recently, with game and console publishers relying on a certain number of console systems being sold, a number of exclusive titles for specific consoles, and the need for large installed bases of "core gamers" to form the basis of the market. Over the years, Nintendo has remained a dominant producer of consoles; Sega provided a key challenge to Nintendo during its SNES phase, but later left the market due to the poor sales of its Dreamcast console; Sony, which unseated Sega, continues with its

PlayStation series; and Microsoft is the most recent successful entrant, with its Xbox line. Yet the "walled garden" style of console systems began to falter and change with the growth of online play, digital distribution, and the emergence of new markets and new technologies for play.

Although the first console to feature online connectivity was actually the ill-fated Sega Dreamcast released in 1998 in Japan and 1999 elsewhere, online play didn't become widely adopted until Microsoft introduced Xbox Live in 2002. At first, such connectivity mostly meant access to servers for multiplayer games such as sports or shooter games, allowing for greater diversity in a player's choice of competitors, or the chance to play a **massively multiplayer online game (MMOG)**, although most of those were played (and continue to be played) via PC. Connectivity also gave console game makers the ability to add new content to previously released games—making them closer to PC-based games in terms of patches and new downloadable content. But, more importantly, services such as Xbox Live and later Sony's Playstation Store became channels for smaller game developers to market their games via services such as Live Arcade. Coupled with the emergence of Valve's Steam service on the PC, digital distribution created new avenues for developers to sell their products outside the traditional game box and retail market, and created new ways to think about pricing and selling games, add-on content, and other extras.

At the same time, developments outside consoles were widening the market for the game industry into demographics largely untouched. One of the biggest—but unforeseen—was the emergence of Apple's iPhone. Prior to it, mobile games were a scattered, largely neglected market. Mobile phones usually featured very different operating systems, screen sizes, and resolutions, and no user-friendly pricing systems or even business models for selling games. That all changed with the release of the iPhone and, more importantly the opening of the App Store to selling games. Less than a year after the opening of the store, more than 10 million apps had been downloaded, and games compose almost three-quarters of all apps, indicating that mobile games are now considered a major revenue source (if not the top source) for app sales on all iOS systems (Consalvo, 2012). In the process, Apple has unwittingly become a key publisher for games, creating a climate conducive for smaller games. That includes quirky titles such as the Finnish best-seller *Angry Birds*

TABLE 12.2 Game Development Costs in Canada by Platform

Platform	Average Cost	Minimum Cost	Maximum Cost	Dev. Days
Traditional Console	$10 million	$150,000	$30 million	380
MMO	$1.1 million	$50,000	$3 million	438
PC	$1 million	$15,000	$15 million	368
Downloadable Console	$604,000	$20,000	$3 million	261
Casual	$462,000	$2,000	$8 million	152
Handheld	$398,000	$32,000	$2.3 million	151
Social	$238,000	$6,000	$1.4 million	197
Mobile	$166,000	$2,000	$3.2 million	96

*Information taken from ESAC "Essential Facts 2011"

Source: Entertainment Software Association of Canada. (2011). *Essential facts about the Canadian computer and video game industry*. Retrieved from http://www.theesa.ca/?page_id=22

and *Superbrothers: Sword & Sworcery*, created by indie studio Capybara Games in Toronto, both of which exploited the **affordances** of—or technological opportunities offered by—Apple's touch screens, and likewise also reached new markets for players, compared to the traditional console market.

THE CANADIAN GAME INDUSTRY

The current state of the game industry in Canada is quite strong. It is currently ranked third in the world as a centre of game production, behind only the United States and Japan. Estimates vary, but approximately 300 to 350 companies employ between 14,000 and16,000 workers coast-to-coast. Developers and publishers generate revenues of $2 billion (Gouglas et al., 2010) and the industry is expected to continue growing by 29 percent over the next five years (SECOR, 2011). Canada is considered a "net exporter" of games, with more than half of Canadian game companies relying on foreign sales for 90 to 100 percent of their revenues (SECOR, 2011). Of the 50 top selling games of 2009 in North America and Europe, 10 were produced by Canadian game development studios (Edge Staff, 2009).

Companies themselves can be quite different, not only in focus but also in size. Currently the majority of companies (43 percent) employ between 6 and 50 workers, with the average size of a firm being 57 employees (Entertainment Software Association of Canada, 2011). However, it is a small group of companies (12 percent of all firms) that employ the most workers: large companies with 151 or more individuals control most of the workers in the industry (Entertainment Software Association of Canada, 2011). And indeed, there are several "mega-companies" such as Ubisoft, which employ thousands of workers across the provinces (Canadian Interactive Alliance, 2009). Where do these companies come from? As Gouglas et al report, "the vast majority of these companies are Canadian owned (85 percent). However, the companies that are owned by foreign parent companies are by far the largest in size. In other words, the Canadian-owned companies tend to be small to mid-sized independent game studios" (2010, p. 6). This means that a small handful of companies, with origins outside Canada, control most of game development in the country, and control most of the profits.

By Province

The game industry isn't spread equally across Canada, but clusters in several regions. The majority of studios are found in Ontario (35 percent), British Columbia (31 percent), and Quebec (21 percent). Quebec is home to the largest studios in Canada, and Montreal employs the largest workforce—estimated at 6,000 to 8,000 employees (Canadian Interactive Alliance, 2009; Entertainment Software Association of Canada, 2011). In addition to game development studios (such as those listed in Table 12.3), Quebec also has middleware and game-engine companies that support the industry

TABLE 12.3 Game Companies by Province

Province	No. of Game-Related Companies	Major Companies
British Columbia	94	EA Games, Koei, Take Two, Radical, Relic
Prairie Provinces	22	BioWare, GamesCafe
Ontario	106	Capcom, Disney, EA, Rockstar, Ubisoft
Quebec	65	EA, Gameloft, Eidos, Funcom, Ubisoft, THQ, Behaviour, WB
Atlantic Provinces	18*	HB Studios, Long Tails, Other Ocean

*All information from this table taken from Gouglas et al., 2010. However, that report does not list the number of game-related companies in the Atlantic Provinces, although it does say the number is "small and comparable" to the number in the Prairies. This number (18) is taken from the Canadian Interactive Alliance 2009 Report, which focuses more broadly on interactive digital media firms, which contains game studios as the majority, but not only, type of firm.

Source: Gouglas, S., J. Della Rocca, J. Jenson, K. Kee, G. Rockwell, J. Schaeffer, B. Simon, & R. Wakkary, (2010). *Computer games and Canada's digital economy: The role of universities in promoting innovation.* Report to the Social Science Humanities Research Council Knowledge Synthesis Grants on Canada's digital economy. Retrieved from http://ra.tapor.ualberta.ca/~circa/wp-content/uploads/2010/03/ComputerGamesAndCanadasDigitalEconomy1.pdf

and facilitate development (Gouglas et al., 2010). Ontario has the largest number of game companies overall (Entertainment Software Association of Canada, 2011; Gouglas et al., 2010), and Toronto is considered to have the strongest indie scene in the country (Gouglas et al., 2010; Woo, 2011). Given their size and budgets, as well as creative interests, many of these companies focus on games that are not "core" console or triple-A titles, instead creating games for the Web, for mobile devices, or to be sold via digital distribution. Notable small companies include Capybara Games, which made the critically acclaimed and best-selling iOS title *Superbrothers: Sword & Sworcery* and Bigpants Games, which won the IndieCade 2011 Audience Choice Award for its game *The Depths to Which I Sink* (Woo, 2011). British Columbia has its game industry centralized around Vancouver, where most companies are small to medium sized, although a few giants, including EA, Radical and Relic are present as well. There are estimated to be almost 4,000 employees in the game industry in British Columbia, although recent layoffs and closures in the region have likely reduced those numbers somewhat (Chapple, 2012; Entertainment Software Association of Canada, 2011; Tipps, 2012). Finally, although it is largely alone geographically, special mention should be made of Alberta-based studio BioWare, founded in Edmonton by physicians who wanted to make video games. A special section of this chapter covers the history and economic situation of this company, which has been particularly successful in the history of the Canadian video game industry.

Tax Credits and Interactive Digital Media

Growth in the Canadian game industry has been rather recent, as it was only in 2010 that Canada overtook the United Kingdom as the third largest developer of games in the world. And tax credits have been acknowledged as one key to that success, particularly in relation to large multinational firms. The practice gained international attention in 1997, when Quebec succeeded in bringing French publisher Ubisoft to its province, based in part on such perks. With no language barrier and labour prices that were lower than in the United States, Quebec (and later the rest of Canada) was a logical choice for the maker of games such as those in the *Assassin's Creed*, *Prince of Persia*, and *Far Cry* series. It was also successful—currently Ubisoft Montreal employs more than 2100 workers, with another 600 in Quebec City, Toronto, and Vancouver. Further, the Toronto branch is expected to expand to 800 employees, in order to produce more triple-A titles, including additional titles in the *Splinter Cell* series (The French Connection, 2011).

Examples of current tax credits that provinces employ include the following:

- The Nova Scotia Digital Media Tax Credit: Businesses can claim a 50 percent tax credit for labour costs or a 25 percent credit for all eligible expenses incurred in the province, whichever is less;
- The PEI Innovation and Development Tax Credit Program gives up to a 150 percent rebate on the first 35 percent of eligible labour costs;
- Newfoundland's Business Attraction Fund provides loans and equity investments to large firms thinking about starting up or expanding in the province;
- The BC Interactive Digital Media Tax Credit provides a refundable 17.5 percent tax credit on eligible salary and wages;
- The Ontario Interactive Digital Media Tax Credit, which offers a 25 to 30 percent credit (depending on company size) for eligible labour expenditures and marketing/distribution expenditures;
- Quebec's Crédit d'impôt remboursable de production des titres multimédia (Production of Multimedia Titles Tax Credit) offers a labour tax credit of up to 37.5 percent for French-language interactive digital media productions;
- Alberta has a Multimedia Development Fund that permits 20 to 29 percent of Alberta production costs to be recovered as a nonrecoupable grant. (Canadian Interactive Alliance, 2009; PWC, 2011)

While such credits have been attractive lures for some companies, there are critics of the practice. Within the industry itself, some fear that provinces will begin to outbid each other with larger and larger credits to lure existing companies away from neighbouring provinces, thus not increasing the actual number of jobs or studios in Canada, but instead merely shifting them around. Others argue the credits drain local economies of needed revenue, offering financial help to those (large firms) who need it least. Some believe that a more important strategy is to build local communities of talented workers, and encourage them to start their own companies, rather than rely on foreign companies to boost revenues. But although some game companies do reference such tax credits in their reasoning for locating in Canada, it remains an open question how beneficial they will be in the long term.

History of BioWare

One way to better understand the history and impact of Canadian studios on the video game industry is through a case study of a particular firm, to illustrate how global shifts and changing technological contexts help to shape the structure of the larger whole in a particular instance. Given its strong roots in Edmonton and global reputation for critically acclaimed games, BioWare is an excellent example on which to expand.

BioWare was founded in 1995 by three students studying medicine at the University of Alberta: Ray Muzyka, Greg Zeschuck, and Augustin Yip. BioWare's name drew on that love of medicine, coming from a combination of "bio," the Greek for "from the chemist" and "ware," for "stuff" (Whitehead, 2007). The three enjoyed practising medicine, but also wanted to make games, and continued to do both in the early years of their studio. To get started as developers they pooled their savings, a total of about $100,000 to make their first game: *Shattered Steel.* The game was a modest hit and was well received critically, and they developed a good relationship with publisher Interplay, a United States–based company best known for its creation of the *Fallout* series of video games.

The next game BioWare created is the one that put the company on the larger game industry map, establishing its reputation for creating immersive and compelling computer role-playing games. With Interplay's assistance BioWare acquired the license to use the *Advanced Dungeons & Dragons* rule set, and the game the company had originally titled *Battleground: Infinity* became *Baldur's Gate,* released in 1998. Receiving widespread acclaim and strong reviews, the game had a 91 percent score on Metacritic, and sold more than two million units. It also led to the release of an expansion pack, *Tales of the Sword Coast,* and later a sequel, *Baldur's Gate II: Shadows of Amn* in 2000 which also sold more than two million units and earned a 95 percent score on Metacritic (Bioware, 2008).

From there, BioWare branched out, creating the action-adventure title *MDK2* in 2000, but then returned to its strength: creating computer-based RPGs. Over the years BioWare has experimented with the form via the creation of very different fictional story worlds, going beyond fantasy and magic to themes including science fiction and Asian lore. The company also began to develop games for console systems in addition to the PC, as the market for PC games began a slow decline. Major titles include *Neverwinter Nights, Star Wars: Knights of the Old Republic, Jade Empire,* games in the *Mass Effect* and *Dragon Age* series, as well as the massively multiplayer online game *Star Wars: The Old Republic.*

Within RPGs, BioWare has constantly innovated in terms of technological advancements and business models. It has also expanded operations and moved beyond a single studio, partnering with multiple international publishers over the years and negotiating opportunities to merge with other studios as well as ultimately be acquired itself. Before discussing how the company has restructured itself to deal with global business concerns, it's also helpful to see how BioWare's games have responded to (or led) changing technological landscapes and increased interaction options for players.

While the strength of the company's games lies in the RPG genre and the engines it has designed and built to run those games, it has also experimented with varying gameplay elements within that genre, helping to expand player expectations for what an RPG should be like. For example, with the release of *Neverwinter Nights* in 2002, BioWare included a toolset for players, that allowed them to "create their own content, build worlds, pen stories, and design quests. This feature alone ensured an almost endless flow of content and a healthy mod scene that continues to this day" (Fahs, 2010). Such elements have become if not required then strongly requested by players who now expect to be able to make their own mods or levels for games such as *Little Big Planet*, *Skyrim*, and *The Sims*. Although debates have ensued about who owns such user-created content, and the ethics of using players to sustain the value and content in a game, the early implementation of that element by BioWare helped it establish such elements as part of a successful digital game, an expectation that continues with contemporary games.

BioWare also innovated with *Neverwinter Nights* via the inclusion of online play. The company offered servers that created online worlds allowing up to 75 players to gather at a time and play together, as well as "the ability to connect multiple servers to create a larger world" (Fahs, 2010). Such instances of *Neverwinter Nights* were not like persistent worlds such as *World of Warcraft*—they could be created and run only via player activation, and once players left, they did not persist. Continuing to grow, BioWare utilized the *Star Wars* license to develop *Star Wars: Knights of the Old Republic* in 2003, which was its first title to be available on console systems. The Xbox version of the game sold more than one million copies, demonstrating the business opportunities in console gameplay (Fahs, 2010). From that point, the company has continued to offer its games on PC, Mac, and consoles, to reach the broadest possible audience.

BioWare has continued to capitalize on Star Wars as a valuable intellectual property (IP) brand, most recently creating the MMOG *Star Wars: The Old Republic*, launched in late 2011 and creating competition for Blizzard's worldwide hit *World of Warcraft* (Rose, 2012). Yet BioWare has also created hit games with original IP, despite industry beliefs that only established licenses will sell titles. Its three *Mass Effect* titles have sold more than 10 million copies so far and been localized into eight languages, while its two *Dragon Age* games have sold six million copies (Kietzmann, 2010; VGChartz, 2012). The games in these series have also been augmented with expansion packs and downloadable content, featuring multiple story add-ons and world augmentations. While such elements do extend the life of a game and create new revenue streams, the company received criticism for its announcement of additional downloadable content (DLC)—effectively an expansion of sorts for *Mass Effect 3*—that would appear on the day of the game's initial release for an additional cost (Kain, 2012). Critics, including industry journalists as well as players, wonder about the value of a new game that is already deemed "incomplete" on its first day, with elements that were perhaps stripped out of the original to be sold for additional profit. Yet the continued success of such DLC ensures the practice will continue in some form for the foreseeable future.

Over the course of this history BioWare has itself expanded to meet the needs of its growing teams as well as multiple constituencies. While still operating its original studio in Edmonton, the group opened BioWare Austin in 2006 in order to create the MMOG *The Old Republic*, hiring industry veterans Gordon Walton and Rich Vogel to lead that group. In 2009 the company opened BioWare Montreal in order to augment efforts on existing projects, including its *Mass Effect* and *Dragon Age* titles. The company has also made strategic moves to expand its revenue and influence in other arenas as well. In 2005 the company formed an alliance with Pandemic Entertainment, best known as the creator of action adventure titles such as *Star Wars: Battlefront II* and *Destroy All Humans*. The alliance was actually a $300 million deal via the venture capital firm Elevation Partners, which combined the two studios yet left BioWare with a "significant level of autonomy" in managing its own studios (www.referenceforbusiness.com). Two years later BioWare agreed to be acquired by EA in a deal valued at more than $600 million (Crecente, 2007). In 2009 BioWare formed BioWare Mythic via the acquisition and merger with Virginia-based Mythic Entertainment; opened BioWare Galway in Ireland in 2011, which is a customer service centre; and later that year created BioWare San Francisco, essentially renaming EA 2D into the BioWare brand. The company continues to expand into new areas, as it did with the release of the social network game *Dragon Age Legends*, which served as a promotional tool for the release of *Dragon Age II*. The game was also hyped as the "first real Facebook game" and as of fall 2011 had more than 200,000 monthly active users (GDC Online Speaker Spotlight, 2011).

BioWare continues to enjoy strong sales for its games, but criticisms of some of its business practices are increasing. In addition to complaints about the downloadable content for *Mass Effect 3*, players have also expressed dissatisfaction with the ending of the game, and some elements of the online multiplayer component (Kain, 2012). However, the company is still doing quite well financially. At the end of 2011 EA reported that BioWare's *Star Wars: The Old Republic* had 1.7 million subscribers, and less than a month after release *Mass Effect 3* had sold more than three million units worldwide (Curtis, 2012; VGChartz, 2012). BioWare also retains an element of control not always accorded companies purchased by larger publishers such as EA, but it does remain beholden to a larger corporation, whose future plans and strategies may occasionally be at odds with its own plans.

The Political Side of the Industry: Ratings, Legislation, Labour Conditions

New media and technological forms usually evoke some fears among groups and individuals, particularly when such forms are directed toward—even partially—at children. For example, echoing fears of pool halls and other potentially "dangerous" establishments, in the 1980s the city of Montreal passed legislation to keep children under the age of 18 out of arcades (Supreme Court of Canada, 1985); it was not alone in doing so—activist parents in the United States did not even want arcades operating near schools (Gonzalez, 2012). Even when municipalities did not prohibit entrance to minors, some did restrict access during school hours, and some arcades themselves took voluntary steps to monitor their customers, to ensure the sites weren't attractive options enticing students to skip school.

With the rise of home console and PC systems, parental control over access could more easily be established with regards to how and when children as well as adults played games, and the focus instead turned to the content of games. Initially there was no legislation in the West or elsewhere that regulated digital game content, and over the years the industry has worked diligently to ensure that voluntary regulations and ratings systems are the norm across the globe, albeit with mixed success.

The first forms of regulation were internal to game developers and producers, which self-regulated what could and could not appear in games. Nintendo in particular saw its role as enforcer of family-friendly content, the better to reintroduce games and console systems into the West. Over the 1980s and early 1990s, Nintendo's internal guidelines were meant to circumvent the need for laws or critique (which also meant potentially lost sales). As Sheff explains, Nintendo had an internal code for its games that "consisted of a set of rules that its licensees had to adhere to when creating a new product; the rules determined what couldn't appear in the game. Specifically, the mandate dictated a prohibition on such taboos as swearing, bloodshed and religious symbols" (1999, p. 459). As a result, some games originally created for the PC and then ported to Nintendo's systems had significant changes to them; and games that were later developed for both Nintendo's and Sega's systems could be quite different.

One of the most significant cases, and ultimately the one receiving the most attention, was Acclaim Entertainment's 1993 title *Mortal Kombat*, which had several "fatality moves" removed from the Nintendo version, but not the Sega Genesis version (Sheff, p. 460). Such moves allowed players to engage in actions such as having character Kano "wrenching his opponents' hearts out of their chests to Scorpion pulling out their spines and skulls" in the Genesis version, which outsold Nintendo's version nearly three to one. Although remembered because of the subsequent legislative attention, the different versions of the games also demonstrated how different companies were positioning their audiences—Nintendo with a family-friendly younger demographic and Sega with an older, edgier group of players (Kent, 2001, p. 464).

Most significantly though, games such as *Mortal Kombat* and *Night Trap* led to U.S. Congressional hearings in 1993 that investigated the marketing of such games to children (Kent, 2001, p. 466). As Kent explains, as a result of those hearings, game industry leaders set up their own trade organization (the Software Publishers Association) and created the **Entertainment Software Rating Board (ESRB)**, which went on to create a voluntary ratings system that was initially adopted by most of the United States and Canada (Kent, 2001, p. 480). The ESRB's ratings are similar to those of the film industry, and have been modified over the years, but remain in active use.

One of the biggest challenges to the voluntary nature of the system came in 2011, when the U.S. Supreme Court ruled that a California law banning the rental or sale of violent video games to minors "violated young people's U.S. Constitutional right to free speech" (Shaw Media, 2011), thus guaranteeing that in the United States, games would be protected by the First Amendment, and game creators accorded free speech rights with respect to their creations. But although Canada utilizes the ratings system of the ESRB, some provinces have enacted legislation, which is still in force, restricting the sale of violent games to children and, as of 2007, Manitoba, Ontario, Nova Scotia, and New Brunswick had such legislation. As a result, when the game *Manhunt* was released in 2004, Ontario's film review board gave it an "R" rating, indicating it could not be sold or rented to anyone under the age of 18, and "fines of up to $25,000 for underage purchasers, and up to $100,000 for retailers who sell or rent a restricted film or game to them" could be awarded (CBC News, 2004).

Overall most games are not subject to restriction in Canada, and the ratings system is relied on by publishers to indicate a game's content. Yet there is past precedent for controlling access to media with respect to children due to section 1 of Canada's *Charter of Rights and Freedoms*, meaning that future challenges to digital games and more provincial control may emerge.

Another area relative to the political aspects of the digital game industry is with respect to workers' rights and workplace conditions. Most attention is usually paid to factory and working conditions in places like China, where companies such as Foxconn produce consoles such as the Xbox 360 and Playstation 3, and individuals work for long hours in sometimes dangerous conditions for relatively little pay (Duhigg & Greenhouse, 2012). Yet the conditions of creative workers in the game industry have begun receiving more attention, due to outcries from the spouses of those workers at companies including EA and Rockstar Games. For example, in 2004 a blog post appeared written by "EA Spouse," documenting how developers at EA studios in California were treated (Hoffman, 2004). Hoffman describes how for workers at EA "the current mandatory hours are 9 am to 10 pm—seven days a week—with the occasional Saturday evening off for good behaviour (at 6:30 pm). This averages out to an eighty-five hour work week" for which "the honor of this treatment EA salaried employees receive a) no overtime; b) no compensation time! ... c) no additional sick or vacation leave. The time just goes away" (Hoffman, 2004). Similarly, Shane Mason writes that EA had its "Vancouver-based Black Box studio on a near constant crunch churning out yearly additions to EA's Need for Speed franchise for five years" (Mason, 2011). Responding to such cases, the International Game Developers Association launched a Quality of Life survey of developers and held a summit to discuss the findings and potential solutions at the 2005 Game Developers Conference. The association found that "crunch time is omnipresent, during which respondents work 65 to 80 hours a week (35.2 percent) ... The average crunch work week exceeds 80 hours" (International Game Developers Association [IGDA], 2004). Not surprisingly, about one-third of developers plan to leave the game industry in five years, and slightly more than half within 10 years (IGDA, 2004). Breaking down the statistics further, Consalvo found that female game developers—who make up approximately 10 percent of the development workforce—were even more likely to want to leave the industry, often citing a desire for greater work–life balance (2008).

Although the IGDA released a list of recommended best practices for studios and EA ultimately settled a lawsuit with some of its employees over unpaid overtime, problems continue, either due to seemingly inflexible deadlines for game releases, management inexperience, or simple disregard for employees' quality of life. If companies can rely on a ready pool of labour from which to draw, there is little impetus for them to change. But if, as recent reports state, the industry has a greater need than ever for experienced workers to lead teams (Gouglas et al., 2010), companies will have to consider such issues as paramount in order to keep a workforce that seems to be looking elsewhere for employment as it ages.

CONCLUSIONS

Games are being played by more people, in more places, than ever before. Some games are relatively inexpensive to produce, while others are more costly than ever. The variety of games on offer—and their styles, genres, and cost structures—is also steadily expanding. Likewise, the game industry itself is rapidly changing, and facing both challenges and opportunities. The Canadian game industry is a key element of the larger global network of game companies. Canada has a strong player base but, more importantly, many companies that contribute to the production of a diversity of titles. Whether tax credits will continue to help grow the industry is an open question; as metropolitan areas such as Montreal and Vancouver solidify their positions as hubs for game production and attract a key number of skilled workers, that may be enough to keep a thriving industry absent government supports (if those are ever scrapped). And workers may eventually start companies of their own, growing more local talent to contribute to game production. But in the meantime, the industry continues to move forward, contributing not only to the larger game industry but to Canadian media offerings as well.

QUESTIONS

1. How do you see the changing demographics of the game-playing public affecting the game industry over the next decade?
2. Will we continue to see dedicated game consoles such as the Xbox 360 and Playstation 3 released every few years from several developers, or will newer models gain greater dominance?
3. How will emerging technologies such as motion-sensing systems such as the Kinect and 3D televisions affect how we play games?
4. Will Canada continue to be an important sector for game development worldwide, or will other countries emerge to challenge its position?
5. How do you see your own game purchasing decisions mirroring (or not) what is happening in the larger game industry?

REFERENCES

BioWare. (2008). About BioWare. Retrieved from www.bioware.com via the way-back machine.

Canadian Interactive Alliance. (2009). 2008 Canadian interactive industry profile. Retrieved August 30, 2012, from http://ciaic.wordpress.com/game-nation

CBC News. (2004). Ontario slaps "R" rating on video game. CBC.ca. Retrieved August 16, 2012, from http://www.cbc.ca/news/story/2004/03/03/game040203.html

Chapple, C. (2012). Ubisoft shuts down Vancouver studio. *Develop Online*. Retrieved August 16, 2012, from http://www.develop-online.net/news/39520/Ubisoft-shuts-down-Vancouver-studio

Consalvo, M. (2008). Crunched by passion. In Y. Kafai, C. Heeter, J. Denner and J. Sun (Eds.) *Beyond Barbie and Mortal Kombat: New perspectives on gender and gaming* (117–192). Cambridge, MA: MIT Press.

———. (2012). Slingshot to victory: Games, play and the iPhone. In P. Snickars and P. Vonderau (Eds.) *Moving data: The iPhone and the future of media* (184–194). New York: Columbia University Press.

Crecente, B. (2007). EA buys BioWare, Pandemic. Kotaku. Retrieved August 16, 2012, from http://kotaku.com/309937/ea-buys-bioware-pandemic

Curtis, T. (2012). Battlefield 3, The Old Republic drive healthy Q3 for EA. *Gamasutra*. Retrieved August 16, 2012, from http://gamasutra.com/view/news/129423/Battlefield_3_The_Ol

Duhigg, C. & S. Greenhouse. (2012). Electronic giant vowing reforms in China plants. *New York Times*. Retrieved August 16, 2012, from http://www.nytimes.com/2012/03/30/business/apple-supplier-in-china-pledges-changes-in-working-conditions.html?hp

Edge Staff. (2009). The 60 biggest selling games of the last 12 months. *Edge Magazine*. Retrieved August 16, 2012, from http://www.edge-online.com/features/60-biggest-selling-games-last-12-months

Entertainment Software Association of Canada. (2011). 2011 Essential facts about the Canadian computer and video game industry. Retrieved August 16, 2012, from http://www.theesa.ca/?page_id=22

Fahs, T. (2010). IGN presents the history of BioWare. *IGN*. Retrieved August 16, 2012, from http://retro.ign.com/articles/106/1062619p1.html

French Connection, the. (2011, November). *Develop*, 32.

GDC Online Speaker Spotlight. (2011). *Gamasutra*. Retrieved August 16, 2012, from http://www.gamasutra.com/view/news/37736/gdc_online_speaker_spotlight_.php

Gonzalez, L. (2012). When two tribes go to war: A history of video game controversy. *Gamespot*. Retrieved August 16, 2012, from http://www.gamespot.com/features/when-two-tribes-go-to-war-a-history-of-video-game-controversy-6090892/p-24.html

Gouglas, S., Della Rocca, J., Jenson, J., Kee, K., Rockwell, G., Schaeffer, J., et al. (2010). Computer games and Canada's digital economy: The role of universities in promoting innovation. Report to the Social Science Humanities Research Council Knowledge Synthesis Grants on Canada's Digital Economy. Retrieved August 16, 2012, from http://ra.tapor.ualberta.ca/~circa/wp-content/uploads/2010/03/ComputerGamesAndCanadasDigitalEconomy1.pdf

Hoffman, Erin/ea_spouse. (2004). EA: The human story. Retrieved August 16, 2012, from http://ea-spouse.livejournal.com/274.html

International Game Developers Association. (2004). Quality of Life White Paper. *IGDA*. Retrieved August 16, 2012, from http://www.igda.org/quality-life-white-paper-info

Ishaan. (2010). Arcades still in decline despite Capcom's revitalization efforts. *Silicon Era*. Retrieved August 16, 2012, from http://www.siliconera.com/2010/05/07/arcades-still-in-decline-despite-capcoms-revitalization-efforts

Kain, E. (2012). BioWare and EA respond to DLC controversy. *Forbes*. Retrieved August 16, 2012, from http://www.forbes.com/sites/erikkain/2012/03/12/bioware-and-ea-respond-to-dlc-controversy/

Kent, S. (2001). *The ultimate history of video games*. Roseville, CA: Prima Publishing.

Mason, S. (2011). Unpaid overtime in gaming industry. *Teamliquid.net*. Retrieved August 16, 2012, from http://www.teamliquid.net/forum/viewmessage.php?topic_id=232476

PWC. (2011). Annual review of tax changes by PwC shows that loopholes have been tightened, corporate rates are on the decline and new personal tax credits introduced. Retrieved August 16, 2012, from http://www.pwc.com/ca/en/media/release/2011-09-12-tax-facts-figures.jhtml

Rose, M. (2012). Blizzard: Drop in WoW subs "attributable" to Star Wars: The Old Republic. *Gamasutra*. Retrieved August 16, 2012, from http://gamasutra.com/view/news/166532/Blizzard_Drop_in_

SECOR Consulting. (2011). Canada's entertainment software industry in 2011. *Entertainment Software Association of Canada*. Retrieved August 16, 2012, from http://www.theesa.ca/?page_id=22

Shaw Media. (2011). Video game law in Canada. *Global Winnipeg*. Retrieved October 13, 2012, from http://www.globalwinnipeg.com/video+game+law+in+canada/300062/story.html

Sheff, D. (1999). *Game over, press start to continue: The maturing of Mario*. Wilton, CT: Game Press.

Supreme Court of Canada. (1985). Montreal v. Arcade Amusements Inc. 1 S. C. R. 368. Retrieved October 13, 2012, from http://scc.lexum.org/en/1985/1985scr1-368/1985scr1-368.html

Tipps, S. (2012). EA confirms Vancouver layoffs. *Develop online*. Retrieved August 16, 2012, from http://www.develop-online.net/news/39757/EA-confirms-Vancouver-layoffs

van Kooten, M. (2010). Top 25 gaming companies 2010. *Software Top 100.* Retrieved August 16, 2012, from http://www.softwaretop100.org/top-25-gaming-companies-2010

VGChartz. (2012). Video game charts. Retrieved August 16, 2012, from http://www.vgchartz.com

Whitehead, D. (2007). The history of BioWare. *Eurogamer.net.* Retrieved August 16, 2012, from http://www.eurogamer.net/articles/the-history-of-bioware-article

Woo, J. (2011). Toronto game developers win at IndieCade. *Torontoist.* Retrieved August 16, 2012, from http://torontoist.com/2011/10/toronto-game-developers-wi-at-indiecade

PART IV
Social Media

Introduction

Leslie Regan Shade
University of Toronto

This section of *Mediascapes* examines various social and policy aspects of social media. Social media refer to a range of internet technologies that allow for participative communicative practices; they consist of tools and platforms that ostensibly empower users to contribute to the development, collaboration, customization, rating, and distribution of a range of internet content. The term "social media" has also superceded the term "new media," popularized in the last decade, and also used alongside and interchangeably with the term "Web 2.0." Social media include social network sites (Facebook), blogs/microblogs (Tumblr), wikis (Wikipedia), and video-sharing sites (YouTube). Social media are also integrally entwined with the "smart" mobile phone. Chapters in this section discuss the surveillance and commodification regimes inherent in the design and terms of service for social media (Werbin), the multifarious methods of mobilities (Nicholson), and attendant policy issues of privacy (Steeves) and copyright especially with respect to fair dealing (Nair).

Kenneth Werbin's chapter examines the paradoxical nature of social media; their convenience factor—used intensely by many of us for mundane activities, communication, community building, research, news, entertainment, and employment—is offset by their architecture of participation and terms of use. These ostensibly "free" sites operate using increasingly sophisticated mechanisms of surveillance to target our personal information. Indeed, as Werbin so persuasively demonstrates, one of the key attributes of social media is their surveillance infrastructure; our personal information is data mined and data aggregated by third-party marketers under the guise of "customizing" our settings and preferences, creating what he describes as a surveillance assemblage that creates a regime of commodification. Social media deployed by activists for mediated mobilization foster collaboration and participation for collective actions. But the flip side is that these commercial social media platforms create a visible record and archive of actions useful for law enforcement, often for social sorting. And as the recent example of the hockey riots in Vancouver demonstrates, evidence is culled directly from citizens themselves. Werbin concludes his chapter by admonishing us to pay attention to how social media impacts our personal privacy and, increasingly, our freedom of expression.

Not surprisingly, just as the mobile phone has become an everyday necessity for work, leisure, and maintaining family ties, scholarship on mobile phone culture situated in the field of mobility studies has been exploding. Judith Nicholson's chapter provides an overview of mobilities wherein theorists from an interdisciplinary perspective examine a range of mobilities: the socioeconomic, political, and cultural dimensions of different forms of human agency, interpersonal and geopolitical connections, modes of transport, and flows of physical and mental spaces. She demonstrates how mobile phone technologies themselves are very much implicated in mobilities, deployed by citizens to organize flash mobs; encourage activism for social justice; and, by citizen journalists, to provide timely photo and video imagery of news events that can then be quickly uploaded to their own websites or those of the mainstream media. Nicholson describes the concept of "constellations of mobility," which is attentive to changing forms, meanings, and practices of mobility. She argues that not everyone enjoys the same access to mobilities; indeed, unequal power relations increase immobilities, which are related very much to race and class.

As Valerie Steeves relates in her chapter, privacy is an inalienable human right that is continuously challenged by technological forces—digitization and new forms of social media—and by post–September 11th political and economic realities. New security regimes in the era of Homeland Security conflict with citizens' rights to personal privacy. Security often trumps privacy. Other definitions of privacy include privacy as intrinsic to democracy, privacy as a social value, and privacy as data protection. As Steeves clearly demonstrates, the privacy balance is continuously tested by a confluence of forces: legal, technological, cultural, and social. And, as new technologies become more ubiquitous, challenges to privacy rights in the public sphere are more prevalent. Canadian privacy legislation makes an effort to keep up with the swift changes engendered by technological developments and citizen/consumer use but, as she describes, this is often difficult to achieve. She also details how social media blurs the lines between public and private, particularly for young people who interact in digital play sites, and who are often unaware of the corporate practices of data mining their personal information for profit.

Intrinsic to social media is their facility in allowing users to upload their own content, reconfigure, and remix. User practices are called "user-created content-(UCC)," or "user-generated content (UGC)." UCC/UGC is characterized by content publicly available over the internet, reflecting some creative component, whether original or adapted. Implicit for UCC/UGC is that content is created outside professional, paid labour, with no industry or institutional affiliation and little to no financial remuneration—hence, UCC/UGC is often referred to as "pro-am" labour (referring to the blurriness between professional and amateur labour). But as Meera Nair discusses in her chapter on copyright in Canada, these contemporary user practices complicate the copyright regime, and copyright policy is rife with ideological differences among industry groups, users, and the legal regime related to what should constitute "fair dealing." Nair argues that we need to understand not only the historical and current legal framework for copyright but also the opposing assumptions surrounding copyright reform, a conflict based on differing sensibilities over how cultural works should be produced and consumed in our present milieu. She situates Canadian copyright legislation and the provisions of very recent copyright "modernization" among the notion of fair dealing and the public domain. The rights of corporations to protect their media properties, and the rights of the public to make fair use of these properties, have been progressively more tested by digitization, global copyright legislation, and normalized social practices—particularly by youth, in the peer-to-peer downloading culture. Nair discusses alternatives to copyright legislation, such as Creative Commons, which allow creators to control their own moral rights related to their works. She concludes by arguing that the essence of fair dealing lies in responsible conduct, which should be the basis for copyright literacy.

13

SOCIAL MEDIA, COMMODIFICATION, AND SURVEILLANCE

Kenneth C. Werbin
Wilfrid Laurier University, Brantford Campus

INTRODUCTION: THE PARADOX OF SOCIAL MEDIA

Have you ever noticed in your Gmail, Hotmail, or Yahoo mail clients, or while logged into Facebook, how the advertising you see tends to very closely correspond to the content you have recently viewed, or are in the process of viewing in your browser? Most likely you have noticed that advertising in **social media** arrangements is customized to your particular interests, tastes and demographics; if you haven't noticed this, log in, and have a look. Such customized advertising is something that social media platforms, such as Facebook, trumpet as one of the many conveniences that you benefit from by allowing these corporations to gather extensive data related to your patterns of interaction and communication. The promise is as follows: The more data you allow social media platforms to gather and share, the more finely tuned are your search results, the more accurate are the friends suggested to you, the more precise are the products recommended for you, the more potential for collaboration and the collective development of knowledge, and the more opportunities that these platforms might open to you in the future.

Instinctively, we might think of Google or Gmail as merely a search engine, or an email service provider, respectively, and not as forms of social media. But in the broadest sense Google and Gmail are media platforms that build on user contributions and facilitate social interaction; hence their designation as "social media." Google not only provides search functionality, but also refines its results and services based on how users interact with its contents. Gmail not only allows users to communicate with contacts anytime and anywhere in email form, but also enables social networking and collective participation in a series of other emerging ways. For example, in addition to the asynchronous service of email, Gmail also provides its users with the potential to socialize in a synchronous manner through its text, audio, and video chat features. This now includes the possibility for making phone calls to land lines and cellular devices. Moreover, Gmail has begun to collectivize the email experience itself, suggesting other people from a user's list of contacts who might be interested in the contents of an email, beyond those who have been included.

More recently, Google has offered seamless integration of all the data users generate into its social networking platform, Google+, offering users "new ways of sharing the right things with the right people" including content, contacts, profiles, photos, videos, physical locations or "hangouts," and mobile services. In that way, the goals of Google, in general, are consistent with the modus operandi of social media: to facilitate social interaction by collectivizing and capitalizing on the interactions and contributions of networks of users through the content they generate, the connections they make, and the data they produce.

For this reason, social media platforms such as Google and Facebook's default settings seek to maximize the capture of user data (Vaidhyanathan, 2011). And the user, in turn, is tacitly and explicitly encouraged to not impede flows of data, lest he or she be deprived of all of the benefits that data capture, monitoring, and analysis enable. As such, participation on social media platforms involves a tradeoff: In exchange for the conveniences and benefits of accurate search results, friend recommendations and networking, finely tuned advertising, and maximized sociability, users agree to give up control over their data, their privacy, how they are monitored and tracked, and the ways in which they are harvested as commodities.

In that sense, the advent of social media is marked by a paradox: On the one hand, social media platforms such as Facebook, Google, YouTube, Wikipedia, and Twitter are celebrated as furthering the democratization of communication and culture by empowering users to participate in the media-making process (Bruns, 2008; Burgess & Green, 2009; Deuze, 2007; Gillmor, 2004; Howe, 2008; Jenkins, 2004, 2006; Shirky, 2008; Tapscott & Williams, 2006). In these participatory arrangements, where the lines between producers and consumers of media are blurred, users are understood to be actively taking control of the means of production: generating, sharing and refining content, connecting with others, creating new ideas and knowledge together, and having their voices heard in ways unparalleled in the history of communication technologies. On the other hand, these same arrangements can also be contextualized as installing intense **commodification** and **surveillance** regimes (Andrejevic, 2004, 2009; Cohen, 2008; Fuchs, 2011; Mosco, 2009; Poster, 2006; Scholz, 2008; Terranova, 2000, 2004; van Dijck, 2009; van Dijck & Nieborg, 2009), wherein the social, political, economic and cultural interactions and communications of people are increasingly monitored and tracked on an up-to-the-minute basis.

Social media as such is a paradoxical beast. Like digital culture in general, it produces strong tendencies in opposing directions. This is what Mark Poster (2006) has characterized as "... an Orwellian extension of governmental and corporate controls or a serious deepening of the democratization of culture" (p. 193). In her book *Privacy in Context*, Helen Nissenbaum (2010) has described digital culture in a similar paradoxical way: "On the one hand it offers individuals the possibility of communicating and interacting with individuals, groups and organizations in the privacy of their homes, while on the other hand it exposes them to unprecedented monitoring and tracking." (p. 27) As Trebor Scholz (2008) succinctly puts it: "The social Web can be defined in terms of creativity, collaboration, courage, collective intelligence, and content as well as commodification, control, consumption and crisis" (p. 356).

In the same vein, this chapter explores the possibilities for participation and connection that social media open with a critical eye on the intense forms of commodification and surveillance they install. It does this by examining the processes that underpin how user data is transformed from a resource into a commodity in social media arrangements, including cloud computing, data mining and aggregation, immanent and external commodification, social sorting, and top-down and bottom-up forms of surveillance. The chapter concludes with a discussion of alternative spaces for imagining social media commodification and surveillance regimes.

SOCIAL MEDIA: A TYRANNY OF CONVENIENCE

The term "social media" goes hand in hand with the term "Web 2.0." **Web 2.0** refers to a shift that has taken place in the last decade on the web, which has moved from being primarily a space of information provision to a space of communication in which **user-generated content**, data sharing, and community building have taken centre stage (Fuchs, 2011). Tim O'Reilly (2005) has posited the most widely accepted definition of Web 2.0:

> Web 2.0 is the network as platform, spanning all connected devices; Web 2.0 applications are those that make the most of the intrinsic advantages of that platform: delivering software as a continually-updated service that gets better the more people use it, consuming and remixing data from multiple sources, including individual users, while providing their own data and services in a form that allows remixing by others, creating network effects through an "architecture of participation," and going beyond the page metaphor of Web 1.0 to deliver rich user experiences. (http://radar.oreilly.com/2005/10/web-20-compact-definition.html)

In these dynamic, networked arrangements, the more that individual users participate on Web 2.0 platforms, generating content and producing data related to their patterns of interaction and communication, the more these interoperable platforms deliver a richer media experience that opens vast potentials for connection, collaboration, and the collective development of knowledge. In that sense, the emergence of Web 2.0 has socialized the media-making process, opening the content generated by individuals, the data produced in their interactions, and the potential for creating community to the masses to build knowledge and culture together in networks; hence the term "social media."

There is little doubt that social media platforms have made sharing our lives, connecting with others, and collaborating around the development of new ideas and knowledge easier than ever. What is less evident about these arrangements is how they also install a technological regime that has the potential to erode the very freedom these platforms are seen as enhancing: freedom of expression.

Ronald Dworkin (1990) first introduced the term "the tyranny of convenience" to describe the way that technological arrangements intended for one purpose gradually take on other functions for which they might not have originally been designed, yet continue to be perceived for their original purpose. According to Dworkin, these processes, which Langdon Winner (1977) first described as "function creep," have the potential to erode rights and freedoms by emphasizing ease of use while obfuscating emergent functionality, like the monitoring, tracking, and surveillance functionality that information and communication technologies (ICTs) enable. It is through the lens of Dworkin's "tyranny of convenience" that we can begin to understand how the majority of people see platforms such as Facebook as open, collaborative spaces, where they are "free" to express themselves and connect with others, and not as the engines of commodification and surveillance that they are equally. As Mark Andrejevic (2009) emphasizes, "it is ... critically important to consider precisely what the cost of these conveniences might end up being, not just in economic terms, but in terms of control over information ... perhaps we are giving up more than we realize ..." (p. 34). Following on Andrejevic's lead, if we are to imagine alternatives to social media as something other than engines of commodification and surveillance, we have to think beyond the conveniences and benefits that are on offer. This begins by developing a critical awareness of the costs associated with their use.

SOCIAL MEDIA AS A REGIME OF COMMODIFICATION

As Vincent Mosco (2009) reminds us in his seminal work on *The Political Economy of Communication*, in a capitalist society, there is no such thing as a "free lunch." Just as bars and taverns once enticed clients into consuming alcohol by offering them a free meal, platforms such as Facebook and Google offer people "free" services involving accessing, creating, and sharing information and connecting with others in exchange for their data and licence to profile their actions and sell them as commodities. In that sense, there is nothing free about social media arrangements. Instead there is a tradeoff that is made between users and these platforms, one that involves granting users "free" access to information, content production services, and the ability to connect with others in exchange for their personal data and exclusive license to transform it into products or commodities. As José van Dijck and David Nieborg (2009) argue,

> To put it bluntly, rather than being in the business of content, Google is in the business of deriving commercially significant data from users and connecting these data to companies which need them for targeted advertising, marketing and sales

> management ... Facebook does not want to link friends to friends, it is in the business of linking people to advertisers and products. Not content, but connections and profiled actions are the new commodities (pp. 865–866).

In a nutshell, the data that users generate are the key ingredient in the economic recipe for "lunch" that makes social media appear to be "free." Where users value their data for its use to them (e.g., the ability to efficiently and effectively help them acquire information and connect with others), corporations such as Google and Facebook are interested in user data for how it can be commodified and the market value that it bears in exchange. In this light, theorists such as Tiziana Terranova (2004) have characterized user-generated content arrangements as exploiting the "free labour" of users, who without wage or monetary compensation produce both content and data for corporations that are in the business of harvesting them as commodities.

User Data: From Resource to Commodity

To begin to approach and understand the commodification and surveillance regimes installed through social media, we must first ask: What is the business model that underpins corporate social media platforms? The answer to this question lies in shifting our attention away from the content that people produce in social media arrangements and instead focusing on the processes of commodification by which user data is captured and combined to reveal patterns of interaction and communication. Google and Facebook are not in the business of content per se; rather, they are in the business of harvesting the **resource** of user data and transforming it into a **commodity** to be sold to advertisers and marketers.

A resource is something of actual or potential use: anything and everything of use anytime, anywhere, to anyone—from what lies beneath and above the soil, to the sea, to the sky, and outward (Schiller, 2007). But not all resources are commodities. It is only under particular conditions that a resource comes to bear the stamp of society through economic exchange and thus becomes a commodity (ibid.). "Commodification is the process of transforming things valued for their use into marketable products that are valued for what they can bring in exchange" (Mosco, 2009, p. 127). In the case of Google, the process of commodification begins with the tracking of search queries. Search data as a resource is useful to Google users who want to more accurately pinpoint the kinds of information they are seeking. But there is a tradeoff for this convenience that involves Google transforming the search data generated by users—this resource—into a commodity that is traded in aggregated forms to advertisers and marketers in exchange for monetary compensation. Search data, which has use value as a resource to information seekers, becomes a commodity that is assigned a market value in exchanges between Google and the advertisers and marketers with whom it does business.

Cloud Computing

The tradeoff between the conveniences that social media platforms provide for users and the profits that corporations accrue through the transformation of data from a resource into a commodity speaks to a broader shift in how applications and data are stored in social media arrangements. Where not long ago the vast majority of the applications that users engaged, as well as the data that they generated, were stored locally on personal computers, today not only are applications increasingly accessed via networked devices (laptops, mobile phones, wireless devices), but also data is stored on commercial servers up in "the cloud." The shift to **cloud computing**—computation and data available to anyone, anytime, anywhere—means that control over information and applications shifts from the user to the corporations that own the servers where applications and data are stored (Andrejevic, 2009). In this way, cloud computing arrangements offer users the convenience of recentralizing their applications and data, thus gaining access anytime, anywhere, on any device (ibid.). But there are costs associated with this convenience: First, users must increasingly rely on privatized, corporate networks for access to their communication resources, and, second, users must give up control of their data and the ways in which it is commodified and monetized.

As such, the business model that underpins corporate social media is based on a tradeoff between users and corporations. In exchange for Google, and more specifically Gmail, offering the convenience of access to its "cloud computing" facilities where users store, read, and write their emails anytime and anywhere, users give up ownership over the emails they compose, making them the property of Google, which controls the servers on which the correspondence is stored (ibid.). But Google is less interested in the contents of user emails, and more interested in how this content can be merged with other data to identify patterns of interaction and communication. Although it may seem counterintuitive, it is important to understand that corporate social media providers are not really in the business of content. Rather, they are in the business of figuring out how the bits and pieces of data that users generate reveal insights into who they are, whom they communicate with, and what they value. Therefore, it is not just the messages that users compose or the content that they produce that are the key resources that are transformed into commodities by corporations like Google and Facebook; rather, it is the data that users generate in their participation and how this data can be combined with other data to further identify patterns of interaction and communication that can be sold to advertisers and marketers. This ability to discern granular patterns of interaction in these arrangements means that the corporations who control, mine, and aggregate user data have the potential to know users better than they know themselves (Nissenbaum, 2010). Given that the business model of corporate social media is based on maximizing the capture of user data, we will now turn to examining the critical role that data mining and aggregation play in the transformation of user data from a resource into a commodity.

Data Mining and Aggregation

Data mining refers to the gathering of information about users and their online behaviours. Data mining seeks to reveal patterns of association between online behaviours and demographic characteristics (Gandy, 2007) in order to uncover patterns of interaction, movement, transaction, and communication (Andrejevic, 2009). As such, data mining can be understood broadly as the extraction of meaningful intelligence about users from their patterns of interaction that emerge over time as they engage with and produce more data in these arrangements. As Oscar Gandy (2007) observes, "these systems learn to become more accurate over time" (p. 151). With every click of the mouse, tap of the keys, snap of a photo, and stream of audio and video that users produce and consume comes the production of data points. These data points are endlessly captured and stored and, in turn, open the door to endless forms of examination, review, and aggregation.

Data aggregation refers to the way that data can be pooled with other data in order to reveal patterns of interaction and communication (Nissenbaum, 2010). Data aggregation operates hand in hand with data mining in the transformation of user data from a resource into a commodity. The products of data aggregation are often referred to as **metadata**. Metadata are valuable to companies such as Google and Facebook, which are in the business of selling this commodity to advertisers and marketers looking to connect users with their goods and services.

In order to more concretely understand how data mining and aggregation factor in the processes of commodification of social media, take the following example: Pat is a student in Toronto in February. Pat is logged into a Gmail account. In the display, Pat sees an advertisement for a cheap spring break vacation package to Florida. This advertisement was generated because Google, through the aggregation of other data, knows that Pat is a student, between the ages of 18 and 25, and is in Toronto in the winter. As such, this aggregated data suggests that Pat might be interested in this kind of winter getaway. Google has mined a variety of data points and aggregated them as a commodity (metadata) that is sold to an advertiser that has an interest in Pat's demographics. Indeed, Pat is interested in a getaway to Florida, so Pat clicks on the advertisement and quickly glances over the offer but does not bite. A minute later, Pat decides to search for information on a film, say *Moneyball*, a film about how data analysis transformed the sport of baseball. A data point is produced that ties Pat to this film. Google then connects Pat to the Internet Movie Database (IMDB) where the trailer is watched. Pat then decides to share the video on Facebook. IMDB, Google, and Facebook now produce data points that indicate that Pat has an interest in the film and baseball in general. Not long after, Pat receives an email from a friend reminding Pat about their yearly Yahoo fantasy baseball league, asking if Pat is going to use the same name for their team, "Pat's Blue Jays." Yet more data points are produced. Seconds later, an advertisement appears in Pat's Gmail interface for cheap winter getaway vacation packages to Florida to see the Toronto Blue Jays at spring training.

Google has connected Pat to this advertisement by aggregating a series of data points that Pat has generated; Pat's location in Toronto, the fact that it is winter, Pat's interest in vacation getaways to Florida, Pat's search for *Moneyball* and watching and sharing of the trailer, Pat's participation in fantasy baseball, and the name of Pat's fantasy team. In this way, "... the analysis of aggregated data sets generates information about people beyond what is given in the individual data sets" (Nissenbaum, 2010, p. 43). Taken together, the sum of the parts of the data that Pat has generated—this metadata—has more value than any of the individual pieces. As an aggregated form, metadata is valuable to advertisers that want to connect with people who are likely interested in their products or services, in this case a vacation getaway.

As such, data mining and data aggregation are the key processes that produce metadata in the commodification processes that underpin social media. Thus it is through these processes that user data as a resource is transformed into the commodity form. Therefore, the more fine grained the bits and pieces of data that Google or Facebook collects, the more they are able to make sense of users and their patterns of interaction and communication, and the more profits they are able to generate by selling the commodity of metadata to advertisers. In that regard, maximizing profits goes hand in hand with maximizing the ways in which users are monitored and tracked; producing endless data points that possess endless potentials to be aggregated with other data points and transformed into the commodity form.

Immanent and External Commodification

There is a sense of immanency in the commodification processes by which user information accrues value through data mining and aggregation in its transformation from a resource to a commodity in social media arrangements. This immanency is directly related to the inherent potential that data possesses for being correlated with other data in the identification of emergent relationships. Let's return to our example: Data, like that collected by IMDB about Pat watching the trailer for *Moneyball* might lay dormant on its servers for days, weeks, months, or even years having not been correlated with other data. But the potential for that data to be established in an emergent relationship with other data is always there. Say Pat now returns to IMDB and watches the trailer for *The Curious Case of Benjamin Button*. Suddenly this data point is aggregated with the *Moneyball* data point, and lo and behold, an advertisement pops up for the new tell-all unauthorized biography of Brad Pitt's life. In this way, the resource of data immanently possesses the potential to be transformed into a commodity when it is pooled with other data. Pat's choices surrounding viewing these trailers mean that Pat is most likely a fan of Brad Pitt and might be interested in purchasing related commodities.

What we can see through this example is how the process of commodification is an immanent or recursive one: it repeats itself indefinitely as commodities beget more commodities (Mosco, 2009). Commodified data inherently possesses the potential to produce more data commodities. Continuing with our example, as it turns out, the advertising broker that captures data and transforms, buys, and sells it as an aggregated commodity is DoubleClick, a company that is owned by Google and provides its services to both IMDB and Facebook. DoubleClick now correlates what it knows about Pat from the other commodities it has produced: that Pat is 18–25, a student who is interested in baseball, spring break vacations, and Brad Pitt. Taken together, this aggregated data suggests that Pat is the perfect demographic to receive a certain kind of advertising. Seconds later an ad for *Maxim Magazine* appears in Gmail's interface, and after that, one for *AXE* deodorant on Facebook. In this way, commodification repeats itself indefinitely as commodities give rise to other commodities, in a process that can be described as cascading.

Mosco (2009) refers to the recursive nature of commodification as "**immanent commodification**," or how "commodities give rise to new commodities" (p. 156). But commodification is not only a recursive process, but also an externalizing one, extending itself into places and practices that we might think are left outside the grip of commodification. Mosco refers to the tendency of commodification to extend itself into noncommodified areas of life as "**external commodification**" (p. 156). A good example of external commodification related to social media is that of privacy. Where once privacy was taken for granted as a right, it has increasingly become a commodity by virtue of its association to the commodification of personal information (ibid.), which has given birth to new commodities and services such as anonymizing software and reputation management.

Classification and Social Sorting

In order to transform data from a resource into a commodity, assumptions must be made about how people will be sorted: by race, gender, religion, nationality, income, etc. As such, to uncover patterns of association between various data points, the operations of data mining and data aggregation are governed by "... rules for the classification of objects" (Gandy, 2007, p. 149). These rules for classifying people tend to mirror those that have proven to be problematic in society (race, gender, ethnicity, class, age, etc.) because of how they inherently exclude people from certain opportunities based on their division into groups (ibid.). As such, the practices of classification on which the commodification of user data are based are inherently political, "rationalizing discrimination in the broadest sense ... in the 'rational pursuit of profits'" (ibid. p. 153).

The processes of classifying and categorizing people are based on sorting populations into groups as a means of helping "... to create the sense of who and what is rightly included and excluded; who is this, that, or other" (Lyon, 2007a, p. 141). David Lyon (2003, 2007a, 2007b) has characterized these processes as "**social sorting**" and has examined how categories and classifications are often invisible, easily taken for granted, and subsumed deep in our social woodwork. According to Lyon, categories are political and call for ethical inspection precisely because social sorting enables forms of exclusion that "... not only cut off certain targeted groups from social participation, but do so in subtle ways that are sometimes scarcely visible" (Lyon, 2007b, p. 372). And yet again, the "tyranny of convenience" rears its head in these arrangements: "All too often, convenience and efficiency are all that get noticed in systems that have surveillance aspects, with the result that data subjects are often unaware of the broader discriminatory and classificatory dimensions of such systems" (Lyon, 2007a, p. 142).

As Colin Bennett (2008) confirms, the causes for how and why people are excluded from opportunities are often invisible and circuitous. And in these hidden operations, exclusion can be "... directly, or indirectly, caused by the collection and processing of inaccurate, obsolete or incomplete personal data" (Bennett, 2008, p. 211). Indeed, the ethical dilemmas associated with the discriminatory practices that are a part of sorting people into groups are compounded by the routine production of errors and inaccuracies in categorization. Kevin Haggerty and Richard Ericson (2006) have argued that the more that data surveillance—**dataveillance**—is integrated into digital infrastructures, and the more that it governs institutional decision making, the greater the likelihood for the routine production of mistakes in the classification of people and their exclusion from opportunities.

To more clearly articulate how social sorting factors in social media arrangements and how the production of errors and inaccuracies are a part of these practices, let's return now for the final time to our example. If you recall, we left off with the appearance of ads for *Maxim Magazine* and *AXE* deodorant. These ads were produced as a result of the aggregation of a series of data points that indicated that Pat, our fictitious user, is a student, in Toronto, in the winter, who is interested in Brad Pitt and the Toronto Blue Jays, and plays fantasy baseball. Taken together, this metadata suggests that Pat is the ideal consumer to target with male-oriented advertising. But Pat is actually short for Patricia, a young woman who has never revealed her gender in her communications, nor when completing her profiles. As a result of this missing piece of data, Pat is inaccurately categorized, and is now not only subject to advertising for males who exhibit certain kinds of patterns of interaction, but also excluded from female-oriented advertising. While the consequences of this inaccuracy are relatively innocuous for Pat, who is only mildly irritated by these ads, when we begin to think through more critical situations involving errors in social sorting, such as the constitution of "terrorists" through the data mining of social media by security and intelligence organizations (Werbin, 2011), we can see how the routine production of mistakes associated with data mining and aggregation can lead to much more problematic and extreme forms of exclusion.

Overall, what we have seen so far is how data is transformed from a resource into a commodity in the processes of commodification associated with social media. In this examination, we have seen how data mining and data aggregation factor in these arrangements. We have also seen how these processes are discriminatory in the broadest sense, in that they are about sorting populations into distinct categories that enforce forms of social inclusion and exclusion. Finally, through this example we began to see how the aggregation and production of metadata as a commodity form involves articulating patterns of interaction and communication through monitoring and tracking operations that can be characterized as forms of surveillance. As such, we will now turn to a more detailed discussion of social media as a regime of surveillance.

SOCIAL MEDIA AS A REGIME OF SURVEILLANCE

> We assume that the benefits—security, efficiency, safety, rewards, convenience—are worth the price of having our personal data recorded, stored, retrieved, cross-checked, traded, and exchanged in surveillance systems. As ordinary subjects go along with surveillance, so the order constructed by the system is reinforced ... (Lyon, 2007b, p. 373).

The tyranny of convenience associated with social media provides a starting point again: this time to a discussion of social media as a regime of surveillance. In the preceding section related to how data is transformed from a resource into a commodity, we touched on how commodification and surveillance operate hand in hand in social media arrangements. "Commodification demands the use of measurement procedures to produce commodities and monitoring techniques to keep track of production, distribution, and consumption" (Mosco, 2009, pp. 141–142). In both the general processes of commodification, and the specific processes of transforming user data from a resource into a commodity, the practice of surveillance is critical. In that sense, the processes of commodification associated with social media not only endlessly produce new commodities, but also create "... powerful surveillance tools that threaten privacy" (ibid., p. 143). The more that social life is captured through data mining, and the more that individuals are constructed and commodified through data aggregation, the more that surveillance becomes a taken-for-granted reality of everyday life, and the more that the order of commodification and surveillance installed through social media arrangements is reinforced. Indeed, it is with regard to the latter that the paradox of social media is revealed to the fullest extent: How a sociotechnical arrangement intended and understood as enhancing the ability to communicate and connect in unprecedented ways might also be construed as impinging on privacy and freedom of expression.

In order to understand the paradox of how privacy and freedom of expression might be limited in social media arrangements, we must first understand how the mere belief that we are being watched, even if we are not being watched, has the potential to alter our words, our behaviours, and our subjectivity (Wacks, 2010). Editing one's speech and altering one's actions with the awareness that one might be watched can manifest in vastly different ways. On the one hand, this might involve limiting the kinds of things one says and does; on the other, it might involve exaggerating one's words and deeds in attempts to be noticed. The common denominator here is that the potential for individuals to alter their words and deeds with the knowledge that they might be watched is ever present.

Over the last years, as participation on social media platforms, such as Facebook, has become taken for granted, stories have emerged about employers increasingly turning to the contents of social media when making employment decisions (Rosen, 2010). There is little doubt that today's youth are increasingly aware of the public nature of their social media profiles that will, in all likelihood, come under scrutiny when they are searching for jobs. More recently, there have even been reports of employers asking potential employees for their Facebook passwords in order to peruse their personal communications before making employment decisions (Palis, 2012). Where the latter story, which represents both an invasion of privacy and a violation of labour laws and codes, generated some outrage in the public, and even some reforms in the United States, it also serves to reinforce the knowledge that what one does or says inside and outside social media contexts might be watched, and therefore one needs to be careful, altering one's words and deeds with this awareness.

SOCIAL MEDIA AS A PANOPTIC REGIME

In order to more fully understand the paradox of how social media threatens privacy and freedom of expression, we turn to the work of French philosopher Michel Foucault (1995) and the concept of the **panopticon** that he wrote about in the seminal text *Discipline and Punish*. Foucault based his articulation of a panoptic society on a plan for the design of buildings such as schools, hospitals, and institutions, and prisons in particular, by the late 18th-century philosopher Jeremy Bentham. The basic concept behind the design is that an observer within the panopticon can observe others without them necessarily knowing that they are being observed. Bentham's design of the prison calls for a circular structure, with the prisoners lining the perimeter in glass-fronted cells. At the centre of the circular prison is a second circular glass tower. From this central point of observation, prison guards can inspect the inmates at any time without them knowing. As Foucault tells it, the idea is:

> ... to induce in the inmate a state of conscious and permanent visibility that assures the automatic functioning of power. So to arrange things that the surveillance is permanent in its effects, even if it is discontinuous in its action ... that the inmates should be caught up in a power situation of which they are themselves the bearers (Foucault, 2007, pp. 70–71).

What matters in this arrangement of power is that the inmate knows that the potential to be observed exists at all times, and at the same time, never knows when or where he or she will be observed. The only certainty for the inmate of the panopticon is the possibility of being watched. As such, the inmate internalizes the panopticon as a form of power and self-regulates his or her behaviour accordingly.

> He [sic] who is subjected to the field of visibility, and who knows it, assumes responsibility for the constraints of power; he makes them play spontaneously upon himself; he inscribes

> in himself the power relation in which he simultaneously plays both roles; he becomes the principle of his own subjection (Foucault, 2007, p. 71).

In extrapolating Bentham's design to think through power and social order more broadly, Foucault expanded access to the central point of observation to all members of society: "... anyone may come and exercise in the central tower the functions of surveillance ... a transparent building in which the exercise of power may be supervised by society as a whole" (Foucault, 2007, p. 73). In positing a social extension of the panopticon, Foucault argues that the more numerous, anonymous, and temporary the observers are, the greater the awareness that one might be observed, and the more the potential to alter what one is and is not willing to do or say, with the knowledge that surveillance might happen everywhere and all the time by authorities and others alike. In this way, people internalize the panopticon as a form of power, assuming responsibility for its exercise.

In order to concretely understand how the panopticon applies to social media, let's consider two recent Canadian events: the Stanley Cup Riots in Vancouver in 2011 and the St. Patrick's Day Riots in London in 2012. The riots in Vancouver happened immediately after the Boston Bruins eliminated the Vancouver Canucks in Game 7 of the Stanley Cup Final. An estimated 100,000 people had gathered to watch the game on big screen TVs in a "secure" zone set up near the Rogers arena. The loss triggered an emotional response in the crowd that led to violence and destruction. Approximately 100 arrests were made that night and over 150 people were injured (CBC News, 2011). The riots in London, Ontario, happened when St. Patrick's Day student parties spilled over into the streets of the downtown core, and celebrations turned ugly. At least 1,000 people participated in the riots, with 11 people arrested that night, and several injured by broken glass and fires (CTV News, 2012).

What differentiated these two events from past riots in Vancouver in 1994 (after the Canucks lost in the Stanley Cup Finals) and Montreal in 1986 and 1993 (after the Canadiens won the Stanley Cup in those years) was that handheld digital devices were everywhere, capturing everything. Indeed, as the riots in Vancouver and London built up, hit an apex, and subsided, streams of data were flowing; images, video, audio, text messages, Facebook updates, and Twitter feeds capturing endless details in documented and time-stamped forms. As these events unfolded, everyday people bore witness in unprecedented ways. And this bearing witness provided a vast stream of evidence for police who turned to social media platforms such as Facebook, Twitter and YouTube to gather evidence and make cases against rioters (Dhillon, 2011; CTV News, 2012).

Of particular note here are the emergence of "identify the rioters" websites that were set up by Vancouver police (https://riot2011.vpd.ca) and concerned citizens (http://www.identifyrioters.com), as well as a Facebook page to identify rioters that was set up by concerned citizens in London (http://www.facebook.com/london ontarioriots). On these sites, users were encouraged to both upload images and video of rioters for others to identify, as well as identify rioters themselves. Herein we can clearly see the social extension of the panopticon that Foucault articulated, how anyone can come and practise the functions of surveillance in the central tower. Everyday people in these events both provided the content to identify rioters and, at the same time, participated in the act of policing by identifying rioters themselves. As such, where we might be inclined to think about surveillance as a top-down practice involving authorities monitoring and tracking everyday people, we can now see how surveillance is both top-down and bottom-up. Bottom-up forms of surveillance are sometimes referred to as *sousveillance* (Dennis, 2008), where the prefix "sous" (French for "below") is substituted for the prefix "sur"' (French for "above, or on top of").

Thomas Mathiesen (1997) first introduced the concept of the "**synopticon**" to speak to how contemporary arrangements of surveillance involve not just the few seeing and supervising the many, but the many seeing and supervising the few. For him, where the gaze of authorities is panoptic, the gaze of citizens is synoptic; they are interlinked, each feeding off the other (Fuchs, 2011). Building on Mathiesen, Haggerty and Ericson (2000) have argued that surveillance is not merely a top-down phenomenon, but a bottom-up one as well in what they articulate as "the **surveillant assemblage**." Sean Hier (2007) has even further argued that the surveillant assemblage possesses the potential to bring about "a partial democratization of surveillance hierarchies" (p. 118). Consistent with such analyses, the vast majority of the images and videos by which rioters were identified were not captured by the closed-circuit television networks of authorities and municipalities. Rather, they were generated from the bottom-up, by the many, captured by participants and bystanders alike and shared across social media. As of this writing, authorities continue to plumb the vast storehouses of social media in continuing efforts to apprehend and charge rioters. Moreover, citizens continue to upload content and identify rioters on these sites, confirming that the many can see and supervise the few, just as the few can see and supervise the many: anyone, citizens and authorities alike, can exercise surveillance in the central tower.

Siva Vaidhyanathan (2011) has critiqued the concept of the panopticon by pointing to the fact that in surveillance arrangements people don't necessarily conform to social conventions or the rule of law based on the knowledge that they are being (or might be) watched; rather, they might not care, or might even play up to the cameras in attempts to get noticed. The latter was clearly on display in the riots. But we are reminded here that the utility of understanding power, surveillance, and social order through the lens of the panopticon is that it provides an understanding of how people might alter what they are or are not willing to do or say, with the awareness that they might be watched. For some people caught up in the riots, the knowledge that their actions could be captured might very well have factored in their decision to obey the rule of law. For others, the knowledge that they were being watched meant that they decided to play up to the cameras, engaging in more extreme forms of behaviour than they might otherwise. In either case, what these people were or were not willing to do during the riots was altered based on the awareness that they might be watched.

Although the example of the riots is an extreme one with respect to developing an understanding of how freedom of expression might be limited in surveillance arrangements, it nonetheless demonstrates how the awareness of surveillance is around us (and in us) all the time. The effects of this awareness are felt across the spectrum of society: in how government operates; in political and economic protest; in our workplaces, schools, and hospitals; in the spaces in which we play; and even in our homes. Indeed, it is in our day-to-day lives, in the minutiae of what we are and are not willing to do or say, on a moment-to-moment basis, where the implications of the awareness of surveillance on freedom of expression are the most pronounced and problematic. As Raymond Wacks (2010) tells it, "the knowledge that our activities are, or even may be, monitored undermines our psychological and emotional autonomy" (p. 4). Indeed, the repeated reinforcement of this knowledge has the potential to fundamentally alter our identities, our relationships, how we organize and socialize; all the while opening the door to possible forms of "totalitarianism" where each and every utterance and interaction of citizens has the potential to be highly scrutinized (ibid.).

DIGITAL ENCLOSURES: SOCIAL MEDIA AS SURVEILLANT ASSEMBLAGE

What we have seen thus far is how corporate ownership and control of social media platforms means that in order to gain access to the conveniences associated with participation, users tacitly accept that they are not only the products of the processes of commodification, but also the subjects of intense forms of surveillance. The more that social media as a corporate controlled communication phenomenon becomes a taken-for-granted reality of social life, the more that the order of commodification and surveillance installed through these arrangements is reinforced.

But contemporary social media arrangements are not discrete, unitary, or exclusive, as the model of the panopticon might suggest. Rather, social media arrangements are more aptly contextualized as an assemblage, or a series of converged enclosures of commodification and surveillance. Social media platforms are designed to work together, as well as with other tracking technologies, such as **global positioning systems**, through an integrated infrastructure where data flows efficiently and seamlessly across platforms that "... are both virtual and physical, with varying spatial reaches and information scopes" (Andrejevic, 2009, p. 23). Each of these platforms, layers, or "digital enclosures" (Andrejevic, 2009), leverages the data capture, mining, and aggregation operations of the others, as well as the capabilities of other surveillance forms operating through cellular, broadband, Wi-Fi and satellite networks.

The contextualization of social media as a series of overlapping digital enclosures echoes what Haggerty and Ericson (2000) have described as "the surveillant assemblage": a highly converged surveillance arrangement that abstracts people as "data doubles," who "... can be scrutinized and targeted for intervention" (p. 606). The idea of surveillance as an assemblage of interoperable layers begins with the work of Gilles Deleuze and Félix Guattari (1987) who broke open traditional notions of phenomenon and structure as being discretely bounded and stable (ibid.). Deleuze and Guattari argue that when we dig below the surface of that which appears to be stable, we find a multiplicity of heterogeneous and ever-evolving operations and processes working together and giving the sense of a functional whole. Indeed, in these arrangements, "... any particular assemblage is itself composed of different discrete assemblages which are themselves multiple" (Haggerty and Ericson, 2000, p. 608).

Let us return to the example of the riots in order to conclude this discussion of social media as surveillant assemblage. More specifically, let us further consider the "identify the rioters" websites and how these particular assemblages are composed of an endless multiplicity of assemblages in their own right. Participants and bystanders in the riots possessed in their hands the key surveillant assemblages that would ultimately result in the "identify the rioters" websites: iPhones, BlackBerrys, smart phones, digital cameras, and the like, each of which are composed of and constituted in more assemblages. Photos and videos taken on smart phones were location-, date-, and time-stamped through the **GPS** surveillant assemblage. Content was uploaded, and data was produced and distributed through the surveillant assemblage of social media, such as Facebook, YouTube and Twitter; each layer contributing its own processes, products, and subjects of surveillance to the others. It is through these multiple, heterogeneous, and integrated layers, both top-down and bottom-up, that the "identify the rioters" websites take shape as surveillant assemblages in their own right. Indeed, it is the contributions of all of these layers, of all of the assemblages discussed throughout this chapter, in addition to endless others, unmentioned and perpetually emerging, that together constitute the regimes of commodification and surveillance on which social media platforms operate.

CONCLUSION: IMAGINING ALTERNATIVES TO SOCIAL MEDIA, COMMODIFICATION AND SURVEILLANCE

> To the extent the resources for communication, expression and interaction are encompassed by a privatized digital enclosure, access to these resources is subject to enhanced forms of monitoring and control ... to the extent that expression becomes increasingly reliant upon private corporations more committed to the realities of the bottom line than to abstract principles of civil liberties, the technology that facilitates the ability to challenge entrenched power could evolve into a breathtakingly efficient tool for monitoring, tracking, and filtering dissident expression (Andrejevic, 2009, p. 35).

The more that communication, expression, and interaction are privatized and enclosed, the more difficult it becomes to not only imagine alternative arrangements, but also challenge the increasingly entrenched form of power reinforced through commodification and surveillance regimes. If we are to continue to value social media for its potential for creation and connection, and begin to find alternatives to the forms of commodification and surveillance installed in these arrangements, we need to find places to have these discussions outside the confines of corporate social media (Scholz, 2008). Indeed, we must value noncommodified spaces, placing our emphasis on how people are to be "... valued as ends in themselves and not for their market value" (Mosco, 2009, pp. 148–149). As Mosco tells it, "there are alternatives to commodification in private life through the cultivation of intimacy, friendship, and kinship" (p. 156), whereas, in public life, finding alternatives to commodification are based on the practices of citizenship:

> ... a set of social processes that carry out democracy, namely advancing equality and the fullest possible participation in the complete range of economic, political, social, and cultural decision-making ... These processes are distinct from those centered in private life, which promote interpersonal intimacy, and those of the marketplace, which advance the creation of exchange and surplus value (p. 152).

Bennett (2008) too insists that the exercise of citizenship is critical to the future of digital culture and privacy advocacy. Indeed, for Bennett, engaged citizenry is a key condition for the possible emergence of a broad-based communication/information rights social movement that might have the resiliency to counter the encroachments of commodification and surveillance in a manner similar to how the environmental, human rights, and feminist movements advocate for their causes. As Bennett concludes, the future of advocacy for communication/information rights and privacy "... lies in the persistent, relentless, and informed articulation of the very simple proposition that individuals have a right to control the information that relates to them. Few would deny this right. Everybody wants it for themselves. The cause is a just one" (p. 225).

As we have seen throughout this chapter, the costs associated with the conveniences and benefits of social media platforms are not only the selling and surveilling of lives, but also the threats that these arrangements pose to privacy and freedom of expression. All of this is not to say that the only alternative to corporate social media is to opt out entirely and do without. Rather, we need to think critically about this form of participation, making informed, tactical, and strategic decisions about what we are and are not willing to do or say in these arrangements. More equitable social media platforms do exist and are increasingly emerging. Platforms such as Diaspora (http://www.joindiaspora.com), Crabgrass (http://crabgrass.riseuplabs.org), Buddycloud (http://www.buddycloud.com) and Thimbl (http://www.thimbl.net), to name but a few, are ones that recognize that users have a right to their privacy, to ownership of their content, as well as control over the circulation, retention, and commodification of their data. Check them out, be on the lookout for more, and talk to your friends and family outside the constraints of corporate controlled platforms about why they should think critically about their participation in social media.

QUESTIONS

1. What is the difference between data as a resource and data as a commodity?
2. Can you identify other examples of social media platforms and cloud computing arrangements? How do these platforms and services engage data mining and data aggregation in the processes of commodification? Describe these examples with regards to immanent and external commodification.
3. Can you identify other examples of social contexts and/or recent events where bottom-up forms of surveillance were at play? Explain these examples with regards to the panopticon.
4. Explain your cell phone, iPhone, BlackBerry, laptop, or any other networked device as surveillant assemblage.
5. Describe your own practice of using platforms such as Facebook, Google, YouTube, and Wikipedia with regards to the paradox of social media. How does your practice leverage the democratic, connective, knowledge sharing and development capacities of social media, and at the same time, play into commodification and surveillance regimes?

REFERENCES

Andrejevic, M. (2004). The webcam subculture and the digital enclosure. In N. Couldry & A. McCarthy (Eds.). *MediaSpace: Place, scale, and culture in a media age* (pp. 193–208). London; New York: Routledge.

———. (2009). Surveillance in the digital enclosure. In S. Magnet & K. Gates (Eds.), *The new media of surveillance* (pp. 18–40). London and New York: Routledge.

Bennett, C. J. (2008). *The privacy advocates*. Cambridge, Massachusetts: The MIT Press.

Bruns, A. (2008). *Blogs, Wikipedia, Second Life, and beyond: From production to produsage*. New York: Peter Lang.

Burgess, J. & J. Green. (2009). *YouTube: Online video and participatory culture*. Cambridge: Polity.

CBC News. (2011, June 16). Vancouver police arrest more than 100 in riot. *CBC News*. Retrieved August 16, 2012, from http://www.cbc.ca/news/canada/british-columbia/story/2011/06/16/bc-riot-thursday.html

Cohen, N. (2008). The valorization of surveillance: Towards a political economy of Facebook. *Democratic Communiqué*, *22*(1), 5–22.

CTV News. (2012, March 18). London, Ont. police turn to social media to find rioters. *CTV News*. Retrieved August 16, 2012, from http://www.ctv.ca/CTVNews/TopStories/20120318/london-ontario-st-patricks-day-party-turned-into-riot-120318/#ixzz1uOGk0nqm

Deleuze, G. & F. Guattari. (1987). *A thousand plateaus*. Minneapolis: University of Minnesota Press.

Dennis, K. (2008). Keeping a close watch—the rise of self-surveillance and the threat of digital exposure. *The Sociological Review*, *56*(3), 347–357.

Deuze, M. (2007). Convergence cultures in the creative industries. *International Journal of Cultural Studies*, *10*(2), 243–263.

Dhillon, S. (2011, December 20). When rioters trashed Vancouver, Twitter fanned the flames—and gathered the evidence. *The Globe and Mail*. Retrieved September 3, 2012, from http://www.theglobeandmail.com/news/national/british-columbia/when-rioters-trashed-vancouver-twitter-fanned-the-flames-and-gathered-the-evidence/article2278581/singlepage

Dworkin, R. (1990). *A bill of rights for Britain*. London: Chatto & Windus.

Foucault, M. (1995). *Discipline and punish: The birth of the prison* (2nd Vintage Books ed.). New York: Vintage Books.

———. (2007). Panopticism. In S.P. Hier & J. Greenberg (Eds.), *The surveillance studies reader* (pp. 67–77). New York: McGraw Hill.

Fuchs, C. (2011). Web 2.0, prosumption, and surveillance. *Surveillance & Society*, *8*(3), 288–309.

Gandy, O. H. (2007). Data mining and surveillance in the post 9/11 environment. In S. P. Hier & J. Greenberg (Eds.), *The surveillance studies reader* (pp. 147–157). New York: Open University Press: McGraw Hill.

Gillmor, D. (2004). *We the media: Grassroots journalism by the people, for the people* (1st ed.). Sebastopol, CA: O'Reilly.

Haggerty, K. D., & R. V. Ericson (2000). The surveillant assemblage. *British Journal of Sociology*, *51*(4), 605–622.

———. (2006). *The new politics of surveillance and visibility*. Toronto: University of Toronto Press.

Hier, S. P. (2007). Probing the surveillant assemblage. In S. P. Hier & J. Greenberg (Eds.), *The surveillance studies reader* (pp. 117–127). New York: McGraw Hill.

Howe, J. (2008). *Crowdsourcing: Why the power of the crowd is driving the future of business*. New York: Crown Business.

Jenkins, H. (2004). The cultural logic of media convergence. *International Journal of Cultural Studies*, 7(1), 33–43.

———. (2006). *Convergence culture*. New York: New York University Press.

Lyon, D. (2003). *Surveillance as social sorting: Privacy, risk and digital discrimination*. London: Routledge.

———. (2007a). Everyday surveillance: Personal data and social classifications. In S. P. Hier & J. Greenberg (Eds.), *The surveillance studies reader* (pp. 136–146). New York: McGraw Hill.

———. (2007b). Resisting surveillance. In S. P. Hier & J. Greenberg (Eds.), *The surveillance studies reader* (pp. 368–377). New York: McGraw Hill.

Mathiesen, T. (1997). The viewer society: Michel Foucault's "panopticon" revisited. *Theoretical Criminology*, *1*(2), 215–234.

Mosco, V. (2009). *The political economy of communication*, 2nd ed. London, UK: Sage Publications.

Nissenbaum, H. (2010). *Privacy in context*. Stanford, California: Stanford University Press.

O'Reilly, T. (2005). Web 2.0: compact definition. Retrieved August 16, 2012, from http://radar.oreilly.com/2005/10/web-20-compact-definition.html

Palis, C. (2012, March 23). Facebook condemns practice of employers demanding employee passwords. *The Huffington Post*. Retrieved August 21, 2012, from http://www.huffingtonpost.com/2012/03/23/facebook-employer-employee-passwords_n_1375020.html

Poster, M. (2006). *Information please! Culture and politics in the age of digital machines*. Durham, NC: Duke University Press.

Rosen, J. (2010, July 21). The web means the end of forgetting. *The New York Times*. Retrieved August 16, 2012, from http://www.nytimes.com/2010/07/25/magazine/25privacy-t2.html?pagewanted=all

Schiller, D. (2007). *How to think about information*. Urbana: University of Illinois Press.

Scholz, T. (2008). Where the activism is. In M. Boler (Ed.) *Digital media and democracy: Tactics in hard times* (pp. 355–365). Cambridge, Mass.: MIT Press.

Shirky, C. (2008). *Here comes everybody: The power of organizing without organizations*. New York: Penguin Books.

Tapscott, D. & A. D. Williams. (2006). *Wikinomics: How mass collaboration changes everything*. London: Penguin.

Terranova, T. (2000). Producing culture for the digital economy. *Social Text*, *63*(18), 33–58.

———. (2004). *Network culture: Politics for the information age*. London: Pluto Press.

Vaidhyanathan, S. (2011). *The Googlization of everything (and why we should worry)*. Berkeley, CA: University of California Press.

Van Dijck, J. (2009). Users like you? Theorizing agency in user-generated content. *Media, Culture & Society*, *31*(1), 41–58.

Van Dijck, J. & Nieborg, D. (2009). Wikinomics and its discontents: A critical analysis of Web 2.0 business manifestos. *New Media & Society*, *11*(5), 855–874.

Wacks, R. (2010). *Privacy*. Oxford, UK: The Oxford University Press.

Werbin, K. C. (2011). Spookipedia: Intelligence, social media, and biopolitics. *Media, Culture & Society*, *33*(8), 1254–1265.

Winner, L. (1977). *Autonomous technology: Technics-out-of-control as a theme in political thought*. Cambridge, Mass.: MIT Press.

14

RECONCEPTUALIZING MOBILITIES AND REMEDIATING THE MOB

Judith Nicholson
Wilfrid Laurier University

Worldwide, billions of us are on the move with cellphones, smartphones, laptops, tablets, and, soon, "augmented reality" glasses (Braiker, 2012). We use our mobile devices for text messaging, TV watching, music listening, video streaming, social networking, phone calling, web surfing, photo sharing, microblogging, navigating, emailing, reading, gaming, and money transfers. These examples of mobile devices and mediated mobile practices, which are only a few among many, hint at a dynamic interplay between different mobilities and between mobilities and mobiles. Even while we move with our handheld mobiles and use them to mediate interpersonal communication and "**post-mass media functions**" (Lemos, 2010), we too are mobiles; we are flesh mobiles. And, we too are mobile media.

We are mobile media when we use our bodies to shape time, spaces, and social interactions while engaging in practices such as **parkouring**, **critical massing**, **vote mobbing**, **flash robbing**, **couchsurfing**, and **citizen journalism**. We experience the world through mobility even when we are engaged in mundane movements such as crawling, running, walking, skipping, or dancing (Cresswell, 2006; de Certeau, 1984; Ingold, 2004). We travel locally, regionally, and globally for migration, work, and leisure, using mediums of mobility such as airplanes, bicycles, boats, trains, trucks, wheelchairs, skateboards, rickshaws, scooters, and, perhaps soon, fully automated driverless cars (Garber, 2012; Vanderbilt, 2012). Using private space shuttles, we even travel to outer space for exploration and shortly, for those who can afford the $200,000 fare, space tourism (see http://www.virgingalactic.com). If physical movement is "the raw material for the production of mobility" (Cresswell, 2010, p. 19), what is mobility?

Mobility is "central to what it is to be human" (Cresswell, 2006, p. 1). However, differences clearly exist across the examples listed above. This chapter explores how mobility or, more accurately, "multiple mobilities" (Sheller & Urry, 2006) are central to our lives by considering how we name and classify mobilities in order to make sense of them, the emergence of "mobilities studies" as a scholarly area of naming and research, and the role we all play in shaping perceptions of mobilities, as well as immobilities, through our everyday practices, which include our use of language.

MOBILITIES AND METAPHORS

The 2011 "BlackBerry riots" in Britain is one of many recent examples of how popularized descriptions reflect a dynamic interplay between multiple mobilities and mobiles. Journalists linked the riots to the Canadian-made smartphone because protestors used the free instant-messaging service named BlackBerry Messenger, or BBM as it is commonly called, to contact one another in order to organize rallies following the police shooting death of a Tottenham resident in August 2011. Protest organizers claimed that police racism had sparked the shooting, which was cited as the latest deadly instance in a history of police bias against blacks in Britain (Halliday, 2011).

While messages of mourning for the victim first appeared via web 2.0 social networking and microblogging, namely Facebook and Twitter, BBM "pinging" (an urgent reminder to the recipient) is credited with quickly transforming peaceful protests into flashpoint moments of rioting, looting, and arson that spread to cities throughout Britain and lasted for nearly a week. Pinging describes the practice of sending a message to another BlackBerry user, or broadcasting a message to several users, utilizing each one's unique BlackBerry PIN. Pings are delivered nearly instantaneously and they are encrypted, which means they are practically untraceable. This encryption is among the reasons business executives and government officials who desired quick and secure transmission of messages were early adopters of the first BlackBerry phones in the late 1990s (Middleton, 2007). The use of smartphones, and particularly SMS (short message services), during the BlackBerry riots appears to link the riots to other recent moments of mobbing that were organized, coordinated, and/or documented using mobiles. Such moments include:

- 2012 **Printemps Érable** (Maple Spring) in Quebec, which was documented widely in photos and videos by mobile-wielding students, who organized months-long protests against tuition hikes, student debt, and a special law against public assembly (Moure, 2012);
- 2011 **vote mobbing** by Canadian university and college students, who used mobiles and social media to organize and document "surprise rallies," which challenged perceptions of voter apathy among youth in the lead-up to a federal election;
- 2011 **Vancouver hockey riot**, which participants and witnesses documented using their mobiles when Vancouverites swept into the streets following the defeat of their Canucks during the Stanley Cup Championship (Staff, 2011);
- 2010 **Arab Spring** mass uprisings against despotic leaders that were fuelled by political tweets and SMS (Allagui & Kuebler, 2011);
- 2010 protests against the **G20 Toronto summit** of world economic issues, during which some protestors used mobiles to coordinate attacks on symbols of capitalism, such as major banks, and to evade police (Byrne, 2010);
- 2007 and 2005 les émeutes des *banlieues* (riots) in France by poor immigrant youth, who used SMS to organize nightly torching of cars following the deaths

of other youth who were in the presence of police (Murray, 2006; Morley, 2000);

- 2004 day of **digital democracy** in Spain when Spaniards used the digits on their hands and the digits on their digital cellphones to create and circulate political text messages in the lead-up to a crucial election (Castells et al., 2007, p. 201);
- a 2003 **flash mobbing** in a New York City department store that would be the first of many fun and brief public performances organized in major cities around the world via cellphone and email (Nicholson, 2006; Walker, 2011);
- 2001 **People Power II** uprisings when Filipinos, who called themselves the "Txt Generation," used text messaging to organize days-long street rallies against a corrupt President (Rafael, 2003)
- 1999 **Battle of Seattle** when antiglobalization protestors used text messaging to coordinate **smart mobbing**, which was also described as organized "flocking" or "swarming," during a meeting of the World Trade Organization in Seattle, Washington (Rheingold, 2003; Townsend, 2000).

There are certainly other recent examples that echo these particular **constellations of mobility**, which are named by participants or by journalists. Constellations of mobility are "historically and geographically specific formations of movements, narratives about mobility, and mobile practices" (Cresswell, 2010, p. 17). Are there advantages to conceptualizing mobilities as existing together in a constellation rather than imagining mobilities as flows of people, things, and ideas moving across vast landscapes (see Appadurai, 1990), or mobilities as routes branching into and out of a system of roads represented on a map (see Adey, 2010; Cresswell, 2006)? Each metaphor is useful because each encourages a relational perspective on mobilities (see Adey, 2006). Constellations, landscapes, and maps can be read differently depending on how they are seen from particular perspectives and locations. Let's consider constellations of mobilities.

CONSTELLATIONS OF MOBILITIES

The notion of constellations encourages a focus on how mobilities are similar, and changed, depending on our perspective in different eras and places. The notion encourages us to pay particular attention to embodied movement across spaces; to representations of movement in oral, written, and visual language; and to everyday sensations and memories of movement (Cresswell, 2006; 2010). Naming of the mediated events listed above reflects attempts to name constellations of mobilities and associated practices, imaginaries, and sensations (Jensen, 2011, p. 268), which are sometimes unique and sometimes familiar. For example, resonances are evident in the naming and quick mobbing performances associated with smart mobbing, flash mobbing, and vote mobbing, and in the naming and protest marches of the Arab Spring and Maple Spring, which imply change and renewal. However, there are also differences, you would likely agree, between the politicized nature of vote mobbing and smart mobbing versus the apolitical focus of flash mobbing and, certainly, differences in the politics and history that inspired the Arab Spring and Maple Spring uprisings. Meanings associated with *mobility* and *mobile* help to highlight significant historical continuities of mobilities in these events and also to suggest how mobilities are different in each event.

Mobility and *mobile* derive from *mobile vulgus*, which was used from about the 16th to the 18th centuries to describe a potentially dangerous or riotous crowd, who used their collective **corporeal mobility** to influence change, most famously during the French Revolution (Hayes, 1992). Over the next two centuries, *mobile* and *vulgus* began to be used separately. *Vulgus* came to mean vulgar or rude. *Mobile* was further shortened to *mob*, which retained the connotation of a potentially dangerous corporeal mobility in the form of a riotous crowd (Hayes, 1992, p. 67). Classification of particular crowds as mobs made them more identifiable for surveillance by state authorities and law enforcement and, by the 19th century, for surveillance and research by scholars (Le Bon, 1960; Canetti, 1962).

By the late 19th century, mobility also acquired positive connotations of adventure and freedom in conjunction with the construction of mediums of mobility such as boulevards, railway stations, and the automobile as well as agency linked to new identities such as flâneur, tourist, and driver (Friedberg, 1993; Benjamin, 2002; Thrift, 2004). "By the 20th century, mobility was right at the heart of what it is to be modern. Modern man, and increasingly modern woman, was mobile ..." (Cresswell, 2010, p. 27). *Mobile* took on the meaning of something that is capable of malleability, movement, or portability, which we see now when describing characteristics of mobile homes, mobile patrols, mobile sculptures, and mobile phones (Jain, 2002, p. 387).

We now use *mobilized* to describe the actions of individuals who organize themselves in order to communicate a message (Berland, 2005, p. 218), as British protestors did in response to the police shooting in Tottenham. We use *immobilized* to describe individuals who are hampered by forces within themselves, like fear or uncertainty (Berland, 2005, p. 218). Individuals may also be immobilized, or thwarted, by external structures, such as poverty, abelism, or racism. For example, it is well known in Canada, the United States, Britain, and other Western nations that black men like the Tottenham victim are "far more likely to be stopped by police due to racial profiling and the mythical crime of 'driving while black' [DWB]" (Cresswell, 2010, p. 26; cf. Gilroy, 2001; Packer, 2008). DWB represents mobility that is deemed to be inappropriate for black men in particular, through certain spaces and, occasionally, in particular expensive vehicles (see Packer, 2008). As this example suggests, immobilities and mobilities are relational. Individuals may also be immobilized, or blocked, by mobile external physical forces, such as a line of police in riot gear as British protestors encountered. In addition to these connotations, newer meanings of *mobility* and *mobile* were discernable in the constellation of mobilities associated with the BlackBerry riots, particularly in the naming of the riots after a handheld mobile.

The word "mobile" is used widely in English-speaking regions of the world for the cellular telephone and the smartphone. Since "mobile" is an old word, does the malleability, or flexibility, of the word make it an apt descriptor also for other handheld communication technologies? For example, should the category of "mobile" include pagers such as the first-generation BlackBerry in the late 1990s, which was more like a one-way radio receiver, PDAs (personal digital assistants) such as the first-generation Palm Pilot in the late 1990s, and even single-function handheld technologies such as the 1990s iPod music players or 1980s Sony Walkman? These technologies could be included in the classification of mobiles, but many people likely would not recognize them as mobiles.

We are encouraged to think of contemporary mobile telephones as the first mobiles through their association with generations, for example, from first-generation analogue phones in the 1980s, to second- and third-generation digital phones in the 1990s, to today's smartphones. Mobiles are significant not because of their technological functions but, rather, because of how we use them to mediate our experiences of mobilities and our social interactions with one another (Slack & Wise, 2006). If mobiles are used similarly in different eras, how do particular ones become iconic in conjunction with certain practices, representations, and sensations that comprise different constellations of mobilities?

Using the Sony Walkman as an example in the 1990s, cultural studies practitioners suggested that five articulated processes contribute to making iconic technologies, which we use to mediate culture, or everyday ways of living together (du Gay et al., 1997). The processes can be posed as five questions. (1) How is the technology represented in oral and visual language, which might include advertising and news stories? (2) What social identities, meaning kinds of people or places, are associated with the technology? (3) How is the technology culturally produced through the telling of stories about its origin and design, inventors and designers, or corporate producer? (4) What particular meanings are associated with the technology through its consumption and everyday uses? (5) What everyday rules or official policies regulate the technology's distribution and use if, for example, its use challenges traditional distinctions between work hours and leisure hours or between public and private spaces?

Key to these processes, which comprise a **circuit of culture**, is an implied movement of a technology, through and between imagining, production, consumption, use and regulation, in no specific order, and a flow of ideas and meanings among designers, advertisers, users, and policy makers. Are these questions useful for interpreting the iconic status of particular contemporary mobiles such as the iPhone or BlackBerry, and how we use them to mediate mobilities and culture? They are relevant questions, but we must now also account for complex articulations between mobilities and a variety of handheld multimodal mobiles.

SCREENNESS

Older handheld mobiles such as walkie-talkies used by military personnel early in the 20th century, the 1970s "brick" cellphone, which earned its nickname for its blocky shape and two-pound weight, and the iPod and Walkman music players, had limited functions, a short battery life and, some, a simple LED screen (Gow & Smith, 2006). Newer mobiles such as the iPad, Kindle, or Kobo tablet, have a longer battery life, increased memory capacity, and a tactile multimodal colour screen that facilitates **screenness** (Richardson, 2007, p. 208).

Screenness describes how screens have increasingly become the focus of our attention and concern (ibid.). Screenness involves an intensified **ocularcentrism**, which describes how visual representations on screens are prioritized as ways of navigating, experiencing, and knowing the world. Screenness is an example of meanings and sensations that seem to distinguish newer mobilities. It is not accounted for explicitly in the circuit of culture because older mobiles did not have a screen. However, this is not to suggest that screenness is completely new or that it is now the major factor in making some mobiles iconic or mobilities contemporary. Humans have long interacted with screens and used them to mediate mobilities.

Our human ancestors used cave walls as screens, which mediated a kind of time travel to the past and future via painted stories (Friedberg, 2006; Packer & Oswald, 2010). The 19th-century train window was a screen that mediated a mobile panomorization of the landscape for passengers who had never experienced such a way of seeing (Schivelbusch, 1986). When we window shop, store windows become screens for our journeys into fantasies just as television or film screens also do (Friedberg, 2002; Morse, 1998). The car windshield is a screen, protecting us from the outside environment and framing our journey (Packer & Oswald, 2010). Screenness is captured also in other key media concepts such as the **gaze** directed at the film screen, the **glance** directed at the domestic television screen, and the **glaze** directed at the screen of the gaming console (Chesher, 2004). In relation to contemporary mobiles, screenness implies the meanings of these other concepts through suggesting how we use our smartphones or tablets for personal screening practices such as photo taking, online shopping, TV watching, and GPS navigating while on the go (see Richardson & Wilken, 2009). Augmented reality glasses, commonly called "Google glasses," bring the screen onto our faces, within inches of our eyes (Braiker, 2012). Perhaps this way of seeing calls for a reconceptualization of screenness.

We use our mobiles to frame our world. However, too much of a focus on screenness can support the myth of technological progress and buttress claims of a devolution in social etiquette. The latter is represented, for example, in complaints about "distracted walking" by mobile users who sway like zombies along city sidewalks while deeply engaged in screening practices such as texting, web surfing, or video watching.[1] Screenness does not mean that mobilities associated, for example with cellphone use, have simply shifted from mouth to thumb to eye, in conjunction with new technological functions that have facilitated talking, then texting, and now screening practices. When we engage with the touch screens on our mobiles, we do so through a combination of haptics, or tactile sensations, textual and visual practices, as well as embodied movements. So, for example, we sometimes use our mobiles to take photos, blog them, and discuss them online while mingling in a mob and while sharing the same photos on the screen of our mobile with other individuals who are co-present in the mob. We use our handheld mobiles to mediate "a material experience of vision ... where hands, eyes, screen, and surroundings interact and blend in a syncopated fashion" (Richardson & Wilken, 2009, p. 22).

The naming of screenness only partially captures the combination of sensations and movements that intersect with representations, identities, and practices and that help to make certain mobiles iconic and certain mobilities contemporary. The concept of screenness only partially characterizes our contemporary propensity for pervasive photography, tweeting, blogging, mobbing, and video making. For example, the constellation of mobilities associated with the BlackBerry riots, namely individuals mobilizing as a mob with their mobiles, were documented in an abundance of photos, videos, texts, and tweets, which mobile users shared via **peer-to-peer communication** (p2p) such as multimedia messaging; via social networks such as YouTube, Facebook and Wikipedia; via micro-blogging to Twitter and Flickr; and via citizen journalism to standard mass media such as television news and TV websites. Tweeting, blogging, and other social networking practices are examples of how we are using our contemporary multimodal mobiles to mediate screenness and associated post–mass media practices. The latter are characterized by "information customization, publication and dissemination worldwide, with multimedia capabilities" (Lemos, 2010, p. 404).

Post–Mass Media Practices

Post–mass media practices are possible not only because of technological developments such as digital mobiles and digital networks, which became available in the early 2000s. Post–mass media practices are also possible because new user identities are emerging in conjunction with screenness, similar to how identities such as flâneur, tourist, and driver emerged in the late 19th century in conjunction with mediums of mobility such as the shopping mall, train, and car. Post–mass media practices include the numerous ways in which users of handheld mobiles make and share content and, thus, become both producer and consumer/user or, **produser** (Luke, 2005), while traditional media content continues to flow mostly unidirectionally from centralized production centres and across a variety of media platforms such as the internet and our handheld mobiles.

Since 2003, we have been using our cellphones and laptops to recontextualize older media such as television, radio, and the internet. We now make digital content for broadcast on TV news, watch TV programs on our mobiles, and use our mobiles to mediate interactivity by sending text messages to call-in radio or TV shows or to cast our vote for contestants in popular TV shows such as *Canadian Idol.* The naming of such practices as post–mass media suggests that they subsume traditional mass media, but they do not. Traditional mass media continue to exist and now rely heavily on produser content. **Citizen journalism** is one example of this reliance, which has been evident in recent constellations of mobilities such as the BlackBerry riots.

Citizen journalism is a post–mass media practice that relies on the mobility of produsers and the digital content they create using their mobiles. Citizen journalism describes when nonjournalists use their mobiles to record images of momentous events and transmit them to commercial media such as TV news and websites for broadcast and publication (Allan, 2002; Snowden, 2007). Citizen journalism gained prominence after witnesses used their mobiles to document the aftermath of the 2001 attacks on the World Trade Center; the 2004 commuter train bombings in Madrid, Spain; the 2004 deadly tsunami in South-East Asia; and the 2005 commuter train bombings in London, England (Allan, 2002; Katz & Rice, 2002; Robinson & Robison, 2006). How does the naming of citizen journalism set up expectations regarding its origins, its makers, and how it is done?

In the early 2000s, citizen journalism gained prominence over other terms such as "amateur newsies," "instant reporters," and "guerilla journalists" (Allan, 2002, 2009). Does "citizen journalist" imply that as mobile users we have a civic duty to bear witness to newsworthy events and that as citizen journalists we perform our duty by documenting and sharing newsworthy events via traditional mass media versus sending content to indymedia, blogging it, or sharing it via peer-to-peer communication? In relational terms, how does citizen journalism redefine standard journalism? While journalists and eyewitnesses have long used landline telephones to call in news (Snowden, 2007), the concept of citizen journalism has been widely popularized in conjunction with a proliferation of digital camera–enabled handheld mobiles, an intensification of screenness, and our contemporary obsession with 24-hour access to news as spectacle, even while on the go (Allan, 2009). The boundaries between traditional journalism and citizen journalism are beginning to blur. For example, mainstream journalists are now using smartphones to file stories and to take "authentic" photos that mirror the amateur aesthetics of photos captured by citizen journalists (Batty, 2011).

Does our perception of citizen journalism, its origins, meanings, and associated mobilities shift if we consider that the roots of citizen journalism may also be located in the 1991 video recording of a group of Los Angeles police assaulting motorist Rodney King? An eyewitness video recording of King's assault on a camcorder was sold, subsequently broadcast worldwide via TV news, and used as evidence in the trial of the police officers, who many viewers accused of profiling King and stopping him for DWB (see Gooding-Williams, 1993).

Does our perception of citizen journalists, and associated connotations of duty, shift if we consider 19th-century antilynching advocates as citizen journalists? Like soldiers at Abu Ghraib, who leaked photos of torture taken by fellow soldiers in 2003, anti-lynching advocates used early portable Kodak cameras to document some of the many thousands of lynching parties that were organized, mostly in the U.S. South, or they purchased photos taken at lynching parties by others. The photos were then sent for publication in magazines and newspapers that were sympathetic to the antilynching campaign (Apel, 2004; Apel & Smith, 2007; Johnson & Pleece, 2008). The actions of these activists mobilized legislators to outlaw lynching.

While the handheld mobiles in used examples above are different, from the 19th-century photographic film camera, to the 1990s tape-based analogue camcorder, to current handheld mobiles, and while the distribution of produser content now flows across multiple media platforms via post–mass media practices, could we argue that the practice we now call citizen journalism has existed for more than a century? Does this perspective influence our perception of this popular mobile practice and how it interpellates us as mobile citizens? Does a more historical perspective on citizen journalism influence our perception of how the naming of mobilities influences their meaning, value, and history; what technologies are counted as mobiles; and how we use mobiles to experience and shape social interactions, justice, and culture?

SOCIAL MOBILITIES

Even when we are not consciously naming mobilities or using our mobiles to mediate various post–mass media practices such as citizen journalism, we use them to mediate mobilities and meanings as suggested by the circuit of culture. Mobiles are associated symbolically with **social mobility** and transformation. Social mobility is discernable in the terms "upward mobility" and "downward mobility," which are relative descriptions of a change in a person's class (Jain, 2002, p. 387). Mobiles can mediate social mobility through being novel, such as in the 1980s when the cellphone was regarded as a "rich man's toy" and a "yuppie accessory" because of a rigorous credit check to acquire one, the $3,000 cost of the phone, and exorbitant rates for unreliable service (Katz & Aspden, 1999; Robbins & Turner, 2002). Cellphone use was exclusive to some people and inaccessible to most.

Today's popular mobiles such as the iPhone and iPad mediate social mobility through being carefully branded by their producer, which in their case is Apple Computers; purchased by millions of consumers, some of whom line up days in advance in order to acquire the latest model; and reviewed by technology journalists and others, whose coverage of each new release is tantamount to a "cultural event" (Pederson, 2008, p. 491). Comparable hype and enthusiasm accompanied the release of some older mobiles too, including Citizen's Band (CB) radios in the 1970s (Blake, 2010; Packer, 2008), and the Walkman in the 1980s (du Gay et al., 1997; Hosokawa, 1984). However, not all new mobiles become iconic and are used to mediate social mobility. In other words, not all mobiles move through the five articulated processes that comprise the circuit of culture. Both the 1970s picturephone, a video telephone system (see Noll, 1992), and the 1980s Sony Watchman, a portable pocket television (see Groening, 2010, p. 1344), were flops for various reasons including that consumers deemed them to be of low social value.

In the 1990s, when BlackBerry use implied upward mobility because it was associated with business executives and government officials, it earned the euphemism of "CrackBerry." The euphemism drew attention to how BlackBerry use challenged the traditional boundary between public and private time and space through suggesting that some users relied on the phone to feed their addiction for **perpetual contact** with a virtual **tele-circle** of family, friends, and professional contacts (Katz & Aakhus 2002; Kopomaa, 2002). The CrackBerry euphemism chastised users for constantly checking email during spare moments, in a practice that has been described as **time slicing** (Middleton, 2007, p. 167). By the 2011 BlackBerry riots, BlackBerry use was less exclusive, in part because of affordable pay-as-you-go services (Ball & Brown, 2011). At the time of the BlackBerry riots, British media reported than an estimated "37 percent of the youth market" were users (ibid.). BlackBerry use by youth is extolled now in British urban music, such as in the song "BB Hype" by Maxwell D, leader of the music group Pay as You Go Cartel (Ball & Brown, 2011). BB Hype extols BlackBerry use along with iPhone, YouTube, and Facebook use as well as connections between these.

Though the circuit of culture poses useful questions, its focus on a limited number of practices and individual technologies hardly accounts now for the complex assemblages of multiple circuits, where remixing occurs regularly between flesh mobiles such as a mob or a concert audience and the multimodal handheld mobiles we use, produser content such as citizen journalism and commercial mass-media content such as TV news, as well as numerous other post–mass media practices such as tweeting and Facebooking (see Richardson, 2011, pp. 427–428). With a BlackBerry or other smartphone, users can listen to BB Hype, watch a video performance of the song on YouTube or other video-sharing website, search and read the lyrics on the internet, and use their mobile to share or comment on this content via SMS, or blogging, even while at a concert where the Pay as You Go Cartel is playing. "BlackBerry riots" names a constellation of historical mobilities, such as mobbing, as well as contemporary mobilities, such as post–mass media practices. This naming by journalists also suggests improper use of the BlackBerry, mostly by youth, through its pairing with "riot," which is synonymous with the mobbing of a riotous crowd.

Mobilities are polysemous. Mobilities and how they are imagined, practised, and experienced can be threatening, liberating, strange, individual, collective, familiar, and new. These paradoxical meanings are captured in the concept of automobilities, which through its naming draws our attention to other constellations of mobilities as well as immobilities.

AUTOMOBILITIES

In November 2007, just outside Paris, two adolescents on a motorbike died in an accidental collision with a police vehicle. Other youth, who blamed police for the deaths, mobilized by forming mobs and engaging in several spectacular nights of arson. Similar to the 2011 BlackBerry riots, and to French riots in 2005, rioters used handheld mobiles to mediate minute-to-minute micro-coordination of their movements, to elude police, and to document their activities via a variety of post–mass media practices (Papenfuss, 2005; Samuel, 2007). The youth who died in the crash and those who rioted were poor, racialized, and living in isolated communities located in outlying French suburbs, or *les banlieues*. The communities, described as "dull and isolated places" (Murray, 2006, p. 29) with apartment buildings that are "concrete monstrosities" (ibid.), represent a ghettoization, or near state incarceration, of first- and second-generation immigrants, mostly African (Hardt & Negri, 2000; Morley, 2000).

Among the institutionalized structures that immobilize residents of the *banlieues* are systemic racism, high unemployment, and police surveillance. These structures are cited as the underlying reasons for the 2007 riots and other moments of civil unrest by *banlieue* residents including a subsequent riot in 2010, and earlier unrest in 2005 and 1997 (Morley 2000; Murray 2006).[2]

"[I]nstitutional racism plus police harassment minus jobs" is said to be the equation that has sparked riots not only in the *banlieus* but also in other racialized and marginalized communities in Britain and in the United States, including the BlackBerry riots (2011) and "Notting Hill (1976), Brixton (1981), Handsworth (1985) and Los Angeles (1992)" riots (Murray, 2006, p. 30).

Another rarely mentioned structure that influences the mobilities and immobilities of *banlieue* residents and other marginalized communities is automobilities (see Morley, 2000). What are automobilities, and how are they relevant to recent uprisings?

In a very broad sense, automobilities describe "a capacity for movement" (Urry, 2004, p. 26), particularly self-propelled forms of mobility such as driving, cycling, and walking. The term is also used more specifically to refer to car culture and to associated, or articulated, driving practices such as the daily commute or special road trips; to positive representations of car ownership and driving as fun, freedom, virility, and the "good life" in cultural products such as songs, films, and advertisements; and to embodied sensations, feelings, and memories linked to the mobility, flexibility, and speed of car travel (Edensor, 2004; Sheller, 2004; Thrift, 2004).

Like mobilities mediated via handheld mobiles, automobilities are also mediated via a mobile. The car is the quintessential mobile of automobilities. It is not the commuter train, public bus, transport truck, moped, bicycle, or skateboard though some of these are also used for transportation and, like handheld mobiles, become iconic by moving through a circuit of culture (see Makagon, 2006). We are moved figuratively by cars, and we use them to move literally through geographic spaces (see Sheller, 2004). Automobilities connote autonomous mobility and autobiography, or being the driver in one's own life and car (Urry, 2007; Sheller, 2004).

The term "automobilities" is also used to describe a complex structure, or assemblage, of contingent practices, representations, and sensations that support car travel, including car manufacturing, sales, repairs and accessories companies; oil refining and distribution processes; construction and maintenance of roads, bridges, parking lots, roadside services such as motels and gas stations, as well as drive-through services such as dining, banking, and drycleaning (Urry, 2004, p. 26). In the context of multiple mobilities in general, and widespread automobilities specifically, not having a car or a driver's licence "may lead to feelings of social exclusion and disempowerment" (Sheller, 2004, p. 230), just as the lack of a handheld mobile might also now elicit such feelings.

For *banlieue* residents, automobilities are not simply empowering; they can be disempowering. In France, where automobilities are as prevalent as in other rich nations (see Ross, 1999), *banlieues* residents are not likely to own a car because of high unemployment (Morley, 2000). Generally, *banlieues* are far from the city centre, underserved by public buses and commuter trains, and surrounded by highways, which run by them but do not service them well (ibid.). In this case, immobilities and mobilities are closely related. The highway, a medium of mobility, which facilitates the movement of drivers, is among the infrastructures that impede the mobility of *banlieue* residents.[3] The *banlieues* have been described as "a series of amorphous and indefinite spaces that promote isolation rather than any interaction or communication" (Hardt & Negri, 2000, p. 188). Here, communication also means transportation (see Peters, 1999; Sterne, 2006). The location and built environment of the *banlieue* makes it an immobilizing technology.

In recent riots, perhaps *banlieue* residents have targeted buses, trains, and particularly the car, because the latter is the central icon of automobilities, which does not deliver to them the "good life" it promises in songs, advertisements, and films. Furthermore, to:

> target more significant symbols of the state would have meant taking a couple of buses and a commuter train in order to first reach them. Which is why, at the height of the uprisings, the police kept a close eye on all major entry points to the French capital and perhaps why some railway stations were actually closed (Murray, 2006: 29–30).

Automobilities mediate car travel, our "predominant global form of quasi-private mobility" (Urry, 2004, p. 26) or **mobile privatization.** For many of us, our car is our mobile sanctuary, our mobile bubble, our surrogate living room (Bull, 2004). We anthropomorphize our car by naming it. We ascribe rebellious and faithful features to our car, and we sympathize with it when it ages or dies (Urry, 2004). Public buses and trains do not offer a similar degree of direct ownership or obvious privacy. In fact, when train travel was still novel in the 19th century, middle- and upper-class passengers had to adjust to sharing a public compartment with other passengers because they were more accustomed to travelling by private coach, which offered seclusion more akin to riding in a car (Schivelbusch, 1986). Some passengers used an existing handheld mobile to mediate their interactions: the book. Some read a novel or a travel guide in order to avoid conversation. Reading eventually became a "surrogate for communication that no longer took place" and a marker of bourgeois status (Schivelbusch, 1986, pp. 66–67). In contrast to first- and second-class carriages, crowding in third- and fourth-class carriages promoted "continuous conversation" among those passengers, who also could not afford to buy books (ibid.).

Using contemporary handheld mobiles, we engage now in practices similar to 19th-century train passengers in order to mediate social relations, proximity, and the boundaries between public and private. For example, we engage in **accompanied solitude** (Bull, 2004; 2005), when we watch TV shows or play games on our Sony PlayStation Portable while in public spaces and, therefore, coincidentally or deliberately, block out other people who are copresent in a space. We enact an **absent presence** (Gergen, 2002; Uy-Tioco, 2007) when we use our BlackBerry to interact with others who are not in the same space but accessible through calling or pinging. We engage in **comobility** (Southern, 2012), and become players—not merely users—when we move virtually with others at a distance through using the GPS (Global Positioning Systems) on our iPhone to share our location and movement with others and, also, to monitor the location of others for locative art and for locative games such as *Dodgeball*, *Mogi*, *FourSquare*, and *Geocaching* (de Souza e Silva & Frith, 2010; Hjorth, 2011; Humphreys, 2010; Lemos, 2010; Licoppe & Inada, 2010). These locative practices simultaneously connect us and separate us, and blur the lines between virtual and physical.

Accompanied solitude, absent presence, and comobility describe how, while performing various communication practices, we combine **virtual mobility** with **embodied mobility** and symbolic mobility. Accompanied solitude, absent presence, and comobility are other ways of describing mobile privatization. Based on how frequently mobile privatization is mentioned now in the new area of study known as **mobilities studies**, Raymond Williams was prescient in coining the neologism in the early 1970s to describe "an at once mobile *and* home-centred way of living" (Williams, 1990, p. 20; cf. Benjamin, 1969). Williams argued that a modern propensity for a paradoxical mix of solitariness and virtual togetherness emerged in the early to mid-20th century in conjunction with the popularization of geographic travel by car and virtual travel via television broadcasting (Williams, 1989, 1990), or what we might now call forms of screenness.

While driving, we are motionless yet move rapidly as a private car–human hybrid (Sheller, 2004) across vast geographic spaces, along an inflexible infrastructure of roadways, in a mass public performance of automobilities with other drivers. While watching television in the privacy of our home, we travel virtually to other places through mass broadcasting that appears on screen, while experiencing a virtual togetherness with other viewers, who watch the screen in their own homes. If we consider the windshield of the car to be like the screen of the television (Friedberg, 2002), both the car and TV can be regarded as mediums "designed to transport the individual or small family group to destinations well beyond the confines of home and neighbourhood, combining privacy with mobility" (Moores, 1993, p. 365).

Mobile privatization describes historically flexible boundaries between public and private spaces; multiple intersecting constellations of mobilities and immobilities, everyday communication practices that are paradoxically individual and collective, and particular ways of seeing, experiencing, and making our world through communication media. It is easy to understand, then, how mobile privatization has become a key concept for theorizing cultural shifts and stasis, which occur in conjunction with our consumption, use, and regulation of mobiles such as the car, Walkman, Citizen's Band radio (CB radio), iPod, cellphone, smartphone, and electronic tablet (see Blake, 2010; Bull, 2005; du Gay et al., 1997; Groening, 2010; Morley, 2000; Morse, 1998; Packer & Oswald, 2010; Slack & Wise, 2006; Sloop & Gunn, 2010; Wiley & Packer, 2010). When Williams coined "mobile privatization," however, "broadcast was the dominant media model ..." (Packer & Oswald, 2010, p. 322). Does the concept now mostly limit or aid our understanding and experiences of mobilities?

MOBILE PRIVATIZATION

Television screens are no longer accessible exclusively in our homes. We can watch streaming TV through mobile and wireless networks to our handheld mobiles; via live or recorded broadcasts on TV screen in airports, food courts, and waiting rooms; and via satellite in our car (see Groening, 2010; Groening, 2011; McCarthy, 2001; Nicholson, 2010; Orgad, 2009; Packer & Oswald, 2010; Spigel, 1992). With the fully automated car, or "driverless car," that Google and major car manufacturers are developing, the windshield becomes an interface more like a TV or computer screen with its overlay of street-view images, maps, and other data. Is our experience of automobilities changed if drivers become viewers?

Currently, smartphones and tablets are sometimes likened to a **third screen** because they can be used to view synchronous or asynchronous content, original programming such as **mobisodes** (mobile episodes of TV programs produced for mobiles), produser content, and web content that we would otherwise watch using the TV screen or computer screen (Goggin, 2006; Nicholson, 2010). Using mobiles, we time-shift and space-shift our viewing practices away from scheduled programming and immobile screens in our homes. Though this suggests an intensified personalization of viewing practices, mobile users also watch collectively by huddling around one mobile screen, for example, while sitting in the stands with other fans at a sports game and using a mobile to watch TV or online coverage of the same game (Orgad, 2009, pp. 202–205). Viewers also sometimes watch TV on their mobile in their homes (ibid.). With the increased informationalization of the car (Packer & Oswald, 2010), will the windshield of the driverless car become a fourth screen?

"The concept of mobile privatization is a powerful and productive way of analyzing a society that is both isolating and connecting, atomizing and cosmopolitan, or inward-dwelling but outward-looking" (Groening, 2010, p. 1335). And much more could be said about the concept, including how it is related to collective forms of sociality and, also, how our quest for mobile privatization feeds consumption of new technologies. For example, how does the desire for mobile privatization "reduce the necessity for shared interests in public resources" (Jain, 2002, p. 399), including public spaces? Because mobile privatization is so closely linked to the consumption and use of electronic communication technologies that mediate mass communication, it does not help us to interpret all mobilities and immobilities, or how they are related. Currently, we regularly exhibit a contemporary penchant for simultaneously using our electronic mobiles and our bodies as flesh mobiles to mediate mobbing as mass communication, for example, during the Maple Spring protests and while flash robbing. Increasingly, we are using mobiles to remediate the mob, which is itself an ancient and powerful mobile medium that requires public space for its mass formation, visibility, and mobility.

Consider flash robbing, which is inspired by flash mobbing and by happy-slapping. The latter involves groups of youth carrying out surprise swarming assaults on strangers and recording the assault using their mobiles. Such attacks have included theft and sexual assault (Goggin, 2006, p. 119; Nightingale, 2007, p. 290). Some happy-slapping videos are shared via p2p communication, and others are posted to blogs and to YouTube. Similarly, flash robbing involves youth using their mobiles to coordinate a scheduled swarming of a store with the purpose of stealing items and, on occasion, recording the flash rob and sharing or posting video of it (Black, 2011). Our contemporary penchant for mobbing was also reflected in *Mobbed*, a short-lived 2011–2012 FOX TV show hosted by Canadian comedian Howie Mandel. *Mobbed* involved strangers staging surprise performances for special occasions such as a marriage proposal (see http://www.fox.com/mobbed). The show was a commercialized representation of flash mobbing that made sense within contemporary constellations of mobilities, which comprise recent moments of flash mobbing, vote mobbing, flash robbing, and riot mobbing. The new mobilities paradigm suggests further how we might classify and interpret singular mobilities and constellations of mobilities (Sheller & Urry, 2006; Urry, 2007).

THE NEW MOBILITIES PARADIGM

Within the mobilities paradigm, mobility is characterized as "the actual and potential movement and flows of people, goods, ideas, images and information from place to place, entangled in networks and in tensions between fixity and motion" (Jensen, 2011, p. 256). In the paradigm, mobilities are classified according to five broad categories.

- The *corporeal* [or *embodied*] travel of people for work, leisure, family life, pleasure, migration and escape, organized in terms of contrasting time-space modalities (from daily commuting to once-in-a-lifetime exile)
- The physical movement of *objects* to producers, consumers and retailers; as well as the sending and receiving of presents and souvenirs
- The *imaginative* travel effected through the images of places and peoples appearing on and moving across multiple print and visual media

- *Virtual* travel often in real time thus transcending geographical and social distance
- The *communicative* travel through person-to-person messages via messages, texts, letters, telegraph, telephone, fax and mobile (Urry, 2007, p. 47, italics in original).

This paradigm has been both praised and criticized for how it encourages further research into mobilities and for how it names mobilities and suggests possible connections between them. It has been praised for taking "the actual fact of movement seriously" (Cresswell, 2010, p. 18), for example, in the category of corporeal movement. This category encourages investigations of mobilities such as *parkouring*, which involves a reinterpretation of urban spaces through freestyle gymnastic running and jumping (Saville, 2008) and couchsurfing, which involves a reinterpretation of tourist mobilities when travellers engage in peer-to-peer networking to find and offer a couch for stays (Molz, 2012). The new mobilities paradigm also encourages interpretations of micro-constellations of mobilities (Vannini, 2011) such as a daily commute to work and why we choose particular routes and mediums of mobility, such as ferries on waterways from a remote island to a mainland instead of living in the city and commuting by car or public transit (Vannini, 2012).

The paradigm also encourages interpretations of large-scale constellations of mobilities, such as links between corporeal travel and communicative travel in the case of the transnational movement of Filipino overseas workers, 75 percent of whom are women (Uy-Tioco, 2007, p. 253), who use their mobile phones to mediate an absent presence known as **remote mothering** (Rakow & Navarro, 1993) and to send money transfers to family at home even as their embodied and communicative mobilities reinforce "patriarchy and the North-South divide" (Uy-Tioco, 2007, p. 254). The mobilities paradigm encourages us to explore how communicative mobilities, such as mobile use for money transfers, intersect with corporeal mobilities, such as North-South movements of workers' bodies that are "fragile, aged, gendered [and] racialized ..." (Urry, 2007, p. 48). The paradigm has been praised and criticized for developing a common language that scholars can use to interpret mobilities. However, even mobilities scholars are asking, "what is 'new' about the new mobilities paradigm" (Cresswell, 2010, p. 18; cf. Jensen, 2011; Wiley & Packer, 2010)? Does it help us to interpret better the practices, representations, and sensations that characterize various and intersecting mobilities? Mobilities scholar Tim Cresswell offers a useful criticism of the language used to name the paradigm.

> First of all the word "paradigm" suggests the Kuhnian notion of normal science being transformed by sudden revolutions where what went previously is unceremoniously tipped into the junkheap of academic history (Kuhn, 1996). We have to be careful about such implications. Any study of mobility runs the risk of suggesting that the (allegedly) immobile notions such as boundaries and borders, place, territory, and

> landscape is of the past and no longer relevant to the dynamic world of the 21st century. This would be wrong and, to be fair, does not seem to be the point of advocates of the new mobilities paradigm where "moorings" are often as important as "mobilities." The second problem concerns the different ways that "new mobilities" can be read. If the emphasis is on the word "new" then this suggests an old mobilities paradigm. If the emphasis is on the word "mobilities; then this suggests that old paradigms were about the immobile or sedentary. The second of these options seems untenable because movements of one kind or another have been at the heart of all kinds of social science (and particularly geography) since their inception (Cresswell, 2010, p. 18).

We could also ask, how long will the new mobilities paradigm remain new, and what comes after it? In addition to the new mobilities paradigm, we might be led to believe that mobilities are new based also on the numerous conferences and workshops that have been organized on mobilities in recent years; the many books, articles, and special issues of journals published in the past decade on mobilities; the new research centres that have been established to study mobilities; and the 2012 launch of the journal *Mobile Media and Communication*, which has set a mandate to examine the "phenomenon of mobility in communication" (see http://www.sagepub.com/journalsProdDesc.nav?prodId=Journal202140), as well as the 2006 launch of the journal *Mobilities*, which has set a mandate to examine "both the large-scale movements of people, objects, capital, and information across the world, as well as more local processes of daily transportation, movement through public and private spaces, and the travel of material things in everyday life" (http://www.tandf.co.uk/journals/RMOB). Mobilities are now seemingly everywhere in our everyday language, in our common communication practices, and in the scholarly emergence of mobilities studies. If mobility is everything, then is it nothing (Adey, 2006)? In other words, what further work needs to be done to differentiate the practices, representations, and sensations that comprise the mobilities that we shape and experience? Also, how do we "illustrate the continuation of the past in the present" (Cresswell, 2010, p. 27) while interpreting mobilities through the new mobilities paradigm and concepts such as constellations of mobilities and mobile privatization? These concepts are related but do not offer identical interpretations of mobilities and immobilities.

CONCLUSION: IMMOBILITIES

Mobilities are made more visible and knowable through the everyday and scholarly language we use to describe and interpret them. However, the euphemisms, phrases, and paradigms we use do not help us to thoroughly understand mobilities. All are inadequate but useful, and so it is prudent to ask, what aspects of mobilities remain largely unscrutinized by users of mobiles and by mobilities scholars? One of several possible answers is the structural immobilities that make mobilities possible.

Among the immobilities that intersect with mobilities, and that are often overlooked, are the many "isms" representing inequalities, such as ableism, racism, sexism and classism. Mobilities are experienced differently based on who is moving, for what purposes, and how their movement is valued, facilitated, or thwarted (Jain, 2002; Massey, 1994). This is discernable in the concept of DWB, in the immobilization and uprising of *banlieue* residents, and in ableist assumptions about mobilities that are built into the very design of handheld mobiles and that are implicit in the new mobilities paradigm, particularly in the category of embodied mobilities (see Cresswell, 2010, p. 29).

Technology divides between users and nonusers continue to be influenced by factors such as "gender, race, socio-economic status, primary language, geographical location, disability, educational level and generational characteristics" (Goode, 2010, p. 498). These divides exist not only at the moment of consumption but also from production to obsolescence and beyond. Civil war, environmental hazards, and health risks are associated with the mining of coltan in the Democractic Republic of the Congo. Coltan is a key mineral used in the production of handheld mobiles and computer chips (see the film *Blood Coltan*). Working conditions are reportedly deadly in the overseas factories where handheld mobiles are made for North American and international markets (Chinese, 2012). When our mobile devices become obsolete, or when we discard them for the newest model, they accumulate as environmental waste and pose a hazard to the workers and pickers who dismantle them in regions outside North America, namely in Asian and African countries (Study, 2002).

Considering structural immobilities such as these is also a way of highlighting how the past continues in our current era of seemingly new and ubiquitous mobilities (see Nicholson, 2008). Our everyday mobililities sometimes further entrench existing social relations with others at home and abroad. However, because mobility entails the capacity for change, and because we shape and define mobilities, we may in the future devise ways to shift some structural immobilities even as we remediate and reconceptualize mobilities.

ACKNOWLEDGEMENT

Thanks to my students in CS400: Mobile Communication for stimulating discussions, which inspired many of the questions and ideas in this chapter.

NOTES

1. The borough of Fort Lee, New Jersey, introduced legislation in May 2012 that will allow an $85 fine to be levied for "distracted walking" (Daidone, 2012).

2. The aftermath of early riots and the hardscrabble conditions of the *banlieues* are portrayed in the award-winning film *La Haine* (1995).
3. For other examples of how automobilities contribute to the immobility of marginalized communities, see Bullard, 2004; Cresswell, 2010; Winner, 1977.

QUESTIONS

1. How many people in Canada, and worldwide, are mobile users? What mobiles will you count (see http://www.cwta.ca, http://www.ctia.org, http://www.itu.int)?
2. How adequately does the new mobilities paradigm capture your everyday mobilities? Based on your experiences of mobilities, are further categories needed?
3. Concepts such as the gaze (for film), glance (for TV), and glaze (for gaming console) interpret how we use particular screening technologies to mediate screenness. Using the alliteration of these concepts as inspiration, which active verbs best theorize how we use our contemporary mobiles, including "augmented reality glasses," to mediate screenness?
4. What mobilities are involved in velomobilities, in which the bicycle is the key mobile (see Aldred, 2010; Furness, 2007), or aeromobilities, in which the airplane is the key mobile (see Adey, 2006; Cwerner, et al., 2009; Salter, 2008), or ferry mobilities, in which the commuter ferry is the key mobile (see Vannini, 2011; 2012)?
5. Does **critical massing** (a type of flash mobbing on bicycles) challenge the hegemony of automobilties (see Furness, 2007)?

REFERENCES

Adey, P. (2006). If mobility is everything then it is nothing: Towards a relational politics of (im)mobilities. *Mobilities*, *1*(1), 75–94.

———. (2010). *Mobility*. London & New York: Routledge.

Aldred, R. (2010). "On the outside": Constructing cycling citizenship. *Social & Cultural Geography*, *11*(1), 35–52.

Allagui, I. & Kuebler, J. (2011). Editorial introduction: The Arab spring and the role of ICTs. *International Journal of Communication*, *5*, 1435–1442.

Allan, S. (2002). Reweaving the internet: Online news of September 11. In B. Zelizer & S. Allan (Eds.), *Journalism after September 11* (pp. 119–140). London; New York: Routledge.

———. (2009). Histories of citizen journalism. In S. Allan & E. Thorsen (Eds.), *Citizen journalism: Global perspectives* (pp. 17–31). New York: Peter Lang.

Apel, D. (2004). *Imagery of lynching: Black men, white women, and the mob*. New Brunswick, NJ: Rutgers University Press.

Apel, D. & Smith, S. (2007). *Lynching photographs*. Berkeley: University of California Press.

Appadurai, A. (1990). Disjuncture and difference in the global cultural economy. *Theory, Culture & Society*, 7, 295–310.

Ball, J. & Brown, S. (2011, Dec. 7). Why Blackberry messenger was rioters' communication method of choice. *The Guardian*. Retrieved August 16, 2012, from http://www.guardian.co.uk/uk/2011/dec/07/bbm-rioters-communication-method-choice

Batty, D. (2011, Dec. 29). Arab spring leads surge in events captured on cameraphones. *The Guardian*. Retrieved August 16, 2012, from http://www.guardian.co.uk/world/2011/dec/29/arab-spring-captured-on-cameraphones

Benjamin, W. (1969). The work of art in the age of mechanical reproduction. In H. Arendt (Ed.), *Illuminations: Walter Benjamin, essays and reflections* (pp. 217–252). New York: Schocken Books.

———. (2002). *The Arcades project* (H. Eiland & K. McLaughlin, Trans.) Cambridge, MA: Harvard University Press.

Berland, J. (2005) Mobile. In T. Bennett, L. Grossberg, & M. Morris (Eds.), *New keywords: A revised vocabulary of culture and society* (pp. 217–229). Malden, MA: Blackwell.

Black, D. (2011). "Flash robs" invade Canada. *Toronto Star*. Retrieved August 16, 2012, from http://www.thestar.com/news/canada/article/1034739--flash-robs-invade-canada

Blake, A. (2010). An audible sense of order: Race, fear and CB radio on Los Angeles freeways in the 1970s. In D. Suisman & S. Strasser (Eds.), *Sound in the age of mechanical reproduction* (pp. 159–178). Philadelphia: University of Pennsylvania Press.

Blood Coltan. (2007). Director, P. Forestier. Production: Tac Presse. http://www.javafilms.fr/spip.php?article8

Braiker, B. (2012, Apr. 5). Google project glass: A new way to see the world. *The Guardian*. Retrieved August 16, 2012, from http://www.guardian.co.uk/world/us-news-blog/2012/apr/05/google

Bull, M. (2004) Automobility and the power of sound. *Theory, Culture & Society*, *21*(4/5), 243–259.

———. (2005). No dead air! The iPod and the culture of mobile listening. *Leisure Studies, 24*(4), 343–355.

Bullard, R. (2004). The anatomy of transportation racism. In R. Bullard, G. Johnson, & A. Torres (Eds.), *Highway robbery* (pp. 15–32). Cambridge: South End Press.

Byrne, C. (2010, June 26). Violent black bloc tactics hit Toronto G20 protest. *CP24*. Retrieved August 16, 2012, from http://www.cp24.com/servlet/an/local/CTVNews/20100626/100626_blackbloc/20100626

Canetti, E. (1962). *Crowds and power*. London: Gollancz.

Castells, M., Fernández-Ardèvol, M., Lichuan Qiu, J., & Sey, A. (2007). *Mobile communication and society: A global perspective*. Cambridge, MA; London: MIT Press.

Chesher, C. (2004). Neither gaze nor glance, but glaze: Relating to console game screens. *Scan: Journal of Media Arts Culture*, *1*(1). Retrieved August 16, 2012, from http://scan.net.au/scan/journal/display.php?journal_id=19

Chinese iPad, iPhone factories pledge to treat workers better. (2012, Mar. 30). CBC News. Retrieved August 16, 2012, from http://www.cbc.ca/news/technology/story/2012/03/30/technology-ipad-iphone-foxconn-china.html

Cresswell, T. (2006). *On the move: Mobility in the modern western world*. New York: Routledge.

———. (2010). Towards a politics of mobility. *Environment and Planning D: Society and Space*, *29*, 17–31.

Cwerner, S., Kesselring, S., & Urry, J. (2009). *Aeromobilities*. New York: Routledge.

Daidone, A. (2012, May 14). Fort Lee, N.J. texting law: Hefty jaywalking fine for the distracted. *NewJerseyNewsroom*. Retrieved August 16, 2012, from http://www.newjerseynewsroom.com/state/fort-lee-nj-texting-law-hefty-jaywalking-fine-for-the-distracted

de Certeau, M. (1984). *The practice of everyday life*. Berkeley: University of California Press.

de Souza e Silva, A. & Frith, J. (2010). Locative mobile social networks: Mapping communication and location in urban spaces. *Mobilities*, *5*(4), 485–505.

du Gay, P., Hall, S., Janes, L., Mackay, H. & Negus, K. (1997). *Doing cultural studies: The story of the Sony Walkman*. London: Sage.

Edensor, T. (2004). Automobility and national identity: Representation, geography and driving practice. *Theory, Culture & Society*, *21*(4/5), 101–120.

Furness, Z. (2007). Critical mass, urban space and vélomobility. *Mobilities*, *2*(2), 299–319.

Friedberg, A. (1993). *Window shopping: Cinema and the postmodern*. Berkeley: University of California Press.

———. (2002). Urban mobility and cinematic visuality: The screens of Los Angeles—endless cinema or private telematics. *Journal of Visual Culture*, *1*(2), 183–204.

———. (2006). *The virtual window: From Alberti to Microsoft*. Cambridge, MA: The MIT Press.

Garber, M. (2012, Apr. 12). Predicting the driverless car (in 1958). *The Atlantic*. Retrieved August 16, 2012, from http://www.theatlantic.com/technology/archive/2012/04/predicting-the-driverless-car-in-1958/255823

Gergen, K. (2002). The challenge of absent presence. In J. E. Katz & M. Aakhus (Eds.), *Perpetual contact: Mobile communication, private talk, public performance* (pp. 227–241). Cambridge, MA, & New York: Cambridge University Press.

Gilroy, P. (2001). Driving while black. In D. Miller (Ed.), *Car Cultures* (pp. 81–104). Oxford: Berg.

Goggin, G. (2006). *Cell phone culture: Mobile technology in everyday life*. New York: Routledge.

Goode, J. (2010). The digital divide: How technology knowledge impacts college students. *New Media & Society, 12*(3), 497–513.

Gooding-Williams, R. (Ed.) (1993). *Reading Rodney King/Reading urban Uprising.* New York: Routledge.

Gow, G. & Smith, R. (2006). *Mobile and wireless communications: An introduction.* New York: Open University Press.

Groening, S. (2010). From "a box in the theater of the world" to "the world as your living room": Cellular phones, television and mobile privatization. *New Media & Society, 12*(8), 1331–1347.

———. (2011). Automobile television, the post-nuclear family and SpongeBob SquarePants. *Visual Studies, 26*(2), 148–153.

Halliday, J. (2011, Aug. 8). London riots: How Blackberry messenger played a key role. *The Guardian.* Retrieved August 16, 2012, from http://www.guardian.co.uk/media/2011/aug/08/london-riots-facebook-twitter-blackberry

Hardt, M. & Negri, A. (2000). *Empire.* London & Cambridge, MA: Harvard University Press.

Hayes, P. (1992). *The people and the mob: The ideology of civil conflict in modern Europe.* Westport, CN: Praeger.

Hjorth, L. (2011). Mobile@game cultures: The place of urban mobile gaming. *Convergence: The International Journal of Research into New Media Technologies, 17*(4), 357–371.

Hosokawa, S. (1984). The Walkman effect. *Popular Music, 4,* 165–180.

Humphreys, L. (2010). Mobile social networks and urban public space. *New Media & Society, 12*(5), 763–778.

Ingold, T. (2004). Culture on the ground: The world perceived through the feet. *Journal of Material Culture, 9*(3), 315–340.

Jain, S. (2002). Urban errands: the means of mobility. *Journal of consumer culture, 2*(3), 385–404.

Jensen, A. (2011). Mobility, space and power: On the multiplicities of seeing mobility. *Mobilities, 6*(2), 255–271.

Johnson, M. & Pleece, W. (2008). *Incognegro: A graphic mystery.* New York: Vertigo Comics.

Katz, J. E. & Aakhus, A. (Eds.) (2002). *Perpetual contact: Mobile communication, private talk, public performance.* New York: Cambridge University Press.

Katz, J. E., & Aspden, P. (1999). Mobile communications: Theories, data, and potential impact. In J. E. Katz (Ed.) *Connections: Social and cultural studies of the telephone in American life* (pp. 41–73). New Brunswick, NJ; London: Transaction Publishers.

Katz, J. E., & Rice, R. E. (2002). The telephone as a medium of faith, hope, terror, and redemption: America, September 11. *Prometheus, 20*(3), 247–253.

Kopomaa, Timo. (2002). The reunited family of the mobile information society. *Receiver: The mobile self.* Retrieved March 22, 2006, from http://www.vodafone.com/flash/receiver/06/articles/index07.html

Kuhn, T. (1996). *The structure of scientific revolutions*. Chicago: University of Chicago Press.

le Bon, G. (1960). *The crowd: A study of the popular mind*. New York: Viking Press.

Lemos, A. (2010). Post-mass media functions, locative media, and informational territories: New ways of thinking about territory, place, and mobility in contemporary society. *Space and Culture, 13*(4), 403–420.

Licoppe, C. & Inada, Y. (2010). Locative media and cultures of mediated proximity: The case of the Mogi game location-aware community. *Environment and Planning D: Society and Space, 28*, 691–709.

Luke, R. (2005). The phoneur: Mobile commerce and the digital pedagogies of the wireless web. In P. P. Trifonas (Ed.) *Communities of difference: Language, culture and the media*, (pp. 185–204). New York: Palgrave Macmillan.

Makagon, D. (2006). Sonic earthquakes. *Communication and Critical/Cultural Studies, 3*(3), 223–239.

Massey, D. (1994). *Space, place, and gender*. Minneapolis: University of Minnesota Press.

McCarthy, A. (2001). *Ambient television: Visual culture and public space*. Durham, NC: Duke University Press.

Middleton, C. (2007). Illusions of balance and control in an always-on environment: A case study of BlackBerry users. *Continuum: Journal of Media & Cultural Studies, 21*(2), 165–178.

Molz, G. (2012). Couchsurfing and network hospitality: "It's not just about the furniture." *Hospitality & Society, 1*(3), 215–225.

Moores, S. (1993). Television, geography and "mobile privatisation." *European Journal of Communication, 8*(3), 365–379.

Morley, D. (2000). Media, mobility, migrancy. In *Home territories: Media, mobility and identity* (pp. 149–170). London: Routledge.

Morse, M. (1998). An ontology of everyday distraction: The freeway, the mall, and television. In *Virtualities: Television, media, art, and cyberculture* (pp. 99–124). Bloomington: Indiana University Press.

Moure, C. (2012, May 18). Photos: Quebec student protests. *The Vancouver Sun*. Retrieved August 16, 2012, from http://www.vancouversun.com/news/Photos+Quebec+student+protests/6644971/story.html

Murray, G. (2006). France: The riots and the republic. *Race & Class, 47*(4), 26–45.

Nicholson, J. (2006, Winter). Flash! Mobs in the age of mobile connectivity. *Fibreculture Journal*. Retrieved August 16, 2012, from http://journal.fibreculture.org/issue6

———. (2008). Calling Dick Tracy! Or, cellphone use, progress, and a racial paradigm. *Canadian Journal of Communication, 33*(3), 379–404.

———. (2010). Third screen as cultural form in North America. In B. Crow, M. Longford & K. Sawchuk (Eds.) *Sampling the spectrum: The politics, practices and poetics of mobile media* (pp. 77–94). Toronto: University of Toronto Press.

Nightingale, V. (2007). The cameraphone and online image sharing. *Continuum: Journal of Media & Cultural Studies, 21*(2), pp. 289–301.

Noll, M. (1992). Anatomy of a failure: Picturephone revisited. *Telecommunications Policy, 16*(4), 307–316.

Orgad, S. (2009). Mobile TV: Old and new in the construction of an emergent technology. *Convergence, 15*(2), 197–214.

Packer, J. (2008). *Mobility without mayhem: Safety, cars and citizenship*. Durham, NC: Duke University Press.

Packer, J. & Oswald, K. (2010). From windscreen to widescreen: Screening technologies and mobile communication. *The Communication Review, 13*(4): 309–339.

Papenfuss, M. (2005). Rioters use cellphones, net to fuel flames. *New York Daily News*. Retrieved August 16, 2012, from http://articles.nydailynews.com/2005-11-09/news/18316296_1_sites-riots-french-youth

Pedersen, I. (2008). "No Apple iPhone? You must be Canadian": Mobile technologies, participatory culture, and rhetorical transformation. *Canadian Journal of Communication, 33*(3), 491–510.

Rafael, V. (2003). The cell phone and the crowd: Messianic politics in the contemporary Philippines. *Public culture, 15*(3), 399–425.

Rakow, L. F. & Navarro, V. (1993). Remote mothering and the parallel shift: Women meet the cellular telephone. *Critical Studies in Mass Communication, 10*(2), 144–157.

Rheingold, H. (2003). *Smart mobs: The next social revolution*. Cambridge, MA: Perseus.

Richardson, I. (2007). Pocket technospaces: The bodily incorporation of mobile media. *Continuum: Journal of Media & Cultural Studies, 21*(2), 205–215.

———. (2011). The hybrid ontology of mobile gaming. *Convergence: The International Journal of Research into New Media Technologies, 17*(4), 419–430.

Richardson, I. & Wilken, R. (2009). Haptic vision, footwork, place-making: A Peripatetic phenomenology of the mobile phone pedestrian. *Second Nature, 2*, 22–40.

Robbins, K. & Turner, M. (2002). United States: Popular, pragmatic and problematic. In J. E. Katz & M. Aakhus (Eds.) *Perpetual contact: Mobile communication, private talk, public performance* (pp. 80–93). Cambridge, UK, and New York: Cambridge University Press.

Robinson, W, & Robison, D. (2006). Tsunami mobilizations: Considering the role of mobile and digital communication devices, citizen journalism, and the mass media. In A. Kavoori & N. Arceneaux (Eds.), *The cell phone reader: Essays in social transformation*, (pp. 85–103). New York: Peter Lang.

Ross, K. (1999). *Fast cars, clean bodies: Decolonization and the reordering of French culture*. Cambridge, MA: The MIT Press.

Salter, M. (Ed.). (2008). *Politics at the airport*. Minneapolis: University of Minnesota Press.

Samuel, H. (2007, Nov. 28). Bloodshed predicted as French riots spread. *National Post*, p. A19.

Saville, S. J. (2008). Playing with fear: Parkour and the mobility of emotion. *Social and Cultural Geography*, *9*(8), 891–914.
Schivelbusch, W. (1986). *The railway journey: The industrialization of time and space in the 19th century*. Berkeley: University of California Press.
Sheller, M. (2004). Automotive emotions: Feeling the car. *Theory, Culture & Society*, *21*(4/5), 221–242.
Sheller, M. & Urry, J. (2006). The new mobilities paradigm. *Environment and Planning A*, *38*, 207–226.
Slack, J.D. & MacGregor Wise, J. (2006). Cultural studies and communication technology. In L. Lievrouw, & S. Livingstone (Eds), *The handbook of new media: Social shaping & consequences of ICTs* (pp. 141–152). London: Sage.
Sloop, J. M. & Gunn, J. (2010). Status control: An admonition concerning the publicized privacy of social networking. *The Communication Review*, *13*, 289–308.
Snowden, C. (2007). Reporting by phone. In C. Acland (Ed.), *Residual media*, (pp. 115–132). Minneapolis; London: University of Minnesota Press.
Southern, J. (2012). Comobility: How proximity and distance travel together in locative media. *Canadian Journal of Communication*, *37*(1), 75–91.
Spigel, L. (1992). *Make room for TV: Television and the family ideal in postwar America*. Chicago: University of Chicago Press.
Staff, *National Post*. (2011). Photos: Riots, fires, destruction after Vancouver's loss. *National Post*. Retrieved August 16, 2012, from http://news.nationalpost.com/2011/06/16/photos-riots-fire-destruction-after-vancouvers-loss
Sterne, J. (2006). Transportation and communication: Together as you've always wanted them. In J. Packer & C. Robertson (Eds), *Thinking with James Carey: Essays on communications, transportation, history* (pp. 117–135). New York: Peter Lang.
Study: Cell phone waste harmful. (2002, May 7). *Wired*. Retrieved August 16, 2012, from http://www.wired.com/science/discoveries/news/2002/05/52375
Thrift, N. (2004). Driving in the city. *Theory, Culture & Society*, *21*(4/5), 41–59.
Townsend, A. (2000). Life in the real-time city: Mobile telephones and urban metabolism. *Journal of Urban Technology*, 7(2), pp. 85–104.
Urry, J. (2004). The "system" of automobility. *Theory, Culture & Society*, *21*(4/5), 25–39.
———. (2007). *Mobilities*. Cambridge. UK: Polity Press.
Uy-Tioco, C. 2007. Overseas Filipino workers and text messaging: Reinventing transnational mothering. *Continuum: Journal of Media & Cultural Studies*, *21*(2), 253–265.
Vanderbilt, T. (2012, Feb.). Let the robot drive: The autonomous car of the future is here. *Wired*, *20*(2), 86–95, 124.
Vannini, P. (2011). Constellations of ferry (im)mobility: Islandness as the performance and politics of insulation and isolation. *Cultural Geographies*, *18*(2), 249–271.

———. (2012). *Ferry tales: Mobility, place and time on Canada's west coast*. New York: Routledge.

Walker, R. A. (2011). Badgering big brother: Spectacle, surveillance, and politics in the flash mob. *Liminalities*, 7(2). Retrieved August 16, 2012, from http://liminalities.net/7-2/flashmob.pdf

Wiley, S. & Packer, J. (2010). Rethinking communication after the mobilities turn. *The Communication Review*, *13*, 263–268.

Williams, R. (1989). *Resources of hope*. London: Verso.

———. (1990; 1974). *Television: Technology and cultural form*. Hanover & London: Wesleyan University Press.

Winner, L. (1977). Technologies as forms of life. In *The whale and the reactor: A search for limits in an age of high technology* (pp. 3–18). Chicago: University of Chicago Press.

15

PRIVACY IN A NETWORKED ENVIRONMENT

Valerie Steeves
University of Ottawa

Conceal your life.
—attributed to Neocles, father of Epicure, 3rd century B.C.

In her novel *The Fountainhead*, author Ayn Rand (1943) wrote "Civilization is the progress toward a society of privacy. The savage's whole existence is public, ruled by the laws of his tribe. Civilization is the process of setting man free from man."

A short 56 years later, a much-read article in *The Economist* argued that privacy is dead. Networked communication technologies, and the surveillance society that flows from them, have enabled a growing legion of bureaucrats, employers, spouses, insurance companies, marketers, and researchers to access and record our commercial transactions, travel arrangements, academic grades, health information, financial records, and personal preferences. *The Economist*'s best advice? "Get used to it" ("End of Privacy," 1999, p. 15).

And yet we have a long history of rejecting surveillance. In 1763, after Englishman John Wilkes criticized a speech given by King George III, the king ordered his agents to break into Wilkes's home and seize his private diaries from his desk drawer. Professor Jeffrey Rosen points out that the king's actions directly influenced the leaders of the American Revolution: "The writers of the U.S. constitution drafted the Fourth Amendment banning unreasonable searches and seizures of persons, houses, papers and effects, with Wilkes' house and Wilkes' papers in mind" (cited in McDougall, 1999, p. 9).

The balance between the individual's right to a private life and the ability of others to invade that privacy is therefore an old and established one. Why is our privacy so beset, then, in a networked society? Part of the answer lies in the enabling effects of networked communications technologies. When the Royal Canadian Mounted Police wanted to investigate whether or not Walter Tessling was growing marijuana in his house, for example, they didn't have to break down Tessling's door. Instead, they flew over his house and used a forward-looking infra-red (FLIR) camera to take a picture of the radiation escaping from the building; the camera was able to "see" the heat generated by grow lights in the basement.

Ordinarily, police are required to obtain a warrant before they enter and search private property. A search warrant is given only if a justice is convinced that the officers have reasonable and probable grounds to support their suspicions that a crime has occurred. In the *Tessling* case, the Supreme Court of Canada decided that no warrant was necessary because the emissions were merely information that was collected by the FLIR camera *after* the emissions left the building. Since the technology did not "enter" the building, there was nothing to stop the police from using that information to make inferences about what was going on inside the home.

The privacy balance has changed precisely because new technologies such as FLIR cameras can watch us without physically intruding into our lives. The technologies we use on a daily basis leave virtual tracks that are collected in the background as we go about chatting with friends, working, and playing. Online examples are legion: Google automatically scans the contents of every Gmail message so it can get a better idea of what to advertise to us; many schools use keystroke-capture software to record everything students do on the school network; Facebook saves every profile and wall post even after the person who created the page has closed his or her Facebook account. In the off-line world, advertisers scan passing cars to see which radio station drivers are listening to, and people walking through a growing number of cities have their faces scanned, digitized, and matched against a database of "criminals" by cameras that can see around corners and hear conversations up to a mile away.[1]

Proponents of surveillance argue that this loss of privacy is justified because surveillance increases security, reduces crime, cuts costs, and fuels the information economy. After all, the argument goes, why worry if you have nothing to hide?

This argument merits close examination. Many of us, for example, trade away our privacy for the convenience of preferred-shopper cards. Companies collect detailed records of our purchase preferences and, in exchange, offer discounts or special offers. How could a list of what we buy at the grocery store harm us?

A shopper in California learned the hard way when he sued a grocery store after slipping on spilled yogurt and shattering his kneecap. The store threatened to expose him as a "falling-down drunk" because his records showed he bought alcohol on a regular basis (Moore, 2004). Another American grocery store was required to hand over its customer records to the Drug Enforcement Agency because, according to the Agency, people who buy lots of plastic bags are more likely to be drug traffickers (ibid).

Technologies such as preferred-shopper cards seem benign, but the information they amass can be used for secondary purposes that may lead to embarrassment, humiliation, manipulation, and discrimination. *The right to privacy is not about secrecy; it's about autonomy.* The right to a private life enables us to enter into relationships of trust and to enjoy a sense of freedom. In the words of Supreme Court Justice La Forest, "[privacy] is at the heart of liberty in a modern state. Grounded in man's physical and moral autonomy, privacy is essential for the well-being of the individual" (*R. v. Dyment,* 1988).

This chapter will examine different definitions of the right to privacy and explore the ways in which Canada and other countries are regulating invasive practices. Throughout, we will examine how the digital environment has changed our experience of privacy and identify the major stakeholders in the emerging privacy debate.

DEFINITIONS OF PRIVACY

The most frequently quoted definition of **privacy** was popularized in 1890 by Samuel Warren and Louis Brandeis. They were concerned about the ways in which new technologies and business practices were changing the modern experience of a private life:

> Recent inventions and business methods call attention to the next step which must be taken for the protection of the person, and for securing to the individual what Judge Cooley calls the right "to be let alone." Instantaneous photographs and newspaper enterprise have invaded the sacred precincts of private and domestic life, and numerous mechanical devices threaten to make good the prediction that "what is whispered in the closet shall be proclaimed from the housetops." (Warren & Brandeis, 1890, p. 195)

Warren and Brandeis's definition of privacy as the "right to be let alone" was not a legalistic one. Their concerns grew from their own experience of personal and social relationships. Like many today, they worried that new technologies were invading established social boundaries and were being fuelled by the commercial value of the information obtained. Underpinning their argument that commerce should not be allowed to overrun the right to privacy was their strong belief in the "inviolate personality" of the individual.

As new communication technologies continued to develop, others built on Warren and Brandeis's vision. During its seminal public consultation on privacy rights and new technologies, the House of Commons Standing Committee on Human Rights and the Status of Persons with Disabilities concluded:

> Classically understood as "the right to be let alone," privacy in today's high-tech world has taken on a multitude of dimensions. According to certain privacy experts, it is the right to enjoy private space, to conduct private communications, to be free from surveillance, and to respect the sanctity of one's body. To the ordinary Canadian, it is about control—the right to control one's personal information and the right to choose to remain anonymous. (Canada House of Commons, 1997, appendix I, p. 1)

Choosing between these definitions is not a neutral process. As the Standing Committee noted, "experience has shown us that the way you ask the question will often determine the type of response you get" (Canada, 1997, p. 33). The current ways to "ask the question" reflect four different ways of looking at privacy:

- privacy as a human right;
- privacy as an essential part of the democratic process;
- privacy as a social value;
- privacy as data protection.

1. Privacy as a Human Right

The dangers inherent in the modern nation-state's ability to seize information about citizens and use it to invade their private lives were exemplified by the Nazi government. When German forces took towns during World War II, the first buildings they seized were often the town halls; Gestapo officers would then search through records to identify the whereabouts of Jewish residents so they could be deported to extermination camps.

The postwar international community responded in 1948 by adopting Article 12 of the *Universal Declaration of Human Rights*, which proclaims that no one "shall be subjected to arbitrary interference with his privacy, family, home or correspondence." This right to privacy, and the other human rights proclaimed in the Declaration, reflected the United Nations' belief that "the inherent dignity ... of all members of the human family is the foundation of freedom, justice and peace in the world" (United Nations, 1948, Preamble).

In the international arena, Canada was a leader in establishing privacy as a fundamental human right. Canadian John Humphrey was one of the authors of the 1948 Declaration; in 1976, Canada ratified the *International Covenant on Civil and Political Rights* (United Nations, 1966), which contains the same guarantee of privacy as the Declaration. However, within Canada, the protection of privacy as a human right is patchy. The Canadian *Charter of Rights and Freedoms* does not include an express right to privacy, despite the fact that the federal government suggested its inclusion as early as 1979. The Supreme Court of Canada has written a limited right to privacy into the *Charter*,[2] but the tests it has developed make it unlikely that this limited right will be able to deal with new invasive technologies.

For example, the Supreme Court has ruled that section 8 of the *Charter*, which protects everyone from unreasonable search and seizure, includes the right to be secure from such a search when the individual has a "reasonable expectation of privacy" (*Hunter v. Southam*, 1984). Under this test, it is unreasonable to videotape what happens in a private hotel room (*R. v. Wong*, 1990), but the police are free to videotape acts of gross indecency in a public washroom because there is no reasonable expectation of privacy in that location (*R. v. LeBeau*, 1988). However, the police are not allowed to "record communications *that the originator expects will not be intercepted* by anyone other than the person intended by its originator to receive them" (*R. v. Duarte*, 1990, emphasis added).

Unfortunately, in a wired environment, new technologies make it extremely easy for others to intercept our communications. Open communications networks are just that—open. Any user can use the technology to capture and read the unencrypted communications of any other user. It is difficult to argue that we have a reasonable expectation of privacy when we send email, participate in an online discussion, or visit a website, because the technology itself gives us *no* expectation of privacy.

It is also hard to enjoy any sense of privacy in public spaces, now that our movements are routinely monitored by closed-caption television security cameras and GPS-enabled smart phones. Moreover, we are increasingly encouraged to share our real-time location data with friends—and with the corporations that collect and publish it—through apps such as Foursquare.

The law has been slow to understand the extent to which communication technologies are changing our experience of privacy. When the police received a Crime Stoppers tip that a Mr. Plant was growing marijuana in the basement of his house, they had no evidence to justify a search warrant. However, they reasoned that growing plants indoors must consume a large amount of electricity. They then used their own computer system to log on to the local utility's computer and pull up Mr. Plant's electricity bills. The Supreme Court of Canada applied the reasonable expectation test, and concluded that:

> Section 8 of the Charter should seek to protect a *biographical core of personal information* which individuals in a free and democratic society would wish to maintain and control from dissemination to the state. This would include *information which tends to reveal intimate details of the lifestyle and personal choices of the individual.* (*R. v. Plant*, 1993, p. 213, emphasis added)

Mr. Plant's electricity bills, they argued, did not reveal intimate details of his personal life; they just showed how much electricity he consumed. But this may not be an accurate conclusion in a wired environment. As Justice McLachlin, who disagreed with her fellow judges, argued:

> The records are capable of telling much about one's personal lifestyle, such as how many people lived in the house and what sort of activities were probably taking place there. The records tell a story about what is happening inside a private dwelling, the most private of places. I think that a reasonable person looking at these facts would conclude that the records should be used only for the purpose for which they were made—the delivery and billing of electricity—and not divulged to strangers without proper legal authorization. (*R. v. Plant*, 1993, p. 219)

Furthermore, in our wired world no single detail, such as a utility bill, exists in isolation. Data-matching software can locate and connect a multitude of personal details: the amount of realty taxes we pay; the kinds of books we buy online; the comments we post on social networking sites. When all these details are linked together, they create an accurate picture of our private lives.

Marketers can use this information to manipulate our purchase choices. For example, a Canadian candy manufacturer used a membership list from a weight-loss organization to mail candy samples to the dieters at Christmas and Easter. Why? Because the company believed that was when the people on the list were most likely to go off their diets.

But marketers are not the only ones interested in the detailed minutiae of our private lives. Universities have disciplined students for underage drinking after they posted pictures of themselves swilling beer on Facebook, and American police officers have used handheld wireless computers to search through commercial databases for information on people they pull over for speeding (Weinberg, 2004). In spite of the fact that the information found can be false or misleading, states increasingly rely on these technologies to combat crime and terrorism. And the consequences can be severe. Based on erroneous information provided to American authorities by the Royal Canadian Mounted Police, Canadian citizen Maher Arar was deported to his native-born Syria, where he was tortured for a year before being allowed to return to Canada (http://www.maherarar.net).

Privacy, the right to be free from being watched, spied upon, and tested, is a human right because it is an essential part of human dignity and autonomy. Life without privacy makes it impossible to enjoy the dignity and freedom that human rights seek to protect.

2. Privacy as a Democratic Value

Because it is so connected to individual freedom, privacy is also an important element of a healthy democracy. As Justice La Forest notes, "[privacy] has profound significance for the public order. The restraints imposed on government to pry into the lives of the citizen go to the essence of a democratic state" (*R. v. Dyment*, 1988, p. 254).

Western governments readily accept that privacy is an important democratic value when authoritarian states such as North Korea or China use invasive practices to suppress political dissidents. They admit that placing video cameras on street corners to scan, record, and identify individuals makes it much less likely that people will participate in a political demonstration (exercising their right to assemble) or even say what they think (exercising their right to free expression). However, when those same practices are used to watch Canadians, officials often justify them because they are efficient and help to reduce risks.

Communication technologies enable the state to process vast amounts of information about citizens; by looking for "patterns" in the "data stream," officials seek to identify those people who pose some "risk." For example, research indicates that certain "types" of people are more likely to commit acts of violence. People filling out a firearms registration form are therefore required to reveal whether or not, in the past five years, they have been treated for depression, substance abuse, or emotional problems; considered suicide; been through a divorce or the dissolution of a significant relationship; lost their jobs; or gone bankrupt. Any of these "factors" indicates the person is "at risk" because they match the profile of a person more likely to commit acts of violence. The trouble is, the profile also catches a much larger number of people who do not pose a risk, but there is no way of distinguishing them from potential criminals.

Public interest groups and privacy advocates argue that this foray into the private lives of applicants puts the innocent citizen in a position in which he or she is forced to defend his or her actions to the state or face the consequences. This process may or may not catch a potentially violent offender, but it will easily catch a bankrupt, depressed, or divorced farmer who, in need of a gun for his livelihood, is forced to reveal intimate details of his life to the state and, even worse, have the state call and discuss his life with his neighbours, boss, and ex-spouse. Moreover, this willingness to invade privacy in the name of risk reduction means that the state is dealing with individuals not as citizens, but as suspects, safety risks, or threats to "secure," "efficient," and "cost-effective" government. In such a situation, the relationships that are essential to our understanding of democracy are undermined.

Similar concerns were raised when the government introduced "lawful access" legislation in Parliament in 2012. Under the proposed bill (*Protecting Children from Internet Predators Act*), telecommunications service providers would be required to give police a subscriber's name, address, telephone number, email address, internet protocol address and device identification numbers "upon request." This would enable the police to put the subscriber under online surveillance without a warrant. The bill would also require service providers to redesign their networks to make it easier for the police to intercept a subscriber's online communications. Citizen outcry to the proposed law was swift and loud; within weeks, over 150,000 Canadians had signed an online petition demanding the government "Stop Online Spying" (see http://stopspying.ca).

The government responded by arguing that it needs this surveillance capacity because criminals can use the internet to commit crimes. The name of the bill itself, *Protecting Children from Internet Predators Act*, indicates that the risk of harm outweighs the democratic benefits of online anonymity. However, this kind of risk reduction is not a neutral exercise. Many have accused governments of using racial profiling to target Arab Muslims and other minorities in order to reduce the risk of terrorism. When Canadian imam Ahamad Kutty flew to Miami on September 11, 2003, he spent 16 hours in jail. After being interrogated by more than 10 officials, he and fellow Canadian Abdool Hamid were declared risks to national security and sent back to Canada. Ironically, Kutty is well known for his strong stand against extremist violence. Nonetheless, American border officials saw him as a security risk because of his religion and ethnic origin (Hall, Shephard, & Harper, 2003).

As former Privacy Commissioner Bruce Phillips notes, the danger—and allure—of the emerging model of risk reduction is that:

> We participate voluntarily, only seeing the obvious advantages—convenience, speed and personal safety—not the less tangible and more complex disadvantages. The most chilling of these is that we will conform because we assume that we are all being watched at all times. Put more starkly: freedom is diminished and, in some cases, disappears. (Privacy Commissioner of Canada, 1999, p. 2)

3. Privacy as a Social Value

Privacy has a strong effect on our social behaviour and organization. Historians suggest that Elizabethan homes, with their kitchens, parlours, and bedrooms, replaced the single medieval common hall because people wanted to enjoy a level of privacy that had previously been available only to the rich. Likewise, in a landmark 1956 study of the Canadian suburb, Crestwood Heights, researchers concluded that:

> increased space, a reason why people buy houses in Crestwood, means increased privacy. ... Privacy for each member of the family is the ideal—but not the isolation of anonymous shelter as offered by a hotel. The essence of the desired privacy is its very presence within the family unit. (McDougall, 1999, p. 8)

Privacy, then, is not the same as withdrawal from social relationships. Rather, it is the power to control and define those relationships.

Contemporary discussions of privacy often focus on this aspect of individual control. We establish social relationships based on different degrees of intimacy; the closer the relationship, the more we share with the other person. When entry into our private lives occurs without our knowledge or consent, this sense of control is lost and we feel violated.

The argument that technology determines the level of privacy we enjoy is dissatisfying because privacy is something we negotiate through our social interaction with others. Children, for example, report that they like online communication because it gives them an opportunity to explore the world outside the watchful eyes of parents and teachers. In spite of the fact the sites they use routinely record their transactions, they report that the internet is *more* private, not less, than other forms of communication, and just because information is posted online does not mean that the people who posted it have no privacy interest in it (Steeves, 2004, p. 12). Facebook learned this the hard way when it tracked Facebook users' purchases and then sent messages about these purchases to all the people on the purchaser's friends list. Within two weeks, over 50,000 Facebook users had signed an online petition protesting the program, and Facebook was forced to allow people to opt out of the "service" (Story & Stone, 2007).

Allowing technology to define the limits of our privacy also fails to account for the fact that technological developments themselves are the result of social choices. Emerging forms of invasion redistribute social power. In the proverbial small town, everyone knows what everyone else is up to. However, this also means that everyone is also called to account for socially harmful actions. Hence, a small-town banker in the 1940s would face social censure if he refused to give someone a loan because the borrower had a family history of cancer. In the modern information society, however, the watchers are invisible. When banks, marketers, drug companies, and insurance companies invade our private lives, we are not even aware of it, and cannot see what they are doing with the information they collect about us. This lack of reciprocity means that it will become increasingly difficult to hold others accountable for decisions that harm us or discriminate against us. And those who have access to the information gain a significant amount of control over us.

The balance between control and accountability is complicated because networked technologies blur the line between private and public. Policymakers typically seek to police online communication because the public nature of the network exposes users to risky contact with strangers and offensive content. But part of the pleasure of online spaces is the publicity they enable; young people in particular report that they like networked technologies because they can use them to try on different identities and experiment with social behaviours in a relatively safe way. By "lurking" on adult sites, "stalking" peers on Facebook, and "flirting" in chat rooms (Livingstone & Bober, 2003), they can pursue what Livingstone calls "the social psychological task of adolescence—to construct, experiment with and present a reflexive project of the self in a social context" (Livingstone, 2008, p. 396).

From this perspective, the ability to watch others, and be watched by them in turn, allows young people "to acquire the cultural capital they use to construct an identity, and then evaluate the authenticity of that identity by monitoring the reactions of peers to their own performance of it" (Steeves, 2012, p. 355). However, this same project of the self requires privacy, both during adolescence and later in life. Privacy, or control over publicity, is what creates fences between the identity that is posted for friends on Facebook and the identity that is performed during a family gathering or a job interview, for example. When the digital traces of our private lives are collected and shared outside our control, it becomes more difficult to negotiate the level of privacy we need to ensure that we do not reveal more of ourselves than we mean to, to the various audiences who are watching us.

4. Privacy as Data Protection

The need to place some limits on the electronic collection, use, and disclosure of personal information was first recognized by the Council of Europe in the 1970s. Europeans, remembering the lessons of World War II, were sensitive to the fact that large organizations such as governments and banks were using mainframe computers to collect and process information about citizens.

Recognizing that this data made individuals vulnerable to human-rights abuses, the Council of Europe passed the *Convention for the Protection of Individuals with Regard to Automatic Processing of Personal Data* in 1980; it set out a framework for the collection, use, access, accuracy, and disposal of personal information. Concerned that national legislation based on the *Convention* might block the international flow of data, the Organisation for Economic Co-operation and Development (OECD) released its *Guidelines Governing the Protection of Privacy and Transborder Flows of Personal Data* in the same year (OECD, 1980). The guidelines contained a set of fair information practices to ensure that personal information is collected openly and that data records are accurate and kept confidential. This approach, which concentrates on protecting the integrity of the data itself rather than the individual who is the subject of the data, is called "data protection."

Data protection made a certain amount of sense in the 1980s, when computing was dominated by mainframe computers. In the mainframe environment, data processing was centralized, so all the data about a particular individual could be easily located and its use regulated. In addition, mainframes were extremely expensive and required constant technical supervision. Accordingly, only large organizations, such as governments, banks, and universities, were able to afford them. This meant that regulation had to apply only to a few, large, easily located organizations. However, as the nature of computing changed in the late 1980s and mainframes were replaced by distributed networks, data storage and processing became highly decentralized. By 1990, the power to collect and manipulate personal information was no longer in the hands of the few. Because of this, the data itself became an extremely valuable commodity.

The fact that personal information is now worth a great deal of money in the electronic marketplace is one of the most complicating features of the new privacy landscape. The sale of personal information is indeed big business, and many corporations have taken advantage of the open environment of the internet in order to capitalize on this trend. For example, Disney's Club Penguin looks like an online playground: children who visit the site create virtual pets, play games, and chat with friends. However, everything the children do on the site—the games they play, the links they click, the stories they post, the conversations they have with each other—are recorded and analyzed, so they can be profiled and targeted with marketing material.

This kind of marketing goes well beyond advertising, and instead seeks to embed the commercial message into the child's social relationships and sense of identity (Steeves, 2007). The pervasive collection of information on which it is based is cast as a form of child protection. Parents are assured that their children can play safely precisely because the corporation is watching them constantly and monitoring their actions. The children themselves are encouraged to participate in monitoring, by becoming "secret agents" who "spy" on other children who swear, bully others, or share personal information (such as name and city) with other children (Marx & Steeves, 2010).

The commercial use of the information, however, is hidden in legalistic terms-of-use agreements. For example, Club Penguin's privacy policy tells children that the site collects their information for "various purposes related to our business" but does not provide a detailed explanation of what those purposes are. The fact that the site is one big advertisement for Disney products is hidden behind the statement that "We do not allow third-party companies to solicit or advertise to our users. Our intention is to keep Club Penguin free from any of this sort of direct advertising" (Steeves, 2012, p. 352). Instead, children are encouraged to play with branded content for hours, which is precisely the kind of "sticky" advertising that is known to dramatically increase sales of offline products (Steeves 2007; Grimes & Shade 2005).

Interestingly, privacy laws have done little to stop the collection of this kind of information from children. Although both Canada and the United States have enacted legislation[3] requiring consent from children and, in certain circumstances, from parents, placing kids under online surveillance remains a multimillion dollar industry. The monetary value of the information collected has done much to shape the legal framework governing privacy.

PRIVACY LEGISLATION

To date, Canadian privacy legislation has been firmly rooted in the language of the marketplace. When Canada drafted its ***Privacy Act*** in 1982, it applied the OECD guidelines to the ways in which the federal government collects, uses, and discloses personal information about citizens and federal employees. The *Privacy Act* was limited in a number of ways. For example, the "exceptions" to the rules were extremely broad, and although the Privacy Commissioner was given the power to investigate complaints, he or she lacks any real enforcement powers. The *Privacy Act*'s greatest limitation was that it focused solely on the public sector, leaving private-sector data collection completely unregulated.

However, as the commercial imperatives of the information economy grew and consumer confidence in the electronic marketplace wavered, the private sector began to lobby for legislation that would encourage consumers to take part in e-commerce by assuaging concerns about privacy. These commercial imperatives were made even more pressing by the European Union in October 1995. Under a European Parliament directive designed to harmonize data protection standards within Europe, member states are required to pass legislation blocking the transfer of information to nonmember states that do not provide an adequate level of data protection (Council of Europe, 1995).

In January 1998, Industry Canada and the Department of Justice released a discussion paper suggesting that data protection legislation should be extended to the private sector but defining privacy solely as a trade issue.

The legislation that grew out of this discussion paper was named the ***Personal Information Protection and Electronic Documents Act*** **(PIPEDA)**. Its purpose is to establish, "in an era in which technology increasingly facilitates the circulation and exchange of information," rules that recognize the individual's right of privacy and "the need of organizations to collect, use or disclose personal information for purposes that a reasonable person would consider appropriate in the circumstances" (PIPEDA, 2000, s. 3). PIPEDA adopts the fair information practices first set out by the Council of Europe, and adds a requirement that personal information should be collected, used, and disclosed only with the individual's consent. However, like the *Privacy Act*, PIPEDA sets out a long list of exceptions to the general rule requiring consent, including investigations into a contravention of the law.

PIPEDA represents an uneasy compromise on the parts of industry, government, and privacy advocates, the latter of whom hoped some protection would be better than none. That compromise began to unravel even before the act was passed on April 13, 2000. Drug companies, pharmacists, and the Ontario Ministry of Health argued before the Senate Committee on Social Affairs that PIPEDA should not apply to personal health information, because it would unduly hamper the efficiency of health-care delivery and research. In spite of the fact that opinion polls and public consultations have consistently indicated that Canadians want more, not less, protection for their health information, a number of provinces have passed health information legislation that makes it easier for the state and "trusted parties" to share medical records without the patient's consent.

PIPEDA has been used to effectively limit some information practices on the part of online corporations such as Facebook and Nexopia. For example, the Privacy Commissioner of Canada, who is responsible for administering PIPEDA, has overturned practices such as setting profiles to public by default and refusing to delete user accounts when asked to do so by the user. However, the Commissioner has also found that PIPEDA cannot stop Canadian firms from outsourcing data management to companies in the United States, even though the data may then be disclosed to the American government under the U.S. *Patriot Act*, so long as the customers are advised of the fact before the information is outsourced. At its heart, PIPEDA relies on informed consent to legitimize the collection, use, and disclosure of personal information; as such, the Commissioner is often limited to requiring that corporations provide users with notice of their practices, leaving it up to the users themselves to decide whether or not to use the service.

Although American legislators have been unwilling to interfere with the private sector in general, relying instead on voluntary standards and privacy policies, there has been a great deal of interest in health privacy and the protection of children. Early attempts to regulate electronic data in the United States were draconian. The *Communications Decency Act*, for example, made it a criminal offence to use a telecommunications device to "knowingly make, create, or solicit ... any comment, request, proposal, image, or other communication which is obscene, lewd, lascivious, filthy, or indecent." In June 1996, a three-judge panel in a Philadelphia court struck down the *Communications Decency Act* for contravening constitutional guarantees of freedom of speech (*Reno v. ACLU*, 1996); a year later, the United States Supreme Court affirmed the lower court decision (*Reno v. ACLU*, 1997). More narrowly drafted was the subsequent *Children's Online Protection Act* (COPA), which made it unlawful to communicate, on the World Wide Web and for commercial purposes, material that is "harmful to minors" unless good-faith efforts are made to prevent children from obtaining access to such materials. On June 22, 2000, COPA was also struck down for unduly restricting freedom of speech (*ACLU v. Reno II*).

The United States continues to follow the privacy debate, although the major concern appears to be the need to avoid trade sanctions because of noncompliance with the 1995 European Union directive. Now that most of the members of the European Union have passed data protection legislation, pressure is mounting for the Americans to act as well. The Federal Trade Commission has set out voluntary standards for online commercial privacy, and the Department of Commerce has developed a "safe harbor" framework under which American firms can "certify" that they comply with a minimum set of fair information standards acceptable to the European Union.

TENSIONS IN THE PRIVACY DEBATE

Many experts argue that European-style fair information practices will ensure that privacy is protected in the new millennium. For example, former British Columbia Privacy Commissioner David Flaherty writes, "I have never met a privacy issue that could not be satisfactorily addressed by the application of fair information practices" (Bennett & Grant, 1999, p. 35). There is, however, a fundamental tension between privacy as a human right and access to information as a tool to enhance competitiveness and control. Fair information practices do not capture the "rights" side of the equation because they were designed by stakeholders to ensure that data will continue to flow into the information marketplace. They create a form of "consensual invasion" whereby the consent process is designed to protect the interests of everyone except the individual who is revealing the information.

In effect, consent is an agreement between the individual disclosing the information and the organization collecting the information. In order for consent to adequately protect the individual's autonomy and freedom of choice, there has to be an equality of bargaining power between the parties to the transaction. But that equality of bargaining power is often absent. If my employer, bank, or insurance company asks me to consent to the release of my personal information, what happens if I refuse? I may find I will lose access to employment, financial services, or insurance coverage.

Consent is also easily sidestepped by legislation and government practices. The United Kingdom has passed a law giving insurance companies the "right" to demand a genetic sample from prospective clients. Iceland sold the genetic records of its entire population to a drug company without first asking its citizens. It is estimated that our images will be captured by 300 surveillance cameras on the way to work in the morning, all of which have been installed and operated without our consent and often without our knowledge. Statistics Canada releases our tax records to epidemiologists conducting medical research because it has decided "it's good for us."

Proponents justify these practices on the grounds that they are efficient and reduce risk. National security, marketplace efficiency, public safety, and the development of new medical treatments are important goals, but not if they are accomplished in ways that sacrifice our individual rights. We have learned—and forgotten—this lesson before. During World War II, the United States Census Bureau released statistical data to the state to assist in the arrest and detainment of Japanese Americans. Even though the detention of Japanese Americans and Canadians has since been condemned, the U.S. Census Bureau released information to the Department of Homeland Security in 2004 detailing the number of Arab Americans living in specific zip-code areas.

The dynamics of national security and the marketplace could not help Japanese Americans and Canadians in the 1940s. To do that, we had to develop a language of human rights. Our choice of language is equally important in the context of the privacy debate. As Franklin (1996) has said: "Ultimately, the level of openness and privacy we enjoy is a social choice. Privacy is not a function of our technological environment or need for security."

In the words of privacy advocate Darrell Evans:

> I think the vanishing of privacy would be a victory of materialism over the human spirit. I find it very hard to picture what kind of room there would be for creativity on the part of human beings in such a world ... We are constantly told it is a more secure world, of course, a more efficient world, a world that catches fraud much better, but to me, that is the victory of bureaucracy over human creativity. ... We want to put individuals in a place of causation rather than being a complete effect of technologies and of a gradual erosion of our privacy. If we are to maintain human freedom, I think that's what we have to do. (cited in Canada, 1997, p. 21)

QUESTIONS

1. Is privacy a fundamental human right? Give reasons for your answer.
2. According to the author, what are the four different ways of understanding privacy?
3. Which do you feel poses the greater threat to privacy—the public sector or the private sector? Give reasons for your answer.

4. In what sense do privacy codes adopt the point of view of business and neglect the rights of citizens?
5. Do websites such as http://www.turnitin.com treat students like suspected criminals? What is the right balance between catching "cheaters" and treating others with respect?

NOTES

1. For example, it is estimated that there are 2.5 million cameras focused on public spaces throughout the United Kingdom. London alone has an estimated 150,000 CCTV cameras monitoring its streets; in 1997, London cameras began to automatically read, recognize, and track automobiles by their licence plates. One year later, the London borough of Newham added face recognition software that scans crowds and matches digitized pictures of the faces of passersby against a database of "known criminals."
2. The major constitutional protection is afforded under section 8, as discussed. Case law suggests that the Court is also willing to interpret section 7 ("the right to life, liberty and security of the person") in ways that will protect privacy (see *Blencoe v. British Columbia*, 2000; *Godbout v. Longueuil*, 1997). However, section 7 rights have also been limited to reasonable expectations of privacy.
3. In Canada, see the *Personal Information Protection and Electronic Documents Act*. In the United States, see *Children's Online Privacy Protection Act* of 1998.

REFERENCES

ACLU v. Reno II (1999), United States Court of Appeal for the Third Circuit, No. 99–1324.

Bennett, C. J., & Grant, R. (1999). *Visions of privacy: Policy choices for the digital age.* Toronto: University of Toronto Press.

Blencoe v. British Columbia (Human Rights Commission), [2000] S.C.J. No. 43.

Canada House of Commons Standing Committee on Human Rights and the Status of Persons with Disabilities. 35th Parliament, 2nd Session. (1997). *Privacy: Where do we draw the line?* Ottawa: Public Works and Government Services Canada.

Children's Online Privacy Protection Act of 1998, 15 U.S.C. §§ 6501–6506.

Council of Europe. (1980). *Convention for the protection of individuals with regard to automatic processing of personal data.* ETS No. 108.

———. (1995, October 24). *Directive on the protection of the individual with respect to the processing of personal data and on the free movement of such data.* 95/46/EC.

End of privacy. (1999). *The Economist, 15.* April 29.

Franklin, U. (1996, September 19). *Stormy weather: Conflicting forces in the information society.* Closing address at the 18th International Privacy and Data Protection Conference, Ottawa.
Godbout v. Longueuil (Ville) (1997), 152 D.L.R. (4th) 577 (S.C.C.).
Grimes, S., & Shade, L. R. (2005). Neopian economics of play: Children's cyberpets and online communities as immersive advertising in Neopets.com. *International Journal of Media and Cultural Politics, 1*(2), 181–198.
Hall, J., Shephard, M., & Harper, T. (2003, September 13). Revered Muslim cleric held in U.S. *The Toronto Star,* A1.
Hunter v. Southam (1984), 11 D.L.R. (4th) 641.
Livingstone, S. (2008). Taking risky opportunities in youthful content creation: Teenagers use of social networking sites for intimacy, privacy and self-expression. *New Media & Society, 10*(30), 393–411.
Livingstone, S., & Bober, M. (2003). UK children go online: Listening to young people's experiences. London: Economic and Social Research Council. Retrieved August 9, 2012, from http://eprints.lse.ac.uk/388
Marx, G., & Steeves, V. (2010). From the beginning: Children as subjects and agents of surveillance. *Surveillance and Society,* 7(3), 6–45.
McDougall, B. (Ed.). (1999). *Perspectives on privacy.* Toronto: Zaxis Publishing.
Moore, L. (2004, July 22). They've got your number: Cutting-edge technologies work as tattle-tales for a surveillance-minded state, Canadian privacy advocates. *The Montreal Gazette,* F1.
OECD (Organisation for Economic Co-operation and Development). (1980, October 1). *OECD recommendation concerning and guidelines governing the protection of privacy and transborder flows of personal data,* OECD Doc. C (80)58 (Final).
PIPEDA (*Personal Information Protection and Electronic Documents Act*), S.C. 2000, c. 5. Retrieved August 10, 2012 from http://laws-lois.justice.gc.ca/eng/acts/P-8.6/index.html.
"Press Kit." Retrieved July 15, 2007, from http://info.neopets.com/presskit/faqs.html#6
Privacy Act, R.S.C. 1985, c. P-21. Retrieved September 30, 2012, from http://laws-lois.justice.gc.ca/eng/acts/P-21/index.html
Privacy Commissioner of Canada. (1999). *Annual report, 1998–1999.* Ottawa: Public Works and Government Services Canada.
Protecting Children from Internet Predators Act, Bill C-30, Part I, 41st Parliament, 1st Session, 2012.
R. v. Duarte (1990), 1 S.C.R. 30 at 46.
R. v. Dyment (1988), 45 C.C.C. (3d) 244.
R. v. LeBeau (1988), 41 C.C.C. (3d) 163 (Ont. C.A.).
R. v. Plant (1993), 84 C.C.C. (3d) 203.
R. v. Tessling (2004), 3 S.C.R. 432, 2004 SCC 67.
R. v. Wong (1990), 3 S.C.R. 36 (S.C.C.).

Rand, Ayn. (1943). *The fountainhead.* Indianapolis, IN: Bobbs-Merrill.

Reno v. ACLU (1996, June 11), United States District Court for the Eastern District of Pennsylvania, No. 96-963. Retrieved August 10, 2012 from http://epic.org/free_speech/cda/#lower.

Reno v. ACLU (1997, June 26), United States Supreme Court, No. 96–511. Retrieved August 10, 2012 from http://epic.org/free_speech/cda/

Steeves, V. (2004). *Young Canadians in a wired world, Phase II: Trends and recommendations.* Ottawa: Media Awareness Network.

———. (2007). "The watched child: Surveillance in three online playgrounds," Proceedings of the International Conference on the Rights of the Child (pp. 119–140). Montreal: Wilson Lafleur.

———. (2012). Hide and seek: Surveillance of young people on the internet. In K. Ball, K. D. Haggerty & D. Lyon (Eds.), *Routledge Handbook of Surveillance Studies* (pp. 352–360). London: Routledge.

Story, L., &. Stone, B. (2007, November 30). Facebook retreats on online tracking. *The New York Times*, C1.

United Nations. (1948, December 10). *Universal declaration of human rights.* Resolution 217 A (III).

———. (1966). *International covenant on civil and political rights.* U.N. Doc. A/6316, 999 U.N.T.S. 302.

Warren, S. & Brandeis, L. (1890). The right to privacy. *Harvard Law Review, 4*, 193–220.

Weinberg, P. (2004, July 16). Big brother comes to Canada. *Inter Press Service.*

16

THE SYSTEM OF COPYRIGHT

Meera Nair
The Hebrew University of Jerusalem

FIVE STORIES

1. It was predicted in the late 1990s that **filesharing** would be the death of the music industry.[1] The industry has changed, but it is alive and well, with online digital sales thriving. In December 2011 music industry associations made arguments to the Supreme Court of Canada that the use of 30-second music previews—as provided to encourage digital music sales—should be subject to payment.
2. In 2006 a Canadian student created the International Music Score Library Project—a legitimate online repository of public domain music. Yet the project has been repeatedly targeted for lawsuit by European music publishers. Those publishers felt it was the student's responsibility to abide by European copyright law, replete as it is with a longer term of copyright.
3. An art student came to me with a question. She had concerns about posting pictures of her work into Facebook; she did not care for the requirement that she grant a non-exclusive licence for Facebook to use her work as it saw fit. Knowing that copyright is imperfect, she still wanted to share her work with family and friends, and promote herself in the art world. But she felt ill equipped to go it alone with the *Copyright Act*.
4. A YouTube work I enjoyed watching was a video about skater Michelle Kwan. With the hope that Kwan would participate in the 2010 Vancouver Winter Olympics, a fan created the promotional video. Composed of excerpts taken from televised sports coverage, set to popular music and interspersed with elegant captions, the effort exemplified how prior work can be incorporated to create something original in its own right. But the video was removed from YouTube on the charge of copyright infringement.
5. A revised edition of Mark Twain's work *Huckleberry Finn* appeared on the market in 2011. Twain's original prose was altered—the word "nigger" was replaced with "slave." Public reaction was not universally favourable[2] but the actions of

the editor and publisher are entirely legitimate; as the term of copyright has long since passed, anyone may edit and republish Twain's work.

Copyright is neither the rogue nor hero of creativity in the digital age. Copyright is only a policy instrument, first enacted to regulate commercial print activity but now also capable of regulating individual behavior. This chapter is not a comprehensive description of the entire realm of copyright; it can only acquaint readers, in broad brushstrokes, with some of the aspects of copyright that touch us in the acts of learning, creating, and sharing.

THE SYSTEM OF COPYRIGHT

The word "copyright" seems intuitively obvious in meaning. Quite simply, copyright is the right to copy. But this literal translation masks an intriguing system of limited rights offered to both copyright holders and copyright users. The rationale for the system is often described as encouragement—that copyright assists in fostering creativity to the benefit of society at large by allowing individual creators to control their work. That claim has both defenders and detractors. Without control, authors, artists and musicians will not be able to support themselves. The rebuttal is that developments in literature, art, and music could not occur but for the tradition of borrowing from, or building upon, past works. The ideal atmosphere for creativity likely resides between these two endpoints.

Copyright falls within the phenomenon known as **intellectual property**. Broadly speaking, intellectual property represents the means by which the rights to intellectual creations are controlled. But the language of "property" is misleading.[3] Those who wish to expand the rights of control argue that since physical property rights grant absolute control, so too should intellectual property rights. Yet an intellectual creation is intrinsically different from a physical entity. And, even if one is willing to overlook the flawed analogy, it remains that physical property rights are limited. The most revered physical property right—land ownership—does not provide complete control to the titleholder. Building codes, zoning requirements, and environmental laws set public well-being ahead of the independence of the landowner.

A structural design element of the notion of "rights" is that of limitation. Said another way, all rights are accompanied by a requirement not to abuse the right to the detriment of society. To determine where to draw the line between rights and limits requires an understanding of what the purpose of the right actually is. This causes some confusion for copyright in Canada—the *Copyright Act* was never given a purpose. This lies in stark contrast to the United States, which has a constitutionally enshrined purpose for intellectual property rights: "To promote the Progress of Science and useful Arts, by securing for limited Times to Authors and Inventors the exclusive Right to their respective Writings." But drawing from the influences of both our English and French forbears,[4] we can informally superimpose an objective upon Canadian copyright: To further the process of creativity to the benefit of creators and society alike.

Yet the contemporary political focus in copyright is about controlling the flow of digital works on the internet. Fortunately, public engagement with the subject of copyright is growing. In 2012, American lawmakers were preparing to adopt legislation known as the *Stop Online Piracy Act* (SOPA). Opposition grew steadily as people became aware that the new law could undermine freedom of expression and legitimate business operations. On January 18, 2012, websites around the world went dark to show support for curbing excessive expansion of copyright.

Within Canada, there is a steady growth in engagement with the subject of copyright. A public consultation on copyright in 2001 netted fewer than 700 letters, including form letters (Canada, 2002); a public consultation in 2009 brought in thousands of independent submissions. Many Canadians are aware of the importance of copyright in the digital age; as our ability to engage with creative effort expands with the reach of the internet, so too does the implication of copyright upon our personal lives.

WHAT DOES COPYRIGHT DO?

Copyright protects the expression of an idea. Ideas themselves cannot be copyrighted, and neither can instrumental building blocks such as facts or data. But for original expressions of literary, dramatic, artistic, or musical nature, copyright is a set of rights that controls the diffusion of those expressions (also known as works). Copyright law also addresses elements beyond these works—broadcast signals, performers' performances, and sound recordings all have special stature under the *Copyright Act*. But the discussion in this chapter pertains only to creative effort that can be written, drawn, composed, or shaped.

Literary works have a wide range, including books and pamphlets, poems and computer programs. Dramatic works can range from a Stratford Festival production to a radio commercial to an amateur video posted on YouTube. Artistic works run the gamut from drawings and paintings to maps and building plans. Finally, musical work includes compositions of music, with or without accompanying lyrics. For all instances of copyright, the protection is immediate—no formal registration or application is required.

The rights embodied in copyright are first granted to the author(s) of eligible works but may be transferred to other parties. The rights are limited in time; when the term of copyright expires, the work is open for any purpose, by any person. The rights are also limited in space—even when a work is protected, there are exceptions that permit some uses of the work under certain circumstances. Said another way, exceptions to the rights of copyright owners are rights in the hands of copyright users.

Copyright in works

3. (1) For the purposes of this Act, "copyright", in relation to a work, means the sole right to produce or reproduce the work or any substantial part thereof in any material form whatever, to perform the work or any substantial part thereof in public or, if the work is unpublished, to publish the work or any substantial part thereof, and includes the sole right:

(a) to produce, reproduce, perform or publish any translation of the work,

(b) in the case of a dramatic work, to convert it into a novel or other nondramatic work

...

(f) in the case of any literary, dramatic, musical or artistic work, to communicate the work to the public by telecommunication,

...

and to authorize any such acts.

Copyright does not arise when copying insubstantial amounts of a work. "Substantial" is not defined.

"Any material form" indicates that the Act applies to any media—the language is technologically neutral.

In total, ten clauses are stipulated in Section 3.1.

"communicate ... to the public by telecommunication" was amended in 2012 to ensure that decisions to make content available online are clearly included in the scope of the exclusive rights of copyright holders.

Authorization need not always be explicit; depending on the situation at hand, authorization could be implicit.

Conditions for subsistence of copyright

5.1 Subject to this Act, copyright shall subsist in Canada, for the term hereinafter mentioned, in every original literary, dramatic, musical and artistic work if any one of the following conditions is met ...

Original is not defined.

Term of copyright

6. The term for which copyright shall subsist shall, except as otherwise expressly provided by this Act, be the life of the author, the remainder of the calendar year in which the author dies, and a period of fifty years following the end of that calendar year.

While Canada enjoys a term of life-plus-50, other jurisdictions have moved to life-plus-70.

Where copyright belongs to Her Majesty

12. Without prejudice to any rights or privileges of the Crown, where any work is, or has been, prepared or published by or under the direction or control of Her Majesty or any government department, the copyright in the work shall, subject to any agreement with the author, belong to Her Majesty ...

Crown copyright is an artifact from copyright's precursor of 16th-century censorship. Not all countries held onto this form of state control; from infancy on the United States resisted Crown copyright.

Ownership of copyright

13. (1) Subject to this Act, the author of a work shall be the first owner of the copyright therein.

Copyright was forged ostensibly to protect authors, yet the figure of the author has little prominence in the act. The author is only a referential point: the first person to own the copyright of a work.

Infringement generally

27. (1) It is an infringement of copyright for any person to do, without the consent of the owner of the copyright, anything that by this Act only the owner of the copyright has the right to do.

The corollary is that copyright owners' scope of control is confined to only those rights defined by law. While section 3.1 is extensive, it does not include the right to negate existing limitations.

Source: From "Copyright and Moral Rights in Works", *Copyright Act* (R.S.C., 1985, c. C-42), Department of Justice, Government of Canada <http://laws-lois.justice.gc.ca/eng/acts/C-42/page-4.html#h-3>

THE PUBLIC DOMAIN

Copyright cannot be explained purely by reference to the language of its law. Copyright takes form only when set against the backdrop of the **public domain**. But no other phrase in the copyright lexicon is more prone to misunderstanding. Credible scholars across many disciplines portray the public domain as composed only of material whose copyright term has expired. This is unnecessarily restrictive. At the other end of the spectrum, the public domain is seen as any material that can be accessed publicly. Whether that access is paid for, or free, is deemed irrelevant. This interpretation is too generous.

Jessica Litman (1990) writes that "... The most important part of the public domain is a part we usually speak of only obliquely: the realm comprising aspects of copyrighted works that copyright does not protect" (p. 976). This means, among other things, that a copyrighted work accessed in accordance with legitimate exceptions is public domain material. The bulk of the public domain comes into existence not by virtue of time, but by the use made of a work.

Think about it. Every book, every image, every film, every strain of music—every creative expression is potentially public domain material.

This conceptual view of the public domain is not confined to Litman's interpretation. For instance, the Center for Study of the Public Domain at Duke University—a highly reputable centre in the world of law—describes the public domain as "... the realm of material—ideas, images, sounds, discoveries, facts, texts—that is unprotected by intellectual property rights and free for all to use or build upon" (Duke University, n.d.). But for those who wish for more forceful institutional support, "Public domain: ... it means from a copyright aspect the realm of all works which can be exploited by everybody without any authorization, *mostly* because of the expiration of the term of protection" (emphasis mine, World Intellectual Property Organization, 1981, p. 207). The inclusion of "mostly" indicates that the World Intellectual Property Organization is aware that there are measures within the law which remove the requirement of authorization. These are known as *exceptions*.

On January 1 of each year, works whose author passed away in the 50th preceding year become unencumbered by copyright in Canada. The website *public-domain* routinely lists the gains.[5] Europeans and Americans are not so fortunate; with copyright terms of life plus 70, coupled with past policy decisions to avoid copyright expiry, fewer works are available in those regions. On December 31, 2011, the avant garde archive *Ubu-Web* celebrated the arrival of James Joyce's work into the EU with a very colourful Tweet to Stephen Joyce, reminding the heir of James Joyce that the work of his grandfather could now be enjoyed by all of Ireland (O'Connell, 2012).

EXCEPTIONS

The rights embodied through copyright are intended to control distribution of both the original form of a work and any re-creation of that work in a different expressional form (*i.e.* through translation, from dramatic work to novel, from literary creation to sound recording, *etc.*). But with the control of distribution rights, the system of copyright offers exceptions to distribution rights. Some allowances of reproduction of copyrighted work are permitted; some allowances are also permitted for reproduction in different formats. Generally speaking, these exceptions are designed to serve institutional distribution, where institutions are entities such as schools or telecommunications providers. Exceptions to distribution are very precisely worded and must be handled with care.

However, there is a very important flexible exception that is designed not to facilitate distribution but to facilitate creativity. This exception is known as fair dealing.

Fair Dealing

Fair dealing permits some unauthorized uses of copyrighted material, under certain conditions. It is not an invitation to copy without restriction. For most of Canada's copyright history, fair dealing applied only to the activities of research, private study, criticism, review, and news reporting.[6] Conditions are attached to fair dealing. For instance, citation is important. So too is careful consideration of the amount copied. Decisions of fair dealing require a two-step process of analysis. First, does the use of the work fall within the accepted list of purposes? Second, is the dealing fair? That second question can be answered only by a comprehensive exploration of each situation. This framework of inquiry was promoted by the Supreme Court of Canada in 2004, via a case often referred to as *CCH Canadian*.

CCH Canadian addressed a number of issues but is best known for its handling of fair dealing. Writing for a unanimous court, Chief Justice Beverley McLachlin stated: "In order to maintain the proper balance between the rights of a copyright owner and users' interests, [fair dealing] must not be interpreted restrictively. ... As an integral part of the scheme of copyright law, the s. 29 fair dealing exception is always available" (*CCH*, 2004, para. 48–49).

In *CCH Canadian* the copying under scrutiny was very modest. Upon request, the Great Library of the Law Society of Upper Canada would reproduce single copies of material related to legal research and convey the material to the patron via print or facsimile. A number of legal publishers claimed this behaviour as infringement, but the Supreme Court found that the library's practices were in accordance with fair dealing. The decision in part rested on the fact that the Great Library had developed a set of internal guidelines whereby patron requests were reviewed against a consideration of fairness.

The legacy of *CCH Canadian* is twofold:

1. The encouragement offered by the Supreme Court of Canada to make good use of the exception of fair dealing (that it is vital to a well-functioning system of copyright).
2. The guidance offered by the Supreme Court of Canada toward a widespread understanding of how to use fair dealing. Each examination of fair dealing must be judged by a comprehensive examination; decisions of fair dealing should include inquiry as to the purpose of the dealing, the character of the dealing, the amount of the dealing, alternatives for the dealing, the nature of the work, and the effect of the dealing on the copyrighted work. The Court also made it clear that not every question will be relevant in all situations and, in some situations other questions may arise. In short—each situation is unique and must be examined on its own merits.

Turning again to the *Copyright Act*, consider the language of fair dealing.

Research or private study

29. Fair dealing for the purpose of research, private study, parody, satire and education does not infringe copyright.

Criticism or review

29.1 Fair dealing for the purpose of criticism or review does not infringe copyright if the following are mentioned:

(a) the source; and

(b) if given in the source, the name of the

(i) author, in the case of a work,

(ii) performer, in the case of a performer's performance,

(iii) maker, in the case of a sound recording, or

(iv) broadcaster, in the case of a communication signal.

News reporting

29.2 Fair dealing for the purpose of news reporting does not infringe copyright if the following are mentioned:

(a) the source; and

(b) if given in the source, the name of the

(i) author, in the case of a work,

(ii) performer, in the case of a performer's performance,

(iii) maker, in the case of a sound recording, or

(iv) broadcaster, in the case of a communication signal.

The inclusion of "education" provoked much discussion before its inclusion in 2012. Yet research, private study, criticism and review are precisely the elements of education.

Fair dealing does not offer easy shelter to artists, authors and musicians who include substantial portions of other works within their own creations. The inclusion may well meet the standard of fairness, but unless the new work falls among the permitted categories, fairness may not be considered.

Canadian creativity should not be obligated to serve a set social purpose in order to enjoy legitimacy. Sometimes art is just art. Fortunately, the Supreme Court of Canada continues to encourage a liberal interpretation of fair dealing

From "Exceptions–Fair Dealing", *Copyright Act* (R.S.C., 1985, c. C-42), Department of Justice, Government of Canada <http://laws-lois.justice.gc.ca/eng/acts/C-42/page-17.html#h-23>

Fair dealing is often decried for its imprecision. People would prefer the comfort of being told precisely what can, or cannot, be done. Yet as no legislator, creator, consumer, or user can precisely define the creative process, it is reasonable that an exception intended to support the creative process should lack precision too. The best the law can do is maintain some degree of flexibility when considering an unauthorized use that may serve the objective of fostering creativity.

Fair Dealing Is Not (Yet) Fair Use

Canada's close relationships with American cultural industries occasionally lead to some confusion in understanding copyright law. While the two countries share the predominantly Anglo-American structure of copyright, there are important differences.

Fair use is the American parallel to fair dealing; both exceptions allow for some unauthorized reproduction of copyrighted material. The critical difference between the two is the elasticity of the American language. Fair use is coded as allowing unauthorized reproduction of copyrighted material "for purposes such as ..." followed by an illustrative set of purposes (*i.e.* criticism, comment, scholarship *etc.*). The merit of the American structure is that it permits all uses an opportunity to be evaluated on fairness. As the Supreme Court of Canada continues to promote a liberal interpretation of fair dealing, Canadian fair dealing may reach the flexibility of American fair use.

Also encoded within American law are four factors that should be considered when determining fair use (17 USC 107):

1. the purpose and character of the use, including whether such use is of a commercial nature or is for nonprofit educational purposes;
2. the nature of the copyrighted work;
3. the amount and substantiality of the portion used in relation to the copyrighted work as a whole; and
4. the effect of the use upon the potential market for or value of the copyrighted work.

These factors are very similar to the framework advocated by the Supreme Court of Canada in *CCH Canadian*. However, what sets Canada apart from the United States is that our Justices emphasized that the framework for consideration may change depending on the situation, and, the effect on the potential market was not the dominant concern (*CCH*, 2004). The prior rigidity of application of the fair-use factors in the United States led to some challenges there (Nair, 2010); with the foresight of our Supreme Court, Canada can avoid those challenges.

More Exceptions

A welcome measure within the *Copyright Act* expressly facilitates documentary work, whether by photograph or film. This allowance relieves Canadian documentarians of some of the excessive clearance demands made of their American counterparts.

Incidental use 30.7 It is not an infringement of copyright to incidentally and not deliberately (a) include a work or other subject-matter in another work or other subject-matter; or (b) do any act in relation to a work or other subject-matter that is incidentally and not deliberately included in another work or other subject-matter	This eliminates the need to clear rights in, for example, logos and trademarks, music (including mobile phone ring tones), and billboards that might appear in a street scene (Documentary Organization of Canada, 2010, p. 6).

Source: From "Incidental Inclusion", *Copyright Act* (R.S.C., 1985, c. C-42), Department of Justice, Government of Canada <http://laws-lois.justice.gc.ca/eng/acts/C-42/page-23.html#h-32>

The Documentary Organization of Canada (DOC) has worked steadily to educate its members about copyright and exceptions, and good practices that facilitate the ability to obtain errors and omissions insurance. DOC began this work in 2005, with a survey of its members and sought to investigate how fair dealing might apply to copyright. In 2006 DOC commissioned a white paper from attorney Howard Knopf that led to collaboration with the University of Ottawa's Canadian Internet Policy and Public Interest Clinic (CIPPIC). DOC published *Copyright and Fair Dealing: Guidelines for Documentary Filmmakers* in May 2010.

DOC astutely recognized that guidelines alone cannot achieve understanding and so in 2011 undertook a Fair Dealing Roadshow across the country. A complete report is available from the DOC website.

And a useful, but little known, exception allows the reproduction of publicly situated art or architecture.

Miscellaneous 32.2 (1b) It is not an infringement of copyright for any person to reproduce, in a painting, drawing, engraving, photograph or cinematographic work (i) an architectural work, provided the copy is not in the nature of an architectural drawing or plan, or (ii) a sculpture or work of artistic craftsmanship or a cast or model of a sculpture or work of artistic craftsmanship, that is permanently situated in a public place or building	Controversy ensued when a Vancouver businessman sold photographs of Ken Lum's work *Monument for Vancouver*. Lum's inspiration came from a cross-word arrangement that has long circulated in Vancouver. Yet as the circulation included use by the Hells Angels, a former associate of the group protested the sale of the photographs and cited copyright registration with the Canadian Intellectual Property Office (Bolan, 2011).

Source: From "Miscellaneous-Permitted Acts", *Copyright Act* (R.S.C., 1985, c. C-42), Department of Justice, Government of Canada <http://laws-lois.justice.gc.ca/eng/acts/C-42/page-26.html#h-37>

User-Generated Content (UGC)

In 2012 the federal government added an exception to the *Copyright Act*. Known as the YouTube exception, this measure appears designed to bolster legitimacy for the individual creativity that is possible through consumer digital technology. The exception permits individuals to incorporate copyrighted material into new works, when those new works are intended for noncommercial purposes. However, Canadians should remember that this provision would not easily apply to YouTube as our *Copyright Act* has no standing outside Canada.

The usefulness of the YouTube exception was questioned from its unveiling. The emphasis that the input components are not a consequence of copyright infringement is likely to be violated by the amateur creators for whom the exception is intended—suggests that the exception is an empty gesture. Moreover, the absence of any support to professional creators cannot be ignored. Martha Rans, Director of Artists' Legal Outreach, said:

> Josh Hite, a Vancouver media artist, made a video "chug chug chug" based on clips he found on YouTube. The exception, as drafted, makes it no easier for him to show the video

Non-commercial User-generated Content

29.21 (1) It is not an infringement of copyright for an individual to use an existing work or other subject-matter or copy of one, which has been published or otherwise made available to the public, in the creation of a new work or other subject-matter in which copyright subsists and for the individual — or, with the individual's authorization, a member of their household — to use the new work or other subject-matter or to authorize an intermediary to disseminate it, if:

(a) the use of, or the authorization to disseminate, the new work or other subject-matter is done solely for non-commercial purposes;

(b) the source — and, if given in the source, the name of the author, performer, maker or broadcaster — of the existing work or other subject-matter or copy of it are mentioned, if it is reasonable in the circumstances to do so;

(c) the individual had reasonable grounds to believe that the existing work or other subject-matter or copy of it, as the case may be, was not infringing copyright; and

(d) the use of, or the authorization to disseminate, the new work or other subject-matter does not have a substantial adverse effect, financial or otherwise, on the exploitation or potential exploitation of the existing work or other subject-matter — or copy of it — or on an existing or potential market for it, including that the new work or other subject-matter is not a substitute for the existing one.

Remember that the "publication" and "making available to the public" are rights afforded to the copyright holder.

The intent of the creation should not carry a profit motive, nor should the creation serve as a substitute in the market for the original.

The citation requirement is similar to that within fair dealing. But as artistic endeavor does not always lend itself to explicit citation, there is flexibility by way of "if it is reasonable ... to do so."

Source: *From Bill C-11, Copyright Modernization Act*, Government of Canada <http://www.parl.gc.ca/HousePublications/Publication.aspx?Language=E&Mode=1&DocId=5144516&File=45#7>

> at a festival. We are, however, seeing best practices emerge that respect the original creators and do not penalize users. It seems to me worthwhile to avoid unnecessary legislative intervention that could slow that process. In the United States, Getty Images, one of the most significant owners of copyrights in visual work, is currently hosting a Mishmash competition. It invites and enables people to upload images from its digital archive and remix them. This suggests to me that copyright holders like Getty have adapted to the new digital landscape. We need a copyright regime that enables artists to create transformative works. ... That is the foundation of much art making. I was recently asked by an internationally respected Canadian painter whether a work of his that transforms images of an 80's pop icon could be exhibited in the public library. The contract required him to represent that there was no potential copyright infringements. He could not sign it and the work was not displayed (Rans, 2012).[*]

Only time will tell if this provision for user-generated content will facilitate or impede creativity. All that can be said now is it offers the potential for emphasizing the collaborative nature of the creative process and acknowledges the growth of such production through digital technology and worldwide networks. For most of copyright's more than 300-year history, battles were fought between rival publishers. But the individual became implicated in the digital age. The UGC exemption is promising action by the federal government to ensure that Canadians who practise creativity are not immediately deemed in violation of copyright. Much will depend on the practices that come forth, and the willingness (or lack thereof) of copyright holders to support creativity among nascent creators.

Also added in 2012 were exceptions for reasonable uses of legitimately acquired content. Consumers are permitted time shifting of television programs, in order that the programs can be enjoyed at times of the consumer's choosing. Similarly, legitimately acquired content may be copied to use on a different device. A general provision to permit creating backup copies of content to guard against damage or loss was also introduced in 2012. But a key theme underwrote the 2012 amendments; infringement was extended to cover the act of circumventing a technological protection measure. This means that content can be locked to a particular media and device, and unlocking the device is considered infringement. It will be to the discretion of copyright holders to determine if Canadians can actually enjoy the exceptions granted by law.

---

*Rans, Martha. Legislative committee on Bill C-11: Text of statement (9 March 2012) <http://artistslegaloutreach.ca/blog/legislative-committee-bill-c-11text-statement> Artists Legal Outreach.

INTERNATIONAL PRESSURES

The introduction of protection for **digital locks** remains a divisive issue in Canada. A public consultation preceded the 2012 amendments; thousands of Canadians expressed opposition on this matter. Protecting a lock distorts any meaningful claim to balance in the *Copyright Act*; exceptions that can exist only on paper are hardly worth the paper they are written on. Eventually, the federal government admitted that such protections do impede legitimate exceptions but justified the protection alternately by reference to Canada's international obligations and the option of consumers to avoid such encumbered products.[7]

A principal motive for amending Canadian law was to enable Canada to ratify two international treaties: the *Copyright Treaty* and the *Performances and Phonograms Treaty*. These treaties were negotiated through the World Intellectual Property Organization (WIPO) in 1996. Canada was under no obligation to ratify the treaties; although there was some political imperative vis-à-vis the United States.

The treaty language surrounding the digital locks was an outcome of intense debate among many countries (Geist, 2010). The treaties themselves allow some measure of individuality in implementation—many countries have limited protection for locks only to actual infringement. However, the federal government sought instead to follow the model provided by the United States in 1998, known as the *Digital Millennium Copyright Act* (DMCA). And although the United States has since repeatedly softened its stance on digital locks, Canada's copyright law does not reflect the broader understanding within the United States today.[8]

The WIPO Treaties must be seen in the context of the atmosphere of the late 1990s. File sharing had emerged and the music industry reacted strongly. This, despite the fact that historically all media developments have brought fear and fortune (in that order) to the entertainment sector (Bettig, 1996; Litman, 2001). Despite the evident growth of the music industry, particularly the growing sales of online music, global policy making efforts to strengthen copyright continues. But where such negotiation previously occurred in an open form such as WIPO, contemporary negotiations are closed-door affairs. At the time of writing, the Anti-Counterfeiting Trade Agreement (ACTA) and the Trans-Pacific Partnership (TPP) are under discussion.

Lost in the perennial global effort to expand copyright is discussion of **moral rights**. Many people are aware of the mechanism of copyright, but are unaware of another set of rights offered to creators of intellectual works: moral rights. The topic does not easily invite interest—"moral rights" sounds distinctly pious. The English translation does not fully capture the meaning of the rights. The term came from France, as *droit moreaux*—which is better translated as *personal or intellectual rights* (Vaver, 2000, p. 158).

MORAL RIGHTS AND CREATIVE COMMONS

Moral Rights

Moral rights arose out of the European civil law approach concerning the protection of intellectual effort and the creators of that effort. Moral rights are rooted in the belief that any kind of intellectual creation carries with it an extension of the creator's soul. When we write, or draw, or compose music, we are giving something of ourselves in that process. Thus an assault on the creation is as reprehensible as an assault on the physical being of the creator. Moral rights were conceived as a means to protect that emotional connection between art and artist.

Moral rights

14.1 (1) The author of a work has subject to Section 28.2 the right to the integrity of the work and ... where reasonable in the circumstances, to be associated with the work as its author by name or under a pseudonym and the right to remain anonymous.

No assignment of moral rights

(2) Moral rights may not be assigned but may be waived in whole or in part.

No waiver by assignment

(3) An assignment of copyright in a work does not by that act alone constitute a waiver of any moral rights.

Term

14.2 (1) Moral rights in respect of a work subsist for the same term as the copyright in the work.

Infringement generally

28.1 Any act or omission that is contrary to any of the moral rights of the author of a work is, in the absence of consent by the author, an infringement of the moral rights.

Nature of right of integrity

28.2 (1) The author's right to the integrity of a work is infringed only if the work is, to the prejudice of the honour or reputation of the author,

(a) distorted, mutilated or otherwise modified; or

(b) used in association with a product, service, cause or institution.

(2) In the case of a painting, sculpture or engraving, the prejudice referred to in subsection (1) shall be deemed to have occurred as a result of any distortion, mutilation or other modification of the work.

(3) For the purposes of this section,

(a) a change in the location of a work, the physical means by which a work is exposed or the physical structure containing a work, or

(b) steps taken in good faith to restore or preserve the work

shall not, by that act alone, constitute a distortion, mutilation or other modification of the work.

The scope of moral rights include integrity, association, and attribution. But the integrity right begins with a caveat of section 28.2 (see below.) Furthermore, attribution is held under the allowance of "where reasonable."

Moral rights differ from copyright—moral rights cannot be assigned to third party. Even if a copyright was explicitly waived, that is insufficient to claim a waiver of moral rights.

Like the term of copyright, moral rights follow the rule of thumb of life plus 50 years.

The challenge for artists to ensure integrity of their work is that diminishment of honour or reputation is the condition. This is not easy to prove, especially for a young artist with no reputation to speak of.

Source: From "Moral Rights Infringment", *Copyright Act* (R.S.C., 1985, c. C-42), Department of Justice, Government of Canada <http://laws-lois.justice.gc.ca/eng/acts/C-42/page-17.html#h-22>

An often used illustration of moral rights is *Flight Stop* by Michael Snow. The work, composed of 60 fibreglass geese, is installed in Toronto Eaton Centre. When the Centre decorated the geese for its 1982 Christmas season, Snow sought redress through the courts. Although the language of the law then was less supportive of artists than our current *Copyright Act*, Snow was successful and the Centre removed the red ribbons added around the geese's necks. The win was surprising; artists had not enjoyed a high success rate with regard to protecting moral rights (Vaver, 2000, p. 162).

Not every country observes moral rights; notably the United States does not. Instead, in 1990, the *Visual Artists Rights Act* added limited moral rights protection in American copyright law. The protection applies to only certain classes of arts; *i.e.*, a photographic image that exists in single copy only or limited edition prints and sculptures. The United States has openly resisted inclusion of moral rights; such control by the artist could interfere with the full gamut of market potential (Murray & Trosow, 2007, p. 65).

Yet, even without widespread formal recognition in law, a development known as Creative Commons (CC) has, perhaps inadvertently, brought one aspect of moral rights closer to universal acceptance.

Creative Commons

Creative Commons (CC) offers individuals an alternative to the contemporary grant of copyright. A CC licence operates under the principal of "Some rights reserved" with individuals free to distribute their work under conditions of their own choosing (*i.e.*, Is commercial reproduction permitted? Is attribution necessary? Is derivative work permitted? And should the conditions be fostered through the derivative work?) As the operation gained followers, it became evident that attribution was a prominent concern. As a consequence, all CC licenses require attribution (unless the author declares otherwise).

Creative Commons suffers from the same challenge as copyright—that the licence can be abused. However, courts have demonstrated that the licenses are enforceable and individuals may opt for legal redress. (That the courts are inaccessible to the broader population is a separate issue.) The movement continues to grow, spanning 70 countries. With participation emanating from the White House, the World Bank, countless academic repositories, and commercial players, the story is worthy of a book unto itself.

CONCLUDING THOUGHTS

"Responsible Communication" Journalists and Bloggers

In a 2009 decision concerning defamation, the Supreme Court of Canada emphasized the importance of "responsible communication on matters of public interest," gave a broad foundation to "public interest," and offered the defence to journalists and nonjournalists alike. The Court did not focus solely on the truth or falsity of information but also upon the conduct of the writer to uncover the truth. In a manner reminiscent of *CCH Canadian*, Chief Justice Beverley McLachlin prescribed a multifaceted inquiry to assess how such stories are produced (*Grant v. Torstar Corp.*, 2009).

Far beyond the concern of defamation, this bodes well for all Canadians. The essence of fair dealing lies in responsible conduct. That our high court places emphasis upon public interest further supports fair dealing in an exercise of journalism, whether by professional journalist or citizen blogger. News reporting already being a category in fair dealing, what must be followed are attribution and a thoughtful assessment of the included material. Fortunately, Canadian case history offers an illustration of fair dealing, both literally and figuratively speaking.

Prior to *CCH Canadian*, a surprising win for fair dealing concerned the reproduction of an image in a contemporary news story. In *Allen v. Toronto Star* (1997), photographer Jim Allen objected to the reproduction of a cover from *Saturday Night Magazine* that included his photograph of then-MP Sheila Copps. The 1985 cover showed Copps attired in black motor cycle leathers and seated astride a Harley Davidson; the *Toronto Star* story used the cover as a contrast with Copps' more sedate image in 1990. Although Allen won at trial, the *Toronto Star* won on appeal. The higher court indicated that the reproduction of the entire cover was fair dealing as it was germane to the purpose of the article and offered no competitive advantage to *The Star* over the original photograph and publication.

Copyright and the Student/Researcher

Fair dealing is eminently suited to learning activities. Four categories of fair dealing—research, private study, criticism, and review—are likely present on a daily basis. And as citation is a foundational practice for academic endeavor, students and researchers usually meet the attribution requirement without any thought. In terms of the fairness of the dealing with the copyrighted work, application of the *CCH Canadian* framework favours fairness.

It is likely that the inclusion is to serve the purpose of criticism or review, as part of the larger expression of the new creator's own ideas. Whether it is a Grade Ten homework assignment posted to a class website or a doctoral dissertation filed in an institutional repository when the individual has chosen an input element appropriate to his or her message and integrated that element in a new creation, such copying is likely to be fair. In our increasingly visual world, quotation may well encompass visual elements. That does not change the legitimacy of fair dealing, provided that reproducing the element is necessary for the larger purpose of the student's expression.

Teachers play a part in helping students choose the amount and type of material needed. In *CCH Canadian*, the justices expressly stated that incumbent practices were germane to a decision of fair dealing. Thus institutions need not worry about setting boundaries on how much material their students can incorporate into projects—that is a decision shaped according to the long-standing practice called teaching.

Copyright and Fair Dealing: Supporting Creativity, Education, and Innovation

Copyright is usually presented as a means to protect artists and enhance their creative output. It is taken as gospel that by expanding copyright, creative people will do better. But the mechanism of copyright does not guarantee income to any creator. A work has to be desired before it might be transacted. And the outcome of a transaction is not always evenly distributed between creator and publisher, or between domestic industries and international conglomerates, or the homegrown superstar as compared to the homegrown neophyte. Those distinctions have less to do with copyright and more to do with education, training, exposure, bargaining power, sheer luck, and the imprecision of creativity itself. However, the system of copyright can contribute to the underlying processes of creativity and innovation, to the benefit of all individuals and industries. Copyright, together with its limits, allows for better chances of prosperity.

On July 12, 2012, the Supreme Court of Canada released five copyright decisions; the outcomes and timing together signalling that copyright's limits are to be taken seriously. These decisions warrant a chapter; however, for a succinct distillation I turn to Michael Geist:

> First, the cases provide an unequivocal affirmation that copyright exceptions such as fair dealing should be treated as users' rights. ...
>
> Second, ... the court has effectively embedded a technology-neutral principle into the law that will extend far beyond these particular cases, as future litigants will undoubtedly argue that existing exceptions can be applied to new uses of copyright works to ensure technological neutrality.
>
> Third, the court continued its expansion of fair dealing by interpreting it in a broad and liberal manner ... When combined with the government's recently enacted Bill C-11 that adds new consumer exceptions and limits damages, Canadian copyright law has undergone an extensive overhaul over the past few weeks with implications that will take years to sort through (Geist, 2012).

Canada's copyright landscape will continue to change. Individuals, industries, and institutions will leave their mark in one form or another. What is noteworthy about Canada's development of the system of copyright in the new millennium is the discernible trend to better understand the nuances of the rights available to all parties. Copyright's first 300 years of life was entirely about control and expansion; this need not be so for the next three hundred years.

QUESTIONS

1. Copyright is a loosely worded prohibition on copying. Yet creative practices are all about copying—we copy implicitly and explicitly when we engage in our own creative effort. Can we reconcile copyright with creative practices?
2. Creative practices adapt with time: mash-ups and fan fiction are illustrations of that progression. However, alterations of works are unsettling to some. While moral rights include protection for the integrity of a work, again, how can this be reconciled against creative practices? And what of works that are in the public domain? Should their integrity be controlled through any measure of intellectual property?
3. By far, the most pervasive myth about copyright is that it is absolute, whereas, copyright is limited in time and space. How can individuals and institutions set about undoing this myth?

NOTES

1. Unfortunately, this inaccurate view still holds today. The story is more complex; the late 1990s saw upheaval in the music industry for many reasons: (1) CD sales were artificially high in their infancy as consumers purchased repertoire *they already owned* in vinyl album format. (2) The retailing structure of the industry changed itself; dedicated music stores could not compete with the rise of large broad-based consumer outlets. Paradoxically, this meant a narrowing of repertoire available to consumers. (3) There was more competition for entertainment dollars; DVD technology became a consumer item and the phenomenon of gaming was on the rise. (4) Finally, with the new millennium came a general economic upheaval via the bursting of the dotcom bubble. Generally speaking, consumer spending declined as people had less money in their pockets.
2. The publisher, New South Books, offers a sample of the range of comments (Seidman, 2011).
3. History enthusiasts may be interested to know that the language of "property" came via Thomas Jefferson during the antebellum years. Jefferson was acutely conscious of the abuse of consumers that occurred when the Crown awarded monopoly privileges as per European and English custom. "... saying there will be no monopolies lessens the incitement to ingenuity ... but the benefit even of limited monopolies is too doubtful to be opposed to that of their general suppression" (cited in Bell 2002, p. 5). As the fledgling United States established systems to encourage creativity, Jefferson steered away from the language of monopoly and the English connotations that went with it. Instead, he opted to refer to the exclusive right of a patent as a property (Walterscheid, 1994).
4. "Where social utility meets with natural rights is in the belief that creativity itself is valued. Otherwise, the underlying purpose of copyright in either tradi-

tion becomes meaningless, raising the question of why have such laws at all?" (Nair, 2009, p. 30).

5. "Such works do not include only 'literary works' in the sense of literature: they also include written works in the pure and applied sciences, humanities, biography and autobiography, as well as musical and artistic works. They include works by presidents and peasants, heroes and villains, from every corner, in every language and medium" (publicdomain, 2012).
6. Canada's first copyright law, the *Copyright Act* (1921), came into effect in 1924 with a fair dealing clause that allowed "any fair dealing with any work for the purposes of private study, research, criticism, review, or newspaper summary." In the late 20th century, the provisions for criticism, review, and news reporting were encumbered with more formal requirements of citation. In 2012, the categories themselves were expanded to include parody, satire and education.
7. Michael Geist, Canada Research Chair for Internet and E-Commerce Law at the University of Ottawa has written extensively on these matters; see http://www.michaelgeist.ca. Through Access to Information, he obtained some key background material prepared for the ministers involved (Geist, 2011, September 21 & 27).
8. For instance, in 2010, the U.S. Librarian of Congress recently relaxed some of the prohibitions upon circumventing technological protection measures. Included was a measure that directly benefits educational uses of copyrighted materials, the extraction of clips from movies encrypted on DVDs, for the purposes of criticism and review, circumscribed by a requirement of good faith. This expands a previous allowance offered only to film and media studies professors; now all college and university professors, together with film and media studies students, have permission. Creation of documentary films and noncommercial videos is also sheltered (Billington, 2010).

REFERENCES

Allen v. Toronto Star Newspapers Ltd., 36 O.R. 3d 201 (Div. Court 1997).

Bell, T. W. (2002). Indelicate imbalancing in copyright and patent law. In A. Thierer & C. W. Crews, Jr. (Eds.), *Copy fights: The future of intellectual property in the information age* (pp. 1–15). Washington, DC: Cato Institute.

Bettig, R. V. (1996). *Copyrighting culture: The political economy of intellectual property.* Boulder, CO: Westview Press.

Billington, J. (2010). Statement of the Librarian of Congress relating to Section 1201 rulemaking. Retrieved August 23, 2012, from http://www.copyright.gov/1201/2010/Librarian-of-Congress-1201-Statement.html

Bolan, K. (2011, July 12). East Van neon cross at centre of copyright dispute. *Vancouver Sun*. Retrieved August 23, 2012, from http://www.canada.com/vancouversun/news/westcoastnews/story.html?id=92d46b7b-ba8f-41bc-af51-8b49309bdd58

Bosman, J. (2011, January 4). Publisher tinkers with Twain. *The New York Times.* Retrieved August 23, 2012, from http://www.nytimes.com/2011/01/05/books/05huck.html?_r=1

Canada. (2002). *An overview of submissions on the consultation paper on digital copyright issues.* Retrieved August 23, 2012, from http://strategis.ic.gc.ca/eic/site/crp-prda.nsf/eng/rp00842.html

CCH Canadian Ltd. v. Law Society of Upper Canada, 1 S.C.R. 339 (SCC 13 2004)

Copyright Act (1921), 1921 Statutes of Canada (1921, c. C-24).

Copyright Act of Canada, Revised Statutes of Canada (1985 c. C-42).

Digital Millennium Copyright Act (DMCA) Pub. L. No. 105-304, 112 Stat. 2860 (1998).

Documentary Organization of Canada. (2010). *Copyright and fair dealing: Guidelines for documentary filmmakers.* Retrieved August 23, 2012, from http://docorg.ca/sites/docorg.ca/files/DOC-FairDealing-EN-v2-web.pdf

Duke University. (n.d.) *Center for the study of the public domain.* Retrieved August 23, 2012, from http://www.law.duke.edu/cspd/

Geist, M. (2010). The case for flexibility in implementing the WIPO internet treaties: An examination of the anti-circumvention requirements. In M. Geist (ed.), *From "radical extremism" to "balanced copyright": Canadian copyright and the digital agenda* (pp. 204–246). Toronto: Irwin Law.

———. (2011, September 21). *Behind the scenes of Bill C-32: The complete ministerial Q&A.* Retrieved August 23, 2012, from http://www.michaelgeist.ca/content/view/6017/125/

———. (2011, September 27). *Behind the scenes of Bill C-32: Govt's clause by clause analysis raises constitutional questions.* Retrieved August 23, 2012, from http://www.michaelgeist.ca/content/view/6026 /125

———. (2012, July 20). Supreme Court shakes the foundations of Canadian copyright law. Retrieved August 24, 2012, http://www.michaelgeist.ca/content/view/6596/135

Grant v. Torstar Corp 3 S.C.R. 640 (SCC 61 2009)

Litman, J. (1990). The public domain. *Emory Law Journal, 39*, 965–1023.

———. (2001). *Digital copyright: Protecting intellectual property on the internet.* Amherst, NY: Prometheus Books.

Murray, L. & Trosow, S. (2007). *Canadian copyright: A citizen's guide.* Toronto: Between the Lines.

Nair, M. (2009). Copyright and ethics—An Innisian exploration. *Global Media Journal—Canadian Edition, 2*(1), 23–39.

———. (2010). Fair dealing at a crossroads. In M. Geist (ed.), *From "radical extremism" to "balanced copyright": Canadian copyright and the digital agenda* (pp. 90–120). Toronto: Irwin Law.

O'Connell, M. (2012, January 11). Has James Joyce been set free? *The New Yorker.* Retrieved from http://www.newyorker.com/online/blogs/books/2012/01/james-joyce-publicdomain.html

Publicdomain. (2012, January 1) Public Domain Day 2012. *publicdomain*. Retrieved August 23, 2012, from http://publicdomain.xanga.com/757968422/public-domain-day-2012

Rans, M. (2012, March 9). Legislative committee on Bill C-11: Text of statement. *Artists Legal Outreach*. Retrieved August 23, 2012, from http://artistslegaloutreach.ca/blog/legislative-committee-bill-c-11text-statement

Reynolds, G. (2010). Towards a right to engage in a fair transformative use. In M. Geist (Ed.), *From "radical extremism" to "balanced copyright": Canadian copyright and the digital agenda* (pp. 395–422). Toronto: Irwin Law.

Seidman, B. (2010). *Conversations on New South's edition of Mark Twain's Tom Sawyer and Huckleberry Finn*. Retrieved August 23, 2012, from http://www.newsouthbooks.com/pages/2011/01/10/conversations-on-newsouths-edition-of-mark-twains-tom-sawyer-and-huckleberry-finn/

17 U.S.C. § 107 (2000 & Supp. IV 2004). Retrieved August 23, 2012, from http://www.law.cornell.edu/uscode/html/uscode17/usc_sec_17_00000107----000-.html

Snow v. Eaton Centre Ltd., 70 C.P.R. 2d 105 (Ontario High Court of Justice 1982).

Vaver, D. (2000). *Copyright law*. Toronto, ON: Irwin Law.

Walterscheid, E.C. (1994). To promote the progress of science and the useful arts: The background and origin of the intellectual property clause of the United States Constitution. *Journal of Intellectual Property Law, 2*. Retrieved from http://www.lawsch.uga.edu/jipl/vol2/waltersc.html

World Intellectual Property Organization (1981). *WIPO glossary of terms of the law of copyright and neighboring rights* (Vol. 827). Geneva: World Intellectual Property Organization.

Media Diversity

Introduction

Leslie Regan Shade
University of Toronto

This final section of *Mediascapes* examines a range of initiatives and issues that focus on media diversity. Media diversity is important so that a diverse Canadian citizenry can effectively communicate, contest existing communicative regimes, and shape policy in the public interest. Chapters discuss the creation of alternative, independent, community and Aboriginal communication mediascapes (Skinner); the development and continuous technological innovation of First Peoples' mediascapes (Roth); various discourses of race and representation in Canadian news media and the politics of racialization (Hirji); and the importance of studying children's media cultures (Coulter).

David Skinner provides an historical and contemporary overview of independent, alternative, and community media in Canada and Quebec, looking at the many definitional dilemmas posed by these myriad nonprofit mediascapes, their varied organizational structures, the role of public policymaking in ensuring the sustainability of commercial-free media in Canada, and the new challenges and opportunities created by digitization. From the early underground newspapers in the 1960s to the resiliency of campus community radio and the student press, to the creation of independent media centres (IndyMedia) after the 1999 antiglobalization demonstrations in Seattle, to new forms of social and mobile media, independent and alternative media continue to strive to allow access to a plurality of voices concerned with local community and cultural issues and events as well as social justice matters at local and global levels, and to foster news and points of view that diverge from mainstream media. However, sustainability for independent and alternative media is problematic on many levels, as funding can be sporadic, and organizations are highly dependent on volunteer labour. Another challenge for Canadian independent and alternative media is ensuring that citizens are aware of these many resources for their information and communication needs.

Lorna Roth provides a panoramic mapping of First Peoples' various mediascapes from the 1960s to now, looking at the particular technologies that motivated the creation of indigenous media and the development of Canadian media policy to support Aboriginal media, from television to social media. As she aptly demonstrates,

Aboriginal people wanted not only access to southern media, but also to create their own media that could be reflective of their issues, their livelihoods, their culture, and their language. Autonomy was key to developing vibrant media; film training projects initiated by the National Film Board's Challenge for Change program kickstarted events; in the 1970s, deployment of the satellite Anik B in the North facilitated the creation of the Inuit Broadcasting Corporation; in the 1980s, Native Communication Societies led to the CRTC Northern Broadcasting Policy, providing not only recognition but also financial support for the creation of programs in First Peoples' native languages. In the 1990s, the *Broadcasting Act* recognized access rights for Aboriginal peoples, and distribution was tackled with Television Northern Canada and the development of a nationwide television network, the Aboriginal Peoples Television Network (APTN). Recent initiatives include successful forays into Inuktitut television production, Isuma (the first independent Inuit production studio in Canada), and innovative content creation on the internet using social media. Roth remarks that youth voices will be important to foster, as they bridge their contemporary culture with the needs and desires of their communities to sustain the knowledge, language, and traditions of their elders.

How Canadian mainstream media portray minority groups, and how the discourse of race and representation is politicized is the subject of Faiza Hirji's chapter. As she illustrates through several case studies regarding immigration, accommodation, and multiculturalism, media discourses reflect questions of power, policy, and representation. As a methodology, critical discourse analysis is one way to analyze the various levels of discursive practices and rhetorical strategies. Another is to look at the political economy of the media itself. Media concentration has not created more diversity in terms of ownership structures; in fact, consolidation has created a more entrenched structure. Competition among media corporations has also made for a less diverse labour force of journalists, with women and ethnic minorities still vastly underrepresented today. Hirji concludes that in order to demand more complex and nuanced accounts of diversity and racialized discourse in the media, educating the public to be critical and savvy consumers is a primary objective.

The increasing commercialization of the children's media landscape is the topic of Natalie Coulter's chapter. Reflecting on her childhood in suburban Canada during the 1980s, she observes how her generation was, to date, the most targeted demographic, due to the deregulation of the U.S. children's advertising industry by neoliberal policies promulgated by then President Ronald Reagan. Integrated marketing through a plethora of media–toy tie-ins, cross licensing, cross-media merchandising, and the introduction of specialty children's cable channels has become the norm, leading some to decry the "carpet-bombing" of children's mediascapes. That children's "consumer power" has reached unprecedented heights in recent years has not gone unnoticed by savvy marketers; the value of the children's cultural marketplace is modestly estimated to be in the billions of dollars. As Coulter documents, children's culture is increasingly dominated and defined by market interests, as the tri-opoly of advertisers, children's media industries, and other producers of consumer goods clamor to capture the hearts, minds, and pocketbooks of this profitable demographic. This also led to the gendering of children's media products, with the tween and girls' market lucrative niches. In Canada there have been notable quality children's programs that have garnered rave reviews and syndication inside and outside Canada; the *Degrassi* franchise is a prime example. But as Coulter points out, there is a scarcity of research to date on the Canadian children's entertainment industry.

17

MEDIA ON THE MARGINS? ALTERNATIVE MEDIA IN CANADA

David Skinner
York University

Alternative media provide a range of perspectives and modes of communication that are not readily available through the profit-driven media that dominate the Canadian mediascape. They include both traditional media forms—newspapers, magazines, television, radio, film—and an increasing range of Web-based media. Some people also include street theatre, murals, postering, music, zines, newsletters, blogs, and culture jamming. However, because the term "alternative media" poses the question "alternative to what?" the field is notoriously difficult to define. Should it be confined to only radical or underground media? Should it include media that operate in languages other than English or French? Should it encompass media directed toward specific ethnic and cultural groups? Should only nonprofit media be considered? At the same time, some argue that because the term "alternative" sets up a dichotomy between "mainstream" and "alternative" forms of media, it serves to help marginalize the latter and shouldn't be used at all (Hamilton, 2008; Clark & Van Slyke, 2006).

There are no easy answers to these questions and concerns. But trying to work through them, this chapter considers some definitions of alternative media, compares and contrasts some of the features of alternative media with those of their corporate cousins, and goes on to look at the history and structure of several different types of alternative media in Canada.

Communication researchers have approached the problem of defining the field of alternative media from several directions. For instance, John Downing (2000, pp. v–xi), one of the research pioneers in this area, limits his focus to what he calls "**radical alternative media,**" that is, media that explicitly challenge dominant institutions, ideas, or values. As he points out, these media "expand the range of information, reflection, and exchange from the often narrow hegemonic limits of mainstream media discourse" (p. 44). They also "often have a close relationship with an ongoing social movement" (p. 44), and, if these "media have one thing in common, it is that they break somebody's rules, although rarely all of them in every respect" (p. xi).

Building on Downing's work, Clemencia Rodriguez (2001) casts her net a little more widely. For Rodriguez, the term "alternative media" traps us in a binary whereby it appears that there are only two types of media: "mainstream (or corporate) media and their alternative, that is, alternative media" (p. 20). Rather than divide media into two camps, she argues that we should instead focus on media that are actively involved in "intervening and transforming the established mediascape" and thereby working to empower the communities with which they are involved. She calls these "citizen's media" and uses that term to describe a broad range of media that are all, to some degree, involved in cultural politics and work to transform established ways of seeing and operating in the world.

While echoing both Downing's and Rodriguez's concerns with the socially transformative elements of media, Chris Atton (2002) retains the term "alternative media" but elaborates on another dimension: organizational structure. As he states, alternative media "typically go beyond simply providing a platform for radical or alternative points of view [to] emphasize the organization of media to enable wider social participation in their creation, production and dissemination than is possible with mass media" (p. 25). He sees this restructuring as enabling alternative media both to provide news and information that are more directly relevant to the communities they serve and to play a communicative role that is more directly responsive to the needs and interests of those communities.

In an effort to offer a frame of reference that "involves no judgments about the empowering effects of the media practices analyzed," Nick Couldry and James Curran (2003, p. 7) define alternative media as "media production that challenges, at least implicitly, actual concentrations of media power." From this point of view, the key feature of media is the "power to represent the reality of others." They argue that the way in which the media portray social groups and events "is an increasingly significant theme of social conflict" and, consequently, the role of alternative media in providing alternative ways of seeing these groups and events is of increasing importance (p. 7).

Examples of what they mean can be found by comparing the ways the ways corporate and alternative media have covered things such as climate change (Gunster, 2011), the early days of the Occupy Movement (Orlowski, 2011), or the U.S. invasion of Iraq (Moyers, 2008).

Working from a perspective that blends those put forward by Rodriguez and Couldry and Curran but focused particularly on what she calls "new media"—that is media that are hybrid, networked, and interactive—Leah Lievrouw (2011, p. 19) offers that alternative media "challenge or alter dominant, expected, or accepted ways of doing society, culture and politics." With this accent on social practices that challenge dominant ways of thinking and doing things, she goes on to describe five different "genres" of "new media projects: *culture jamming*, *alternative computing*, *participatory journalism*, *mediated mobilization*, and *commons knowledge*" (Lievrouw, 2011, p. 19 [italics in original]).

So what are we to glean from these different definitions?

First, they provide important insight into the role alternative media play in the promotion of public dialogue, the exchange of ideas, and the promotion of social action. They share the concern that media are a key means for how we come to understand the world and our place within it and that, in particular, alternative media are key means of both building community and animating social change. As Downing (2000, pp. 43–45) puts it, alternative media are agents of "developmental power."

Second, and perhaps more importantly, these definitions are all based on a concern that the dominant corporate media do not adequately represent the interests of all members of society. This is not to say that corporate media do not sometimes contain radical perspectives or opinions. However the concern is that, in many ways, they tend to support dominant ideas and patterns of social behaviour over others. Alternative media then, represent the perspectives of the socially, politically and culturally excluded (c.f. Lievrouw, 2011; Coyer et al., 2007). Consequently, before more closely considering examples of alternative media, it is useful to review some of the ways in which the range of perspectives contained in corporate media is constrained.

WHY ALTERNATIVE MEDIA?

While it would generally be a mistake to say that journalists, editors, or the media outlets where they work conspire with big business to exclude particular ideas or perspectives, there is ample evidence of gaps and omissions in the news offered by large, profit-driven media corporations. For instance, NewsWatch Canada has documented the media's "apparent unwillingness or inability to adequately cover" issues in the areas of labour, social inequality, and corporate power, as well as gaps in coverage around issues such as "environmental degradation as a systemic and ongoing problem," "human rights abuses by Canada's 'friends,'" and "gender-related stereotypes" (Hackett and Gruneau, 2000, p. 166). Other studies illustrate problems in the way the media cover issues and events concerning poverty, gender, race, ethnicity, and Aboriginal peoples (Jiwani & Young, 2006; Roth, 2005; Alia, 1999).

In both traditional and internet-based media, these problems stem from a number of complex factors. For instance, the push to wring increasing profits from Canada's major media outlets has driven their ownership into fewer and fewer hands. Such concentration of ownership can lead to a narrowing of perspectives in at least two ways: (a) owners may try to use the same news, columnists, and other information products in as many of their media outlets as possible (e.g., in newspapers, on the Web, TV, radio, etc.); and (b) owners may impose common editorial policies on the media outlets under their control, which, in turn, leads to similar perspectives or points of view in those products (cf. Senate of Canada, 2006; Hackett and Gruneau, 2000).

Other problems with corporate media can be traced to the fact that "news and commentary ... are shaped by a consumerist orientation" and the drive to capture audiences with particular demographic qualities (Hackett, Pinet, and Ruggles, 1992, p. 14). For instance, large portions of the newspaper such as the "Home," Lifestyles," and "Automotive" sections—are devoted to showcasing and reviewing consumer products, and throughout the paper, most of the pages are laid out so that the eye lands first on the advertising and not the news. Information presented by corporate media on television and on the Web suffers similar problems, often focusing on celebrities, entertainment news, and product reviews. Even new media sites such as Google and Facebook work to focus their users' attention on advertising tailored to what those corporations perceive as their interests and desires (Marlow, 2012).

The narrative form of news stories is also shaped by economic concerns. For instance, most hard news is written in the "inverted pyramid style," where the story has no particular conclusion and the facts are laid out in what the author perceives is a descending order of importance (Hackett et al., 1992, p. 14). This way the story can be easily edited to fit the "news hole"—the space allotted to the news after the ads have been placed on the newspaper or Web page. Moreover, whether presented in newspapers or on television, radio, or the internet, news stories often take the perspective of the consumer, analyzing conflicts and events such as labour strife, tax increases, and rising oil prices in terms of their impact on the wallets of readers and audience members, rather than their larger impact on social justice, equality, and the environment. Meanwhile, news and opinions that are not of direct import to the target audience, or information and ideas that might prove too controversial or offensive to that group, may be left out (cf. Hackett and Gruneau, 2000, pp. 63–64).

The codes and practices of professional journalism can also often lead to the marginalization of particular voices and perspectives. Source selection, news values (that is, the kinds of people and events that qualify as news), and story form—all of these professional choices affect the diversity of perspectives and ideas found in the news. For instance, when developing their stories, journalists seek the opinions and perspectives of official sources—that is, politicians, business people, and community leaders (Hackett and Zhao, 1996, p. 50, 1998). Consequently, within news narratives the significance of events is often judged and framed by "those in charge," and news stories tend to reinforce dominant ideas and existing relations of social power. By the same token, stories are often written from an "objective" point of view, seemingly taking no particular side but in fact representing only a narrow range of perspectives. News that doesn't meet with professional and institutional standards often isn't published (White Eye, 1996). While journalists may be aware of the constraints professional values impose upon the products they produce, pressures on time and resources often make such choices difficult to avoid.

Alternative media generally follow a different logic.

Alternative media are guided by a purpose or mandate other than profit, such as providing a range of ideas and opinions that are not readily available in the corporate press or serving the needs of a particular group or community that is poorly served by commercial media outlets. They are generally independently owned, and usually operated on a not-for-profit or cooperative basis. In some instances, they do not accept advertising, and, when they do, the income it provides is seen as secondary to serving specific community or social purposes.

While corporate media are structured to promote consumption of the products they advertise, alternative media are more about "mobilizing" their audiences to other than economic ends. It is because alternative media often act to forward and champion the interests of the communities they serve rather than sell their audiences products that writers such as Rodriguez argue that alternative media are socially "empowering." Moreover, to the extent that these media are part of a cultural milieu that offers a place in which "experiences, critiques, and alternatives" to dominant social patterns and relationships might be developed, they can also be seen as helping animate autonomous or alternative "public spheres"—that is, communities in which traditions, ideas, and values that differ from the dominant culture might develop and flourish (Downing, 2000, pp. 29–30). This points to a possible distinction between "radical alternative media," which look to be active agents of social change, and alternative "community media," which either explicitly or implicitly challenge dominant ideas and values but do not necessarily advocate for change. Because both these types of media work to challenge concentrations of media power, for our purposes they will both be considered alternative media.

In terms of structure, alternative media sometimes replicate the hierarchy of "the mainstream press, with an owner and editor overseeing reporters, staff writers and technical production staff" (Atton, 2003, p. 42). However, in an effort to decentralize organizational power and create an inclusive production process, they also often reject "hierarchical methods of doing business" and instead operate collectively, sharing tasks and roles among the people working there (Atton, 2003, p. 43).

Out of a concern for the ways in which some of the values of "professional" journalism tend to marginalize and silence particular perspectives, some alternative media outlets put on workshops to educate people in how to craft their own stories. The point here is to try and establish a "horizontal" relationship between writers and readers, that is, a situation where there is as little filtering of news and information as possible.

Based upon this short discussion, we can see that alternative media work to challenge concentrations of media power, and particularly corporate media, in several ways. Rather than tailor content, organizational structure, and production practices to maximize return on investment, alternative media foreground specific social issues and values. In terms of organizational structure, they often purposefully shun traditional hierarchical models of organization to facilitate as much input into production as possible. And in terms of production, in order to countermand the tendency to have professional values dictate the subjects, structure, and sources of content, they often seek participation and contributions from members of the communities they serve rather than rely on professional journalists.

But difference from corporate media has its price. Because alternative media are guided by purposes other than profit, they often lack economic stability. Because of their small size and reach they have few economies of scale, and staff and contributors often work for little or no pay (Cohen, 2012). The size and demographics of their audiences are often unknown, making advertising and subscription sales difficult. And even when audience information is available and audience demographics amenable to advertising sales, the small size of their audiences and/or ideological concerns over the impact of advertising revenue on content often mitigate against this form of financing. Moreover, there is little in the way of government support to help promote the development of these kinds of organizations, and some of the infrastructure that did exist has been eroded over the last decade.

ALTERNATIVE MEDIA THEN AND NOW

Publishing

While the term "underground newspaper" may now seem like an anachronism, it had real currency in the heat of the protests and social upheaval that characterized the 1960s and early 1970s. In 1969, 22 charges were laid against Vancouver's *Georgia Straight* and its employees. They ranged from libel, to publishing obscene material, to "counseling another person to commit an indictable offense," which stemmed from publication of an article on how to grow marijuana (Sullivan, 1970, pp. 280–283). Across the country both producers and vendors of underground papers were often harassed by police.

Content of these papers varied, but recalling Downing's dictum, they all had "one thing in common" in that they broke "somebody's rules." While some papers' key themes were sex, drugs, and rock and roll, they were also on the edge of shifting cultural politics and carried news and opinion pieces on the antiwar movement, Aboriginal rights, the women's movement, justice for workers, and environmental and antinuclear issues (Verzuh, 1986). Others were more focused in their concerns. For instance, Toronto's *Body Politic* addressed the concerns of the gay movement. Vancouver's *Kinesis*; Toronto's *Broadside*; and Halifax's *Pandora* focused on feminist concerns (Freeman, 2012); and the politics of Quebec nationalism was a key issue for papers in that province (Raboy, 1984).

While most of these papers accepted advertising, commercial imperatives did not rule the production process. As for organizational form, some operated as collectives, while others had more traditional hierarchical structures (Ladner, 1986; Lipton, 1980). Financing was a problem for almost all of them.

By the mid-1980s, shifting social currents sank most of these papers, and a new genre of glossy, business-savvy "news and entertainment" weeklies such as Toronto's *Now*, the *Montreal Mirror*, and a revamped *Georgia Straight* had taken their place. While, at times, these papers still engage with radical politics, their focus is generally on the bottom line. As Dan McLeod, editor of the *Georgia Straight* puts it, "We haven't survived with our ideals and principles intact" (Verzuh, 1986, p. 3).

However, set between the principles of community service and the imperatives of the marketplace, a broad range of alternative newspapers and magazines continue to be published across the country. Although too numerous to enumerate here, they range from papers focused on local or regional politics, to gay and lesbian papers, to publications focused on feminist and environmental concerns. Similarly, there are also a small number of magazines such as *This Magazine*, *Canadian Dimension*, and

Briar Patch that carry on the progressive political tradition of alternative newspapers. *Megaphone*, a magazine sold on the streets of Vancouver by low-income and homeless vendors, strives "to provide a voice and an economic opportunity for homeless and low-income people while building grassroots support to end poverty" (Megaphone, n/d). The internet has given rise to a range of publications with similar content to what are sometimes called these "legacy" media and, at the same time, many of these long established publications are making growing use of the internet and websites to develop audiences. Still, financial difficulties continue to haunt them.

In Quebec, the alternative press has historically been better funded and organized than in the rest of the country. For over 20 years the Quebec government has offered varying degrees of support to l'Association des médias écrits communautaires (AMECQ), an association representing 87 not-for-profit newspapers and magazines that provides a range of support services and training to its members. To be a member of AMECQ, publications must be collectively owned and democratically managed. Unlike other provinces, the Quebec provincial government has several programs to support this kind of publication, including a 1995 guarantee that it will spend 4 percent of its advertising budget with its members. However, in 2011 provincial funding became the target of budget cuts and AMECQ claims the 4 percent target has never been reached (AMECQ 2011). Moreover, publications found only online are not eligible for government programs. While only a few of AMECQ's members actively advocate for social change, insofar as they provide perspectives on community and community relationships not available in the corporate press, they are to a degree "alternative" publications.

The Student Press

The 1960s were a key turning point for the student press in Canada as students across the country became engaged with the social activism that characterized that time. Out of a concern for the biases inherent in corporate journalism, many papers began to shun both the idea of objectivity in news reporting and the use of the inverted-pyramid style of news writing. Over the years, however, experiments with alternative story forms and writing styles met with mixed results, and the activist politics of the student press have themselves been the subject of debate.

An important organization in the historical development of the student press is the Canadian University Press (CUP). Established in 1938, CUP is a nonprofit cooperative news-gathering organization with over 70 member papers. Its 1977 Statement of Principles declares that "the major role of the student press is to act as an agent of social change," that it should "support [other] groups serving as agents of social change," and that "the student press must use its freedom from commercial and other controls to ensure that all it does is consistent with its major role and to examine issues which other media avoid" (Canadian University Press, 1977). To encourage diversity in perspectives in news, CUP has also encouraged its members to seek "alternative" rather than "official" news sources, and until recently their constitution required that member papers be "democratically run," meaning that all members of a newspaper's staff could share in business and editorial decisions. Today CUP offers its members a number of services including a national news wire that provides stories from across the country, access to a national advertising agency, and business and legal advice (CUP, n/d).

Broadcasting

Under the terms of the 1991 *Broadcasting Act*, the Canadian Radio-television and Telecommunications Commission (CRTC) maintains a range of policies in the areas of community, student, ethnic, and Aboriginal broadcasting that provides the framework for many small radio and television operations. To varying degrees, these outlets can be seen as alternatives to commercial broadcasters.

Television

Inspired by the social movements of the time, the National Film Board launched *Challenge for Change* in the late 1960s. The program was designed to create film and videos that would help animate positive social change, particularly for disadvantaged social groups. It provided an example of how ordinary people might use film and television to develop and strengthen their communities, and inspired people across North America to get involved in video production (Halleck, 2002, pp. 146–147).

Responding to people who wanted to take up video as a means of community development, the CRTC encouraged cable companies to provide a community channel where these types of productions might be aired and, in 1975, the CRTC made the provision of a community channel—complete with a small studio and equipment—a condition of licence for most cable operators. In 2010, there were 120 community channels operating in Canada (CRTC, 2011. But as Goldberg (1990, p. 18) points out, outside Quebec "control over programming decisions, productions, and equipment use was gradually shift[ed] out of the hands of community members and into the hands of the cable licensee and its employees hired to 'run' the community station." This ownership structure made it particularly difficult for community groups to gain access to the channel and "programming and the types of users ... [became] more conventional." This situation was exacerbated in 1997 when the CRTC ruled that cable companies would no longer be required to fund a community channel.

Recognizing that ongoing concentration of ownership has resulted in "reduced representation of local voices," the CRTC announced a new community media policy in 2002 (CRTC, 2010). That policy was designed to increase public involvement and reinvigorate the community channel as a means of public expression. While it did result in the creation of a few independent community stations, by and large control over community television—in terms of both production and distribution—generally remained in the hands of large cable companies and other program distributors. In turn, these corporations generally have a choice to either put funding into a community channel or a program production fund for commercial television. The financial incentives point them toward the latter. There were also numerous complaints that despite the new policy large cable companies cut back on community programming and moved to create program formats that mimicked those of commercial broadcasters (Lithgow, 2012; Lederman, 2008; Vallantin, 2008; Canada, 2003, pp. 337–341).

In April 2010 the CRTC held a review of the 2002 policy and a new community television policy was announced in August of that year (CRTC, 2010). Leading up to that review, a new organization—the Canadian Association of Community Television Users and Stations (CACTUS)—was formed to represent the interests of the different groups using cable-owned community channels and the handful of independent community stations that developed out of the 2002 policy. During the hearings CACTUS presented a new model for community broadcasting. This plan would have largely taken control out of the hands of cable companies and set community broadcasting on new independent footing. The centrepiece of the plan was an independent community media fund to seed the development new "multi-platform community-access production and distribution centres" across the country (Edwards, 2010). While this plan garnered strong public support at the hearings, in the end the CRTC left control of community channels in the hands of cable companies, and while some minor changes were made to the 2002 policy, the concerns voiced by intervenors at the hearings went largely unaddressed (Lithgow, 2012; Edwards, n/d).

In Quebec, community television broadcasting is structured differently than in the rest of the country. While in some instances the community channel is operated and managed by cable companies, in others, programming the channel is the responsibility of nonprofit, community-based associations. There are about 50 such associations in Quebec, 44 of which are represented by the Fédération des télévisions communautaires autonomes du Québec (FEDETVC). The cable operator provides associations with access to the channel but has little or no control over programming. Each association is administered by a council that is elected annually by the association's members, and membership is made up of people and groups who use the channel as well as members of the local community. The associations provide training, and production is undertaken by a combination of employees and volunteers. They are financed by a combination of advertising, bingo revenues, fundraising and membership campaigns, and government funding.

Programming varies but is generally focused to cast light on events and issues of local concern. While for the most part it is not "radical," it puts the power of representation in local hands and, in that way, challenges the power of nationally and regionally focused corporate media. With the CRTC's 1997 decision, some associations complained that cable companies cut back on their access to the community channel and some had their access to the channel cut off altogether (FEDETVC, n.d.).

New technologies have also presented challenges to community television, as satellite broadcasters are not required to carry a community channel. Regulations also limit the community channels' access to advertising revenue. Perhaps the best hope for the future of community television in Canada is the development of non-profit community-based television associations—something similar to the Quebec model—or independent community media centres like those proposed by CACTUS coupled with reliable sources of income and guaranteed access to the basic program packages offered by cable, satellite, and other distributors.

Community Radio

The goal of community radio is to be a "participatory" mode of communication that works to "respond to the priorities set by the community, to facilitate their discussion, to reinforce them, and to challenge them" (Girard, 1992, p. 3). Toward this end, the CRTC defines a "community radio station" as a station that is "owned and controlled by a not-for-profit organization, the structure of which provides for membership, management and programming primarily by members of the community at large" (CRTC, 2000). In 2010 there were 117 community stations operating in Canada (CRTC, 2011). Licensees are expected to help promote community access by informing the public of opportunities for participation and providing training to those who wish to participate. Outside Quebec, stations have one or two generally part-time paid staff members but are programmed by volunteers. Stations raise funds through a variety of means including membership fees, fundraising drives, and advertising. Regulations generally impose much stronger limits on advertising by community stations than commercial stations, particularly in urban centres.

Not all community radio stations operate in the same manner. Delivering programming in seven languages to the neighbourhood of Quartier St-Louis in downtown Montreal, Radio Centre-Ville's statement of principles declares that its "programming will, first and foremost, be oriented towards promoting the interests of low income residents of our area" (Radio Centre-Ville, n.d.). Vancouver's CFRO tends to be more radical in focus. As its mandate states, "We provide news and perspectives that are not otherwise accessible—information that is not covered by the conventional media or perspectives that challenge mainstream media coverage" (Vancouver Co-operative Radio, n.d.). More rural stations, like CHMM in Mackenzie—a town of about 5,000 people in the interior of British Columbia—take a more centrist approach in their efforts to build community by providing opportunities for high-school students, promoting tourism, and helping local businesses reach potential customers via reasonably priced radio advertising (c.f. http://www.chmm.ca).

Community stations based on university campuses are classified in regulation as another form of community radio. In 2010, there were 41 of these stations operating in Canada. Like their community station cousins, campus community stations carry a range of programming and their political affiliations can vary.

A number of both community and campus-based community stations are members of the National Campus and Community Radio Association/Association nationale des radios étudiantes et communautaires (NCRA/ANREC). Founded in 1981, the NCRA represents 82 stations across the country and works with government and related industry groups on issues such as licensing, regulatory fairness, and copyright. The NCRA defines community radio as "community-owned, democratically-governed, non-share not-for-profit corporations ... [that] are structurally bound to the communities that they serve" (NCRA, n.d.). The organization also has a Statement of Principles that recognizes "that mainstream media fails to recognize or in many instances reinforces social and economic inequities that oppress women and minority groups of our society" and commits members to "providing alternative radio to an audience that is recognized as being diverse in ethnicity, culture, gender, sexual orientation, age, and physical and mental ability." The NCRA also distributes *Groundwire*, a community radio sector news program that is produced by NCRA member stations and shared among NCRA members and other independent media sites (Groundwire, n.d.).

Like community television, community radio is somewhat better organized and has played a larger political role in Quebec than in the rest of the country. It also enjoys some support from the Quebec government. The Association des radiodiffuseurs communautaires du Québec (ARCQ) has 35 member stations in 17 regions of the province. Each station is managed by a board of citizen volunteers and, together, these stations have 226 employees, 1,561 volunteers, and 22,572 members. The stations attract about 500,000 listeners over the age of 18 each week. Fifty-three percent of the revenue of these stations comes from advertising, 21 percent from government, and 26 percent from community contributions (ARCQ, n.d.).

In 2007 Canada's largest community radio associations founded the Community Radio Fund of Canada/Fonds canadien de la radio communautaire (CRFC), an independent not-for-profit funding organization focused on the community radio sector. Seeded by a $1.4 million commitment by Astral media as part of an ownership transfer community benefits package, it has continued to benefit from transfers of corporate ownership in the broadcasting sector. The purpose of the fund is to "facilitate the development of high quality and accessible community-oriented and not-for-profit audio programming and related services for all Canadians" (CRFC/FCRC, n.d.) Funds from the CRFC are available to community stations across the country to bolster programming and other services they deliver. While the CFRC is bringing an important and very much needed source of revenue to community radio in Canada, its funding is largely derived from the proceeds of transfers of ownership in the corporate sector. Not only are such proceeds dependent upon the idea that the new ownership arrangements will be profitable, but also under current regulations who or what organizations benefit from such largesse is left up to the corporation undertaking the purchase. Hence this is a fickle and undependable funding mechanism, not well suited to the long-term stability or growth of this sector.

Aboriginal Media

Canada's First Peoples have long existed on the margins of the media system (Bredin, 2012; Roth, 2005; Alia, 1999). But poor treatment by the established press has not been the only media-related problem. Particularly in the North, many Aboriginal people live in small, remote settlements, making communication within their communities difficult. In the 1970s and 1980s a number of efforts were made to address these problems.

Starting in 1970, federal support through the Secretary of State's Native Communication Program helped fuel the development of Aboriginal newspapers. These papers offered a wide range of news and information particularly relevant to the communities they served, such as debates over constitutional and self-government issues, and education and health concerns. But budget cuts in 1990 hit these publications hard, and, by 2000, only 5 of the 12 newspapers that had been funded by the program survived (Molnar and Meadows, 2001, pp. 154–157). Today there are numerous Aboriginal newspapers and magazines serving national, regional, and local audiences (cf. AMMSA, n/d; Canada—Aboriginal Canada Portal, n/d.).

In 1983 the federal government created the Northern Native Broadcast Access Program (NNBAP) to help fund the production and distribution of Aboriginal television and radio programming in the north. Radio was a particularly welcome addition to isolated communities. As Mohr (1992, p. 36) points out, "Programmes focus on international, national, and regional news, culture and traditions, children and youth, and important issues such as native self government, the education system and the extremely high suicide rate among their young. Weather, birthdays, and sports (hockey is played with a passion in the North) are not forgotten." Programming in Aboriginal languages encourages their use and survival. In 2005 NNBAP was folded into the Aboriginal Peoples Program (APP)—a larger policy package designed to support Aboriginal culture and language. Today, one program, Northern Aboriginal Broadcasting covers all Aboriginal broadcasting north of the 55th parallel, which demarcates Canada's north for policy purposes (Canada—Aboriginal Canada Portal n.d.). In 1999 Aboriginal broadcasters were given the opportunity to share their stories with all of Canada with the launch of the Aboriginal Peoples Television Network (APTN). Carried on all program distributors, today APTN reaches over 10 million Canadian households and is in part financed by a small mandatory subscription fee. Its network links both large metropolitan centres in Canada's south and small northern communities. Eighty percent of APTN programming is Canadian in origin, and it is broadcast in English, French, and a variety of Aboriginal languages.

While the wide range of Aboriginal media outlets operating in Canada today are generally not overtly political, through serving and developing the interests of Aboriginal peoples, they operate as agents of cultural power and provide both Aboriginal people and the public at large alternative perspectives on Aboriginal communities.

The Internet

The internet has changed the face of media, but its promise of myriad sources of news and information has not been fulfilled. Producing quality content is costly and time consuming, and access to the Web is still a problem for many people, particularly those outside urban centres. Still, it is a growing source of innovative alternative media.

One of the first and most innovative alternative media sites on the Web were Independent Media Centers (IMCs) or Indymedia. The first IMC was set up in Seattle in 1999 to offer a counterpoint to corporate media reports of the protests at the World Trade Organization meetings (Atton, 2007). Utilizing streaming technologies, the IMC's website provided real-time distribution of reports from the frontlines of the protest, reports that often contradicted those issued by corporate media. During the protest, the IMC's website received an estimated 1.5 million hits, and, by the time the WTO meetings drew to a close, the anticorporate globalization movement had established a new media voice.

The success of the IMC in countering corporate media quickly led to a network of centres being established around the world. Generally operated by volunteers and run as collectives, by July 2004 there were 12 centres listed as operating in Canada. Some provided coverage and support for protests against corporate globalization; others focused on more local concerns (Skinner et al., 2010).

Perhaps the key feature of the Indymedia project was the principle of **open publishing (OP)**, which allowed anyone with access to the Web to instantly publish work on a globally accessible website using open-source software. IMC websites were touted as a kind of information commons and encouraged people "to become the media" by posting their articles, videos, audio clips, and other work directly to their websites. The point was to have as few editorial decisions as possible between the content creator and the readers or viewers and thereby create a "horizontal" relationship between them.

While some IMCs continue to operate, there is very little activity on Canadian IMC websites. Dependence on volunteer labour and commitment to open publishing eventually led to volunteer exhaustion, as a small number of dedicated citizen journalists struggled to keep their sites free of racist posts and spam while, at the same time, trying to find the time and energy to report local news. Moreover, the proliferation of blogs and websites where people could post news and opinion undermined the uniqueness of IMCs and fragmented their audiences. For a time, however, IMCs highlighted the power of alternative media, particularly in the context of the internet, and helped spark what is now sometimes seen as a "citizens'" or "participatory" journalism movement. (Lievrouw, 2011).

The passing of Canadian IMCs highlights the difficulty of sustaining alternative media projects. While the internet provides an easy means to distribute media content, as with other mediums developing quality content—whether in terms of writing, researching, editing, or maintaining a website—it is both time consuming and requires considerable skills. Consequently, maintaining operations solely on volunteer labour is an extremely difficult task (Cohen, 2012). Consistent quality generally requires at least some paid staff to help create content and coordinate training efforts and volunteers if nothing else.

Elements of the self-publishing legacy of IMC's lives on in Canada, however, in several forms. For instance, some pages on Facebook, clips found on YouTube, or blogs found on Tumblr might meet some of the criteria of alternative media. But while these sites do enable some forms of social organizing that help animate social change and provide venues for the circulation of ideas and perspectives not found in dominant media, given their varied content, as well as their developing commercial character, it would be a stretch to call them "alternative" as the term has been defined in this article. Similarly, while a number of blogs might meet the definitions of alternative media offered here, by and large they are as varied as the people who post them and few actually meet those definitions.

At the same time, there are also a number of commercial news companies that draw on the IMC legacy. For instance, Now Public—a Vancouver-based company—draws upon the idea of citizen's journalism. It offers people the opportunity to upload news stories, photographs and video clips to its website, with the possibility of having them distributed to the "global community" (Now Public, n/d/). Unlike IMCs, however, Now Public is a commercial enterprise whose business model is based upon selling these contributions to mainstream commercial media such as Associated Press. Working in another direction, OpenFile foregrounds citizen journalism's concern over creating a more horizontal relationship between journalists and readers or audiences. Employing what it calls "community powered journalism," it links professional journalists with people who suggest news story topics to them. Linking professionals with citizens helps ensure the quality of the end product while, at the same time, working to increase the range of ideas and perspectives found in the media. As its website states, "By connecting citizens to the reporters who cover their communities, OpenFile gets answers to important local questions, enables citizens to participate in gathering and sharing the news and ensures Canadians are informed about issues that affect where we live and work" (OpenFile (a), n/d) Again, however, OpenFile is a commercial organization that also touts its form of journalism as offering advertisers "a targeted and more intimate relationship with our readers by delivering unique branding opportunities" (OpenFile (b), n/d). In what ways the commercial logic underlying these organizations might affect the range and character of their news reporting is not known at this time. However, as we have seen, the principles on which these businesses are based—citizen-based journalism and developing a more horizontal relationship between audiences and media producers—are the very principles that motivated media activists and others to create alternatives to corporate media in the first place.

There are however, a number of innovative Web-based alternative media organizations operating in Canada. For instance, one organization that has utilized the basic principles upon which IMCs were founded to build a noncommercial operation is the Media Co-op. The Co-op has three types of members—readers, contributors, and editors—each with their own interest and role in the association. Designed as a venue for independent citizen journalists, as well as vehicle for developing a closer relationship between new producers and readers, the Co-op has "locals" in Halifax, Montreal, Toronto, and Vancouver. It also publishes *The Dominion*—a national newspaper that is produced both electronically and in hard copy (c.f. http://www.mediacoop.ca). Deploying a somewhat different structure, rabble.ca combines news with activist tools and resources, operates through a combination of paid and volunteer labour, and publishes both original and reprinted materials. Thetyee.ca provides a relatively comprehensive independent news alternative in Vancouver, one of the most heavily concentrated media markets in Canada. The Tyee is a private for-profit company and its content is not alternative in the radical sense of the term. Rather, it has an emphasis on investigative journalism and goes head to head with corporate media. However, given the generally conservative tone of the dominant media in the Lower Mainland, it does challenge the dominant media in that area. But while Web-based alternative media such as these three may present well on the screen, the economics of such operations are a challenge, particularly in light of the fact that in Canada there are no government programs and few charitable foundations to help support online news organizations.

CONCLUSION

To a large extent, alternative media function in a different manner than conventional corporate media. They are guided by a purpose or mandate other than the profit motive, and they are often organized to facilitate a broader range of input into production than their corporate cousins. They generally operate under a different set of news values than the dominant media, and they provide ways of seeing and understanding events that are marginalized or not available there. In some cases, as with some forms of community radio and media that are tied to activist groups, they also work to facilitate modes of social organization and social action that are generally beyond the purview of corporate media. In all these ways, alternative media work to challenge concentrations of media power.

However it would be a mistake to see media as divided into two camps: "corporate" or "mainstream" versus "alternative." The range of media available in Canada should be viewed as a continuum rather than as a dichotomy, with alternative media working to engender modes of communication that are circumscribed by dominant, market-driven media forms (c.f. Hamilton, 2008: p. 4). But much needs to be done to support the development of alternative media if they are to continue to increase the range of perspectives and modes of communication that comprise Canada's mediascape.

In recent years, a growing number of activist voices have attempted to raise public awareness of media issues related to alternative media (Hackett & Carroll, 2006). For instance, in 2001 activists in Toronto and Vancouver organized Media Democracy Day (MDD) celebrations. These events were designed to increase public awareness of issues such as concentration of ownership, publicize alternatives to mainstream media, and challenge the existing media system. MDD events continue today and have been organized in cities and towns across Canada and the United States as well as in Argentina, Brazil, Germany, Indonesia, Spain, and the United Kingdom. On another front, a 2007 conference at the University of Windsor celebrating the 20th anniversary of the publishing of Edward Herman and Noam Chomsky's *Manufacturing Consent*, laid the ground for Openmedia.ca—a media advocacy group that has been quite successful in building public awareness of issues important to the development and well-being of alternative media such as media diversity, net neutrality, and affordable internet. And a May 2010 conference at York University—Making Media Public—set the task to keep these concerns alive and raise public awareness and discussion of the issues facing alternative and public media.

But despite their increasing profile, by and large the economic circumstances of alternative media organizations remain uncertain at best. More information is needed on the range of alternative media that are currently operating in this country, and the kinds of programs and policies that would help them become more economically viable and give the public greater access to them. Only through understanding and strengthening the mechanisms that support these media can we create the infrastructure needed to maintain vibrant and diverse avenues of public expression.

QUESTIONS

1. Is media content simply a mirror image of society, or is the relationship more complex than that metaphor allows? What are some of the factors that influence the way in which media represent the world?
2. How would you define the term "alternative media"? What are some of the problems you encounter in trying to come up with a definition?
3. Some definitions of alternative media include zines, culture jamming, and street theatre. Do you think these should be included?
4. What are some of the differences in the ways in which community radio and commercial radio envision their audiences?
5. Should regulation be used to ensure that the public have access to community television?
6. What does it mean to say that a media outlet has a "horizontal" rather than a "vertical" relationship with its audience?
7. Given the increasing profile of internet-based media, should we be concerned about the development of alternative media?

ACKNOWLEDGMENTS

The author would like to thank Megan Humphrey, Frédéric Dubois, Kathe Lemon, Scott Uzelman, and Kristiana Clemens for their help in researching this article. This work was made possible by a York University Faculty of Arts Research Award and a grant from the Canadian Media Research Consortium.

REFERENCES

Alia, V. (1999). *Un/Covering the north: News, media and Aboriginal people.* Vancouver: UBC Press.

AMECQ (l'Association des médias écrits communautaires). *Présentation du mémoire de l'AMECQ à la ministre Christine St-Pierre le 11 novembre 2011 par Daniel Pezat et Yvan Noé Girouard.* Retrieved August 22, 2012, from http://www.amecq.ca/nouvelles_de_l_association/2011/11/11/presentation_du_memoire_de_l_amecq_a_la_ministre_christine_st_pierre_le_11_novembre_2011_par_daniel_pezat_et_yvan_noe_girouard

AMMSA (Aboriginal Multi-Media Society). (n/d). Publications. Retrieved September 16, 2009, from http://www.ammsa.com/publications

ARCQ (Association des radiodiffuseurs communautaires du Québec). (n/d). Portrait. Retrieved August 22, 2012, from http://radiovision.ca/arcq

Atton, C. (2002). *Alternative media.* Thousand Oaks, CA: Sage Publications.

———. (2003). Organization and production in alternative media. In S. Cottle (Ed.), *Media organization and production* (pp. 41–56). Thousand Oaks, CA: Sage Publications.

———. (2007). Alternative media in practice. In K. Coyer, T. Dowmunt, & A. Fountain (Eds.), *The alternative media handbook* (pp. 71–76). New York: Routledge.

Bredin, M. (2012). Indigenous media as alternative media: Participation and cultural production. In K. Kozolanka, P. Mazepa, & D. Skinner (Eds.) *Alternative media in Canada* (pp. 184–204). Vancouver: UBC Press.

Canada. Aboriginal Canada Portal. (n/d). Media and multimedia. Retrieved August 22, 2012, from http://www.aboriginalcanada.gc.ca/acp/site.nsf/eng/ao26714.html#news

———. Department of Heritage. (n/d). Northern Aboriginal Broadcasting. Retrieved August 22, 2012, from http://www.pch.gc.ca/eng/1267292195109/1305897413896#a1

———. House of Commons. (2003). *Our cultural sovereignty: The second century of Canadian broadcasting: Report of the standing committee on Canadian heritage.* Ottawa: Canadian Government Publishing.

Canadian University Press. (1977). *CUP editor's manual* (2nd ed.). Ottawa: Canadian University Press.

Clark, J. & Van Slyke, T. (2006). Welcome to the media revolution. *In these times.* Retrieved August 22, 2012, from http://www.inthesetimes.com/article/2687/welcome_to_the_media_revolution/

Cohen, N. (2012). From alienation to autonomy: The labour of alternative media. In K. Kozolanka, P. Mazepa, & D. Skinner (Eds.) *Alternative media in Canada* (pp. 207–225).Vancouver: UBC Press.

Couldry, N. & Curran, J. (2003). *Contesting media power: Alternative media in a networked world.* New York: Rowman and Littlefield.

Coyer, K., Dowmunt, T., & Fountain, A. (Eds.) (2007). *The alternative media handbook.* New York: Routledge.

CRFC/FCRC. Community Radio Fund of Canada/Fonds canadien de la radio communautaire (n/d). Mandate. Retrieved August 22, 2012, from http://www.communityradiofund.org/index.php?option=com_content&view=article&id=65&Itemid=53&lang=en

CRTC. (2000). Community radio policy, Public Notice CRTC 2000-13. Retrieved September 25, 2009, from http://www.crtc.gc.ca/archive/ENG/Notices/2000/PB2000-13.HTM

———. (2010). Community television policy. CRTC 2010-622. Retrieved August 22, 2012, from http://www.crtc.gc.ca/eng/archive/2010/2010-622.htm

———. (2011). Communications monitoring report. Retrieved August 22, 2012, from http://www.crtc.gc.ca/eng/publications/reports/PolicyMonitoring/2011/cmr4.htm#n3

CUP (Canadian University Press). (n/d). Services. Retrieved August 22, 2012, from http://cup.ca/services

Downing, John D. H. (with Ford, G., Villarreal, G., & Stein, L.). (2000). *Radical media: Rebellious communication and social movements.* Thousand Oaks, CA: Sage Publications.

Edwards, C. (2010). A new vision for community TV. Retrieved August 22, 2012, from http://cactus.independentmedia.ca/node/401

———. (n/d). New CRTC community TV policy little better than previous one. Retrieved August 22, 2012, from http://cactus.independentmedia.ca/node/436

FEDETVC (Fédération des télévisions communautaires autonomes du Québec). (n.d.). Présentation. Retrieved September 22, 2009, from http://www.fedetvc.qc.ca/ accueil.html

Freeman, B. M. (2012). One part creativity and nine parts hardwork: The legacy of feminist periodicals. In K. Kozolanka, P. Mazepa, & D. Skinner (Eds.) *Alternative media in Canada* (pp. 85–103).Vancouver: UBC Press.

Girard, B. (Ed.). (1992). *A passion for radio: Radio waves and community.* Montreal: Black Rose Books.

Goldberg, K. (1990). *The barefoot channel: Community television as a tool for social change.* Vancouver: New Star Books.

Groundwire. (n/d). Mandate. Retrieved August 22, 2012, from http://groundwire.ncra.ca/page.cfm/Mandate

Gunster, S. (2011). Covering Copenhagen: Climate politics in B.C. media. *Canadian Journal of Communication,36,* 477–502.

Hackett, R. A. & Carroll, W. F. (2006.) *Remaking media: The struggle to democratize public communication.* Routledge: New York.

Hackett, R. A., & Gruneau, R. (2000). *The missing news: Filters and blind spots in Canada's press.* Ottawa: Canadian Centre for Policy Alternatives and Garamond Press.

Hackett, R. A., Pinet, R. & Ruggles, M. (1992). From audience commodity to audience community: Mass media in B.C. In H. Holmes & D. Taras (Eds.), *Seeing ourselves: Media power and policy in Canada* (pp. 10–20). Toronto: Harcourt, Brace, Jovanovich.

Hackett, R. A., & Zhao, Y. (1996). Are ethics enough? Objective journalism versus sustainable democracy. In V. Alia, B. Brennan, & B. Hoffmaster (Eds.), *Deadlines and diversity: Journalism ethics in a changing world* (pp. 44–58). Halifax, NS: Fernwood Publishing.

Halleck, D. D. (2002). *Hand held visions: The impossible possibilities of community media.* New York: Fordham University Press.

Hamilton, J. F. (2008). *Democratic communications.* MD: Lexington Books.

Jiwani, J. and Young, M. L. (2006). Missing and murdered women: Reproducing marginality in news discourse. *Canadian Journal of Communication 31*, 895–917.

Ladner, P. (1986, March–April). A case study in alternates. *Content*, 7–8.

Lederman, M. (2008, April 10). Is community TV facing its Waterloo? *The Globe and Mail.* Retrieved September 5, 2009, from http://democraticmedia.ca/news-item/community-tv-facing-its-waterloo

Lievrouw, L. A. (2011). *Alternative and activist new media.* Malden, MA: Polity Press.

Lipton, B. (1980, May). Prairie fire history illustrates struggles of the alternate press. *Briarpatch*, *9*(4), 31–35.

Lithgow, M. (2012). Transformations of practice, policy, and cultural citizenships in community television. In K. Kozolanka, P. Mazepa, & D. Skinner (Eds.) *Alternative media in Canada* (pp. 125–144).Vancouver: UBC Press.

Marlow, I. (2012, March 1). Google, Facebook get personal by revamping their advertising tactics. *The Globe and Mail*, B1.

Megaphone (n/d). About. Retrieved August 24, 2012 from http://megaphonemagazine.com/about/2/about

Mohr, L. (1992). To tell the people. In B. Girard (Ed.), *A passion for radio: Radio waves and community* (pp. 23–38). Montreal: Black Rose Books.

Molnar, H. & M. Meadows. (2001). *Songlines to satellites: Indigenous communication in Australia, the South Pacific, and Canada.* Sydney, Australia: Pluto Press.

Moyers, B. (2008, July 11). Is the fourth estate a fifth column? Corporate media colludes with democracy's demise. *In these times.* Retrieved August 22, 2012, from http://www.inthesetimes.com/article/3790/is_the_fourth_estate_a_fifth_column

NCRA (The National Campus and Community Radio Association). (n/d). *About c/c radio.* Retrieved August 22, 2012, from http://www.ncra.ca/about-cc-radio

Now Public. (n/d). *What is Now Public?* Retrieved August 22, 2012, from http://www.nowpublic.com

OpenFile (a). (n/d). About OpenFile. Retrieved August 22, 2012, from http://www.openfile.ca/about-openfile

OpenFile (b). (n/d). Associate your brand with a growing and highly engaged audience. Retrieved August 22, 2012, from http://www.openfile.ca/advertise-openfile

Orlowski, K. (2011). Big media afraid to take Wall Street protest seriously. *The Tyee.* Retrieved August 22, 2012, from http://thetyee.ca/Mediacheck/2011/09/26/Occupy-Wall-Street-Coverage

Raboy, M. (1984). *Movements and messages: Media and radical politics in Québec.* Toronto: Between the Lines Press.

Radio Centre-Ville. (n.d.). Who are we? Retrieved from http://www.radiocentreville.com

Rodriguez, C. (2001). *Fissures in the mediascape: An international study of citizens' media.* Cresskill, NJ: Hampton Press.

Roth, L. (2005). *Something new in the air.* Montreal & Kingston: McGill-Queen's University Press.

Senate of Canada. (2006, June). Final report on the Canadian News media, vol. 1 of 2. Retrieved September 3, 2012, from http://www.parl.gc.ca/Content/SEN/Committee/391/TRAN/rep/repfinjun06vol1-e.htm

Skinner, D., Uzelman, S., Langlois, A., & Dubois, F. (2010). Independent media centres in Canada: Three case studies. In D. Kidd, C. Rodriguez, & L. Stein (Eds.), *Making our media: Mapping global initiatives toward a democratic public sphere* (pp. 275–293). NJ: Hampton Press.

Vallantin, C. (2008, June 19). Fade to black: How cable companies and the CRTC's lenience are killing what's left of community TV. *Fast Forward Weekly.* Retrieved September 3, 2012, from http://www.ffwdweekly.com/article/screen/television/fade-black

Vancouver Co-operative Radio. (n.d.). About Co-op. Retrieved September 3, 2012, from http://www.coopradio.org

Verzuh, R. (1986, March–April). Alternates: Moving uptown? *Content,* 2–6.

White Eye, B. (1996). Journalism and First Nations. In V. Alia, B. Brennan, & B. Hoffmaster (Eds.), *Deadlines and diversity: Journalism ethics in a changing world* (pp. 92–97). Halifax, NS: Fernwood Publishing.

18

CANADIAN FIRST PEOPLES' MEDIASCAPES: REFRAMING A SNAPSHOT WITH THREE CORNERS*

Lorna Roth
Concordia University

INTRODUCTION

In this chapter, I argue that Canadian Aboriginal media are now well immersed in a process of cultural and social networking transformations that have opened up global venues of public access and participation. Independent film production and digital Aboriginal media arts and culture have taken hold of the imaginaries of actual and potential audiences for **First Peoples**' media output. Original media objectives of preserving First Peoples' languages and cultures, initially associated exclusively with broadcasting, are no longer of as much interest as they were in the past to Aboriginal constituency groups in Canada. For those nations that consider this a broadcasting priority, there seems to be a turn to the establishment of specialty channels or Web-TV in their native languages.

As the **internet** has become more available and less costly in small, rural, and remote communities across this vast land, independently funded Aboriginal media sites that identify more with independent media and social networking initiatives and services than with existing First Peoples broadcasting are forming. How are these social, cultural, and infrastructural shifts reshaping the Aboriginal mediascape? Can the present Aboriginal mediascape enable better dialogue to take place with other First Peoples global actors and non-native users of the internet? What are the implications of being "out there" with the other "others"?

For illustrative purposes, I use the visual metaphor of a snapshot (see Figure 18.1) in this essay to describe and analyze the historical context out of which current Aboriginal mediascapes have emerged.[1] In three of the snapshot's corners, I review some of the key moments of First Peoples' media pathways to the present. After historically situating early film initiatives in the debates around media process and product originating in the **National Film Board's Challenge for Change Program** in the 1960s (Mediascape Snapshot, Corner I), as well as describing two historical cases of broadcasting services and independent feature film production (Mediascape Snapshot, Corner II), I proceed to create an initial picture (Mediascape Snapshot, Corner III) of the Aboriginal digital mediasphere and its processual challenges in the early part of the 21st century. In a previous version of this essay, Corner IV was

FIGURE 18.1 Snapshot with Three Corners

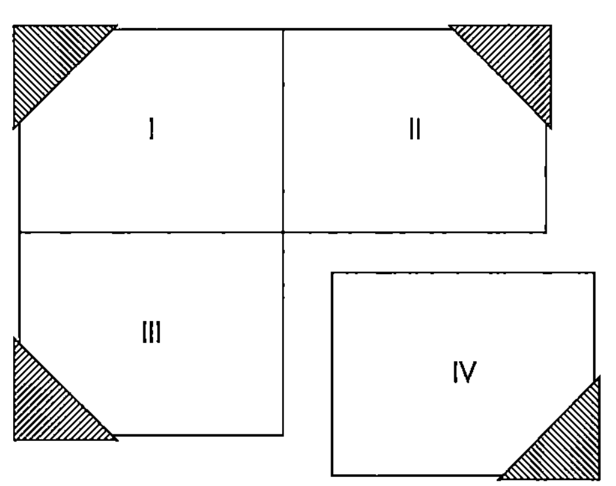

empty, characterized as a not-yet-constructed, unknown territory of the future in which we could not predict the configuration of connections that might emerge. What appeared outside, but in proximity to, the empty Corner IV was a box containing words from which a combination of new culturally convergent patterns (that could be relevant to First Peoples' media development) could be assembled or designed. These were for the open consideration of the reader as he or she logged the choices and routes that the next generation of Aboriginal media makers seemed to be following. In this revised iteration, the box has additional keywords to account for the ever-transforming digital environment (emergent new infrastructures, digital social experiments, and social media practices, among other modifications). Corner IV is no longer as indescribable and unpredictable as it was in the initial writing of this text.

MEDIASCAPE SNAPSHOT, CORNER I

The Little-Known Root Behind Inuit Television Culture[2]

> A democratic civilization will save itself only if it makes the language of the image into a stimulus for critical reflection, not an invitation to hypnosis. (Eco, 1961).

In 1965, in response to requests for television in the Canadian North coming mainly from administrative, industrial, military, and resource centres' employees and supported by managers who wished to maintain a stable labour force, the Canadian Broadcasting Corporation (CBC) established an interim service called the **Frontier Coverage Package.** This was a temporary pre-satellite service of four hours per day of prerecorded videotapes of Southern-selected programming that was shipped by air to one community and from there, cycled on a one-week delayed basis to various towns around the North. In 1968, the *Telesat Act* was passed and created a domestic satellite service for all of Canada that would substantially improve the quality and access of telecom services across the country. It was particularly relevant for the remote and Northern communities that had been deprived of basic services until the satellite became operational in 1973. At this time, CBC and Radio Canada television programming originated in the South and was merely "parachuted" into the Arctic and remote Northern communities on the assumption that what was good for the South was good for the North.

Radio was inclusive of indigenous voices right from the beginning in 1958, with the commencement of CBC Northern Services: network broadcasters were always open to incorporating native-language programming on a local and regional basis. Furthermore, very early in the 1960s, many communities discovered the cost effectiveness and ease with which local community radio could be produced. Currently, there are approximately 120 native community radio stations across the country. This article will not discuss community radio other than to state that it should be a recognized part of the local aspect of the First Peoples' mediascape. It is popular, highly regarded in the communities, and the source of much utilitarian information. It is often self-financed through Radio Bingo and other local fundraising activities.

The extension of national broadcasting services to all communities with a population of 500 or more, known under the policy name, **Accelerated Coverage Plan**, began in 1974 and continued until pretty much every community in Canada that wished to have CBC and Radio Canada became connected.[3] Although there was a demand for a broader range of broadcasting services by Northern and remote community residents, including some First Peoples, the way in which this was done turned out to be a major error in judgment on the part of federal government bureaucrats. Many First Peoples considered the process in the same vein as a national colonial project: television blatantly confirmed their absence both in front of and behind the screen—other than in films highlighting the stereotype of a cowboy facing off with an Indian, an "Eskimo" savage, or an Indian princess. What national network services did do, however, was trigger the recognition in First Peoples themselves that they *had* to have access to media production and distribution processes in order to create their own presence on the airwaves. This would be key to their national identity being made apparent to viewers Canada-wide.

While evidence for this conclusion was being gathered and deliberated around the country, in the Eastern Arctic something important was about to take place that would support Aboriginal television development in the early 1970s. Interestingly, early video initiatives were tied to film production in that it was a National Film Board Executive Producer, **Wolf Koenig**, who helped establish two film-training centres in the Eastern Arctic in 1972 and 1974. Out of the initial organization, infrastructure, and films emergent from these two workshops came the dream of a much broader set of media and, in particular, television possibilities that would drive the Inuit and First Nations to further their objectives of establishing a broadcasting system to meet their multiple cultural, linguistic, and educational needs.

Although the Eastern Arctic was not the sole site for early media projects, the two cases described here are particularly relevant because they provided the roots for an ongoing debate about media arts as cultural products versus media use as stimulating processes of consciousness raising and community development. Furthermore, they framed the way in which visual culture was mobilized in the discourses about community development tools in indigenous Canada.

The National Film Board—Product versus Process Debates in the 1970s

In 1972, Executive Producer of the Animation Department of the National Film Board of Canada Wolf Koenig arrived in Cape Dorset, Baffin Island, to work on a documentary entitled *Pitseolak: Pictures out of My Life*. While waiting for the plane in Frobisher Bay, his exposure to Frontier Coverage Package programming confirmed to him that television did not adequately reflect native concerns. Curious as to how television might have modified the cognitive structures and reordered the perceptions of the Inuit people, Koenig interviewed residents of Frobisher Bay and Cape Dorset (Thorvaldson, 1976, p. 2). His informal research led him to the following suppositions: (1) television had indeed transformed the Inuit cultural base—for instance, anecdotal information provided by teachers suggested that English language use and comprehension among children had improved but that these newly acquired skills were gradually eroding interest in learning Inuktitut grammar and writing syllabics; (2) interest in Inuit culture was on the decline; (3) an increase in consumerism was conspicuous; (4) family ties were loosening due to generational gaps; (5) social interaction patterns were shifting (personal interview with Wolf Koenig, June 9, 1975). Although Koenig was aware that television was not the only factor influencing these transformations, he suspected that it was the one that could be appropriated most effectively by First Peoples (Thorvaldson 1976, 2). Anticipating a more intelligent use of television that would also serve the interests of the Inuit, he visualized a project in which they would have access to their own community transmitter:

> When in Frobisher Bay, we saw television that was totally irrelevant. We thought it was insane to see white faces. The Inuit saw none of themselves on TV; what they saw had no relation to their world.
>
> Communications is a way people get to know who they are. If there's no identification in dramatic terms, then an individual becomes depersonalized. This results in what they see on TV becoming normal. Normality is outside. "What I see in the mirror becomes abnormal." Your own image tells you lies.
>
> So, we thought about Dorset as a community. It has a tremendous artistic tradition and the people have lots of time. Why not set up a 16 mm camera to find its way onto the tube. The psychology is "We could share that same magic box," which means ... "We can be persons." (Koenig, June 10, 1975)

While in Cape Dorset, Koenig committed the NFB to establishing a film training project in which Inuit youth could learn to produce culturally relevant material appropriate for eventual broadcasting on Northern television. Discussions with key community members and funding agency representatives in Frobisher Bay before his return trip to Montreal succeeded in establishing the appropriate funding. Arrangements for the Sikusilarmiut workshop were finalized by October 1972, at which point an animator/producer with the NFB Vancouver studio moved North to install equipment in the Cape Dorset work space and to begin the training program.

Over the next three years, about six talented Inuit animators emerged out of the community population of 700. A collection of short fascinating films highlighting Inuit heritage, cultural patterns and indigenous subjects (shamans, animal spirits, and historic individual biographies, such as that of Peter Pitseolak, the first Inuit photographer) were assembled into a reel entitled *Animation from Cape Dorset*. This was awarded first prize at the Zagreb International Animation Film Festival (1974). Innovative techniques such as sand animation and double-exposure pixilation of a human were created for the first time ever. The films riveted the attention of local and international publics.

Though relatively little was produced beyond this one reel, a most important outcome of the Sikusilarmiut venture was that Inuit youth learned film production skills. It also planted ideas about future possibilities for the development of the arts beyond Inuit print making, which had already become a well-established means of expression.

An evaluation of the Dorset undertaking at the time suggested the need for rethinking NFB media training in the Arctic. For technical, transportation, economic, and administrative reasons, the NFB decided to close the Dorset workshop and open a live-action, Super 8 film studio in Frobisher Bay (1974–1976). Super 8 meant lower film costs, lighter and more portable equipment, and total automation with high quality results. It was also a responsive and practical medium, capable of withstanding extreme temperatures. In addition, general access to Super 8 equipment in Northern settlements, via the Hudson's Bay Company stores, had already made it into a familiar, hence approachable, medium.

Dorset filmmakers did not move to Frobisher; instead, several went on to film school for more advanced training; others used their training in personalized ways and didn't make a career of filmmaking. Editing equipment was transferred to Frobisher.

Two key points prevailed in the NFB's decision:[4] the Animation Department wanted to keep indigenous film training projects within the North itself, hoping to be able to provide both financial support for trainees and Northern job opportunities for those who had completed their training. The latter considerations were designed to render credible the "job" of filmmaker—an occupation that was at that time foreign to Inuit culture—and to promote the idea that it could lead to employment for Inuit.

Funding was negotiated for infrastructure and personnel but, unfortunately, not for trainee salaries. This caused resentment, and resulted in erratic commitments to the training process as time went on. Nor were there any systematic trainee recruitment procedures other than a few announcements made over the local radio asking for volunteers. No matter what their age or skills, anyone who responded was accepted as a trainee (children as young as ten signed up). It was later recognized that curiosity was not an adequate criterion for participation (personal conversation with Wolf Koenig, January 6, 1981).

By the winter of 1975, one interesting and well-edited film entitled *Natsik Hunting* (about a family seal hunt), had been produced by Mosha Michael. Natsik Hunting was blown up to 16 mm for NFB distribution purposes (Thorvaldson, 1976, p. 4). Other than this, no concrete products were finalized during the lifespan of this workshop. The fact that these workshops tended to recruit village "drifters" had an important impact on what happened within the workshops: originally drawn by the novel aspects of filmmaking, interest often tended to lag once it became apparent that an ongoing commitment, as well as a lot of hard work, was expected. Nonetheless, those Inuit who participated benefited from learning another way of seeing and framing reality. Moreover, the workshops became a context within which local artistic talent could be discovered and supported.

Impact of the NFB Media Workshops

The workshops served mainly to establish a relationship between the National Film Board Animation Department and Inuit people with an expressed interest in the visual arts. As the first direct effort on the part of a federal media institution to stimulate Inuit film production, they played an important role in shaping visual culture and aesthetic practices in the North. The Animation Department approached film as a specialized and professional activity. Its interest in the Arctic was thus basically artistic. A secondary concern was to facilitate cultural preservation by providing the opportunity to develop a set of historical and cultural records for the Inuit people that could then be broadcast—if in a form that met the technical broadcasting quality standards. The NFB was there to guide them in conforming to those standards.

Those few trainees with an ongoing commitment to the projects temporarily became the communication professionals of the Eastern Arctic. However, because the workshops had not evolved from within a grassroots context, they operated without strong linkages to relevant community organizations and were perceived by the local population as an outside agency's project that had been randomly located within their communities.

Although they were only of passing interest to most departments in the NFB, the workshops elicited active responses from the Media Research Department and Challenge for Change. The Media Research department, preoccupied as it was with philosophical questions regarding media use, turned to the workshops to bolster its argument regarding the negative impact of television on indigenous culture. The department was also interested in accumulating data on alternative forms of communications appropriate for native peoples (Cruickshank and Martin, 1974–75: personal interviews).

The Challenge for Change program showed interest for other reasons. Created in 1966 in response to a government policy directive, it was coordinated by an interdepartmental committee comprising of seven federal government departments and the National Film Board. Challenge for Change was differentiated from other NFB programs because it considered film, and later video, to be not only a tool for community development and consciousness raising, not just a means to create an artistic product that could be marketed in the international economy. Using film as a basis for generating dialogue, filmmakers would become engaged with a constituency group seeking empowerment, often in a confrontational situation, and would show members of this organization or group how to use the technologies themselves to create a credible collective voice, a mediating force that could enable the resolution of a conflict by helping people "save face" and "gain voice."

Concerned about the relationship between the media, community organizations, and participatory development, the program's stated objectives were to improve communications, create greater understanding, promote new ideas, and provoke social change (Hénaut, 1971–1972, p. 3). To this end, portable media—usually videotape recorders but sometimes Super 8 film—were seen as tools that could be used by a social animator to diffuse conflict, resolve problems, and assure promised action. The uses to which the media were put were process-oriented, with final products being seen as nothing more than documentary evidence of the process undergone by a given community. Projects supported by this program depended largely on community initiative, leadership, and support at the local level. The NFB acted merely as a media/technical service in this context and ideally perceived its involvement as a consultative body available at a community's request only. As for the medium and the producers, they were regarded as technically supportive elements in the movement toward the resolution of sociopolitical conflicts; they were seen as catalysts for social change. This radical departure from the notion of the film producer/director as a professional specialist to a resource person/technician offended many institutionalized filmmakers, who were accustomed to having full artistic and editorial control over their productions.

The emphasis on experiment, innovation, and sociopolitical transformation processes within the Challenge for Change team suggested that projects would not take on characteristics of permanency, that they were visualized as having an end-point where they could be evaluated, changed, terminated, or recycled, but not fixed within the NFB's permanent collection of "completed" films. Consequently, funds were limited for each project (Driscoll, 1972, p. 23).

Challenge for Change and the Animation Department clearly did not share the same film philosophy. The concern of the former was whether or not the random participants in the program would come to recognize the project as their own and attempt to take control of its direction by developing strong linkages within the community. In 1976, the NFB reduced its support. Consequently, several trainees decided to transform the studio into a small, community drama unit called Nunatsiakmiut. Team members negotiated local access with CBC Northern Service for their short productions, which were broadcast weekly for 15 minutes for many years, as a stand-alone project. They eventually became absorbed into the Inuit Broadcasting Corporation team. Nunatsiakmiut independently produced the first set of Inuit live-action dramatic narratives that differed from all previous productions undertaken by them with the assistance of the NFB.

Though it is difficult to evaluate the precise degree to which academic research and early demonstration projects such as the NFB's influenced Inuit public opinion, it is likely that they played a significant part in motivating Inuit leaders to begin a comprehensive (re)assessment of their communication priorities in the mid-1970s. What is clear is that First Peoples (mostly the Inuit) recognized that data collected about media effects and the results of the NFB pilot projects would not, in itself, bring about the desired changes to the broadcasting system. Well aware that it was only through viewing communications as *interaction and representation*, as opposed to technological *extension*, that they could move the struggle from a technical to a politically based challenge to the ruling relations within the media in Canada, it became important to First Peoples' representatives that they enter into critical political and cultural dialogues with federal government policy-makers and bureaucrats. To this end, "**bridge discourses**"—to borrow Nancy Fraser's (1989) term—that could mediate relations between unilingual Aboriginal communities and the federal government, would have to be initiated and developed. "Go-betweens"—natives who could speak their own and at least one of the official languages of Canada and/or non-native "interested parties" (activists, media researchers) who were acceptable to First Peoples' community leadership—would play this bridging role. By situating themselves between the two worlds, the task of these go-betweens would be to knit together the disparate discourses of governmental regulatory policies, results of early media experiments, and Inuit and First Nations' cultural and infrastructural concerns. The NFB stimulated the beginning of this process, as well as trained several key people who could become mediators.

MEDIASCAPE SNAPSHOT, CORNER II

The Cultural and Linguistic Salvage Paradigm

Case I: First Peoples' Television—Indigenous Self-Production

In the late 1970s, Terry Turner took up a position critical of cultural survival and pure culturalist approaches to an emerging and transforming indigenous politics. He particularly took issue with the model that identified indigenous futures only with cultural preservation, ossifying such life-worlds into unchanging

> enclaves. Instead, he proposed a focus on indigenous self-production. Turner argued that one should not substitute the past products of people's actions (their culture) with the values people themselves sought to bring into being under constantly changing conditions. (Ginsberg and Myers, 2006, pp. 27–28)

In 1976, after the coming into operation of the **Anik B satellite**, the federal government issued calls for a competitive bid for community access time in which to experiment with intercommunity video/audio communications. In the Eastern Arctic, two grants of over a million dollars each were awarded and became known as *Project Inukshuk* and *Nalaakvik Project* (1978–1981). Under the auspices of the Inuit Tapirisat of Canada and the Northern Quebec Inuit Association, the teams demonstrated to Canadian funding agencies that the establishment of accessible communications infrastructures designed to link isolated communities together would make good economic, cultural, and political sense. They provided evidence that ordinary citizens could appropriate the satellite's technical potential to communicate their own (inter)cultural, sociopolitical, and economic development goals to others within and beyond their own territories. Their publicly mediated voices could contribute to their constituency groups' politicization. The politics of communications and the communication of politics were seen to be integrally tied together in the development of First Peoples' media. The Inuit's positive evaluation led to their being granted a network licence to operate a regional television broadcasting service in the Inuktitut language. It was named the Inuit Broadcasting Corporation and still operates today as one of the contributors of programming to the **Aboriginal Peoples Television Network (APTN)**. Recently, it has been rumoured that the IBC is seeking to form a separate and distinct broadcasting channel dedicated to Inuktitut (Inuit language) programming over and above its contributions to APTN.

In the early 1980s, a total of 13 regional communications groups were organized and became the mediating vehicles through which their populations could engage conversationally among themselves and with members of the federal government. The 13 Native Communications Societies (NCS) (as they were called), all located above the 55th line of latitude, proceeded through several stages of development, culminating in their official acknowledgment by a federal policy framework announced on March 10, 1983.[5] The Northern Broadcasting Policy recognized the value of native participation in the production and distribution process and, along with its implementation vehicle (**Northern Native Broadcast Access Program**), provided financial support[6] for the weekly production of 20 hours of radio and 5 hours of television in First Peoples' languages, reflecting their own cultures. Programming focus was to be restricted to this paradigm and funding renewal was tied to the NCS' success at achieving this objective.

After this de facto recognition through the establishment and practice of these two initiatives for almost a decade, NCS leaders banded together to demand consistent funding and distribution capacity under their own control. Several of them applied for and received licences from the Canadian Radio-television Telecommunications Commission (Canada's regulatory agency) to become network broadcasters. From 1983 to 1986, federally funded programming from the NCSs was intraregional, with minor exceptions of occasional "outside" contract work.

In the late 1980s, Northern Native Broadcasting, Yukon (NNBY) took the bold initiative to move beyond the cultural, territorial, and political borderlines to negotiate a contract for a half-hour program *Nedaa* (Your Eye on the Yukon) on Canadian Broadcasting Corporation's *Newsworld* service. This had the long-range consequence of opening small spaces for Aboriginal broadcasting within the mainstream of Canadian media and of stimulating debate over how one goes about building cross-cultural alignments for political, social, and cultural activist purposes. The NNBY decision to push the limits deserves special mention, as it was one of the first strategic uses of First Peoples' programming to initiate a public relations strategy. Going beyond the salvage paradigm opened up First Peoples' media discourses and practices for experimentation and analysis by others working in and around the industry. Had they been too controlled by federal government objectives because these converged with their own? Did they not have other objectives for their broadcasting services as well that went beyond those of the government?

Funding Northern broadcasting was not a problem by the end of the 1980s—the challenges were exhibition and distribution. A major federal lobbying strategy was undertaken and **Television Northern Canada (TVNC)** was established as a Pan-Northern distribution service in 1991, the year in which communications access rights for Aboriginal peoples were enshrined in Canada's *Broadcasting Act*. TVNC became the vehicle through which they would publicly represent their Northern perspectives.

Not surprisingly, exposure to each others' NCS programming stimulated critical public debates. First Peoples wanted multidirectional communication flows; they also wanted feature films and independent producers' work from other parts of Canada integrated within their scheduled programming. This could not happen on TVNC, given its restricted funding, hours of broadcasting, and its mandate restrictions to act as distributor for the 13 NCSs.

By 1997, TVNC's Pan-Northern successes convinced its Board and staff to pursue the establishment of a nationwide network. Though controversial due to the resistance on the part of cable operators to carry it on their analogue services as a mandatory national channel, the CRTC approved TVNC's application on February 22, 1999, and granted Aboriginal Peoples Television Network carriage on basic cable and satellite services throughout Canada with a small monthly subscription fee in the South.[7] APTN has been operating since September 1, 1999, the same year Nunavut, Canada's first Inuit-governed territory, was created. In August 2005, APTN had its licence renewed for another seven years. In 2011, APTN received $32,575,942 in mandatory subscriber fees from its viewers.

Indigenous broadcasting sites have become pivotal tools and outlets for the expression of First Peoples' cultural, social, and political imaginaries. Indigenous broadcasting has opened up frontier audiovisual spaces, improving the information structures, sources, and conditions for the renegotiation of their power relations in Canadian society. First Peoples have become national broadcasting citizens in control of their own information services and public intellectual perspectives.

APTN has enabled indigenous messages to be heard by constituency groups that might never have had access to a live person of Aboriginal descent; it provides bonding opportunities to share national imageries and histories, to build bridges of understanding, and to bridge cultural borders. Equally important, however, is that it *exists:* it is on the air, is one of many services competing for audience attention, is now a performer on the electronic power grid, and, to a great extent, has transformed the roles that were anticipated for public media since its early days.

APTN is a hybrid between what has traditionally been defined as public and private broadcasting. It carries advertising, yet it addresses public issues and models itself after public-service television. It is multilingual, multicultural, and multiracial in content, production staff, and management. It attempts to be both local and global and attracts niche, not mass, audiences.

It does very little original production on its own; rather, it shares a collaborative relationship with other independent feature film producers on an ad hoc basis. Furthermore, indigenous programming that originates in the North is now complemented by an expanded range of programs derived from Southern Canada and international sources. These include documentaries, dramas, comedy shows, variety shows, talk shows, a cooking show, and children's programming. Beginning in 2000, APTN introduced live news and current affairs programming that provides an Aboriginal lens through which to view (inter)national news and public affairs. Thus, it distributes locally and regionally produced cultural programming to a national audience from a native perspective.

The fact that APTN is already integrating international programming and is considering expansion of its service to become a Global First Peoples' television network comparable to TV5 or the BBC World Service indicates clearly its intention of international constituency group building across national borders. At a New Zealand meeting of all the indigenous television station presidents in the world (2007), there was a first serious discussion of this possibility for the future. This objective continues to be on APTN's agenda.

The practical reality of APTN's program mandate to serve all Aboriginal and Canadian communities, North and South, is extremely complex to manage, especially in this period when digital media has become so popular and competitive with the more traditional medium of television. However, the network has served its constituency groups well in that it has Northernized and indigenized Canadian television programming and provided First Peoples' viewers with a multicultural snapshot of their communities and interests from coast to coast to coast. To motivate the interest of the next generation in this media-transformative period, APTN is offering apprenticeships and internships to recruit future journalists currently involved in college training programs. It is live-streaming its news and current affairs programming, and trying to create appealing Web materials. More and more focus is being placed on web program access and interactivity, blogs, etc. Discussions are taking place at all levels of the organization about how to maintain a strong audience from within a social media-competitive environment.

Case II: Igloolik Isuma Productions, Inc.: The Independent Feature Film Initiative, the Dramatic Turn, and Migration to the Web

Igloolik Isuma Productions was founded in 1988 by former employees of Inuit Broadcasting Corporation, Zacharias Kunuk and Paul Apak Angilirq[8] who, together with Norman Cohn (New York video artist) and elder Pauloosie Qulitallik, sought a more independent approach to media production. Their mission was "to create a distinctive Inuit style of community-based film-making that preserves and enhances Inuit culture, creates needed employment, and offers a uniquely Inuit point of view to the global media audience" (Soukup, 2006, p. 241). More interested in drama than in public service broadcasting, they envisioned docu-drama and historical fiction film as a means to illustrate Igloolik community elders' stories and oral histories (ibid.).

Given their focus, NNBAP funding was not accessible to them. Unintentionally, the NNBAP restricted the development of an Aboriginal feature film industry, as it did not conform to government criteria for Northern media development. Nor was there much other financing around for Aboriginal dramatic media through dedicated arts agencies such as Telefilm, the NFB, and Canada Council which all seemed to require a "special" program for First Peoples who did not fall within predefined Canadian film funding categories. One would have assumed that the Northwest Territories, and later Nunavut, would have been more forthcoming financially, but neither were very generous. In looking back at Isuma's financial woes, Norman Cohn recently commented: "If Bill Gates were creating Microsoft in Nunavut right now, he'd be under 'arts and crafts' in the [Nunavut government's] economic development strategy. You can't compete nationally if your film industry is under arts and crafts" (CBC News North, July 8, 2011). Consequently, to attain adequate production funding, Isuma needed to lobby consistently and strategically as an "exceptional" case, figure out the loopholes in existing policies at the various cultural funding agencies, argue for a more generous funding formula at the national and provincial levels, all this while simultaneously fundraising within the private sector. This was no easy set of tasks.

As the first independent Inuit production studio in Canada, Isuma somehow figured out a fundraising process that has resulted in the completion of over 40 films in Inuktitut. These have been highly acclaimed by (inter)national audiences and have been awarded many distinctions (six Genies), including the Camera d'or Prize at Cannes in 2001 for *Atanarjuat, The Fast Runner*. Likely due to Isuma's persistent and successful lobbying, support funds for Aboriginal feature films in Canada increased slightly for a short time before more severe cutbacks took place, the most recent having been announced on March 29, 2012.

As a consequence of repeated cuts, Igloolik Isuma Productions (the original production company) was unable to stabilize its internal finances and was "placed in receivership following a Quebec Superior Court decision" in June 2011 "to appoint a receiver to wind up the company and sell off its assets" (ibid.). This branch of Isuma apparently owed about $1.2 million to 15 creditors and had to cease operation due to financial insolvency (ibid.). Fortunately, Atuqtuarvik Corporation, the company to which Isuma owed $500,000 and that initiated the action, claimed it would make "all reasonable efforts ... to locate a suitable Nunavut purchaser of the culturally relevant assets of [Isuma] to protect such property for future generations of Inuit" (ibid.) This is a very sensitive cultural issue with the only consolation being that digitally archived materials can be easily retained and reproduced.

To bypass some of the challenges of production/exhibition costs and challenging distribution logistics in the North and to popularize the work of indigenous filmmakers from around the world, Isuma launched a website, IsumaTV, in 2008 with support from two relatively new players in the field: the Canada New Media Fund and Partnerships Fund of Canadian Culture Online. IsumaTV is a video internet portal that provides free and easy access to a growing international collection of Aboriginal feature and documentary films. As a web platform located in cyberspace, IsumaTV holds the archive for approximately 800 Inuktitut media files (Cohn, personal interview, May 2, 2012) and 2,000 other films in 41 languages. It is steadily making available increased amounts of international Aboriginal programs through its uploading features available to First Peoples' makers from around the world. It also carries on-line radio programming and a television channel. It is owned by Isuma Distribution International, a private corporation. IsumaTV is innovative and cross-culturally instructive, visionary, and *very* engaging. It is utilizing a transmedia story-telling approach with great success.

Other holdings of Isuma seem to be faring well, despite the financial woes mentioned above. Isuma Distribution International is running the Digital Indigenous Democracy (DID) project, that:

> "installs in each slow-speed community a low-cost, innovative package of community-based technology that allows users to jump the Digital Divide and use interactive media at high-speed" (Isuma Creative Materials 2). It is anticipated that DID will facilitate the participation and empowerment of Inuit to make decisions in the seven communities effected by externally-driven mining development that they do not necessarily support. A new Nunavut-based production company called Kingulliit (Those Who Came After) Productions has been formed to replace the old "Isuma" now closed. NITV (Nunavut Independent Television Network) local servers are also moving forward as part of the Digital Indigenous Democracy project." (Cohn, email correspondence, May 2, 2012)

Consequently, despite the negative publicity about the closure of Isuma Igloolik Productions, IsumaTV and its sister companies continue to be available to the international viewing community. They are excellent sources of worldwide Aboriginal information, news, features, and artistic productions, and are invaluable to the process of recognizing First Peoples as significant (inter)national media citizens.

MEDIASCAPE SNAPSHOT, CORNER III

The Digitization of First Peoples' Arts and Cultures

> When the time came a few years ago to find an Inuktitut term for the word "internet," Nunavut's former Official Languages Commissioner, Eva Aariak, chose ikiaqqivik, or "travelling through layers" (Minogue, 2005). The word comes from the concept describing what a shaman does when asked to find out about living or deceased relatives or where animals have disappeared to: travel across time and space to find answers.
>
> According to the elders, shamans used to travel all over the world: to the bottom of the ocean, to the stratosphere, and even to the moon. In fact, the 1969 moon landing did not impress Inuit elders. They simply said, "We've already been there!" (Minogue, 2005). The word is also an example of how Inuit are mapping traditional concepts, values, and metaphors to make sense of contemporary realities and technologies. (Soukup, 2006, p. 239)

Telephone and internet access, affordable broadband costs, and Web 2.0/3.0 have technically and socially changed First Peoples' mediascapes. Aboriginal broadcasting is no longer the singular, most powerful tool of information dissemination, entertainment, and cultural reinforcement it once was. Although it is still popular among elders and young children, teenagers and young adults watch it only periodically and have complained that they are not interested in listening to elders lament the loss of their languages and cultures. They prefer to do their identity building over the internet with various social networking services, such as Facebook (the most popular site in the North), Flickr, and Bebo. In particular, Aboriginal youth are attracted to the internet as a way of joining postmodernity; of building virtual local, regional, and (inter)national social networks; and of participating in gaming activities. Many are attracted to the possibility of producing their own videos, films, and music entertainment that they can post on YouTube and Flickr. Writing their own blogs and accessing innumerable websites such as Second Life satisfies their hunger for stimulation, novelty, virtual travel, and identiplay.[9] Essentially, the drive to use the Web for the current generation of Aboriginal youth is little different from that of other ethnic youth around the world.

Although there are fascinating sites to explore around First Peoples' issues and interests, even more interesting is how the internet has brought together, into one technology, multiple First Peoples' cultural and communication forms, genres, and networks. It has offered the possibility of recirculating native media content in unique ways (such as that of IsumaTV) and has opened up creative options and fascinating images never before considered on other media (see http://sermitsiaq.gl/icecam/?lang=EN to watch Greenlandic icebergs melt in real time).

Medi-escapes bypass regulation and make tools accessible for the social engagement of people across (inter)national territories (see http://usmob.com.au)—to develop pseudo-intimate relationships without ever being co-present, and to construct knowledge and picture archives that show off interesting features of their (sub)cultures to the international community. As Aboriginal youth navigate through their favourite internet sites, the process of participating and collaborating in the production of meaning leads them to the creation of their own medi-escape strategies. It is within their minds that unique intercultural and media convergence and divergence patterns are etched into their personal mediascapes. It's on their websites that these perceptions and interpretive views of the world add to the collective intelligence of their affinity communities.

There is no doubt that First Peoples in urban areas have well located themselves within the internet using Web 2.0 and are in the process of building their individual identities, their social and professional networks, and their (inter)national personae, as almost everyone in the world with "access" is doing. As the next generation of mediaforms appear on their horizon, we can expect urban First Peoples to be appropriating and transforming them for their pleasures and purposes in a most original and culturally unique fashion.

A cautionary note is warranted here, however. What I have been describing above is only a partial snapshot taken with a metropolitan-biased lens. The missing fragments consist of Northern First Peoples whose access to digital media is by no means as ubiquitous as in the Southern and more populated regions of the county.

Rural and Remote Broadband Challenges

The national requirement for universal telephone service access in Canada does not pertain to the internet. Consequently, Canadian internet service providers do not have a legal obligation to develop broadband infrastructure in rural and remote communities and will likely not do so voluntarily unless they see it as a profitable business case, in support of their own interests. In the past, they have insisted on government investment and subsidies to assist rural and remote populations. In 2009, the federal government announced Industry Canada's Broadband Canada program, which had designated $10.6 million to match investments from Nunavut Broadband's Yellowknife-based internet provider SSi Micro. Eighty percent was to be used for satellite bandwidth for the following three years and was to compensate for the Nunavut government's initial underestimation of the demand for internet access in previous years (Zarate, 2010). Nunavut's error in projection of its bandwidth needs had resulted in the rationing of satellite bandwidth, the use of caps, and lower transmission speeds, especially during peak business hours. The amount of money allocated to the **Qiniq** network[10] (the name of the Nunavut broadband network) was by no means enough to accommodate the local community and regional conditions in Nunavut: remote and rural communities are often isolated due to permafrost, bog, island locations, poor or no roads, and an antiquated infrastructure incapable of carrying multiple signals simultaneously. Consequently, there are still very serious access issues with which to contend at both the Canadian-wide and Nunavut governmental levels (ibid.).

This, along with the lack of clarity around the scope of First Peoples minority communication and cultural rights enshrined in formal documents such as section 35 of the Canadian *Constitution* (1982), presents multiple challenges facing indigenous control over telecommunications policy development and service delivery (McMahon, O'Donnell et al., 2011, 8). Specifically, these include: "funding constraints, fragmented government policies, and a policy development process typically developed in centralized, urban institutional environments" (ibid.).

Broadband connectivity at the community level on Baffin Island, for instance, is well below access levels in Aboriginal communities in the urban South or mid-Canada and its cost is much more expensive. Furthermore, usage caps make Northwestel service (the main internet provider in the North) more profitable to the company, while increasing the cost for users. Looking more deeply at the complexities, let's return to the IsumaTV case. IsumaTV has been viewable all around the world via its website since its inception. However, people in small communities in the Arctic still cannot have high-speed access to its programs, films, and videos because of both the lack of bandwidth and the high cost of its rental. Nor are these problems of access limited to the High Arctic. As noted in an article on Nunatsiaq Online (June 9, 2010), internet downloading speed "is still many times slower in Nunavik than in southern Quebec. For example, a 90-minute movie takes five hours to download in Nunavik, but only three minutes in Montreal," according to Jean-Francois Dumoulin. "Many communities are still using dialup access, as the expense of ordinary internet service that we take for granted in the South is too prohibitive in the North. For an idea of the cost, let's take the example of high-speed Ultra internet service to Northwestel customers. In 2010, this cost $100 per month with a 10 gigabyte limit on downloading and a penalty of $10 for every gigabyte that is downloaded over that limit" (Windeyer, April 8, 2010). "To offer Nunavimmiut the same speed of internet via satellite that people in Montreal receive would cost $8,800 a month" (op cit. Nunatsiaq Online, June 9, 2010). The inequity of these costs is economically unjust and has made serious impact on the level of information availability to the communities of the region.

Another key impact is the continued process of **marginalization** of First Peoples to the sociopolitical and communicative peripheries. In June 2010, Tom Axtell,

Northern communications consultant, described this technological alienation in a personal interview with me:

> I believe that satellite bandwidth in the North actually costs 100 times what bandwidth costs in the South. In under 10 years, we in the South will be living in a 100 MB, or 500 MB download world like they do in Japan. If you think we are addicted to the Web now!!!! I predict that the gap will grow so great that people from the South will refuse to work in the Arctic under those low bandwidth conditions. It will seem as severe as the extreme cold temperatures which can hover at minus 30 for weeks.

What solutions to these dilemmas have been proposed? There are two levels of solutions being debated: macro/top-down approaches and grass-roots/bottom-up perspectives.

The Top/Down Approach

In January 2010, the Kodiak Kenai Cable Company of Alaska proposed the construction of an "ArcticLink, a massive 15,000-kilometre, US$1.2 billion cable connecting London and Tokyo" (Windeyer, January 25, 2010). The idea was to create a suboceanic fibre optical cable that would have to pass through the Northwest Passage, via the Parry Channel, down Baffin Bay and the Davis Strait, past southern Greenland (ibid.). The placement of the cable had become possible because of thinning Arctic ice due to global warming and climate change. However, the company would have to pass through Canadian territorial waters and would thus need federal approval from Industry Canada, as well as an environmental assessment. This infrastructure would have bypassed the existing satellite-based telecom system on which the North has been dependent since the 1970s. Northwestel had not responded to repeated requests to negotiate with the Kodiak Kenai Cable Company at the time; nor had the federal government.

Affordable connectivity and its sustainable local maintenance and management is central to the successful expansion of broadband and fibre optical systems in the North. The Kodiak Kenai Cable Company has not yet gained access to the area. However, recently Arctic Fibre Inc., a Canadian competitor of the Alaskan company and of Telesat (which currently delivers telecom services) announced that is has raised $640 million in financing, and will commence construction in 2013 for a 15,000 km. undersea fibre-optic cable linking London and Tokyo via Canada's Northwest Passage (Rogers, 2012). Will this kind of infrastructure incidentally enable the development of improved access to meet the needs of local community members whose lives are lived adjacent to the Arctic waters within which these optical fibres will be located? Will this be an affordable solution for people living in the communities? What will be the cost to the consumer? How much bandwidth equivalent will be provided? On the skeptical side, will these top-down plans provide false hope to Northern residents that a systemic solution will be arriving in the North as soon as the fibre optical infrastructure is set up? Where will small local companies such as Isuma be placed in relation to Arctic Fibre Inc.? Who from the local communities will be delegated to establish formal working relationships with the Arctic Fibre administration? How will this potential infrastructure impact on the First Peoples and their next generations—economically, culturally, and politically?

Local Independent Solutions: The "First Mile" Approach from the Bottom Up

Access issues in relation to the internet and other digital services are currently as appalling as they were in the 1960s and 1970s in relation to broadcasting. It doesn't appear that federal or private business solutions from outside the communities will resolve these inequities in the near future. First Nations and Inuit are aware of this and have been taking important self-driven initiatives to control ICT development and access within their own jurisdictions. For example, in July 2008, the Assembly of First Nations (AFN) passed resolution 16/2008, which "mandates the AFN National Technical Working Group to develop and implement an ICT Strategic Plan to address the issues of connectivity, hardware and software, and information management to serve First Nations in Canada" (Draft Resolutions, 2011).

This strategy supports a model that is driven, owned, and controlled by First Nations and prioritizes infrastructure, connectivity, and indigenous human resources (ibid.). In this context, the AFN has mobilized the notion of the "First Mile/Last Mile" (Paisley and Richardson, 1998), a concept that frames a continuum of control, involvement, and resource ownership levels. In relation to broadband or ICT access for remote communities, the Last Mile would refer to a process of connectivity established by and linked to centralized institutions located in metropolitan areas. In this case, the idea, product, process, and outcome would be designed and controlled by "outsiders," linking underserved communities to already existing systems and structures. In contrast to this, the First Mile approach would argue for a ground-up method of engaging local citizens in all aspects of the project. In other words, the latter is a process in which community members can "articulate and address their needs, before technical development and planning take place" at the initiation of outsiders (McMahon, O'Donnell et al., 2011, 1). The position seeks to "re-frame solutions to the 'digital divide' in ways that support community-based involvement, control, and ownership" (ibid.). McMahan, O'Donnell et al offer two case-study descriptions in which First Mile initiatives are taking place in First Nations communities. The first case is Fort Severn First Nation in Ontario, which is using the approach for both the development of broadband networks and a new cell phone service for its community (ibid., 3). The second case is being undertaken in doctoral research on the Northern Indigenous Community Satellite Network (NICSN) (ibid). For further information about this latter project, see National C-Band Benefit User Group (2005).

Another case that is utilizing the First Mile approach, though the project is not framed within this terminology, is that of IsumaTV, which has initiated media activity on both local and global levels. On the global level, it provides an internationally accessible service via its various projects carried on IsumaTV. On the local and regional levels, in trying to make the internet an "equal-access" distribution technology for Inuit and Aboriginal communities, IsumaTV has developed a system (on the same site) with two levels of compression to meet the needs of its users. This allows low-speed users in the North to choose videos on IsumaTV in moderate quality low-bandwidth versions specially designed to download ten times faster than other sites. At the same time, IsumaTV delivers video quality equal or superior to mainstream sites such as YouTube and up to full HD 1080p through Video on Demand (Kunuk & Cohn, 2010, p. 2). Isuma developers have gone even further in providing fair access to small and remote communities; they have established a:

> Nunavut Internet TV Network (NITV) which is a low-cost high speed network of local servers installed in remote low-bandwidth communities. NITV local servers cache IsumaTV's best-quality videos in hard drives in each participating community, allowing local users to choose large media files as if these were already downloaded at high-speed. Local new production uploaded to NITV plays immediately in each community while gradually updating all other servers in the NITV network. NITV allows schools complete high-speed access to all archives and other media on IsumaTV as well as curriculum resources to support their use for teaching. By connecting the NITV local server to its cable TV system, any community can broadcast a daily playlist 24/7 of programming selected from IsumaTV specifically for its local community channel. (Kunuk & Cohen, 2010)

NITV initially set up local servers in six Nunavut communities in 2010–2011. These systems are administered by community-based trained technicians who are less dependent for service from outsiders as are those working with mainstream satellite-based services. Within the next five years, the plan is to have the system installed in 26 Inuit communities (Cohn, personal interview, May 2, 2012). Working at the grassroots level with community participation, this is another example of the way in which the First Mile approach can be implemented and sustained.

More research on the ways in which these three projects are evolving and expanding would surely provide scholars and practitioners with models of indigenous community-based and controlled ICT development that would be a worthy contribution to this growing literature. Where might these projects fit into the fourth corner of our Mediascape snapshot?

MEDIASCAPE SNAPSHOT, CORNER IV

Whither the Next Generation?

> Ready or not, we're already living in a convergence culture.
> (Jenkins, 2008, p. 16)

In my previous version of this article, Corner IV was an empty page but for a box of floating keywords, which, alone and without context, best described the particularities from which the Aboriginal digital mediasphere (Web 2.0) of the future could be constructed. Assuming appropriate broadband/fibre optical access, Mediascape Snapshot, Corner IV would represent the next generation of Aboriginal media, the unknown, uncharted territory of mediaspace and makers that were still unpredictable, wild, and always in motion. Its meaning and direction could not yet be grasped.

Some of the words from which Corner IV was to be constructed were displayed in the box for the reader's deliberation. Here were some focalizing questions from which a contemplative framework could be built: Where is this next generation of First Peoples' media makers heading? What are their visions for the future? What

FIGURE 18.2 Snapshot Corner IV

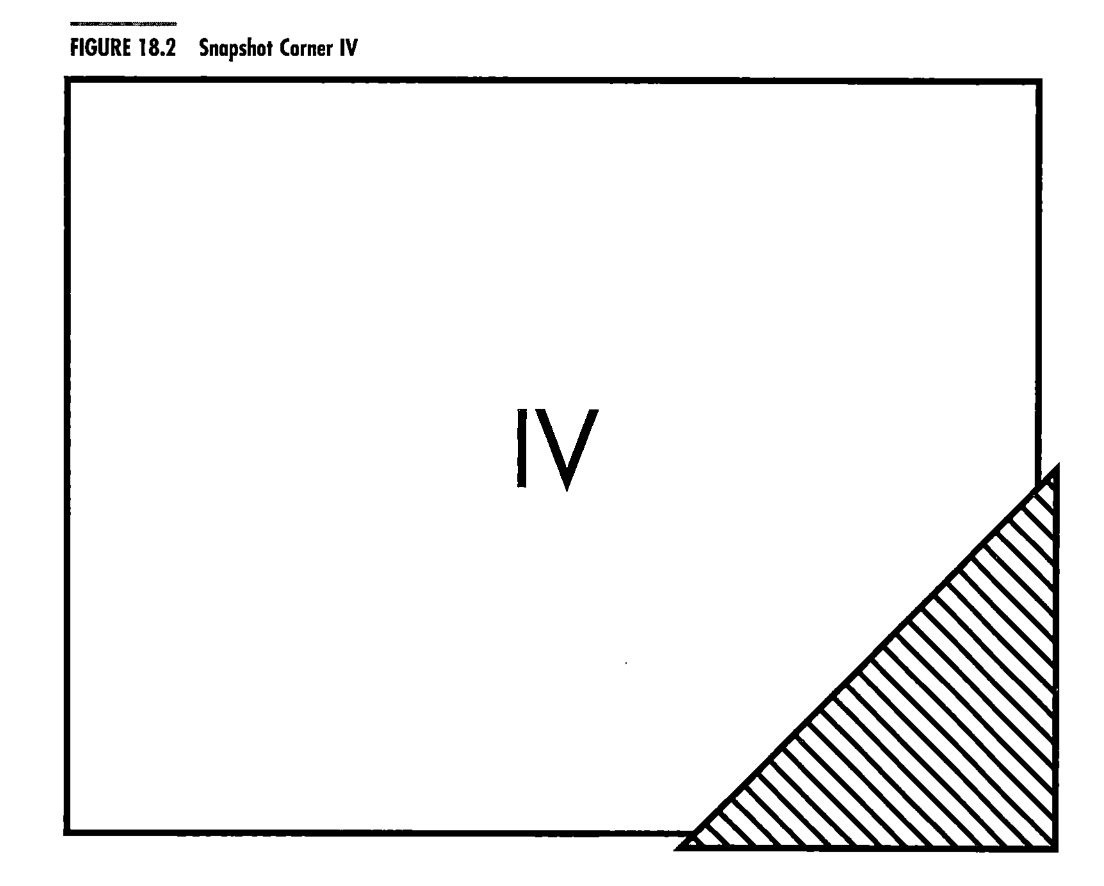

FIGURE 18.3 Keywords—Participatory and Convergent Media Culture

Open source, Linux, open systems, remix culture, transmedia storytelling, the visual archive, the traditional archive, social networking, adhocracies, collective intelligence, collective knowledge, wikis, Flickr, Bebo, Facebook, MySpace,YouTube, online radio, iTunes, bulletin boards, mp3, mp4, iPhone, participatory culture, participation gaps, digital divide, connectivity, digitextuality, technology extension, convergence culture, media generations, surveillance technologies, culture jamming, residual media, blogging, blogosphere, mobile media, generation gaps, polysemy, palimpsist, open text, multimedia, intermedia, affinity spaces, co-creation, collaborative authorship, gaming, digital cinema, websites, ethical protocols, privatization of cultures, cultural privacy, non-linear narrative, hypermedia, html, intertextuality, interactivity, media mix, MMORPGs (massively multiplayer on-line role-playing games), Second Life, MUDs (multiple user domains), multiplatform entertainment, skins, identiplay, smart mobs, globalization, glocalization, synergy, timeshift, transcreation, Web 2.0, avatars, Kindle, webcam, justin tv, Twitter, community-based media, piracy, copyright, scene culture, social mapping, bedroom culture, hyperlinking, satellite radio, homogeneity, heterogeneity, diversity, soundscapes, sonic identities, self-publication, virtual ethnography, auditory epistemology, habitus, satellites, user-generated content, new media nation, polyphony, quality, autoethnography, audience fragmentation, fractal, multiple voices, poetics, capacity building, infrastructure, cultural commons, (re)branding, Google Earth, inter-generational knowledge transfer, hacking, message clutter, marketing, messaging, collaboration, participation, relational aesthetics

might be the potential impact of current convergence culture on the identities of the next generation of Aboriginal media makers? How can First Peoples participate in making connections among dispersed media content?

How do digital media models like those described as First Mile projects fit into this imaginary empty corner in a state of flux? To where can models like these lead in terms of thinking about the democratization of media infrastructures and practices? Whose claims for the design of the context and content of this empty corner will be validated and legitimized?

CONCLUDING COMMENTS

In reflecting upon the history of First Peoples' media in Canada, what strikes me is the current revival of NFB debates about product, process, access, infrastructure, grass-roots community participation, and how important it has become for First

Peoples to be actively engaged in a range of political, cultural, and economic self-expressive activities in order to have a public identity. APTN is a product-oriented institution under CRTC regulation. The number of voices it broadcasts is restricted due to time constraints; production is costly; response to feedback is not immediate. In the feature film industry, limitations on the number of stories told are directly related to the financial status of a given production. Again, stories reflect a restricted number of characters and perspectives. With inexpensive digital cameras, recorders, and the internet (especially Facebook, YouTube, blogging, easy website construction and social networking), voices marginalized and excluded on television, radio, or film can privately gain public access to huge audiences at a reasonable cost and with long-lasting impact because of the Web's archiving features. There is more room for individual and collective differences in computer space than on the televisual and in the film industry. This, of course, is both its asset and liability.

Who among First Peoples actually listens to Web-based voices? Who engages in interactive conversations? What is the impact of this engagement on persons living in remote and isolated communities? Is there still a value to traditional media such as television, radio, and print? How are new media affecting old media markets, users, and producers? What are the political implications of the responses to these questions? These are questions that call for concrete, empirical research in the future.

The movement toward the digitization of almost everything will no doubt continue among First Peoples participating in the Web 2.0 and 3.0 worlds as long as they can obtain and retain affordable access to appropriate media delivery infrastructures. How the next generation of Aboriginal youth will collectively contribute to a shifting international mediascape will be of great interest to those involved in more traditional media, who are seeking ways to draw them back to First Peoples' existing cultural, social, and political corridors of power. The impact of the next generation's alternative mediated explorations on the positive transformation of the quality of life in their communities remains to be seen. Much of this impact will be reliant on an accessible and sustainable infrastructure that is financially and technically affordable, locally controlled, and available for the expression of a range of content relevant to all First Peoples and their neighbours living in remote and rural communities.

QUESTIONS

1. How does APTN serve as a television broadcasting model for other indigenous communities around the world?
2. Do you prefer to think of media as an art product or as part of a larger process of consciousness raising—or as something else? Describe your views and give reasons for your opinions.
3. Describe the images in your snapshot of Corner IV displaying indigenous media.

4. Does indigenous media represent a political tool in the ongoing dialogue between First Peoples and the dominant settler population? Does control of cultural production and consumption have implications for political solidarity?
5. How do you think digital convergence culture will impact the next generation of media makers in First Peoples' urban and remote communities?

NOTES

I would like to thank Alexa Conradi for her research assistance in the first version of this essay.

*"First Peoples" refers to all of Canada's indigenous/Aboriginal peoples: Amerindian, Métis, Inuit, and Inuvialuktun (Inuit who live in the area of Inuvik). The term "First Nations" and "native" refers only to Amerindians, Métis, and mixed-blood Amerindians. However, the word "native" is often mistakenly used by the general public to refer to all indigenous peoples. Consequently, the name "Native Communications Societies" has become the generic way of describing the communications organizations created by indigenous peoples for government administrative purposes. Although the most current term used by aboriginal peoples to refer to themselves varies, I believe that First Peoples is the most inclusive term and therefore use it most frequently.

1. Here, I make no claims to be comprehensive and take full responsibility for the selectivity and partiality of the evidence in this essay. Mine is an outsider's view of Aboriginal media history based on textual research, on-site interviews, visual research, and my personal experience of having been involved as witness and participant in the process in various capacities over a long period of time—from the early 1970s until very recently.
2. Parts of this section have been taken from my book, *Something New in the Air*, 2005 (pp. 97–106) and are reprinted with the permission of McGill Queen's University Press. It has been modified to make it relevant to this essay.
3. For readers interested in those First Peoples who protested the imposition of "outside" broadcasting services before local language programming was in place, see Roth (2005), for details.
4. These points were the result of the lessons learned from the NFB's first attempt to engage the interest of Aboriginal people in the filmmaking process. Until the Dorset project, the most direct relationship between the NFB and First Peoples took place in the training of an Indian film crew between 1968 and 1970. A team of First Nations' trainees from across Canada received production training and practice for two years while living in Montreal. Although expecting to receive employment with the NFB after the training terminated, this did not happen, and the crew ended up becoming freelancers, picking up production contracts here and there when possible and creating their own projects, often using the Challenge for Change approach.

5. For a history of their evolution, please see Roth, 2005.
6. Their first four years of funding was for $1.4 million to be shared among the 13 NCSs for both radio and television production.
7. At its commencement, the cost was 15 cents per household per month. In its 2005 licence renewal, this was raised by ten cents. The money secures their long-term funding and is used as a production fund in communities that are not economically viable enough to sustain media economies. It also pays for licence and program fees. In this regard, APTN may be a prototype for other states interested in assuring the sponsorship and sustenance of public service programming for minorities.
8. Unfortunately, Paul Apak passed away in 1998.
9. "Identiplay" is a term I first used in 1999 in an article entitled "Reflections on the Colour of the Internet" in Steve Hicks and Ed Halpin (eds.). (2000), *Human Rights and the Internet*, London: MacMillan and Company. It refers to the multiple ways in which users play with a range of false identities or personae as they navigate through the internet. It is what one does when taking on the identity of an avatar.
10. "QINIQ" means "to search." The Qiniq network is an advanced satellite and wireless network, delivering broadband internet services to all communities in Nunavut, Canada. The network spans 25 communities, servicing a total population of approximately 29,000 people across 2 million square kilometers." Retrieved August 22, 2012, from http://www.qiniq.com/about

REFERENCES

APTN Fact Sheet. (1999). Aboriginal Peoples Television Network. Retrieved on September 6, 2012, from http://www.aptn.ca/corporate/facts.php

APTN Milestones. (2003). Aboriginal Peoples Television Network. Retrieved on September 6, 2012 from http://www.aptn.ca/corporate/milestones.php

Assembly of First Nations. (2011, December 6). Draft Resolutions. AFN Special Chiefs Assembly. Retrieved August 22, 2012, from http://www.afn.ca/uploads/files/sca/draft_2011_sca_resolutions_fe.pdf

Boswell, R. (2012, March 27). Undersea fibre-optic cable would boost communications in far north. *Postmedia News*. Retrieved April 28, 2012, from Canada.com

———. (2012, March 28). Northern Cable Plan Gains Steam. Retrieved September 3, 2012, from http://www.nunatsiaqonline.ca/stories/article/65674northern_cable_plan_gains_steam

CBC News North. (2011, July 8). Igloolik Isuma productions going out of business. Retrieved September 1, 2012, from http://www.cbc.ca/news/story/2011/07/08/isuma-productions-business.html

Christen, K. (2005). Gone digital: Aboriginal remix and the cultural commons. *International Journal of Cultural Property 12*, 315–345.

Draft Resolutions. AFN Special Chiefs Assembly December 6–8, 2011. Retrieved September 3, 2012, from http://www.afn.ca/uploads/files/sca/draft_2011_sca_resolutions_fe.pdf

Driscoll, D. (1972). Can we evaluate Challenge for Change? *Access: Challenge for Change Newsletter*, *10*, 22–23.

Eco, U. (1961, January/February). Verso una civiltà della visione? *Pirelli: Rivista Bimestrale d'Informazione e di Tecnica*, 32–41.

Fraser, N. (1989). *Unruly practices: Power, discourse and gender in contemporary social theory*. Minneapolis: University of Minnesota Press, 11–12.

Ginsburg, F. & F. Myers. (2006). A history of Aboriginal futures. *Critique of Anthropology 26* (1), 27–45.

Hénaut, D. T. (1971–72). Powerful catalyst. *Access*, 7, 3–7.

Jenkins, H. (2008). *Convergence culture: Where old and new media collide*. New York: New York University Press.

Kunuk, Z. & Cohn, N. (2010, October 1). CRTC Intervention Letter. National Aboriginal Broadcasting.

McMahon, R., O'Donnell, S., et al. (2011). Digital divides and the "first mile": Framing First Nations broadband development in Canada. *The International Indigenous Policy Journal*, 2 (2). Retrieved August 22, 2012, from http://ir.lib.uwo.ca/iipj/vol2/iss2/2

National C-Band Benefit User Group. (2005). Indigenous community leaders from the north in three provinces to attend opening of satellite broadband network in Sioux Lookout, Ontario. [Press Release]. Retrieved August 22, 2012, from http://smart.knet.ca/satellite/press_release.html

Nunatsiaq Online. (June 9, 2010). "Internet speeds doomed to lag." Retrieved September 1, 2012 from http://www.nunatsiaqonline.ca/stories/article/98789_nunavik_internet_speeds_doomed_to_lag

Nunavut Fibre Optic Feasibility Study. (March 2012). Retrieved September 1, 2012, from http://www.qfile.ca/p/42424/Workspaces/NBDC%20Fibre%20Report/Nunavut%20Fibre%20Optic%20Feasibility%20Study%20-%20Final%20Report.pdf

Paisley, L. & Richardson, D. (1998). Why the *first* mile and not the last? In L. Paisley & D. Richardson (Eds.). The first mile of connectivity: Advancing telecommunications for rural development through a participatory communication approach. *Communication for Development*. Rome: Food and Agriculture Organization of the United Nations (FAO). Retrieved August 22, 2012, from http://www.fao.org/sd/CDdirect/CDre0025.htm

Rogers, S. (2012, January 24) "Fibre optic cable headed for Canadian Arctic?" Nunatsiaq Online. Retrieved September 6, 2012, from http://www.nunatsiaqonline.ca/stories/article/65674is_fibre_optic_cable_on_its_way_to_the_canadian_arctic

Roth, L. (2005). *Something new in the air: The story of First Peoples television broadcasting in Canada*. Montreal: McGill-Queens University Press.

Soukup, K. (2006). Report: travelling through layers: Inuit artists appropriate new technologies. *Canadian Journal of Communication 31*, 239–246.

Thorvaldson, P. (1976). The NFB film workshops. *Pot Pourri* (NFBNewsletter), Spring, 2–8.

Windeyer, Chris. (2010, January 25). "Alaska company eyes cable through Northwest Passage." Nunatsiaq Online. Retrieved September 1, 2012, from http://www.nunatsiaqonline.ca/stories/article/250110_alaska_company_eyes_cable_through_northwest_passage

———. (2010, April 8). "Norwestel Puts Squeeze on Iqualuit High-speed Customers," *Nunatsiaq Online*. Retrieved September 5, 2012, from http://www.nunatsiaqonline.ca/stories/article/8796_northwestel_puts_squeeze_on_iqaluit_high_speed_customers/

Zarate, G. (2010, May 28). Qiniq promises true broadband for Nunavut. *NunatsiaqOnLine*. Retrieved August 22, 2012, from http://www.nunatsiaqonline.ca/stories/article/98789_qiniq_promises_true_broadband_for_nunavut

PERSONAL INTERVIEWS

Tom Axtell, Northern Communications Trainer and Consultant, June 2010.

Ron Blumer, NFB Producer and Trainer. 1974, 1975. Multiple conversations.

Norman Cohn, President, Isuma Distributional International and IsumaTV. May 2, 2012.

Lyle Cruickshank (Director) and Gordon Martin (Researcher), NFB, Media Research Department. Several interviews, 1974–75.

Wolf Koenig, Executive Producer, Animation Studio. NFB. June 9, 10, 1975; January 6, 1981.

Jean Larose, President and CEO of APTN. September 23, 2008.

Peter Raymont, NFB Executive Producer, Animation Studio. 1974–75. Multiple conversations.

19

THE COLOUR OF DIFFERENCE: RACE, DIVERSITY, AND JOURNALISM IN CANADA

Faiza Hirji
McMaster University

TELLING THE STORIES

In 2002, Canadian news media reported on the story of a Syrian-Canadian man who had been detained by immigration officials in the United States and then sent to Syria on suspicion of terrorism. The reasons for this detention and subsequent rendition were not disclosed due to security concerns. However, prominent media outlets such as *The Ottawa Citizen* reported that there was reason for considering the man a security risk, citing unnamed government sources (O'Neill, 2003). The detention of that man, and the subsequent coverage of it, confirmed the suspicions of many Canadians that citizens of Middle Eastern ancestry were not to be trusted during this politically fraught time. The same coverage made Canadians of Middle Eastern ancestry feel frightened and under attack. The man, Maher Arar, was returned to Canada after enduring months of torture in Syria. He continued to assert his innocence, and a federal inquiry went on to agree, suggesting that there was no evidence to indicate that Arar was ever a security threat to Canada or to the United States (O'Connor, 2006). Upon his release, Arar argued that the media were partly to blame for his trials. He proclaimed his disappointment that the media continued to portray him as a guilty man when there were no data to support this.

In 2010, Canadian media covered the story of Tamil migrants who had arrived in British Columbia on a ship. Government officials were quick to react, casting suspicion on the motives of the migrants, questioning their right to set foot on Canadian soil, and suggesting that there might be a connection between the migrants and the Tamil Tigers, an alleged terrorist organization. The media repeated these comments, with one article referring to "illegal migrants," the need to screen for "potential terrorists or smugglers," and to government allegations that "the passengers include human traffickers and people linked to the Tamil Tigers terrorist group" (Chase, Youssef, & Lindell, 2010, p. A1). The Canadian Border Services Agency later revealed, following the detention and investigation of the migrants, that more than 300 migrants had been released and only 12 were facing litigation over their refugee claims.

In 2011, Canadian media covered the story of the *niqab* ban, a new rule introduced by Immigration Minister Jason Kenney to ensure that women who wear the *niqab*, a garment covering the entire body and all of the face except for the eyes, must uncover their faces in order to take a citizenship oath in Canada. CBC News quoted Kenney as saying that it was "bizarre" that women would have been allowed previously to wear the face covering. He added that "he doesn't accept that it's a religious obligation to wear the veil" (Payton, 2011, para. 4–5).

In 2011 and 2012, the media reported on the alleged murder of three Canadian sisters and their father's first wife. Their car was discovered submerged in the canal in Kingston, Ontario. Police arrested the girls' father, mother and brother, suggesting that the killing was motivated by anger over the young women's desire to date and their refusal to comport themselves in accordance with their father's notion of modesty. The media regularly referred to the trial of the suspects as the "honour killings" trial, suggesting that the concept of honour killing was well known in Afghanistan, where the father was born. A *Toronto Star* article following the guilty verdict for the three accused emphasized the theme that such killings are unknown in civilized countries such as Canada, recounting the verdicts and then stating, "In our country, men and women are equal. A female's life is worth as much as a male's. In our country, femicide is homicide" (DiManno & Chung, 2012, p. A1).

Why is the representation of these cases problematic, and why does it matter? In a country as multicultural as Canada, the media must cover a variety of cases involving people of varying backgrounds. The information they provide, and the manner in which they provide it, help to educate the public. For some members of the public, media exposure may be the only venue that they have to learn about certain minority groups. This is particularly true for those citizens who live in areas that are not especially diverse (Mahtani, 2008, p. 232). As Mahtani comments, "media scholars have thoroughly documented how the Canadian media have the power to create social agendas, construct **ideologies**, and frame social issues, providing the lens through which Canadians view themselves and their fellow citizens" (2008, p. 232). In cases such as those described above, the Canadian public may be left with a misleading impression, and this can have very real consequences.

This is clearly problematic when the media are openly racist, meaning that they attribute negative qualities to members of a particular race, however that race is being defined (Miles and Brown, 2003, p. 8). More often, however, the media are not overtly or intentionally racist. However, they do not always know how to address cases involving minorities: in such cases, **racialized discourses** tend to emerge, where individuals or groups will be defined—sometimes subtly—by difference, whether that difference takes the form of race, religion, or culture.

In the first case mentioned above, Maher Arar was painted by government officials and by the media as being different on a number of levels: a Muslim man, of Syrian origin and Canadian citizenship, who was unable to renounce his Syrian citizenship due to the laws of that country. He has argued that the media tarnished his reputation and advanced the impression that he was a threat to national security.

They did this in the absence of any convincing evidence, he claimed, and this continued as recently as 2009, when the media reported on allegations that alleged terrorist Omar Khadr had seen Arar in terrorist safe houses in Afghanistan. With the media and government forces aligned against him, it was an uphill battle to convince Canadians to advocate for his freedom. Reflecting on his ordeal during a panel organized by the Canadian Journalism Foundation on the subject of media coverage of his case, Arar said, "I want reporters to consider who they serve, the powerful and the anonymous or the weak and the vulnerable ... Err on the side of the weak not the strong" (Gombu, 2009, p. A3).

While the coverage of the Arar case certainly did hurt one individual's reputation, it may be seen as part of a larger pattern in which the media demonstrated difficulty in covering stories related to Muslims, Islam, the Middle East, or Afghanistan. In the wake of September 11, 2001, one media poll did find that Canadians were more suspicious of Muslims (Blanchfield, 2002; also see Walton & Kennedy, 2002), and comments posted on media blogs on stories about Muslims seem to reflect both that suspicion and a distinct degree of xenophobia. Naturally, it is not media coverage alone that creates hostility toward minorities, but it is certainly a key contributor. In the case of Maher Arar, he was eventually cleared, but months of allegations that he was guilty likely left an impression on citizens exposed to stories about his case.

Similarly, in the case of the Tamil migrants, it seems likely that the coverage of the story would affect public opinion. Although the Tamil migrants constituted a very small percentage of the approximately 19,000 refugee claims made in Canada that year, the coverage made it appear far more significant and the negative impact was emphasized on several levels: in addition to the alleged terrorist links, there were also stories about the possibility that the migrants were infected with tuberculosis (Fong, 2010, p. A1). Moreover, although there were no legal grounds for detaining or deporting the migrants, the initial smear on their reputation is difficult to forget. Such cases are not uncommon in Canada: previous cases involving Tamil migrants provoked similar consternation in the media and the same allegations of terrorism (Henry & Tator, 2002). In 1999, a ship filled with Chinese migrants that attempted to dock in British Columbia elicited a similarly heated reaction, with commentary about the strain on the Canadian public (see Hier & Greenberg, 2002). In that case, as in the Tamil case, due process was followed and legitimate claimants were permitted to stay while unsuccessful claimants were deported. Media coverage of this kind tends to create negative feelings about refugee claims in general, rather than generating compassion for people in desperate circumstances. However, Mahtani indicates that some refugees and immigrants tend to be depicted more negatively than others, depending on their racial heritage. As an example, she notes that refugees from Kosovo have been portrayed positively in past media coverage, but "migrants from China were portrayed as problematic and unwelcome" (2008, p. 236).

With the coverage of the *niqab* ban, there is again a sense of imposition on the Canadian public. In actual fact, the number of women wearing *niqab* in Canada is quite small, and there are alternative methods of ensuring that a woman wearing *niqab* is reciting the citizenship oath, such as asking the woman to uncover her face in a private setting with another woman. However, the notion of a *niqab* ban—which, in some countries, took the form of a complete ban—was acquiring popular currency at the time that Canada introduced it. Extensive media emphasis on women who cover themselves for religious purposes, beginning with stories of oppressed burqa-clad women in Afghanistan in 2001, attracted widespread attention to this practice in Canada, and often made it seem problematic (see Alvi, Hoodfar, & McDonough, 2003; Khan, 1995). Realistically, *niqab* wearers pose no threat to others and their numbers are so small that most of the Canadian public is unlikely to be affected, in any case. While Smith's (2011) article notes that *niqab* wearers constitute perhaps 300 members of the Canadian public, the title of her article ("Veiled Threat") and the amount of overall media exposure made this practice seem as though many citizens would be in contact with *niqab* wearers and as though these citizens would be at risk. Some of the media stories on this topic were quite even handed, but others, simply by dwelling on the government's comments or on the general subject with an intensity that seemed disproportionate to the number of people affected, emphasized the notion that Muslim women are different and that they refuse to conform to Canadian societal norms. Minister Kenney's remarks about his refusal to accept the notion of religious obligation in regard to the *niqab* (Payton, 2011), in fact, left a strong impression that women who wear the *niqab* have no religious reason for doing so, when in fact their interpretation may simply differ from his.

In the case of the Shafia murders, again, a combination of government commentary and media coverage left a misleading and powerful impression. The emphasis on the family's Afghan roots, and the repeated use of the term "honour killing," gave weight to the idea that honour killings were common among people of Afghan origin. This is arguable in itself; more problematic, perhaps, the term "honour killing" exoticized a practice that is sadly not uncommon. Domestic violence, and the attempt to control women's bodies, is not limited to a specific group of people. Referring to this case as an honour killing case helped provide a powerful and easily understood narrative for the prosecutors in the case, but reproducing that narrative over and over again in the media may have distracted the public from the fact that violence against women is a widespread and deeply disturbing problem throughout Canadian society. When journalists emphasized the fact that this was a crime committed by people with values foreign to Canadian society, they were validating longstanding notions that Western societies are more progressive, developed and civilized, while societies in other parts of the world may be backwards, barbaric and bogged down in incomprehensible traditions. This tendency to normatize the Self, and to condemn the Other, is documented in Edward Said's book on **Orientalism** (1978) in which he notes the ways in which Western travellers and writers have historically set up dichotomies where their society is valourized at the expense of another. In the Shafia case, it is perhaps not surprising that journalists tended to explain such an utterly repugnant crime by focusing on culture, and the difference between the Shafias and the average Canadian.

The coverage of these cases matters, given that questions of policy, power, and representation are involved. This chapter discusses these questions, and the importance of responsible and equitable media coverage wherever possible. The following sections provide further detail about the ways in which racial bias manifests itself in the media, the structural and sociocultural reasons why this may occur, and possible solutions. Eliminating racial bias in the media should not be considered an impossible ideal. It is crucial to represent all groups in society as fairly as possible. Understanding of complex societal issues around multiculturalism, immigration and accommodation is involved in the cases I mention here, and there are many other such examples. Many citizens do not spend extensive hours studying immigration practices or multiculturalism policies in detail. They rely on the media for their information. Sometimes, the media will be their only or primary source of information on the practices of particular ethnic groups, or on the implications of immigration, or on national security issues. The impressions they gain from watching or reading these stories may remain with them as they vote on related issues, or as they interact with other Canadians. What the media say, then, matters.

THE RACE PROBLEM: POWER AND DISCOURSE

If the media do exercise significant influence over public opinion, one may wonder about the specifics of how they do this. After all, the role of journalists, one might suggest, is to report the truth, as accurately and factually as possible. This is indeed the way many reporters understand their profession, and certainly the way many citizens understand it, hence their faith in what they read or see. However, some might argue that the truth depends on one's perspective. Objectivity is virtually impossible to achieve. Most individuals carry biases of some kind with them, born of their upbringing, education, or interactions with others. These biases are important when they are reflected in the work of journalists, but also equally important from the perspective of media consumers. Certain words in headlines ("threat," "honour") or images in pictures (the woman in *niqab*) may speak to existing beliefs, whether these are conscious or subconscious.

Language and images are not neutral. As the Dutch scholar Teun van Dijk (1988, 1991, 1993, 1996, 1998) has explained, ideology infuses language. If there is a dominant narrative about a particular story or group, that narrative is likely informed by power relations: who has it, who does not have it, who wants to keep the status quo. Often, powerful individuals or groups tend to shape media narratives, even if their influence is indirect or goes unrecognized. These power relations are reflected in the way a media story is represented, in terms of who has a voice and how that voice is permitted to speak. In a sense, journalists belong to a societal elite and they contribute, however unconsciously, to reinforcing existing notions about the way the world is. Alternatives do exist to the dominant discourse—in this case, a discourse that normalizes the behaviour of the white majority and emphasizes the difference represented by minorities—but their effectiveness can be diminished. Even a short media story, whether broadcast or printed, has a particular undercurrent that can be transmitted to the public, through techniques such as placement or framing (see Karim, 2003, p. x for his suggestion that alternative efforts are often subverted).

Racialized Discourses and Critical Discourse Analysis

Framing allows the media to present a story in a particular way, emphasizing specific aspects. A story about a *niqab* ban may have various aspects that can be highlighted; the journalist or editor presenting the story will decide if this should be framed as a story about religious freedom, objectification of women, women's rights, or the need for assimilation. Framing is one key technique found in the media as a general rule, but may be especially worth examining in stories about race or religion. Similarly, with placement, stories that contradict the dominant discourse are frequently found toward the end of newspaper sections or broadcasts, or they are outnumbered by stories arguing the dominant view. Sometimes the means of silencing alternative or oppositional voices are quite blatant, as when journalists are fired, rebuked, or edited until their pieces lose much of their political vigour. Placement is one of the more subtle methods of downplaying or undercutting alternative voices (Karim, 2003, pp. 161–165; Shoemaker & Reese, 1996, p. 37). For instance, a positive story about a minority group may be juxtaposed with stories about criminal activity by migrants, leaving an overall negative impression. Placement may also be important with respect to the themes that are emphasized in a viewer's mind.

These techniques work only when they are affirming beliefs that are already held by media viewers or readers. The pre-existing stereotypes identified by Jiwani (1993, p. 10) are explained by van Dijk as models, "mental structures of information which, besides the new information offered in a news report, feature information about such a situation as inferred from general knowledge scripts" (1991, p. 74). He suggests many ways in which features of news reports, such as lexical choice, placement, and structure combine to create and reinforce notions of "white superiority" (1993, p. 128). Analyzing these features, using a technique called **critical discourse analysis**, allows researchers to deconstruct the type of language used in the description of minorities, assessing some of the biases that may be embedded within a discursive sample, e.g., a news article.

Van Dijk suggests that discourse has to be analyzed at two levels, the more specific "local, micro level" and the "higher level, societal orders of discursive practices" (1993, p. 122). The latter issue is addressed, at least partially, by the problem of bias in the newsroom. In terms of the actual news articles themselves, headlines serve as a significant starting point for analysis, given that many readers consult headlines and first paragraphs in order to determine their interest in a particular article. This is especially true now, with the large number of media sources (broadcast, online, print) available to the public. With so much information available, media consumers may be especially prone to rely on headlines to decide whether or not to probe further. After absorbing information supplied in the headlines and first paragraphs, they may cease reading for lack of interest or conversely because they feel they have already grasped the essential facts of the article (van Dijk, 1991, pp. 50–51). That being the case, headlines are significant in that they serve as a type of filter for readers determining which articles are of interest. However, they are also significant because the words in the headlines may leave a lasting impression, even if the actual story provides an entirely different context than that supplied by the headline.

This allots special emphasis to headlines in the Shafia case such as "In a crime based on honour, court finds nothing more 'honourless'" (Appleby, 2012), and "Yes, Shafia murders were honour killings" (Lakritz, 2012), or in a different case, "Veiled threat: Niqab ban has some fearing a less tolerant Canada" (Smith, 2011). For those who do not read more detail about these cases, the notion of honour killing appears to be the central aspect of the Shafia case, and seems to be entangled inextricably with religion. Similarly, the story about the *niqab* ban, which is about new rules prohibiting women from wearing face coverings during citizenship ceremonies, is headlined in such a way that it implies *niqab* wearers present a threat to society. In fact, the story is really about changes to the *niqab* wearers' way of life, not vice versa. The story text is thoughtful, but the effect may be lost because the headline seeks to create a sense of danger.

Within a story itself:

> rhetorical structures are studied as means to emphasize or de-emphasize meanings as a function of ideological opinions. Metaphors may be chosen that highlight the negative character of our enemies, comparisons in order to mitigate the blame of our own people, and irony to challenge the negative models of our opponents. (van Dijk, 1998, p. 208)

Tarek Fatah, head of the Muslim Canadian Congress and an oft-quoted commentator on Islamic culture, spoke in a *Toronto Star* article about the Shafia case: "If these four women were white women, they would still be alive today ... These girls went to the school, the cops, child services and everyone wanted to protect multiculturalism—not the lives of these young women" (Findlay, 2012, p. A10). This quote manages to isolate murderous tendencies to minorities and suggests that multiculturalism promotes a cultural relativism that prevented these young women from securing assistance. Fatah may be correct, but it is not clear that this is the case from the facts that were disclosed in their trial. As in many cases of domestic violence, some individuals did try to intervene on behalf of the young women but failed. Multiculturalism is not the chief culprit in what is clearly a heinous case. As a policy, **multiculturalism** promotes acceptance of diversity but not at the expense of citizens' security.

The tactics used in the *Toronto Star* article are a direct expression of ideology and a more specific evolution of group members expressing "our" beliefs (van Dijk, 1998, p. 239). The use of words such as "we," "us" and "our" is frequently found in articles arguing a firm ideological standpoint and attempting to minimize resistance to that point of view (Cottle, 2000, p. 2; see Deacon, Pickering, Golding, & Murdock, 1999, p. 324; van Dijk, 1998, p. 203). Some of the news reports on the Shafia killings and the *niqab* ban honed in on this difference by clearly articulating the difference between what "we" think, as opposed to what detractors may wish to say. DiManno and Chung (2012) highlighted this difference as explicitly as possible by referring to "our country" and the fact that the Shafias brought their own beliefs into it, and by emphasizing repeatedly that cultural misogyny and violence are Afghan constructs, not Canadian ones: "Bad Afghan boys can stay out till 3 a.m. with their little brothers and not get slapped across the face for it." Van Dijk posits that "the social others, as part of the targeted outgroup, may be talked *about* but at the same time indirectly, socially and ideologically *addressed*" (1998, p. 225, italics in original).

In theory, interviews with social others who are generally not given a voice would mitigate the damage that uninformed reporting about others might inflict. If words spoken in an interview are taken out of context, this may be difficult to assess here with any degree of exactitude. However, by looking at the selections of text that are provided, it is possible to apply, to some extent, van Dijk's theory that "most forms of quotation ... are indirect or a mixture of direct and indirect speech. This allows varying degrees of distance, marked in different linguistic ways, between the quotation and what was actually said" (1991, p. 152). It is often the case that the quotation provided will have been selectively edited in order to provide a particular impression. For instance, in her critique of a letter writer who tried to separate the notion of violence against women from specific religions, and of a politician who protested the use of words such as "barbaric" to describe cultural practices, Lakritz left out the larger explanation behind these attempts, ridiculing them with the following oversimplification:

> Nice try, letter writer, but your attempt to tarnish other cultures so as to avoid singling out the culpable ones, doesn't wash. Christians and Jews may be guilty of spousal abuse and domestic violence, but the premeditated killing of sisters, daughters and wives to preserve some primitive sense of male "honour" doesn't happen. (2012, p. A10)

This is one area in which "relative incompleteness," the omission of relevant information, may occur (van Dijk, 1998, p. 268). In the case of the *niqab* ban, some media outlets actually did a very good job of interviewing *niqab* wearers, some of whom spoke articulately and clearly about their reasons for wearing *niqab* and their belief that they did not pose any threat to Canadians. However, this was also juxtaposed with comments such as the one cited earlier by Minister Kenney, where he implies that women who wear *niqab* do not really understand their own religion.

Lexical style can be suggestive of many aspects of position and power, van Dijk says, adding that the "choice of words will also reveal who is in control and what the relations are between writers and readers, or between writers and the people they speak about" (van Dijk, 1991, p. 211). Some of those people can be represented in ways that indicate the groups in which they hold membership and their corresponding norms and values (van Dijk, 1998, p. 259): this was clearly the case with the coverage of the Shafias and the *niqab* wearers. The Tamil migrants were assigned, in the absence of any other contextual information, to a number of groups: refugees, possible terrorists, menace to Canadian society. Such indications of power relations are typical in what van Dijk refers to as an **"ideological square"** consisting of four main strategies. These strategies involve placing emphasis on any positive information regarding the in-group and, conversely, on negative information related to the out-group, while suppressing positive information about the latter as well as negative information about the former (1998, p. 267).

While lexical style focuses on specific presentation of subject matter, topic selection can also "influence the representation readers construct in their mind of specific ethnic events and situations" (van Dijk, 1991, p. 74). Another way of minimizing the impact of statements or movements by minorities is the use of a divide-and-conquer strategy, wherein ethnic groups appear to be plagued by internal rivalries (van Dijk, 1991, p. 197). The quoting of Tarek Fatah in the article about the Shafia case is one way of suggesting, first of all, that Muslims have peculiar beliefs and practices, particular only to themselves, and then condemning those practices (and by extension those individuals) all the more vigorously because another Muslim has spoken out against them and suggested that faith is the chief motivation for a shocking murder.

FROM THE TOP DOWN: WHY THE MEDIA LACK DIVERSITY

The vast majority of journalists in Canada work diligently to provide balanced and fair coverage of current events. Nonetheless, as I have already suggested, the outcome is not always ideal. There are a number of reasons this may be the case: some are economic and others are sociocultural, and many times they overlap. One reason relates to the political economy of the media. In other words, while journalists may have every intention of providing the most accurate and informative coverage possible, they work within an economic system that has constraints. The news media are part of an industry, and ownership matters within this industry. Owners, such as the conservative former media baron Conrad Black or the late pro-Liberal Izzy Asper, may impose their views upon the editors and journalists who work within their media outlets.

Even in cases where owners may define themselves as being apolitical, ownership can still affect media diversity. As McChesney (1999) and McChesney and Pickard (2011) have demonstrated, the last few years have seen increased concentration in the ownership of the media, not only in North America, but also around the world. This places more and more media outlets under the ownership of a few individuals. Perhaps more importantly, these conglomerates tend to employ considerable economies of scale in order to maximize profits. This can involve relying on a smaller number of journalists whose opinions are then reprinted or rebroadcast across several media outlets. In converged companies that operate several media platforms, as nearly all of the major media companies now do, the same journalist's opinion may be reproduced in several different formats, saving time and money, but reducing diversity and originality.

If concentrated ownership is the problem, one might perceive public, or state-operated media as the solution. While this is true in theory, it is less so in practice. In Canada, the Canadian Broadcasting Corporation (CBC), is intended to provide a public alternative to the media. To some extent it does so: as a Crown corporation operated at arm's length from the government the CBC is not subject to editorial interference from its owners. However, it operates on increasingly slender funding amounts that may be altered any time at the behest of Parliament. Indeed, as funding cuts have continued to beleaguer the CBC, there have often been rumours that public broadcasting will eventually be phased out in Canada. In this uncertain environment, the CBC must continue to compete with those same large media corporations that have the advantage of collecting advertising dollars and savings across multiple platforms, as in the case of companies that draw revenue from television and radio networks as well as mobile telephone and computing units. The CBC, in contrast to these large private-sector competitors, does not have the budget or a mandate to purchase various media outlets and disseminate content through them. It is also expected to support and promote Canadian programming, which is a culturally important goal but one that does have financial repercussions when a private-sector competitor can derive large profits from popular American television programs or from sales of mobile telephone services. To its credit, the CBC continues to draw audiences for news, but it is pressed to do so with fewer resources than its private-sector competitors.

In Canada, the increasingly lean budgets of news media outlets have fostered a dependence on European and American news agencies and wire services (Karim, 2003, p. 14; see Shoemaker & Reese, 1996, p. 118), which has the effect of ensuring that stories are mediated by another source prior to publication in the Canadian press, and also propagates the trend of delivering a limited number of stories which receive coverage in all the major media sources, since most are drawing on the same pool of information. This trend is further exacerbated by "pack" or "copy-cat" journalism, in which a large number of reporters pursue the same leads in order to ensure that their respective outlets do not miss a major story (Shoemaker & Reese, 1996, p. 123; Ungerleider, 1991, p. 159). Given the economic pressures on Canadian newspapers, in particular, some of which already operate on slim profit margins due to rising newsprint costs, it is unsurprising that no editor wishes to risk losing the major story of the day. Related to these competitive pressures is the stress of filing a story quickly, which may not allow sufficient time for in-depth research (Cottle, 2000, p. 20; Shoemaker & Reese, 1996, p. 119). Whether public or private, many media outlets tend to rely on the same easily accessible sources for their stories, which also dilutes the diversity of the news. These sources include official proceedings, news releases, press conferences, leaks, and reports from other news organizations, with markedly less emphasis on alternatives such as interviews, firsthand accounts, and independent research and analysis (Shoemaker & Reese, 1996, p. 128).

All media outlets, in fact, even those that are profitable, feel the pinch of competition acutely in the digital age. In the era of print and basic cable, major newspapers and a few major broadcasters competed with one another to provide stories to the public in the evening edition or the news hour at dinnertime. The 24-hour news channel, exemplified by CNN, altered this format completely. No longer was it sufficient to chase a big news story all day and provide the details to the public by the evening. Instead, viewers, readers, and listeners came to expect breaking news instantly, at any time of day. As digital media, such as websites and satellite stations, have increasingly begun to provide an alternative to news consumers, the traditional media have had to keep up with the new model. Some have attempted to cope by borrowing from the techniques of the ever-growing competition, such as the use of social media (e.g., Twitter, live blogging) and even borrowing the media productions themselves. For instance, some news outlets now ask for citizens to provide photographs or video of stories they have witnessed, a nod to the important role that citizens' media has played in breaking or adding to news stories through a conveniently placed camera phone at the scene of an event, such as the uprisings of the so-called Arab Spring, or the Stanley Cup riots. While these attempts at adaptation do help to make traditional media more flexible, the fast pace and the use of multiple different sources makes it difficult to authenticate stories.

Increasing our expectations of the speed with which a story is transmitted may sound entirely positive. No longer would a citizen have to wait to be informed of matters of importance. The problem, however, is that much of the news that feeds the 24-hour news cycle is arguably not news. A great deal of the "news" coverage is actually devoted to so-called experts who analyze every event endlessly. This tendency can now be seen across the news spectrum. As Thussu (2007) notes, the 24-hour news cycle is demanding, but its requirements do not include a substantial amount of hard news. Rather, with so many competitors crowding the market, news outlets must seek out the highest number of consumers in order to attract advertising dollars, and this may be accomplished through attention-getting headlines, frames that emphasize conflict, and simplistic summaries of events and problems.

Of course, the news business has always been fiercely competitive and this is in part because advertising dollars, which fund the industry, are never a guaranteed source of revenue. However, the combination of numerous new media outlets, including blogs and celebrity coverage sites, with convergence and concentration of ownership sometimes mean that profits are prioritized before the notion of public service that has historically guided—and still guides some—media owners. In a fast-paced environment with fewer staff and higher expectations, journalists must do more with less. Time pressures may limit the ability to perform research or to learn more about very complex issues—and stories that concern race, ethnicity, and religion are almost always more complex than a 500-word story can convey.

In the absence of time and freedom to learn more about an issue, journalists may fall back upon their pre-existing beliefs or assumed knowledge. In a newsroom that tends to be dominated by white, middle-class members, as many North American newsrooms are, it is reasonable to suggest that the existing base of knowledge about minorities will be insufficient. Underrepresentation of women and ethnic minorities in the media production process has been repeatedly noted as one of the possible culprits of unbalanced coverage (Cottle, 2000; International Women's Media Foundation, 2011). Fleras and Kunz (2001) note that visible minorities are woefully underrepresented in many sectors of the Canadian news industry, in particular. This being the case, it is perhaps unsurprising that coverage of visible minorities is often skewed or misleading.

This is not to say that minorities are automatically more knowledgeable about issues of race and ethnicity. In a country as diverse as Canada, minority groups are very different from one another and also demonstrate considerable differences within their own groups. However, their different experiences may help bring a new lens to a story, or expand the knowledge base within a newsroom. At the moment, however, too many newsrooms continue to be populated by people who lack basic knowledge about some of the minority groups in Canadian society.

Gunther Kress argues that a "truly equitable society is one in which the mainstream groups see it as essential to have access to the linguistic and cultural resources of minority groups and demand such access as a matter of equity" (1996, p. 18). Van Dijk agrees that this is the goal of an equitable society, but suggests that his own comprehensive analyses of news over the years have resulted in the finding that mainstream media demonstrate inherently racist behaviour. This is not, for the most part, the result of deliberate action or policy, but rather the natural outcome of a system that minorities often cannot access. The reasons for this vary but may include limited social and financial resources that would otherwise permit organized action such as press releases and conferences, persistent perceptions held by journalists of minorities as less credible sources than white institutional sources, and differences in communication styles between reporters and minorities (van Dijk, 1996, p. 93; also see Cottle, 2000; Poole, 2002). Van Dijk argues that journalists may see themselves as holding relatively liberal viewpoints, but such an interpretation ignores the fact that "lack of media access by minorities is one of the most conspicuous properties of the symbolic dominance of white elites" (1996, p. 92).

Van Dijk's findings in European media are similar to those of researchers of the Canadian press, including Karim H. Karim (1993), who notes the tendency in Canadian media to call attention to immigrant status, even if this is not necessarily relevant in the context of a story, and to emphasize non-Canadian birth if the person under discussion is being portrayed in a negative light. For example, sprinter Ben Johnson quickly lost his status as a Canadian hero and was represented instead as Jamaican-born following the discovery that he had used steroids in winning his 1988

Olympic race (Karim, 1993, p. 205). Ungerleider confirms that Canadian journalists generally prefer to affirm the existing social order, minimizing potential threats by characterizing minorities as villain or victim, in contrast to the perennially superior Anglo-Saxon white male (1991, pp. 159–161). As Jiwani suggests, visible minorities are most likely to be featured in the media when they "fit prevailing stereotypes of their groups" (1993, p. 10), with a tendency towards criminal behaviour serving as one of the primary stereotypes (also see Henry & Tator, 2002; Karim, 2003; Jiwani, 2006, pp. 30–62).

Another problem involves the treatment of minorities as monolithic groups. For example, different sects within Islam, Hinduism, etc., are not discussed or are not explained in sufficient detail. Instead of explaining that South Asians, for instance, are a diverse and large group practising many different religions and observing different traditions, journalists often tend to simplify by treating minorities as members of loosely defined groups (Scanlon, 1977, p. 252). Such inattention to detail only serves to further confuse, or as Jiwani terms it, dehistoricize, relevant issues (1993, p. 123). Karim (2003) documents a similar tendency with coverage of Islam. As Poole notes, reporting on Islam is no easy task for the media, even the more conscientious members, "given that actors do claim religious motives for their actions," but she adds that "failing to make a distinction between Islam and Islamists has negative implications for all Muslims because it implies that the problem resides in the religion and in the people who follow it, rather than in alternative factors" (2002, p. 9).

Questions of racism in the media are often treated as merely academic, but Poole, among others, argues that distorted portrayals of Muslims have very real and dangerous consequences. She notes that there appeared to be an increase in crimes directed at British South Asians during the Gulf War (p. 20), an observation that is also true of Canadian Muslims following September 11, 2001 (Foss, 2001). Poole further adds that "the media as an instrument of public ideology demonizes Islam, portraying it as a threat to Western interests, thus reproducing, producing, and sustaining the ideology necessary to subjugate Muslims both internationally and domestically" (2002, p. 17).

I would agree, noting that certain characteristics recur in depictions of Islam—for instance, the perception of the religion as extreme and as perpetuating inequity—and would suggest that the range of images available for the Muslim man, from oil sheikh to gun-toting terrorist, does not represent a linear trajectory so much as a handful of convenient characterizations that can be summoned depending upon circumstance. A similar series of stereotypes exists for Muslim women, including black-clad Iranian women marching on behalf of anti-Western figures such as Khomeini, members of the harem presenting themselves sensually, and meek wives expected to conform at all times to strict Muslim law (see Alvi, Hoodfar, & McDonough, 2003; Karim, 1997; Karim, 2003; Khan, 1995). *Niqab* wearers constitute a small portion of the Canadian population yet they are depicted in media with a frequency that implies a much greater influence. Photographs or televised images of these women emphasize their difference from an assumed norm; *niqab* wearers, or rival wives in polygamous marriages, are discussed in the media as a conflation of two stereotypes: the extremist religious figure and the oppressed woman.

These stereotypes are especially potent because of the ease with which they are absorbed and accepted into popular consciousness. As Said points out, copious coverage on Islam leads many observers to believe that they know a great deal about the subject when, in fact, they are often hearing from journalists and experts whose own knowledge may be limited or may consistently conform to particular political interpretations (1997, p. 1). The same may be true when applied to coverage of Tamils, or any group whose difference is emphasized in the media.

IN CONCLUSION: MAKING A CHANGE

The presence of racialized discourses in the media does not attest to the claim that the media join forces with the government in a conscious conspiracy, but the fact that the upper ranks of North America's major newspapers are staffed by some of the same elites who dictate economic and political policy helps to ensure a certain ideological consensus (van Dijk, 1988, pp. 155–157). The voices lacking in the media, then, are arguably those of the most affected. They may not have access to the media and may not speak of issues most journalists are equipped to understand. For instance, while some argue that media tend to favour the Judeo-Christian tradition when they cover religion, there is also an argument to be made that the media are staffed by journalists who are by and large trained to operate within a secular tradition. Thus, North American reporters do not always possess the appropriate credentials for covering religious issues, a major handicap when so many of the world's major modern conflicts have cultural, historical, and religious underpinnings (Karim, 2003, p. 184).

In recognition of this fact, groups such as the Canadian Journalism Foundation and the Centre for Faith and the Media work to critically examine the conduct of the media in certain situations, as with the Arar case. Community groups have also sought to educate journalists, conducting awareness workshops, providing background on their ethnicity or faith, and suggesting alternatives to terms that may be considered offensive. In the wake of the attacks of September 11, 2001, for example, the Council on American Islamic Relations-Canada (CAIR-CAN) has made considerable progress in sensitizing journalists and editors about Islam and has also reminded the media of their responsibility to cover the news in a way that is thorough and balanced. CAIR-CAN monitors the news for stereotypes, provides accurate information, meets with editorial boards, and also produces publications such as "A Journalist's Guide to Islam." Not all researchers believe that this activism makes a difference: as Mahtani explains, some antiracism scholars support this line of intervention while "others insist that such practices will never fully derail the deeply saturated forms of hegemony that exist in media organizations" (2008, p. 245). Some columnists have protested the kind of advocacy practised by CAIR-CAN, the Canadian Islamic Congress and others, opining that the resulting political correctness prevents them from saying what they would like to. For instance, Margaret Wente, longtime *Globe and Mail* columnist, complains about organizations that have achieved an attention to "correct speech," leading "to the awkward spot where it's permissible (in Canada, at any rate) to say any terrible thing you want about the United States, but not permissible to be critical of any aspects of Muslim societies or cultures" (2001, p. A17). Others, however, seem to welcome the opportunity to engage meaningfully with these groups, and some individuals who are well informed about diversity, such as Haroon Siddiqui, the former *Toronto Star* editor, speak frankly and consistently about the need to provide balanced coverage (for examples, see Siddiqui, 2000, 2002).

These conversations in themselves can contribute significantly to the impression left by the media. Those who consume the media can engage in these debates, and can look critically at the material they read or watch. Media production is an immense part of the equation when examining representation, but it is nonetheless important for individuals to consider how they should approach the media reports they encounter.

Due in large part to the intervention of determined individuals and organizations, change is indeed possible, however slow it may seem at times. Many journalists are committed to ensuring equitable coverage, even if they continue to operate within considerable constraints. The news business remains competitive; the pace is only becoming faster, rather than slowing down; media owners must compete for attention at a time when advertising dollars are divided between growing numbers of outlets. Education for journalists does not routinely include exposure to the principles of diversity and the history of religious traditions. All the same, many journalists want to do the best job that they can of informing the Canadian public. For that reason, while many stories about the *niqab* ban did employ stereotypes and images that emphasize difference, some journalists also made an attempt to obtain firsthand accounts from women who wear *niqab*. Some of the accounts of the Shafia case probed carefully into the question of whether culture was the chief reason for the deaths of the Shafia women (for one example, see Allemang, 2012).

Beyond the individual responsibility of journalists, a new configuration to the media industry may also provide more equitable coverage through an increased attention to stories about minority groups, whether this occurs by way of specialized units or an enhancement of mainstream outlets' daily activities. In addition to ethnic media, Mahtani argues that mainstream media organizations "are recognizing the need to cover stories that are of interest to the ever-growing multicultural population in Canada in order to improve their market share" (2008, p. 239). The motive for this, she notes, is economic, not altruistic. All the same, it is the outcome that matters.

Finally, while journalists and citizens may disagree among themselves about the extent to which the media should acknowledge diversity, such debate is healthy. At the very least, it brings notions of difference to the forefront, and causes media users to think more carefully about the content they consume. It is unlikely, at least in the near future, that mainstream media organizations will have the resources to ensure that every piece they write about a minority group will be thoroughly researched and will appropriately explain every relevant cultural nuance. Whatever their race or religion, people are complex, and so are their stories. A realistic hope might be to educate the public to be critical about these stories, and to understand that every story involving racialized discourses also involves unequal power relations. Until the day—perhaps a mythical one—when equality arrives, the power to be critical consumers of the media may be the most important one we have.

QUESTIONS

1. This chapter provides examples of cases where race, ethnicity, and/or religion may not have been represented accurately. Can you think of other examples?
2. The focus of this chapter is race, ethnicity, and religion, but are there other characteristics of individuals or groups that may lead to inaccurate reporting? What are they? Can you give examples of cases where this can be seen?
3. What steps should journalists take to ensure that they are reporting fairly and accurately on stories involving visible minorities?
4. What can readers and viewers do to ensure that they are receiving complete and accurate information about stories that involve visible minorities?
5. Why is media coverage of stories involving race, ethnicity, or religion important to Canadian citizens? Why does it matter?

REFERENCES

Allemang, J. (2012, January 28). Could child services have stopped the deaths? *The Globe and Mail*, A6.

Alvi, S., Hoodfar, H., & McDonough, S. (2003). *The Muslim veil in North America: Issues and debates*. Toronto: Women's Press.

Appleby, T. (2012, January 30). In a crime based on honour, court finds 'nothing more honourless.'" *The Globe and Mail*, A8.

Blanchfield, M. (2002, December 21). Canadian attitudes toward Muslims, immigration harden in wake of Sept. 11. *The Montreal Gazette*, A1, A12.

Chase, S., Youssef, M., & Lindell, R. (2010, August 14). Tamil boat testing Canada's response, Ottawa says. *The Globe and Mail*, A1.

Cottle, S. (Ed.) (2000). *Ethnic minorities and the media: Changing cultural boundaries*. Buckingham, UK: Open University Press.

Deacon, D., Pickering, M., Golding, P., & Murdock, G. (1999). *Researching communications*. London: Arnold.

DiManno, R., & Chung, A. (2012, January 30). Shafia family members guilty of first-degree murder. *The Toronto Star*, A1.

Findlay, S. (2012, January 30). No "honour" in these killings. *The Toronto Star*, A10.

Fleras, A., & Kunz, J. L. (2001). *Media and minorities: Representing diversity in a multicultural Canada*. Toronto: Thompson Educational Publishing.

Fong, P. (2010, August 12). Tamil migrants sick with TB. *The Toronto Star*, p. A1.

Gombu, P. (2009, January 30). Arar shocked, depressed by testimony tying him to Khadr. *The Toronto Star*, A3.

Henry, F., & Tator, C. (Eds.) (2002). *Discourses of domination: Racial bias in the Canadian English-language press*. Toronto: University of Toronto Press.

International Women's Media Foundation. (2011). Global report on the status of women in the news media. Retrieved August 22, 2012, from http://iwmf.org/pdfs/IWMF-Global-Report.pdf

Jiwani, Y. (1993). *By omission and commission: "Race" and representation in Canadian television news*. Unpublished doctoral dissertation, Simon Fraser University, Burnaby, British Columbia.

———. (2006). *Discourses of denial: Mediations of race, gender, and violence*. Vancouver: University of British Columbia Press.

Karim, K. H. (1993). Constructions, deconstructions, and reconstructions: Competing Canadian discourses on ethnocultural terminology. *Canadian Journal of Communication, 18*(2), 197–218.

———. (1997). The historical resilience of primary stereotypes: Core images of the Muslim Other. In S. H. Riggins (Ed.), *The language and politics of exclusion: Others in discourse* (pp. 153–182). Thousand Oaks, CA: Sage Publications.

———. (2003). *The Islamic peril: Media and global violence*. Montréal: Black Rose Books.

Khan, S. (1995). The veil as a site of struggle: The *hejab* in Quebec. *Canadian Woman Studies, 15*(2), 146–151.

Kress, G. (1996). Representational resources and the production of subjectivity: Questions for the theoretical development of critical discourse analysis in a multicultural society. In C. R. Caldas-Coulthard & M. Coulthard (Eds.), *Texts and practices: Readings in critical discourse analysis* (pp. 15–31). London and New York: Routledge.

Lakritz, N. (2012, January 31). Yes, Shafia murders were honour killings. *The Calgary Herald*, A10.

Mahtani, M. (2008). How are immigrants seen—and what do they want to see? Contemporary research on the representation of immigrants in the Canadian English-language media. In J. Biles, M. Burstein, and J. Frideres (Eds.), *Immigration and integration in Canada in the twenty-first century* (pp. 231–251). Montreal and Kingston: McGill-Queen's University Press.

McChesney, R. (1999). *Rich media, poor democracy: Communication politics in dubious times*. Urbana: University of Illinois Press.

McChesney, R., & Pickard, V. (Eds.). (2011). *Will the last reporter please turn out the lights? The collapse of journalism and what can be done to fix it.* New York: The New Press.

Miles, R., & Brown, M. (2003). *Racism* (2nd ed.). London and New York: Routledge.

O'Connor, D. (2006). Report of the Events Relating to Maher Arar. Ottawa: Government of Canada. Retrieved August 22, 2012, from http://www.sirc-csars.gc.ca/pdfs/cm_arar_rec-eng.pdf

O'Neill, J. (2003, November 7). Security services anxious to protect investigation of al-Qaida cell in Ottawa, sources say. *Ottawa Citizen*, A1.

Payton, L. (2011, December 12). Face veils banned for citizenship oaths. CBC News. Retrieved August 22, 2012, from http://www.cbc.ca/news/canada/montreal/story/2011/12/12/pol-kenney-citizenship-rules.html

Poole, E. (2002). *Reporting Islam: Media representations of British Muslims.* London: I.B. Tauris & Co.

Said, E. W. (1978). *Orientalism.* New York: Vintage Books.

———. (1997). *Covering Islam: How the media and the experts determine how we see the rest of the world* (Rev. Ed). New York: Vintage Books.

Scanlon, J. (1977). The Sikhs of Vancouver: A case study of the role of media in ethnic relations. In *Ethnicity and the media: An analysis of media reporting in the United Kingdom, Canada and Ireland* (pp. 193–261). Paris: United Nations Educational, Scientific and Cultural Organization (UNESCO).

Shoemaker, P., & Reese, S. (1996). *Mediating the message: Theories of influence on mass media content* (2nd ed.). White Plains, NY: Longman.

Siddiqui, H. (2000, April 16). Canadian media view from the right. *The Toronto Star*, A13.

———. (2002, November 24). Four telltale themes: Anti-Muslim bigotry "spreading like wildfire." *The Toronto Star*, B1–B2.

Smith, G. (2002, December 18). Muslim garb a liability in job market, study finds. *The Globe and Mail*, A10.

Smith, T. (2011, December 23). Controversy grows over veiled threat: Government talk of banning the niqab has some fearing a less tolerant Canada. *Regina Leader Post*, C9.

Thussu, D. K. (2007). *News as entertainment: The rise of global infotainment.* Thousand Oaks, CA: Sage Publications.

Ungerleider, C. S. (1991). Media, minorities and misconceptions: The portrayal by and representation of minorities in the Canadian news media. *Canadian Ethnic Studies, 23*(3), 158–164.

Van Dijk, T. A. (1988). *News analysis: Case studies of international and national news in the press.* Hillsdale, NJ: Lawrence Erlbaum.

———. (1991). *Racism and the press.* London and New York: Routledge.

———. (1993). Stories and racism. In D. K. Mumby (Ed.), *Narrative and social control: Critical perspectives* (pp. 121–142). Newbury Park, CA: Sage Publications.

———. (1996). Discourse, power and access. In C. R. Caldas-Coulthard & M. Coulthard (Eds.), *Texts and practices: Readings in critical discourse analysis* (pp. 84–104). London and New York: Routledge.

———. (1998). *Ideology: A multidisciplinary approach*. Thousand Oaks, CA: Sage Publications.

Walton, D., & Kennedy, P. (2002, September 7). Muslims feel forced to explain their faith. *The Globe and Mail*, A11.

Wente, M. (2001, October 2). Tipetoeing through Islam. *The Globe and Mail*, A17.

20

FROM THE TOP DRAWER TO THE BOTTOM LINE: THE COMMODIFICATION OF CHILDREN'S CULTURES

Natalie Coulter
York University

INTRODUCTION

A few years ago my parents gave me an old dresser. It's a pretty standard dresser, it has four deep drawers and stands about four feet tall. There is nothing really interesting about the dresser except that it was in my father's bedroom when he was a child growing up in a middle-class family in Scarborough, Ontario, in the 1950s. My dad shared the dresser with his two brothers. They each had a drawer for their clothes and they used the fourth drawer for the various odds and ends that young boys like to hide away. Almost 70 years later, in a similar middle-class neighbourhood, the same dresser is in my daughter's room and it is stuffed. The top drawers hold her pajamas and her socks, tights and underwear, the bottom two house her T-shirts—short and long sleeved—her pants, her skirts, her sweaters, and her sweatshirts. The dresser is so full that her summer clothes are in storage boxes under her bed. And when I open the drawers to look inside, all I see are a dizzying array of purples and pinks festooned with character licences; there are sparkly Disney princess pajamas, shimmery Hanna Montana T-shirts, frilly Barbie socks, and colourful Strawberry Shortcake underwear.

To me, as someone who researches children and consumer culture, this dresser and the stacks of clothes in it is much more than a reminder of how much laundry has to be done, it is emblematic of the changes in children's culture. This beat-up old dresser reveals the intensification of children as consumers. Children have become little commercial engines that drive much of a family's spending. And the girly clothes in the drawers reveal the strong interconnections between the media content and merchandise, as well as the strict gender divisions in the children's marketplace.

Now this story about the dresser isn't to lament the loss of an imaginary "good ol' days" when there wasn't massive shopping and Disney princesses didn't dominate our daughter's closet. Such a narrative is derivative and falsely assumes that things were simpler and better back then. My father lived in a commercial world as well, but it was different, very different, from the commercial world my daughter occupies. Comparing my father's experiences to my daughter's opens up opportunities to reflect on how children's culture has changed and the role of the marketplace in that shift. It also allows us to think critically about the ways in which young peoples' cultures have become intertwined with consumer culture in the past seven decades.

So what can this dresser tell us? It reflects the changing relationship that children and families have with consumer culture. Throughout the 20th century the marketplace has become more tightly enmeshed with children and their culture. In the 1930s the children's clothing industry began to design and organize children's clothes into departments based on age and gender instead of by the type of clothing. As a result, toddlers and teenagers became distinctive merchandising categories (Cook, 2004; Schrum, 2004). In the 1940s and 1950s companies such as Walt Disney began to produce media content solely for a child audience who was watching television alone, at the same time magazines such as *Seventeen* spoke specifically to teenage girl audiences. A whole range of companies began to realize the value of gearing their products directly to factions of the youth market instead of the family as a whole. And the aesthetics and values of the teenager began to drive the fashion and music industries. Then in the 1980s and 1990s there was a dramatic intensification in the connection between consumer culture and children's culture. This period signalled the arrival of department-sized toy stores, specialty television channels for youth markets such as MuchMusic and YTV, and the development of transmedia texts.

This situation has not let up in the early decades of the 21st century; on top of the wide range of products and media that are pushed on young people, babies are even marketed to directly with products such as Baby Einstein, while companies use digital media to further entrench young people into the values of consumer culture (Wasko, 2010).

In light of this history, scholars of children's culture struggle to articulate the relationship between children's culture and consumer culture. Locating the distinction between where children's culture ends and consumer culture begins is a slippery endeavour. Daniel Cook, a key scholar in the field of childhood studies, argues that children's culture is indistinguishable from consumer culture (2000), Harvard economist Juliet Schor suggests that "kids and teens are now the epicenter of American consumer culture" (2004, p. 9), and media expert David Buckingham states that in the 20th century childhood became "inextricably entwined with consumer culture. Children's social and cultural needs are unavoidably expressed and defined through their relationships with material commodities and through the commercially produced media texts that permeate their lives" (Buckingham, 1993, p. 166).

But what does all of this mean? How is children's culture at the "epicenter" or "entwined" with consumer culture? What these scholars are suggesting is that the commercial world is interwoven with children's culture. It is not an add-on or an invasion of childhood where childhood is a time of innocence that has been corrupted by greedy commercial forces. Instead, consumer culture has become an inevitable part of children's culture. The historical development of consumer culture over the course of the past 70 years has been symbiotically interwoven with the development of children's culture.

The goal of this chapter is to begin to understand the evolution of the dresser. How did the dresser go from housing the clothes of three boys in the 1950s to being crammed with only some of the clothes of a girl in the 2010s? Really what we are exploring is the wider shifts in children's consumer culture as marketers, advertisers, and the media began to conceptualize children in ways that respond to changes in the media marketplace. The chapter concludes with an analysis of children's culture in the digital age.

THE CHANGING MEDIASCAPE IN THE 1980S

To explore these connections between children's culture and consumer culture, I will begin with the 1980s since this was a period characterized by a dramatic intensification of the connection between the two. It was in the 1980s that young people became targeted more explicitly and more intensely as consumers by the media marketplace. Up until this period the marketing of youth products "was more or less haphazard" (Wasko, 2008, p. 461). The reason for this new intensity can be traced to three radical changes in the mediascape: deregulation, character licensing, and a new approach to market segmentation.

Deregulation Legitimizes the Child as a Consumer

The media landscape underwent a radical overhaul in the 1980s, with children and teens caught up in the mechanics of such changes. One of the more poignant changes in the North American mediascape was the repositioning of the child consumer/audience. During the mid- and late-1970s concern over the increasing commercialization of children's culture led to highly contested public debates over the social acceptability of treating the child as a consumer. The battleground for such debates was television. In both Canada and in the United States, public battles over the effects of television advertising on children were waged between the triangular adversaries of governmental regulatory bodies (in the United States, the Federal Communications Commission [FCC] and the Federal Trade Commission [FTC], and in Canada the Canadian Radio-television and Telecommunications Commission [CRTC]) on one side; child advocates on another; and the entertainment industry on the third. Each side had its own agenda in the fight. On the one side the governmental regulatory bodies were largely unwilling to take on the media industry and fight for media regulation; instead they opted to have the industry regulate itself. This was a double bind for governments, which wanted to avoid forcing the media to regulate but did not want to be seen as abandoning children's rights. Child advocates, on the other hand, argued that advertising to children was detrimental to a child's mental health and pushed for increased governmental regulation of the media. Self-regulation by the media, they argued, had largely been ineffective in the past and they urged the government to legislate children's media (Kline, 1993, p. 215). On the third side, the entertainment industry, desperately hoping to avoid governmental regulation, urged for self-regulatory structures that would allow it to police itself.

In the United States the fight between the three adversaries began in the early 1970s when Action for Children's Television (ACT), a public interest organization, began to petition the government to devise policies to protect innocent, gullible children from the manipulative pressures of the corporate media (Montgomery, 1990). This instigated a national debate on the moral validity of advertising to children. In 1974 the FCC imposed guidelines limiting children's advertising, acknowledging children's vulnerability to advertising. These regulations prohibited program-length commercials by mandating distinct separations between television shows and commercials and also restricted advertising time to nine and a half minutes per hour on weekends and 12 minutes on weekdays (Schor, 2004, p. 177). Four years later in 1978 the FTC published a report declaring that children's advertising was "inherently unfair and deceptive" because children were "too young to understand the selling and purpose of, or otherwise comprehend or evaluate the advertising" (FTC Staff Report, 1978, as cited in Kline, 1993, p. 213). Corporations fought back by arguing that governmental agencies did not have the authority to operate as the "National Nannies" (Quart, 2003, p. 57).

But by the 1980s many of these debates were of little relevance and the arguments of child advocates and public interest organizations proved to carry little weight as the FTC and FCC swayed under the leadership of the neoliberal Reagan administration and offloaded the responsibility of regulating children's media onto the free market. In 1981 Congress stripped the FTC of many of its duties to regulate the media, with President Ronald Reagan appointing Mark Fowler as chair of the FCC. In his new position, Fowler contended that it was the marketplace, not governmental regulation, that could best control children's television. By 1984 the FCC relaxed many of the policies that regulated children's advertising and completely deregulated the limits on the amount of commercial minutes permitted during children's television shows (Kunkel, 2001, p. 385).[1] The FCC asserted that "marketplace forces can better determine appropriate commercial levels than our own rules" (as cited in Kunkel, 2001, p. 385).

Similar debates on the regulation of children's media and advertising were waged in Canada, and with the exception of Quebec, regulation was offloaded onto the industry. Quebec, on the other hand, imposed tighter laws and legislated a provincial ban on advertising to children under the age of 12. In the rest of Canada, in an attempt to circumvent further governmental regulation, individual television stations such as the CBC experimented with their own policies that limited advertising to children. Fearful of the prospect of government regulation, the industry lobby group, the **Canadian Association of Broadcasters (CAB)**, proposed the **Broadcast Code for Advertising to Children**. The code was governed by the self-regulatory body, **Advertising Standards Canada (ASC)**. While this was not governmental regulation but the industry regulating itself, broadcasters did have to indicate that they would comply with the codes in order to be granted their licence by the CRTC. Unfortunately, the ASC code was (and still is) vague with lots of wiggle room, while the ASC itself had no real regulatory strength (Coulter & Murray, 2001).

Clearly, Pandora had opened the proverbial box; the deregulation of children's media in the mid-1980s by the United States, which both produced and influenced tremendous amounts of the world's media products, proved to lead to a dramatic increase in the global commercialization of children's culture. The outcome of Reagan's deregulation of the media was that it legitimized children as competent consumers. By the mid-1980s, children were seen as consumers in their own right with access to a disposable, expandable income in the billions (Pecora, 1998, p. 24), leading *Marketing Magazine* to proclaim in 1990 that the child was considered the "dream consumer" (Marney, 1990, p. 15). With a regulated media, the child was allotted special status to be protected from being treated in the same manner as adult consumers; but with deregulation, children were positioned as competent consumers and considered to be market savvy instead of needing protection. Delegating the responsibility of media regulation to the marketplace, away from the protective embrace of the government, further entrenched the child as a legitimate, bona fide consumer. Children were able to engage in the fantasy of democratic choice offered by the rationality of a free market that was supposedly simply responding to children's needs and wants.

Strawberry Shortcake Opens Up the Girl Market

The second radical shift is a change in character licensing. Before Reagan's deregulation of children's media in the 1980s there were very few shows that catered specifically to the girl audience (Seiter, 1993). The assumed audience of children's television shows was the boy audience. Seiter asks us to think about children's media prior to the 1980s; most of Disney's animated characters were male: Bambi, Dumbo, Peter Pan, Jiminy Cricket, Mickey Mouse, Donald Duck, and Goofy. The situation was not much different at Warner Brothers and Hanna-Barbera with Porky Pig, Tom and Jerry, Daffy Duck, Elmer Fudd, Bugs Bunny, Coyote and the Road Runner, Sylvester, and Tweety. The female characters that did appear, Minnie Mouse, Daisy Duck, and Petunia Pig, for example, were all comic foils for male characters. Even the seemingly progressive *Sesame Street* (1969–current) was dominated by male characters, as was the *Muppet Show* (1976–1981).

Girls were ignored because it was assumed that they were not a large enough market to justify the expense of programming. While the media did not want to directly alienate the girl audience, the preferred market was the boy audience. It was thought that having shows that specifically catered to girls would drive away boys. Girls, it was believed, would still consume media products designed for boys, but boys would not consume what was intended for girls (Seiter, 1993, p. 147; Kenway and Bullen, 2001, p. 49). Up until the 1980s this strategy had been true for most children's media with perhaps the exception of the teen magazine market.[2] Most media favoured male characters and privileged boy audiences, while girls were left to identify with token female characters that were designed to maintain the interest of the girl audience without being central enough characters to drive away the boy audience.

Things began to change in the 1980s in the deregulated mediascape of Reagan's America. The shift to **deregulation** opened up new spaces for the girl audience to be a lucrative, viable market. Under deregulation, the industry-friendly FCC lifted its restrictions on program-length commercials. This meant that the promotion of products could now occur within the content of a television show (Kunkel, 2001, p. 385). Taking advantage of this situation, the toy industry began to aggressively push toys that were based on television shows. The result was that half-hour television shows such as *The Smurfs* (1981–1990), *The Transformers* (1984–1987), *Jem and the Holograms* (1985–1988) *He-Man* (1983–1985) and *Strawberry Shortcake* (1980–1985) became half-hour advertisements that peddled toys built around the characters of the shows, something that would not have been allowed under the old FCC regulations. The success of a show could be parlayed well beyond the toy department of stores. With the magic of character licensing, children could acquire a whole range of consumer products adorned with their favourite characters. Clothing, bedding, furniture, party favours; the possibilities of character licensing proved to be endless.[3] By the 1980s, television shows and characters were designed based on their ability to translate into lucrative licensing opportunities (Englehardt, 1986; Kline, 1993; Seiter, 1993). These programs began to form what Buckingham calls "trans-media intertextuality" which increasingly connected television with films, comics, books, records, and computer games (Buckingham, 1993, p. 156).

With the potential of selling media content alongside an enormous amount of licensed merchandise, the girl market suddenly became a viable market. It was no longer the size of an audience that mattered to the children's cultural industry; instead, it was the ability of the audience to buy character merchandise that dictated the value of an audience. It was in this commercial space that, according to Seiter (1993), girls and boys came to be "sold separately.". Up until this point the market for girls' television shows and girls' toys was largely untapped, but character licensing opened up the floodgates and made the girls' market worth it.

The first truly successful character licence was Strawberry Shortcake. In the late 1970s a small firm called Those Characters from Cleveland (TCFC) attempted to get to know the girls' market using focus groups, interviews, and storyboards of character designs (Englehardt, 1986, pp. 72–73; Kline, 1993, p. 139; Seiter, 1993, p. 150). Based on the girls' responses, the company designed the Strawberry Shortcake characters and subsequently produced a series of television specials that featured Strawberry Shortcake and her "berry nice friends" who all lived in Strawberryland.[4]

With the deregulation of the media, Strawberry quickly became America's number-one-selling toy doll and appeared on hundreds of products selling more than $1 billion (US) worth of merchandise by the time she was four years old

(Englehardt, 1986, p. 73). The astronomical success of Strawberry Shortcake led critic Tom Englehardt to dub the process of designing characters based on extensive market research and the ability to translate the characters into licences "The Shortcake Strategy."

Toy companies even advertised to merchandisers the financial opportunities in becoming a licensee. Strawberry Shortcake, Hasbro's Jem, and Mattel's Princes of Power and Barbie lines for example, all had full-page advertisements in the children's apparel trade publication *Earnshaws* in an attempt to peddle their licences to potential merchandisers, hoping that a children's clothing company or an underwear manufacturer would buy the licence to sell Strawberry Shortcake jeans, or Barbie underwear.

With Strawberry Shortcake, the girls' market had arrived. Seiter notes that prior to Strawberry Shortcake, the only successful girls' licences were Barbie and Mary Poppins (Seiter, 1993, p. 150). The girls' toy market had been underdeveloped and there was little innovation in girls' toys. Strawberry and her friends had proven the incredible power of the girls' market. The Shortcake Strategy of utilizing extensive market research to create characters that would lend themselves to licensed merchandise was successfully adopted by other companies that produced characters solely for a girls' market such as Rainbow Bright, The Care Bears, and My Little Pony.[5] The development of such characters in the 1980s was essentially the development of a girls' market. In collusion with the media production companies, the toy industry leveraged the findings from market research to create characters and products designed to cater to a solely female audience.

This gender division is even more entrenched today. For example, the megasized toy store Toys "R" Us is virtually divided down the middle between boys' and girls' toys. Toy lines such as the Disney Princess line, Mattel's Barbie and the Littlest Pet Shop dominate one side of the store while Disney's Cars, Star Wars and Hot Wheels dominate the other. This division extends into media as well and the same situation can be viewed on the television set with *Thomas & Friends* (1984–present) for boys and *Dora the Explorer* (2000–present) for girls. Children's websites are also divided by gender as some are clearly geared to boys and others to girls.

Narrowcasting to Children and Teens

The third dramatic shift in the mediascape that led to a profound repositioning of children's media was the wider trend wherein audiences were niched out into smaller, more homogenous segments. This segmentation and niching was due to the proliferation of cable television stations. The 1980s was a period of dramatic expansion in which both the FCC and FTC in the United States and the CRTC in Canada embarked on a rapid diversification of channels, ultimately challenging the commercial hegemony of both countries' major network stations and marking the beginning of cable television. The expansion of the television dial was both a result of new technologies combined with a lax regulatory environment.

With the expansion of the television dial and buoyed by the legitimization of the child as a consumer, the entertainment industry began to consider children and teens lucrative enough markets to have entire stations geared specifically to them. The first station to cater solely to the child consumer was Nickelodeon, launched on April 1, 1979 by Warner Communications. It was, according to Cy Schneider, one of the station's first heads, "an idea that came along at exactly the right time" (Schneider, 1989, p. 193). Nickelodeon's mandate was to do something different from the stock cartoons that were on the commercial networks and the reruns of *Sesame Street* (1969–present) that were on public television. It developed a whole lineup of entertaining, child-centred, character-driven, television shows.

While Nickelodeon was catering to the children's market, its corporate parent reached out to the teen market. In August 1981 Warner Communications and American Express (Warner Amex) debuted Music Television (MTV) headed by a vibrant, young 28-year-old named Robert Putman. The goal of MTV was to target its programming to the under 25-year-old who was supposedly ignored by radio (Szatmary, 1991, p. 252). MTV proved to be a very successful format. In 1981 MTV was broadcast into 2.5 million American households. According to its own statistics by 1983 there were 14 million MTV households that watched MTV an average of 63 minutes every weekday and 91 minutes a day on weekends (MTV 1983, p. M-19). Witnessing the success of MTV, and the genre of music television in general, CHUM Limited launched a Canadian version of the station in 1984 called MuchMusic. MuchMusic was Canada's first 24-hour music specialty station. Originally it was offered as pay-TV but in 1987 it moved to basic cable to a bigger audience.

Despite MuchMusic's success in adapting the American station MTV to the Canadian market, it was almost an entire decade before a station similar to Nickelodeon would be made available in Canada. Buoyed by the success of Nickelodeon in the United States, YTV began on September 1, 1988, in Canada. Owned by Rogers and CUC Limited, it was the first specialty channel for Canadian "children and youth." The daily content of the station was aimed at 40 percent for preschoolers, 40 percent for teens aged 12–17, and 20 percent for families (Bream, 1988, p. 14). YTV's mandate was to "provide full time access to Canada's young people of youth-oriented fare" (CRTC, 1987, vol. 13). Kevin Shea, president of YTV, argued in a CRTC public hearing that "with 35 channels available in most urban markets within the broadcasting system it is time that one of them (was) dedicated to children. That's the ingredient that's missing" (as quoted in CRTC 1987, vol. 13).

Each of these four stations—Nickelodeon, MTV, Much Music, and YTV—offered advertisers direct access to the child and teen markets on a full-time basis. Youth were no longer isolated to Saturday morning slots or during the dinner hour. In the fractured televisual landscape with little regulation, youth were a serious market and a pure audience that made its own purchasing decisions. Broadcasting to youth was not a social service and the content of youth media was not educational; instead, youth were treated as sophisticated consumers with their own resources to spend.

Clearly, things have dramatically changed since Kevin Shea declared that children's content was missing from broadcasting. Currently, there is a whole plethora of stations available on cable for various youth markets. In 1997, feeling that its audience was too bulky, YTV segmented the preschooler to a new channel called Treehouse. In 2006, Rogers acquired the rights for BabyTV, a 24-hour commercial-free programming station geared to babies and toddlers available on the Rogers cable package for only $4.99 per month. And if BabyTV, Treehouse, YTV, and MuchMusic do not provide enough stimulation for the Canadian child, young Canadians can also watch BabyFirst, Nickelodeon, BBC Kids, Teletoon, Disney Junior, and Disney XD (a network for tween boys that launched in March 2012 in Canada).

Youth is Fractured into Smaller and Smaller Marketing Niches

The current reality of the television market for children is a plethora of stations catering to a narrow segment of the youth market based on children's ages and genders. Children can graduate through television channels as they age from Baby TV, to Treehouse (preschooler), to YTV (young tween), to Disney XD (male tween) and then to MuchMusic (teen). Each of these stations cater to a narrow segment of the children's market as the life course of young people is divided into smaller, tighter marketing niches. Marketers, for example, talk about the baby market, the preschool market, the pre-tween market, the tween market, and the teen market. Each of these markets is further subdivided based on gender; there are strict distinctions between the boy tween and the girl tween markets, for example.

Political economist Dallas Smythe tells us that the media exists to sell audiences to advertisers. He suggests that the audience is a commodity that is sold to advertisers (Smythe 1994). The value in segmenting children into narrow television audiences means that television stations can deliver a tight and precise audience to advertisers. Media companies try to appeal to advertisers by claiming that they can deliver a desirable group of consumers, one so narrow and precise that the advertiser will not waste money paying to reach audience members not interested in the product (Leiss, Kline, Jhally, & Botterill, 2005; Turow, 1997). Media firms sell their audiences to advertisers by claiming that virtually every audience member is a potential customer for the advertiser.

With the children's market, it is not just a child's ability to pay attention to the commercials (many children's stations have very limited commercial breaks) it is also a child's ability to purchase the whole spectrum of character-licensed products. It is hoped that the child who is watching *Dora the Explorer* on Treehouse is also buying Dora Band-Aids®, Dora pajamas, and Dora books, as well as maybe even attending a Dora concert. As one industry observer has astutely noted "children's programming has been quite simply the engine that drives young customers and their parents to the toy, video game and apparel markets" (as quoted in Wasko 2008, p. 464).

This market segmentation goes well beyond the television dial. Young people are not only audiences, but also customers. Advertisers such as Coca-Cola or

McDonalds speak specifically to narrow market segments in commercials, retail stores such as Baby Gap or Abercrombie Kids are designed to cater to specific market segments, and companies design products for specific market segments; for example, McCain Pizza Pockets for tween boys or Listerine Cool Blue for pre-tweens.

These market segments are not random divisions, nor are they reflections of natural stages of children's development. Instead these market segments are organized and defined to meet the needs of the marketplace. Market research companies such as Yankelovich's Youth Monitor or Child Research (whose clients include CBC and Kraft) spend huge amounts of money gathering data on children's views, preferences, and consumption habits in order to be able to categorize childhood into these separate markets. These market researchers conduct focus groups, survey young people at shopping malls, and even observe children in their own homes.

All of this research on children is geared to knowing children as potential customers and audiences. The goal is to understand them as consumers instead of in ways that can empower young people as citizens. In the commercial marketplace, young people are understood according to the logics and needs of the marketplace. The market research conducted on children is interested in youth only as a pattern of consumption and not as a social demographic or as citizens (Davies et al., 2000; Danesi, 2003). The problem with this is that in segmenting youth into categories constructed purely in market terms, young people are often reduced to objects where they are "commodified and marketed back to themselves, stripped of any history, individual identity or power" (Grioux cited in Brooks 2003, p. 13). In colonizing youth markets, the baby, the preschooler, the pre-tween, the tween, and the teen have all been constructed as specific segments of the market that are legitimated, defined, and contained according to the logics of the marketplace.

The segmentation of young people has taken place within a rigid set of dominant discourses that has failed to address a wide range of demographics and subjectivities. Age and gender are privileged above other subjectivities in the division of the children's market while distinctions in class, race, and sexuality are overlooked. The child consumer is most often assumed to be white, middle class, heterosexual, and able bodied. However, this is slowly beginning to change in terms of race/ethnicity as some advertisers and media companies are attempting to diversify the market and reach out to young consumers of colour; for instance, *Dora the Explorer* as a Latina character or Disney's attempts to broaden its princess pantheon by including Mulan (1998) or Tiana from *Princess and the Frog* (2009). My favourite example of this would be the Canadian show *How to be Indie* (2009–present) on the YTV network, which follows the quirky antics of a 13-year-old Indian Canadian teenager named Indira "Indie" Mehta as she tries to navigate the demands of her strict, but loving, Indian parents. Although there is some movement toward diversity in terms of race/ethnicity; representations of diversity with sexuality, ability, and class are still largely ignored in the children's market.

YOUNG PEOPLE IN THE DIGITALSCAPE

The expansion of children's culture into the online world has opened up new opportunities for market researchers to gather information on young people. New media erodes the traditional barriers between commerce and culture (Montgomery, 2001) as advertising and market research are increasingly woven in with content. Take, for example, websites such as Webkinz.com, or Neopets.com, or the current hot trend in children's online gaming, Moshimonsters.com. In the case of WebKinz and Moshi Monster, children can gain access to these websites by buying a WebKinz or Moshi Monster plush toy and entering the special code called a "unique activation code" that accompanies the toy. This code gives them access to the virtual online playground called WebKinz World or Monstro City. Other websites such as Club Penguin, require memberships in order to upgrade to the VIP status, which allows players to access a much wider range of services than if they only played for free. The number of visitors to all of these sites is massive. By the end of 2011 there were 70 million registered accounts for Moshi Monster, 72 million for NeoPets, and 150 million for Disney's Club Penguin; teen social networking site Habbo had 255 million (KZero, 2011).

Most children's television stations (Nickelodeon, Disney, Treehouse) also have websites where children can play a multitude of games or watch clips from their favourite episodes, as do toy companies such as Barbie or Strawberry Shortcake. All of these sites deliver what the industry calls "multi-platform content," content that crosses over many media platforms. Each of these websites is designed to keep a child occupied for hours so that he or she never leaves the website to go to a new one.

These websites generate revenue in multiple ways. One of the most obvious means is to link toys and the virtual world together. Children can either buy the toys to enter the websites or, by just being on the website, they are engaged in a branded experience of the toy. Their online time is basically commercial time where there is no distinction between content and an advertisement for the toy. Whether is it designing "glamtastic" outfits for Barbie's fashion show, or finding Dora's best friend Boots on the Treehouse website, the distinction between play and advertising is blurred. The motivation for companies to blur these boundaries is simple, according to a representative for K Zero, a market research firm catering to the virtual world, "it's an extension of the real world toy play and keeps the children in a 'branded' frame of mind" (as quoted in Wasko 2010, p. 116).

Another way that these online games generate revenue is by "immersive advertising," a strategy similar to product placement in which advertisements are integrated right into a site's content instead of being a pop-up or banner ad. In a study conducted on Neopets it was found companies such as Mattel, Kraft, and Proctor and Gamble integrated their products and brand names right into the games and features of the website (Grimes & Shade, 2005). The immersive advertising campaigns for General Mills cereals such as Lucky Charms and Trix were so successful that the two companies signed a multi-year partnership to continue their relationship (Grimes & Shade, 2005, p. 187).

A third means by which these websites generate revenue is through market research. Websites gather data through the information given when a player registers for a site, by tracking cookies and also, in the case of Neopets, players earning Neopoints by entering the "Survey Shack" and filling out surveys. Neopets has an intimate connection with market research company the Dohring Company, which was founded by Doug C. Dohring, who at one point was also the chair/CEO of Neopets. With this information Neopets produces a plethora of marketing research and publishes various reports (Grimes & Shade, 2005, p. 183). Its annual youth survey is used by numerous companies including *Advertising Age* (Wasko, 2008, p. 471). Similar, but subtler, opportunities occur on the WebKinz website and also on Moshi Monster but it is unclear as to how this information is actually used (Wasko, 2010, p. 123).

YOUNG PEOPLE AS CULTURAL PRODUCERS

In reading this chapter so far, you would not be wrong to assume that young people are manipulated by a crass media machine that organizes and defines youth according to its own agenda while young people mindlessly participate in this production. In much of the literature in the fields of sociology, psychology, marketing, and communication, childhood and adolescence are often conceptualized as periods of vulnerability. Young people are perceived as malleable and gullible to corporate pressures. Adults in this equation are immune to this influence, but the young with their seemingly "tender minds" are at risk of manipulation. Although such arguments may seem slightly absurd, they remain at the heart of much of the concern over young people's use of the media.

Obviously, such a reading is too narrow and "neglects the diverse and complex ways in which youth use and relate to cultural commodities" (Buckingham, 1993, p. 166). While we can't deny the incredible power of media culture to shape and influence youth culture, young people do have a certain power and agency in their relationship to the media. For one thing, children, as Buckingham (1993) has shown, are often much more intelligent viewers than they are given credit for and can make thoughtful, critical, and often cynical assessments of the mass media. For another, young people have found ways to respond and engage with the media in ways that resonate with them. There are numerous examples of young people producing their own media, particularly those disenfranchised by the mainstream media. For example, in the 1980s and 1990s, young people published their own magazines called zines, which flourished as an alternative to the mainstream press. This form of expression was particularly popular with young feminists who produced a plethora of titles including *riot grrrl*, *FanGirl*, and *Action Girl*. In the 1990s the internet began to open up new possibilities for young people to develop their own media content. Not surprisingly, in the 1990s many zines morphed into webzines. *New Moon*, first published in 1995, is now a webzine created by and for 8- to 14-year-old girls.

These productions allowed girls to move beyond simply being consumers of media to being producers of media texts unconstrained by the commercial demands of the mainstream press.

The web has allowed for a space in which the lines of production and consumption are blurred, giving young people more opportunities to engage with and create media. In the past decade sites such as YouTube have created spaces for young people to share their own digital productions and respond to others. A good example of this is a YouTube video called "Webkinz Pool Party" produced by Starrystarr33 and analyzed by Cheryl Cowdy, a scholar of children's studies. Cowdy notes how in the video two girls play subversively with their WebKinz toys in a pool. The toys get sucked into the filtration system of the pool and ride around on flip-flops that become "stylin boats." The girls parody the KinzCash economy of Webkinz as their toys try to purchase items found on the pool deck. Cowdy suggests that the girls have produced an alternative online community to the official WebKinz World: "What is perhaps most striking about the continuing popularity of Starrystarr33's YouTube production (note that it has had over 348,000 hits since it was re-uploaded in August of 2010) is its representation of the children's play with their WebKinz as physical, material objects in actual rather than virtual spaces" (Cowdy, 2012).

Digital media such as Starrystarr33's production remind us that children are not simply passive victims in a commercialized world. Young people can act as producers of alternative media in ways that "challenge and contest the limited and limiting options provided by their corporate creators" (Cowdy, 2012).

Children's Media and the Canadian Mediascape

In this discussion you may have noticed that Canada has a really rich media presence in the children's entertainment industry. In fact, Canadian television shows have been trailblazers in providing edgy, youth-centred content. One of the best examples of this is the sensational hit *Degrassi* franchise. The series started in 1979 with *The Kids of Degrassi Street* (1979–86), then *Degrassi Junior High* (1987–89), and later as *Degrassi High* (1989–91). *Degrassi* was produced by Playing with Time Productions. It originally aired on the CBC in Canada and was broadcast in the United States on the Public Broadcasting Service (PBS). The series was one of Canada's most successful exports of the 1980s, broadcasting in over 40 countries with over 10 million viewers weekly in Great Britain and the United States alone (Byers, 2005). In 2001 the series returned as *Degrassi: The Next Generation*. It is still in production and is now just called *Degrassi*.

There is a long history of successful Canadian children's and youth programming. On CBC television the shows the *Friendly Giant* (1958–1985) and *Mr. Dressup* (1967–1996) both had nearly 30-year runs on the public broadcaster and are reflective of the fact that Canadian children like to watch Canadian programming. While Canadian shows have faced tough competition from American programming in the past few decades, they still gather large audiences. According to a report titled "The Case for Kids Programming," in the 2007/2008 television season in Canada three of the top-ten children's television programs in the English-language market were Canadian, and six in the French-language market. Not only were Canadian shows in the top ten, 55 percent of all viewing time on children's television shows in English Canada was of Canadian shows. Furthermore, Canadian shows made up an astounding 82 percent of all of the shows watched in the French-language children's market. Shows that were popular included *Degrassi: Next Generation* (2001–present), *Instant Star* (2004–2008), *Life with Derek* (2005–2009), *Ramdam* (2001–2008) and *Kaboum* (2007–present) (Nordicity Group, 2009).

Canadian children's and youth programming is a successful export as well. In 2007/08 Canadian children's and youth programming generated an estimated $103 million in international export revenues and was watched on channels such as ABC (Australia), Disney Channel (United States, France, Italy, Japan, Latin America, Brazil); Nickelodeon (United States, United Kingdom, Australia, Spain, Asia and Germany), TF1 (France), Pyramid Entertainment (Kuwait), Nick Jr. (United Kingdom) and Al Jazzera (United Arab Emirates). This provides great economic value for Canadians. In 2007/08 the industry was worth over $257 million in production volume and was responsible for over 2500 production jobs and an additional 3900 spinoff jobs (Nordicity Group, 2009).

But the success of this industry is a story that is often not told. As Canadians we are not fully aware of the incredible international success of our Canadian children's media or its presence on the world stage. Unfortunately, this oversight extends to the field of communication studies as well. With a few notable exceptions (e.g., André H. Caron's work with the Centre for Youth and Media Studies on how Canadian children and families appreciate and interpret media content in their daily lives (2010) and Michelle Byers's scholarship on the *Degrassi* franchise (2005), to name two), there is very little scholarship on the Canadian children's entertainment industry.

CONCLUSION

Today, children's relationships with consumer culture have changed radically since my father's childhood but it is important to remember that adults' relationships with it have changed as well. The purpose of comparing my father's experiences with my daughter's is not to romanticize a false notion of the past when childhood was free from the pressures of the marketplace. Instead, the comparison allows us to connect the growth of the children's market with the broader social and historical contexts of the development of consumer culture.

In the past few decades, children have increasingly been understood and defined according to logics of the marketplace, particularly since the 1980s with media deregulation, character merchandising, and market segmentation. But as

Starrystarr33 reminds us, young people have new opportunities to create their own texts that overtly challenge the messages of the mass media on gender, sexuality, race, and generation. But we need to look beyond the polarized views of hapless consumers or savvy empowered consumers and instead think about the ways that consumption is embedded in the practices of children's everyday lives (Buckingham, 2011, p. 66).

Of course, we must always remember that the marketplace does not provide the same opportunities to all children. Both here at home, but also globally, many young people live in conditions of poverty and do not have access to the technologies to produce their own media and have their voices heard. They often remain invisible in the media and they are alienated as consumers. For some children, the only connection they have to consumer culture is as cheap labourers producing the clothes, the technologies, and the toys that North Americans consume. One can only wonder how many children were involved in making the clothes that fill my daughter's dresser. Were they the young students removed from school and forced to work under the blazing suns in the cotton fields of Uzbekistan?[6] Or were they in the dusty factories sewing sequins on a Gap blouse?[7] These are the forgotten children of children's consumer culture; the children in foreign lands who make the spoils of consumer culture available at an affordable cost for my daughter. My daughter's dresser drawers are crammed full because children's clothes are cheap for her middle-class parents (and grandparents) to buy. But, in buying these clothes, we fail to see the cost of them on the children who actually produce the clothes.

QUESTIONS

1. How has consumer culture shaped how we define and understand children, childhood, and youth?
2. Look at the ASC's Broadcast Code for Advertising to Children at http://www.adstandards.com/en/clearance/childrens/broadcastCodeForAdvertisingToChildren-TheCode.aspx What do you think is the ideology behind such codes? Do you think these codes are valuable? Do you think they work? How would you regulate children's advertising?
3. How are youth targeted as specific market niches? What are some examples of how youth are targeted as these niches?
4. Does the internet provide an alternative space for young people to produce their own cultural content? What are some examples of this? Or is it really just a space for the further commercialization of youth culture?
5. Do you think Canada produces its own specific brand of media for children and youth? Why do you think Canadian productions have been so successful internationally? Why do you think that few Canadians know about this international success?

6. Do online gaming sites geared for young people work to sell the values of consumerism or do they offer a space for young people to be empowered? Look at some of the online sites such as WebKinz, Club Penguin, Habbo, Poptropica, Stardoll, and Moshi Monsters, and explore how they work. How does the website make money? What are the tasks or goals of the players? How do the players engage with each other?
7. Ask your parents or grandparents about their childhood experiences with the media, consumer goods, and the marketplace. Begin by asking them to describe their bedrooms, or the toys they played with. What types of clothes did they wear and how did they acquire such items? Ask them how they spent their free time. How many items of clothes did they have? What did they do when they came home from school? How did they spend their weekends? Reflect on these questions yourself. What were your experiences like? In asking these types of questions, you can begin to get a picture of the changing relationship of young people to consumer culture. Explore what was different and what was the same. Think about the changing ways that consumption is embedded in the practices of children's everyday lives.

NOTES

1. However, the FCC reinstated this in 1990, limiting the number of commercial minutes per hour to 10.5 minutes on weekdays and 12 minutes on weekends.
2. Attempts at co-ed magazines for teens do not have a history of being very successful.
3. See Stephen Kline's work *Out of the Garden* (1993) for a further analysis of character licensing.
4. Part of this strategy was that it also offered "line extensions" as a way to increase sales; Strawberry Shortcake had friends that could also be bought, and there was an entire line of My Little Ponies.
5. Character licensing also created more opportunities for obsolescence. Children got rid of goods not when they wore out but when the characters were no longer cool. According to a 1996 report in *Advertising Age*, the licensing business was about creating the "here-today, gone-tomorrow lunch bucket" (Fitzgerald, 1996, p. S10).
6. In a gross violation of human rights, the government of Uzbekistan forcibly removes children from schools to pick cotton during the harvest season. This cotton is then used by companies such as Carters and Gymboree to make children's clothes cheaply. See http://www.cottoncampaign.org [February 10, 2012]
7. In 2007 it was reported by the British newspaper the *Guardian* that children as young as 10 were found to be working in conditions "close to slavery" to produce clothes for Gap Kids. See http://www.guardian.co.uk/world/2007/oct/28/ethicalbusiness.retail (retrieved February 10, 2012).

REFERENCES

Banet-Weiser, S. (2007). *Kids rule! Nickleodeon and consumer citizenship*. Durham, N.C.: Duke University Press.

Bream, M. (1988, October 24). Kids' television: Vive la difference. *Marketing Magazine*, p. 14.

Brooks, K. (2003). Nothing sells like teen spirit: The commodification of youth culture. In K. Mallan and S. Pearce (Eds.), *Youth cultures: Texts, images and identities*. Westport, Connecticut: Praeger.

Buckingham, D. (1993). *Reading audiences: Young people and the media*. Manchester UK: Manchester University Press.

———. (2011). *The material child: Growing up in consumer culture*. Cambridge UK, Polity Press.

Byers, M. (2005). *Growing up Degrassi: Television, identity, and youth cultures*. Toronto ON: Sumach Press.

Centre for Youth and Media Studies. (2010). *A National Study on Children's Television Programming in Canada*. Prepared for Alliance for Children and Television. Retrieved from http://www.ymamj.org/pdf/nationalstudy.pdf

Chung, G. & S. M. Grimes. (2005). Data mining the kids. Surveillance and market research strategies in children's online games. *Canadian Journal of Communication*. 30, 527-548.

Cook, D. (2004b). *The commodification of childhood: The children's clothing industry and the rise of the child consumer*. Durham NC: Duke University Press.

Coulter, N., & C. Murray. (2001) *Watching the watchers: Gender justice and co-regulation in the new media marketplace*. Toronto ON: MediaWatch.

Cowdy, C. (2012, October 21). Pool Parties and Renegade WebKinz™: The Materiality and Immateriality of Online Play. Paper Presented at ARCYP Symposium—Children's Material Cultures, York University.

CRTC. (1987, April 30). Application by YTV Canada Inc., vol 13.

Danesi, M. (2003). *Forever young: The teen-aging of modern culture*. Toronto: University of Toronto Press.

Davies, H., Buckingham, D., & Kelley, P. (2000, January). In the worst possible taste: Children, television and cultural value. *European Journal of Cultural Studies*. 3, 5–25.

Englehardt, Tom. (1986). The Strawberry Shortcake strategy. In Todd Gitlin (Ed.), *Watching television*. New York: Pantheon Books.

Ewen, S. (1976). *Captains of consciousness: Advertising and the social roots of the consumer culture*. New York: McGraw-Hill.

Fitzgerald, K. (1996, February 12). Licensed to sell. *Advertising Age*, pp. S1–S10.

Grimes, S. M. & Shade, L. R. (2005). Neopian economics of play: children's cyberpets and online communities as immersive advertising in NeoPets.com. *International Journal of Media and Cultural Politics*. 1(2), 181–198.

Kenway, J. & Bullen, E. (2001). *Consuming children: Education, entertainment, advertising*. Buckingham, UK: Open University Press.

Kline, S. (1993). *Out of the garden: Toys, TV and children's culture in the age of marketing*. London, UK: Verso.

Kunkel, D. (2001). Children and television advertising. In D.G. Singer and J.L. Singer (Eds.), *Handbook of children and the media*. Thousand Oaks, CA.: Sage Publications.

KZero, (2011). Virtual Worlds: Industry and user data chart: Universe chart for Q4 2011. Retrieved from www.kzero.co.uk/blog [February 22, 2012].

Leiss, W., Kline, S., & Jhally, S. (1986). *Social communication in advertising: Persons, products & images of well-being*. Toronto, New York: Methuen.

Marney, J. (1990, January 29). Children: The powerful new consumers. *Marketing Magazine*, p. 15.

Montgomery, K. (1990). *Target prime time: Advocacy groups and the struggle over entertainment television*. NY: Oxford University Press.

Montgomery, K. (2001). Digital Kids: The new-online children's consumer culture. In D. G. Singer and J. L. Singer (Eds.), *Handbook of children and the media*. Thousand Oaks, CA.: Sage Publications.

MTV. (1983, August 1). Advertisement. *Advertising Age*, p. M-19.

Nordicity Group Ltd. (2009). *The case for kids programming*. Retrieved from http://www.ymamj.org/pdf/thecase2009.pdf

Pecora, N. O. (1998). *The business of children's entertainment*. New York: The Guilford Press.

Quart, A. (2003). *Branded: The buying and selling of teenagers*. London: Arrow.

Schneider, C. (1989). *Children's television*. New York: NTC Business Books.

Schor, J. (2004). *Born to buy: The commercialized child and the new consumer culture*. New York: Scribner.

Schrum, Kelly. (2004). *Some wore bobby sox: The emergence of teenage girls' culture 1920–1945*. New York: Palgrave Macmillan.

Seiter, E. (1993). *Sold separately: Children and parents in consumer culture*. New Brunswick, N.J.: Rutgers University Press.

Smythe, D. W. (1994). Communications: Blindspot of western marxism. In T. Guback (Ed.). *Counterclockwise: Perspectives on communication*. Boulder, CO: Westview Press.

Szatmary, D. P. (1991). *Rocking in time: A social history of rock and roll* (2nd ed.). New Jersey: Prentice Hall.

Turow, J. (1997). *Breaking up America: Advertisers and the new media world*. Chicago: University of Chicago Press.

Wasko, J. (2008). The commodification of youth culture. In K. Drotner and S. Livingstone (Eds.). *The international handbook of children, media and culture*. Los Angeles: Sage.

———. (2010). Children's virtual worlds: The latest commercialization of children's culture. In D. Buckingham and V. Tingstad (Eds.). *Childhood and consumer culture*. Hampshire, UK: Palgrave MacMillan.

CONTRIBUTORS

Amin Alhassan (PhD) is an associate professor of Communication Studies. He previously taught at York University, Toronto, for several years and is currently teaching at the University for Development Studies, Nyanpkala, Ghana. His research interest is in the area of development communication theory and practice. He is also a strategic communication consultant to a number of nongovernmental organizations in development practice in Africa.

Sylvia Blake is a PhD candidate at Simon Fraser University's School of Communication. Her research interests include communication policy and regulation, globalization and cultural policy, and cultural trade.

Mia Consalvo is Canada Research Chair in Game Studies and Design at Concordia University in Montreal. She is the author *of Cheating: Gaining Advantage of Videogames* (MIT Press, 2007), and is currently writing a book about Japan's influence on the video game industry and game culture. Mia has published her work in *Critical Studies in Media Communication*, *Games and Culture*, *Game Studies*, *Convergence*, and many other journals. She has presented her work at professional as well as academic conferences including regular presentations at the Game Developers Conference. She is the past president of the Association of Internet Researchers, and has held positions at MIT, Ohio University, Chubu University in Japan, and the University of Wisconsin—Milwaukee.

Natalie Coulter is currently an assistant professor at York University in the Department of Communication Studies. Her research interests are in girls' studies and in critical advertising studies. Her book *Tweening the Girl: The Crystallization of the Tween Market* is forthcoming from Peter Lang's Mediated Youth series. She has published in the *Canadian Journal of Communication* and *Jeunesse*. She is a founding member of ARCYP (Association for Research on the Cultures of Young People). She is currently researching the history of children's cultural industries in Canada.

Zoë Druick is an associate professor in the School of Communication at Simon Fraser University. Her books include *Projecting Canada: Documentary Film and Government Policy at the National Film Board* (McGill-Queen's University Press, 2007), *Programming Reality: Perspectives on English-Canadian Television* (Wilfrid Laurier University Press, 2008), and *Allan King's A Married Couple* (University of Toronto Press, 2010). She has also published numerous articles on reality-based and educational media in journals such as *Screen*, *Television and New Media*, *Canadian Journal of Communication*, *Canadian Journal of Film Studies*, and *Studies in Documentary*, as well as a number of anthologies.

Josh Greenberg is an associate professor of Communication Studies at Carleton University, where he is cross-appointed in the Department of Sociology and Anthropology. He is the director of the Crisis and Emergency-Risk Communication Research Unit at Carleton University. His areas of research interest include public relations, risk and emergency communication, media representations of social problems, media and civil society (nonprofits and social movements), surveillance, and qualitative methods. His work appears in numerous journals and books. He is co-editor of *Communication in Question* (Nelson Canada, 2008; Second Edition, 2013); The *Surveillance Studies Reader* (Open University Press, 2007); and *Surveillance: Power, Problems and Politics* (UBC Press, 2009).

Sheryl N. Hamilton is the Canada Research Chair in Communication, Law and Governance at Carleton University. She is an associate professor in the School of Journalism and Communication, and in the Department of Law. She is the author of *Impersonations: Troubling the Person in Law and Culture* (University of Toronto Press, 2009) and *Law's Expression: Communication, Law and Media in Canada* (LexisNexis, 2009). She is the coauthor of *Becoming Biosubjects: Bodies. Systems. Technologies.* (University of Toronto Press, 2011). She has published articles in a variety of international journals and chapters in edited collections exploring issues of gender and technology, science and media, social science fiction, intellectual property, and communication theory. She is currently completing a project exploring the emotional publics constituted in the media's treatment of significant legal decisions in Canada and is simultaneously beginning a new project examining the cultural anxiety of living in pandemic culture. She is the director of the Canadian Initiative in Law, Culture, and Humanities and is currently co-editing a collection of essays on law and the senses.

Faiza Hirji is an assistant professor in the Department of Communication Studies and Multimedia at McMaster University. She specializes in research exploring media representation of race, religion, ethnicity, and gender; use of media in the construction of identity; popular culture and youth; and the importance of media within diasporic/transnational communities. She is currently working on two research projects, one investigating overlapping musical cultures and their associated politics within South Asian and black diasporas, and the other looking at media representations of Muslim women. Her recent book, *Dreaming in Canadian: South Asian Youth, Bollywood and Belonging* (2010, UBC Press), details her work on audience readings of nationalism and religion in Bollywood cinema. She has published articles on the formation of online communities by Muslim Canadians, the depiction of Islam in Indian cinema, e-health, and feminism in television, film, and music. Her work has appeared in *Global Media Journal; Journal of Communication Inquiry; Information, Communication and Society*, *Canadian Journal of Communication*; and *TOPIA*.

Russell Johnston is associate professor in the Department of Communication, Popular Culture & Film and the graduate program in Popular Culture at Brock University. His research on Canadian media history has appeared in journals such as *Media,*

Culture & Society, *Journalism & Mass Communication Quarterly*, *Historical Journal of Film, Radio & Television*, the trade paper *Marketing*, and the book *Selling Themselves: The Emergence of Canadian Advertising* (University of Toronto Press, 2001).

Mark Lipton is an associate professor in the School of English and Theatre Studies at the University of Guelph. He also teaches in the Media Studies program at Guelph-Humber. In the classroom he strikes a balance between theory and practice by employing alternative pedagogical models from multidisciplinary perspectives. He is an advocate for media literacy and works with social media to advocate for Ontario public school teachers. His work with the Media Education Project was funded by the Canadian Council on Learning and the Social Sciences and Humanities Research Council of Canada. He is the author of the media literacy textbook *Smoke Screens: From Tobacco Outrage to Media Activism* (with M. Dewing and Children's Media Project, Children's Health Initiative, NY State Dutchess County Executive's Office, W. Steinhaus, 2002), has written numerous monographs on the subject of media education, and is a co-editor of *Visualizing the Web: Evaluating Online Design from a Visual Communication Perspective* (Peter Lang, 2010). In 2009, as a result of his work with the *Media Education Project*, Lipton was awarded the Jacques Ellul Award for Outstanding Media Ecology Activism.

Michael Andrew Lithgow received his PhD from Carleton University in the School of Journalism and Communication in 2012. His research explores the tensions between aesthetics, power, and knowledge in popular cultures. He has worked as a community media advocate and journalist in radio, print, and television; and he is currently a research associate with the Canadian Alternative Media Archive. He is a contributing editor at *Art Threat Magazine*, and his first collection of poems, *Waking in the Tree House*, was published by Cormorant Books in 2012.

Meera Nair received her PhD from the School of Communication at Simon Fraser University in March 2009. Her interest in intellectual property law stemmed from a BSc in mathematics and 10 years as a private consultant working on technology transfer projects between academia and industry. She is currently an Azrieli international postdoctoral fellow at Hebrew University in Jerusalem. A list of her publications can be found at her blog, Fair Duty (http://fairduty.wordpress.com/) together with an eclectic mix of commentary on copyright, innovation, and culture.

Judith Nicholson is an assistant professor in the Department of Communication Studies at Wilfrid Laurier University. Her research interests include narratives of innovation and progress in the history of mediated mobilities and intersections of race, gender, and mediated mobilities. She has published articles and reviews in the *Canadian Journal of Communication*, *Fibreculture Journal*, *M/C: A Journal of Media and Culture*, and *Topia: Canadian Journal of Cultural Studies*.

Lorna Roth is a professor and former chairperson of the Department of Communication Studies, Concordia University in Montréal. She is author of *Something New in the Air: The Story of First Peoples Television Broadcasting in Canada* (McGill-Queen's

University Press, 2005) and is currently working on her second book entitled *Colour-Balance: Race, Technologies, and "Intelligent Design."* She has a long-standing interest in minorities in public and private media sectors, and has written extensively about the (de)construction of cultural and racial diversity in the media, identity persistence, and the ways in which technologies, race, and culturally inflected design decisions are linked.

Philip Savage, PhD, lectures and writes on the history and changing role of audiences in Canada and around the world. He is an assistant professor at McMaster University, where he teaches research methodologies, political economy of media, communication law and policy, and professional communication practice.

A long career in community media, public broadcasting, and professional media research includes roles as Audience Research Head for CBC Radio (1990s) and Senior Manager, Planning and Regulatory Affairs for CBC Television and cbc.ca (early 2000s). Savage continues to be involved in public policy formation and has worked as a consultant and expert witness with the House of Commons, CRTC, Commissioner of Official Languages, and the Canadian Media Research Consortium. He is a leader in the Europe-based RIPE group (Re-Visionary Interpretations of the Public Enterprise) and has contributed to major publications on developments in broadcasting and its digital transformation around the world.

Savage is cofounder of McMaster University's Communication Metrics Laboratory (COMM-Lab), a collaborative research space for theorizing and conducting communication measurement and audience analysis. He publishes interdisciplinary pedagogical research and presents instructional workshops with the Centre for Leadership in Learning (CLL) at McMaster University, and the Society for Teaching and Learning in Higher Education (STLHE).

Kim Sawchuk is a professor in the Department of Communication Studies, Concordia University, Montreal, where she teaches courses on research methodology, communication theory, feminist theory, and mobility studies. Kim is the cofounder of studioXX, a feminist digital media production centre located in Montreal, a cofounder of the Mobile Media Lab—Montreal, the "Fembot" Research Network, and *Wi: Journal of Mobile Media.* Her most recent research explores ageing with respect to digital media environments. She is also conducting a number of research-creation projects that use location-based technologies for digital story telling, curatorial collaborations, and media activism. She currently holds a Concordia University Research Chair in Mobile Media Studies.

Leslie Regan Shade is an associate professor at the University of Toronto in the Faculty of Information. Previously she taught at Concordia University in the Department of Communication Studies (2003–2012) and at the University of Ottawa in the Department of Communication (1997–2003). Her research focus since the mid-1990s has been on the social, policy, and ethical aspects of information and communication technologies (ICTs), with particular concerns toward issues of gender, youth, and political economy. Research contributions straddle the line between academic and nonacademic audiences, including policymakers and nonprofit groups. She is the author of *Gender and Community in the Social Construction of the Internet* (Peter Lang, 2002), and co-editor of *Feminist Interventions in International Communication* (with Katharine Sarikakis, Rowman, & Littlefield, 2008), three volumes in *Communications in the Public Interest* (edited with Marita Moll, Canadian Centre for Policy Alternatives, 2001, 2004, and 2008) and also for CCPA, *For Sale to the Highest Bidder: Telecom Policy in Canada* (with Moll, 2008) and *The Internet Tree: The State of Telecom Policy in Canada 3.0* (with Moll, 2011). A recent co-edited collection is *Connecting Canadians: Investigations in Community Informatics* (with Clement, Gurstein, Longford, and Moll, Athabasca University Press, 2012). Shade's articles have also appeared in *Continuum*, *The Gazette*, *Canadian Journal of Communication*, *Government Information Quarterly*, and *Feminist Media Studies*. She is a former president of the Canadian Communication Association.

Jeremy Shtern is an assistant professor in the Department of Communication, University of Ottawa. His research program focuses on the impacts of digital technologies and globalization on communication governance, creative labour, and cultural industries. Among various research contributions, Jeremy has coauthored two recent books, *Media Divides: Communication Rights and the Right to Communicate in Canada* (with Marc Raboy, UBC Press, 2010) and *Digital Solidarities, Communication Policy and Multi-stakeholder Global Governance* (with Marc Raboy and Normand Landry, Peter Lang, 2010). Jeremy holds an honors BA in Film Studies from Queen's University (CA), an MSc in New Media, Information and Society from the London School of Economics and Political Science (United Kingdom), a PhD in Communication from the Université de Montréal (Canada), and has previously held research affiliations with CNRS SciencePo (France); McGill University (Canada) and Ryerson University (Canada).

David Skinner is an associate professor in the Department of Communication Studies at York University. Most recently, he is coauthor of *Mass Communication in Canada*, 7th ed. (Oxford University Press, 2012) and co-editor of *Alternative Media in Canada* (UBC Press, 2012).

Valerie Steeves, JD, PhD, is an associate professor in the Department of Criminology at the University of Ottawa in Ottawa. She has written and spoken extensively on online issues, and worked with Industry Canada, Health Canada, Heritage Canada, the Department of Justice, and the Office of the Privacy Commissioner of Canada on online policy. She is also a frequent intervener before parliamentary committees, and has worked with a number of policy groups, including the International Council on Human Rights Policy (Geneva, Switzerland), the House of Lords Constitution Committee on The Impact of Surveillance upon the Privacy of Citizens (United Kingdom), and the Children's Online Privacy Working Group of the Canadian Privacy and Information Commissioners and Youth Advocates.

Steeves's current research focuses on young people's use of networked technologies. She is the principal investigator of the eGirls Project, funded by the Social

Sciences and Humanities Research Council of Canada, which is examining the performance of gender on social networking sites. She is also the lead researcher on the Young Canadians in a Wired World project, funded by the Office of the Privacy Commissioner of Canada, which has been tracking young people's use of new media since 1999.

Ira Wagman is an associate professor of Communication Studies in the School of Journalism and Communication at Carleton University with research interests in cultural policy, media history, and the history of communication research. He has published essays and reviews in a number of scholarly journals, including the *Canadian Journal of Communication*, the *Velvet Light Trap*, and the *Journal of Canadian Studies*. He is currently at work on a book on the history of Canadian audiovisual policy, as well as new research on the role of media technologies in multilateral institutions, with a particular emphasis on UNESCO.

Kenneth C. Werbin is an assistant professor of Contemporary Studies and Journalism at Wilfrid Laurier University's Brantford Campus. Like the title of his chapter in this textbook, his research focuses on intersections of social media, commodification, and surveillance. His research and scholarly contributions have appeared in edited collections and national and international journals including the *Canadian Journal of Communication; Media, Culture & Society;* and *The International Review of Information Ethics*. His current SSHRC funded research project is titled "Auto-Biopolitics: Privacy, Surveillance and Self-Representational Forms of Digital Media."

Ezra Winton is pursuing a PhD (ABD) in Communication Studies at Carleton University where his research and teaching interests include alternative media, social movements, communication networks, and documentary cinema, institutions, and events. His dissertation looks at the cultural politics of documentary as seen through the lens of Toronto's Hot Docs film festival. Ezra is the cofounder and director of Programming of Cinema Politica, the world's largest grassroots documentary screening network, and is the cofounder of Art Threat, a cultural policy and political art blog.

GLOSSARY

A

AC Nielsen. In Canada, Nielsen Media Research provides people meter results on a national basis and for major markets—a national sample of about 3,500 homes. Nielsen is privately owned and sells the data to networks, local stations, and advertisers. Nielsen, the largest media measuring company in the world, is owned by parent company VNU, a leading market research and information company headquartered in The Netherlands. (7)

Aboriginal Peoples Television Network (APTN). A television network launched in 1999, with headquarters in Winnipeg. APTN is devoted to the stories and culture of Canada's First Peoples and is available nationally on basic cable and satellite. See http://www.aptn.ca (18)

Absent presence. The absorption of people's attention and consciousness by a focus on communication technologies such as the mobile phone. While people are co-present with others, their attention is focused on their personal means of communication to the absence of other human interactions. (14)

Accelerated Coverage Plan. Extension of national broadcasting to Northern communities, initiated in 1974. (14)

Accompanied solitude. Refers to the act of engaging in solitary activities such as talking and texting on a mobile phone or listening to music with headphones on while in public spaces. (14)

Administrative research. A term first used by Lazarsfeld (1941) to describe the type of research he himself conducted and frequently also called "dominant," "mainstream," or "noncritical." This approach is more characteristic of U.S. research, which produces knowledge useful to media corporations and state agencies. It is often funded by the media industry, uses primarily quantitative and empirical methods (such as opinion polling), and seeks to answer clearly defined problems (e.g., who watches TV, how effective are messages, etc.). (1)

Advertising. Commercial speech whose function is to place products and attitudes in the mind of the public with the eventual goal of persuading members of the public to buy products. Advertising is organized industrially on a large scale. (8)

Advertising Standards Canada (ASC). The ASC is the Canadian advertising industry self-regulatory body. It manages the Canadian Code of Advertising Standards, established in 1963, which sets the standards for acceptable, responsible, truthful, fair, and ethical advertising. See http://www.adstandards.com (8, 20)

Affordances. Refers to the qualities of objects and technologies and the capabalities enhanced or limited (afforded) by them for interaction and engagement. (12)

Alternative media. Media that provide a range of perspectives and/or modes of communication that aren't readily available through the corporate, profit-driven media that dominate the Canadian mediascape. (17)

Anik B Satellite. Anik, which in Inuit means "little brother," was the first commercial Direct Broadcast Satellite Service (DBS) launched in 1978 by Telesat Canada for television in Canada. (18)

Arab Spring. A name given to the political uprising and dissent of citizens in the Middle East and Northern African (MENA) region against their authoritarian or repressive regimes; it started in December 2010. Using a variety of social media tools, street demonstrations, and other forms of civil resistance, citizens protested governments and in some instances—Tunisia, Egypt, Libya, and Yemen—forced power from the government. Youth have been particularly active and vocal in this social reform movement. (14)

Audience. Derived from the Latin word "audire" ("to hear"), it refers to any group of people united around a common experience. The experience usually offers itself as pleasurable and worthy of repetition. Some audiences—such as those for sporting events, movies, concerts, etc.—are physically co-present. Other audiences—such as those for novels, television, radio, etc.—are not physically co-present. Additionally, audience members need not undergo the experience at the same time (i.e., not everyone reads the book or sees the movie at the same time). (7)

Audience engagment measures. Methods to assess the connection between audiences and their exposure to media messages and their behaviour. Engagement is assessed by recall, attitudes, appreciation, and emotional response. (7)

Audience massage model. The rhetorical strategies employed by professional audience researchers to influence favourable outcomes by decision-making bodies that fund or regulate broadcasting. The model consists of rhetoric, frames, and structure. (7)

Audience ratings. The measurement of how many people are viewing or listening to particular broadcasting, film, or theatrical events. Ratings are compiled by various methods, such as diaries, electronic recording, and telephone or internet surveys. (7)

Audience research. The use of social science and market research techniques to study the traits of actual and potential audiences. (7)

B

Battle of Seattle. Refers to a massive antiglobalization protest that took place in Seattle, Washington, in November 1999 against the World Trade Organization

(WTO) Minsterial Conference. Activists consisting of citizen's groups, unions, educators, and anarchists protested widening global socioeconomic gaps and neoliberal policies, including free trade, and effectively shut down the talks. (14)

BBM. Used to stand for Bureau of Broadcast Measurement (but now the organization uses only the acronym). BBM is the Canadian cooperative of member broadcasters and advertising agencies. BBM surveys smaller local TV markets with diaries—two major sweeps per year, and from 2010 offered a national metered TV ratings system using PPMs. BBM is the only major supplier of radio data; it supplies ratings based on a combination of PPMs and diary research in two major surveys per year. (7)

BDU. Refers to broadcasting distribution undertakings. This can be a cable, satellite or microwave distributor. (5, 9)

Bricolage. Combining and recombining facets of texts to render new ideological meanings. Appropriating and remixing media forms is one practice. (2)

Bridge discourses. Discourses that mediate relations between social movements and the state, adapted from Nancy Fraser in *Unruly Practices: Power, Discourse, and Gender in Contemporary Social Theory* (University of Minnesota Press, 1989). (18)

Broadcast Code for Advertising to Children. Developed by the Canadian Association of Broadcasters (CAB) and the Advertising Standards Canada (ASC), the code complements the Canadian Code of Advertising Standards regarding appropriate and ethical advertising for children. See http://www.adstandards.com/en/clearance/childrens/broadcastCodeForAdvertisingToChildren.aspx. (20)

Broadcasting Act. In 1932 the Government of Canada introduced the first *Broadcasting Act*. It was revised in 1936, 1958, 1968, 1988, and 1991. The *Broadcasting Act* sets out objectives for Canadian broadcasting generally and for the Canadian Broadcasting Corporation (CBC) specifically. It specifies the composition of the CBC's board of governors, the creation of the broadcasting regulatory agency (CRTC), content rules, and so on. See http://laws.justice.gc.ca/en/B-9.01 (8)

C

Canadian Association of Broadcasters (CAB). Created in 1926 as a lobby group for private radio broadcasters. It expanded to include private television broadcasters in the 1950s. It is concerned with all aspects of broadcasting and specialty services and has long demanded a separate regulatory agency for public and private broadcasting in Canada. See http://www.cab-acr.ca (20)

Canadian Code of Advertising Standards. Administered by Advertising Standards Canada to promote the professional practice of advertising. Initially established in 1963, periodic reviews update the Code. See http://www.adstandards.com/en/standards/thecode.aspx (8)

***Canadian Journal of Communication* (CJC).** Founded in 1975, the leading English-language scholarly journal devoted to communication in Canada. Currently edited by Michael Dorland at Carleton University. See http://www.cjc-online.ca (1)

Canadian Radio-television and Telecommunications Commission (CRTC). Federal regulatory agency created by the *Broadcasting Act* of 1968 as the Canadian Radio-television Commission. Its name was changed in 1975 when its mandate was expanded to include telecommunications. Its first and best known chairman was Pierre Juneau. The CRTC grants and may revoke licences for radio, television stations, television networks, cable companies, specialty and pay channels, satellite distribution systems, and multipoint microwave distribution systems. Since 1975 it has also overseen the telephone and telecommunications industries. The CRTC has established Canadian-content rules for both radio and television and has set forth numerous regulations on such issues as sex-role stereotyping, television violence, editorial independence, etc. The CRTC may also approve and regulate media ownership issues, and also rules on digital policy issues such as net neutrality and usage-based billing (how internet service providers meter and price internet use). The CRTC consists of up to 13 full-time and 6 part-time commissioners appointed by Orders-in-Council. Cabinet maintains the right to -give directions to the CRTC, to set aside its decisions, and to refer decisions back to it. See http://www.crtc.gc.ca/eng/welcome.htm (5)

Can-con. Refers to CRTC provisions to ensure appropriate levels of Canadian content in radio and broadcasting programming in order to promote Canadian musical performers, singers, and songwriters. MAPL is the quota system used to designate songs as Canadian; this refers to music, artist, performance, and lyrics. See http://www.crtc.gc.ca/eng/cancon.htm and http://www.crtc.gc.ca/eng/info_sht/r1.htm (5)

Challenge for Change Program. Initiated in 1966 and lasting until 1980 by the National Film Board of Canada, *Challenge for Change* popularized film and video production in various communities across Canada to highlight social concerns and, through the use of film effectuate change at local and national levels. See http://www3.nfb.ca/collection/films/fiche/?id=11410 (18)

Chicago School. A school of philosophical inquiry at the University of Chicago between 1894 and 1904. Founded by John Dewey, its notable members included George H. Mead, James H. Tufts, James R. Angell, Edward Scribner Ames, and Addison W. Moore. The Chicago School sought to apply the principles of pragmatism to social inquiry. As such, it rejected strictly empirical approaches and attempted to understand the ways in which human groups shaped meanings collectively and interactively. This implied a systematic questioning of received notions and standard explanations that makes the Chicago School representative of critical inquiry. A leading modern-day exponent of Chicago School pragmatism is philosopher Richard Rorty. (1)

Circuit of culture. A theoretical construct to understand how technologies impact on everyday life and culture. The circuit looks at how technology is represented through news media and marketing; the forms of social identities engendered by technology; the cultural production and reception of the technology; the everyday meanings and uses of the technology; and the policies and rules governing the use of the technology. (14)

Citizen journalism. The practice of citizens who are amateur journalists collecting, reporting, analyzing, and disseminating news and information, typically online through personal blogs, social media, or through online venues of established news organizations. (22)

Cloud computing. Remote storage of internet-based services that allow businesses and individuals to access software and hardware managed by third parties. These services include file sharing and storing, webmail, social network sites, and business applications. (13)

Commodification. Rendering products and services that are often noncommercial and transforming them into entities valuable for their market exchange and function. (13)

Commodity. Items that are marketable and intended to produce economic or emotional needs. (13)

Communication. The exchange of ideas and symbols between people, and later between institutions or between machines. It is linked etymologically to words such as "community" and "common," and in its oldest acceptance means "to make common," therefore to share, to exchange, or to make public. It was often associated with means of transportation, and prior to the 20th century the railway, waterways, and public roads were often thought of as means of communication. After the 20th century, communication was increasingly used to refer to media of communication, such as film, radio, television, and the internet. In this more modern meaning, the word is often pluralized (communications) to underline clearly that it refers to media or systems or technologies of communication. As a field of study, communication refers to the way in which the various phenomena of communication (i.e., the fact of interpersonal exchange, the existence of technologies, their social and cultural uses) came into being, have evolved in various contexts, have affected or been affected by the circumstances of their use and development, have been constrained or encouraged, and have been understood, misunderstood, theorized, and thought about. (1)

Comobility. The ability of people to be mobile with each other at a distance because of mobile devices and apps that facilitate locational finding such as GPS (global positioning systems). (14)

Concepts. A unit of knowledge built from particular characteristics. Can be an abstract idea that resides in certain disciplines. Can be intersubjective and performative, moving between disciplines and people. (4)

Conglomeration. A term that refers to the process by which one company in a field buys up other companies in the same field. For example, when one newspaper or newspaper chain buys other newspapers, the press industry is undergoing conglomeration. The process is characterized by fewer and fewer owners and larger and larger corporations. Supporters of conglomeration claim that it is a desirable business practice that protects jobs and brings stability to the marketplace. Opponents claim that it confers too much power on dominant owners who can shape our knowledge of events to suit their interests. (9)

Constellations of mobility. A theoretical concept that refers to the various historical and geographic formations of movements, mobile practices, and mobility narratives. (14)

Convergence. The process by which formerly separate technologies such as television and the telephone are brought together by a common technological base (digitization) or a common industrial strategy. The internet is the most outstanding example of technological convergence, because it can deliver digitized print, images, sound, voice, data, etc., equally well. One example of industrial convergence is the large corporation BCE (Bell Canada Enterprises) because it brings together under a single corporate umbrella television broadcasting, telephony (fixed and mobile), newspapers, etc., and uses each to cross-promote and to provide content for the others. (9)

Corporate media. Generally, these are large, privately owned media corporations that are operated on a for-profit basis. (9)

Corporeal mobility. Mobilities that are determined by bodily actions: walking, running, and travel by automotive or air transportation. (14)

Couchsurfing. Use of social networking by travellers to connect to free places to stay that are offered by volunteers. Couchsurfing.org is one of the first social network sites to offer such a service. (14)

Creative Commons. An alternative form of copyright that allows creators to legally amend standard copyright in order to give them a wide range of rights that they choose. See http://creativecommons.org (16)

Critical. To engage in criticism. As applied to communication studies, critical entails looking at media institutions and policies from a political economic or cultural studies perspective. (2)

Critical discourse analysis. An approach to studying written and spoken media texts to analyze the structures and nuances of language that can reveal sources of bias, power, and dominance. Typically, CDA analyzes social problems or policy issues. (19).

Critical massing. A type of flash mob that involves bicycles. Critical mass events have been held since 1992 in global cities on the last Friday of every month. Operating in a decentralized fashion, critical massing can be for fun and for protest. See http://criticalmass.wikia.com/wiki/Main_Page (14)

Critical race theory. Emanating from critical legal studies, critical race theory considers the social construction of race, and is concerned with issues of race and representation, subordination and discrimination. (4)

Critical research. A term first used by Lazarsfeld in 1941 to describe research that (1) takes as its proper object of study the relationship between communication and power, (2) sees power as unequally distributed, (3) believes theory (social critique) is more important than method (objective knowledge), (4) argues that researchers must acknowledge their own value orientations, (5) is inspired by European Marxist (Frankfurt School) or American radical (pragmatism) approaches, and (6) seeks to bring about positive social change. It is often assumed that communication study in Canada is naturally or spontaneously critical. (1)

Critical thinking. A rigourous process of skilful and active interpretation, evaluation, and reflection of media texts. (2)

Cross-media ownership. Cross-media ownership occurs when a firm in one industry acquires a firm in another similar but not directly related industry; an example is when a television broadcaster purchases a newspaper. (9)

Cultivation analysis. Developed by the late Professor George Gerbner through his 1960s Cultural Indicators research project, which studied the impact and influence of television viewing on viewers, cultivation research examines the mass media as a socializing agent. It is part of the "effects" tradition in communication theory. (3)

Cultural imperialism. The process whereby the cultural artifacts of a politically and economically dominant power—usually the United States—enter into another country and eventually dominate it, thereby spreading the cultural, political, and other values of the dominant power, to the exclusion of indigenous values and voices. (3)

Cultural industries. In the Frankfurt School specifically, and political economy generally, cultural industries refers to the fact that culture has been debased by being turned into a commodity controlled by profit-making enterprises. In this view, the function of culture is not to enrich or enlighten but to manipulate and indoctrinate. Since roughly the 1970s, a new and more optimistic definition has arisen, which sees culture as an occasion for economic expansion, employment opportunities, and the development of individual preference. (6)

Cultural sovereignty. The ability of nation-states to control and promote their national culture. Enacted through various strategies such as communications policy and legislation, funding packages to encourage media and cultural development, and educational and public outreach activities. (9)

D

Data aggregation. The many ways that data can be combined with other data in order to reveal patterns of interaction and communication. (13)

Data mining. The retrieval, accummulation, monitoring, and compilation of discrete forms of data through sophisticated e-commerce and online surveillance technologies. Data mining can be used to track consumer behaviour on the internet. (13)

Dataveillance. The act of surveilling personal information through data mining and aggregation. (13)

Decoding. The symbolic work that readers of media texts engage in to arrive at a meaning. (2)

Demographics (Demos). A term used to describe audience classification (for a specific population group) by characteristics such as age, sex, education, and occupation. (7)

Dependency theory. A critique of modernization theory, dependency theory emanates from Marxist and critical theories, arguing that underdevelopment in less developed countries was not due to internal factors but, rather, external factors related to the global capitalist political economy. (3)

Deregulation. Refers to governmental withdrawal or reduction of services to allow the private market to take over. Ostensibly to allow for market efficiency and innovation, critics contend that deregulation further erodes the provision of services for a welfare state and the public good. (9, 20)

Development communication. The use of communication—whether through technologies or practices of social persuasion—to stimulate development in less developed countries. Highly critiqued by dependency theorists, who question its ideological assumptions and cultural imperialist focus. (3)

Dialectical. A position on social determination that suggests that historical change is produced through the coming into conflict of oppositional forces. Key scholars exploring a dialectical approach are G. W. F. Hegel and Karl Marx. (1)

Diaries. A method of measuring the television and cable viewing habits of audience members. Users recorded their viewing habits in a paper diary. Because of human fallibility in recording in the diary, the electronic People Meter was later initiated as a more reliable measure. (7)

Digital democracy. The use of information and communication technologies to encourage, create, and propagate democratic modes of communication and to stimulate social democracy. (14)

Digital divide. Refers to the fact that socioeconomic factors, including income and educational levels, geographical location, gender, and age, influence participation in the new media environment. As a result, richer people and countries have greater access to, and make greater use of, new media and the internet than do poorer people and countries, a situation that has led to the creation of the categories of the "information rich" and the "information poor." "Digital divide" also refers to the view held by many that digital technologies not only confer benefits but also contribute to social inequalities. For example, not everyone has equal access to digital technology and, even among those who do, not everyone is equally competent in using it. (3)

Digital locks. Anticircumvention measures, including restrictions against the manufacture, sale, and distribution of code-cracking devices to illegally copy software, that are used by media corporations so that users do not illegally download or pirate their media content. In the United States, the *Digital Millennium Copyright Act* (DMCA), passed by the U.S. Congress in 1998, was controversial because of its measures protecting digital locks. The DMCA is intended to implement the 1996 treaties signed at the World Intellectual Property Organization (WIPO) Geneva conference. The *Canadian Copyright Act* also allows for digital locks, despite controversies and resistance against their implementation by the public. The government claims it needs to respect international laws such as those in the United States and internationally, such as WIPO. See http://thomas.loc.gov/cgi-bin/query/z?c105:H.R.2281.ENR (16)

Digitization. Refers to the process, applicable to any medium, whereby the content of that medium is converted into computer-readable format and can be manipulated and transmitted electronically. This allows the content of formerly separate media—for example, newsprint, radio sound, television images, and hypertext links—to exist side by side on the internet in a way that was previously impossible. Digital media also possess greater storage capacity and higher transmission speeds and permit infinite nondegraded reproduction of the original content. They tend also to be more user-friendly and to heighten the opportunity for individual creation, manipulation, storage, and transmission of content. In so doing, digitization has raised questions about copyright control and the ownership of intellectual property that have pitted individuals against corporations. (6)

Discriminatory. A nuanced and precise way of engaging with and thinking critically about media texts. (2)

DIY. Short for "do it yourself," referring to the creation of diverse media by amateurs, or nonprofessionals not out for commercial gain. (6)

Docudrama. Dramatizations of actual historical events. (10)

Documentary. Nonfictional film intended to document some aspect (historical or contemporary) of life for education and political and social impact. (10)

E

Embodied mobility. Mobilities that involve the use of bodies, such as walking and bicycling, or the use of transportation technologies or communication technologies to extend bodily reach. (14)

Empirical. An approach to research that focuses on the analysis of social phenomena through their observation and analysis in accordance with accepted principles and methods. For empirical scholars, observation precedes theoretical analysis. (1)

Entertainment Software Rating Board (ESRB). Established in 1994 by the Entertainment Software Association, the ESRB is a nonprofit, self-regulatory organization whose mandate is to assign age and content ratings for video games and mobile apps.

Most videogames sold in the United States and Canada are rated by the ESRB. See http://www.esrb.org/index-js.jsp (12)

Epistemology. An element in the construction of knowledge that focuses on the question, How is it that we know what we know? Epistemological debates ask whether we can produce objective truth about our reality or whether our knowledge is always subjective. (1)

Ethnographic research. A type of research methodology that uses fieldwork to provide a description of human societies, subcultures, or organizations. Often conducted over a considerable period of time, this research methodology involves a high degree of trust between the researcher and his or her research participants. (4)

External commodification. When commodification extends into noncommodified spaces. For instance, in social media, privacy has become a commodity as it increasingly relates to the commodification of personal information. (13)

F

Fair dealing. A limited exception to the exclusivity of intellectual property in the Canadian context. Fair dealing refers to mechanisms for fair critique, private study, and public information on material protected by copyright. Fair dealing requires acknowledgment of the author or creator of the protected material, and is intended for noncommercial use. (16)

Fair use. Emanating from U.S. copyright law, fair use refers to the limited use of copyrighted materials without the permission of the rights holder for purposes of scholarship and review. See http://fairusenetwork.com (6)

Fee for carriage/value for signal. A proposed regulatory policy for Canadian television to require cable and satellite television to compensate over-the-air television stations for their right to carry their local signals. (5)

Feminism. Belief in the political, social, economic, and cultural equality of all women. Feminism is a social movement, a theory, and a philosophy. (4)

File sharing. Distributing or providing access to digital files such as movies, television shows, and music, The legality of file sharing is widely debated, especially with respect to copyright laws and concern over illegal pirating practices. (16)

First Peoples. Refers to Aboriginal peoples in Canada, also known as First Nations, Inuit, and Métis, recognized under the Canadian *Constitution Act* of 1982 (s. 25 and 35). See the *Royal Commission Report on Aboriginal Peoples* at http://www.aadnc-aandc.gc.ca/eng/1307458586498/1307458751962 (18)

Flash mobbing. The organization, via electronic media such as mobile phones, of a group of strangers so that they can gather in a public place at a specific time for purposes of public performance, which is then determined once they get to the predetermined location. Flash mobs became popularized in the early 2000s. (14)

Flash robbing. A flash mob whose purpose is to quickly rob a store. Often flash robbing incidences are filmed and uploaded to YouTube. (14)

Focus groups. Small (from 4–12 people) informal groups who are led through a focused discussion by a moderator. Used in audience research to get nonrepresentative reactions to programming or advertising content or ideas; exploring how people think about things; and get reactions and ideas in people's own words. (7)

Fogo Process. Using media as a tool of participatory community development. Named for its first use in Fogo Island, Newfoundland, when Donald Snowden, then director of the Extension Department at Memorial University of Newfoundland, decided to use media to allow community members to respond to an Economic Council of Canada "Report on Poverty in Canada," which he felt was derogatory of community members. See http://www.uoguelph.ca/~snowden/fogo.htm (3)

Foucauldian analysis. An analysis derived from Michel Foucault (1926–1984), a French philosopher and historian whose structuralist and poststructuralist analyses focused on discourses of power, knowledge, and regimes of governmentality. See http://plato.stanford.edu/entries/foucault (3)

Framework. Identification of the specific epistemological or ontological assumptions that lie beneath subcategories, in order to provide an analysis or an argument. (4)

Framing. In media studies, framing refers to how the news media covers events or people to influence behaviours or attitudes. Frame building is impacted by the political and ideological orientation of journalists and the news organizations they work with, wider public opinion, organizational pressures and influences, and input from external groups such as public interest groups, lobbyists, and governments. (19)

Frankfurt School. A school of critical inquiry founded at the University of Frankfurt in 1922. It was the world's first clearly Marxist institute of social research, and its leading members included Theodor Adorno, Max Horkheimer, Herbert Marcuse, Erich Fromm, and Leo Lowenthal. Its aim was to understand the way in which human groups create meaning collectively under the impact of modern technology, instrumental or means–ends rationality, authoritarian social structures, and the increasing absorption of the formerly autonomous individual into the culture industries. The Frankfurt School was highly pessimistic about the possibility of genuine individuality under modern capitalism and condemned most forms of popular or mass culture as a type of incessant propaganda that indoctrinated the masses and disguised genuine social inequalities. (1)

Freedom of information legislation. Legislation by the Government of Canada, provinces, and territories that establishes a citizen's right to ask for and receive information held by government bodies. Information can be exempted from disclosure, such as personal information about third parties, information that could affect the security of individuals and groups, and information provided to the federal government by other countries or provinces that could impact governmental relations. (11)

Frontier Coverage Package. From 1967 to the mid-1970s, the CBC provided limited television service to remote and northern communities. Transmitters in selected communities carried a four-hour selection of black-and-white videotaped programs that were flown into communities. (18)

G

G20 Toronto summit. In June 2010, Toronto hosted the fourth annual international meeting of the heads of state for their discussion of global economic trade and cooperation. Toronto police, anticipating massive social protests, instituted a large security and surveillance apparatus that led to many critiques from activists and civil liberties groups concerning police violence and infringement against freedom of assembly. (14)

Gaze. In film and media theory, a term derived from psychoanalyis to refer to the relationship of subjects toward the objects and people they view and desire. (14)

Genre. A category of literature, art, drama, film, music, or videogame. (10)

Glance. A cursory look at something, whether televisual, human, or object. (14)

Glaze. Referring to undivided and persistent attention to a media object, such as a videogame or a mobile screen. (14)

Global positioning systems (GPS). Radio-identified technologies that enable controlling, tracking and geographical positioning. (13)

Global South. Refers to African, Asian, and Latin American countries in the southern hemisphere of the globe. (3)

Globalization. A term that refers to the process in which formerly separate, discrete, or local phenomena are brought into contact with one another and with new groups of people. This contact generates the idea that the world is a single place. Supporters of globalization claim that it liberates populations from local or particularistic rules, generates wealth, makes possible the movement of people and ideas, and contributes to the development of human rights by putting all people in touch with all other people. Critics of globalization claim that it flattens out cultural differences, spreads a single culture (usually American) to all areas of the world, and strengthens capitalism and unequal property relations. (9)

Guerrilla marketing. Unconventional, spontaneous marketing targeting consumers when they least expect. (8)

H

Hetero-normativity. The implied assumption that heterosexuality is a given, including values associated with male–female coupledom. (4)

Hoax. A deliberate attempt to fool an audience. (10)

Horizontal concentration of ownership. When a firm in one line of media buys a major interest in another media operation not directly related to the original business, or when it takes a major stake in a nonmedia company. (9)

I

Ideological square. As used in critical discourse analysis, a concept that organizes people and society into polarized terms: "us" versus "them," "positive" versus "negative." (19)

Ideology. A frequently used word with two main definitions. From Marx, ideology refers first to false consciousness, the fact that people fail to understand their genuine interests and instead adopt values and ideas that are opposed to their interests. Second, it refers to a system of ideas and values, specifically those of the ruling classes. The ideas of the ruling classes are contained within and reproduced by the dominant social institutions (the law, the family, religion, education, etc.). Ideology is that which appears to be common sense, unchallengeable, natural, good, and desirable but which is actually socially constructed and contingent. (1)

Immanent commodification. The development of intensive measurement and surveillance technologies that produce detailed demographic portraits of social network users. (13)

Information poverty. An approach to development communication that sees modernization as an issue of "information poverty" that needs to be remedied via the diffusion of information and communication technologies. (3)

Information subsidies. Refers to the information sources provided to the news media, such as press releases, letters to the editor, and opinion pieces. (11)

Institutionalization. The process, involving government, universities, and individual scholars, by which the field of communication came to be recognized as an autonomous field of study, with its own departments, research agendas and funds, scholarly publications, debates, etc. In Canada, this process largely occurred in the 1960s and 1970s and involved the coming together of administrative research, political economy, and cultural studies. (1)

Instrumentalist. An approach to media literacy in which media texts are used as mere instruments or tools to supplement learning. (2)

Intellectual property. Intellectual or creative work that can be owned by an individual, institution, or company. The thing owned can be an actual artifact (e.g., a machine or device), an artistic or intellectual expression (e.g., a novel, a painting, a film, a mathematical formula, etc.), a process (i.e., a specific method of producing that artifact), and so on. The main methods used to protect intellectual property are trademarks, patents, and copyright. (16)

International Development Research Center (IDRC). IDRC is a Canadian crown corporation established by the Canadian Parliament in 1970 to aid developing countries in the use of science and technology to ameliorate poverty and develop practical and sustainable solutions to social, economic, cultural, and environmental problems. See http://www.idrc.ca (3)

Internet. The internet is a "network of networks" that connects millions of computers around the world. Networks connected to the internet use a common protocol, TCP/IP (Transmission Control Protocol/Internet Protocol). This allows networks to have unique addresses and to communicate seamlessly with one another. Internet services include email, email lists, Usenet, the web, FTP, Telnet, chat, streaming video, and radio. The internet is available through computers and smart phones. The origins of the internet are found in the late 1950s and early 1960s, when it was decided to construct a communication system that could withstand thermonuclear attack. The goal was to build a decentralized system that could continue to operate and route messages even if part or parts of it were destroyed. This involved devising a method for splitting messages into smaller parts (packet switching) so that each part could find its own path to its destination, where all the parts would be reassembled. Much credit is often given to Paul Baran, Vinton Cerf, the Rand Corporation, and DARPA (Defense Advanced Research Projects Agency), but the true list of contributors is extremely long. Virtually identical efforts were undertaken at the same time in the Soviet Union, Britain, and Australia. See http://www.isoc.org/internet (18)

Intervention. A critical approach to media studies and media literacy that encourages the active involvement of students to further activism and social justice for the public good. (2)

K

Kill screen. A term used in video games to describe an error in the game coding that halts a player's actions and progress in the game at a certain stage or level of gameplay, wherein games crash, freeze, or end abruptly. (12)

M

Marginality. The fact of being on the margins, not being at the centre, not being the focus of attention. It is sometimes claimed that marginality affords perspective, distance, and the luxury of contemplation. As such, it is sometimes claimed marginal thinkers can discover insights that thinkers at the centre of things could never attain. (1)

Marginalization. Relegating communities and individuals to the sidelines of political and social life because of their race, ethnicity, gender, or socioeconomics. (18)

Mash-ups. A web application that combines data (sound, images) from more than one source into a new integrated product. (6)

Media. The plural form of the word "medium" that makes explicit that one form or mode of communication is necessary in order to convey a message. (2)

Medium. Any form of communication that conveys meaning. (2)

Meme. A popular image that is repurposed and remixed and spreads virally through social media. Memes can often be newsworthy events, or objects from popular culture, such as popular cat memes. (6)

Metadata. Products (such as personal information and personal preferences) distilled from data aggregation in social media. They are valuable to marketers and advertisers who wish to link to users. (13)

Meter. An electronic media monitoring system where minute-by-minute viewing behaviour is tracked. A panel-based system, with groups in designated market areas across the country. Panelists are all volunteers. The television set is measured for channel selection, and viewers report who is watching by a push button system. See also *People Meter*. (7)

Methodology. An element in the construction of knowledge that focuses on the processes through which questions are framed and research is conducted. Examples of methodologies include ethnography, science, and discourse analysis. (1)

Methods. An element in the construction of knowledge that involves the actual techniques through which knowledge is produced. Examples of methods include interviews, surveys, narrative analysis, content analysis, and focus groups. (1)

MMOG (massively multiplayer online game). A multiplayer video game that can support hundreds of online players at once. Some of the more popular games played over the internet include EverQuest, Final Fantasy series, and World of Warcraft. Newer game consoles such as the Xbox 360, PlayStation3, Wii, and Nintendo DS also support MMOGs. (12)

Mobile privatization. A term coined by cultural theorist Raymond Williams to describe the way that communication and transportation technologies (or technologies of mobility) render our experiences private, even when we are in public. (14)

Mobilities studies. Social science research that explores the various social, economic, and policy aspects in the intersection of people with communication and transportation technologies (or technologies of mobility). (14)

Mobisodes. Mobile episodes of television programs produced for mobile phones. (14)

Mockumentaries. Fictional films that imitate documentary conventions in order to pay homage to, parody, and/or reinforce the production of factual discourse. (10)

Modernity. Refers to a type of society in which individuals are deemed to be fundamentally rational and therefore capable of determining their own forms of social organization. Societies that are modern, therefore, also tend to value freedom of speech and of association, democratic forms of government, increasing knowledge, variety of cultural forms, and so on. They reject the notion that forms of social organization and individual behaviour are predetermined or unalterable. As a result, in modern societies, norms of behaviour are the object of constant debate. Societies that place less emphasis on the individual and more on divine transcendence (the view that social forms are given by a divinity outside human society) are often called premodern, or traditional, societies. Societies that value the individual but also doubt the value of rationality are often called postmodern societies. The fundamental characteristic of modernity, therefore, is the central role granted to reason or rationality in the determination of norms for individual and collective behaviour. (3)

Moral rights. An intrinsic element of Canadian copyright law that protects the original creation and intention of a creator's output. (16)

Multiculturalism. This refers to communities containing many diverse cultures. Adopted as an official policy of the Canadian federal government under Prime Minister Pierre Trudeau in the 1970–80s, multiculturalism is legislated by the *Multiculturalism Act* (1988), which recognizes and promotes the racial, ethnic, cultural, and linguistic diversity of Canadian society. Multiculturalism is also enshrined in the *Canadian Charter of Rights and Freedoms* in section 27. See http://laws-lois.justice.gc.ca/eng/acts/c-18.7 (19)

Multimodalities. A term that facilitates the many ways that media work within communication systems. (2)

N

National Film Board (NFB). A film-production unit established by the federal government in 1939, originally to make wartime propaganda films. Its first and most famous commissioner was John Grierson (1898–1972). After World War II, the NFB abandoned propaganda in favour of documentaries, travelogues, social issue films, etc. In the 1950s and 1960s, the NFB spawned the *Cinéma direct* movement and was instrumental in launching the Quebec film industry. The NFB was intended to serve as a foil to American film distribution and production. NFB films have won 11 Academy Awards and numerous other international awards. The board has served as a training school for some of Canada's most successful film directors. (10)

Neoliberalism. Economic and social movement that promotes policies for a free and open marketplace. In the communication sector, it is characterized by privatization, commercialization, and the deregulation of media industries. (9)

Net neutrality. The principle that all traffic on the internet be treated equally and without discrimination by network service providers, regardless of its source, ownership, content, or destination. A contested policy debate in North America started in 2007, with a CRTC hearing on net neutrality, or as they called it, traffic management, in July 2009. In its decision the CRTC adopted new guidelines for traffic management that put the onus on citizens to complain about discriminatory practices by internet service providers. (6, 9)

New media. Refers to communicative forms that are interactive, digital, related to the internet, and characterized by a convergence of "old" and "new" media. The result of social, political, economic, and technical forces, they can engender changes in everyday practices, our experience of reality, and our experience of ourselves. Now interchanged with the term "social media." (18)

New World Information and Communication Order (NWICO). During the 1970s the Movement of the Non-Aligned Nations (NAM), which comprised over 90 member nations, questioned the rise of commercial transnational media systems (TNCs) in terms of (1) the global economic imbalance between the North and the South; (2) the Western monopoly of global news services with their content focused mainly on developed countries; and (3) the dominance of news and entertainment programming that, because it reflected often-alien Western values, was deemed imperialist. These issues culminated in the call for a New World Information and Communication Order (NWICO). In 1976 UNESCO (United Nations Educational, Scientific, and Cultural Organization) convened the MacBride Commission to study global communication issues and develop solutions for ameliorating the North–South divide. Its final report, *Many Voices, One World*, was issued in 1980. Among its 82 recommendations were those devoted to eliminating the media imbalances between countries; protecting the rights of journalists; reducing commercialism in the media; use of the media to aid oppressed peoples; and recognition of the freedom of the press and freedom of information. (3)

Non-Aligned Movement. Refers to the coalition of developing countries who demanded a global agreement curbing the dominance of Western media during the NWICO debates. See also *NWICO*. (3)

Northern Native Broadcast Access Program. This program encouraged Aboriginal participation in the production and distribution of broadcasting under the Northern Broadcasting Policy. (18)

O

Ocularcentrism. A term used to describe how diverse visual representations on screens are prioritized as ways of navigating, experiencing, and knowing the world. (14)

Open publishing (OP). A system of publishing popularized by Indymedia, which allowed anyone with internet access to publish work on Indymedia using open-source software. (17)

Open source (OS). An alternative to commercial and proprietary software such as that developed by Microsoft, OS is the development of computer software that allows many developers to share in the source code and create licences for distribution. Examples of popular OS software include the operating system Linux, Apache (a program that runs 50 percent of the web servers in the world), and perl, (a language for interactive webpages). See http:// opensource.org/history (6)

Orientalism. A term used to describe the false depiction, imitation, assumptions or prejudices about Middle Eastern or East Asian cultures. Popularized by cultural scholar Edward Said, the term has been used widely in postcolonialist scholarship. (19)

Over-the-top services. Video services streamed over the internet. An example is the subscription-based service Netflix, which allows subscribers to access a multitude of films streamed to their computer from the centralized Netflix servers. (5)

P

Panopticon. Designed by the late–18th century philosopher Jeremy Bentham, the panopticon was a prison whose circular design enabled the observation of the prisoners by guards without the prisoners knowing exactly when they were being observed. As used by philosopher Michel Foucault, the pantopicon refers to a form of power and self-regulation. It is also a term widely used in surveillance studies and refers to the widespread and often invisible uses of surveillance technologies by governments and corporations. (13)

Paradigm. From science historian Thomas Kuhn in his *The Structure of Scientific Revolutions* (1962), paradigms refer to intellectual worldviews that offer everyday and scientific explanations of how things operate. (4)

Parkouring. Engaging in freestyle gymnastic running and jumping in urban spaces. (14)

Participatory theories and approaches. A methodological approach to communication research that involves, at the onset of the research, the participation of the communities that are being researched in the design, development, and diffusion of the research. (3)

Peer-to-peer communication. The use of mobile technologies to communicate with other people both synchronously (in real time) and asynchronously (not in real time). (14)

People meter. A small electronic device, attached to randomly selected Nielsen Research households, which detects TV station and length of tuning. Viewers are asked to use a remote control device to record their presence as they watch. Data is automatically downloaded via phone lines at the end of each day from the people meter to the Nielsen central computer, allowing for "overnight" ratings to be provided the next day to broadcasting and advertising clients. People meters were introduced to Canada in 1989 and replaced by PPMs in 2010. The Portable People Meter (PPM) is a pager-sized device carried by a representative panel of television viewers. It automatically detects inaudible codes that broadcasters embed in the audio portion of their programming using encoders provided by the ratings company. In Canada, BBM started market tests of PPM in Quebec in 2002, using technology jointly developed with Arbitron, the major radio ratings company based in the United States. By 2010, the bulk of radio and TV audience listening and viewing data were collected by PPM. (7)

People Power II. In 2001 Filipino citizens deployed SMS (text messaging) through their mobile phones to coordinate citizen engagment and activism against a corrupt president. (14)

Perpetual contact. Refers to the habitual ways that mobile technologies allow for constant and persistent contact with others. (14)

***Personal Information Protection and Electronic Documents Act* (PIPEDA).** Initiated in 2000 and updated in 2006, PIPEDA is one of two pieces of federal privacy legislation. PIPEDA establishes rules for the collection, use, and disclosure of personal information by private-sector organizations in the course of commercial activities. The law gives individuals the right to access and request correction of the personal information these organizations may have collected about them. It provides for the use of electronic means to communicate or record information or transactions and amends the *Canada Evidence Act*, the *Statutory Instruments Act*, and *the Statute Revision Act*. (See *Privacy Act*.) See http://www.privcom.gc.ca/legislation/ 02_06_01_e.asp (8, 15)

Positivist. A stream within an empirical approach to research that is highly indebted to science. It seeks to produce verifiable data through the application of strict scientific methods to any social phenomenon. (1)

Post–mass media functions. The qualities of mobile technologies that allow for interpersonal and peer-to-peer communication that are distinct from the traditional broadcast model of communication, which involves a centralized transmission model to many. (14)

Printemps Érable. See *Arab Spring*. (14)

Privacy. The right to be let alone, to be free from surveillance by the state, institutions, or one's fellow citizens; the right to control the disclosure of personal information; the right to determine the use of information disclosed; respect for the dignity of the person. (15)

***Privacy Act*.** One of two federal privacy laws, the *Privacy Act*, first established in 1983, obliges federal government departments and agencies to respect privacy rights by limiting the collection, use, and disclosure of personal information. Individuals have the right to access and request the correction of personal information about themselves held by these federal government organizations. See http://laws-lois.justice.gc.ca/eng/acts/P-21/index.html and *Personal Information Protection and Electronic Documents Act*. (15)

Program Tests. Limited survey analysis of audience reaction to video or audio programming (existing content or pilots). Usually involves mailing out content and following up with a survey. Involves using a small sample of people (100–200) in which people listen/watch in their homes and then answer a structured survey. (7)

Propaganda. Communication whose goal is to influence the attitudes of individuals and audience members about a particular cause or issue. (11)

Prosumers. Combination of the words "consumer" and "producer" to refer to independent and innovative media creation. (7)

Protectionist. An approach to media literacy that seeks to protect children and young people from harmful and powerful influencers in the media. These harmful effects can be content that is deemed to be violent or sexual in nature. Early media literacy education was protectionist in nature while more contemporary media literacy education is more nuanced and discriminatory. However, protectionist discourses are prevalent in current debates and policies about regulating the internet and social media for children and young people. (2)

Public domain. Intellectual material that is not protected by copyright legislation, and thus available freely for the public to access and reuse. Some material passes into the public domain once copyright expires, while other material is created with the explicit intention to remain public. (16)

Public opinion. The aggregation of attitudes or opinions held by the public. Public opinion is gathered through quantititive measures: surveys, polls, and the study of communication media. Public opinion measurement is culled by governments, political parties, and private and public polling and survey organizations. (7)

Q

Qiniq. Nunavut broadband network. (18)

Queer theory. A type of theory that claims gender is a fluid category and people are not limited to just masculinity/femininity or homosexuality/heterosexuality. (1, 4)

Quotidian. Referring to the everyday. (2)

R

Racialized discourses. Spoken, written, and visual texts and language that categorizes and sorts people, places, and things into constructs of race. Such discourse can reveal assumptions, beliefs and practices that are racist in nature in their privileging of whiteness, and their challenging of equity and rights for all peoples. (19)

Radical alternative media. Media that explicitly challenge dominant institutions, ideas, and values. (17)

Ratings. In common parlance, all quantitative measurements of audience size, including shares, reach, and average audience applied to radio and television. It is contrasted with qualitative audience research, which comprises survey work about audience attitudes or a range of nonsurvey-based, nongeneralizable study techniques such as focus groups, ethnography, and textual analysis. "Rating" refers to the average audience to a program, web page, or advertisement expressed as a percentage of the total population in a country. (7)

Razor and blades model. A business model that refers to manufacturers initially selling at a low price a product in order to entice consumers to purchase other ancillary products that are necessary for the product to be useful. In this case, shaving razors are sold cheaper than the blades necessary to make the shaver work. In the case of video gaming, game consoles are sold at an initial loss for the manufacturer, but the games themselves at a higher margin. This creates an installed base of users, and games can then be sold at a fixed price, with license fees paid to the console company in order to offset the initially high costs of manufacturing. (12)

Reception research. Qualitative studies of how media are integrated into everyday life and various institutionalized processes. (4)

Remote mothering. A term coined by Rakow and Navarro in the 1990s to refer to the early use of the mobile phone by women and mothers to manage household responsibilities while at work. It has also been taken up as a term to refer to the transnational labour practices of women from the South and developing countries who must support their families by pursuing employment as nannies in Western countries; the money they make is sent home to support their extended families and children. (14).

Reputation management. As used in PR, this refers to understanding and influencing a company brand. Increasingly, it is used to refer to the management and cultivation of one's personal online presence in social media. (11)

Resource. Something of actual or potential use in a variety of circumstances and situations. Resources that are economically exchanged become commodities, whereas other resources can remain noncommodified and be considered public goods. (13)

S

Scientific method. A method of inquiry aimed at producing empirically verifiable certainty. To be scientific, a method must be (1) objective (it must not depend on the nature or status of the person conducting the experiment, and it must not be influenced by ideology, personal preference, desire for gain, etc.); (2) reproducible (it must not be the result of chance and must therefore be infinitely repeatable); and (3) falsifiable (it must be stable in a way that allows it to be subjected to experimentation; hence, statements concerning parapsychology, for example, are not scientific because they are not subject to experimentation). Further, various experiments must be internally consistent and work together in support of an overall hypothesis. (1)

Screenness. A term used to describe the pervasiveness of multiple screens in our everyday lives—television and video screens, computer screens, mobile phone screens, and tablet screens. (14)

Semiotic analysis. The study of signs or signifying practices, also known as semiology. Semiotics attempts to explain the meanings of objects, actions, images, etc., in the world around us by showing how they fit into, and express, larger systems and patterns of belief and meanings of which we are frequently unaware. For example, semioticians will attempt to explain the success (or failure) of an advertising campaign by showing how its imagery or musical theme or catch line, etc., fit into and draw on older patterns of meaning and symbolism with which we are all familiar but whose far-reaching nature might be unknown to us. For years, the leading exponent of semiotics was Roland Barthes (1915–1980). (1)

Simulations substitution. Broadcasting policy that allows Canadian networks to sell advertising on American network programming. (5)

Smart mobbing. Popularized by Howard Rheingold, this refers to technologically mediated forms of self-structuring social organization. See http://www.smartmobs.com (14)

Social media. Internet and mobile media whose characteristics include the ability for social networking and participatory communication. Popular applications and services include Facebook, Tumblr, Wikipedia, YouTube, and Twitter. (13)

Social mobility. The ability of individuals and families to shift across classes and cultures. (14)

Social sorting. The processes of classifying and categorizing people based on sorting populations into groups. Social sorting can be used for discriminatory purposes, such as excluding people based on their race, ethnicity, socieconomic status, age, or gender. (13)

Surveillance. The monitoring, tracking, and control of people and populations by governments and corporations for the purposes of informational control. (13)

Surveillant assemblage. The many technologies (physical and human) that comprise surveillance regimes. (13)

Surveys. Attitudinal and behavioural data generated by the administering of in-person telephone, mail or internet questionnaires. Used in audience research to measure programming tastes, attitudes, and motivations for using media; how people react to current and proposed programs; and related demographic and lifestyle phenomena. (7)

Synopticon. A term used in surveillance studies to indicate that contemporary arrangements of surveillance involve not just the few seeing and supervising the many, but the many seeing and supervising the few. (13)

T

Tele-circle. A term that refers to intimate contact and communication with friends, families, peers, and colleagues through social media. (14)

Television Northern Canada (TVNC). A Pan-Northern distribution service implemented in 1991, the year that communications access rights for Aboriginal peoples were enshrined in Canada's *Broadcasting Act*. (18)

Text. A term broadly defined to acknowledge how all media construct and carry meaning; as a result, all media (books, films, television, radio, social media) can be subject to analysis and critical thinking. (2)

Third screen. A term that refers to mobile screens; the first and second screens are film and computer screens. (14)

Throttling. A term that refers to the slowing down of internet services by internet service providers to manage traffic on their network. See also *Net Neutrality*. (6)

Time slicing. A habit of constantly checking one's email on the computer or smart phone. (14)

Torrent. Open-source file-sharing applications for sharing and distributing large software and media files. (6)

Truman Doctrine. A 1947 proclamation by Harry S. Truman that lent U.S. economic support to Greece and Turkey to prevent their falling under Soviet control. (3)

U

Universal service. A telecommunications policy that affirms that Canadians living in rural and remote regions of the country should be able to receive the same services as Canadians in more populous urban regions through subsidies provided to service providers by the government to be used to offset the high costs of deployment. (5)

User-generated content. Internet content that is created by users, typically but not always in a nonrenumerative fashion. User-generated content includes the use of social media and posting original content on social media. (13)

V

Value neutrality. A sociological term derived from scholar Max Weber that refers to the objectivity of social scientists in their interpretation of data. (1)

Vancouver hockey riot. In 2011 following the defeat of the Vancouver Canucks in the Stanley Cup playoffs, fans rioted in the streets of Vancouver; mobiles and social media were widely used to document the event. This documentation was also used by police to convict some of the rioters. (14)

Vertical concentration of ownership. A concentration of firms within a line of business that extends a company's control over the process of production and/or distribution. (9)

Vertical integration. In media ownership, a process in which a single company gains ownership or control over several aspects of a product or service's production and distribution process. The most common form of vertical integration is when the same media firm controls both content creation and distribution properties. (5)

Virtual mobility. The use of mobile technologies to allow for communication at a distance. (14)

Vote mobbing. A form of activism facilitated by social media that was used during the Canadian federal elections of 2011 by students to encourage young people to vote. (14)

W

Web 2.0. A term that designates internet content and services that allow for participatory uses; used interchangeably and now often replaced by the term social media. (13)

Wolf Koenig. A National Film Board of Canada filmmaker who made substantial contributions to documentary film. An overview of his films can be found at http://www.imdb.com/name/nm0462860 (18)

World Summit on the Information Society (WSIS). The World Summit on the Information Society (WSIS) (http://www.itu.int/wsis) took part in two phases. The first culminated in a Geneva Summit in December 2003, with the goal to develop core principles and a common vision toward an understanding of the information society, particularly for developing countries, and to develop a Declaration of Principles and a Plan of Action for coordinated global development. Phase 2 took place in November 2005 in Tunis, focusing on refinement of Phase 1 development themes, assessment of progress made to date, and a clearer focus on the nature of internet governance. WSIS was coordinated by the International Telecommunications Union (ITU) with interested UN organizations, including UNESCO, and brought together most "developed," "developing," and "least developed" countries along with private industry and civil society groups. This model of multistakeholder participation was unique in being the first such high-level global summit to bring together civil society groups to discuss and debate their issues and concerns alongside governments and industry. See http://www.itu.int/wsis/index.html (9)

INDEX

B

C

D

E

F

H

I

N

T

U

Y

Z